Ovid's *Heroides*

Howard Jacobson

Ovid's
Heroides

Princeton University Press

Princeton, New Jersey

COPYRIGHT © 1974 BY PRINCETON UNIVERSITY PRESS
ALL RIGHTS RESERVED

LIBRARY OF CONGRESS CATALOGING IN PUBLICATION DATA WILL
BE FOUND ON THE LAST PRINTED PAGE OF THIS BOOK
CHAPTER I APPEARED ORIGINALLY IN *Phoenix* (VOL. 25,
1971) AND IS GIVEN HERE IN SOMEWHAT REVISED FORM,
WITH THE KIND PERMISSION OF THE EDITORS.

PUBLICATION OF THIS BOOK HAS BEEN AIDED BY THE ANDREW W. MELLON FOUNDATION
AND THE RESEARCH BOARD, UNIVERSITY OF ILLINOIS
THIS BOOK HAS BEEN COMPOSED IN LINOTYPE BASKERVILLE

PRINTED IN THE UNITED STATES OF AMERICA
BY PRINCETON UNIVERSITY PRESS, PRINCETON, NEW JERSEY

For My Parents

אשרי אדם שזכו לו אבותיו

אשרי אדם שיש לו יתד להתלות בה

Contents

Preface

This book is an interpretive study of Ovid's *Epistulae Heroidum,* by which title I signify the first fifteen letters in the corpus of twenty-one commonly called the *Heroides.* I do consider the last six poems genuine, but have nonetheless ignored them here for a simple reason: the first fifteen *epistulae* and the last six are two distinct works. Not only were 16-21 written at a different time in the poet's life from 1-15, but they are quite different in their form, scope, and nature. These so-called "double letters" are a work unto themselves and would demand separate and thorough treatment. It was the superficial similarities between the two works which made it possible and easy for them to be joined together and transmitted as one. My study, however, is concerned solely with the *Epistulae Heroidum* that Ovid wrote and published as his first great venture into the world of myth, namely, *Heroides* 1-15, the "single letters."

For simplicity's sake I regularly use the term *Heroides* rather than *Epistulae Heroidum* to refer to these fifteen letters.

I have arranged the chapters on the individual poems in a rather idiosyncratic order so as to juxtapose certain epistles which in various ways lend themselves to illuminating contrast and comparison. The reader who wishes to follow the traditional order (or to read selectively) will find no difficulty in so doing since each of these essays is intended to stand equally well on its own.

For the text of the *Heroides* I have used H. Dörrie's recent edition (Berlin and New York 1971). Citations of Dörrie's text do not invariably signify that I agree at all points with the readings quoted.

I have been able to make only very limited reference in footnotes to the following works, since the book was already at the printer's when I incorporated the material: Della Corte's article

"I Miti . . . ," Döpp's dissertation, and Thraede's monograph (full citations can be found in the Select Bibliography). The article by Paratore, "L'influenza . . ." and the study by Cugusi I have not seen.

It was only when this book was in the final stage of production that I read Professor W. S. Anderson's fine essay on the *Heroides* in *Ovid*, ed. J. W. Binns (London and Boston 1973), and the third part of Professor Dörrie's invaluable *Untersuchungen* (*NAkG* 1972), which the author so kindly sent to me. Unfortunately, I have not been able to take into account either of these works.

Acknowledgements

I am greatly indebted to Professor William M. Calder III and Professor Gilbert Highet. Professor Highet read my whole manuscript, Professor Calder most of it. I have benefitted immensely from their criticisms and suggestions. This is not to say that they would agree with all my arguments and interpretations or that they are in any way responsible for errors of fact or judgment that may persist.

The Graduate College of the University of Illinois awarded me Summer Fellowships in 1969 and 1970, and appointed me to the University's Center for Advanced Study as an Associate Member in the spring semester of the year 1971-1972. The Graduate College's Research Board provided me with a research assistant in 1970-1971 and contributed funds to help subsidize the publication of this volume. All this support immeasurably facilitated its completion and production.

The National Endowment for the Humanities awarded me a Fellowship for the year 1971-1972. This enabled me to devote my energies during that year to research and writing. In this period most of the writing of the book was done.

Professor John J. Bateman, who was Head of the Classics Department in the years that I did most of the work on this book, provided help and support in many ways.

Mr. Charles Eberline, who served as my research assistant for a year, was wonderfully competent and responsible in carrying out various difficult and unpleasant tasks.

To the staffs of the Classics Library (headed by Mrs. Suzanne Griffiths) and the Reference Library at the University of Illinois I am very grateful.

I am also indebted to Mrs. Polly Hanford of Princeton University Press for her expert editing.

Last, and as the proverb goes, most precious: Elaine was always Elaine. ואת עלית על כלנה

xi

Abbreviations and Short Titles

For abbreviations of ancient authors and works consult *The Oxford Classical Dictionary*, 2d ed. (Oxford 1970), pp. ix-xxii; Lewis and Short's *A Latin Dictionary* (repr. Oxford 1962), pp. vii-xi; Liddell-Scott-Jones' *A Greek-English Lexicon* (repr. Oxford 1968), pp. xvi-xxxviii. Occasionally I have preferred abbreviations that seemed to me clearer (e.g., Aristoph. rather than Ar. for Aristophanes).

For abbreviations of standard works (e.g., Nauck's *Tragicorum Graecorum Fragmenta*) consult *The Oxford Classical Dictionary* and *American Journal of Archaeology* 74 (1970) 3-8.

For abbreviations of periodicals consult *American Journal of Archaeology*, and the lists in the annual volumes of *L'Année Philologique*.

The following works recurring throughout the volume are cited by author's name or in other abbreviated form. Additional works recurring within a specific chapter will be similarly treated, with abbreviations listed usually in the first footnote of the chapter.

Anderson, J. N. *On the Sources of Ovid's Heroides I, III, VII, X, XII* (Berlin 1896).

Atti del Convegno Internazionale Ovidiano. Two vols. (Rome 1959). Cited as "Atti."

Dörrie, H. "Untersuchungen zur Überlieferungsgeschichte von Ovids Epistulae Heroidum," *NAkG* (1960).

Eggerding, F. "De Heroidum Ovidianarum Epistulis quae vocantur commentationes," *DPhH* 18 (1911) 133-252.

Elia, S. d'. *Ovidio* (Naples 1959).

Fraenkel, E. *Horace* (Oxford 1957).

Fränkel, H. *Ovid: A Poet Between Two Worlds* (Berkeley and Los Angeles 1945).

Giomini, R. *P. Ovidi Nasonis Heroides* I (Rome 1963²); II (Rome 1965).

Huxley, G. L. *Greek Epic Poetry* (Cambridge, Mass. 1969).

Kirfel, E.-A. *Untersuchungen zur Briefform der Heroides Ovids* (Bern and Stuttgart 1969).

Loers, V. *P. Ovidii Nasonis Heroides* (Köln 1829-1830).

Luck, G. *Untersuchungen zur Textgeschichte Ovids* (Heidelberg 1969).

Mette, H. J. *Der Verlorene Aischylos* (Berlin 1963).

Oppel, E. *Ovids Heroides: Studien zur inneren Form und zur Motivation* (Diss. Erlangen-Nürnberg 1968).

Otis, B. *Ovid as an Epic Poet* (Cambridge 1966; 2d ed. 1970).

Ovidiana, ed. N. I. Herescu (Paris 1958). Cited by title alone.

Page, D. L. *Poetae Melici Graeci* (Oxford 1962). Cited as *PMG*.

Palmer, A. *P. Ovidi Nasonis Heroides* (Oxford 1898).

Tolkiehn, J. *Quaestionum ad Heroides Ovidianas spectantium capita VII* (Leipzig 1888).

Webster, T.B.L. *The Tragedies of Euripides* (London 1967).

Wilkinson, L. P. *Ovid Recalled* (Cambridge 1955).

Ovid's *Heroides*

"I haven't opened it yet," said the White Rabbit, "but it seems to be a letter, written by the prisoner to—to somebody."

"It must have been that," said the King, "unless it was written to nobody, which isn't usual, you know."

"Who is it directed to?" said one of the jurymen.

"It isn't directed at all," said the White Rabbit; "in fact, there's nothing written on the outside." He unfolded the paper as he spoke, and added, "It isn't a letter after all: it's a set of verses."

"Are they in the prisoner's handwriting?" asked another of the jurymen.

"No, they're not," said the White Rabbit, "and that's the queerest thing about it." (The jury all looked puzzled.)

"He must have imitated somebody else's hand," said the King.

Alice's Adventures in Wonderland

Introduction

Few would now agree with Willa Cather's Niel who "read the *Heroides* over and over, and felt that they were the most glowing love stories ever told."[1] Yet similar opinions have periodically been expressed from the Renaissance to the present century. J. C. Scaliger called them *politissimae* of all Ovid's works and the seventeenth century scholar, Rapin, thought them *florem elegantiae Romanae.*[2] Of equal or greater significance is the high valuation set on the *Heroides* by eminent poets: Seneca's plays are heavily influenced by them; Chaucer's *Legend of Good Women* is nearly a re-creation of the *Heroides,* and many other authors, including Gower, Ariosto, Drayton, Racine, Pope, and probably Shakespeare, clearly knew and liked them. Moreover, Dörrie's recent book on the history of the heroic epistle[3] has demonstrated vividly that the *Heroides* are the progenitor of a long and often distinguished line of descendants. Unfortunately, the nineteenth century did Ovid and particularly the *Heroides* serious injury that has only of late and with difficulty begun to be repaired and redressed.[4] On the one hand, the poems were attacked as inferior works of art; on the other, the text was treated with irresponsible and reckless disdain. It became, so to speak, an arena for scholars eager to discover interpolations or to condemn poems as spurious. One need not totally deny the existence of interpolated passages here and there to gladly agree with Owen's barbed words: "The presumed interpolator, who derived enjoyment from inserting copy of his own into other people's works, that critics in a far-off future might exercise their ingenu-

[1] *A Lost Lady* (New York 1939) 81.
[2] Both cited by Loers in his *Prooemium*, p. LXVIII.
[3] *Der heroische Brief* (Berlin 1968).
[4] For a brief but valuable account of the critical fortunes of the *Heroides* in the last two centuries, see H. Dörrie, *A&A* 13 (1967) 41-42.

3

ity by scenting out these irrelevancies, is an ill-supported fantasy which flourished in the last century, and still dies hard."[5]

Happily, such trends are passing. The major problem with *Heroides*-criticism (and Ovid-criticism in general) lies now elsewhere. It is the habit of believing that, in one critic's candid words, "Ovid è sempre un poeta superficiale."[6] This view, too, is slowly dying, as the work of, among others, Fränkel, Otis, Ludwig, Dörrie, and Segal indicates. We are now often told, though with a certain degree of defensiveness, that, after all, Ovid was a serious poet. This is all to the good. For, if our understanding of the *Metamorphoses* was gravely hampered by the judgment that it was a simple and shallow poem—we must, in Fränkel's words, be "patient and curious enough to search on with a mind responsive to anything, unexpected as it may be, then we shall be rewarded by startling finds"[7]—the *Heroides* have suffered even more on this score. The largest obstacle to a proper understanding and appreciation has been the tendency to see them as simple poems; for, taken as a simple work, the *Heroides* cannot but be judged a failure—and a boring failure at that. But the truth is quite the opposite. As Büchner wrote a decade ago, the *Heroides* "offenbaren ihre Vielfalt immer mehr, je länger man sich in sie vertieft."[8] Or as Dörrie has recently put it: "Die *epistulae Heroidum* sind eine sehr komplexe Dichtung, und ihre Interpretation muss von vielen Gesichtspunkten her unternommen werden."[9]

These are, indeed, complex poems and they repay the reader as he deserves of them. A cursory reader will find no more than superficial and casual poems. But the fault will not be the poet's. Ovid himself, we can be fairly certain, thought these epistles important and successful poems. His elaborate catalogue of them in *Amores* 2.18 and the proud claim *ille novavit opus* at *AA* 3.346 are testimony. When he cites *Her.* 7.197-198 at *Fast.* 3.549-550, we may take it as an unspoken assertion that his Dido, not Ver-

---

[5] S. G. Owen, *P. Ovidi Nasonis Tristium Liber Secundus* (Oxford 1924) p. VI. Equally cogent and biting are the observations of R. P. Oliver in *Classical Studies Presented to Ben Edwin Perry* (Urbana 1969 = *Illinois Studies in Language and Literature* 58) 154-155, n. 43.

[6] G. Carugno, *GIF* 4 (1951) 152. See also 155 for remarks on the *Heroides* in particular.

[7] P. 73.

[8] K. Büchner, *Römische Literaturgeschichte* (Stuttgart 1962³) 380.

[9] *Op. cit.* (supra n. 4) 42.

4

gil's, is the standard or definitive portrait of that heroine. And the *Heroides* themselves reflect an enormous amount of expended time, labor, and energy.[10]

While still young, Ovid perceived, with an insight into the viability and flexibility of the genres of poetry that remained characteristic of him throughout his life, that Elegy, as it had been taken over from the Greeks with such brilliance by the Latin poets of the first century, had reached the end of its road or—at the least—that he was not the person to continue its journey down traditional and well-worn paths. To be sure, by the year 25 or thereabouts, Propertius and Tibullus had evidently begun to feel similar qualms, as evident in their experimentations that lie outside the realm of personal erotic elegy. Most striking in this respect is Propertius' fourth book, a series of conscious attempts to break away from what had by now become the hackneyed mold of Latin elegy, and to renounce the kind of poems that make up most of his first three books. Ovid entered the elegists' world with what on the surface appeared little more than his own imitation of Propertius' erotic elegies, but was in fact a radical adaptation. The *Amores* are, in one respect, a burlesque of the traditional. But they are also an amazing transformation of subjective elegy, for while the format is first-personal, no different from Tibullus' and Propertius', yet the tone of the poems denies this subjectivity. He brings, as Parker neatly observes, "subjective erotic elegy outside the subject."[11] Somehow, first-person composition becomes an objective mode of writing. Ovid stands outside the poems while at the same time being part of them.[12] It was, years later, an unimaginative extension of this technique,

---

[10] Recent estimates of the *Heroides* have been mixed. Wilkinson (see esp. 97 and 106) and Otis (16-18) are by and large negatively disposed, while Dörrie and Fränkel (36-46) think well of them. Aside from Fränkel's chapter and Dörrie's essay (supra n. 4, 41-55), there are illuminating general discussions of the *Heroides* by Loers (*Prooemium*, pp. LXIX-LXXV) and W. Kraus, *WS* 65 (1950-51) 57-63. E. Oppel's 1968 dissertation is a study of much insight and value.

[11] D. Parker, *Arion* 8 (1969) 96.

[12] I have no intention of becoming embroiled in the recent controversy over whether the distinction between subjective and objective elegy really has any meaning. See, for instance, J. K. Newman, *Augustus and the New Poetry* (Brussels 1967 = *Coll. Lat.* 88) 265-269, 365-371, and D. O. Ross, Jr., *Style and Tradition in Catullus* (Cambridge, Mass. 1969) 163ff. Certainly, as a purely descriptive distinction it is useful.

5

when in the *Ars* the very form made concrete the distance between the poet as poet and the poet as lover. When Ovid turned from the *Amores* to the *Heroides*, he was again working within the framework of traditional subjective elegy while rejecting it at the same time. For here the dichotomy between the subjective "I" and the poet, merely implicit in the *Amores*, becomes a necessary function of the form. Put another way, Ovid transfers the subjective element to his heroines, a stroke essentially paradoxical. In a manner of speaking, the *Heroides* are the turning of the "empathetic" technique (to use Otis' fruitful phrase) in upon itself: the poet does not read his character's mind, he becomes it. There can be no question that much of the wit and parody that is present—though subservient to more important considerations—is often the function (sometimes, I feel, unintentional and infelicitous) of this "split."

But Ovid had other reasons for rejecting traditional forms. Erotic elegy, even in the new guise of the *Amores*, was insulated. Its scope was very narrow. Its world was only love, the lovers, and poetry. The range and scope of its psychology is restricted. In addition, love elegy has no history aside from the love relationship of the lovers. It is almost unidimensional. Ovid changes all this by incorporating elegy into the world of myth—indeed, by making elegy the world of myth—and thus giving it range and relationships other than lover-beloved, and psychological dimensions other than the erotic.

Further, the *Heroides* are Ovid's initial attempt—the culmination comes some years later in the *Metamorphoses*—at revitalizing myth as subject of literature. When Rome's creative artists of the third century adopted Greek myth, they were directing their attention not really at myth, but at that literature (and art) which embodied myth—literature which, of course, was not even their own. Their choice was tantamount to preferring literature to myth and the alien to the native. Under such circumstances, it is not surprising that the myths finally turned into paradigmatic matter and the use of myth as a major subject of poetry withered away. The *Aeneid* is a great and suggestive exception, successful largely because Vergil was able to see the myth as a mythic structure and as native Roman in its essence. The elegists had been content to utilize, in varying degrees and ways, myth as *exemplum*. Ovid, however, re-creates the myth by forcibly projecting it into a new world: of elegy, of the erotic, of an idiosyncratic psychology.

Emotional monologues of mythical women in love, betrayed or otherwise, had a long history before the *Heroides*. Ovid would have known Catullus' Ariadne, possibly Scylla's speech in the *Ciris* (404-458) or a Greek original of it, and undoubtedly many in Hellenistic literature. But it is Euripides who, so to speak, created and popularized the passionate female monologue. And it is Euripides who must be considered the distant ancestor of the *Heroides*, not merely because he so effectively and influentially utilized women's speeches, but also because in the *Heroides* Ovid —whether consciously or not—inherited many of the intellectual and moral attitudes that were Euripides'. Like the Greek tragedian, he had a remarkable ability to see through the eyes of women. He too was interested in the erotic, in the psychopathology of love, and in human psychology in general. Both show unusual affection for generalizations; their intrusive *sententiae* can be annoying at times. Both were apt to consider originality and novelty virtues in themselves. Finally, we can be quite sure that Euripides' moral relativism made a major impact on Ovid's thought and sensibility. Trapped in an age of deliberate and imposed puritanism, himself by disposition a liberal spirit, Ovid was only too ready to adopt a Euripidean pose in opposition to Augustan policy and dogma. The *Heroides*, a spectrum of love and lovers, is almost *ipso facto*, in its deheroization of the mythic material and in its rejection of the male viewpoint, a denial of the Augustan (and Vergilian, at least as envisioned in the *Aeneid*) ideal. Ovid's relativism, no less than it effected the transformation of the sense of words which were highly charged for Augustus (like *rusticus*; consider especially the *princeps'* moral and rural programs), was able to deflect the meaning of whole myths. It is an irony which Ovid would have understood that while his contemporaries condemned his poetry as immoral, later ages saw it (including the *Heroides*) not only as highly moral, but as paradigmatic.

The faults which detract from the achievement of the *Heroides* are generally those which seem, one might say, congenital to Ovid and are recurrent in most of his work. Here as elsewhere *nescit quod bene cessit relinquere*: points are made and made again, poems carried on further than taste and need dictate. In

7

a manner typical of Ovid's narrative elegy, pentameters are sometimes weak, tending to obstruct the fluidity of movement, or repetitious, almost "fillers," generated by his usual reluctance to begin a coherent and continuing sense-unit with the second half of the distich. On rare occasions, conventions are not personalized and become obtrusive or, at the least, uninteresting. The wit and humor that now and then are present in the *Heroides* degenerate at times into little else than cleverness, sometimes rather ludicrous cleverness.[13] Many of Ovid's faults, both in the *Heroides* and elsewhere, reside in that very instinct which is at the same time responsible for much excellence in his poetry, namely, his close attention to language. Ovid's perception of the correspondences between language and the reality represented—the way the same word can relate to different realities or, conversely, different words to the same reality—is acute, and when exploited as an insight into the nature of reality, perception, and representation is a valuable and critical asset of his work. But when points of language take precedence over points of sense, when plays on words prove no more than a substitute for substance, then his failure is manifest.

* * *

Wilamowitz was essentially correct when he wrote that there is no reason to search out Greek poetic models for most of the *Heroides*.[14] Neither in form nor in poetic treatment of the myths was Ovid imitating his predecessors. Yet, certain though it be that the *Heroides* are uniquely the product of Ovid's creative

[13] I am in almost complete disagreement with E. J. Winsor, *A Study in the Sources and Rhetoric of Chaucer's Legend of Good Women and Ovid's Heroides* (Diss. Yale 1963) 360, who thinks that the *Heroides* are "mock-declamations so conducted as to ridicule the formalities of declamation and to render them absurd. Thus the style of the poems is contrived to be comic and filled with such passages as the critics have called breaches of taste." Such an approach seems to avoid the problem rather than to meet it. One can always defend failure by claiming that it is deliberate and therefore, in a way, successful. If the *Heroides* are essentially parody of declamatory rhetoric, surely Ovid did not need fifteen poems to make the point. At any rate, even if such burlesque is occasionally present in the *Heroides*, to see it as the main thrust of these poems is surely inadmissible.

[14] U. von Wilamowitz-Moellendorff, *Aischylos: Interpretationen* (Berlin 1914) 20, n. 1.

powers, *Quellenforschung* remains a valuable resource for understanding these poems. For it speaks nothing against their originality that they grow out of a literary tradition.

Rohde went to a strange extreme in denying the role of Greek tragedy as source material for the *Heroides*, suggesting that Ovid's inventiveness and what he derived from the rhetorical schools sufficed. (Paradoxically, he then argued that one should see in a number of the *Heroides* Hellenistic poetic models. Why one should make so clear-cut a distinction between fifth century tragedy and Hellenistic poetry he did not explain.)[15] But common sense and substantial evidence demonstrate that Ovid knew and utilized many literary versions of these myths. It is, as Wilamowitz knew, rather meaningless merely to pinpoint the sources. But comparative analysis can be fundamental. It allows us often to determine precisely where Ovid's originality lies and thereby to understand what his particular aims were. The path, however, is rarely smooth: it is not always immediately clear what literary source Ovid was using. And all too often the unfortunate loss of classical and Hellenistic works compels us to attempt reconstruction on the basis of the mythographers or later Greek poets like Quintus and Nonnus, a risky business indeed. An added complexity is presented by the problem of the relationship of classical Latin poetry to late Greek literature. Traditionally, similarities between two works belonging one to each of these periods has been explained by dependence on some common earlier Greek source—a methodological approach of obvious importance to the *Heroides*. Recently, however, the heretical view that late Greek authors knew and utilized Latin poetry has been gaining ground.[16] This, of course, matters a great deal. For instance, the occurrence of a peculiar version of a myth in only Ovid and Quintus is usually offered as evidence for its preexistence in earlier Greek literature. But if we allow for the possibility that

---

15 E. Rohde, *Der griechische Roman* (Leipzig 1914³) 137, n. 1. The view of E. J. Winsor (supra n. 13) 213, n. 1, that "Roman sources can be suggested for nearly all the letters" and therefore we need not think Ovid used Greek sources is bizarre and misguided.

16 W. Kroll, *Studien zum Verständnis der römischen Literatur* (Stuttgart 1924) 10, argued strongly against the possibility that late Greek writers utilized classical Latin poetry. In contrast, A. Lesky, *A History of Greek Literature*, tr. Willis and de Heer (New York 1966) 815, n. 5, cautiously suggests that they may have and J. Diggle, *Euripides: Phaethon* (Cambridge 1970) 180ff, believes that they definitely did.

9

Quintus was reading Ovid, we may then feel justified in crediting Ovid with an innovation in the myth.

So much for the mythic material. We must never forget that the *Heroides* belong not only to the mythic tradition, but equally to the Latin elegiac one. No matter that Ovid broke decisively with his predecessors; his debt to them can scarcely be overestimated. In his language, meter, and thematic matter he constantly betrays their influence. The most cursory reading of Propertius and Tibullus alongside the *Heroides* will reveal numerous parallel passages, often with differences that illuminate Ovid's special reshaping of erotic elegy. Obvious as this may appear, it needs mention, for many areas of real interest have gone unnoticed. Propertius, for instance. Everywhere we are told that 4.3 is the precursor of the *Heroides*. With that, the discussion of Propertius' influence on the *Heroides* usually comes to an end. In fact, insofar as the genre of the *Heroides* is concerned, other poems of Propertius may be equally important as stimuli to Ovid.[17] In narrower areas, e.g., language and themes, Propertius' enormous influence goes largely without recognition. Hosius' collection[18] of Propertian echoes in Ovid is quite inadequate vis-à-vis the *Heroides*, nor is Zingerle's (for Propertius and Tibullus)[19] any better.[20] I suspect that Ovid knew much of Propertius' poetry by heart and had it, consciously or unconsciously, immediately available at any moment.

[17] See chapter XVII, "The Nature of the Genre."

[18] In his Teubner edition of Propertius (1932[8]), pp. xxiii-xxviii.

[19] A. Zingerle, *Ovidius und sein Verhältnis zu den Vorgängern*, vol. 1 (Innsbruck 1869).

[20] One might remark, for example, the possible influence of Prop. 2.9 on the *Heroides*, especially on *Heroides* 1 and 3. Note the references to Penelope and Briseis (3.9), the verbal and thematic similarities: 8/1.116; Achilles called *dominus*: 11/3.5-6; the picture of Briseis with her dead man: 11-12/3.49-50 (note *cruentum/cruenta*); she is *captiva*: 11/3.69. Might the description of Achilles being embraced by his girl (3.114) be a gruesome and ironic recollection of Propertius' picture of the dead hero "embraced" by Briseis (2.9.14)? Then again I doubt that enough attention has been paid to the relationship between the *Heroides* and the *corpus Tibullianum*. Compare, e.g., Sulpicia 4.7.9-10/ *Her.* 4.33, 133ff; also, Sulp. 4.11.1/ *Her.* 14.123. The latter is particularly striking since the one small change Ovid makes, transferring the epithet from its common association with *cura* to *soror*, marks the very keynote of his characterization. Compare also pseudo-Sulp. 4.3.11ff/ *Her.* 4.41ff. Some possible parallels between Ovid's poetry and the *corpus Tibullianum* (esp. Book Four) have been noted by R. S. Radford, *AJP* 44 (1923) 230-259.

At all events, there is much room for furthering our understanding of Ovid's poetry in general and the *Heroides* in particular by inspecting more carefully than has been done his relationship to the Latin elegists who preceded him. Though my chief interests and goals lie elsewhere, I hope that occasional light will be shed in the following pages on this aspect of the *Heroides*.

I

Heroides 3: Briseis

Two of the first three *epistulae* come from the pens of Homeric heroines, the one illustrious, the other of small repute. It is with the letter of Briseis that I shall begin, a poem which exquisitely exhibits Ovid's purposes and aims, his achievements and failings, while at the same time being free of the burden that too often oppresses the student of both the *Heroides* and the *Metamorphoses*, the problem of lost sources.[1]

There is no arguing that Vergil's familiarity with the *Iliad* and the *Odyssey* was extraordinary.[2] Nevertheless, the role of Homer in the educational curriculum and his great stature as poet would have made his two epics all but second nature to any Roman with an interest in literature. Ovid did not know the *Iliad* and *Odyssey* by heart, but it is difficult to determine, when his imitation is exact and deliberate, whether in fact he had Homer by heart selectively or simply composed with a text at his side. Whichever is the case, it is indisputable that Ovid was drawing heavily and directly on the *Iliad* in this poem. Note the following passage in which Briseis recounts the many gifts Agamemnon has offered Achilles:[3]

> (auxerunt blandas grandia dona preces):
> Viginti fulvos operoso ex aere lebetas
>   et tripodas septem pondere et arte pares.

[1] The following works are cited in this chapter by author's name alone: B. Döhle, "Die 'Achilleis' des Aischylos in ihrer Auswirkung auf die attische Vasenmalerei des 5. Jahrhunderts," *Klio* 49 (1967) 63-149; Z. K. Vysoký, "Aischylova Achilleis," *Listy Filologické* 82 (1959) 8-34. *ARV²* = J. D. Beazley, *Attic Red-Figure Vase-Painters²* (Oxford 1963).

[2] Though in the classical age of Greece such expert knowledge may not have been too unusual. See Xen. *Symp.* 3.5-6.

[3] Tolkiehn (49-50) has pointed out many of the correspondences between this passage and its Homeric counterpart.

3. Briseis

Addita sunt illis auri bis quinque talenta,
  bis sex adsueti vincere semper equi,
quodque supervacuum est, forma praestante puellae
  Lesbides, eversa corpora capta domo;
cumque tot his—sed non opus est tibi coniuge—coniunx
  ex Agamemnoniis una puella tribus.

(30-38)

Compare the Homeric account:

ἕπτ' ἀπύρους τρίποδας, δέκα δὲ χρυσοῖο τάλαντα,
αἴθωνας δὲ λέβητας ἐείκοσι, δώδεκα δ' ἵππους
πηγοὺς ἀθλοφόρους, οἳ ἀέθλια ποσσὶν ἄροντο.
οὔ κεν ἀλήϊος εἴη ἀνὴρ ᾧ τόσσα γένοιτο,
οὐδέ κεν ἀκτήμων ἐριτίμοιο χρυσοῖο,
ὅσσα μοι ἠνείκαντο ἀέθλια μώνυχες ἵπποι.
δώσω δ' ἑπτὰ γυναῖκας, ἀμύμονα ἔργ' εἰδυίας,
Λεσβίδας, ἃς, ὅτε Λέσβον ἐϋκτιμένην ἕλεν αὐτὸς,
ἐξελόμην, αἳ κάλλει ἐνίκων φῦλα γυναικῶν.

(Il. 9.122-130)

ταῦτα μὲν αὐτίκα πάντα παρέσσεται. εἰ δέ κεν αὖτε
ἄστυ μέγα Πριάμοιο θεοὶ δώωσ' ἀλαπάξαι,
νῆα ἅλις χρυσοῦ καὶ χαλκοῦ νηησάσθω
εἰσελθών, ὅτε κεν δατεώμεθα ληΐδ' Ἀχαιοί,
Τρωϊάδας δὲ γυναῖκας ἐείκοσιν αὐτὸς ἑλέσθω,
αἵ κε μετ' Ἀργείην Ἑλένην κάλλισται ἔωσιν.
εἰ δέ κεν Ἄργος ἱκοίμεθ' Ἀχαιϊκόν, οὖθαρ ἀρούρης,
γαμβρός κέν μοι ἔοι· τίσω δέ μιν ἶσον Ὀρέστῃ,
ὅς μοι τηλύγετος τρέφεται θαλίῃ ἔνι πολλῇ.
τρεῖς δέ μοί εἰσι θύγατρες ἐνὶ μεγάρῳ εὐπήκτῳ,
Χρυσόθεμις καὶ Λαοδίκη καὶ Ἰφιάνασσα.
τάων ἥν κ' ἐθέλῃσι φίλην ἀνάεδνον ἀγέσθω
πρὸς οἶκον Πηλῆος.

(Il. 9.135-147)

Though Ovid has not taken over the description intact and indeed has in places made careful modifications, the influence could hardly be clearer. So too at line 85 where Briseis' plea, *vince animos iramque tuam*, echoes Phoenix' δάμασον θυμὸν μέγαν (9.496)[4] (the two-edged Greek noun receiving its full equiva-

---

[4] This echo is noted by Anderson (42).

lence),[5] and probably at 43, *an miseros tristis fortuna tenaciter urget*, an echo of 19.290, ὥς μοι δέχεται κακὸν ἐκ κακοῦ αἰεί. Ovid's heroine recalls her past in language that derives from Homer:[6]

Vidi consortes pariter generisque necisque
　　tres cecidisse: Tribus, quae mihi, mater erat.
Vidi, quantus erat, fusum tellure cruenta
　　pectora iactantem sanguinolenta virum.

(47-50)

ἄνδρα μὲν ᾧ ἔδοσάν με πατὴρ καὶ πότνια μήτηρ
εἶδον πρὸ πτόλιος δεδαϊγμένον ὀξέϊ χαλκῷ,
τρεῖς τε κασιγνήτους, τούς μοι μία γείνατο μήτηρ,
κηδείους, οἳ πάντες ὀλέθριον ἦμαρ ἐπέσπον.
οὐδὲ μὲν οὐδέ μ᾽ ἔασκες, ὅτ᾽ ἄνδρ᾽ ἐμὸν ὠκὺς Ἀχιλλεὺς
ἔκτεινεν, πέρσεν δὲ πόλιν θείοιο Μύνητος,
κλαίειν.

(*Il.* 19.291-297)

Throughout this poem one hears such Homeric voices, sometimes with sharp clarity, more often dimly.[7] To these we shall re-

---

[5] See August. *Ennar. in Ps.* 87 (Migne 37.1113) and *Ennar. in Ps.* 105 (Migne 37.1415), two passages highly instructive on the various ways of translating θυμός into Latin (cited *ThLL* s.v. *ira*, vol. 7² cols. 361-362).

[6] The similarities are noted by Tolkiehn (54).

[7] Thus, at 57-58, *quin etiam fama est, cum crastina fulserit Eos, | te dare nubiferis lintea plena Notis*, Tolkiehn's suggestion (52) that we have an echo of *Il.* 9.682f seems supported by the similar sense, the common mention of *Eos*, and by Ovid's strange usage of the present infinitive, possibly modeled on the Homeric construction. E. Merone, *Studi sulle Eroidi di Ovidio* (Naples 1964) 37-38, however, would emphasize its expressive purpose; i.e., Briseis is so certain that Achilles will leave that she sees his departure as virtually taking place already. This seems dubious, both because there is no indication that she is certain and also because *fama est* on the one hand contradicts certainty, and on the other removes the responsibility for the thought from Briseis. It is probably more likely (if we are unwilling to see here Homeric influence, and if the text is correct) that this is simply a colloquialism (present for future seems most common with the verb *dare*; see *Met.* 7.739 which, according to Merone, may be the only other instance in Ovid of this construction). *Achaeiadas* (71) also seems a verbal echo of Homer (so Tolkiehn 52), who uses Ἀχαιίδες in precisely the same context (*Il.* 9.395), the forthcoming (hypothetical) marriage of Achilles in Greece. Ovid seems to have limited his use of Ἀχαίς to strictly geographical notions, as in *Achaidas urbes* or *Achais = Graecia* (e.g., *Met.* 3.511; 5.306, 577; 7.504), though perhaps metrical considerations also had something to do with his choice of Ἀχαιάς here (a Homeric form that does not seem to occur elsewhere in Latin litera-

turn. For the present one small but perhaps significant point. Again, Ovid's Briseis:

> Nam simul Eurybates me Talthybiusque vocarunt,
> Eurybati data sum Talthybioque comes.
>
> (9-10)

The mission of Talthybius and Eurybates to take Briseis from Achilles is drawn, of course, from the *Iliad's* first book. It is unlikely that a handbook would have perpetuated their names in this connection. Most strikingly, there is reason to believe that Ovid might have known the names of Agamemnon's two heralds only from the *Iliad*, or rather of the one, Eurybates, who in contrast to his famous colleague Talthybius appears to have all but vanished after his one brief mission.[8] Excepting scholia on the relevant Homeric passages (and on Aeschylus, discussed below), the only ancient reference to him appears in Hyginus' catalogue of Homeric personages, *Eurybates et Talthybius internuntii* (*Fab.* 97.15), probably drawn, directly or indirectly, from the Homeric mention in Book One. Further, according to Pausanias, Polygnotus' *Iliupersis* depicted Eurybates, *the herald of Odysseus* (cf. *Il.* 2.184; *Od.* 19.247), performing a mission for Agamemnon (10.25.4, 8), a circumstance which, no matter how we understand it, remains instructive. Either Polygnotus (or his "source," be it artistic or literary) was unaware that Agamemnon had a herald by this name and unwittingly ran the risk of potential confusion (unless he assumed that his audience's ignorance would preclude this possibility) or else, as Frazer believes, Pausanias, notwithstanding his usual familiarity with myth, has gone astray through his ignorance of the existence of an Agamemnonian Eurybates.

A peculiar scholium on Aesch. *PV* 440 reports that ἡ Νιόβη διὰ τὴν

---

ture). When Briseis refers to herself as *munus* (20, 149), we may wonder whether Ovid plays upon her designation as γέρας (1.185). Finally, we might consider the possibility that the description of Achilles as *immitis matrisque ferocior undis* (133) has as its point of departure *Il.* 16.34f.

[8] I exclude the possibility that the Eurybates coupled with Odios at *Il.* 9.170 is Agamemnon's herald, but even if he were this would not affect the question of this herald's appearance outside of the *Iliad*. As for Talthybius, he becomes the herald *par excellence*. He is a character in, e.g., Euripides' *Hecuba* and *Trojan Women*, and is mentioned at Eur. *IA* 95, 1563; Plaut. *Stich.* 305. Seneca (*Apocol.* 13) neatly calls Hermes *Talthybius deorum*.

ὑπερβάλλουσαν λύπην ἐσιώπα, καὶ οἷον τὸ τοῦ Ἀχιλλέως, ὅταν ἐστάλησαν πρὸς ἐκεῖνον ὁ Ταλθύβιος καὶ Εὐρυβάτης καλοῦντες εἰς μάχην. What this alludes to is anyone's guess, and confusion and conflation may be likely authors of a worthless statement. So in fact many scholars have judged it. If, however, the scholium is reliable, we may have to think of some scene in a tragedy (e.g., Aeschylus' *Myrmidons*) where the Greeks send the two heralds to seek Achilles' return to battle. Even so, the lesser herald (Eurybates) would probably have been a mute and rather inconspicuous.[9] There seems only one probable conclusion. Ovid would have known Eurybates as Talthybius' comrade from the *Iliad* and nowhere else.[10]

It is of little surprise that Ovid made extensive use of the *Iliad* in this letter. But what of the non-Homeric matter that abounds? Ovidian? Perhaps, but can we attain a modicum of certainty? Might Ovid have been drawing on some other Briseis-source as well as the *Iliad*? Such a question can never be finally answered, but the evidence, as far as it goes, suggests that the Greeks never elaborated the brief Homeric episodes concerning Briseis. Mentions of her are rather few, and she seems never to have been made a heroine—or even major character—of any large-scale work. Extant references seem to descend directly from the *Iliad*. Now the number of lost tragedies dealing with Achilles is great—some we know of, e.g., those by Astydamas, Aristarchus of Tegea, Carcinus, Livius, Accius, Ennius; others have undoubtedly passed into oblivion, titles and all—and any one of these might have found Briseis a large and important role. But we must think this doubtful when we consider that no play—with which we have some familiarity—does. Beyond this, we have not one secure item of evidence that Briseis ever spoke a word in a tragedy, though she surely must have. An obscure reference to Mynes in Sophocles' *Aichmalotides* may bear witness to her presence in

---

[9] This is essentially the view of T. Bergk, "Die Myrmidonen des Aeschylus," *Hermes* 18 (1883) 484ff; M. Croiset, "Eschyle Imitateur d'Homère," *REG* 7 (1894) 152-158; V. Di Benedetto, "Il Silenzio di Achille nei *Mirmidoni* di Eschilo," *Maia* 19 (1967) 381; L. Ferrari, *I Drammi Perduti di Eschilo* (Palermo 1968) 95; Döhle 82. Mette (114) also seems inclined to accept it. For a conjectural attempt to see the reflection of some such scene from the *Myrmidons* in a vase-painting by Polygnotus, see L. Massei, *Studi Classici e Orientali* 18 (1969) 171-172.

[10] Ovid could have been familiar with Eurybates from one of the many paintings of the abduction. But it seems much more likely that he drew the actual name from a literary source.

this play, while an unsure reading might—no more—testify to her appearance in Aeschylus' *Phrygians*. That is all.[11]

The *Cypria* (p. 20K), which recounted how Achilles sacked Briseis' land and won her as his prize, probably went into no further detail, while there is no evidence that Briseis appeared in the *Aithiopis*, though probability suggests that she must have.

Two passages, one in Quintus of Smyrna (3.544ff), the other in Propertius (2.9.9ff), combine to suggest that there may have existed, perhaps of Hellenistic origin, a non-Homeric Briseis episode in which she was seen mourning Achilles. This is a disputed matter, and the critical question—would this have been an isolated scene or was Briseis given a role of prominence?—cannot be answered, even if such a poem did exist.[12]

The unusual tales Dictys tells about Briseis we can attribute to his unique mythopoeic style, but one episode should perhaps give us pause. Both Dictys (4.15) and Quintus (7.709-727) describe how Neoptolemus, after Achilles' death, visits his father's

11 A. von Blumenthal, "Sophokles," *RE* 3 A (1927) 1052, has suggested that the title *Aichmalotides* refers to Briseis and her fellow captives, and that the tragedy dramatized the opening of the *Iliad*. Sophocles' *Chryses* probably dealt with the beginning of the *Iliad* only tangentially. The view that Briseis' seizure was depicted in Aeschylus' Achilles trilogy (see H. Brunn, "Troische Miscellen: Dritte Abtheilung," *S B Mun* 1880, 179) has been abandoned, but it is still possible that Briseis did have a role, perhaps in the episode of the reconciliation of Agamemnon and Achilles or in that of Priam's ransom of Hector's body (the latter conceivably receiving its impetus from the mention of Briseis at *Il.* 24.676). Of special note is Aesch. fr. 267N² which may be a direct address to Briseis or at least a reference to her (see H. W. Smyth, *Aeschylus* 2 [Cambridge, Mass. 1963] 472-473; O. Werner, *Aischylos: Tragödien und Fragmente* [Munich 1959] 570-571; L. Ferrari [supra n. 9] 107-108). Vysoký (22, 34) believes that, while there is no direct reference to Briseis here, Aeschylus is playing on the audience's ability to recognize the name of her homeland. Mette (119), however, does not see any reference to Briseis here at all.

12 Enk observes on the Propertius passage, *Propertius et Quintus Smyrnaeus meminerunt poetae aetatis Hellenisticae nobis ignoti.* There is, however, no evidence for this, and Enk's own remark, *sed Homerus de Briseide Patroclum lugente narrat similia,* seems to show his own doubt. The view implicit in Enk's latter words, that Quintus adopted the mourning scene for Patroclus and transferred it to Achilles' death, seems to be that of F. Vian, *Quintus de Smyrne* 1 (Paris 1963) *ad loc.* R. Keydell, "Quintus v. Smyrna," *RE* 24.1 (1963) 1278, rejects the theory of a common Hellenistic source. If one is willing to accept Keydell's view that Quintus used Latin sources, it is even possible that his account was influenced by this very letter of Ovid's.

tent and there finds Briseis. Unless Quintus is echoing Dictys, both may be utilizing one source,[13] perhaps the same shared by Quintus and Propertius, which might mean the existence of some poem which treated the death of Achilles, the reaction to it, and the ensuing arrival of Neoptolemus.

But all this remains very tenuous hypothesis. And even if there did exist a small body of poetry which involved Briseis, it was surely insignificant, for Homer's Briseis, small a role as she plays in the *Iliad*, seems to have held the day.[14]

Briseis did not fare much better among the Romans. In general, she underwent the transformation reserved by the Romans for Greek mythological characters. Isolating out two facets of the Briseis tale which seemed to them essential or most striking, the Romans made Briseis—or rather, the relationship between her and Achilles—their *exemplum* for (1) the power of love and (2) the love of a man for a social inferior.[15]

Thus, Propertius finds consolation for his own sufferings in love in the example of Achilles who let his arms grow idle, saw his fellow Greeks routed, and his closest friend slain

> omnia formosam propter Briseida passus.
> tantus in erepto saevit amore dolor.
>
> (2.8.35-36)

And Ovid observes that even great heroes were susceptible to love and points to Achilles, *ardet in abducta Briseide maestus Achilles (Am.* 1.9.33).

The other common motif is the love of an inferior. Thus, Hor-

---

[13] Such indeed is Vian's view, *Quintus de Smyrne* 2 (Paris 1966) 50-51.

[14] See Dion. Hal. *Rhet.* 9.13; Lucian, *Im.* 8, *Pr. Imag.* 24; Strab. 13.584. For a discussion of the conflicting reports on Briseis' homeland, which could conceivably reflect different Briseis traditions, see F. Vian, *Recherches sur les Posthomerica de Quintus de Smyrne* (Paris 1959) 125-126.

[15] The latter interpretation may be a Roman innovation. The actual relation of Briseis to Achilles in the *Iliad* is ambiguous. Since she is a captive, one expects her to be a slave, or at least an inferior (witness the position of Eumaeus in the *Odyssey*). However, the statement that Briseis could become Achilles' wife points to her equal status (*Il.* 19.297-299), although one might object that this remark, made by Briseis and in the name of Patroclus, has little objective validity. We may, however, compare Sophocles' Tecmessa, who seems to be both captive slave and respected wife at one and the same time. For discussions of this problem see J. W. Jones, *The Law and Legal Theory of the Greeks* (Oxford 1956) 186 and n. 2, and A.R.W. Harrison, *The Law of Athens* (Oxford 1968) 13.

ace advises a friend not to be ashamed of loving a servant, and looks toward Achilles, *prius insolentem serva Briseis niveo colore movit Achillem* (*C.* 2.4.2-4), and in similar fashion Ovid excuses his own love of a slave, *Thessalus ancillae facie Briseidos arsit* (*Am.* 2.8.11). One can well see that the emphasis in all these passages is on the role played in the relationship by Achilles, and that Briseis is but a secondary and colorless, though necessary, partner.

This of course goes nowhere. If anything, it is regression, in typical Roman fashion—a concession to the death of myth and the *coup de grâce* for the terminal patient.

At any rate, these and the few other allusions to Briseis in Latin poetry are all either derivative from the *Iliad* (e.g., Prop. 2.8.29f; Ov. *Rem. Am.* 475ff) or clearly original with the particular poet (e.g., *Rem. Am.* 777ff).[16]

The iconographic evidence is still harder to interpret. Drawing lines between tradition and individual creativity is often impossible, and it is equally difficult to ascertain where representational and literary traditions coincide. But in certain areas we can see clearly. Briseis is most often shown in scenes of the abduction, the Homeric source being apparent, though individual styles account for a variety of portrayal.[17] A natural extension can be discerned in paintings depicting Briseis brought to Agamemnon, an event implicit, though not described, in the *Iliad*.[18]

In rejecting the traditional interpretation that the *bouclier de Scipion* depicts the restoration of Briseis to Achilles, Bulas rests his case partially on the "fact" that such a scene is never depicted in extant ancient art.[19] Such an argument, not very compelling under any circumstances, proves self-fulfilling when every possible instance is rejected on these grounds. While it may be true

[16] *AA* 3.189-190, however, is a little puzzling. Is the description of Briseis' habit drawn from a painting? There was evidently some kind of tradition of the "fair-skinned" Briseis. See Hor. *C.* 2.4.3; Prop. 2.9.10; Dares 13. Does this go back to the epithet καλλιπάρηος that is usually attached to Briseis' name by Homer?

[17] The most notable deviation from the "standard" abduction scene occurs in Macron's painting (*ARV²* 458.2), which shows Agamemnon himself leading Briseis away from Achilles. There is probably no reason to postulate a literary source, but we should note the possibility that αὐτὸς ἀπούρας (*Il.* 1.356) may imply an alternative version of the tale.

[18] E.g., *ARV²* 406.1.

[19] K. Bulas, *Les Illustrations Antiques de L'Iliade* (Lwow 1929) 82-84.

that we know of no work of art which unquestionably shows Briseis' return to Achilles, there are a few possibilities which suggest that such a scene was not unknown in the ancient iconographic repertoire.[20] Does this attest a tradition other than the *Iliad,* since the latter does not actually describe the delivery of Briseis to Achilles? Perhaps, but it is much more likely that we have here another artistic elaboration of the elliptical scene in Homer.[21]

There is one scene that does not seem explicable in terms of expansion on the Homeric text: Briseis serving wine to Phoenix.[22] One could explain this solely within the Iliadic context since Phoenix, who remains with Achilles after the failure of the embassy in Book Nine, is presumably in his tent when Briseis returns there in Book Nineteen. But this stretches credulity, and one might with some reason think here of an episode from a lost tragedy.

I pass over in silence a few paintings in which Briseis appears only peripherally or as the sole character, for these offer us no help.[23] Indeed, the artistic evidence must point us in the same di-

[20] C. Robert, *Archaeologische Hermeneutik* (Berlin 1919) 358-359, interprets a scene on a black-figure sherd as the restoration of Briseis; see B. Graef, *Die antiken Vasen von der Akropolis zu Athen* 1 (Berlin 1909) nr. 1174; 2 (Berlin 1911) pl. 67. Most likely is *ARV²* 1030.33, a painting by Polygnotus often taken simply as a mourning scene but just as easily understood as the returning of Briseis to Achilles by Talthybius, as indeed Vysoký 27-28 and 34 and Döhle 128 and 131-132 have recently interpreted it. See too A. D. Trendall and T.B.L. Webster, *Illustrations of Greek Drama* (London 1971) 54-55. K. Schauenburg, *BonnJbb* 161 (1961) 221, thinks that *CVA* Lecce 1.4. D r 1 may represent Agamemnon handing over Briseis to Achilles.

[21] Döhle, to be sure, thinks the scene may derive from Aeschylus' *Nereides.* Even were this true, she would have been merely a mute character.

[22] *ARV²* 369.1, 4 according to Beazley. Actually, only 369.1 is inscribed with the names of Briseis and Phoenix. Beazley understands 369.4, a similar scene, as also depicting Briseis and Phoenix, but tentatively interprets 386.3 as Hebe serving Zeus. R. Hampe, in *Corolla L. Curtius*, ed. H. Bulle (Stuttgart 1937) 142ff, thinks the characters in 369.4 more likely to be Priam and Helen.

[23] E.g., *ARV²* 183.8; Polygnotus' Iliupersis (see Paus. 10.25.4). Massei (supra n. 9) 166-167, thinks the woman present in Oltos' representation of Priam ransoming Hector's body (*ARV²* 61.74) may be Briseis. This is no more than conjecture and even if the lady is Briseis this would simply be, as Massei observes, expansion on the Iliadic text. As for the scene on black-figure vases which represents a woman receiving Ajax as he returns with the body of Achilles, there seems no reason to think here of Briseis. See M. Robertson, *CQ* n.s. 19 (1969) 217.

rection as the literary. Briseis undoubtedly had a secure place in representations of the Achilles myth even outside the immediate Homeric context, but evidently never achieved any independent significance in the mythic tradition aside from her role in the *Iliad*.[24]

After much examination we may therefore conclude, with good reason and some confidence, what others have asserted on the basis of little more than intuition and faith in the authority of Homer, that Ovid had no other source than the *Iliad* and that material which does not derive from the epic originates with Ovid himself.

* * *

Though the characters and myths of the *Heroides* are in the main those of tragedy and epic, the language, meter, themes, and motifs are *grosso modo* those of erotic elegy. Though it is in part true that often the success of a particular poem varies in direct proportion to the facility with which Ovid finds a balance between these disparate styles or fuses them into a coherent and blended unity, nevertheless this is a judgment which must not be exaggerated, since many times Ovid deliberately plays off the two styles against each other and the wit, the sense of remove that are found at times in the *Heroides*—though with not nearly the same frequency as in some of his other works—are partially produced by the incompatible juxtaposition of the tragic crisis and the elegiac viewpoint.

The poetic conception of the Briseis letter is among the best in the corpus. Whether execution completely matches conception may be doubted and, if it does not, we shall not go far astray in attributing the failure to the way the erotic element obtrudes upon the tragic, not vice versa. Yet, to observe this and therefore dismiss the poem in abrupt terms (as D'Elia does),[25] is to miss what Ovid *has* accomplished; in fact, it is to ignore what Ovid was trying to achieve.

24 The suggestion of R. Bianchi-Bandinelli, *Hellenistic-Byzantine Miniatures of the Iliad* (Olten 1955) 117-118, that there may have been a "romance of Briseis" in existence in late antiquity goes beyond the evidence. The iconography of Briseis is so limited in its variety that we have reason to believe that she was almost always depicted in connection with the conflict between Achilles and Agamemnon.

25 D'Elia 134.

21

Echoes from erotic elegy are numerous. Some grate on our sensibilities, others do not. What we ought not to miss is how Ovid tries to adapt them to the non-elegiac matter. For the moment a brief survey of the more obvious elegiac elements will suffice.

The tear-stained letter recalls the lovers in Catullus and Propertius (3-4).[26] *Mora* (13) must make the ear attuned to the elegiac vocabulary hear the lover who would stay longer but is unable.[27] At 17 Ovid has wittily turned the hostile *custos* of elegy into a flesh-and-blood soldier who is not quite as easy to deceive (*decepto*) as the traditional *ianitor*.[28] Time viewed as the passage of nights (21) possesses, as Loers has observed, erotic innuendo. Line 26 jars, no matter how often we tell ourselves that this is, after all, elegy. As if Achilles would want *cupidi nomen amantis!* (Are we to think of that one brief section in the *Iliad* where Achilles professes his ability to love a woman, 9.340-343?) Verse 42, at least, is more in keeping with the general circumstances. Again, at 111ff, Briseis accuses Achilles, *inter alia*, of being faithless to her. The fact is indeed imbedded in the *Iliad* (9.186ff, 664f), but the evaluation, perspective and judgment are elegiac. The phraseology, vocabulary, and sense of 138, *nec miseram lenta ferreus ure mora*, are elegiac, and fortunately not unsuited to the situation.

Granted that this elegiac matter is substantial, it remains true that most of the poem cannot, strictly speaking, be designated simply as erotic elegy. To be sure, had Ovid wanted to reshape the Achilles-Briseis tale, psychologically and poetically, as elegy, he could have done so easily—the basic plan of the rejection of one lover by the other was accessible in the myth—but the end product would not have been this poem.

In spite of her pivotal role in the *Iliad*, as a character Briseis remains vague and undeveloped. Since Greek poets seem to have ignored her potential for fuller realization and their Roman counterparts by and large saw her as a paradigm, Ovid had virgin soil to sow, little standing between him and Homer. He may well have seen himself as the creator of Briseis by virtue of his endowing her with a complete and psychologically suitable character that she lacks in the *Iliad*. In so doing it is remarkable how

[26] See Prop. 4.3.3-4; Cat. 68.2; Ov. *Tr.* 1.1.13-14.
[27] See Tib. 1.3.16, 1.8.74; Prop. 1.13.6.
[28] See Plaut. *Mil.* 146; Tib. 1.2.15, 1.6.9-10; Prop. 2.6.37; Ov. *AA* 2.635.

he utilizes (one might say, exhausts) every event, every remark in the *Iliad* which bears, even indirectly, on Briseis.

Quam legis, a rapta Briseide littera venit (1). We become immediately aware of the personal involvement of the writer and realize that the perspective from which the Homeric events will unfold is far different from that of the *Iliad*.[29] We will be viewing those familiar events of the epic not through the eyes of the objective poet but through those of one intimately, though in a sense tangentially, involved. As Fränkel well remarks,[30] "The perspective is changed by causing the glorious events to be seen from the point of view of a mere accessory, a person who in the ancient epic played only a minor and passive part; in the *Iliad*, Briseis had nothing to say and was no more than an object of transactions between the great kings."

It is in their tone that the opening verses are remarkable, for the anger that one anticipates—Briseis is after all *rapta*—is lacking, and in its stead we sense rather a defensive posture. Apologies dominate. *Vix bene barbarica Graeca notata manu* (2), "My Greek is none too good; I am after all a foreigner" (writing a Greek letter in Latin and calling attention to the fact is typical of Ovid's wit. If we recall Plautus' use of *barbarus*, this may even be a slap against himself—humorous, of course—on Ovid's part). The juxtaposition of *barbarica Graeca* reveals her consciousness of the gap between herself and Achilles. Her inability to write well in his language because she is a non-Greek is a manifestation of the difference between them. He is a Greek and a ruler, she a barbarian and a slave.

Quascumque adspicies lacrimae fecere lituras (3), "excuse me if anything is blotted; I've been crying." Such a paraphrase seems to represent the force of this line. More follows. Complaint is tempered by reservation. *Si mihi . . . fas est* (5-6), "if you don't mind, I'd like to complain"—but only a bit (*pauca*). She knows her place; Achilles is addressed as *dominoque viroque* (5, 6). He is first and foremost her *dominus*, only secondarily her *vir*.[31]

---

[29] Note *rapta*. Briseis is usually *abducta* (Prop. 2.20.1; Ov. *Rem. Am.* 777, *Am.* 1.9.33; but cf. *AA* 3.190), a description more suitable for the Homeric scene.

[30] Fränkel 43.

[31] We ought to note how purposeful is the epanalepsis (5-10), for which Lachmann condemned the epistle. The verbatim repetition of the *si* clause in the apodosis displays her meekness: if she is allowed, she will do *this*,

The substance of her complaint is revealing in its contorted phraseology:

> non, ego poscenti quod sum cito tradita regi,
>> culpa tua est—quamvis haec quoque culpa tua est.
>>> (7-8)

She again wavers between her desire to condemn Achilles and her realization that her status does not allow her to do so. This inner confusion and conflict is reflected in her confused expression. What she wants to say is clear: "it is not your fault for turning me over to Agamemnon, but you should not have done it so quickly." Thus, we might have expected something like (unmetrically) *non culpa tua est quod sum tradita regi, sed quod cito tradita sum*. But she is perplexed and upset and so lets slip too early what disturbs her most, *cito*. Thus, she has in fact stated what she does not mean, that she does not think it Achilles' fault for giving her up so readily. She is then compelled to backtrack, and this she does by adding *quamvis haec quoque culpa tua est*. But the complexity goes further. Why does *ego* anticipate its clause and, indeed, what is the emphatic pronoun doing here at all? The answer is that *ego* "goes with" *sum tradita* only to satisfy rules of syntax.[32] In point of fact, we should not consider *ego* the subject of the subordinate clause. We have here an anacoluthon. *Ego* begins as the subject of the main clause, which Briseis intends as a strong statement, e.g. (unmetrically) *non ego te culpo, quamquam alii te culpant* (a variation of the sentiment expressed at *Her.* 12.133), but she feels the pressures and tones down her remarks to the mild *non ... /culpa tua est—quamvis haec quoque culpa tua est.*

---

precisely this, and no more; repetition reflects in line 8 her hesitant change of mind and in lines 9-10 the immediacy of the event, without interruption or wavering on Achilles' part.

[32] It is surprising that no one has observed the strange and meaningful position of *ego*. Though I have noticed many examples of sentences beginning with *non ego*, I do not know a single instance in which the *non* does not go with the *ego*. A number of examples from Latin poetry can be found in Pease's note *ad Aen.* 4.425. A similar placement of the pronoun at 7.33, *aut ego quem coepi—neque enim dedignor—amare,/ materiam curae praebeat ille meae*, on which Dörrie (137), has appropriately commented, "man müsste erwarten, dass *ego* Subject im folgenden Hauptsatze wäre," has (*inter alia*) caused that eminent scholar to consider the verse corrupt.

24

3. Briseis

In such a way are the tone of the letter and the character of Briseis set early. Although the apologetic disposition is softened in the rest of the letter, it is still present, especially in the concessions Briseis constantly makes in her complaints and pleas. "If you go, take me with you," she cries (67-68), but immediately qualifies this, *victorem captiva sequar, non nupta maritum* (69), "I'll even go as a captive slave." Another demand, *exagitet ne me tantum tua, deprecor, uxor* (77) is again retracted, *vel patiare licet*. Later, a plea for Achilles to heed her as his wife (91-92, 97-98) is followed by her admission that she is not his *coniunx*, only his *serva* (99-100). Her oath of fidelity (103-110) again shows Briseis on the defensive, for it is clearly on Agamemnon that guilt must fall, and it is on his shoulders that the burden of an oath must rest (as it does in the *Iliad*). The self-deprecating *hoc animae* (142) is also characteristic. Finally, the last line sounds familiar notes with its threefold emphasis: *domini iure . . . iube*. She remains no more than a helpless and utterly dependent slave, her very life at the whim of her master's legitimate command.

Ovid manipulates the Homeric material, adding, eliminating, and modifying as he sees fit. Eight lines embrace the departure scene, and viewed through Briseis' eyes it is rather different from that of the *Iliad*:

> Nam simul Eurybates me Talthybiusque vocarunt,
> Eurybati data sum Talthybioque comes.
> Alter in alterius iactantes lumina vultum
> Quaerebant taciti, noster ubi esset amor.
> Differri potui; poenae mora grata fuisset.
> Ei mihi! discedens oscula nulla dedi!
> At lacrimas sine fine dedi rupique capillos;
> infelix iterum sum mihi visa capi.

(9-16)

Verses 11-12 are among the best known in the *Heroides*. Wilkinson calls the couplet a "good and characteristic touch," and Tolkiehn has perceptively understood the Ovidian technique here operative.[33] Homer describes no such occurrence, but Ovid's invention is nevertheless firmly founded in the Iliadic text, where Achilles does not object (1.298f), and the heralds are perhaps surprised, for they must be urged on (329ff). We ought to

---

[33] Wilkinson 90; Tolkiehn 54.

note in passing that, although this surely is, as Wilkinson says, "a characteristic touch," the pictorial element may be significant, for it appears that there were artists who in much the same way invested the heralds with more life than Homer had given them.[34] But what is truly interesting here is that this remark, Briseis' interpretation of the nonverbal behavior of others, represents in fact her own feelings. As a psychologist would say, she projects. More, Ovid's Briseis does not appear as the stolid, impassive, and resigned heroine who goes from Achilles ἀέκουσα, but she graphically and physically displays her feelings of helplessness, loss, and insecurity.[35]

These verses begin to point up Briseis' personality and her relationship to Achilles. We get a glimpse of the depths of her helplessness and her need for him. She dreads life without Achilles. Ovid has with subtlety and insight molded Briseis' character in accord with her personal history. Her homeland has been destroyed and sacked, her family, including brothers and husband, wiped out, she herself taken captive. Her one comfort and solace was Achilles' kindness and support (51-54). But Ovid is well aware that such an experience must have been a traumatic one, with permanent scars left on Briseis' heart and in her memory. Indeed, he portrays her throughout as a ghost-haunted and past-obsessed personality. The ways she talks, feels, thinks, and acts are all determined by certain ineradicable events of her past. She conceives of her very existence as an offshoot of that horrible experience, *nostram, tua munera, vitam* (149). Her dead kin recur in dissimilar contexts (47ff, 103ff, 143). In fact, the extraordinary frequency of occurrence of nouns denoting one form of kinship or another may be attributable to *ethopoeia*. The loss of her kin makes Briseis especially sensitive to familial relationships and their value. A brief glance will reveal, among others, the nouns *natus, satus, coniunx, mater, vir, maritus, socer, nepos, prosocer* (only here in Ovid), *uxor, frater, parens, pater,* some more than

---

[34] The famous Pompeian wall painting of the abduction scene (see E. Pfuhl, *Malerei und Zeichnung der Griechen* 3 [Munich 1923] pl. 655; Engl. tr. [London 1926] fig. 122) shows the heralds, in Pfuhl's words, "looking . . . with puzzled expression" (Engl. tr. 102).

[35] At *Il.* 1.348 Briseis goes ἀέκουσα, while Achilles is described as weeping after she leaves. Homer is basically interested in Achilles, Ovid however in Briseis. Thus, when Achilles cries, Thetis comes to comfort him and asks, τί κλαίεις; (362). In Ovid it is Briseis who needs solace, and so Patroclus comes and consoles her, beginning *quid fles?* (24).

once. Noteworthy too is the emphatic *parens* (94), where stress is gained both by position and by the apparent superfluity of the noun. Here our attention is focused at beginning, middle, and end of the scene on the act as a perverted relationship, *fratribus . . . nati . . . parens*. Earlier, the legates were described in strange terms,

> Telamone et Amyntore nati,
> ille gradu propior sanguinis, ille comes,
> Laertaque satus.

(27-29)

None are named, all are designated "children of," with the added exposition of Ajax' kinship to Achilles. In Book Nine of the *Iliad* both Odysseus and Ajax are referred to by their patronymics and Phoenix mentions his father Amyntor,[36] but this will not do to explain Ovid's phrasing, for were he simply echoing or imitating the epic he would surely have used the patronymics (as he does elsewhere).[37] We should, I venture to suggest, understand the explicit terms *nati* and *satus* as a manner of speaking characteristic of Briseis, who tends to see people in their roles as kin.[38]

To return: When Briseis is taken from Achilles she sees her past repeating itself, *infelix iterum sum mihi visa capi* (16). Just as she had once lost everything that had significance for her in the destruction of her city and the murder of her family, so now she is again deprived of all that has meaning for her by her abduction from Achilles. Even her physical response, *at lacrimas sine fine dedi rupique capillos* (15), is appropriate to the tragedy of loss of home and family.[39] For a second time she is cut off from

[36] *Il.* 9.308, 448, 623, 644.

[37] *Amyntorides* (*AA* 1.337), *Telamoniades* (*Met.* 13.231), *Telamonius* (*AA* 2.737), *Laertiades* (*Met* 13.48).

[38] *Satus*, indeed, is found only here in the *Heroides*. However, in the *armorum iudicium* episode of the *Metamorphoses* Ajax and Odysseus are introduced with these words: *solis Telamone creato/ Laerteque fuit tantae fiducia laudis* (12.624-625), and a little later Ajax is referred to as *Telamone satus* (13.123) and *Telamone creatus* (13.346). These examples suffice to demonstrate that there may be no ethopoeic significance in these three verses, and if they were isolated instances I would hesitate to build upon them. But given the "extraneous" *ille gradu propior sanguinis* (28) and the numerous kinship nouns throughout the poem we are perhaps entitled to see in these verses something more than a stylistic habit of Ovid's.

[39] See, e.g., *Il.* 22.405-411; Eur. *Tro.* 793ff. Briseis' perception of her life as tragic history repeating itself may account for the non-Homeric scene at 23-24

the people and places which lend her life meaning and security. Her largest feeling is that of fear, fear that she will again be deserted, and she appeals to Achilles as one on whom she can be dependent, one who, she feels, has a real interest in her. In some sense her anger toward Achilles for giving her up so casually is a corollary of this: she feels betrayed (53-54).

Briseis' disposition to visualize the events of her life in terms of her original captivity accounts for the manner of expression—often misunderstood—in verses 17-20. Naylor has observed that *custode* refers to her Greek guard, *hostis* to a Greek soldier, and *caperer* to capture by a Trojan.[40] True, but what is crucial here and determines Briseis' choice of words is her continuing fear of once again undergoing that—for her—archetypal trauma, capture (*prenderet, caperer*). And so, in this self-contained world, Briseis sees even the Greeks as her enemy. These verses have been condemned by Palmer as feeble, and his objection has some merit. But the feebleness is Briseis', not Ovid's. For these remarks on her frustrated desire to escape are fitting, almost necessary, products of her character. Her weakness compels her to see a potential, if ridiculous, objection to her position: "If you are so interested in being with me, why haven't you escaped and returned to me?" In defense, she claims that she has intended to escape, but cannot do so.

Let us return to the enumeration of gifts (31-38 and *Il.* 9.122ff). In Briseis' mouth it rings of her character. *Operoso ex aere* and *pondere et arte pares* reflect her feminine awe and wonder at the quality of these items, while *quodque supervacuum est* and *sed non opus est tibi coniuge* represent a reaction which is partly jealous anger and partly earnest pleading. Her confusion is strikingly present in the juxtaposition of *quodque supervacuum est* and *forma praestante puellae*, the former phrase necessitated by her role as rival, the latter by her role as advocate. On 35-38 Amar's remarks (quoted by Loers) are worth repeating: "muliebriter, nec sine invidia: terrent enim Lesbides puellae, quae

---

where Patroclus, on Briseis' abduction, tries to comfort and cheer her. In the *Iliad* he does indeed do so, but on the occasion of her capture by Achilles. Since, however, Patroclus' words of comfort have become indelibly etched in Briseis' mind as an integral part of that event, so here, when tragedy repeats itself, Patroclus is again present to offer words of consolation.

[40] H. D. Naylor, "The Alleged Hyperbaton of *Heroides* 3.19," *CR* 25 (1911) 42.

forma praestant, terret magis *ex Agamemnoniis una puella tribus,* quae *coniux* Achilli ab Atrida offertur; quia non opus est illi *coniuge,* qui habeat Briseida. Omnia haec ingeniose et vere atque e natura loquentis."

Finally, the description of the Lesbian girls in Homer[41] is accompanied by a straightforward and perfectly factual description of their capture by Achilles: Λεσβίδας, ἃς, ὅτε Λέσβον ἐϋκτιμένην ἕλεν αὐτός, / ἐξελόμην (*Il.* 9.129-130). In Briseis' mouth this becomes a pathetic and tragic observation, filled with emotional overtones: *eversa corpora capta domo* (36). The homes and families of these girls have been destroyed, they are no longer people, just bodies. As Burman rightly remarks, "In servitutem enim redacti vix hominum nomine digni, *corpora* tantum vocabantur" (quoted by Loers). Although these girls are her potential rivals, Briseis can regard them with such broad sympathy and understanding because she feels herself at one with them. Both she and they have undergone the same tragedy at Achilles' hands—loss of home, captivity, and treatment as pawns in the affairs of kings.[42]

Briseis' autobiographical remarks, also adapted from the *Iliad,* are preceded by a series of questions, or rather accusations cloaked in question form, for again she hesitates to attack Achilles directly. The final question,

> an miseros tristis fortuna tenaciter urget
> nec venit inceptis mollior hora meis?
>
> (43-44)

serving as transition from her present to her past misfortune, comes from *Il.* 19.290, ὥς μοι δέχεται κακὸν ἐκ κακοῦ αἰεί, where it also immediately precedes Briseis' account of her past. The verbal imitations are notable: εἶδον (292)/*vidi* (45, 47, 49), the last two, like their Greek model, at the beginning of the verse; τρεῖς τε κασιγνήτους, τούς μοι μία γείνατο μήτηρ (293)/*tres cecidisse: Tribus, quae mihi, mater erat* (48). Yet Ovid, again concerned with the characterization of Briseis, has reshaped the Homeric verses.

---

41 A familiar passage in antiquity. Witness Pherecrates' parody (Kock, *Com. Att. Frag.* 1.192, fr. 149) and Philostratus' reminiscence (*Imag.* 2.2).

42 Verses 39-40 have, strangely, been misunderstood by Wilkinson (91), who writes, "Could he not have accepted the other gifts and used them to ransom her?" The meaning is rather that Achilles should even have been willing to give all these gifts to Agamemnon to recover her.

In this account of the destruction of her city and the slaying of her family the emphasis throughout is on her direct and personal experience of the catastrophe: *vidi* (45), *fueram* (46), *vidi* (47), *vidi* (49). That she saw all this occur right before her eyes greatly increased her suffering,[43] and in *Marte tuo* (45) she casts the blame on Achilles, and thereby suggests his great obligation to her. Though the note of pride in line 46, *et fueram patriae pars ego magna meae*, does not seem to suit the tone of the letter, its purpose is clear. By emphasizing her close relationship to her country, she magnifies her pain and suffering at its fall. Further, the line is, as has often been noted,[44] an imitation of Verg. *Aen.* 2.5f, *quaeque ipse miserrima vidi/ et quorum pars magna fui.* Briseis (anachronistically) is aligned with Aeneas, for they both lose spouse, home, and country at the hands of the Greeks.

In her description (45-51), marked by a series of first-person verbs to stress her own involvement, there is an emotional progression: she moves from the destruction of her city (45-46) to the slaying of her brothers (47-48) to the murder of her husband (49-50). Though the scope of the catastrophe narrows with each succeeding distich, the personal horror for Briseis correspondingly increases.

An explicit declaration of her feelings reveals Briseis' conception of her relationship to Achilles (51-52). Till now it had only been implicit. Achilles is a substitute for all her losses, he is the only person or thing she can depend on, he keeps her from feeling totally alone and abandoned. Further, if in line 46 Briseis finds a connection between herself and Aeneas, in lines 51-52 she finds one between herself and Andromache, and with good reasons, though with ironic differences. The verbal reminiscence is clear and deliberate.[45] Both Briseis and Andromache can make this kind of declaration because they have both lost their families in war; indeed, they have both had their families destroyed by Achilles. But the irony in Briseis' adopting Andromache's position is all too evident, for whereas Andromache finds consolation in Hector, Briseis must find solace in the very man who has caused all her sorrows. Moreover, Andromache is afraid of losing her husband and tries to draw him away from the fighting, while

---

[43] The idea of visual experience as intensifying suffering occurs again at line 66: *et videam puppes ire relicta tuas.*

[44] See Palmer *ad loc.*

[45] *Il.* 6.429-430. The echo is noted by, among others, Loers *ad loc.*

Briseis fears being deserted by Achilles, and tries to persuade him to return to the battle.

The influence of the Iliadic restoration scene is yet more extensive. In the *Iliad* it is Briseis' big, virtually only, scene, and Ovid takes care to utilize it to maximum effect. We mentioned earlier Briseis' agony and self-mutilation on being torn from Achilles, a scene which has no parallel in Homer. Actually, this is the way Briseis acts upon viewing Patroclus' corpse, and Ovid has transferred this behavior of hers to a different context. In that Homeric mourning episode Briseis concludes by describing Patroclus' kindness to her at the time of her city's fall. He comforted her, told her not to cry, and promised to make her Achilles' wife (*Il.* 19.295-299). Ovid has taken this occurrence also and made it part of the abduction scene (24), representing Patroclus as comforting her, telling her not to cry, and assuring her that she will soon be back with Achilles. Ovid echoes Homer's οὐδὲ μὲν οὐδέ μ' ἔασκες . . . κλαίειν (*Il.* 19.295-297) in direct speech, *quid fles?* (24). Furthermore, by moving this scene of consolation from the time of her city's destruction to the moment of her abduction from Achilles, Ovid has left open the conclusion of the former episode. He then gives it a different ending. Briseis, after seeing her family destroyed, is indeed consoled, but it is by Achilles himself, not by Patroclus: *utile dicebas ipse fuisse capi* (54). Ovid—or Briseis—has deliberately given this act of kindness to Achilles because it emphasizes, by contrast, the baseness of his present behavior. It stresses his responsibility to her as established by his own actions and words.

For perhaps the most striking and artful manipulation of Homer we return to the embassy episode. Briseis identifies and empathizes with the ambassadors because she and they are striving toward the same end, the persuasion of Achilles. Like Phoenix, she tells the Meleager story to convince him. It is with good and insightful reason that Ovid has Briseis align herself most closely with Phoenix, of the three men. For he is closest to Achilles (cf. *Il.* 9.438-443 and *Her.* 3.28, *comes*, which is echoed by *comitata* at 3.29). He will accomplish what Briseis wants, should Achilles resolve to return to Greece. *Si tibi iam reditusque placent patriique Penates,/ non ego sum classi sarcina magna tuae* (67-68) echoes the sentiments of Phoenix, who, when Achilles declares his intentions of going home, says that he desires to go with him (*Il.* 9.434-438). But, perhaps most important, Phoenix, like

Briseis, has experienced deep tragedy within the confines of his own family (*Il.* 9.447-457), and for Phoenix, as for Briseis, Achilles represents a surrogate kin (cf. *Il.* 9.494-495; *Her.* 3.52).[46]

Before beginning the Meleager narrative, Phoenix urges Achilles: δάμασον θυμὸν μέγαν (*Il.* 9.496). Briseis, in imitation, also anticipates the Meleager tale with the words: *vince animos iramque tuam* (85). On the Meleager section Wilkinson well remarks,[47] "Ovid has an advantage, for the tale is doubly effective in the mouth of a 'wife' herself." But one can go further. Ovid has not simply taken the same tale and put it in Briseis' mouth. He has changed the point, the essence, the whole purpose of the narrative of the Meleager story. Phoenix' "moral" of the story is that Achilles should learn from the example and not act as Meleager did, for Meleager delayed too long and lost all the gifts he could have received. Phoenix thinks Achilles should allow himself to be persuaded by the prospect of great material benefits (602-605). Briseis takes the same story and makes a completely different point. In effect, she proclaims that Achilles *should* follow the example of Meleager, and she strengthens her advice by focusing on aspects of the story which for Phoenix were secondary, and by ignoring the parts of the story which are irrelevant to her purpose. Thus, she does not mention that Meleager forfeited his gifts by the long delay, and strongly emphasizes the fact that it was his wife who finally persuaded him to fight (*sola*, 97), even though in Phoenix' tale it is clear that the extreme circumstances (the burning of the city) influenced Meleager to return to the battle as much as did his wife's pleas. Moreover, Briseis, though magnifying the role of Meleager's wife, must avoid mentioning the latter's arguments, for they are calculated to spur on the defense of one's own city, while she desires Achilles to adopt the part of aggressor. Also, whereas Phoenix points to potential advantage,

[46] I so interpret in spite of the fact that Ovid only alludes to Phoenix' past in the reference to Amyntor. Ovid's reading of the embassy episode is clearly close and careful, and Phoenix' autobiographical narrative would not have been without its effect on him. Further, Phoenix' family tragedy was so well known, both through the *Iliad* and through many plays written on this subject (by Sophocles, Astydamas, Ion, Euripides, and Ennius; witness the echo of Euripides' debate scene between Phoenix and Amyntor in Menander's *Samia*. See Webster 85 and C. Dedoussi, *The Samia of Menander* [Athens 1965] 48-49) that Ovid may have virtually taken the reader's response for granted.

[47] P. 92.

Briseis must remind Achilles that there is no disgrace involved in heeding her (*nec tibi turpe puta*, 91). There are still other variations in the Ovidian version, these stemming from differences in characterization. Phoenix' description of Althaea is lengthy and perhaps a bit harsh (566-572), while Briseis' is more sympathetic, as can be seen by the solitary descriptive phrase *fratribus orba* (93). Briseis can sympathize with Althaea, since she knows what it means to lose one's brothers. Meleager, on the other hand, whom she identifies with Achilles, is described much more harshly than in Phoenix' speech (e.g., *ferox, rigida mente, patriae . . . negavit opem*, 95-96).

We should not see these alterations of fact and emphasis purely as persuasive devices. We shall be closer to the truth if, rather than asserting that Briseis changes the tale to suit her purposes, we realize that in a sense Briseis' version represents how she hears the story, how it impresses itself upon the mind of a person in her circumstances.

The oath which Agamemnon is prepared to take, that he has not slept with Briseis, also forms part of the embassy episode (*Il.* 9.274-276). It is rather straightforward and direct.[48] In Briseis' mouth it becomes elaborate, and symbolizes the paradox and tragedy of her life. She is the mistress of the very man who murdered her husband and brothers. She swears to him by their bones and souls, but they are dead only because of him. Moreover, their bones by which she swears have not received a proper burial, again because of Achilles. She reveres her husband's bones, but she lives with his murderer. Her brothers *bene pro patria cum patriaque iacent* (106) at the hands of a man who refuses to fight on behalf of his people. She swears by his sword, the very sword with which he destroyed her family. One can scarcely refrain from thinking that Briseis is here identified with another victim of Achilles, Priam, who in pleading with Achilles finds himself compelled to kiss the hands which slew his son (*Il.* 24.505f).[49]

[48] The actual oath is more involved (*Il.* 19.258ff).

[49] This comparison is made by L. P. Wilkinson, "Greek Influence on the Poetry of Ovid," in *L'influence Grecque sur la Poésie Latine de Catulle à Ovide* (Fond. Hardt, *Entretiens* 2 [1953]) 230. It is instructive to compare Sophocles' Tecmessa, another captive who identifies with Andromache and dreads the future without her master/husband (see esp. *Aj.* 485-524). But Ovid sees the heart of Briseis' tragedy in her living with the very man who

The same pathos is present in her plea to Achilles (135-138), qualified by a conditional prayer, *sic omnes Peleus pater impleat annos,/ sic eat auspiciis Pyrrhus ad arma tuis.* She prays for the welfare of his closest relatives, for she, having lost hers, fully appreciates their import.[50]

* * *

Although Briseis is not depicted as thoroughly weak and inept, still her attempts at assertiveness and her expressions of anger are few and usually reserved, as we have seen, for example, at verses 5ff. In verses 21-42 she comes closest to outright anger, though even here it is tempered. *Pugnas ne reddar, Achille* (25) is beautifully and bitterly sarcastic, since this would then appear to be the only fighting Achilles does. The catalogue of gifts serves as an integral part of her condemnation of Achilles, who now, it seems, cares so little for her that he refuses such a wealth of gifts and Briseis as well. This is another interesting twist given to Homeric material; in the *Iliad* the recounting of gifts is part of an attempt to persuade Achilles. Here, in Briseis' mouth and following on Achilles' rejection, they serve to intensify his guilt.

At mea pro nullo pondere verba cadunt (98). In these words is summed up Briseis' sense of utter helplessness. Nor can she even become angry (*nec tamen indignor*); after all, she is but a slave (*serva*), a point hammered home by the ironic juxtaposition of *dominam captiva* (101).

In verses 111ff Briseis seems to wax bolder and to accuse Achilles. But Fränkel's remarks get to the heart of the matter: "Seizing upon his immense pride, she tries to rouse him to action by taunts of which she does not mean one word seriously."[51]

---

has slain her family, while Sophocles seems to go out of his way to represent Ajax as innocent of the murder of Tecmessa's kin (see Jebb on 516-517 and Stanford on 515-516). Consider, too, Eur. *Andr.* 170-173, where Hermione rebukes Andromache for living with the son of her husband's murderer. Another Euripidean heroine, Merope (in the *Cresphontes*), is apparently married, like Briseis, to her former husband's murderer. She, however, hates him and in the end helps in the plot to kill him.

[50] Strikingly, at *Il.* 19.321ff, Achilles laments that the loss of Patroclus afflicts him more than the death of his father or son would. I think it likely Ovid had these lines in his mind when writing lines 135-136, especially since they follow hard upon the mourning scene of Briseis which he utilized so fully in this poem.

[51] P. 44.

These are not accusations arising from jealousy. They are re-proofs designed to shame Achilles into returning to the war. The language renders this perfectly clear. Note the sarcastic *fortissime* (111), a bitter and ironic contrast to the *fortes animas* of 105, *pugnare recuses* (115), *pugna nocet* (116), *tutius est* (117), *placebant* (121) and *dulcis erat* (122), both bitter past tenses, *laus tua victa iacet* (124). All this is a stratagem in Briseis' attempt to persuade Achilles.

There is no real feeling of affection or concern in this letter, in spite of references to *amor* (42, 139) and superficially jealous accusations (111ff).[52] The key to the relationship between Achilles and Briseis must be sought in such language as *o miseram!—cui me, violente, relinquis* (61), *quis mihi desertae mite levamen erit?* (62), in *relicta* (66) and the whole section 67-76. Briseis fears abandonment; she needs a *levamen*,[53] someone to furnish her with a sense of security and attachment, someone tied to her in a bond of warmth and concern. Though she would prefer Achilles as husband or lover, she views him as essentially a support, and so is willing to go as a household slave.[54] But she has one reservation: neither Achilles nor his wife may mock her (77-80). Line 78, *quae mihi nescio quo non erit aequa modo*, with its brilliant, almost paranoid, *nescio quo modo*, subtly reveals Briseis' feeling that she is always mistreated. But this added sense of pride and desire for recognition as a person gives way in line 81 to her primary concern, not to be deserted. Thus fear, not jealousy or anger, is her predominant emotion.[55]

[52] Fränkel's observation (44) on lines 57ff, "Her genuine devotion comes into the open in a passage where she tells of the cruel shock she received when she learned that Achilles had threatened to sail the next morning," is surely a misinterpretation. Briseis has very little devotion to Achilles. Her interest is mostly self-interest, and her concern is for herself. It is not love or devotion to Achilles which causes her shock on hearing that he intends to leave, but rather her fear that she will be deserted.

[53] *Levamen* is instructive. It is not part of the erotic-elegiac vocabulary, but is rather associated with serious loss and suffering. In elegy it is found only at Cat. 68.61 (in a simile) and at Prop. 4.11.63, where it is used of the comfort the dead Cornelia finds in her children.

[54] What seems like a topos or mere rhetoric (cf. Cat. 64.158ff; Eur. fr. 132N²; *Il.* 3.409; *Ciris* 443ff—the latter references from Kroll *ad* Cat. 64.158-163) abruptly comes to life when we pause and realize that this is of course a statement of fact. Briseis is *captiva* to Achilles' *victor*.

[55] Note *timidam* (18), *timebam* (19), *pavidas* (59), *metus* (82), *sollicitam* (137).

Her final attempts at persuasion are founded on threats (139ff).
If he fails to reclaim her, he will be responsible for her death. She
will fade away and die (141-142), or will commit suicide (143-
144), or will bid him to kill her (145-148). This last is important.
Why does Briseis call upon Achilles to kill her? Suicide will do
well enough. The motivation is that which governs all her hopes,
wishes, and actions, her desire not to feel alone and meaningless.
Even the act of killing her would show that he does have some
feelings toward her. Line 146, *est mihi qui fosso pectore sanguis
eat*, demonstrates her fear that Achilles no longer knows or cares
that she is "alive." It is an assertion of the existence of her person,
of her reality. The emphatic placing of *me* (147) is to the same
end, as is also the description of Achilles' sword as the one which
threatened Agamemnon, for to be slain by that famous sword
(note *ille*, 147) which almost killed the leader of the Greeks
would be a strong affirmation of her existence and significance as
a human being.[56]

Perhaps the most vivid indication of how Ovid has avoided an
essentially amatory relationship within an erotic-elegiac context
comes in lines 113-122, a passage which has in fact many erotic
elements. In these lines Briseis tries to shame Achilles into returning to the battle by accusing him of unseemly behavior—playing
the lyre, enjoying himself with his mistress, and in sum preferring these activities because they are safer than warfare, for
whose glory and honor he no longer cares. Could one get farther
from the world of love elegy? It is, quite naturally, one of the
most common and important motifs of this genre that war is the
antithesis of love, and that the lover scorns the fame of war for
the safety and joy of a quiet life at home with his girl and other
amusements.[57] A true *puella* of elegy would never want her lover

[56] We might compare Achaemenides' request to be slain in the *Aeneid*;
for him death by human hands will serve to restore his dignity (3.606). Since
I have been at pains to show how well Ovid knew his Homer and how
carefully and purposefully he utilized him, I deem it only fair to point out
in line 147 what may be a slip on Ovid's part: *si dea passa fuisset*. In the
Iliad (1.198) only Achilles sees Athene; no one else, including Briseis, is aware
of her intervention. A small point, and Ovid seems to have forgotten it. Unless, of course, this is Ovid's witty way of informing us that Achilles told
Briseis about the goddess' intervention.

[57] See e.g., Tib. 1.1.53-58, 1.10.25-32; Prop. 1.6.29-30, 3.5.1-2. That Ovid
here effectively inverts the elegiac motif to underscore the necessary abnormality of a "love" relationship between Achilles and Briseis can best be seen

to go off to war and fight. Briseis, however, must call upon war, the enemy of love, to reestablish her relationship with Achilles.

As noted earlier, the letter ends with a return to Briseis' prime concern. It matters little whether Achilles stays or goes, or whether he restores Briseis to her position as mistress and again loves her. Her single abiding concern is not to be abandoned: *domini iure venire iube* (154). Palmer translates, "by an owner's right." She will gladly go as a slave. Her only wish is that he take her with him.

In so characterizing Briseis Ovid has remained within the limits, and built upon the foundation, of the *Iliad*. Achilles has been her solace and comfort, her one source of security since her family and home were destroyed, so it is natural for her to feel dependent on him. But what kind of love could she feel for the man who ravaged her land, murdered her closest kin, and turned her into a slave? Little, and certainly not unalloyed.

We ought not to miss the possibility that Briseis' defensiveness, her obsession with kin, and her "death-wish" at the poem's end are all indications of a sense of guilt, understandable in one who has survived when all her family has been slain, and who has then served and loved the man responsible for the tragedy.[58]

* * *

As so often in Ovid, formal elements of the poetry contribute to the overall purpose, here the characterization of Briseis. Briseis strongly feels that she never acts, but is constantly acted upon, that she is not treated as a person, but as a tool, a pawn in the affairs of others. This is brought out by the frequent use of passive verb forms, which repeatedly suggest that she is invariably an object acted upon. Note, e.g., *tradita* (7), *visa capi* (16),

---

by comparing 117-118 with *Am.* 2.11.31-32, *tutius est fovisse torum, legisse libellos,/ Threiciam digitis increpuisse lyram.* The lines are virtually the same, but they make points that are diametrically opposed. In the *Amores* the sentiment is direct and means what it says, whereas in Briseis' mouth the sarcasm reverses the natural sense of the words. For the general incompatibility of love and war see *Am.* 3.8.9-22.

58 For a brief summary of the concept of survival-guilt as evidenced in the survivors of Hiroshima and the concentration camps see R. J. Lifton, *Death in Life* (New York 1967) 56. As guilt attaching itself to a person who forms ties with an enemy of the family, see again Eur. *Andr.* 170-173.

data, danda (21), *repetor* (22), *tradebar* (23), *reddar* (25), *redimenda* (39), *fieri* (41), *scindi* (79), *relinquar* (81). When in lines 129-134 she waxes bolder for a moment, it is Achilles' verb that is in the passive *(comminuere,* 134). But we end, as we began, in the earlier vein: *destituor* (143), *iussa* (144).[59]

The unusual frequency with which *me* and *mihi* recur in this epistle also points up her existence as an object acted upon, rather than as an acting person. This sense of being a thing, not a person, is illustrated at line 152, where Briseis implicitly refers to herself as *materia,* and probably best of all at line 68, where she designates herself mere *sarcina.* Finally, the many questions that are posed in the poem manifest the fear, insecurity, and helplessness which characterize her.

We have yet to touch on an important theme of the letter, one which is complex and varied. This is the conflict or discrepancy between words and action, speech and behavior, the verbal and the concrete. It is largely concerned with the futility and deceitfulness of verbal expression and the truth and power of actions and deeds. One can readily understand why this is of such relevance and importance to Briseis. The most significant events of her life have been uniquely and totally embodiments of actions devoid of reason and impervious to persuasion: her home destroyed, her family murdered, she herself captured and taken prisoner. Further, she has seen how little efficacy and truth words have. The embassy could not persuade Achilles, though their arguments seemed good. She had received a promise from Achilles that she would enjoy life with him (53-54), but he turned her over to Agamemnon. Patroclus told her that she would soon return to Achilles' tent (23-24), but this has not come true. She knows from experience the great difference between word and deed.

The opening paragraph (1-4) makes the point clearly, vividly, and effectively. She apologizes for her inability to write well, but notes *lacrimae pondera vocis habent.* Her words, she knows, will be ineffectual, but her tears, the concrete result of a physical act which discloses her inner emotions, do have weight, and she hopes they will have effect. At lines 11-12, the heralds do not say

---

[59] In two places *(tradebar,* 23; *repellar,* 55) this characteristic makes clear that the MSS readings, which have come under attack (at 23 Palmer thinks *tradebat* may be right, at 55 he, Giomini, and Dörrie read *repellas*), are perfectly sound.

a word, but their thoughts and feelings are clear (*quaerebant taciti, noster ubi esset amor*) because of their behavior (*alter in alterius iactantes lumina vultum*). Words are unnecessary to convey truth.

In lines 91ff it seems, at first glance, that the Meleager tale introduced by Briseis points to the power of words. But this is not so. The real power in the Meleager story resides in the relationship between husband and wife. This is brought out by the juxtaposition *virum coniunx* (97) and by lines 97-100, in which Briseis concedes that she is not actually in the same position as Meleager's wife, because she is not really Achilles' wife. Words will avail her nothing: *at mea pro nullo pondere verba cadunt* (98).

But Briseis does know the power of the concrete, and this gives her one hope. The embassy failed with their pleas,[60] but she can call upon her tears and the fact that she knows physical contact with Achilles (131-134). This will mean something. Once again, words are unnecessary: *ut taceam, lacrimis comminuere meis* (134).

* * *

A few words on the poem's structure. Obvious as it is that the Iliadic embassy episode constitutes a very important source, we should notice how Ovid reshapes what is a single, unified, and coherent action in Homer into several separate and individually pointed segments.

The first (27-38) consists mainly of the list of gifts the ambassadors proffer. It highlights Achilles' lack of concern for Briseis, and is broken off at line 39 by her emotional response. At lines 57-58 the embassy scene returns in Achilles' threat to leave Troy, here designed to show how far he has gone in his base behavior. This, too, is followed by Briseis' emotional comments (59ff). At lines 92ff we meet Phoenix' Meleager narrative, utilized by Briseis to persuade Achilles. Again, her reaction interrupts (97-98). Finally, she returns to the embassy at lines 129-130, noting its failure and claiming that she herself could be more readily successful. Thus, Ovid has divided the one episode into vari-

[60] Compare also the two legations, which Ovid may be tying together by his echoing of final *comes* (10) in 28. The one comes to Achilles, says nothing, but accomplishes its mission; the other speaks at length, and elaborately, but gets nowhere.

ous parts and given each portion its own purpose and effect in terms of the emotional and dramatic development of the letter.

In the structure of the letter Ovid has cleverly dovetailed chronology and rhetoric. The argument builds in seriousness and intensity while at the same time preserving the chronological sequence of the *Iliad*, thus giving us, as it were, a step-by-step documentation of the feelings and reactions of Briseis to the events as they take place in the *Iliad*.

The letter opens as if the embassy had not yet taken place, as if Briseis were writing immediately after her abduction (*rapta*, 1). There is no indication of a lapse of time, and she is completely involved with Achilles' lack of resistance in giving her up. On reading through line 16, one could scarcely think that an even more insulting and injurious event had come upon Briseis since her abduction. The poem then moves forward in dramatic fashion. Time passes in lines 17-20, and in lines 21-22 a new accusation consonant with the chronological movement is put forth: why has Achilles made no attempt to recover her? This cry comes at a specific moment in time, the moment before the arrival of the embassy, for if Achilles had already rejected an opportunity to get her back she would not simply be complaining of his unwillingness to reclaim her. Finally, at line 25, we reach the time when the embassy has already come and gone, and Briseis now complains of his rejection of their terms. It is only at lines 57-58 that we come to the dramatic and rhetorical high point at which Achilles not only scorns the gifts but also threatens to leave Troy. And it is at this temporal point that Briseis focuses her pleas and arguments, ultimately moving from the present into the future via a series of threats, hopes, wishes, and imaginative constructions of the future (69ff, 125ff).

In sum, Ovid has seen the chronological sequence of the *Iliad* as an emotional crescendo for Briseis, and conceives it in the poem as a rhetorical movement toward a climax.

As is his custom in the *Heroides*, Ovid has depicted his heroine at the moment of highest crisis. Like Ariadne, who wakes and finds herself abandoned, like Phyllis, who finally understands that Demophoon will not return, Briseis begins to suspect the worst, that Achilles has no intention of seeking her back and is preparing to return home. By locking this letter into that critical moment Ovid would seem to have cut himself off from the chronologically later material which bears most directly on Briseis.

3. Briseis

But, as we have noticed time and again, this is not so. For it is characteristic of these poems that though, strictly speaking, they exist at only a very specific and brief moment in time they constantly partake of the entire myth, present, past, and even future. In this poem past, present, and future merge at one point in time, and Briseis' tragedy, from the moment of the first capture till the time of the final restoration, comes vividly to life, shaped by her own words and psyche.[61]

If I have emphasized the poem's virtues this is largely to counter the superficial criticism, such as D'Elia's, which it has suffered. It is, however, true that, in spite of Ovid's frequent attempts to weave the erotic elements into the texture of the epic, he is not always successful, and that at times even his successes must be deemed artificial. In addition, that sense of remove, of distance, which so often informs Ovid's poetry, lurks here sometimes as well, and this we can only regret. Ovid and his audience were undoubtedly delighted and amused to hear the words of the great Homeric heroes in the mouth of a mere girl, in an elegiac format and a partially amatory context, and, to top it all, with a very different sense and put to quite distinct purposes, but this delight and amusement is one thing the poem could well do without, especially since it invests the character of Briseis with an element of unconscious self-parody. Unfortunately, even when Ovid fully sympathizes, he is incapable of fully empathizing, though this is perhaps more a function of his art than of his character.

In spite of this, the poem is a notable achievement. In its brilliant command of the epic material and its transformation of it into "subjective" elegy it impressively breaks new ground for Latin elegy. But it is most striking for its full-blown and insightful development of the character of Briseis out of a few isolated hints in the *Iliad*, and in its Euripidean understanding of and sympathy for the female victim of war, bereft of home and family.[62] Simone Weil, in her perceptive essay on war which utilizes

[61] When Ovid involves Patroclus in the life of Briseis (anachronistically, as far as the Homeric account is concerned) he is in a sense calling to the reader's mind that Briseis will undergo yet another catastrophe of the same order (Patroclus' death), and that indeed her miseries do not and will not end.

[62] Documentation is unnecessary, but I should like to point out two places in the letter where the sense of tragedy and the insight into it could virtually have been modeled on Euripides. At lines 45ff the horrors of death and devastation are magnified by the direct visual experience (*vidi . . . vidi . . . vidi*), as at *Tro.* 479ff (though this is a theme with a long history. Cf.

41

—sometimes, granted, very loosely—the *Iliad* as a starting point, describes Homer's Briseis in words that would probably do better for Ovid's:

> If, by some miracle, in the slave's breast a hope is born, the hope of becoming, some day, through somebody's influence, *someone* once again, how far won't these captives go to show love and thankfulness, even though these emotions are addressed to the very men who should, considering the very recent past, still reek with horror for them. . . . [The slave] loses his whole inner life.[63]

For Ovid, living in a time of relative calm, prosperity, and peace, to have perceived the inner spiritual plight of the captive of war which Weil learned from her own unspeakable experiences and Euripides appreciated from living in another war-torn age is no small feat of insight and sensitivity. Insofar as erotic elegy could bear the weight of tragedy and pathos, it has done so here, molded by the skillful, if sometimes erratic, hands of the last great Latin elegist.

Οἰχαλίας ἅλωσις, *EGF*, 61K, fr. 1; Verg. *Aen.* 2.499-502 [with Austin and Servius *ad* 499]. See A. Turyn, *Studia Sapphica* [Leopoli 1929 = *Eos* suppl. 6], 67-68); and at line 46 the tragedy is heightened by the awareness of the gulf between one's present status (slave, captive) and one's former greatness, as is the case at *Tro.* 489ff.

[63] *The Iliad or the Poem of Force* (Wallingford, Pa. 1967) 9-10.

II

Heroides 8: Hermione

To read Hermione's letter hard upon Euripides' *Androm-ache* is at once a shocking and illuminating experience. There is no trace in Ovid of Euripides' arrogant and villainous bitch, no hint of the wanton shrew and unconscionable murderess.[1] The fairly neutral statement, *parcius Andromachen vexavit Achaia victrix* (13), even if Ovid intends some irony here, shows just how far we are from Euripides' play with its stridently emotional invective and its bitter conflict between Hermione and Andromache. It is almost as if Euripides' play never existed, at least insofar as the conception of Hermione goes (to be sure, the poem does seem to bear some verbal traces of the play), and here, strange to say, is the rub. The mishaps of survival have left us with but one full-scale treatment of Hermione in Greek literature, and from secondary allusions and fragmentary remains we can appreciate how little we do know about the character Hermione in ancient poetry. It is beyond my purposes and abilities to unravel the skeins which by now seem hopelessly entangled or even to establish with some degree of surety what sources Ovid knew, and, of these, which he used, which he ignored. It takes, however, no exacting research to conclude that Ovid is willfully ignoring Euripides' Hermione, who, one may reasonably suggest, was a product pure and simple of that tragedian's imagination, being elsewhere depicted in a totally dissimilar vein. The anti-Spartan bias is obvious and familiar, and the association of Orestes with a female relative in gruesome acts of violence is well remembered from Euripides' peculiar version of the slaying of Clytemnestra and Aegisthus in his *Electra*. There is no evidence that anyone, prior to Euripides, represented Hermione acting in

[1] For a treatment of Euripides' Hermione more sympathetic than is common, see G. Pagani, *Dioniso* 42 (1968) 200-210.

43

complicity with Orestes to effect the dastardly murder of Neoptolemus, nor that the nasty rivalry between Hermione and Andromache existed before Euripides. And it is in precisely these two areas that Hermione's contemptible nature is made manifest in the *Andromache*.

Unfortunately, the bits and pieces of information that survive document facts, not characterization, and consequently there is little to be said about the depiction of Hermione in other literary works. But facts are important, and we can safely say that on the evidence of extant material there is no indication that any poet, aside from Euripides, assigned to her actions that would have made her a condemnable character.

About all we know comes from scholia and mythographers. Of primary poetic material there is little and it is none too helpful. Homer's references at *Il.* 3.174-175 and *Od.* 4.4ff appear to be irrelevant to the tradition of the antagonism between Orestes and Neoptolemus. Nor are Hesiod's (frs. 175.1, 204.94MW) and Sappho's (23.3ff LP; see Page, *Sappho and Alcaeus* 138-139) mentions of any use. While we can learn nothing from a few allusions in Propertius and Ovid, Vergil does provide a brief epitome of the Neoptolemus-Orestes-Hermione-Andromache relationship (*Aen.* 3.325ff). The most extensive remains of a single work which dealt with Hermione are those of Pacuvius' play (Ribbeck³, 161-190), but even these are so incoherent and fragmentary—and with regard to Hermione herself so uninformative—that only tenuous hypotheses may be constructed on so flimsy a foundation.

What we do understand—and this perhaps more complicates than simplifies the problems—is that very many writers handled or mentioned one aspect or another of the myth and with quite a few variations.² Sophocles' *Hermione* is commonly held the

2 See schol. Eur. *Andr.* 32 (Philocles and Theognis); *FGrHist* 382F10 (Lysimachus); *FGrHist* 3F63-64 (Pherecydes); perhaps schol. Pind. *Nem.* 10.12 (= Ibycus, *PMG* 294) and *POxy* 2619, fr. 16. 10 (Stesichorus). For Theodorus' play *Hermione* (first century B.C.?), see Dittenberger *Syll.*² no. 699. I do not know why, in discussions of the literary treatments of the Hermione-myth, this tragedy is invariably ignored. See too Christ-Schmid-Stählin II.1⁶ (1920) 333. For Livius' play, see Ribbeck, *TRF*³ 23. For Sophocles', see Pearson 1, pp. 141-144. It would be interesting to see how Hermione was depicted in comedy, but unfortunately Theophilus' *Neoptolemus*, if indeed it was a parody of the myth and included Hermione within its framework, is lost beyond recall, and Menecrates' lost *Hermioneus*, unless with Meineke (*FCG* 1.493-494) we assume, on no evidence, that this is a corruption of the correct

source of Ovid's letter, but it is safer to say that Ovid's treatment seems, on the whole, merely compatible with the little we know of Sophocles'—and little it is, for in fact we do not know for certain even what the basic plot was.[3] We can only be sure that Sophocles' drama was built on the conflict of promises between Tyndareus and Menelaus concerning the marriage of Hermione, and this is indeed a critical point in Ovid's poem (31-34). It is reasonable conjecture, not much more, that in general Sophocles treated the same events as Euripides, but the existence of only two inconsequential fragments contributes to our ignorance. What complicates the problem is that our secondary sources concentrate on certain factual details (too often anonymously: "some say," "others say") which have little or no relevance to the situation presented by Ovid and so fail to clarify the relationship between Ovid and his predecessors. Thus, for example, the questions of whether Hermione has any siblings, whether she and Orestes (or she and Neoptolemus) have any children and what their names are, who kills Neoptolemus and how are commonly matters of discussion, issues which are of little import to the context of this letter. Reviews of the following questions prove only a bit more fruitful: (A) How does the dual "marriage" come about and exactly what is the relationship of Orestes to Hermione before she passes to Neoptolemus? (1a) Menelaus first betroths Hermione to Orestes, then later (at Troy) to Neoptolemus. (1b) Menelaus betroths her to Neoptolemus at Troy, Tyndareus to Orestes in Greece; this is Ovid's version and was apparently Sophocles' too. (2a) Hermione is engaged, not married, to Orestes (so Euripides). (2b) Hermione is married to Orestes (so seemingly Ovid, line 35), and according to some already pregnant when given to Neoptolemus.[4] (B) How does Hermione pass into Neop-

---

title *Hermione*, had nothing to do with her. Some additional information on Hermione, irrelevant to our aims, can be found at schol. *Andr.* 32. For a discussion of some interesting aspects of Hermione's representation in art, concerned mainly with Kalamis' sculpture of Hermione, see J. Dörig, *JDAI* 80 (1965) 166-177.

[3] Zieliński's discussion (*Tragodumenon Libri Tres* [Cracow 1925] 114-117) is valuable, but his theory that Sophocles' heroine wrote a letter to Orestes asking for his help (much like Ovid's Hermione) is ingenious, not convincing. For a cautious and very brief survey of the legend of Hermione through the fifth century, see P. T. Stevens, *Euripides: Andromache* (Oxford 1971) 1-5.

[4] (1a) See Eur. *Andr.* 966-970. (1b) Ovid *Her.* 8.31-34; Eustath. *Od.* 1479.10ff. (2b) For a pregnant Hermione, see schol. *Andr.* 32.

tolemus' possession? (1) Menelaus takes her from Orestes and turns her over (so, it seems, Euripides, Sophocles, Philocles, Theognis).⁵ (2) Neoptolemus seizes Hermione by force. This version is attested by Servius, Apollodorus, and perhaps by Vergil, but without any primary source specified, and is followed by Ovid (9-12, 18, 66, 82, 103).⁶ Thus, even these data fail to pinpoint a "source" for Ovid. In fact, I would venture to say that even were our knowledge of Ovid's literary antecedents here full and precise, we would still find ourselves unable to point to one work as Ovid's source, or even primary source, for it is highly unlikely that any single work would have incorporated the elements which have, by virtue of the unique nature of the *Heroides*, been fused here into a coherent whole. The introduction of autobiographical matter and quasi-historical data, the repetition of pleas and attempts at persuasion, the "legal" argumentation, these are the poet's innovations, and, though it is possible that a number of these elements were present in various works, it would be perverse to attribute to Ovid an eclectic plagiarism that could account for the total substance of the poem. The dynamics of this poem are generated by the peculiar nature of the genre, while the characterization of Hermione, the precedents for which are almost completely unknown to us, must surely be Ovid's own.⁷

This poem bears many resemblances to the letter of Briseis

⁵ *Andr.* 969-981; Eustath. *Od.* 1479.10ff; schol. *Andr.* 32.

⁶ Serv. *Aen.* 3.330; Apollod. *Epit.* 6.14 (ἁρπάζει); *Aen.* 3.330-331. Vergil's *ereptae . . . coniugis* is ambiguous. *Eripio* need not involve physical violence (cf. Prop. 2.8.1; Lygd. 2.2,4 = Tib. 3.2.2,4). We do not know who originated the forceful abduction. I wonder whether it may have been conceived under the influence of literary and artistic depictions of Pyrrhus' violent slaughter of Priam, a favorite theme of poetry and painting (e.g., Lesches, F16 Allen; Pind., *Paean* 6.112-117; *Aen.* 2.506-558, where see Austin for artistic examples). It does seem likely that Ovid's description of the rape of Hermione by Pyrrhus was influenced by Vergil's account of Pyrrhus' murder of Priam. Note *trementem traxit* (550-551)/ *clamantem traxit* (9-10), *implicuitque comam* (552)/ *inornatis . . . comis* (10). Earlier, Vergil had adopted the motif of Pyrrhus' failure to meet Achilles' standards (540-543), as Ovid does here (3-4, 83-86). To go in another direction, the influence may be Euripidean. At *Andr.* 709-710 Peleus threatens that Pyrrhus will drag Hermione through the halls by her hair.

⁷ Colluthus' account (328-388) of Hermione's grief on Helen's departure recalls Ovid 75-80, though the details are rather different. It is possible, though by no means necessary, that such a scene was found in an earlier Greek poem. See Norden *ad Aen.* 6.14 (p. 121).

and is playfully conscious of the fact. One realizes immediately that the situations virtually duplicate each other, acted out by the succeeding generations of the same families. In both the seizure of one man's woman by another, in both the direct conflict between a Peleid and an Atreid. But Ovid, as is his wont, cherishes and relishes such similarities because they allow him to turn sameness into variety and they heighten and enhance the status of his achievement by the vivid contrast between external likeness and the essential individuality of each poem and each heroine.

The similarities are effectively—and with no attempt at subtlety—called to our attention. Alone of Ovid's heroines do they call themselves *sarcina* (3.68; 8.94). Both of them evince a strange defensiveness, virtually a compulsive need to justify themselves when there is no question as to the rights and wrongs of the situation. If Briseis defends herself by asserting that she has indeed tried to escape from Agamemnon, Hermione does much the same by proclaiming her resistance when Neoptolemus abducted her: *quod potui renui, ne non invita tenerer,/ cetera femineae non valuere manus* (5-6).

The interaction is present from the beginning with the evocation of the memory of Achilles in *Pyrrhus Achillides, animosus imagine patris* (3),[8] in the continuing allusions to both Achilles and Agamemnon, especially in contrast one to the other (recalling their bitter rivalry in *Iliad* 1),[9] in the similar self-pity for unremitting misfortune (3.43-44; 8.87-88), and, most decisively, in the explicit recollection of the abduction of Briseis (85-86). But such bare correlations never satisfy Ovid. In a sense the whole set of circumstances in which Hermione and Orestes find themselves trapped is viewed as a kind of scenario in which the participants or actors are playing roles—indeed, a multiplicity of

[8] The theme of Pyrrhus as son carrying on the tradition of a great father is, however, an old one, going back to Odysseus' account of Pyrrhus' accomplishments to his proud father in the underworld (*Od.* 11.504-540), receiving its most outstanding treatment in Sophocles' *Philoctetes*, and recurring in various forms afterward (e.g., *Aen.* 2.540-550; Quintus of Smyrna, 7.176ff). Whether this theme is related to the original identity of Achilles and Neoptolemus I cannot say. See J. Fontenrose, "The Cult and Myth of Pyrros at Delphi," *UCalPubClArch* 4, no. 3 (1960) 207ff.

[9] Verses 43-46 seem a clear recollection of *Il.* 1.278-281. Compare especially *hic pars militiae, dux erat ille ducum* with εἰ δὲ σὺ κάρτερός ἐσσι . . . ἀλλ' ὅγε φέρτερός ἐστιν, ἐπεὶ πλεόνεσσιν ἀνάσσει.

47

roles—whose parts have in large already been written and played. Beyond the fact that Hermione is reenacting Briseis lies the striking perception that the roles of Achilles and Agamemnon have in this generation been reversed, for the scion of Achilles is presently the villainous abductor while Agamemnon's son proves to be innocent victim. Hermione is quick to see and utilize this in her attack on Pyrrhus, but tactfully abstains from recalling Agamemnon's part in the crime against Achilles:

> Pelides utinam vitasset Apollinis arcus!
>   Damnaret nati facta proterva pater.
> Nec quondam placuit nec nunc placuisset Achilli
>   abducta viduum coniuge flere virum.

> (83-86)

Ovid, however, realizes an even more complex role-playing. For if Pyrrhus is seen both in the image of his father (*animosus imagine patris*, 3) and as failing that image (84), he is also this generation's surrogate for Paris, the primal rapist. Correspondingly, Hermione must play not only Briseis, but also a virtuous version of her mother, Helen, and poor Orestes must take the part of the wounded Menelaus, while also living up to the example of Agamemnon, his father. Hermione sums it all up concisely: *Tu mihi quod matri pater est. Quas egerat olim/ Dardanius partes advena, Pyrrhus agit* (41-42).[10]

In a variety of ways this poem stands apart from the other letters: for example, in the sympathy and understanding the writer reveals for the addressee. In no other poem do we find so clear a picture of the workings of the *man's* mind. In part, this is a result of the sharply calculated arguments, so marshaled as to be directed precisely at Orestes' psychological state. This is perhaps the only letter wherein it is sometimes hard to determine whether a particular remark is occasioned by the emotional condition of the writer or by that of the recipient. Hermione's arguments

10 Why the choice of cattle-thievery at 17-18: *An si quis rapiat stabulis armenta reclusis,/ arma feres, rapta coniuge lentus eris?* Was there a tradition of Orestes performing some such feat? If so, it seems not to have survived. But *Paris* was famous for just such a deed, as Ovid notes at *Her.* 16.359-360: *Paene puer caesis abducta armenta recepi/ hostibus et causam nominis inde tuli.* Is this irony or humorous play on the confusion of roles again? *Rapta coniuge* also recalls, in inverted form, Paris.

are clearly intended to shore up Orestes' courage and often tacit-
ly assume a cowardly Orestes. Thus, she must show Orestes that
his ancestry is as distinguished and courageous as is Pyrrhus'
(43-48).[11] In addition, she utilizes rather traditional forms of argument: *facile* (23-24; coincidentally or otherwise, this is what
Apollo's oracle enjoins Orestes to do (Soph. *Electra* 35-37),
though Ovid, in maintaining the theme of role-playing, uses language applicable to Menelaus), *honestum* (25-26), *pium* (27-30),
iustum (31-34), *utile* (35-36). But this rhetorical regimentation
does not completely preclude elements of particular relevance
to the drama here being played out. Thus, *at pater Aeacidae pro-
miserat inscius acti* (33), though possibly a manifestation of Hermione's defensive nature, may however reflect more on Orestes,
for perhaps by professing such an objection he seeks to avoid taking action. A similar note at 36: *si iungar Pyrrho, tu mihi laesus
eris*. There must be significance in the assertion of what Orestes
more than anyone should know, that his own interests are at
stake.

As is usually the case in the *Heroides*, behavior, especially
strange behavior, is psychologically motivated. After this lengthy
—for the *Heroides*—attempt at persuasion, the final lines clarify
the portrait: *Nec virtute cares. Arma invidiosa tulisti* (49). What
begins as encouragement, *nec virtute cares*, ends as illuminatingly disturbing apology. The implicit connection between lines 49
and 50 is crucial. That act of courage, rather than serving Orestes
as a model for continued boldness and as an example of his ability to act strongly and decisively, has turned him into a vegeta-
ble, paralyzed by the deed of matricide and rendered incapable
of bold action, even in his own behalf.[12] And so, Hermione must
shift her ground and seek to rationalize away that murder:
Induit illa pater. . . . non lecta est operi, sed data causa tuo
(50-52). Still, she salvages something by concluding on a note
which ignores the murder of Clytemnestra and focuses only on
Aegisthus' death, *Hanc tamen implesti, iuguloque Aegisthus*

---

[11] Typical of D'Elia's cursory reading of the *Heroides* is his careless classifica-
tion of these lines among passages in which the heroine proclaims the nobility
of *her* lineage (139, with n. 71).

[12] There is a fine touch at 102, *ni pro se pugnet*, where *se* comes παρὰ
προσδοκίαν instead of *me*. Along similar lines is the striking litotes *non timidas*
(for *audaces*) at 16.

aperto/ tecta cruentavit, quae pater ante tuus (53-54).[13] The last four words return us to the arena of roles and recurrence. Aegisthus, in death, replays the gruesome part of Agamemnon.

It is rare in these letters for the hero to be characterized in any significant degree. If Ovid does so here, it is not only because he is striving for variety in technique but also because he realizes that in this particular couple there exists in the hero's past, as well as in the heroine's, that kind of traumatic event which can easily be responsible for long-lasting, even permanent, changes in the character.[14] To be sure, it is hard to say whether this conception of Orestes is Ovid's personal creation; this may well be, but we must allow for the possibility of Euripidean influence (though not the *Andromache*), an Orestes free from supernatural persecution but plagued by his own conscience and reluctant to take bold measures.[15] In this regard we may observe in passing that Hermione's next remarks *Increpat Aeacides laudemque in crimina vertit* (55) recall *Andromache* 977-978: ὃ δ' ἦν ὑβριστὴς εἴς τ' ἐμῆς μητρὸς φόνον / τάς θ' αἱματωποὺς θεὰς ὀνειδίζων ἐμοί, though in Hermione's mouth the additional *laudem* continues to encourage Orestes.[16]

Strange to say, this poem, though perhaps containing more insight into the character of the recipient than any other (a full six lines [49-54] recount an event in the hero's life which has no direct bearing on the heroine), nevertheless quantitatively possesses as little direct address to him as any. Though epistolary in form, the *Heroides* commonly break the formal bounds of the letter and partake of the nature of various other literary modes of expression. On the broad implications of this more will be said elsewhere. Here we are concerned with its relevance to this poem.

[13] Again at 120 Clytemnestra's death is tactfully ignored; and the key word is *fortiter*.

[14] *Malis stupeo* (111) might do as byword for Orestes!

[15] M. Platnauer, *Euripides' Iphigeneia in Tauris* (Oxford 1938) p. vi, speaks of "Orestes' initial moments of misgivings, not to say cowardice." Even more to the point is the portrait of Orestes at the beginning of *Orestes*, where, as D. J. Conacher, *Euripidean Drama* (Toronto 1967) 216, writes, Euripides subtly depicts "the crippling power of guilty conscience." Is Ovid's an extension of the Euripidean characterization?

[16] Similarly, Aegisthus torments Electra with his nasty remarks about Orestes (Eur. *Electra* 329-331). Pacuvius may have shown Pyrrhus comparing his acts of bravery with Orestes' (*TRF*[3] fr. 6).

A glance at second-person terms, pronouns, and verbs, is instructive. The first twelve lines (3-14) contain only two, *facis* (7) and *tibi* (8), both, however, of Pyrrhus, as Hermione reports her pleas when he carried her off. *At tu* (15) abruptly brings Orestes into the picture and introduces a lengthy passage of persuasion (15-56) with second-person notices in abundance. Then, the second person vanishes once more, occurring but once in the next 34 lines, again in Hermione's recollection of a past utterance: *Sine me, me sine, mater abis?* Ten lines follow (91-100) in which nine second-person terms are present, but all refer to Helen, as Hermione graphically relives her past. The frame of reference changes and another long stretch ensues marked by the absence of the second person (101-118). Finally, four lines from the poem's end, *tui* and *tibi* restore the second person, and for the first time in some 65 lines (54-119) it belongs to Orestes! Thus, the "direction" of Hermione's words serves as a sort of barometer for her emotional state and her aims, and helps to clarify for the reader the varying tones of the poem.

Much of this poem is conceived as a dreamlike reverie, a shadowy internalized monologue in which Hermione confronts her past and present and passes her life in review. Thus, the initial portion (3-14) reproduces her abduction in language that is addressed to no one in particular, indeed to no one at all. Orestes himself, the presumed recipient, is no more than another third-person outsider (*clamantem nomen Orestis* [9], not *nomen tuum* or the like). The next section (15-54) has greater external orientation and is more strictly appropriate to the letter-form, an attempt to convince Orestes to bring her aid. This done, Hermione withdraws into herself (55-116) and proffers a rather self-indulgent rehearsal of her plight which is at once a description of her misery and her misery itself:

> Flere licet certe; flendo diffundimus iram
> perque sinum lacrimae fluminis instar eunt.
> Has semper solas habeo semperque profundo;
> ument incultae fonte perenne genae.
>
> (61-64)

Orestes has again become a bystander: *Hermione coram quisquamne obiecit Oresti?* (59). But the immediacy of her present misfortune fades away into dim recollections of the calamitous past, sorrows experienced by her forebears (65-72) and by herself

51

(73-80) which, for the moment, overshadow her present suffering and put Orestes and Pyrrhus out of mind. Even when the chronological narrative reaches the present, there is no sense of a second person, only Hermione absorbed in her thoughts (81-88). Abruptly, another return to her childhood. Movingly Hermione recounts the emptiness of those years, addressing her mother who, as it were, materializes before her mind, in some of the most effective verses in the poem. Even the final return to the present, Hermione's portrait of her unhappy union with Pyrrhus, is more inner-than outer-directed (101-116). With the last six verses the earlier pleas to Orestes are finally resumed and the letter ends with a masked request framed in the language of asseveration.

Thus, this letter persistently shifts planes, both in its modes of expression and in its temporal dimensions. Beginning with a rather straight description of the present and immediate past, it moves to urgent argumentation and direct entreaties, only to withdraw inward in self-pity and then to proceed backward in time to agonize misfortunes of kin and self, re-creating the past so vividly as to mentally visualize the presence of her neglectful mother. A return to the present prepares for the final redirection of her words to the outside world in the form of Orestes, the oft-absent addressee. Yet, even the last words of the poem leave us wondering whether Hermione's mind strays again, for she does not say *tua uxor ero*, but rather *Tantalidae Tantalis uxor ero* (122)—has Orestes once more become the distant third person?

This kind of movement is by no means unusual in the *Heroides*; but it is rarely so neatly delineated and executed in such extreme fashion. Here it is both product and manifestation of a woman lost in the maze of horrors that has afflicted her and her ancestors, mind wandering from present to past and back, almost detached from herself as she views and reconstructs her life in dreamlike fashion. Her own misfortunes are described in a manner not very different from the way she recounts those of others, as she sees her own life merge into the history of her family. There is, I think, one queer linguistic feature of the letter which is calculated to reinforce this impression. *Pyrrhus Achillides, animosus imagine patris,/ inclusam contra iusque piumque tenet* (3-4). Palmer suggests *Hermionen* or *me clausam*, for surely we miss an explicit object here. But seemingly unnoticed have gone two recurrences of this elliptical usage: *Surdior ille freto clamantem nomen Orestis/ traxit* (9-10); *Pyrrhus habet captam* (103). In each case the accusative participle demands the epexegetical note *"scilicet me."* Three times in one poem is, however, too much to explain by coincidence or textual corruption.[17] The absence of the pronoun creates an effect of vagueness. Certainly, it limits precision. No matter that on each occasion we say, *"scilicet me"*; the plain fact is that *me* is not there. The interwoven effects are at least two: the diffusion of sense (Pyrrhus holds [someone] shut in; Pyrrhus dragged [someone] shouting; Pyrrhus holds [someone] captive), and the conversion of Hermione into a spectator of her own life, both aspects of the poem promoted in different ways throughout.

Ovid strikes two other notes in regard to the character of Hermione. There is an undertone of childlike feminine vanity, a taste perchance of the female who will populate works like the *Ars* and *Medicamina*, especially in the strange, almost humorous, excessive concern for her external appearance. *Traxit* (sc. *me*) *inornatis in sua tecta comis* (10). Is the adjective merely descriptive or ornamental? It occurs only here in the *Heroides*. And what shall we say of *incultae . . . genae* (64), this adjective only twice in all the *Heroides* (9.125)? What then of the young girl *non longos etiam tunc scissa capillos* (77) and her concern for her *cultus* (95)? Here too we almost sense Hermione watching Hermione—or at least looking in a mirror.

Mentions of her hair (10, 79) in connection with the two crises in her life, the rapes of her mother and herself, coincide with the duplication of another motif, this of greater import. *Clamantem nomen Orestis* (9) is echoed in *clamabam "Sine me, me sine, mater abis?"* (80). On the one occasion Hermione calls upon her mother, on the other upon her husband. The former event has left its mark upon the latter. When calamity strikes and Hermione cries for help, there is no answer. Helen does not respond and, to compound her difficulties, Menelaus also goes off. *Surdior ille freto* (9); to be sure, this phrase describes Pyrrhus, but we need no explicit declaration to understand that it applies equally well to Orestes. Again, Hermione cries out; again, no answer. As with Briseis there is the perception of history—or tragedy—repeating itself. When Hermione pathetically condemns Helen, *non*

---

[17] In itself a single occurrence is of little consequence. We can point elsewhere to isolated instances of the absence of direct object *me*, e.g., *Her.* 7.127, 12.65, 14.83. But the threefold recurrence in one poem seems deliberate and significant.

cultus tibi cura mei (95)—a deficiency of her childhood which may be for Ovid the motivating factor of her concern with appearances in her maturity—the verbal echo of verse 15, *At tu, cura mei si te pia tangit, Oreste*, proves to be also historical repetition. There was no *cura* for Hermione on Helen's part, there is, evidently, none on Orestes'. In a sense, Hermione has less hope than Briseis. The latter sees a chance to persuade Achilles, if she can only confront him. Hermione's voice cries vainly, falling upon ears that are deaf; she possesses recourse only to tears, futile tears: *Has semper solas habeo semperque profundo* (63); we ought not to miss the illuminating *semper*.

As often, Ovid's precision in defining his heroine is grounded in an understanding of the events of her life. Although Briseis has constantly played the part of victim, still, she has, at least once, been treated generously (after the fall of her country). More important, the separations she has suffered have been inflicted upon her by strangers, while Hermione has had the critical blow of abandonment dealt her by those who least should have done it, her parents: *et duo cum vivant, orba duobus eram* (90).

Herein we have the essence and the originality of Ovid's conception of Hermione, in his association of the child Hermione deserted by her parents with the grown woman, wife of Orestes; in his realization that the fragmented mythological tradition ignores the developmental unity of the individual. To speak of what Greek poets did *not* write is of course a risky business, but if Euripides did not create his mature Hermione as a reflection of the young girl, we may well doubt whether anyone did. With Ovid's Hermione, the child is truly father of the man. Again, however, we must notice how Ovid extends a pattern present in Briseis' letter. The latter sees her present adversity as personal history repeating itself. For Hermione personal history merges with family history; her past embraces not merely the years of her own life, but also the decades and generations of her ancestors.[18] Her

---

[18] I am puzzled by the phrase *Tantalides matres* (66). Hermione is justified in calling her female ancestors *apta rapina*: Helen is her mother, Leda her grandmother, Hippodamia her great-grandmother. But to designate them *Tantalides* seems inexact, to say the least. None of them descends from Tantalus. Helen and Hippodamia, to be sure, marry descendants of Tantalus. Yet, even here there is some absence of logic. For the rapes of Helen (by Theseus) and Hippodamia (by Peleus) take place before they marry into the Tantalid family. And Leda cannot be called Tantalid no matter how far we stretch

misfortune represents the renewal of family, as well as personal, tragedy.

There are, of course, typically Ovidian touches. Witness the predilection for the double relationship, confused and confusing: *si non esses vir mihi, frater eras./ Vir, precor, uxori, frater succurre sorori* (28-29), the witty and ironic understatement, *orabat superos Leda suumque Iovem* (78), a grandeur of humor and irony wrapped up in one small possessive adjective: Leda, on the occasion of her daughter's rape, calls upon her own personal rapist for aid (cf. 67-68). The description, *et duo cum vivant, orba duobus eram* (90), is just neatly pointed enough to lose the poignancy it should otherwise have had, while the pathos of the oxymoron *sarcina grata* (94) does have a winning charm.

This poem, though it reveals various facets of Ovidian technique in the *Heroides*, is not very successful. The neatly manicured structure hinders the movement of the poem, and the lengthy argumentation with its formally rhetorical construction is rather boring, not to say sometimes silly and annoying (e.g., 36-38, 40, 48). But there are fine moments and in them the poem finds its raison d'être: the sketchy but illuminating account of the turmoil at the court of Menelaus; the simple but exquisite statement, *vix equidem memini, memini tamen* (75), where the first clause suggests the distant childhood of Hermione—she was too young when this happened to remember it—while the corrective second mirrors the gravity of Helen's deed. This her daughter cannot forget, no matter how young she was at the time. It is almost as if the memory is painfully called forth from the deepest recesses of her mind. And the following words prove almost equally effective in their concise vagueness: *omnia luctus,/ omnia solliciti plena timoris erant* (75-76).[19] Finally, the picture of Hermione (79-80), charming in its pathetic and childlike *non longos etiam tunc scissa capillos* and curiously moving in the chiastic reiteration *sine me, me sine*.

But undoubtedly the high point of the poem is the sympathetic and effective account by Hermione of her life without parents, a brilliantly evocative delineation of a young woman mourning

---

the embrace of the term. Her only connection with the Tantalids (as Burman *ad* 8.67 noted) is as mother of Helen, the wife of Menelaus. See too Loers *ad* 8.66.

[19] Are these words an unconscious recollection of Cat. 64.186-187: *omnia muta/ omnia sunt deserta, ostentant omnia letum?*

her lost childhood. The reverberating negatives, which sound the note of deprivation powerfully clear (91-96), the apostrophe to a heartless mother, and the marvelous choice of words render this passage wonderfully striking in its longing for a childhood that never was.[20] The adjectives are skillfully selected to suggest a tiny and helpless child: *parva* (in the *Heroides* only here and at 15.70 of a person); *primis . . . in annis* (a note pointedly reiterated at the poem's end, *primo in aevo*, 121), *incerto . . . ore*, *brevibus lacertis*. Well chosen too are the suggestive words, *blanditias*, the immature utterances of an appealing child,[21] and *captavi*, with its implication of futile grasping. Throughout, the importunate addresses to Helen are bitterly pathetic: *tibi, mea mater, tua, tuo, tibi, tibi, te, tua*, the second person who was never there. Fine also are the last lines of this section, the return of Helen. Mother does not recognize daughter, nor daughter mother. But, as Hermione resentfully observes, she correctly sensed who Helen was—the most beautiful woman, of course.

Finally, we should not ignore the good psychological insight at 111-116, especially 115-116: *Saepe Neoptolemi pro nomine nomen Orestis/ exit et errorem vocis ut omen amo*. Not only is the slip Freudian, but it is, in its own way, acknowledged as such.[22]

---

[20] If Ovid was familiar with Euripides' *Orestes*, then it is noteworthy that he ignores Clytemnestra's rearing of Hermione in Helen's absence (62-66). Ovid's description should be contrasted with Euripides' account of Iphigeneia's childhood (*IA* 1220-1230).

[21] Similar uses of *blanditiae* at Lucr. 5.1018; Sen. *Cons. Marc.* 5.4.

[22] In his commentary Palmer observes the legal terminology present in the poem, e.g., *non sum sine vindice* (7), *sub domino* (8), the *manus iniectio* of 16. Presumably too the argument of 31-35, though the matter would probably be clearer if the text were certain. I am not sure whether we can establish if this argument falls under Roman law, Greek law, or Ovidian invention, but it would be of value if we could. For if it is Greek law, we can rest assured that Ovid has taken it from a Greek source; while, if Roman, we can be equally sure that it does not come from a Greek model. On the other hand, it may be an *ad hoc* figment of Ovid's imagination, just as the marital circumstances in Plautus' *Trinummus* appear to be, from a legal perspective, the invention of the playwright (See A. Watson, *The Law of Persons in the Later Roman Republic* [Oxford 1967] 5). I also wonder whether Hermione's early remarks, *quod potui renui, ne non invita tenerer* (5), *clamantem nomen Orestis/ traxit* (9-10), may carry some legal implications. Perhaps Roman or Greek law or custom required a woman, when raped, to produce some evidence that she was not in fact a consenting partner, e.g., a struggle or a call for help. Though I know of no extant source that reports such a law in ex-

8. Hermione

All in all, the poem must stand or fall on the characterization of Hermione, a woman helpless and without hope, childlike in compensation for having never been a child, burdened by the feeling that her life is fated to be marked by betrayal on the part of those she loves most and hence having little trust or faith in them, too disillusioned to raise her voice in anger or invective. Ovid has departed intensely from Euripides' heroine. He has magnified her plight, adopting a version of the myth, neither Euripidean nor Sophoclean, which had Pyrrhus violently seize Hermione, already Orestes' wife, and, going one step further, has Hermione represent herself as a virtual prisoner.[23] She refuses, it appears, to have intercourse with Pyrrhus (*si iungar Pyrrho*, 36), and is filled with revulsion and disgust toward him (110-114),[24] both features of Ovid's treatment which seem to have no precedent in any prior version of the myth. And all these features serve, for Hermione, to aggravate her predicament, intensify Orestes' delay, and increase her need for immediate help.

---

plicit terms, the argument at Eur. *Tro.* 998-1001 (used, coincidentally, with respect to Hermione's mother Helen) suggests that some such existed. (See W. Schulze, *Kleine Schriften* [Göttingen 1934] 183-185.) We do know of Roman laws in other areas where a person's shout is of critical legal importance, e.g., *Leg. XII Tab.* 8.13. We should compare the Biblical injunction at *Deut.* 22.23-27, which (as Professor Reuven Yaron points out to me) also has a parallel in Hittite law. If there were a similar Roman or Greek law, then Hermione here offers a legal argument to support her virtue and her case. For discussions of the role of the law in Ovid's poetry, see two recent articles by E. J. Kenney, *Philologus* 111 (1967) 212-232, and *YCS* 21 (1969) 243-263. Cf. too R. Düll, "*Ovidius Iudex*: Rechtshistorische Studien zu Ovids Werken," in *Studi in Onore di B. Biondi* (Milan 1965) vol. 1, 73-93.

[23] Palmer thinks that *inclusam* (4) at the least needs defensive apology, but may even be corrupt. His suspicions are unwarranted and fail to take note of *captam* (103). The point is simply that, as far as Hermione is concerned, she *is* a prisoner.

[24] Hermione's dissatisfaction with Pyrrhus in the *Andromache* is totally different.

III

Heroides 2: Phyllis

Comparison is fruitful, as we have seen from setting
Homer's Briseis and Euripides' Hermione by Ovid's singular cre-
ations. Theoretically, perhaps, the critic should be dependent
only on the substance of the poem, without recourse to anything
external. But, in fact, having a second treatment greatly facili-
tates the discrimination of highlights, emphases, techniques,
shadings, and nuances, which might otherwise be missed. With
Phyllis, however, no such work exists, which is doubly unfortunate since it seems that this myth—or perhaps Callimachus' rendition of it—was of great popularity in antiquity,[1] a fact especially noteworthy if, as seems likely, the tale has its roots neither
in early epic nor in fifth century drama, but only in the politiciz-
ing mythology of the late fifth century. To the best of our meager
knowledge, the only pre-Roman literary treatment of the myth
in Greek was Callimachus', of which all of four words survive. To
be sure, there is no solid evidence that Callimachus told the tale

---

[1] There are many mentions of Phyllis in Ovid and a few in Propertius.
Ovid's contemporary Tuscus wrote a "Phyllis" (see Ov. *Pont.* 4.16.20) of
which we know nothing. Lucian lists the tale of Phyllis among those myths
that should be familiar to the performer of the pantomime (*Salt.* 40). Especially valuable testimony are Persius' painful acknowledgement of the myth's
popularity in his day (1.34) and, centuries later, references whose very casual
aspect suggests an immediate recognition by the reader, e.g., Colluthus 214ff
(though here the possibility of a copied Hellenistic original is present) and
Procopius *ep.* 18, p. 539 Her., *ep.* 86, p. 565 Her. (Of interest too is a ninth
century composition by Cometas Chartularius, *AP* 5.265.) The view held by
Knaack and Kiessling-Heinze that Hor. *C.* 4.5.9-12 and Oppian *Hal.* 4.335-
342 derive from Callimachus' Phyllis is without foundation. They may even
be true-to-life descriptions of what happened when travel by sea was a real
danger. We might perhaps think of Monnica when Augustine leaves her
(*Conf.* 5.8).

at any great length, though the hypothesis seems likely.[2] The mythographers, scholia, and Latin poets offer us help but do not make good the loss of a full-scale primary source. At any rate, the bare outlines of the legend are, up to a point, neatly delimited and quite familiar. The journeying hero comes to the land of the royal heroine who receives him hospitably, falls in love and sleeps with him, only to have the idyllic relationship interrupted by his need to attend to pressing business. So he departs, swearing love and promising to return. Here, however, we are at the fork in the mythological road. Phyllis and Demophoon part company and so do our sources. When Demophoon is slow in returning, Phyllis dies (usually by suicide). According to some sources, she succeeds in putting a curse on Demophoon before dying and he, as a result of this curse and a magical box which Phyllis had earlier given him, also dies.[3] A different tradition, of note for its maudlin romanticism, has Phyllis slay herself in her impatience, only to frustrate Demophoon who, though late, does return and finds Phyllis transformed into a leafless tree which he forthwith embraces. As a gesture of reciprocal love and sympathy, the tree puts forth leaves to match his tears.[4] Now what has Ovid done with the raw material? From a broad perspective he seems to have maintained the essential thrust of the tradition, though he does ignore the common tale of Phyllis' nine trips to the seashore —or rather he ignores the number, for the episode itself is quite clearly present (121-124)—presumably because he felt that the *Heroides* were no place for aetiology. Elsewhere he is quite happy to make such reference: *quaere, Novem cur una Viae*

[2] See Callim. fr. 556Pf. G. Knaack's reconstruction of Callimachus' version (*Analecta Alexandrino-Romana* [Greifswald 1880] 29-48) is interesting, but unconvincing, going far beyond the evidence. M. de Cola, *Callimaco e Ovidio* (Palermo 1937) 15-17, is much more cautious in her evaluation of Ovid's worth as a basis for reconstructing Callimachus. For a discussion of some of the problems pertinent to the development of the myth, particularly on Demophoon's side, see Jacoby *ad FGrHist* 323a F20-21, pp. 41-42, with the extensive notes in vol. two.

[3] See Apollod. *Epit.* 6.16; Tzetzes ad Lycoph. *Alex.* 496 (with Acamas as the male). The Suda (s.v. Αἰγαῖον Πέλαγος) peculiarly reports that Theseus, after killing the Minotaur, begged leave from Ariadne to return home to inform his father of his success. Once home, he decided not to go back to her. This sounds more like the usual stories of Demophoon (Theseus' son) and Phyllis than like those of Theseus and Ariadne.

[4] See Serv. *Ecl.* 5.10; schol. *Ecl.* 5.10; schol. Persius 1.34.

dicatur, et audi/ depositis silvas Phyllida flesse comis (AA 3.37-
38; see too *Rem. Am.* 55-56, 601). Insofar as the myth's climax
goes, there is clear allusion to Phyllis' forthcoming suicide

> Saepe venenorum sitis est mihi, saepe cruenta
>   traiectam gladio morte perire iuvat.
> Colla quoque, infidis quia se nectenda lacertis
>   praebuerunt, laqueis implicuisse iuvat.
> Stat nece matura tenerum pensare pudorem;
>   in necis electu parva futura mora est
>
> (139-144),

which was, of course, a constant in all versions,[5] but nothing
which gives us a clue as to Demophoon's behavior and fate. We
can, however, recognize that:

1. The two factors crucial to the version in which Demophoon
dies are lacking: the magic box which ultimately causes his death
—in the scheme of the *Heroides* in general and of this letter in
particular there is plenty of opportunity to mention it—and the
curses which Phyllis invokes against Demophoon, though again
opportunity is scarcely missing (and such curses are found elsewhere in the *Heroides*); closest are verses 43-44, *si de tot laesis
sua numina quisque deorum/vindicet, in poenas non satis unus
eris!* But curses they are not.

2. Those detailed sources which add that Demophoon was to
receive (or did receive), along with Phyllis, the Thracian kingdom as dowry (so Ovid 111-114 also)[6] make it clear that this was
not Phyllis' doing, but the responsibility and action of her father.
Ovid differs: *quae tibi subieci latissima regna Lycurgi,* etc.

3. In no source is Demophoon described as landing *shipwrecked* on Thrace; in fact, no reason is ever given. Presumably,
he simply stops there as a matter of course on his journey from
Troy homeward. Ovid depicts him as long-wandering and shipwrecked: *At laceras etiam puppes furiosa refeci* (45), *quae tibi,
Demophoon, longis erroribus acto/ Threicios portus hospitium-
que dedi* (107-108).[7]

---

[5] Hyg. *Fab.* 59 appears to be the only exception: *ob desiderium Demo-
phoontis spiritum emisit.* At Hyg. *Fab.* 243.6 she is a suicide.

[6] See Apollod. *Epit.* 6.16; Tzetzes *ad* Lycoph. *Alex.* 496. Cf. also *Anec.
Bekk.* 1.251.

[7] The possibility of damage to the text of Philostr. *ep.* 28 is particularly
unfortunate. As things stand now, we can only say that if something is miss-

2. Phyllis

With no more than this we can see how and to what end Ovid reshaped the very skeleton of the myth. No matter how wronged Phyllis may have been represented as being, nevertheless the sympathy that would naturally accrue to her must of necessity have been dulled by her initiative in precipitating Demophoon's doom. Though the differences are large and obvious, we would think perhaps of Medea, treated badly, yes, but losing our sympathy when she proves a greater villain than her betrayer. Ovid has avoided this trap, not only by eliminating the two aspects of the myth which were integrally involved with Phyllis' act of revenge, but by toning down Phyllis' anger and vituperation throughout. Anger, of course; regret, of course; even some harsh words, but nothing incompatible with a delicate and injured nature, calculated to win and merit our sympathy on all counts. The two other large-scale adaptations which Ovid makes are interwoven. Whether Ovid invented the shipwreck of Demophoon or adopted it from some minor tradition, his purpose is clear. In the usual version Demophoon comes, loves, and leaves; that is all. Ovid manufactures a perilous situation and thereby enhances Phyllis' generosity. This was not merely a love affair, but a benefaction on the part of Phyllis, who condescended to love the shipwrecked sailor and, in addition, gave him much concrete aid. Once again, the effect is to increase the sympathy for Phyllis by magnifying the ingratitude of Demophoon's behavior toward her, an effect achieved not merely by the statement of bare fact, but also by the constant juxtaposition of Phyllis and Demophoon, "I" and "you," first person and second person. The contrast between the host who acted beyond the call of duty and the guest who could not maintain minimal standards of decency reverberates through the letter. The note is struck in the first words of the poem, as the mingling of adjectives, nouns, names, and pronouns produces this significant juxtaposition: *hospita* (I), *Demophoon*

---

ing then there is room for the possibility of a shipwrecked Demophoon. If such was Philostratus' version, we would then be faced with the problem of evaluating it as evidence for much earlier treatments of the myth. The interesting report at *POxy* 2506, fr. 26, col. i, 17ff (= *PMG* 193) that Stesichorus represented Demophoon as carried to Egypt on his way home from Troy offers no direct help. But it does indicate that Demophoon did, at least according to one poet and on one occasion, make a stop dictated evidently by adverse conditions of sea and weather (such, I imagine, must be the implication of ἀπενεχ[θῆναι]) on his voyage home.

61

(you), *tua* (I), *te* (you), *Rhodopeia Phyllis* (I).[8] The opening is on the keynote word *hospita*, introducing a motif to be repeated often, e.g., *te, scelerate, recepi* (29), and notably at 109-110, *cuius opes auxere meae, cui dives egenti/ munera multa dedi, multa datura fui*, where the contrast is most vividly stamped in the juxtaposition *dives egenti*—son of Theseus, king of Athens, *egenti!* Inextricably tied up here is Ovid's third change. Those sources which are explicit about the kingdom of Thrace as dowry for Demophoon are all agreed that Phyllis is a princess. It is conceivable that an alternate tradition made her queen, but it is more likely that the *regina Thracum* of some sources is an inadvertent ambiguity deriving from vagueness in the use of *regina* (either queen or princess).[9] Ovid eliminates Phyllis' father and puts her in power. It is she who offers Demophoon the kingdom. Again, we have a change made to widen the gulf between Phyllis' behavior and Demophoon's. It is not her father who treats him well and proffers the generous dowry, but Phyllis herself; and, in spite of this kindness, he betrays her.

As I have indicated earlier, we simply do not know how often and how extensively Phyllis had been drawn in Greek literature, and so we are on dangerous, nay fatal, ground, if we try to talk about sources, especially since the little we know of earlier treatments makes it clear how greatly Ovid deviated. Yet, in a strange fashion, we can talk about a "source." There can be almost no doubt that this whole poem represents a kind of literary game Ovid is playing with Vergil's Dido and Aeneas. Examine the motifs which Ovid introduced into the myth: First, there is the shipwrecked sailor, much traveled, in need of help. This is an *alter Aeneas*, not only in the bare facts but in the very phraseology: *longis erroribus acto* (107) // *erroresque tuos; nam te iam septima portat/ omnibus errantem terris et fluctibus aestas* (*A.* 1.755-756); *te iuvi portuque locoque* (55), *cuius opes auxere meae, cui dives egenti/ munera multa dedi, multa datura fui* (109-110) // *eiectum litore, egentem/ excepi et regni demens in parte locavi* (*A.* 4.373-374), *opibusque iuvabo* (*A.* 1.571), *omnibus exhaustos iam casibus, omnium egenos* (*A.* 1.599).

Ovid's second innovation is Phyllis' royal power. It is fairly obvious that this emanates from the position of Dido in the *Aeneid*.

---

[8] For a less elaborate but equally brilliant use of the juxtaposition of "I" and "you" see *Aen.* 4.333.

[9] See schol. *Ecl.* 5.10; Serv. *Ecl.* 5.10.

For the rest, the love affair, the departure and apparent betrayal, this was, of course, the myth as it came down to Ovid—but it is still striking how, in terms of language, poetry, and rhetoric Ovid has re-created the tale on the model of Vergil's.

When Phyllis complains that if Demophoon abandons her she will have no one to marry, for the lords she has scorned in his favor now reject her, this is Dido all over again.

> At mea despecti fugiunt conubia Thraces,
>   quod ferar externum praeposuisse meis
>   (81-82)

>   despectus Iarbas
> ductoresque alii, quos Africa terra triumphis
> dives alit.
>   (*A.* 4.36-38)

> te propter Libycae gentes Nomadumque tyranni
> odere, infensi Tyrii
>   (*A.* 4.320-321)

> en, quid ago? rursusne procos inrisa priores
> experiar, Nomadumque petam conubia supplex,
> quos ego sim totiens iam dedignata maritos?
>   (*A.* 4.534-536)[10]

And this scarcely makes sense for Phyllis, while it perfectly suits the beleaguered Dido in need of a political marriage and alliance.

Similarly the guilt Phyllis manifests (note e.g., *turpiter*, 57, *dum potui Phyllis honesta mori*, 60) is much more in place for Dido, who, by receiving Aeneas as her lover, has (she believes) betrayed her commitment to her dead husband (cf. *A.* 4.550-552).

When Phyllis invokes the justice of the gods with a *si* clause, *si de tot laesis sua numina quisque deorum/ vindicet* (43-44), we again recall Dido, *si quid pia numina possunt* (4.382). Numerous references to *fides* and similar concepts are common to both (e.g., Ovid 21, 26, 31, 102; *A.* 4.373, 552, 597).

---

[10] Ovid's elaboration of this Vergilian passage seems to have other literary antecedents too. Verses 83-84, both in context and tone, call to mind Nausicaa's remarks at *Od.* 6.282-284, and verses 85-86, with their condemnation of the pragmatic justification, resemble Eur. *Hipp.* 700-701 (might 67ff also recall the *Hippolytus*, 976-980?).

Citations are unnecessary to establish that in both *Heroides* 2 and *Aeneid* Four there is much emphasis on and repetition of the notions embodied in the words *amans, fallo, dolus, perfidus, spes, crimen, dextra* (as oath),[11] *pudor*. But I would like to point out a few similarities which, if not thematically quite as important, render Ovid's "dependence" on Vergil (if there exists any doubt at this point) certain. *Lectus iugalis* (57) echoes *A.* 4.496. This collocation, strange to say, is found nowhere else before Ovid. *Remigium*, fairly common in the *Aeneid*, occurs only here in the *Heroides* (47). *Turicremus* (18) is a Lucretian invention found but twice before Ovid, in Lucretius and at *A.* 4.453. Like Vergil, Ovid uses it of the altar on which his heroine sacrifices. The description of Neptune, *concita qui ventis aequora mulcet* (38), recalls Vergil's Aeolus, *et mulcere dedit fluctus et tollere vento* (*A.* 1.66). The ecphrasis at 131ff, *est sinus . . . hinc* is Vergilian in its shape, though, to be sure, perfectly common in Ovid (see Austin *ad A.* 4.483; cf. too *A.* 1.161-164). Verses 63-65 are a variation of *A.* 4.93-95, lines which Ovid liked and adapted elsewhere as well. The motif of the ill-omened wedding-night conflates several Vergilian passages (115-120): the attendant deities and the *pronuba* motif from 4.166-168, the sinister owl from 4.462, the baleful goddesses and hideous Allecto from 7.318ff.[12] Like Dido before her (*A.* 4.391-392), Phyllis collapses and must be helped by her maidservants (129-130). Dido's last words, *sic, sic iuvat ire sub umbras*, etc. (660-662) may find an echo in Phyllis' penultimate remarks, also a profession of suicide with the word *iuvat* playing an important part (140, 142).[13]

Ovid has the habit, whenever doing something novel or striking, of calling attention to it rather than leaving it completely to the imagination of his reader. If, after reading through the poem, we still had our doubts as to its relation to Vergil's epic, Ovid

---

[11] Verses 31-32 seem virtually to be Eur. *Medea* 21-22 turned into direct discourse.

[12] For further discussion, see chapter XXI, "*Variatio.*"

[13] To my knowledge, recognition of the *Aeneid's* influence on *Heroides* 2 is limited to brief notices by H. Tescari, *Convivium* 6 (1934) 80, n. 3, who points out similarities between a few passages, and Eggerding (170-172, n. 3) who calls attention to Ovid's use here of Vergil's "Dido and Aeneas." Eggerding alone has observed how Ovid makes Demophoon shipwrecked, like Aeneas. I must now call attention to the dissertation of S. Döpp, *Virgilischer Einfluss im Werk Ovids* (Munich 1968) 51ff, which argues the influence of the *Aeneid* here in detail.

lights a beacon for us in the final distich: *Phyllida Demophoon
leto dedit, hospes amantem;/ ille necis causam praebuit, ipsa
manum.* Listen now to Ovid's Dido (7.197-198): *Praebuit Aeneas
et causam mortis et ensem./ Ipsa sua Dido concidit usa manu.*
Not only are the sentiments and much of the language the same,
but these are the only poems in the corpus which end with self-
composed epitaphs (*Heroides* 14 does not). In other words, Ovid
deliberately connects the letters of Phyllis and Dido and thereby
invites the reader to see not only in the similar epitaphs or in the
similar situations but also in the poems and the myths themselves
a calculated interplay. Now the blending of myths or of mythical
characters is nothing new. We can trace it from antiquity to the
twentieth century with little trouble. Consider how the *Odyssey*
transfers to Odysseus a whole cycle of adventures previously
tied to the Argonauts. Remember Vergil's Dido, herself a blend
of Dido, Medea, Calypso, Circe, Helen, or Callimachus' Theseus
(Odysseus and Telemachus) or several contaminated personalities in Silius (e.g., Scipio) or any number of such characters in
Joyce's *Ulysses.*[14] What Ovid intends here is a tour de force
of a different order—to compete twice with Vergil, or, in effect,
with both Vergil and himself. For he approaches Vergil's Dido
episode and adapts it two times in two different ways, once
in the person of Dido herself, a second time in the guise of
the Thracian heroine, Phyllis. The *Heroides* in general are a
proclamation by Ovid of his ability to tell and retell the same
story in a multitude of colors, but on this level he crowns his
achievement when he intentionally redesigns one tale to make
it externally as close as possible to a second and within that
framework seeks to differentiate the two myths and the two
characters.[15]

[14] On the *Odyssey*, see D. L. Page, *The Homeric Odyssey* (Oxford 1955) 2.
For Silius, see E. L. Bassett in *The Classical Tradition*, ed. L. Wallach (New
York 1966) 264-265. The examples of Dido and Theseus I owe to Professor
J. K. Newman.

[15] I had originally thought that the similarities between Phyllis' letter
and the *Aeneid* might indicate a common source, perhaps Callimachus' treatment of Phyllis. Recently Fr. Della Corte in *Coll. Latomus*, vol. 101 (1969)
312-321 has gone down this path on the basis of the similar story-lines.
Years ago Anderson (49) noticed points of resemblance between *Heroides*
2 and 7 and, from this, suggested that Callimachus' Phyllis had provided
material for both Ovid and Vergil. The evidence, however, argues strongly
against this view. Much of the similarity between Vergil and Ovid inheres

But this poem is a game not only vis-à-vis its models, but also
in its play on literary motifs. It is, to a large extent, a study in
paradox, not the least of which is the Catullian *odi et amo*, with
the *odium*, however, sharply toned down to *ira*. It would not
have been the only time Ovid trespassed on this territory of
Catullus. *Amores* 3.11b is little more than an extended exaggeration of Catullus' famous couplet.[16] (Of course, we cannot forget
that Vergil's Dido is not free of this vacillatory and paradoxical
behavior.) Broadly speaking, the poem revolves around the co-
existence of apparently incompatible and (*logically*) mutually
exclusive emotions: sincere love/ genuine anger; hope/ despair.
We move easily from one to the other. Verses can function on
two levels at once, e.g., 7-12 which explicitly make reference to
her affection and implicitly to her anger. We move from concern
(15-16) to tempered love (17-22) to anger (23-54). Later, the
movement is reversed as the indignation of 99-100 is dissipated
in a virtual affirmation of lasting love (101-102). Similarly, declarations of hope die off in despair, and despair is conquered by
glimmers of hope. The despondency of 11-26 is at two points brilliantly contradicted by unconscious flashes of hope. *Thesea
devovi quia te dimittere nollet;/ nec tenuit cursus forsitan ille
tuos* (13-14). Regard that superb *forsitan* which discloses hope in
the midst of hopelessness, which subtly reverses the tenor of the
whole sentence. *Denique fidus amor, quidquid properantibus
obstat,/ finxit et ad causas ingeniosa fui* (21-22). *Properantibus*,
not merely, e.g., *venientibus*; we detect, below the surface of her
professed despair, a faint persistent hope in Demophoon's good
faith.

The long tones of despair are again broken at 87-88, *At si
nostra tuo spumescant aequora remo,/ iam mihi, iam dicar con-*

---

in the Latin itself and can in no way be accounted for by a common Greek
source. Further, Della Corte persists in seeing basic similarities between
Vergil's Dido-tale and the Phyllis myth (e.g., shipwrecked sailors aided by
royal heroines), even when all the evidence points to Ovidian innovation
in the story of Phyllis.

[16] There are a number of vague parallels between this letter and Catullus
64, mostly pertaining to the vigils maintained by Ariadne and Phyllis at
the seashore: 2.121/ 64.126; 2.127/ 64.128; 2.124/ 64.52, 62, 249. These do
not have the appearance of direct influence. They could be coincidence. But
they might reflect a common source. F. Klingner, *Studien zur Griechischen
und Römischen Literatur* (Zurich 1964) 195ff, thinks of Callimachus' Phyllis.

suluisse meis, but quickly renewed at 89, *Sed neque consului nec te mea regia tanget*; again broken at 101-102, *Et tamen expecto*, but resumed at 103, *quid precor infelix?* The discordant emotions reside together in 121, *Maesta tamen scopulos fruticosaque litora calco*; in *maesta* despair, in *tamen* and the behavior described (through 128) residual hope.[17]

But the sense of paradox is by no means limited to the confused emotions of Phyllis. We hear of a crime that is a good deed, a crime which counts to her merit:

> Dic mihi, quid feci, nisi non sapienter amavi?
> Crimine te potui demeruisse meo?
> Unum in me scelus est, quod te, scelerate, recepi;
> sed scelus hoc meriti pondus et instar habet.
>
> (27-30),[18]

of tears that are no sign of sincere feeling, *Credidimus lacrimis. An et hae simulare docentur? / Hae quoque habent artes, quaque iubentur, eunt?* (51-52), of kindness that proves self-destructive,

> At laceras etiam puppes furiosa refeci,
> ut, qua desererer, firma carina foret;
> remigiumque dedi, quo me fugiturus abires.
> Heu, patior telis vulnera facta meis!
>
> (45-48)

The last line, whether ultimately derivative from Aeschylus[19] or just proverbial, is phrased in language that lends it more than surface meaning. For the expectation produced by the erotic vocabulary is destroyed by the context. The three key words, *patior telis vulnera*, are traditionally elegiac-erotic with reference to the blow of Love, but here the context frustrates our expectations, for the referent is in fact not erotic and the context ultimately is the abandonment of love.

More: a monument erected to testify to villainy (73-74), a nearly oxymoronic death-wish, *venenorum sitis* (139), an epitaph which reports that a guest caused the death of his host, who, in

---

[17] We ought to note the brilliant manner in which explicit and implicit contradict each other at 79, *illa—nec invideo—fruitur meliore marito. Nec invideo* of course means *invideo*, as the pregnant *fruitur* (rather than, e.g., *habet*) confirms.

[18] See additional discussion in chapter xxi, "*Variatio.*"

[19] Nauck[2] 139, cited by Palmer.

67

addition, was in love with him.[20] Finally, and of large import, the role of wind and water:

nec vehit Actaeas Sithonis unda rates
(6)

alba procellosos vela referre notos
(12)

mersa foret cana naufraga puppis aqua
(16)

Demophoon, ventis et verba et vela dedisti;
vela queror reditu, verba carere fide.
(25-26)

Per mare, quod totum ventis agitatur et undis,
per quod saepe ieras, per quod iturus eras
(35-36)

(nec) fessaque Bistonia membra lavabis aqua
(90)

... prospicio, quis freta ventus agat
(124)

Ad tua me fluctus proiectam litora portent
(135)

Repeatedly, we are reminded that Phyllis' hope lies in the seas and the winds, which, she prays, will return Demophoon to her. And so, we should not condemn (as e.g., Wilkinson, 89, does) the glib rhetorical wit of 25-26. Far more than being a momentary display of surprising sophistication, it is a reminder to us that the reliance which Phyllis, with rare exception, places on wind and water throughout the poem betrays a grim paradox, for it is these two forces of nature which are traditionally the poet's metaphor for falsehood, fickleness, and perfidy.[21]

It will not escape the reader's notice that this poem is filled with allusions to natural forces and natural phenomena. From the opening designation of the passage of time by the risings and wanings of the moon (3-5) to the differentiation of night and day

[20] *Hospes* implies *hospitam*, but *amantem* does not imply *amans*. Throughout Phyllis describes herself as *amans*, but never Demophoon. Cf. 24 and note 93, 104.

[21] Even in this poem note the occasional allusion to the destructive potential of the sea: 16, 35, 38.

by their distinct phenomena (123-124) we perceive a theme whose instances are multiplied in the numerous references to water and wind (not all of which were cited above) and in the descriptions, sometimes elaborate, of geographical and topographical scenes (111-114, 121-122, 131-132). In a poem whose keynote is fraud (*dolus, fallo, fallax, perfidus,* etc.) and which is constantly punctuated by cries of *credidimus* and *putavi,* "I was gullible; I was naïve; I was taken in,"[22] this is more than coincidence. On the one hand, Nature: consistent, reliable, permanent, honest; on the other, Man (Demophoon): hypocritical, false, deceitful, untrustworthy.[23] What is uniquely human is particularly false. Man communicates—lies: *Credidimus blandis, quorum tibi copia, verbis* (49). He holds on to his past and makes it important to his present—only to pervert it: *credidimus generi nominibusque tuis* (50). He weeps to express his feelings—falsely (51-52). He establishes the gods as his guarantors—and then plays them false (31-42; 53). He speaks through kisses and tears—and then betrays them (93-96).

We mentioned earlier how the *hospes/ hospita* theme, which introduces and ends the poem, serves to build a contrast between the behavior of the two, which is reinforced throughout by reiterations of the "I helped you in your need" motif. This is subserved by the repeated juxtaposition of first- and second-person words (1, 11, 24, 29, 37, 47, 95, 105, 106, 135, 136, 145, 147). But the opposition is muted, for Phyllis is seen not only as the foil to Demophoon, but also as his partner. This is clearest in the opening 22 lines, especially at 9-10: *Spes quoque lenta fuit. Tarde quae credita laedunt/ credimus. Invita nunc et amante nocent,* at 11: *Saepe fui mendax pro te mihi,* and at 21-22: *Denique fidus amor, quidquid properantibus obstat,/ finxit et ad causas ingeniosa fui.* If Demophoon has engaged in deceit, Phyllis is quite ready

---

22 Note *non sapienter* (27), *credentem puellam* (63), *simplicitas* (64), *amans et femina* (65).

23 A contrast perhaps played on at 37f where Phyllis hesitates to believe that Demophoon is kin to Neptune, here represented virtually as a force of Nature. Perhaps such objections to divine origins are not rare (again one immediately thinks of Vergil's Dido and Aeneas: *Nec tibi diva parens,* 4.365). I note, however, without offering any suggestion as to implications, that the paternity of Neptune is also disclaimed at Callim. *H.* 6.98 and in Bacchylides' sixteenth Ode. The latter reference is striking because it is the claim of Theseus, Demophoon's father, that is challenged (33-36, 57-60, 77-80).

to practice self-deceit.[24] Consequently, the recurrent hope against hope. Phyllis was gullible enough to be easily deceived; she remains sufficiently naïve to deceive herself. Hand in hand with this goes her indecisiveness, which appears vividly at the critical moment, when she ponders suicide and turns over in her mind various options. It is not so much her turning from plan to plan that is worth note; this kind of deliberation is traditional— we think of Medea plotting murder, or Dido, or Aeneas himself —but rather the language of her excogitation, a series of periphrases not quite as decisive as a simple "I will." *Mens fuit—et . . . erit* (134), *sitis est mihi* (139), *iuvat* (140, 142). Her irresolution, rather than her decisiveness, is intensified by the repeated *saepe* (139). There is more of a sense of resolve in the final *stat* (143). But the force is somewhat blunted in the preface to her epitaph, *aut hoc aut simili carmine notus eris* (146). *Hoc* would settle matters, once and for all; the afterthought *aut simili* leaves us wondering whether after all Phyllis has incontrovertibly reached a decision. The epitaph itself seals and closes the poem.

What are we to make of the frequent second-person periphrases? Though Phyllis has no reluctance to address Demophoon by name, she utilizes an unusual number of virtually periphrastic expressions: *ancora tua* (4) = *tu; Actaeas rates* (6) = *te; alba vela* (12) = *te;*[25] *cursus tuos* (14) = *te; puppis* (16) = *tu; tuo remo* (87) = *te; tua litora* (135) = *te.* Now there is no lack of *te*'s in the letter and so this may be an attempt at stylistic variation. Further, the association of Demophoon with his ship is perfectly natural since he must return by sea. If there is more here than meets the eye, perhaps we may discern in this usage a reflection of Phyllis' despair and mistrust. In Demophoon there is little hope, perhaps some may be found in the impersonal ship, sea and winds. Let us not, however, press the point.

Certain passages and their role in making the poem work merit attention. Why does Phyllis call herself *Rhodopeia Phyllis* in the opening verse? To be sure, this is consonant with the recurring geographical themes, but I believe there is more. The clue comes

---

[24] Thus, she by and large exonerates herself: her *crimen* is a *meritum* (28-30). He, not she, is *scelerate* (29). Phyllis' self-deceit has been noticed by Fränkel (190-191, n. 3) and Oppel (83-85).

[25] Are we to detect in *alba vela* a memory of Demophoon's father, whose failure to raise white sails proved disastrous?

at 105-106, *utque tibi excidimus, nullam, puto, Phyllida nosti./ Ei mihi, si, quae sim Phyllis et unde, rogas!* Phyllis identifies herself precisely, because she fears that Demophoon may no longer even remember her. This of itself is not unusual, but *et unde* is strange and is clearly answered in anticipation by the *Rhodopeia* of the first verse and by the geography lesson at 113-114 (which I suspect ultimately derives from some Atthidographer's account of the extent of the kingdom). The reason may be simple. Phyllis worries that Thrace may seem like the end of the world to a Prince of Athens. Therefore, she must be exact in recalling it and herself to his mind.[26]

The next few lines are a rather well-known crux:

> Cornua cum lunae pleno semel orbe coissent,
>   litoribus nostris ancora pacta tua est.
> Luna quater latuit, toto quater orbe recrevit
>   nec vehit Actaeas Sithonis unda rates.
> Tempora si numeres bene quae numeramus amantes,
>   non venit ante suam nostra querela diem.
>
>   (3-8)

Burman's argument, that it makes sense for Phyllis to write immediately when the appointed day passes, not to wait three months, and his suggestion to follow two manuscripts in reading *quater* for *semel* (so too N. Heinsius) are to the point—but misguided. Rather than involve ourselves with the logic of the situation, better to consider what the strange text does for the poem. Ovid has Phyllis write three months after Demophoon's return came due. That the text is correct is borne out by the subsequent lines (9-22), all of which imply a lengthy period of time following the day of Demophoon's anticipated return, e.g., *lenta, tarde, saepe, saepe, interdum, saepe, denique.*[27] This is purposeful. By delaying the letter for three months Ovid magnifies her plight and her credulousness; even now that Demophoon is three months late and evidently not about to return, Phyllis retains an element of hope. In this passage we are struck by the present

---

26 Palmer's reference to the Homeric τίς καὶ πόθεν is apt, but he fails to consider why the motif occurs here and how it is adapted to the needs of the poem.

27 As so often, the best remarks on this problematic passage lie buried in Loers' commentary *ad loc.*

tense, *nec vehit* (6): she is still waiting; and by the remarkable *forsitan* (14).[28]

The modified epanalepsis, *Cornua cum lunae pleno semel orbe coissent,/ . . . Luna quater latuit, toto quater orbe recrevit* (3-5), effectively communicates a sense of the inexorable roll of time, impervious to external intervention: Demophoon does nothing to break its—for Phyllis—monotonous movement.

Iturus (36) is the first of several future participles in the poem. *Fugiturus* (47), *itura* (92), *visurus* (99), *datura* (110), *futura* (144). Is this more than chance? In *fugiturus* and *numquam visurus* at least there is a note of condemnation. Phyllis assumes Demophoon's intent to betray was already present when he left her.

There is a neat trick at 73, *hoc tua post illos titulo signetur imago*. In face of the difficult *illos*, emendation has been suggested. N. Heinsius' suggestion points in the expected direction, *illum*. Your statue will stand behind Theseus'. The alternative is to understand *titulos*, which is possible but difficult. It is not readily understood from either *titulis* (68) or *titulo* (73). Further, *post titulos* is strange, since *titulus* is the inscription, not the statue. I suggest that *illos* here recapitulates all the aforementioned villains whom Theseus has overcome. The implication ("You Demophoon come right after them") is that Demophoon is being enlisted in a rogue's gallery—where he indeed belongs. We must observe that the wrongdoers whom Phyllis enumerates are, with perhaps one exception, like Demophoon violators of the laws of hospitality: Sciron, Sinis, and Procrustes, the traditional trio; the Thebans who rejected the common right of burial, the Centaurs who violated the sanctity of the wedding-feast, Pluto himself, the over-tenacious host who keeps all his guests (in this case, Pirithous whom Theseus cannot liberate). It is among these malefactors that Demophoon belongs and it is among them where Phyllis implicitly sets him.[29]

Though anger and love are expressed in rather moderate tones, there is a current of low-pitched emotion effected in stylistic terms. The names of the lovers, the betrayer and the victim,

---

[28] Verses 7-8 are bitterly ironic. Are they a play on the Catullian motif of lovers' count (5 and 7)?

[29] When Ovid writes, *hoc tua post illos titulo signetur imago*: "*Hic est cuius amans hospita capta dolo est*" (73-74), he alludes at once to the statuary and to the poem itself, for the poem is the *imago* of Demophoon branded for his deceit of Phyllis.

resound with a frequency unparalleled in the *Heroides*. Vocatives, interjections, imperatives, and rhetorical questions abound. Anaphora, polyptoton, and other forms of repetition are particularly effective: 3 and 5, 5, 7, 9 and 10, 11,[30] 17 and 19, 25 and 26, 29 and 30, 31 and 33, 35-39 (*per*), 40, 49-53,[31] 58, 62, 77, 88, 88 and 89, 95, 98-101, 110, 139, 140 and 142.

If the poem moves around the dominating contrast between the false Demophoon and the trusting Phyllis, generated in the main by way of bare fact and constant juxtaposition, it is also served by calculated suggestive echoes. Clearest perhaps is the parallel between 74 and the final distich. In the first Phyllis imaginatively constructs a monument for Demophoon, in the latter a tomb for herself, and for each she composes an inscription. But in fact this is but two-thirds of a pattern, the missing link being the opening distich, which is in effect a prefatory inscription. Thus, the poem is punctuated at three critical points, beginning, precise midpoint, and end by epigraphs which accentuate the twofold relationship (guest-host, lovers) and the betrayal perpetrated by Demophoon: *hospita-hospita-hospes*; *amans-amantem*; *ultra promissum tempus abesse—capta dolo—leto dedit* (note the progression here).

Corresponding to the opening sincere *queror* of Phyllis come Demophoon's deceitful plaints: *Ausus es ... queri ... "Phylli, fac expectes Demophoonta tuum!"* (93-98). Phyllis' *meriti summa* (56) is matched by Demophoon's *laudis summa* (66). If she is *lenta* (9) in her persistent hope, he is *lentus* (23) in his willingness to stay away. Finally, verses 11-12 reverberate in two ways toward the poem's end. First, the doubling of *saepe* repeated in 139-140 graphically brings to mind how far Phyllis has come since the poem's beginning, from simple self-deceit to the verge of suicide. Second, this progression, if such it be, is underscored by the the-

---

30 Note the progression in 13-22. First, a rationalization for his not having started out, then for his failure to arrive. In 15 she imagines him coming (*tendis*), by 21 he is hastening (*properantibus*).

31 Observe how the last *credidimus* comes, contrary to expectation, not first but third in its line, probably Ovid's way of achieving climax. Lines 49-52 represent simple deceit on an interhuman level, 53 involves a violation of deity. For heightened effect *dis* is placed first, which also enhances the double-entendre here. From the context we realize that *dis quoque credidimus* means, "I trusted you when you swore by the gods," but the Latin is so phrased that we must also understand "I had faith in the gods," i.e., I thought the gods punish those who abuse their deity (much as in 43-44).

73

matic material. In 11-12 Phyllis hopes for the aid of natural forces
in carrying Demophoon to her shores. At 135-136 her prayer is
that these forces bear her dead body to his shores. In passing, we
must not miss the brilliant word order in 135-136. *Ad tua me*
leaves us in the dark; *fluctus proiectam litora* shocks with its sudden horror. The same technique is repeated (with less effect) in
the next line. *Occurramque oculis* suggests a meeting, *intumulata*
completes the gruesome picture (of course, in this case the effect
is blunted by our knowledge of the preceding verse).

It is difficult to talk about this poem's structure because it is a
reflection of the character of Phyllis, hesitant, indecisive, angry
and loving, confused. Though many of the *Heroides* are dis-
jointed and repetitive in their narrative sections, none goes quite
as far as this one. Most of the heroines are more or less set in one
attitude, unlike Phyllis, who is torn and wavering. Thus, she constantly reverts to the theme of her love since she still loves and
still hopes, but she returns as well to her great service to
Demophoon and his faithlessness because of her anger and despair. Consequently, the movement of the poem is, so to speak,
musical, slowed by recurrences of the same themes, propelled
forward by some slight variations. Thus, after the opening account of her circumstances and feelings, we learn for the first
time of her kindnesses to Demophoon in vague and general terms
(27-30). There ensues a lengthy passage in which she chastizes
him for his lies (31-44). Then we move back again to Phyllis' benefaction, but now in somewhat more specific terms (45-48). Again
this theme leads into that of Demophoon's treachery, now joined
by the first explicit allusions to her gullibility (49-54). Once more
we return to Phyllis' kindness, in a section which combines a
slightly new account of the facts with her present emotions
(55-62). Two couplets on her credulity (63-66) are followed by a
lengthy passage which introduces in new ways the themes of
Demophoon's perfidy and Phyllis' naïve generosity (67-90). Yet
again recurs Demophoon's falseness, but in a new context, the departure scene, which concludes with an explicit declaration of
persistent hope (91-102). The *perfidus Demophoon* motif is given
a new twist in 103-106: a rival love; but it leads directly back to
the old tune of Phyllis' kindness (107-116), a final recollection of
the whole affair which recapitulates for Phyllis her relationship
with Demophoon. Not unexpectedly it ends on the note of his
guile (115-116) which is continued in the familiar mythic meta-

74

phor (117-120). At this point, the poem moves out of the past, into the present and future with descriptions of her daily activities and her plan to commit suicide.

The musical analogy seems apt.[32] Three or four themes are stated and recur in varied patterns, usually with some novel turn; there is a kind of oscillating movement, progressing forward at some slightly greater speed than that at which it periodically moves backward. In a sense, the poem struggles against itself to move ahead, fighting the internal forces which persist in drawing it back, just as Phyllis struggles to move from naïveté, hope, and indecision to firmness, realistic perception, and decision.

There are, as always, verses and passages which contribute little. Line 47, not much more than a repetition of the prior distich, serves merely to prepare for the pentameter's pointed paradox. Lines 67-74 seem needlessly bathetic, as do 138 and 141-142. The grandiose finish is overdone, with its elaborate descriptions of the methods of suicide (note especially *cruenta*, 139; this will be a bloody mess) and the dramatic epitaph.

In sum, important as the characterization is, Ovid's concern here is with much else too. As far as Phyllis goes, Ovid seeks to so emend the traditional myth as to make Phyllis an even more sympathetic character than she may already have been, by rendering her as indecisive and naïve, kind and hospitable, still in love and hoping for the best, and by introducing the plan of her suicide, which, as the reader knows, she does perpetrate. Quite unlike heroines of the same cast, Vergil's Dido, Apollonius' Medea, Catullus' Ariadne, there is no excessive passion, no love at first glance, no wild raving. Her emotion is genuine, but moderated, sincere but composed. To be sure, we must recognize, as always in the *Heroides*, that differentiation may be necessary between Ovid's conception of his heroine and Ovid's conception of his heroine's self-portrait. Drawing the requisite lines of demarcation is, in *Heroides* 2, particularly difficult.[33] But over and beyond the characterization, the poem is a witty literary game, playing on its relationship to Vergil's "Dido and Aeneas," on traditional literary themes, on the language and metaphor of Latin poetry. We might say that Ovid here fulfills, in an extended sense, his role as *tenerorum lusor amorum*.

[32] The point is made by D'Elia (143) and *Atti* 2.386.

[33] It may be relevant to observe that Phyllis at *Rem.Am.* 591ff seems more in the mold of the raving heroine.

IV

Heroides 7: Dido

One need not agree with Austin's dismissal of this poem as a "bland rehash" of *Aeneid* Four (*ad Aen.* 4.305-330) to be surprised by A. G. Lee's laudatory evaluation, "In the *Heroides* Ovid was not afraid to put his Dido in competition with Virgil's, and to my mind in that competition the honours are even."[1] But lest one be seduced by the thought that Ovid's poem could not but pale before Vergil's masterpiece and that we would view it in a much more favorable light did it not, standing in the shadow of *Aeneid* Four, suffer invidious comparison, let us be quick to admit that this letter is a failure in its own right and would be so judged whether the *Aeneid* existed or not. We need go no further than place it side by side with most of the poems in the corpus, of which this is certainly one of the least successful. But it will nevertheless repay study, both for the light it sheds on Ovid's understanding of and attitude toward Vergil's work, and because it gives us rare insights into the nature and causes of Ovid's poetic failure.[2]

In no other poem of the *Heroides* is there less of a problem regarding sources. Whether or not Vergil invented the love affair of Dido and Aeneas is a question on which scholars have not yet reached full accord, but there is no doubt that his was, at the

---

[1] *Atti* 2.408. Seneca's interesting observation (*Ep.* 79.5) on how Ovid repeated a particular Vergilian theme with success cannot, unfortunately, be extended to Ovid's treatment of Vergil's Dido.

[2] For good remarks on the differences between the two Didos, see T. Means, *CW* 23 (1929) 41-44 and Oppel 45-51, 98-100; cf. too R. Lamacchia, *Maia* 12 (1960) 321ff. Eggerding 133-178, has a few valuable points buried under a mass of poor argumentation and unreadable Latin. R. Amerio, "De Ovidi Didone cum Vergili comparata disputatio," *Mondo Classico* suppl. 5 (1936) 1-39, has a few interesting comments in an excessively lengthy essay. I have not seen J. H. Bergmann, *De Didonis epistula Ovidiana* (Diss. Leipzig 1922).

least, the first elaborate treatment of the relationship.[3] We rest assured that Ovid was following one model, the *Aeneid*.

A statistic leads the way. In the climactic section of Book Four, from Dido's awakening to the end (about 400 lines) Dido's many brilliant and memorable speeches encompass approximately 170 lines. Ovid's Dido, in one monologue, goes on and on for over 190 lines, a length attained, by the way, in only two other poems (*Heroides* 12 and 15). Length alone does not necessarily mean a fiasco, but it helps, especially in this poem where tedium and weariness for the reader set in long before the poem happily draws to an end.

With the *Aeneid* and *Heroides* 7 both before our eyes, we must begin by analyzing some of the many echoes and adaptations of Vergilian material.[4] We start with the most obvious:

> Forsitan et gravidam Didon, scelerate, relinquas
> parsque tui lateat corpore clausa meo.
> Accedet fatis matris miserabilis infans
> et nondum nati funeris auctor eris
>
> (*Her.* 7.135-138)

> saltem si qua mihi de te suscepta fuisset
> ante fugam suboles, si quis mihi parvulus aula
> luderet Aeneas, qui te tamen ore referret,
> non equidem omnino capta ac deserta viderer.
>
> (*Aen.* 4.327-330)

Here Austin misreads and then condemns Ovid: "Ovid, in some vulgar lines, makes Dido already with child" (*ad* 4.329). In fact, Dido only says she may be pregnant, a tactical change intended to arouse sympathy, paternal feelings, and even greater remorse, should she threaten suicide.[5] Vergil's lines are not calculated to

---

[3] See Jacoby *ad FGrHist* 566F82, with n. 424 in particular.

[4] Many parallels have been noted by Loers and Palmer in their commentaries, and by Anderson (48-76), and Eggerding (133, n. 3). I think that some I have brought in the text are my own.

This poem is a fine example of the dangers involved in the reconstruction of lost sources on the basis of Ovid. Imagine if the *Aeneid* were lost. We might argue from *Heroides* 7 that in the *Aeneid* (1) Dido is pregnant. (2) Dido doesn't curse Aeneas. (3) Aeneas is responsible for Creusa's death. (4) Aeneas' men do not wish to leave Carthage.

[5] Compare Apollonius' Hysipyle, who also, though with much more taste, suggests that she may be pregnant (1.897-898).

induce Aeneas to change his mind (i.e., to stay permanently), Ovid's are.

Another modification of the same order:

> Et socii requiem poscunt laniataque classis
> postulat exiguas semirefecta moras.
>
> (*H.* 7.177-178)

Two points are made. Aeneas' men would prefer to stay and his ships are in no condition to take to the seas. Here is Vergil.

> classem aptent taciti sociosque ad litora cogant
>
> (4.289)
>
> ocius omnes
> imperio laeti parent et iussa facessunt.
>
> (294-295)
>
> fugae studio
>
> (400)
>
> laeti nautae
>
> (418)

It is a brilliant touch of Vergil's to suddenly present us with Aeneas' long-forgotten men eager and yearning to depart. That Aeneas' ships have by now been repaired is clear. The version of the Ovidian Dido is a last resort, a desperate attempt to salvage the situation.

A similar purpose is evident in these lines:

> Nec nova Karthago nec te crescentia tangunt
> moenia nec sceptro tradita summa tuo.
> Facta fugis, facienda petis. Quaerenda per orbem
> altera, quaesita est altera terra tibi.
>
> (13-16)

First, the city is *crescentia* (perhaps an echo of *Aen.* 1.366: *moenia surgentemque novae Karthaginis arcem*), then becomes *facta*, an exaggeration at the least. Recollection, however, of the *Aeneid* may compel us to suspect even *crescentia*:

> non coeptae adsurgunt turres, non arma iuventus
> exercet portusve aut propugnacula bello
> tuta parant: pendent opera interrupta minaeque
> murorum ingentes aequataque machina caelo
>
> (4.86-89)

(4.260 scarcely speaks to the contrary). The high-keyed rhetoric of the Ovidian passage is characteristic of the whole poem. Note the tricolon of 13-14, each item more specific and more alluring than the preceding; the chiasm extending through 15-16 and embracing the inner polyptoton; and the clever use of participles in 13-20. Present and past denote the accessible Dido and Carthage, while the recurring gerundives suggest the remoteness in time and space of Aeneas' goals.

> Nec mihi tu curae; puero parcatur Iulo!
> Te satis est titulum mortis habere meae.
> Quid puer Ascanius, quid di meruere Penates?
> Ignibus ereptos obruet unda deos?
>
> (75-78)

Whence this argument? Certainly not from Vergil's Dido. It is, however, eminently reasonable and taken up again in 155-158. In fact, it derives from the instructions given Aeneas by Jupiter and Mercury:

> si nulla accendit tantarum gloria rerum
> nec super ipse sua molitur laude laborem,
> Ascanione pater Romanas invidet arces?
>
> (232-234)
> si te nulla movet tantarum gloria rerum
> [nec super ipse tua moliris laude laborem,]
> Ascanium surgentem et spes heredis Iuli
> respice. . . .
>
> (272-275)

Ovid, in typical fashion, has taken the same essential argument, "think of Ascanius," and reversed its purpose. To the gods Ascanius is the heir to Aeneas' fate and must not be deprived of his destiny; to Dido, Ascanius and his well-being are subjects of Aeneas' paternal concern.

Dido seeks to elicit Aeneas' sympathy by narrating the horrors she has experienced and may yet be subjected to:

> Occidit ut Tyrias coniunx mactatus ad aras
> et sceleris tanti praemia frater habet.
> exul agor cineresque viri patriamque relinquo
> et feror in duras hoste sequente vias;
> adplicor ignotis fratrique elapsa fretoque;
> quod tibi donavi, perfide, litus emo.

Urbem constitui lateque patentia fixi
  moenia finitimis invidiosa locis.
Bella tument. Bellis peregrina et femina temptor
  vixque rudes portas urbis et arma paro.
Mille procis placui, qui me coiere querentes
  nescio quem thalamis praeposuisse suis.

(115-126)

In most ways this follows the *Aeneid* quite exactly, but the variations are striking. Vergil's Dido is not driven out into exile, but
leaves of her own choice. Nor is she pursued by anyone.[6] Ovid's
heroine ignores her theft of much treasure. She underplays the
magnitude of her purchase by calling it *litus* (the very word
Iarbas uses in scorn, 4.212; cf. too *Her.* 5.116). She neglects her
negotiation of the escape and her cunning in winning much territory. We have here no *dux femina facti*. Verses 123-124 exag-
gerate. In the *Aeneid* the potential for attack exists, no more
(4.39-44). Similarly 125-126, a conflation of 4.36-37 and 4.213-
214, imply that Dido has rejected her suitors in favor of Aeneas.
But in the *Aeneid* she had refused them before Aeneas arrived
in Carthage.

The preceding examples all display Ovid's modification of Vergilian material for the purpose of building a good rhetorical case
for Dido. Other changes are also present. For instance: Ovid
draws on Vergil who in his turn was utilizing an old tradition.

Fallor et ista mihi falso iactatur imago:
  Matris ab ingenio dissidet ille suae.
Te lapis et montes innataque rupibus altis
  robora, te saevae progenuere ferae
aut mare, quale vides agitari nunc quoque ventis:

(35-39)

The essence of the Homeric version (*Il.* 16.33-35), in spite of
Thetis, is that Achilles' behavior marks him as less than human
and so his parents could not be human beings. Vergil goes a step
beyond, placing the emphasis on divine parentage:

nec tibi diva parens generis nec Dardanus auctor, etc.

(4.365)

---

6 At least in the *Aeneid*. Servius (*Aen.* 1.363) has a strange report to the
effect that Pygmalion's men did pursue her.

"Far from being of divine lineage, you are not even a member of the human race." Ovid goes his own way, ready to infuse an erotic element no matter how alien to the tradition. His Dido calls Aeneas' parentage into question because he proves to be insufficiently devoted to love; as such he could scarcely be Venus' son.[7] Funny, yes; witty, perhaps; suitable, one wonders. Unfortunately, *nescit quod bene cessit relinquere*. Ovid tries again from a different angle. To the long-standing notion of the sea as punisher of sinners (57-58) he appends an erotic twist:

> praecipue cum laesus amor, quia mater Amorum
> nuda Cytheriacis edita fertur aquis
>
> (59-60)

which appears ludicrous in light of the kinship mentioned at 31-32 and 35-38 (the latter passage, by the way, vitiating the point of the former). The *mater Amorum* is *mater Aeneae* as well. Is she to punish her own son? (Consider the role of Venus in the *Aeneid*).

> Si pudet uxoris, non nupta, sed hospita dicar;
> dum tua sit Dido, quidlibet esse feret.
>
> (169-170)

Though but a variation on a common topos, it has its own point here. Ovid's Dido goes one step beyond Vergil's in her willingness to make concessions. The latter is unhappy with a mere *hospes-hospita* relationship (4.323-324); the former willing to have at least that much.

> Audieram voces, nymphas ululasse putavi:
> Eumenides fatis signa dedere meis.
>
> (95-96)

Here Ovid, so to speak, corrects Vergil: *summoque ulularunt vertice Nymphae* (4.168).[8] *Putavi* is the key. Dido thought, as Vergil says, that the omens were good. In fact, they were dire.

---

[7] It is remarkable that Ennodius, in his paraphrase of the Vergilian lines (*Dictio* 28), adopts what is in effect an Ovidian interpretation: *constat Veneris non esse filium, nil amantem* and *edidit ergo Venus fugientem nomen amoris?*

[8] In spite of Pease (*ad Aen.* 4.168), I find it difficult to avoid the conclusion that Ovid understood Vergil's *ulularunt Nymphae* as a good omen.

81

In an outpouring of anger Dido recalls the rescue of the *Penates*.

> Sed neque fers tecum nec quae mihi, perfide, iactas
>   presserunt umeros sacra paterque tuos.
> Omnia mentiris; neque enim tua fallere lingua
>   incipit a nobis primaque plector ego:
> Si quaeras ubi sit formosi mater Iuli—
>   occidit a duro sola relicta viro

(79-84)

These are amusing lines, particularly so the allusion to Creusa which is more in tone than in fact a distortion of the *Aeneid* (cf. *Aen.* 2.711, 725, 736-740). Here it is well to stop and observe how rhetorical ends constantly lead Dido into "contradictions." At 77-78 she makes her point by reference to the rescue of the Penates by Aeneas. At 79-80, in a display of anger, she claims this was all a lie.[9] But come 107-110, when Dido must defend her own behavior, then Aeneas is *pius* all over again and his rescue of Anchises once more a fact. The same is true for 131-134[10] and 159-160, where the rhetoric is of a different sort.[11]

Much the same is the manner in which the theme of divine parentage fluctuates according to rhetorical needs. What was forcefully denied at 37-39 is taken for granted as the truth at 109 and 159. So, too, at 115ff it is advantageous to Dido to assiduously avoid all mention of the treasure she has accumulated. But contextual exigencies change and at 152 she offers Aeneas the *advectas Pygmalionis opes*.

Dido kills herself with Aeneas' sword, a concrete symbol of the failure of their love and of the future enmity between their descendants. Unlike Vergil, Ovid belabors the drama of the situation (185-198), throwing in a modification of the tear-stained letter topos (letter-sword, tears-blood)[12] and adding one of the most bathetic lines in all his work (190).[13]

---

[9] Does Ovid take a hint from *Aen.* 4.597-599?

[10] Loers notes, without elaboration, that 131-132 echo *Aen.* 2.717-720. The parallel is worth comment. Ovid turns the deeply religious sentiment into the rationale of the betrayed lover.

[11] It is possible, though certainly not necessary, that this coloring of Aeneas' dutiful and heroic acts toward his father and the Penates to his discredit may be related to similar "distortions" in an anti-Aeneas tradition. See e.g., Serv. *Aen.* 2.636, schol. Lycoph. *Alex.* 1268.

[12] Further discussion in chapter XXI, "*Variatio.*"

[13] I find H. Akbar Khan's laudatory remarks on this passage (*CP* 63 [1968]

7. Dido

The vision of the dead Sychaeus (4.460ff) is similarly elaborated (101ff).[14] The haunting quality of Sychaeus' ghostly voice in association with other evil omens is in direct contrast to Ovid's precise delineation of the frequency and nature of his address to Dido.

From the moment Vergil's Dido confronts Aeneas with his betrayal she refers to herself as *moritura* (308, 415, 519, 604). Ovid follows suit, *moriturae* (1),[15] in unfortunately typical (for this letter) expansiveness (1-4).[16] Here, however, his failure to perceive the subtlety of Vergil's Dido defeats him. As Austin well remarks, "Dido, in all her impulsiveness, at once envisages her death—not suicide as yet, for it is not till later, when all her hope has gone, that the idea of self-destruction comes upon her and then grows inexorably in her mind" (*ad* 4.308). Ovid, by expanding the Vergilian text, portrays a Dido on the verge of death—note the swan song simile, *ultima, fata vocant*, which naturally lead to the dec-

---

283-285) incredible. Strangest is his observation that "the picture of her (sc. the pregnant Dido) with the unsheathed sword of Aeneas in her *gremium* becomes all the more packed with pathos" (sc. because of her pregnant figure?). Suffice it to say in Ovid's defense that he does not represent Dido as certainly pregnant. If he did, then surely to call attention to her pregnant belly with the sword adjacent to it would be not pathetic but ludicrous.

[14] I do not find the feminine *quas* (100) as puzzling as most editors. After all, *Manes* does occur in inscriptions some half-dozen times as feminine (and perhaps once or twice in literary texts. See *ThLL* s.v.), even with reference to a dead male (see *CIL* 5.6710). *Cinis* in the singular is fairly often feminine and its occurrence in the plural as masculine in 98 does not really argue against the possibility of its being feminine in the singular here. We might compare Catullus 68, where in line 90 *cinis* (sing.) is feminine, eight lines later (98) *cineres* is masculine. In association with *animae* I do not see any cogent reason for not taking *Manes* and *cinis* as feminine, especially when the manuscripts come down so decisively for *quas*. The lines, I suspect, recall *Aen.* 4.25-27; *ad quas* is virtual adaptation of *ad umbras*.

[15] It makes no difference whether we begin the letter at 1 (*Accipe*) or at 3 (*Sic ubi*). In either case the poem open on a note of imminent death. I tend to agree with Kirfel (61-64) and Dörrie (209; he seems to have changed his mind in his edition) who accept the authenticity of 1-2. To their arguments I would add the following: The relationship between this opening distich and the poem's final distich is striking. In each the names of both lovers are mentioned, but the opening *Dardanide* and *Elissae* tie them both to their pasts, him to Troy, her to Tyre, while the concluding references, as he departs and she plans suicide, tie them to their present and future (*Aeneas*—Rome; *Dido*—Carthage). Further, the echo of *carmen* in 196 (*hoc tamen in tumuli marmore carmen erit*) may stamp this whole poem as one long epitaph.

[16] Compare Vergil's *decrevit mori* (4.475).

laration of total despair at 5-6. As we shall see, this does not serve the poem's advantage.[17]

Satis superque. Over and over Ovid modifies Vergil to achieve some rhetorical play, often to outdo his predecessor, and almost each time shows himself inferior. This competition with Vergil is the genesis of one aspect of the poem. It is a commonplace of Ovidian criticism (quite wrong, but a commonplace nonetheless) that the *Heroides* are *suasoriae* in verse. The Dido-letter comes closest to falling into that category. Virtually from beginning to end, Dido seeks to persuade Aeneas. Arguments of all sorts gush out in a never-ending cascade. Why, then, when most of the poems in the *Heroides* contain varying but small doses of persuasion, does Ovid fill this poem with rhetorical argumentation? The answer has two parts. In the first place, the situation is suitable for it.[18] The proximity of the two people involved and their relationship make an attempt at persuasion at least plausible. Think of Penelope, Phyllis, Hypsipyle, Ariadne, so separated from their men as to make communication, not to mention persuasion, impossible. Think of the nymph Oenone and the captive-slave Briseis, scarcely in positions to affect their noble or royal lovers. But Dido is royalty, at least on an equal plane with Aeneas; more important, she is almost face-to-face with him. Thus, attempts at persuasion are virtually inevitable. In the second place, Ovid is following in the steps of Vergil, for *Aeneid* Four is filled with rhetorical argumentation on Dido's part. Ovid expands, elaborates and adds to it. But if it works in Vergil, it falters in Ovid. In part, this is a matter of degree. Ovid works the rhetoric harder than Vergil ever did; and, coming all at once, as it does in this letter, it is wearisome. In addition, Ovid has undercut the element of persuasion right at the beginning. Following upon the Vergilian *moritura*, his Dido, unlike Vergil's, appears set on suicide from the start. But to declare one's resignation and realization that persuasion is impossible and then to proceed with attempt after attempt of persuasion is damaging to the rhetoric of the situation, no matter what it may contribute to the psychological characterization of the writer.[19]

[17] More parallels between *Heroides* 7 and the *Aeneid* could be adduced, but the point has been made.

[18] For some good observations on the relationship between the situation and the content of this poem, see Oppel 45ff.

[19] Hope and persuasion persist virtually to the end. Note the surface

7. Dido

Let us not, however, pretend that Ovid was aimlessly wandering, tallying point after point in his contest with Vergil. His Dido is, after all, a unique creation, sharply distinguished from Vergil's. A number of his alterations of the material serve to differentiate the character of his Dido.

Ovid's Dido is not capable of the extreme anger and hatred which mark Vergil's heroine. She is gentler. But with the fire and intensity she has lost what made Vergil's character interesting as well as sympathetic. Vergil's Dido hopes for the shipwreck of Aeneas:

> i, sequere Italiam ventis, pete regna per undas.
> spero equidem mediis, si quid pia numina possunt,
> supplicia hausurum scopulis et nomine Dido
> saepe vocaturum.
>
> (4.381-384)

In clearly reminiscent words Ovid's Dido ponders the possibility of shipwreck for Aeneas and his men and prays against it (61-72; note *bibat/hausurum*; 67-72 elaborates 383-384). But there is an underlying element that is absent in Vergil. The latter's Dido lets loose the fury of her feelings, disregarding the potential consequences. Ovid's, still hoping to persuade, demonstrates her concern and at the same time enumerates the ills that will befall Aeneas should he desert her (note *finge* rather than *spero*): he will lose his reputation, be punished by the gods, will come to repent. But by a counterpoint not unusual in the *Heroides*, the thoughts flow in two directions at the same time. Though she imagines all these horrors afflicting Aeneas, she hopes for quite the opposite: *Perdita ne perdam, timeo, noceamve nocenti/ neu bibat aequoreas naufragus hostis aquas* (61-62) or *nullum sit in omine pondus* (65). Verses 69-70 are interesting: *coniugis ante oculos deceptae stabit imago/ tristis et effusis sanguinolenta comis.* This, I think, intentionally calls to mind the scene at the end of *Aeneid* Two,

> infelix simulacrum atque ipsius umbra Creusae
> visa mihi ante oculos et nota maior imago
>
> (772-773),

---

optimism implied by *si minus* (183). To the pattern of this letter one might contrast Phyllis', where the decision to commit suicide does not come till the letter's end. For further discussion, see chapter XIX "Dramatic Structure."

thereby identifying Dido in the role of Creusa, i.e., destined to be a lost wife of Aeneas'. This will, of course, take on additional coloring a few lines hence when Dido accuses Aeneas of deserting Creusa, just as he now abandons her (83-84).[20]

Nothing in this letter matches Dido's vicious regrets that she did not kill Aeneas, his men and even Ascanius (4.600-602) or her grand imprecations against Aeneas and his descendants (612-629). Even the arguments that Aeneas stay or delay are invested by Ovid's Dido with more concern for Aeneas himself than are the very similar pleas of Vergil's queen. The latter expresses shock and anger that Aeneas would depart in such inclement weather (4.309-314). *Crudelis*, she cries, *mene fugis?* Ovid, who expands the statements in rhetorical fashion, also tones down the emotion (41-48).

Both heroines request the favor of a brief delay:

> extremum hoc miserae det munus amanti:
> exspectet facilemque fugam ventosque ferentis.
> non iam coniugium antiquum, quod prodidit, oro,
> nec pulchro ut Latio careat regnumque relinquat:
> tempus inane peto, requiem spatiumque furori,
> dum mea me victam doceat fortuna dolere.
>
> (4.429-434)

> Da breve saevitiae spatium pelagique tuaeque;
>   grande morae pretium tuta futura via est.
> Nec mihi tu curae; puero parcatur Iulo!
>   Te satis est titulum mortis habere meae.
>
> (73-76)

> Pro meritis et siqua tibi debebimus ultra,
>   pro spe coniugii tempora parva peto:
> Dum freta mitescunt et † amor dum temperat usum†,
>   fortiter ediscam tristia posse pati.
>
> (179-182)

Ovid maintains the theme of delay as a means to psychological recovery, but renders it also a way of preserving Aeneas and his family, a concern which again displays Dido's love.

---

[20] I cannot agree with Dörrie (140) who thinks that 67-68 refer to Dido's ghost, 69-70 to Creusa's. Rather, all four lines allude to Dido's shade and have as point of departure *Aen.* 4.384-387. The memory of Creusa in 69-70 serves to color Dido's self-portrait. That 69-70 do, however, refer to Dido's ghost is supported by *Fast.* 3.639-640, lines which clearly echo these and describe the ghost of Dido.

Whether Ovid's toning-down of Dido in these passages is a matter of Ovidian modification of her character or rather part and parcel of creating a more effective argument is hard to determine.

Though Ovid's Dido never reaches a point of hate, she is perfectly capable of intense and sometimes nasty anger. In varying degrees all the following passages are motivated by her wrath: 19-20, 27-30, 79-86, 131-134, 141-150. As a result the situation sometimes appears subtly different from that in Vergil. Thus, Dido acts as if Aeneas deceived her in regard to his lineage and his past (35, 79-86). But the presupposition here is only half true. While there is no doubt that Aeneas' narrative has great impact on her, it is equally clear in the *Aeneid* (1.561-578, 613-630) that Dido is well informed about Aeneas' deeds and lineage even before his arrival and already has a high opinion of him.

Verse 90, *vixque bene audito nomine regna dedi*, modifies Dido's generous offer at *Aen.* 1.572-574. For, whereas the implication is that Dido offered Aeneas the kingdom as soon as meeting him, in the *Aeneid* she offered it to his men even before he revealed himself. Of course, Dido is interested in stressing her kindness to Aeneas personally.[21]

Something of an inconsistency exists between 85-86 and 89-90.

> Haec mihi narraras, † at me movere merentem.†
> Inde minor culpa poena futura tua est.

> Fluctibus eiectum tuta statione recepi
> vixque bene audito nomine regna dedi.

The former passage is calculated to condemn Aeneas for elaborate deception, the latter to enhance Dido's kindness; and so, in the latter Aeneas need say only a few words to win her over, in the former large speeches.

I want to focus on the quality and nature of Dido's arguments, for they will provide us with the key to Ovid's conception of the queen and her relationship to Aeneas. Almost all the points are derived from the *Aeneid*, but are intensified, exaggerated, and given additional rhetorical color. The first arguments, posed as questions, make the following points: Aeneas has a land, a kingdom, and a loving wife; why should he go to a place unknown to

---

21 I think it impossible to assume that Ovid's lines describe what actually happens in the *Aeneid*, where Dido offers a share of her kingdom to Aeneas' men almost immediately upon hearing Aeneas' name from them. The singular *eiectum* (89) is decisive.

him, be compelled to seek a new wife, who will never match Dido's devotion anyway?[22] Though Vergil's Dido hints at the first point (Aeneas has a kingdom at hand [4.311-313]), she nowhere makes it an important or even an explicit argument; the second aspect (Dido as wife, etc.) is never even hinted at. Ovid not only makes the points elaborately here, but comes back to them again (145-166).[23] One observation. Whether we enjoy the rhetoric here or not, the fact remains that the argument is a good one.

Dido argues next from the weather (41-50), then expresses a faint hope (51-52), proceeds to an a fortiori argument (53-54) and to the ludicrous introduction of the sea-born Venus (55-60). Again, much of this is embellished rhetoric: the essential point is hinted at in Vergil (4.309-313, 430), but not developed as here, whereas the peripheral facets—the sea as avenger and the erotic character of Venus—are added. Again, we must admit: the basic argument is a good one (and repeated at 73-74 and 171-176).

The argument from Ascanius' welfare is once more an Ovidian innovation and quite in contrast to Dido's wish in the *Aeneid* (4.601-602) that she had served his flesh as dinner for Aeneas. *Puero parcatur Iulo* (75) is taken up from a different perspective at 155-158,

> Si tibi mens avida est belli, si quaerit Iulus,
>   unde suo partus Marte triumphus eat,
> quem superet, nequid desit praebebimus hostem;
>   hic pacis leges, hic locus arma capit,

a passage which plays not only upon Mercury's message to Aeneas (4.272-276), but also—and more significantly—upon the great theme of Rome's dual mission in the world, *pax* and *arma*. We cannot but hear the words of Anchises:

> tu regere imperio populos, Romane, memento
> (hae tibi erunt artes), pacique imponere morem,
> parcere subiectis et debellare superbos.
>
> > (6.851-853)

"Why go all the way to Italy for this," pleads Dido; "you (and

---

[22] These lines ironically recall for us the prophecy of the sibyl, *Aen.* 6.83-94. Ovid's Dido has the advantage of having read the *Aeneid* and knows what is coming!

[23] The play between the concrete kingdom at hand and the hypothetical remote one is sharpened in the way 165 echoes 17.

Ascanius) can achieve these goals right here!" Who will deny that the argument is a sharp one?

Lines 167-170 begin as an imitation of 4.424-426, but end with a twist all their own (169-170). The latter distich contrasts markedly with *Aen.* 4.537-539, where Vergil's Dido characteristically dismisses a similar thought.

There can be little question that, as argumentation, this letter far surpasses the speeches of Dido in the *Aeneid*. Not only are the arguments persuasive but—above all—they are reasonable, both in their content and in the manner of presentation. Here is the essence of Ovid's Dido; she is reasonable. An example: *Nec mihi mens dubia est, quin te tua numina damnent:/ Per mare per terras septima iactat hiems* (87-88); *Hoc duce nempe deo ventis agitaris iniquis/ et teris in rapido tempora longa freto* (143-144). The logic is unassailable. Is she to believe that Aeneas is guided by the gods when all he has met with is suffering, wandering, catastrophe? It might be more reasonable to assume that Aeneas is persecuted by wrathful deities! So too the conclusion at 149-150 is sound. Aeneas would be better staying in Carthage, for at his present rate he will be an old man by the time he reaches his destination, if ever.[24] Dido's cynical remarks at *Aen.* 4.376-380, superficially similar, reflect a totally different perspective and attitude.

Dido's talent at disputation is displayed by her ability to argue a point, concede some hypothetical objection, and then counter it by introducing a new argument. Thus, at 11-24, the argument builds upon itself: (1) Aeneas does not know where he is going. (2) Granted that he does reach his destination, who will give him his land? (3) Even if he gets the land, how long will it take him to build a city like Carthage? (4) Even should he succeed in all this, where will he find a wife like Dido?

Again, at 53ff: (1) The weather is bad; do not leave. (2) Granted that at some time the weather will clear, do not go then either; the sea is particularly dangerous for someone like you at all times!

Finally, there is Dido's tendency to give her arguments erotic shades, a quality totally absent in Vergil's Dido who mentions *noster amor* (4.307; cf. 370, 429, 479) and feels no need to harp on the obvious. Ovid's utilizes every erotic conceit she can marshal (25-26, 29-34, 59-60, 159-160, 166, 191-192).

24 Dido's apologia at 107ff is also typically reasonable.

With the evidence assembled we can gauge what Ovid was trying to do. His Dido is a model of common sense in the erotic-elegiac vein. She is no ranting epic heroine but a lover with a repertoire of traditional elegiac poses and arguments, capable of seeing the immediate realities and coping with them. But common sense and reason do little good here. The notion of a divine mission that must override personal considerations, the ability to perceive and appreciate the strange ways in which the supernatural hand operates—all this is beyond Ovid's Dido. If this, however, were merely a matter of how Ovid characterizes Dido, he might have made this poem a success by ironically playing it off against Vergil, by investing it with a sense of parody and by suggesting an aloofness, a sense of distance between himself and the poem (or its heroine).[25] But I suspect that Dido's attitude is essentially Ovid's and that the inability to separate out his personal feelings from the mythical situation is one reason why this poem fails. Ovid was congenitally averse to the Vergilian world-view and quite unable to sympathize with a Weltanschauung that could exalt grand, abstract—not to mention divine—undertakings over simple individual, human and personal considerations, and could dictate the sacrifice of the self for "higher ends." In this poem we hear not simply Dido struggling with Aeneas, but Ovid waging war against Vergil; and he is doomed to defeat from the start because of his incapacity and unwillingness to appreciate the Vergilian position.[26] One reason why Phyllis' letter is so much better—there is no "philosophical" question involved: Demophoon simply betrays Phyllis. Here too is part explanation for the absence of those great curses which Vergil's Dido invokes

[25] One could actually argue that this is precisely what Ovid is doing. Such a view would have the singular advantage of explaining away much of what appears ludicrous or humorous in the poem. I do not, however, think it would be right.

[26] I. K. Horváth, *Acta Antiqua* 6 (1958) 385-393, argues that Ovid's version of an *impius Aeneas* predisposed Augustus against him and the *ars* was, as it were, the straw that broke the camel's back. Be this as it may, the essential insight here is crucial. *Heroides* 7 represents a serious attack on the Vergilian and Augustan philosophy of life and society. We can also observe this in the parody of the Roman ideals at 158. Moreover, Ovid could never have been sympathetic to Vergil's restoration of the divine and supernatural to serious prominence in literature, especially when Roman poetry had been going by and large in the opposite direction. This will account for the playful treatment of the divine agents in this poem (e.g., 31ff).

against Aeneas' descendants, allied to perpetual hatred between their two peoples. For such imprecations demand a willingness to see the personal conflict between Dido and Aeneas *sub specie aeternitatis*; this Ovid will not do.

The brilliance of Vergil's Fourth *Aeneid* lies in his ability to understand and appreciate the dilemma of both people involved and through this the book becomes the tragedies of both Aeneas and Dido. Ovid simply cannot work himself into the tragedy of Aeneas, but understands and sympathizes with Dido's plight. Dido's tragedy, however, loses more than half its meaning without Aeneas'. She becomes in this letter little more than a persuasive betrayed lover out of the world of elegy. One trouble is that the balance of the Vergilian tragedy is completely lost. Throughout Book Four we move from Dido to Aeneas and back. To the rhetoric and high-pitched emotion of Dido there is constantly opposed Aeneas' cool sorrow. The stony resolve and the buried grief of the hero offer repeated counterpoint to the screams of Dido, achieving a twofold effect: emotionally, it is a change of pace; dramatically, it provides the realization that there is a second side, a side that also suffers, loves, and follows the logic of its convictions. But to hear Dido's side alone and all at once is tedious and shallow, especially when Vergil's brilliant, heartfelt descriptions of the unmoved Aeneas (4.331-332, 438-449), particularly the great simile of the battered oak, turn into pale interspersed comments like *ad mea munera surdus* (27) and *Tu quoque cum ventis utinam mutabilis esses/ et nisi duritia robora vincis—eris* (51-52, clearly an echo of the oak simile).[27]

But there is also a technical problem here which Ovid has failed to resolve. The structure of the epic makes possible the segmentation of Dido's thoughts and words. From speech to speech we can perceive the passage of time, the effects of Aeneas' reactions on her, and we can appreciate the changes Dido undergoes, so that we fully understand how it is that the Dido at the end of Book Four is quite different from the one who approaches Aeneas at line 305. The movement is clear and well-defined. But to pull off a similar achievement within the constraining limits of the *Heroides*-genre is more difficult. True, this is a problem Ovid

[27] Ovid's justification of Dido within the context and framework of the *Aeneid* is quite different from those which exonerate her by denying her affair with Aeneas outright, e.g., *Anth. Plan.* 151 (= *AP* 16.151); Priscian, *Perieg.* 185-186.

faces in virtually every letter in the corpus, for the formal nature of the letter-poem is static and tends to inhibit character development, but never perhaps so seriously as here. Ovid seeks to incorporate into one moment, one speech, elements from a whole series of speeches made at different times, under changing circumstances and displaying Dido's resultant changes of mood and feeling: In effect, to blend into one static characterization elements that belong to varying characterizations. The broad problem—the difficulty of having a character grow, change and develop when she is captured at one moment and no external movements can be introduced to motivate internal changes—Ovid strives to solve in various ways throughout the *Heroides*, as, e.g., in *Her.* 3, where he succeeds in giving the poem the objective structure of the whole *Iliad* and manages to incorporate the sense of external movement to parallel, or rather induce, the internal development of Briseis.[28]

Ovid was not blind to the problem here and he did make some attempt—however futile—at circumventing it. Throughout the *Heroides* Ovid seeks various kinds of effects by shifting the second person to the third person. In this poem a very unusual set of assumptions gives this technique new purpose. For Ovid's model, *Aeneid* Four, displays a constant movement from second to third person, as Dido alternately confronts Aeneas and speaks of him to others and to herself. Thus, the sense of physical proximity that inheres in the opening 24 lines is suddenly broken off and 27-28 give the impression of conversation come to an end, with Dido describing the response of Aeneas. It is a kind of signpost, as if Ovid here says, "End scene one, the first confrontation between the lovers."[29] With the resumption of the second person at 37, the next meeting, as it were, begins (just as in the *Aeneid*, with the "wild beasts begot you" motif, 4.365). Verses 61-62, with Aeneas again the third person, may serve the same function; certainly 97 through at least 112 do: all sense of face-to-face encounter is gone; we feel Dido all alone—or accompanied only by her husband's ghost. Similarly, the final lines which create the image of Dido solitary with pen and sword at hand (185-198), with their address to Anna and the epitaph, seek to again manufacture a sense of concrete and substantial distance between Dido and

[28] For a discussion of the problem in general, see chapter 1 "*Heroides* 3."
[29] It is interesting that Vergil uses this kind of shift to endow Dido's words at 4.369-370 with a tone of scorn.

Aeneas. All in all, however, one may doubt whether even Ovid thought that these artificial shifts on Dido's part could effectively replace the moving "interludes" between Dido's speeches which also provide a real sense of the passage of time.

In sum, Ovid has tried to create a new Dido out of his feeling of outrage at the *Aeneid*, out of, if you will, a moral stance quite different from Vergil's, a Dido whose "case" is promoted in the most advantageous ways and whose position is justified while Aeneas' is blackened.[30] Vergil vindicates Aeneas, Ovid vindicates Dido. In *Heroides* 7 all Aeneas' positions seem untenable. In contrast, Dido is reasonable, loving, sensible, and without malice. There can be no question here as to who is right and who is wrong. The conflict is drawn in black and white.

---

[30] If we can take *AA* 3.39-40 seriously and personally (which we probably cannot do), it would be evidence of Ovid's own distaste for Aeneas. What is, at any rate, particularly striking is how Ovid, here and at *Fast.* 3.549-550, by citing *Heroides* 7, implies that his version, not Vergil's, is the definitive treatment of the story of Dido and Aeneas.

V

Heroides 6: Hypsipyle

The short-lived romance of Hypsipyle and Jason exists at
the point of convergence of two myths of remote antiquity, those
of the Lemnian women and of the Argonautic expedition, each
rich in its many tellings with variation upon variation. Three distinct areas interest us: (1) Hypsipyle and Jason; (2) Hypsipyle's
life before Jason; (3) Hypsipyle's life after Jason (accounts of
which are often important for the story of Jason and Hypsipyle,
by virtue of recollections and "flashbacks," e.g., in Statius'
Thebaid and Euripides' *Hypsipyle*). Unfortunately, the large
number of treatments makes source-hunting a rather futile task,
especially considering the relative obscurity of many of those
who wrote, in prose and poetry, of Hypsipyle.[1] Scholia and
mythographers do preserve small details which at least make it
possible to see what kinds of options were available to Ovid and
to evaluate the choices that he made. We will not, I think, be surprised that, in the midst of a plethora of versions, Ovid has nevertheless managed to conceive the myth and the characters involved in a novel fashion, partly the result of the new genre into

[1] Herodorus *FGrHist* 31F6, Asclepiades *FGrHist* 12F14, Kaukalus *FGrHist*
38F2 (zweifelhaftes), Myrsilus *FGrHist* 477F1a, Theolytus *FGrHist* 478F3.
Sophocles, see Pearson 2.51ff; Aeschylus, Mette, frs. 39-42. Callimachus, frs.
226 and 668Pf. Perhaps also Simonides *PMG* 547. Whether many comedies
called *Lemniai* (Aristophanes, Nicochares, Antiphanes, Diphilus, Turpilius,
and a *Lemnia* by Alexis) are relevant is impossible to tell. Whether Ennius'
Nemea traversed the same ground as Euripides' *Hypsipyle* is open to question.
The extent of Hypsipyle's role in early epics like the *Argonautica* and the
Naupaktia is impossible to determine (see Huxley 60 and 68ff).

F. Zoellner, *Analecta Ovidiana* (Leipzig 1892) 7-23, has an interesting
chapter on the relationship between *Heroides* 6 and Apollonius. For the text
of and commentary on Euripides' *Hypsipyle*, see the edition by G. W. Bond
(Oxford 1963) and the article by F. Görschen in *Archiv f. Papyrusforschung*
(19) 1969, 5-61.

which he has incorporated the elements of the old tale, but partly because of his peculiar psychological insights into myth.

In broad terms Ovid has maintained the external structure presented in Apollonius of Rhodes. Thus, the Argo arrives at Lemnos on its outgoing voyage, not on its return (as in Pindar and apparently in Myrsilus),[2] and the affair between Hypsipyle and Jason follows the massacre by the Lemnian women of the male population.[3]

[2] *Pyth.* 4.251ff; Myrsilus (supra n. 1).

[3] See 53-54 and 135-140. This is usual; Myrsilus reverses the order. I think it impossible that Ovid would conceive of the massacre as occurring in the interval between the departure of Jason and the writing of this letter. Whenever his heroines recount or mention events that have taken place since the hero left they make it perfectly clear that this is the case and usually describe the happening in some detail. Hypsipyle's allusions here take for granted Jason's familiarity with the slaughter. Robert's reconstruction of Euripides' *Hypsipyle* (*Hermes* 44 [1909], 376-402; *Heldensage*, 857) founders, *inter alia* (see J. P. Mahaffy, *Hermathena* 35 [1909] 347-352), on his misreading of Ovid. He argues (and Bond tends to agree) that Euripides conceived the massacre after the Argo's departure, basing himself chiefly on what seems to me a flawed understanding of the Euripidean text. At fr. 64, col. ii, lines 72-87, Hypsipyle, the argument runs (see esp. Bond 128-129), mentions first her exile from Lemnos, then the fact that she did not kill her father, and finally her flight from the island. Given the traditional order of events, this would be, in chronological terms: post-Jason, pre-Jason, post-Jason. Such temporal leaps are avoided by assuming that the massacre took place only after Jason left. This, however, is poor argument, based on the introduction of the Jason-episode which is not mentioned at all in the text. The passage under consideration is one of question and answer, a dialogue concerned with cause and effect. The temporal interval during which Jason appeared is totally irrelevant to the conversation. Hypsipyle explains: I went into exile. Why? Because I did not kill my father; consequently, I was compelled to flee. There is nothing unusual here whatsoever, even if we assume Jason appeared on Lemnos after the massacre and before Hypsipyle's flight. Bond begins his discussion by saying that Robert's order is "strongly supported by Hypsipyle's narrative" and ends it with the observation, "the argument from 72ff is not cogent." This is still understatement. The argument is no argument at all. Robert then supports this position by noting *Her.* 6.43-44, taking it to prove that Thoas married Hypsipyle to Jason. This too will not do. First, because it fails to consider sufficiently the lines in their role as "typically" Heroidean motif (see, however, Robert 381): Hypsipyle seeks to reinforce her claim to Jason's devotion by asserting the respectability of their relationship (which certainly did not require the intermediacy of Thoas, especially if he was absent or presumed dead) and by contrasting her position to Medea's. Second, because it completely ignores Hypsipyle's explicit remarks (53-54, 135-140) which establish, as I've in-

Equally clear are the deliberate divergences from Apollonius. Thus, Hypsipyle has evidently told Jason of the massacre, unlike Apollonius' heroine who concocts an elaborate fiction to conceal the deed from Jason (1.793-833). Ovid may have originated this change, perhaps to make possible the telling contrast between Hypsipyle and Medea (133-136), or may have adopted it from sources which had Hypsipyle (or the women) confess the truth,[4] because this suited his ends. Similarly, Apollonius' Argonauts tarry in Lemnos, it appears, but a few days (1.861-862), Ovid's stay over two years (Statius has about a year, 5.459-460). Lennep's view,[5] that Ovid here follows some lost source, should be rejected; Loers is surely correct in his judgment that Ovid deliberately lengthens the period to strengthen the ties between Jason and Hypsipyle. This chronological alteration has complications. Ovid has an affection for the maternity motif[6] and here takes it from Apollonius whose Hypsipyle is presumably pregnant at Jason's departure (1.897-898; cf. *Her.* 6.61-62. See too schol. Stat. *Theb.* 5.403). But when Ovid extends the residence of Jason in Lemnos from a few days to two years, he must do one of two things, either have the children born during Jason's stay in Lemnos (which is exactly how Statius handles the problem, 5.463-465);[7] this he hesitated to do because it would have deprived him of (a) the pregnancy situation at departure time and (b) the opportunity for Hypsipyle to throw out at Jason the news of the birth of twins; or else simply ignore the biological logic of the situation and assume conception had not occurred till approximately a year and a half after Jason's arrival. This is, of course, what he does.

Just as Ovid revises Apollonius' chronology to increase the depth of Jason's commitment to Hypsipyle, so he revises Apollonius' departure scene to the same end. In the epic Jason is the first to board the departing Argo, in Ovid he is the last.

A few other points of agreement and difference merit brief

---

dicated above, the priority of the massacre. The *Heroides* have too often been subjected to this kind of pick-and-choose reading. Finally, the assumption that *Heroides* 6 reflects Euripides' play is, to say the least, not guaranteed.

[4] Such seems to be the situation in Valerius Flaccus (2.326-328, cf. 2.408ff); is certainly so in Statius (5.452). What we know of Aeschylus' play leaves room for the possibility there.

[5] Cited by Loers. So too Robert, *Hermes* 44 (1909) 385-386.

[6] See T. Zieliński in *Conferenze Virgiliane* (Milan 1931) 50-54.

[7] So, it seems, Euripides too.

mention. The whole concept of marriage (41-44) has no place in Apollonius; more on this later. The Lemnians' response to the arrival of the Argo (51-54) is vague enough to suit Apollonius' account, where the women prepare to do battle, then change their mind, but is certainly alien to Sophocles', in which the Lemnians do fight (so too Statius), and to Aeschylus', wherein the storm-driven Argo is prevented from landing by the women until the Argonauts swear to have intercourse with them. It is no surprise that the elaborate description of Hypsipyle's behavior on the ship's departure (67-74) is absent in the epic. Apollonius follows the Argo, not the Lemnian queen. In both poems, however, the queen offers Jason the rule of Lemnos, and in a similarity that must be more than coincidence each queen emphasizes the fertility of the land (A.R. 1.827-831; *H.* 6.117).[8]

One must be struck, even on first reading, by the distinctive tone and mood of Hypsipyle's letter. There is but little of the tender plaint, the querulous lament, the soft colors that so often inhabit the *Heroides*. The opening lines are revelatory.[9] The abrupt shock of being thrust *in medias res* stands in sharp contrast to most—though not all—of the letters, which tend to start more slowly and with some mode of "introductory" matter. The tightly packed sentence is laden with fact (note, e.g., how much is embraced in the word *reduci*), but no mention is made specifically of either writer or recipient. Still, behind the facade of sheer fact we sense contained emotion, especially in *diceris* (which will prove a kind of leitmotif). In *Gratulor incolumi* (3) the sarcasm, perhaps bitterness, is not hard to detect (cf. *H.* 9.1). With *quantum sinis* the screen is partially withdrawn and in the following words the point of *diceris* is made explicit: *hoc tamen ipso/ debueram scripto certior esse tuo* (4). She must rely on hearsay; Jason has not had the decency even to send her a letter. Underplayed insult is also subtly incorporated into the rationalization of Jason's failure to return,

> Nam ne pacta tibi praeter mea regna redires,
> cum cuperes, ventos non habuisse potes.
>
> (5-6)

[8] Is the description of the stranger at 25-26 just by chance so similar to that of Jason at A.R. 1.784?

[9] The accepted opinion that the distich a-b is spurious is surely correct. The outsider's comment *et in verbis pars quota mentis erat* can in no way be justified. See esp. Kirfel 59-61.

Note *praeter*, as if she merely expected Jason to pass her way and perhaps stop by on his way home.[10] Thus, an informing characteristic of this poem, unique indeed to this one, is the sense of insult and injury. Hypsipyle's feelings are not typically those of the lover who has loved and lost; she is hurt, by and large, because Jason has had the nerve to treat her in an unbecoming and insulting manner. The motif of "merit" (*digna* or *merita*) is common in the *Heroides*, but nowhere else do we hear such a remark, *Hypsipyle missa digna salute fui!*, "I deserved a letter." The sense of self-importance is enhanced by the aloof and impersonal declaration of her name and by its place as first in the verse. Lines 3-4 are expanded in more angry form at 9, *Cur mihi fama prior quam littera nuntia venit*. To the following description of Jason's feats Hypsipyle characteristically appends,

> Hoc ego si possem timide credentibus "Ista
>   ipse mihi scripsit" dicere, quanta forem!
>
> (15-16),

a reflection of her concern for her image, for public opinion, for her pride. We may sense this same feeling of insult in the way she speaks of Medea

> Argolidas timui—nocuit mihi barbara paelex!
>   Non expectato vulnus ab hoste tuli.
>
> (81-82),

almost as if she does not mind losing Jason quite so much as she does losing him to this kind of rival; had a respectable Greek woman won him, that would be one thing; it is quite another matter to lose him to a foreign woman and such a "low-class" one at that (this theme is repeated at 131-138). Do not Hypsipyle's arguments (97-108), founded in appeals to Jason's concern for public opinion and his image, reflect in fact *her own* concern for such things? Again, the balanced question of 111-112, with its deliberate echo of Jason's own words (60), and the ensuing emphasis on the distinction of her own blood-line are products of a proud nature.[11]

---

[10] I assume, though not with the confident ease of all the editors, that the text of 5-6 is correct.

[11] I am not so sure that at 118 we should prefer the emendation *dotales* to the attested *res tales* (see Dörrie 129 for a strong affirmation of the emendation), prosaic as it may appear. Perhaps *res tales* is disparaging. My lineage, my fertile land—all this is trivial compared to me. You Jason can have me

6. Hypsipyle

The *diceris* motif, enunciated in verse 2 as a simple statement of fact that manifests, in Hypsipyle's opinion, an insult to her person, adumbrates a widening theme of "telling, saying" which sheds light in different ways on this sense of affront. *Fama . . . venit* (9), *narratur* (19), *narrat* (32, 39), *diceris* (132). When she writes,

> Hanc, o tu demens Colchisque ablate venenis,
> diceris Hypsipyles praeposuisse toro?
>
> (131-132),

it is no question here of primary and secondary sources of information. *Diceris* represents Hypsipyle's refusal to believe (or more accurately, her desire not to believe) that Jason could prefer someone like Medea to herself. Once again, her aloof arrogance is evoked by her designation of herself as "Hypsipyle" while, in cutting contrast, Medea is reduced to a nameless pronoun, *hanc*. Here and elsewhere in the poem she claims that Medea has won Jason by magic potions and spells (83-84, 97-98, 131), the underlying assumption being that Jason would only desert her under such circumstances.[12]

The narrative sections of this poem are among the most successful in the *Heroides*. The first, however, is clouded by difficulties. Lines 31-38 have often been called into question both because of a few problems of language and because, as Giomini puts it, "inepte sententia renovetur quae est in vv. 10-14."[13] The two chief linguistic difficulties are, I think, of little note. *Diurna* (36), it is true, is used strangely. But the identical phrase, *fata diurna*, with the same sense (enduring for but one day) at Manil. 1.184 is more than sufficient support for the text. The shift, at 37, from *oratio obliqua* to *oratio recta* can be explained and, perhaps, paralleled. We are suddenly presented with the scene as

---

—that is what is worth considering. The emphatic position of *me* supports this tone of self-importance.

12 Though Hypsipyle's references to the bewitching of Jason by Medea are clearly a product of her character and situation, there evidently was a tradition of Medea winning his love through her magic. See Val. Fl. 7.488-489. Ellendt (*Soph. Lex.* s.v. ἀϊστόω) suggests that Soph. fr. 536P. alludes to Medea's casting a spell on Jason, but this is doubtful. Strangely enough, quite the opposite tradition also existed, that Jason bewitched Medea. See Pind. *Pyth.* 4.213-219; Tzetzes Lycoph. *Alex.* 310; Hyg. *Fab.* 22.

13 Recently, Luck (21) has repeated the traditional arguments and condemned the whole passage.

99

live occurrence, with Hypsipyle and the stranger standing before us (note too the shift now to the present tense in 37-40), and are prepared for the abrupt break in the middle of the line as the eager and anxious girl interrupts the stranger's speech.[14] Nor is the objection that these verses are an inept rehash of 10-14 any more tenable. In fact, these two accounts complement, not repeat, each other. Verse 10 is filled out and continued by 32, 11 is expanded, clarified and, as it were, corrected by 33-34, 12 is explained in greater detail in 35-36, while 13-14 serve to complete, by anticipation, the account which is cut off in the middle of 37. Finally, the second recapitulation maintains a critical characteristic of the first which only the most insightful interpolator could have recognized. Witness the verbal phraseology of 10-14: *isse boves, seminibus iactis, segetes adolesse, dextra non eguisse tua, rapta vellera*. Where, we will do well to ask, is Jason in all this? The oxen seem to move of their own accord (*isse*, not, e.g., *te misisse*), *iactis*, but by whom, *rapta forti manu*, but whose? The only clear reference to Jason is to his superfluity in the accomplishment of these great feats, *inque necem dextra non eguisse tua*.[15] This strange pattern is maintained in the later narrative. Again, the oxen seem to act on their own, *arasse boves; dentes iactos*, again, we ask, by whom? Once more, the warriors achieve Jason's desires for him, *arma tulisse viros*; and again, on hearing *devictus serpens*, we wonder, by whom? Thus, in each account of the deeds, Jason's role is completely ignored. This is not the doing of some clever interpolator.

Hypsipyle wields a sharp pen. Jason gets no credit because, she imagines, he deserves no credit. Only through Medea were the acts of heroism accomplished. As often in the *Heroides*, Ovid makes a point implicitly and then throws out later a larger hint lest the earlier subtlety evade his reader. So it is here. In these narrative sections three feats were discussed: the bulls, the soldiers, the dragon. Jason's role in the slaying of the warriors was immediately rejected (12). The implicit denial of his part in the other two labors is later clarified:

> Scilicet ut tauros, ita te iuga ferre coegit:
> quaque feros angues te quoque mulcet ope.
>
> (97-98)

[14] Compare, though the text is problematic, Lucr. 3.84. See *CP* 61 (1966) 154-155.

[15] In fact, according to Apollonius (3.1380ff) and Apollodorus (1.9.23), Jason does enter the fray and kill the warriors.

6. Hypsipyle

Thus, it was Medea who, in effect, yoked the bulls. And that fearful dragon *pervigilem* scarcely required a *forti manu* to overwhelm it; In fact, it was fast asleep, courtesy of Medea, when Jason walked off with the fleece.[16]

The meeting of Hypsipyle and the stranger is a stroke of good insight, for it introduces (as but rarely in the *Heroides*) a third person who acts or talks, and thus, in giving the poem a touch of the dramatic, lends it a sense of movement. And the encounter is finely wrought, with the reluctant hesitation of the man on one side, and the eager anxiety of Hypsipyle on the other.[17] Especially good is her response, *"Vivit? An" exclamo "me quoque fata vocant?"* (28). Her natural concern for Jason's welfare sets off even more sharply his act of betrayal. And *me quoque* is fine for all it leaves unsaid.

Finally, the shift to present tenses focuses all attention on the encounter. It becomes, so to speak, present to us and to Hypsipyle. When she cries out,

> Heus, ubi pacta fides? Ubi conubialia iura
> faxque sub arsuros dignior ire rogos?
>
> (41-42),

we are not able to distinguish temporal lines. Is this her response when the stranger reveals the truth? Is it her reaction now, at the moment of writing? Is it both? Past and present merge in the emotions, in the mind.

Revealing also is the way in which Medea is worked in and comes to the fore. First, Jason's successes and return home are presented. Then, Medea is mentioned, but simply as Jason's new consort (19-20). Hypsipyle scorns to call her by name and refers to her by two nasty and vile adjectives (*barbara . . . venefica*). Only at 75, in a moment of anger, does Medea's name cross her lips, but is shortly replaced again by pejorative epithets, *barbara paelex* (81), immediately followed by a lengthy description, in traditional terms, of Medea as witch.[18] Finally, Hypsipyle turns to Medea's active role in her partnership with Jason, proceeding

---

16 For parallels in the *Heroides* to (1) the scornful narrative of the hero's exploits and (2) the retrospective illumination of an earlier passage by a later one which reveals the writer's knowledge of certain facts, see my discussion of *Heroides* 1.41ff and 75-78.

17 Compare the messenger scene in the *Antigone* (223ff).

18 Cf. A. R. 3.528ff. The section on voodoo (91-92) sounds a bit like Soph. fr. 536P., which may refer to Medea's witchcraft.

with ever increasing intensity to her portrait of Medea as criminal murderer and traitor (97ff).

A corresponding progression can be detected in Hypsipyle herself. She opens with what seems to be little more than injured pride: Jason has failed to write her of his achievements. Soon it becomes manifest that the injury to her pride is larger than a matter of one letter (17-20) and her cool complaints turn into mild anger (41ff), then heated wrath and scorn (75ff, 123ff), finally, violent anger, hate, and curses (145ff). Thus, Ovid attempts to construct a development in his characterization of Hypsipyle, her emotions directed and motivated by her recollections of various aspects of the intertwined lives of herself, Jason, and Medea.

We are often told that the *Heroides* utilize irony as a frequent and effective technique. In fact, this is not true. On the contrary, it is striking how little a role, given the opportunity in a static mythological construct, irony plays in these poems. This letter, however, is one of the major exceptions. Irony is so pervasive, so informing a factor that one is almost inclined to suggest that the poem exists for the irony in it.

> Male quaeritur herbis
> moribus et forma conciliandus amor.
> Hanc potes amplecti thalamoque relictus in uno
> impavidus somno nocte silente frui?
> Scilicet ut tauros, ita te iuga ferre coegit:
> quaque feros angues te quoque mulcet ope
>
> (93-98).[19]

Nothing explicit here, just the shadow of disaster. The implication that a love won by magic spells must turn out badly is suggestive. Verses 125-130 are more specific:

> legatos quos paene dedi pro matre ferendos;
> sed tenuit coeptas saeva noverca vias.
> Medeam timui—plus est Medea noverca—
> Medeae faciunt ad scelus omne manus.
> Spargere quae fratris potuit lacerata per agros
> corpora, pignoribus parceret illa meis?

Hypsipyle hesitates to send her children as *legati* to "plead" their mother's case (*legatos ferendos* is neat; it is a strange set of ambassadors that must be carried to their destination!). Immedi-

---

[19] Is not verse 97 an unconscious remembrance of Eur. *Medea* 242?

ately, Euripides' Medea comes to mind, compelled to act out *Hypsipyle's* plan and send her children as *legati*. Hypsipyle's rationale strikes us as unerring—would Medea spare Hypsipyle's children when ultimately she will not even spare her own? Finally, the curses which Hypsipyle calls down upon Medea's head (151-164). These are so strikingly accurate in their fulfillment that one scarcely restrains a smile; it is quite as if Hypsipyle had read Euripides' *Medea*. Medea will lose husband and children,[20] will prove *acerba* to them, she will be forced to take flight in exile and seek refuge, she will take the sky-road as her last resort and will be blood-stained through her own act of terror.[21] But there is, I think, a secondary layer of irony also. For the catastrophes that Hypsipyle wishes upon Medea will, in large measure, befall herself too. She will be bereft of her children (though not permanently), she will become an exile.[22] If, it is true, line 160 will not suit Hypsipyle at all, in turn line 158 and the adjectives *inops, exspes* may do better for her coming fate than for Medea's.[23]

It is attractive to conclude that the factual progress of the myth with its potential for irony so clear and large is the motivating

[20] The text of 156 is problematic. The manuscripts are basically divided between *illa* and *atque*. One can argue both ways. Madvig, *Adv. Crit.* 2.73-74, defending *illa*, well points out that Hypsipyle claims to be cursing Medea measure for measure and, since Hypsipyle possesses her children, she must only curse Medea with loss of husband. But against this we can observe that Hypsipyle goes on to wish upon Medea far greater disasters than she has suffered and there is no reason why she cannot begin to do so here. She has experienced loss of husband; upon Medea she wishes loss of husband and children. Most decisively, we want here (as Dörrie 134 implies) the irony of the accurate prophecy that Medea will indeed lose husband and sons. The precise parallelism between 156 and 160, with the key words *natis* and *viro* repeated in the same positions, suggests that 156, like 160, alludes to the loss of her children. To Kenney's objections (*Gnomon* [1961] 482) that unelided *atque* does not occur in Ovid's elegiac verse and that *orbus a* is impossible, one responds: for *atque*, read *aque* (as Dörrie now does). *Orbus a* at Cic. *Flacc.* 54 seems sufficient justification for the construction here.

[21] The sentiment of 162, a favorite of Ovid's, may be compared especially to Eur. *Hipp.* 1028-1031 (if 1029 is genuine), where the inaccessibility of sea and land is also an important theme, and to Accius *Medea* 415R³, *exul inter hostis, exspes expers desertus vagus*, probably Medea threatening Jason. Cf. Cat. 64.197.

[22] Is there further double irony at 95-96, given the fact that the Lemnian women murdered their men in the bedrooms, and at 136, *me mea Lemnos habet*, since she will soon be compelled to flee the island?

[23] Presumably 160 and *caede cruenta* (162) are not designed to call to mind the death of Archemorus.

factor for the kind of heroine Ovid has here drawn; in other words, that the characterization is subordinated to and in fact grows out of the play on irony. The future fate of Medea would have been adumbrated most readily by some kind of prophecy and this most easily effected in the desires or wishes of the rejected lover, embodied in curses. And so, Hypsipyle utters curses, not because this is a necessary product of her character and the situation, but because it enables Ovid to exploit the potential for irony. This is not, however, the case, as I hope to show. Rather, the character of Hypsipyle is shaped for intrinsic, not external, reasons.

Hypsipyle moves from proud and scornful anger to the depths of violence and hate. In this she is virtually unique among Ovid's heroines. Though there is a sum of material in the poem which may fall into the category of "persuasive" (esp. 95-140), it is not (as *contra* in *Her.* 7) basically persuasive, for most of it reflects as much on Hypsipyle as it does seek to convince Jason. Although Hypsipyle wants Jason back, she never asks him to return (cf. 111-112). Most of her arguments are self-unveiling or in a sense self-persuading. They vindicate her own position or affirm her own importance—to herself. When she hints that she is prepared to take violent measures against Medea and, pursuant to this, viciously curses her, she goes, in her speech, farther beyond the bounds of "decency" than any heroine in Ovid, including Medea herself. When she cries, *Medeae Medea forem* (151), she does herself no favor, especially just moments after she has described Medea in the most vile and villainous terms. Thereby, she unwittingly condemns herself out of her own mouth.[24] More, she describes Medea pejoratively *devovet absentes* (91) and then proceeds to follow Medea's example. Indeed, with her final curse she even echoes that language: *Vivite devoto nuptaque virque toro!* (164). By the time we reach the last stages of the poem (139-164) there is no longer the slightest attempt to obtain Jason's return, only an all-consuming desire for revenge.

But revenge on whom? If we look closely at the main body of the curse (149-162), we are startled to realize that Jason has disappeared, only to make a perfunctory reappearance in the poem's last line. Hypsipyle vents her anger and hatred upon Medea; the poem becomes more a confrontation between Hypsipyle and

---

[24] A trick Ovid learned from Euripides. Cf. e.g., *Electra* 1094ff, *Hipp.* 1364ff.

Medea than between Jason and Hypsipyle. And herein lies a clue to the poem's key.

There are in this letter surprisingly few allusions to the notorious Λήμνιον κακόν, but enough to ensure that it not escape our minds and that it had not escaped Ovid's (51-54, 135, 139-140). Ovid has shaped his Hypsipyle within the determining context of the chronological juxtaposition of the Lemnians' terrible crime and Jason's betrayal. Hypsipyle, alone of the Lemnian women, did not kill her designated male (piety or cowardice?). Shortly thereafter she loves a man who then betrays her. In other words, for a second time she finds herself unable to act successfully in a confrontation with a man. But—the severest blow—she once again finds herself opposed and in a sense bested by a woman. If she has failed to win Jason, Medea has not. This is why pride plays so vital a role in the poem. Her betrayal by Jason represents not simply a personal slight, but a blow to her female identity. Sexual role-reversal lies at the heart of the matter. The Lemnian women, after the fashion of the Amazons, have betrayed, nay, abandoned, their female identity (note the virtual oxymorons in *feminea pellere manu*,[25] 52, *milite forti* of the women, 54). Hypsipyle has been unwilling—or unable—to do so. But she finds that she, as woman, cannot cope with the male, while in contrast to her a second woman who is herself almost another example of the masculine female has succeeded in defeating Jason. The sense of sexual role conflict is manifest at 97-104, where Medea acts the male part, plays the conquering hero and, most explicitly, seeks to usurp the honors and titles of the male. It is for this especially that Hypsipyle hates Medea, not simply because she has stolen Jason from her, but because she has succeeded in accomplishing what Hypsipyle has not, the defeat of the male, or perhaps better, the assumption of the male role.[26] This is also why the word *vinco* is so important in this poem, for deep-down Hypsipyle

---

[25] *Femineus* four other times in the *Heroides*, once neutral (5.68), three times in contexts of weakness and helplessness.

[26] It is unfortunate that Aeschylus' treatment is lost. One wonders, in light of his unique version that the women made the Argonauts agree to sleep with them and particularly in light of his concern elsewhere with the sexual role conflict (consider, e.g., the masculine Clytemnestra of the *Oresteia*; see R. P. Winnington-Ingram, *JHS* 68 (1948) 130-147; and the central problem of the Danaid Trilogy: see A. F. Garvie, *Aeschylus' Supplices: Play and Trilogy* [Cambridge 1969] 221-224), whether he may have focused on similar themes here.

knows she is engaged in a war between the sexes and she is losing. The Lemnian women, being more than women, can prove superior to the male, *Lemniadesque viros—nimium quoque—vincere norunt* (53), but Hypsipyle, having lost Jason, sees herself now beaten by Medea, *scelerata piam vincit* (137), who in turn has herself defeated Jason, *Scilicet ut tauros, ita te iuga ferre coegit/ quaque feros angues te quoque mulcet ope* (97-98). It is surely this sexual question which is the causative factor for the numerous occurrences of the word *vir* in the poem (more than in any other in the *Heroides*). So, too, perhaps, the greater frequency of *nosco* and *cognosco*,[27] twice with explicit sexual meaning. At 133, *turpiter illa virum cognovit adultera virgo*, the explicit sexual content is suggestively colored by the paradoxical *adultera virgo* and the auditory reverberation of *virum/ virgo*.[28] Finally, when Hypsipyle declares, *Medeae Medea forem* (151), she, in psychological jargon, identifies with her oppressor. As Hypsipyle, she has maintained her female nature and failed. Perhaps "as Medea" she will prove more successful.[29]

Why, then, is Ovid's Hypsipyle so different from—in fact, alien to—all other characterizations of this heroine, whom, for example, Hyginus classifies among the *piissimae*, who in Apollonius is rather modest and soft-spoken, and who seems to have always been drawn in gentle and sympathetic colors? First, as we have seen, there is the, so to speak, psychological factor. Ovid appears to be the only ancient author who has attempted to make a connection between the Hypsipyle of the Lemnian women episode and the Hypsipyle of the Jason-Hypsipyle relationship. For Ovid, the latter must surely be a reflection of the former. As a result of her "noble" act, she has isolated and excluded herself from the way of the masses. Psychologically, she stands alone. To inflict upon such a character the slight of Jason and the defeat by Medea would produce, as Ovid sees it, the kind of pathological response that this letter and this Hypsipyle is.[30]

[27] Excluding forms of *notus, cognosco* here three times, never more than once in the other letters. *Nosco*, here two or three times (depending on the reading of 83), nowhere else more than once.

[28] Given the theme of sexual role conflict in the poem, it would be delightfully apt for the letter to end with *femina virque* (164). Though many manuscripts attest this reading, the correct one seems to be *nuptaque virque*.

[29] That Ovid's treatment of the Hypsipyle myth reflects any awareness on his part of the profound sexual roots of the Lemnian myth and ritual is not likely. On the subject, see W. Burkert, *CQ* 64 (1970) 1-16.

[30] If H. Fränkel (*AJP* 64 [1943] 473) is right, Apollonius may have made

6. Hypsipyle

Second, Ovid has looked forward as well as backward and therein created a betrayed Hypsipyle. There is no indication of any other Hypsipyle confronted with the knowledge of Jason's future escapades. Jason leaves Lemnos, Hypsipyle is later compelled to flee and her life goes on from there, with never any knowledge of Jason's affair with Medea. Euripides' *Hypsipyle* is relevant. Hypsipyle is often presented wistfully thinking of the Argonauts, with presumably no knowledge of what has happened to Jason after he left Lemnos.[31] When she hears of Jason's death, she is quite obviously shocked and grieved—she has no awareness of Medea's existence.[32] Moreover, if Apollonius is representative, Jason never expressed undying love, never told Hypsipyle he would return to her; in fact, Hypsipyle does not expect him to come back! Now we cannot be sure that this was traditional. So many treatments of the myth are lost. Thus, Aeschylus or Sophocles may have ended his play with some such separation and declarations of eternal faith and love (so Pearson indicates for Sophocles' play, but with no evidence), but this seems most unlikely. Whereas Ovid, to deepen the sense of betrayal, has extended Apollonius' stay of days to two years and has enacted a departure scene[33] with prayers for return and assertions of enduring love.[34]

---

a small attempt at showing the psychological results of their crime on the Lemnians by depicting their confused activity on the shore, but in general no full-scale attempt is made. In essence, the Lemnian episode is used (as, it seems, in all treatments of the Argonauts at Lemnos) as necessary factual background and motivation for what happens between the Argonauts and the women.

[31] Note esp. φρουρεῖ (fr. i ii 25) which Robert, subtly and perhaps rightly, sees as a true present, displaying Hypsipyle's ignorance.

[32] This does not support Robert's view that underlying Euripides' play was a tradition of the Jason myth which had no Medea in it, but is simply the result of immediate exigencies. Euripides does not want Hypsipyle to know of Medea, that is all.

[33] Verse 68 is strikingly effective. The distance between the two is concisely embodied in the vocabulary and structure of the line. *Terra*, where she stands, comes first; *aquae*, where he is, last, and the two are separated by the lengthy word, *adspiciuntur*. We almost feel the strain of the eyes (which is, indeed, described in 71-72, lines notable for Ovid's typically good insight into the physiological effects of psychological states). D'Elia (158) can see nothing more in verse 68 than a "contrapposizione spiritosa."

[34] The only possible sources for a sense of betrayal on Hypsipyle's part outside this poem are schol. Pers. 1.34, who reports that on learning of Jason's return home Hypsipyle lamented his ungrateful love, and perhaps the moderate complaints of Hypsipyle in Statius (5.472-474), which may be either

Through his realization that the myth of Hypsipyle and Jason could be seen within the frame of the erotic-elegiac tradition as a miscarried love affair (a potential that almost no one perceived; witness the small number of allusions to the tale in Latin elegy. Cf. Prop. 1.15.17-20), Ovid was able to shape the story into the mold of the *Heroides*,[35] and, more important, to give the character of Hypsipyle a uniquely new and understandable look. But he also achieved one further goal that ought not be missed, a completely novel insight into the myth of Jason and *Medea*. While Euripides (and Ovid himself) had presented that myth from two perspectives, those of Jason and Medea, here now is a third. The meeting at Colchis, the great feats, the marriage, the future destinies of this couple are seen from the viewpoint of an involved outsider. Also, this is a kind of tour de force, for Ovid thus manages to present within the *Heroides* two very different versions of the same events and peoples, seen as they are through the eyes of two women involved in quite different ways, Hypsipyle (*Her.* 6) and Medea (*Her.* 12).

Statius' own twist or, more likely, a memory of Ovid. As for the scholiast on Persius, I suspect that he is simply in error here. It is possible that Persius' *Phyllidas, Hypsipylas* is simply a reference to the *Heroides*, but I doubt it. The scholiast correctly refers the allusion to Phyllis to her metamorphosis, a portion of the myth not in the *Heroides*. The Hypsipyle reference probably concerns the story of Hypsipyle and Archemorus, a more popular part of the myth and one which Lucian prescribes as requisite knowledge for the pantomime (*Salt.* 44). In other words, Persius' reference to Hypsipyle probably has naught to do with her relationship to Jason. Whether the scholiast himself was thinking of *Heroides* 6 or simply using his own imaginative powers is hard to say.

[35] There are abundant similarities between *Heroides* 6 and 2 (first references to *H.* 6, second to *H.* 2): 41-42/ 31-34; 43-46/ 117-120; 59-62/ 98; 63-64/ 95-96; 69ff/ 121ff; 74-75/ 98-99; 117/ 111-112; 141ff/ 135ff; 95/ 93; 137-138/ 28.

VI

Heroides 12: Medea

Ovid returned to Medea again and again in his poetic career. The loss of his tragedy *Medea* is likely one of the most significant gaps in our treasure of works from antiquity and is but scarcely repaired by the relatively extensive treatments of Medea in the *Heroides* and *Metamorphoses* and the numerous allusions to her in virtually every work Ovid wrote. Ovid's willingness, nay tendency, to repeat legends and to reintroduce heroes and heroines in his poetry in completely different, even contradictory, fashions makes it foolhardy to attempt an evaluation of his lost *Medea* on the basis of his handling of the myth elsewhere. In general, the problem is compounded by Medea's extraordinary popularity among both Greek and Latin authors,[1] with the result that differences in traditions are further complicated by individual literary idiosyncrasies.[2] If we tend to think of the pre-Ovidian Medea only in terms of Euripides' and Apollonius' heroines, we will do well to remember Gilbert Murray's observation, which seems today virtually as justified as it was half a century ago, that "the most authoritative form of the Medea-Argo epic, in Alexandrian times and later, was the Corinthian

---

[1] In epic we note Eumelus and the *Nostoi*. Among innumerable dramas, plays by Euripides, Aeschylus (*Trophoi*), Neophron, Euripides the younger, Carcinus, Sophocles, Dicaiogenes, Deinolochus, Diphilus, Antiphanes, Eubulus, Ennius, Pacuvius, Accius. Callimachus treated aspects of the myth too. This list scarcely exhausts the versions of the myth we know of. Even the fresh papyri add to it; *POxy* 2426 testifies to a *Medea* by Epicharmus.

[2] For general treatments of the Medea myth in antiquity and later, see the following: W. H. Friedrich in *NAkG* (1960) 67-111 (repr. in *Vorbild und Neugestaltung* [Göttingen 1967] 7-56); K. von Fritz, *A&A* 8 (1959) 33-106 (repr. in *Antike und moderne Tragödie* [Berlin 1962] 322-429); A. Lesky, s.v. *Medeia* in *RE* 15.29ff; U. von Wilamowitz-Moellendorff, *Hellenistische Dichtung* (Berlin 1924) 2.165ff.

epic of 'Eumelos,"[3] the fragments of which are, unfortunately, too meager to give us much of an idea as to how Medea was portrayed. To note but one problem among dozens: Ovid was surely familiar with the *Argonautica* of Varro Atacinus. But the fragments are insufficient to tell us whether Varro faithfully followed Apollonius or went his own way and produced a work of some depth and originality. Consequently, scholars have been compelled, in studying *Heroides* 12, to act as if Apollonius and Euripides were Ovid's sole sources. To be sure, the work of Zoellner, Anderson, Birt, and Tolkiehn has established beyond a shadow of a doubt that Ovid did make use of both these works.[4] More interesting, however, than the many parallel passages they adduce are those parts of the epistle which find no correspondence in Euripides and Apollonius or go directly against them. Here we are faced with the competing claims of "lost sources" and "Ovidian originality." When Otis breaks down the poem into two sections, the Apollonian (1-130) and the Euripidean (131-214),[5] we must consider the analysis not so much superficial as unhelpful, especially since it implies (deliberately or not) a kind of disjointedness between the two parts of the poem, which is certainly not the case. If the first half is Apollonian, it is so only in that the events described happen to be those recounted in the *Argonautica*; similarly, the latter half is Euripidean merely in that the events narrated and foreshadowed are, by and large, those of the *Medea*. But even this neat factual and chronological bisection will not hold water, since Euripidean events are present in the first half and Apollonian in the second. An objection of still more consequence is that both halves are informed by a spirit which one can only call Ovidian. It will be one of our goals here to examine how Ovid incorporates the quite different Medeas of Apollonius and Euripides into a character of his own creation.[6]

I begin with a point of obvious weight, a severe divergence in the "Apollonian" section from Apollonius' narrative:

[3] *The Rise of the Greek Epic*[3] (Oxford 1924) 176, n. 1.

[4] F. Zoellner, *Analecta Ovidiana* (Leipzig 1892) 23-54; Anderson 91-133; T. Birt, *RhM* 32 (1877) 400-403; J. Tolkiehn, *WKPh* 23 (1906) 1208-1214.

[5] *TAPA* 69 (1938) 214, n. 89.

[6] There is a somewhat useful chapter on *Heroides* 12 in H. Hross, *Die Klagen der verlassenen Heroinen in der lateinischen Dichtung* (Diss. München 1958), esp. 144ff.

At non te fugiens sine me, germane, reliqui.
Deficit hoc uno littera nostra loco:
Quod facere ausa mea est, non audet scribere dextra.
Sic ego, sed tecum, dilaceranda fui!

(115-118)

That is, Medea herself killed her brother Apsyrtus. Not so Apollonius, who, though he represents Medea as betraying him to Jason, nevertheless does not allow her to perform the actual murder. There were clearly two traditions, in one Medea was the killer,[7] in the other Jason or the Argonauts.[8] Pherekydes' evidently made Medea's share in the murder even less than it is in Apollonius: Jason directs Medea to bring Apsyrtus from his bed and the Argonauts then kill him.[9] Who the actual murderer was in Sophocles' *Scythai* and *Colchides* and in Callimachus' *Aetia* is not known. Thus, with Apollonius' version of the murder of Apsyrtus by Jason before him, Ovid turns to the alternative tradition. Moreover, Apsyrtus was sometimes represented as Medea's half-brother, born of the same father but of a different mother. So Sophocles' *Scythai* (fr. 546P.). This was, it seems likely, an attempt to extenuate Medea's guilt. Ovid, on the contrary, offers no such palliative and repeats the *germane* of 115 in 162, *Inferias umbrae fratris habete mei!* We cannot be certain that Ovid knew the other version, but it would be strange if he did not. Thus, simply put, the story of the death of Apsyrtus offers variants at two points, each of which tends to mitigate Medea's guilt. Ovid chooses neither, preferring to adopt on each occasion the version which gives full prominence to Medea's criminal activity. This should put us on our guard against views that Ovid depicts his Medea in a relatively favorable light.[10]

In fact, he does not stint in his enumeration of her crimes. The murder of Pelias is introduced (of course, not in Apollonius and only touched on in Euripides), and, although it would be going too far to argue that here too Ovid adopts a version which blackens Medea over one which does not (do Cic. *Sen.* 23.83 and Plaut.

[7] E.g., Eur. *Medea* 167; a Roman tragedy (perhaps Accius' *Medea*), *TRF*[3] fab. inc. xciii; Lycoph. *Alex.* 1318. See too Tzetz. Lycoph. *Alex.* 175; Apollod. 1.9.24.

[8] E.g., Apollonius 4.464-481; Hyg. *Fab.* 23; schol. Eur. *Medea* 167.

[9] *FGrHist* 3F32a.

[10] See e.g., Anderson 131, 133.

Pseud. 868-872 bear witness to a tradition in which Medea did indeed rejuvenate Pelias?), still the moving phraseology is conspicuous, for Medea is condemned not merely for the murder of Pelias but also for the corruption of his faithful daughters (131-132). Even the initial relationship between Medea and Jason seems less innocent than it customarily is, *virginitas facta est peregrini praeda latronis* (113); they invariably share a perfectly respectable relationship until, under compulsion, they sleep together to effect a marriage (e.g., A.R. 4.1098ff). Of course, Ovid does not hesitate to make considerable allusion to the forthcoming murder of her children, veiled though it be (211-214). In comparison we might notice Dionysius Skytobrachion's Medea[11] (and even Apollonius' to a degree) to understand how it were possible to put Medea in a moderately positive light; Ovid's creation is worlds apart.

Additional indices. After the traditional wish that she had died before meeting Jason, Medea goes on: *tum potui Medea mori bene. Quidquid ab illo/ produxi vitae tempore, poena fuit* (7-8). Palmer translates *poena* "misery," but this seems doubtful. First, *poena* almost never lacks a punitive notion before Seneca (*Her.* 5.8 seems an exception). Second, such an interpretation deprives the poem here of a motif of much importance and it vitiates the force of the antithesis, *tum potui mori bene // poena fuit*; the contrast is not weakly honor/ suffering, but honor/ shame, crime, punishment. When Medea describes that period of her life as one of punishment, she means precisely what she says. For the crimes that she has perpetrated she recognizes the misery she has experienced as deserved recompense. When later she invokes the justice of the gods, retribution is due not only herself but Jason as well, *Numen ubi est? Ubi di? Meritas subeamus in alto,/ tu fraudis poenas, credulitatis ego* (121-122). By the poem's end, consciousness of her own guilt has dissolved in the face of her recognition and condemnation of Jason's crimes, *sed quid praedicere poenam/ attinet?* (209-210). Merited punishment is still uppermost in her mind, as it was at the beginning, but it is now the punishment she will inflict upon Jason, no longer that which she deservedly suffers. But lines 121-122 should not be passed over so quickly. The pentameter has, after all, shocked many readers. Listen to Palmer: "No two verses of the *Heroides* are

[11] *FGrHist* 32F14.45ff.

more frigid and absurd; that a woman should assign her credulity as a reason for her deserving retribution from heaven, after mentioning that she has murdered her brother, is laughable. Verily bonus Ovidius dormitat. Is it too wild to suppose these lines spurious?" Now this manages to miss the point precisely as it hits it on the head. Medea recognizes her guilt—after a fashion. She was guilty of gullibility, credulity, naïveté, of allowing herself to be taken in by Jason. It is the very triviality of the remark following hard upon her admission of fratricide that makes the juxtaposition so horrifying. To be so concerned with her own image, her pride, her power when she recognizes herself as a fratricide brands her character and her values in the most sinister and blackest tones. More: three times in the letter she makes explicit and legalistic reference to her guilt (nocens, 108, 120, 134), language that no other heroine in the corpus utilizes.

Self-incriminating also is the distich 133-134:[12] *Ut culpent alii, tibi me laudare necesse est,/ pro quo sum totiens esse coacta nocens.* Jason is, as Medea herself knows perhaps better than anyone, the last person to serve as a point of reference for judging moral behavior; but when Medea describes herself as *coacta nocens*, which is justified neither by any account of the myth we know nor by Medea's own descriptions of the events in this letter —she may claim naïveté, coercion is quite another matter—we identify a weak attempt at softening the guilt of which she herself is cognizant. We wonder too at the nearly paranoiac outburst at 161-164,

> Laese pater, gaude! Colchi gaudete relicti!
> Inferias umbrae fratris habete mei!
> Deseror amissis regno patriaque domoque
> coniuge, qui nobis omnia solus erat,

especially *amissis*, etc., a far cry from the more accurate *Proditus est genitor, regnum patriamque reliqui* (111), and another instance of Medea's revaluation. When she follows these four lines not with regret or remorse but with expressions of disappointment at her own weaknesses and failures, we realize that there is no hope for this dastardly villain, an impression reinforced in the semi-Euripidean lines 177-182 with their fear of ridicule en-

---

12 This distich serves an interesting structural function. By standing between references to the murder of Pelias and Jason's divorce of Medea, it enables Medea to bridge some ten years of happy marriage in silence.

hanced by the implication that Jason will have to invent new accusations against her—as if the present ones do not suffice!

In its abrupt (*at*), nasty (I was not inconsiderate, as you are), and somewhat arrogant tone (*Colchorum . . . regina*, especially since *regina* more usually means queen), the opening distich introduces us to Ovid's Medea.[13] The past unfolds through a series of rhetorical questions, taking us unobtrusively from the sailing of the Argo (9-10) to its arrival in Colchis (11-12) to the first appearance of Jason before Medea (13-14). Thence to the yoking of the bulls (17-18) and the sowing of the seeds (19-20). This skillful narrative not only advances the chronological movement but also progressively narrows the focus, an almost cinematic technique, as if the perspective narrows from a panoramic one to an isolated close-up: from the view of the ship Argo (9-10) to that of the masses of individual Colchians and Greeks (11-12) to that of the single protagonists, Jason and Medea (13ff). Most important—and typical of the *Heroides*—is the fusion of narrative with emotional response: the rhetorical questions simultaneously present the events and implicitly wish that they had never taken place; the wishes become explicit at 17-20. This instance of the rather common motif, "would that these events had never happened" is set off by the uniqueness of its substance. Nowhere else in the *Heroides* does a heroine phrase such a wish in these terms, i.e., that the hero had died (contrast, e.g., 10.103-104). This is Medea.

To turn more closely to the so-called Apollonian portion of the poem, much in the epic narrative is missing here, certainly in large part owing to the relative capacities of the two genres.[14] Thus, the meeting of Aeetes and Argos and the dialogue between Jason and Aeetes are ignored. But this is also the product of the perspective. Apollonius is concerned in an objective fashion with his hero Jason, while Ovid presents Medea's responses and reac-

---

[13] See Kirfel (74-77), who argues convincingly that the poem begins with *At tibi Colchorum—memini—regina vacavi*. I cannot but wonder whether this is, conscious or otherwise, a reminiscence of another opening verse of a famous ill-fated love story, *Aen.* 4.1, *At regina*.

[14] I argue from Apollonius' version not simply because I do think that Ovid was using it and deliberately diverging from it, but also because it offers (regardless of Quellenforschung) a very good point of comparative reference and, under any circumstances, can illuminate Ovid's treatment by virtue of its different emphases, focal points, and aims.

tions. Jason enters the palace at 31-32, and at 41 the labors are imposed upon him. In the interval, instead of the speeches of Argos and Jason, we get only a description of Medea's infatuation (quite different from Apollonius', 3.275-298, though 33 is an echo of 3.454, precisely because of the subjective and hindsighted perspective), which falsifies Jason's role: *Perfide, sensisti! Quis enim bene celat amorem?* (39).[15]

The description of the labors is brilliant. Lines 41-52 at once do and do not recount the orders as Aeetes proffers them. First, the yoking of the fire-breathing bulls (41-46), next, the sowing of the seeds (47-50), finally, the confrontation with the sleepless dragon (51-52). Yet, the most cursory comparison with the relevant lines in Apollonius testifies to enormous differences. (1) Ovid leaves out Aeetes' account of his own ability to perform these feats and adds *insolito,* in contradiction to the facts in Apollonius. (2) Apollonius does not mention the combat with the dragon as one of the tasks. (3) The difference in tone is remarkable. Apollonius describes the bulls in direct factual language (3.409-410) and so too the "seeds," with one qualifier ὄφιος δεινοῖο . . . ὀδόντας (414). Ovid's account is filled with emotive adjectives: *dura, ferorum, insolito, saevi, terribilis, nigra, devota, iniqua.* In other words, we hear not the language of Aeetes (clearly he does not tell Jason, *qui peterent natis secum tua corpora telis,* 49), but his commands filtered through the mind of the anxious spectator, Medea. This anxiety, conveyed in dark and somber tones, is that of the love-struck girl who ponders the terrible hidden realities of her father's words. Understanding the passage in this light il-

---

15 Two items of note in this passage. (1) Is *perii* (35) two-edged? "I fell madly in love," "I was doomed." (2) Verse 38 seems to echo Apollonius 3.1018-1019. But this does not, in my opinion, satisfactorily account for the differences in Ovid's text and especially for the peculiarity of the Latin: *abstulerant oculi lumina nostra tui. Aufero* + "eyes" in the accusative usually means "avert one's gaze," e.g., Stat. *Theb.* 7.508, or, if the eyes belong to someone else, "turn another person's gaze upon oneself" (e.g., Stat. *Theb.* 6.669). No parallel exists for Ovid's extended metaphorical use of the phrase. I wonder whether Ovid's usage implies or reflects the notion of a magical spell. Medea hints that through the contact of eyes Jason bewitched her, a manner of witchcraft, interestingly enough, not unused by Medea herself. Recall how she bewitches Talos by gazing into his eyes, by giving him, in effect, the evil eye (A.R. 4.1669-1670). And to be sure, there was a tradition that Jason did win Medea's love through magic (e.g., Pind. *Pyth.* 4.213-219), though not this sort of sorcery. Finally, I note that at *Her.* 6.131 *aufero* is used of enchantment, coincidentally or not, this time of Jason's by Medea.

luminates the problem of the third labor. Scholars have either assumed that 51-52 is an interpolation[16] or that Ovid follows a tradition in which the conquest of the dragon was one of the assigned labors.[17] The former is foolish, the latter unnecessary. The account is Medea's reminiscence and the difference is due to the perspective. When Medea hears her father prescribe the tasks, *she* knows that even should Jason succeed he must in the end face the dangerous dragon; the thought is in her mind, not necessarily in the commands of Aeetes.

Jason's departure in gloom is similarly compressed, with again the addition of Medea's emotional involvement: *Tristis abis. Oculis abeuntem prosequor udis/ et dixit tenui murmure lingua: "Vale!"* (57-58).[18] At this point some 500 lines in Apollonius, from Jason's departure till his meeting with Medea, are condensed into ten lines (59-68), with the inevitable result that much material is left out and some drastic changes in the sequence of events are effected. But Ovid does incorporate from Apollonius Medea's anxiety, her waking nightmares, her insomnia, the mediation of her sister and her agreement to help the Argonauts. What is, however, most significant is what Apollonius has emphasized and Ovid has left out, Medea's indecision and internal conflict. Her inability to understand her own feelings, the fears that her emotions are—or will prove to be—betrayal of her family and country, her hesitation as shame (αἰδώς, 652) and desire (ἵμερος, 653) battle within her, the roundabout manner in which Chalciope asks and Medea agrees to help Jason (contrast the directness and immediacy of 67-68), the ensuing guilt which afflicts her and the remorse with thoughts of suicide—all this is nowhere in Ovid. One might suspect that Ovid's Medea ignores all this because it is in her interest to show Jason how unwavering she was in lending him aid, but even if this is so (and I doubt it),[19] another effect

[16] E.g., Zoellner (supra n. 4) 24-25.

[17] As in Pind. *Pyth.* 4.241-246 and Herodorus *FGrHist* 31F52.

[18] Note the circular composition of the passage (25-58):

    25-26 / 57-58—Jason comes to the palace; he leaves it.

    27-30 / 55-56—References to Creusa and Creon.

    31-32 / 53-54—Jason sits down; Jason rises from his seat.

    33-38 / 41-52—Medea sees a strange vision; Jason hears a strange report.

[19] I am doubtful because Medea makes scarcely any attempt to reclaim Jason. It is not till 185 that there is any indication that she even wants him back. And then one wonders whether she is not really interested in

is much more powerful. Medea is deprived of the moral stature and integrity which Apollonius is at such pains to endow her with. Ovid's Medea has no concern for parents and country, no sense that she may be performing an act of disloyalty. For whatever reason (overpowering love?) she is unable to glimpse the ethics of the situation.[20]

Consider the meeting-scene. The locale is described in sinister tones absent in Apollonius, *nemus . . . atrum* (68); *vix illuc radiis solis adire licet* (70), the latter verse significant, I suspect, in a way modern orthography must obscure; we should think, as the ancients would have thought, of *solis* and *Solis*, and understand the allusion in light of both Medea's descent from *Sol* and the common motif of the "all-seeing sun," as here ten lines later, *cuncta videntis avi* (80). Medea betrays her origin from *Sol* by adopting the evil ways of the nocturnal deity, Hecate.[21] At any rate, once again the modest and hesitant girl of Apollonius is nowhere to be seen. Jason's speech bears little resemblance to the hero's in Apollonius, in part because the latter's responds to the shy and reserved demeanor of Apollonius' heroine. Ovid's is a gem of understated rhetoric, highly persuasive in its direct simplicity, making effective use of the promise of marriage which Apollonius' Jason does not propose until Medea, in her childlike and appealing way, virtually puts it in his mouth (1128-1130).[22] Ovid's Medea, by turning the dialogue between herself and Jason into one abbreviated speech, distorts the course of that meeting

---

her office, her status, *redde torum* (195). In this and many other of the *Heroides* persuasion is of tiny import. Birt's description of Medea as a suppliant trying to revive Jason's love is far off the mark, relevant to but a few verses in the whole poem—and even in these we may question the "love" element.

20 Quite different is the Medea of the *Metamorphoses*, who is, for a while at least, torn between the conflicting claims of honor and love (7.1-73).

21 The poem abounds in references to fire, heat, flames. Does this have something to do with (a) Medea's relation to *Sol*, (b) fire as the weapon of Hecate (cf. Soph. *Rhizotomoi* fr. 535P.) and the ultimate burning deaths of Creusa and Creon (as surely at 182)?

22 It is a cunning and clever speech. Jason begins by stressing the glory Medea will earn by saving him, then presents himself as suppliant begging pity. Finally—in lines noteworthy for the inversion of the Euripidean theme of Jason's, the Greek's, condescension toward Medea, the barbarian (*Quodsi forte virum non dedignare Pelasgum*, 85)—he offers marriage.

to make it appear as if Jason smooth-talked her into giving him aid. And the following lines corroborate this:

> Haec animum—et quota pars poterat?—movere puellae
>   simplicis et dextra dextera iuncta meae.
> Vidi etiam lacrimas,—an pars est fraudis in illis?
>   Sic cito sum verbis capta puella tuis.

(91-94)

Jason sheds no tears in Apollonius; in fact, it is Medea who does (1064, 1077, 1118-1119)! Further, when she claims that Jason's words persuaded her, she not only ignores the situation in Apollonius, but also her own earlier admission that she promised Chalciope to aid Jason, even before meeting him.[23] She is condemned out of her own mouth.

In passing we note a nice touch at 99-100: *Ipsa ego, quae dederam medicamina, pallida sedi,/ cum vidi subitos arma tenere viros.* Medea is not spectator to the labors in Apollonius.

If Apollonius offers us a young girl, modest and naïve, innocent and devout, who is at length corrupted only under the influence of an unexpected and abrupt crisis,[24] Ovid presents a villainous creature, a fratricide, a corruptor of the innocent, about to become a child-murderer, who, though always aware of her crimes and her guilt, seeks to represent herself as a girl, once innocent and pure, corrupted by a treacherous criminal.[25] Besides Medea, only Hermione of the heroines calls herself twice a *puella*, and, shockingly, Medea alone refers to herself as *simplex*. At every point in the letter where we are presented with a virtuous or a naïve young Medea, we are abruptly and immediately returned to the present and set face-to-face with Medea as she is, a technique which ensures that we never get carried away by the picture of the gullible maid or forget the traitor and murderer. The Medea of the distant past is constantly opposed by the Medea of the present, and we are never allowed to separate the one from the other. As soon as we get the first view of the innocent love-

---

[23] Again, comparison with the *Metamorphoses* is fruitful. There, Chalciope is left out and it is indeed Jason's personal request that wins Medea over.

[24] See the discussion in H. Fränkel, *Noten zu den Argonautika des Apollonios* (Munich 1968) 487ff.

[25] One thinks of the reference in the *Auct. ad Her.* (2.25.40) to a passage in some Roman tragedy (Pacuvius' *Medus?*) wherein Medea tries to whitewash an obvious crime she has committed, of course, to no avail.

sick girl (33-38), we immediately see too the hard-hearted Medea seeking to deflect responsibility from where it properly rests (39-40). No sooner do we glimpse the anxious girl, worried about the plight of Jason, than we recognize the rival of Creusa (55-56) and the enemy of Creon—and we know what this foreshadows. Lines 59-94, which tend in the same direction, have already been discussed.

Awestruck and concerned Medea awaits the outcome of Jason's labors (95-104). But immediately Creusa returns (105-108) and, but one distich later, Medea acknowledges herself as traitor and murderer (111-118). Moreover, when she claims (108) that Jason now rejects her for being *nocens*, this is, of course, projection. Jason (at least in Euripides' play) never indicates he divorces Medea for her character and actions; this is rather Medea's inner sense of guilt receiving external expression.

All this is to say that Ovid advances a Medea who makes a futile attempt at "apologia," a whitewash which does not prevent us from seeing that the naïve but virtuous Medea never existed; she appears as such only in Medea's distorted self-image. We may guess that Ovid was unwilling to allow for a youthful Medea like Apollonius' because he found it difficult to conceive such a person proceeding to commit deeds of such gruesome violence as Medea did. To turn this around, we might say that Ovid re-creates Apollonius' Medea in terms of the Euripidean Medea. By which I mean, at the least, that the villainous heroine of Euripides' play is introduced into the earlier Medea, though it is likely that a play like Euripides' *Peliades* had treated the earlier Medea in a similarly negative fashion.[26] One step further: Even Euripides' Medea wavers when contemplating her revenge against Jason. Ovid ignores this. The conflict between reason and passion is nowhere in sight. This Medea has no such qualms; she is resolved to follow her passion wherever it leads, *quo feret ira sequar. Facti fortasse pigebit* (211); just as in the past, Medea remains ready to act first and regret later. All her experience has taught her nothing, changed her not a whit.

There is little good to be said for Ovid's Medea. Over and above everything already said, her contemptible personality is sharpened by a sense of superiority (e.g., 3, which scarcely jibes with her later claim that she was but a naïve girl), nasty vitupera-

---

[26] See Webster 32-36.

tion and enjoyment of it (23-24), self-concern, arrogance (e.g., 183-184), a casual propensity for violence (211-214), her lack of sincere feeling for Jason (even her "love" is self-serving, possessive, and grasping, 175-176, 199-200).[27]

Ovid sets a countervailing background to the icily cold, clear-thinking Medea, an ambience full of the sinister, the mysterious, the unknown, and the unusual. To an extent this was an integral part of the Argo-Medea tale—a sorceress of the remote East, fire-breathing oxen, a vigilant dragon, the novelty of the Argo itself.[28] Still, Ovid takes special pains to depict the initial situation in terms of its strangeness. Jason is preternaturally attractive (13-14), the Argo is novel (15, 25), Medea is shocked by the queer pangs of love (35), the plough is *insolito* (42), the oxen are unique (43), seeds are sown for destruction, a crop that harms its own cultivator (47-50), eyes do not close (51-52). Soon after we are taken into the sunless grove (68ff). Thus, we apprehend the sense of darkness and mystery which not only enfold the events described but also enshroud the final lines of the poem.

Ovid plays on the "dramatic" theme of reversal. Medea begins as the regal personage from whom Jason must beg favors (*regina*, 3; *peteres*, 4), and ends as the suppliant throwing herself before him (187-188). In time gone by it was Jason who was under another's thumb (*iussus*, 25), now it is she (*iussa*, 137). Once it was Jason who passed from the palace in gloom (57), now it is Medea (137, 150). Once Jason came to Medea, took an oath in the name of *Sol* and other deities, begged her aid and offered marriage (75-90); now Medea takes a similar oath, ironically beseeching Jason to restore that marriage of old (193-196). Finally, a keynote is sounded in line 8 with *poena*. Till now Medea's life of torment has been punishment for her sins, but now the final *poena* (209) will be the recompense Jason will pay for his betrayal.[29]

---

[27] The language of 199 seems significant, *te peto, quem merui*. Not, I have earned your love, but I have earned you. Medea is possessive. *Mereo* + a personal accusative (not a god) seems to have no classical parallels (*ThLL* s.v. cites only Mart. Cap. 9.907 and *Anth.* 53.1. *Her.* 2.61 would be another instance if, as is not at all likely, *te*, not *me*, is the right reading). If the usage of *emereo* can shed light, we ought to note that *emereo* + a personal accusative is usually not a "nice" phrase, most often denoting nothing but sexual favors.

[28] For the novelty of the Argo, most illuminating is Accius' famous description (*Medea*; *TRF*³ 391-402).

[29] The thematic reversal produces a concomitant structural balance whereby

The elaborate description of the wedding procession which awakens Medea to the intensity of her plight, a scene with no precedent in, at any rate, Euripides' *Medea*, affords the poem a moment in which, to a degree, the static mold is broken. After lengthy accounts of past events, we suddenly, as it were, are thrust into the very present, almost as if action and writing coincide. But this is only seeming, as is made manifest on the one hand by the past tenses which here mingle with the present (e.g., 143-146) and on the other by the earlier outbursts which had already defined the moment (27-28, 55-56, 105-106). From the beginning of the letter Medea was aware that Jason was abandoning her for another woman.

There is, however, one area of genuine development. Early, Medea remarks, echoing Euripides' heroine,[30] *Est aliqua ingrato meritum exprobrare voluptas;/ hac fruar, haec de te gaudia sola feram* (23-24). The implication, especially in *sola*, is that Medea is content to chastize Jason, but has no intentions of going any further. By the final stages of the letter, we are witness to Medea contriving her terrible plans. No longer is she satisfied with bitter words, active revenge is now in her mind. The trouble here is that the tone and language of the poem leave us unprepared for the shock of the ending. In spite of all the explicit allusions throughout to Medea's proclivity for acts of gross violence, there is nothing in her hostile words to Jason that prepare us for a horrifying conclusion. She is nasty, supercilious, condescending, malicious, paranoid, but she never reaches any peaks of passion that foreshadow so drastic a turn. Perhaps Kraus is right when he suggests that it is the idea of Jason and Creusa mocking her that bends Medea toward thoughts of violence (179-182),[31] but we need only recall Euripides to realize how pale a development this is. Where is Euripides' high-keyed, tense, passionate woman? Ovid's Medea has no thoughts of suicide, no dreams of starving

themes of the first half of the poem are reproduced with different colors in the second half. To the examples already noted in the text, we may add: the description of the Argonauts, the labors, and Medea's help which begin the poem return again toward the end (197-208); the insomnia that afflicts Medea in her anxiety for Jason (60) ironically recurs in her distress over his rejection of her (171-172).

[30] *Medea* 473-474. In each case the following lines recount Jason's feats, Medea's help, her betrayal of her father, and the murder of Pelias.

[31] *WS* 65 (1950-51) 61.

herself. She is coolly, in fact, coldly rational and alert. Perhaps this is the only way a cold-blooded murderer can be.[32] It is important that Ovid has actually set the stage before the opening of Euripides' play—or perhaps at its very outset. For it is clear that his Medea knows nothing of her imposed exile. Now it is simply possible that Ovid did not want to clutter his poetic landscape with one more complication, but it surely would have been easy enough—one distich could have done the job perfectly well. There is purpose in his refusal. In Euripides, while Medea seemingly intends to avenge herself on Jason from the start, it takes Creon's dictate of exile to spur her on to do so. Ovid's Medea does not need any such added inducements. She is ready to take violent vengeance even under these milder circumstances.

If on the level of character-development we may wonder whether Ovid has been successful, we can have no such doubts as to the effectiveness of the emotive-narrative sections in conveying a sense of the passage of time. Some instances we have already observed. The opening set of rhetorical questions and wishes takes us from the Argo's launching to its arrival in Colchis and then to the feats of Jason. Similarly, the account of the labors set Jason in terms of Medea's anxiety unobtrusively moves us through the whole palace-scene and the confrontation between Aeetes and Jason. Again, at 109ff, Medea's self-rebuke is at the same time a chronological account of her crimes and strikingly

---

[32] Though Ovid does not have Medea explicitly decide to kill her sons, the murder is present to the reader not only through his acquaintance with Euripides, but also in the allusions, by way of irony, to it in the poem. Most striking are verses 189-192:

> Si tibi sum vilis, communes respice natos:
> Saeviet in partus dira noverca meos.
> Et nimium similes tibi sunt et imagine tangor
> et quotiens video, lumina nostra madent.

The irony in 189-190 is obvious; she argues that her children will be endangered by their stepmother. In fact, it is she who will kill them. Beyond this, these lines are rich in their pregnant implications. Observe how Medea is compelled to utilize the very arguments Hypsipyle, from whom she stole Jason, made use of: think of the children, they look just like you, beware their stepmother (cf. 6.123-130). Finally, *et nimium similes tibi sunt*. Why *nimium*? I suspect that Ovid mirrors in these words a brilliant psychological insight into Medea's unconscious motivation in murdering her children. When she kills them, she sees herself killing Jason. In them, Jason dies.

the wish at 123-128 is in fact an emotion-charged record of the Argo's itinerary on its return trip to Iolcus.[33]

Though interesting in what it tries to achieve, this letter, or more to the point, Ovid's Medea, must in the end face relentless and odious comparison with, at the least, Euripides' play and Apollonius' epic—and, strange enough, though it comes as no great shock that Ovid is found lacking, what diminishes Ovid's version in our eyes is its lack of excitement, its frigidity, the absence of spontaneity and passion, those elements which are so crucial in both Apollonius' and Euripides' successes, different though they be. If Ovid felt the need to mediate between the impassioned naïveté of Apollonius' heroine and the complex emotional sophistication of Euripides', he has so done, producing a rather clear-headed villain not terribly concerned with questions of conscience, but the result is unfortunately dull. To a degree, this must be the fault of the poem's preoccupation with the description of events, brilliant though some of it is. But it makes for a sameness and a simplicity which plague hardly any other of the *Heroides*. As usual with Ovid, the generating idea is a good one: to present virtually the whole career of Medea from her own point of view, a kind of *apologia pro vita sua* set out by a classic and notorious purveyor of crime, a defense which Ovid believes must inevitably fail because of the severity of the deeds perpetrated and because of the obvious willingness of the person to continue down the same path, adding even more horrible crimes to those already on her record.

[33] Whether the Argo returned by the same route it came varies according to different authors and traditions. See *FGrHist* 1F18a, with Jacoby's comments, and *FGrHist* 566F84-88, with Jacoby's discussion and notes. The matter is complicated by occasional confusion of the *Symplegades* and the *Planctai*; see D. L. Page *ad* Eur. *Medea* 2.

VII

Heroides 14: Hypermestra

Everyone, Pausanias points out (2.16.1), knows of the crime
of the Danaids. And, we might want to add, nearly everyone had
his own peculiar version of what happened. Disagreement exists
at almost every point. Why do Danaus and Aegyptus quarrel?
Why do the Danaids and Danaus object to the marriage? What
does Danaus instruct his daughters to do? Why does Hypermestra spare Lynceus? What happens to Hypermestra and
Lynceus after the infamous night? Depending upon where one
looks, each of these questions can be answered in a variety of
ways.[1] Unfortunately, almost all our information comes in the
form of notices in the scholia and accounts in the mythographers,
so it is quite impossible to establish whether Ovid had in mind
any particular antecedent treatment or treatments, of which
there were probably many.[2] But the simple availability of so
much factual data is valuable because it reveals the options
which lay before Ovid or—better—the potential of the myth, and
thereby enables us to perceive the individuality of Ovid's version, his motives and aims.[3]

[1] For an exhaustive treatment of virtually all questions pertinent to the
Danaid myth, see A. F. Garvie, *Aeschylus' Supplices* (Cambridge 1969).

[2] *Pace* T. Birt, *RhM* 32 (1877) 408-409, and R. Ehwald, *Exegetischer Kommentar zur xiv. Heroide Ovids* (Gotha 1900) 3, who assert that only a few
treatments existed.

[3] Our most grievous losses are the epic poem *Danaides* and the two Aeschylean plays that follow the *Supplices*. Of the latter loss it is worth noting,
especially since we shall refer later to attempts at reconstruction, that Lloyd-
Jones has observed, "almost everything concerning the last two plays of the
trilogy remains uncertain" (*Gnomon* 34 [1962] 740), and Garvie's recent
study tends to confirm this. Theodectes wrote a *Lynceus*, which presumably
had something to do with the myth; Phrynichus wrote an *Aigyptioi* and
Danaides, Timesitheos a *Danaides*. Other works with revealing titles are
Melanippides' *Danaides*, Hecataeus' *Danaides*, several comedies, e.g., Aristophanes' and Diphilus' *Danaides*, Menander's *Dactylius* (one fragment refers

We may begin with two complementary points, each no less illuminating for being obvious. There are two notions, two classes of words, which provide, one by its presence, the other by its absence, a clue for an understanding of this poem. Striking for its absence in this "love letter" is love, no *amo*, no *amor* (only *Her.* 10 shares this characteristic);[4] and, to anticipate a bit, this bare statistic is reinforced by the tone of the whole poem. There is no evidence of affection.[5] On the other hand, we are constantly put in the presence of great and devout virtue, piety, if you will allow the extended use of the English cognate.[6] *Pietas*, in its nominal and adjectival forms, occurs no less than seven times in the 132 verses of the poem, while no more than three times in any other of the *Heroides*. More important is the fact that all these

to Danaus. Play's subject is unknown), perhaps Nicochares' *Amymone*. Euripides treated the myth, but to what extent we do not know. See Nauck² fr. 846 and *adesp.* fr. 454. Also Pap. Hamb. 118a col. II *apud* C. Austin, *Nova Fragmenta Euripidea* (Berlin 1968) 13, not to mention allusions in the extant plays. Pap. Hibeh #221, of the third century B.C., may be an argument to a tragedy which dealt with the Danaids. Perhaps the Hesiodic *Catalogus* treated the myth. Dionysius of Samos (*FGrHist* 15F6) also did. When we further consider how closely the Io myth is interwoven with the Danaid legend (witness this Ovidian epistle and the extant plays of Aeschylus), we recognize the need to include in this list works like Sophocles' *Inachus*, Callimachus' *Ious Aphixis*, Chaeremon's *Io*, Accius' *Io*, Calvus' *Io*, and perhaps even early epics like the *Phoronis*, and the *Aigimios*. We know that Archilochus at the least mentioned the Danaus-daughter-Lynceus syndrome (fr. 150B.), though in what detail is unknown, and of course Pindar has several passing references. To carry the complications to an unexpected extreme, we may even have to consider the possibility that Hypermestra was an important figure in early Greek lyric. This W. H. Friedrich has suggested (*A&A* 12 [1966] 6), with only reasonableness, not evidence, on his side, conjecturing that Hypermestra may have gained her fame in sixth century lyric. Be this as it may, there is plenty of substantiated literature on the Danaids and Hypermestra that is lost to us without having to seek out additional problems.

Insofar as *Heroides* 14 goes, three studies must be mentioned. Birt's (supra n. 2) 408-430; Ehwald's (supra, n. 2), and Oppel (68-76). Birt's suffers from excessively subtle source analysis often helped along by emendations or strained interpretations of the text, while Ehwald's labors under his overemphasis on rhetoric, being an attempt to prove the letter a *controversia*.

4 A point made by Birt and repeated by Ehwald, Purser, and many others.

5 Friedrich (supra n. 3) 7, seeks vainly to get around this by identifying Hypermestra's pity with awakening affection.

6 The precise nature of Hypermestra's *pietas*, as Ehwald remarks (10), is never made clear. See, however, Oppel 126, n. 9.

instances of "piety" in *Her.* 14 refer to Hypermestra herself (line
14 is a generalization which applies to her), while only two of the
other heroines mention their own piety, each once (*H.* 1.85,
6.137). If nothing else, this sets off the letter from many of its sisters wherein *amor*, sometimes pure and whole, sometimes mixed
with anger or hate, sometimes rejected, regretted and abandoned, plays so central a role. We are keyed in by the opening
line: *Mittit Hypermestra de tot modo fratribus uni.*[7] Whether *de
tot modo fratribus uni* is used of Lynceus with respect to his
brothers, i.e., "one of so many brothers" or of Lynceus and his
brethren vis-à-vis Hypermestra, i.e., "one of so many cousins," the
address remains peculiar. She addresses her husband in a manner which is at best straightforward and matter-of-fact, at worst
formal and impersonal.[8] He is not her lover, not her husband, just
one of her cousins (or the one survivor of a group of brothers).
And this strange view of their relationship repeats itself over and
again. But once does Lynceus receive the appellation *vir* (12) and
once *maritus* (19). When, on the fatal night, she awakens him and

[7] Objections can be—and have been—lodged against the opening distich.
Most recently Luck (32) has declared it spurious. *De tot modo fratribus uni*
is a strange and ambiguous phrase which, one could argue, has been built
on the basis of verse 73. In addition, one points to the third-person statement, the use of *mitto* with no explicit object, and finally the effectiveness
of beginning with line 3, *clausa domo teneor*. Still, the objections, though of
some number, are not individually cogent. The opening third-person declaration is found also at *Heroides* 13. Moreover, the third person here may be
intentionally designed to balance the third-person epitaph in the poem's
penultimate distich. Further balance of this sort between the beginning and
the end is evident in the references to her chains at 3 and 131. *Mitto* is commonly used without explicit objects, especially in reference to the writing
and posting of letters (see *ThLL* s.v. *mitto* col. 1184-1185 and Kirfel 99).
The occurrence of *de tot modo fratribus unus* at 73 does not preclude its
presence here. Indeed, one might take *de tot modo fratribus uni* as a significant quotation by Hypermestra of her words to Lynceus at that critical
nocturnal moment. The fact that the letter could open perfectly well at 3 does
not speak against its opening at 1. Finally, the distich is universally attested.
I think, moreover, that the distich evidences subtle characteristics which
serve to initially define the tone of the poem: the sense of solemn and
staid remove, the distance from Lynceus, especially promoted by the third
person and by *de fratribus uni* instead of, e.g., *tibi* or *viro* or *Lynceo*.

[8] I can in no way understand how Fränkel reaches the notion that Hypermestra calls Lynceus "cousin" instead of "husband" because she is "too bash-
ful to betray her love" (191, n. 9).

urges him to flight, he is *Belide, de tot modo fratribus unus* (73), though here we must take into account the fact that this is a horrifyingly brilliant way of having Hypermestra tell Lynceus what has happened. But there is no explaining away the *uno fratre manente* (122) and Hypermestra's ultimate refusal, even in her own epitaph, to grant Lynceus the status of lover and husband, *mortem fratri depulit* (130).[9]

If the manner in which Hypermestra addresses Lynceus offers a quality of distant and aloof formality, so do the tone and the formal elements of the poem. We have noticed elsewhere and often how Ovid effectively makes intermittent use of shifts from the second to the third person. But in this poem we might say that the sporadic and therefore striking introduction of the addressee as the object of the writer's thought rather than as the recipient of her communication becomes the normal state of affairs. The letter opens with a description of Hypermestra's plight, declarations of her virtue and willingness to accept whatever ills may befall her as a consequence of her heroic act. Where, one might question, is Lynceus? Palmer finds him in verse 5, *quod manus extimuit iugulo demittere ferrum*, "scil. *tuo*; this poem presents many marks of want of finish." I cannot agree with either observation. That there is no *tuo* here is deliberate and calculated. Examine the lines that precede and follow. There is no sense whatsoever of a second person addressee. We are in no way entitled to supply *tuo* with *iugulo*. What Hypermestra says is this, "because my hand was afraid to plunge a sword into a throat."[10] In the next distich, *Esse ream praestat, quam sic placuisse parenti;/ non piget immunes caedis habere manus,* where we might have had a remark to the effect, "I do not regret having saved you," we again descry the total absence of Lynceus, "I do not regret not having committed a crime." When Hypermestra's account of the crime finally presents us with two people, herself and the potential victim, what do we hear but *qua non cecidit vir nece* (12)? Lynceus is simply a character out of her past life, not someone to whom she is presently addressing her thoughts and pleas, not *qua cecidisti* or the like. He seemingly

---

[9] It is fruitful to compare how Hermione, who, like Hypermestra, has a twofold relationship to her lover, makes ample use of both those relations. See e.g., 8.27-30.

[10] See Ehwald 12.

exists for Hypermestra as nothing more than an integral component of her heroic act. Remarkably striking is verse 19 which
seems not to have troubled many commentators, but, I think,
should have, *quam tu caede putes fungi potuisse mariti*. Who is
tu? Can this really be Lynceus? Why should he, of all people, be
the one to think that Hypermestra could have committed an act
of murder? Moreover, does not the third person *mariti* in the
same line make it rather unlikely that *tu* is Lynceus?[11] Perhaps,
if the text is sound, *tu* is vaguely general. (I have little faith in this
view. Might Ulitius' *ne* for *tu* be worth considering?) At any
rate, I suspect that Lynceus is again in this verse but a third
person.

Only at 41, in the midst of the description of the wedding-
night, is it clear that Lynceus is addressed. Yet, even here qualification is in order. It is hard to detect communication, interpersonal contact. First, of course, this is direct narrative, no pleas,
wishes or even thoughts. Moreover, it is direct and straightforward in a way few, if any, narratives in the *Heroides* are. Hardly
any interjections break the flow. Hypermestra sees the whole
event taking place before her mind's eye (note the marvelous
ecce, 29). Present tenses dominate; she virtually relives the experience. Thus, when her account finally narrows to a view of
Lynceus and herself alone, she almost sees him sleeping by her
side. When she says, *ipse iacebas* (41), she is addressing in retrospect the image of Lynceus present to her mind, not the Lynceus
to whom she is (supposedly) sending a letter. Even though the
sense of communication increases with the course of the narrative
(e.g., 47-48), by its end we can only feel that Lynceus has here
existed only (or, at least, mostly) for his role in that event. There
are no emotional interjections, no outbursts directed at him,
nothing really said to him. At 78, he flees; at 80, he is found
absent (*abes*), and then both he and the second person of the recipient disappear until the poem's conclusion. It is quite as if, for
Hypermestra, Lynceus' existence begins and ends with that one
night. It is only at 119 that we sense a genuine address to
Lynceus and, in fact, his name is first mentioned at 123. These
last verses, 123-128, are the sole reflection of this poem as letter,
as communication.

---

[11] Ehwald (13) retracted his Teubner reading *mariti* and adopted *marito*,
but this strikes me as impossible.

The emphasis on *pietas,* the conspicuous absence of *amor,* and the peculiar formal elements just described,[12] all interact toward one end. Uppermost here is an act, not a human relationship, an act whose magnitude has created or re-created the personality of its doer, an act which can be embodied in one word, *pietas.* No love, no warmth, no affection; just a cold and removed dedication of one's being to a principle which appears to have been the motive factor in the greatest deed of one's life. Persons no longer count. Lynceus' importance to Hypermestra resides in his having played a role of essential significance in that great event of her life.

Still, I suspect that a closer examination of details will repay our efforts and modify—or at least amplify—our earlier observations. The whole *pietas* motif and what it entails merits scrutiny. *Est mihi supplicii causa fuisse piam* (4). Of course, our initial response is to the paradox, repeated in the letter (e.g., 83-84), of suffering punishment for virtuous behavior,[13] an interesting paradox if for no other reason than that it inverts another found in the *Heroides,* that of the "meritorious crime." Hypermestra's *supplicii* stands in contrast to Medea's *poena.* The latter recognizes her guilt, the former her suffering. Paradox aside, we must notice the unemotional quality of the line. In the following verses, the motif expands to a breadth which it maintains through the letter; Hypermestra glories in her piety. She presents herself, one might say, as a heroic martyr. She enjoys being virtuous (8); she will withstand heaven and hell, but will not betray her virtue (9-14). The self-righteousness of *non est quam piget esse piam* (14) is almost unbearable; "someone else might give in and say 'I'm sorry,' but not me. I'm a truly virtuous person." And so the letter continues. The horror of the murder-night is so great that she cannot even speak of it (17-20); but (heroine that she is), she will make an attempt: *Sed tamen experiar* (21).[14] In the ensuing

---

[12] To which we may add the persistent use of impersonal verbal notions (7, 8, 9, 13, 14, 15, 64, 87, 131). Do these further the impression of emotional sterility and absence of will?

[13] *Clausa domo* (3), prisoner in one's home, is a virtual paradox too (cf. *carcer* 84). Brilliant is the oxymoron *rea laudis* (120). Cf. *Antigone* 74, 923ff. It is interesting that the "identification" of bedchamber with tomb (31) is also found in the *Antigone* (891).

[14] For whose benefit is the narrative? Lynceus knows what has happened. This sort of unnecessary narrative of information is common in the *Heroides,* where the narratives are often for the benefit of the inner self; what strains

description she again portrays herself as the self-sacrificing martyr in grand style: *Si manus haec aliquam posset committere caedem,/ morte foret dominae sanguinolenta suae* (59-60). Her concern with *pietas, quo mihi commisso non licet esse piam* (64) is not merely excessive, it is obsessive.[15] Then, the grandiose climax of her epitaph, with its emphasis on her piety, her undeserved suffering, and her heroic action (129-130). She calls her epitaph a *titulus* (128) ; this is suggestive. The terminology is essentially masculine—or rather, heroic. *Titulus* is fairly common in the *Heroides*, but, with the exception of this verse and 5.24, is always used of the male. Hypsipyle's description of Medea's encroachment on Jason's prerogatives is illuminating, *titulo coniugis uxor obest* (6.100). When here Hypermestra allows herself a *titulus* in the heroic fashion, it is to impress upon us the heroic nature of her behavior.[16]

---

matters here is the *sed tamen experiar*, as if someone wants her to recount the events and she consciously agrees.

[15] I think the interpretation of 115-118 is relevant. It revolves around our understanding of 117, *Nam mihi quot fratres, totidem periere sorores*. Palmer sees in *periere sorores* a reference to the murder by Lynceus of the guilty sisters, attested at schol. Eur. *Hec.* 886. Garvie (supra n. 1) 165 and 170, agrees. But this is clearly wrong. First, this scholium is the only source for the story and it includes Danaus as well as the Danaids as Lynceus' victim. As Danaus is obviously alive in *Heroides* 14, Ovid is not following this tradition. Anyway, in the context of the letter, Lynceus has not had any opportunity to kill them; he fled immediately. More, from verse 15 it is manifest that the sisters are still alive, *paeniteat sceleris Danaum saevasque sorores*. The key to the clause lies in its parallelism to the preceding verse, *quique dati leto quaeque dedere, fleo*. She then proceeds to explain (*nam*) why she mourns both groups; *quique dati leto* is taken up by *fratres, quaeque dedere* by *sorores*. The sisters *periere* precisely because they *dedere*. This is a moral valuation, typical of Hypermestra. The sisters are ethically ruined by their crime (as Ehwald 25-26, Loers *ad loc.*, and, after a fashion, Birt 428 have briefly noted). Even earlier Hypermestra had made this equation of moral failure and death: *Finge viros meruisse mori; quid fecimus ipsae?/ Quo mihi commisso non licet esse piam* (63-64). As for the use of *pereo*, we should think of the common ethical sense of *perditus* (which is virtually the participle of *pereo*). *Mihi* in 117 hovers, I suspect, between a *dativus incommodi* and a *dativus iudicantis*. I note a very similar use of *obeo* at Sen. *Phaedra* 998, where Theseus rejects Hippolytus as his son with the remark, *gnatum parens obisse iam pridem scio*. Perhaps the vague similarity of "I've lost my . . ." makes it relevant to cite Prop. 3.23.1, *nobis periere tabellae*.

[16] To be sure, *titulus* is regularly used in the sense of "inscription" and there is, consequently, nothing strange in its application to an epitaph. The

But it is all a pose. Ovid means us to see through the screen. The proclamations of piety are one too many. "The lady doth protest too much." We cannot but be skeptical. More, the unswerving fortitude and self-sacrifice, even in the face of death, dissolves somewhat toward the end. Do we detect here a twinge of regret?

> En ego, quod vivis, poenae crucianda reservor:
>   Quid fiet sonti, cum rea laudis agar?
> Et consanguineae quondam centesima turbae
>   infelix uno fratre manente cadam.
>
> (119-122)

She does, after all, wish to be saved, *vel fer opem vel dede neci* (125; presumably he will not follow *dede neci*[17]). But it is the final distich that seals the case. It comes unexpectedly. After *Heroides* 2 and 7 we are prepared for a heroine to conclude her letter with an autobiographical epitaph. When, at 129-130, Hypermestra follows the lead of Dido and Phyllis, especially in terms that so decisively echo and enhance language and motifs that have been crucial for the whole poem, we feel that this is the tonic on which the poem must end.[18] But, to our shock, there is more, one last distich, quite distinct in tone from all that has preceded: *Scribere plura libet. Sed pondere lassa catenae/ est manus et vires subtrahit ipse timor.* Herewith a sense of heavy weariness, of girlish helplessness.[19] Now we discern the real Hypermestra, the young girl who has acted bravely, who may be even a little overwhelmed by the magnitude of her own behavior. She is, in fact, afraid of the consequences of her action, but strives to live up to her imagined role as courageous and selfless heroine. Underneath her mask she is weary, anxious, fearful. The final distich thus lowers the key of the whole letter. Not heroic martyrdom here, but a physical and psychological weakness. The *vires* (132) which perhaps sufficed her in that one critical moment

---

peculiar and suggestive usage of the word here is revealed by its rather uniform connotations elsewhere in the *Heroides* and by the fact that Ovid's other heroines designate their epitaphs *carmen* (2.146; 7.196).

17 For *dede neci*, "put to death," cf. Verg. G. 4.90; Ov. *Fasti* 4.840.

18 Is this why Dilthey, *De Callimachi Cydippa* (Leipzig 1863), 147, in his *apparatus criticus* to *Her.* 20.241-242, declares the next distich (131-132), the poem's last, spurious?

19 The motif of weariness is not rare. See Kirfel 80.

now fail her. Earlier we had hints. Her *pietas* was not enough to keep her from actively contemplating murder,

> Non ego falsa loquar. Ter acutum sustulit ensem,
>   ter male sublato reccidit ense manus.
> Tandem victa mei saeva formidine patris
>   admovi iugulo tela paterna tuo.

(45-48)

She made no secret that *pietas* was not the sole constituent of her reluctance, *sed timor et pietas crudelibus obstitit ausis* (49).[20] And even earlier, *manus extimuit iugulo demittere ferrum* (5). Also, chinks in her armor of piety are visible in her complaints, rare though they be (e.g., 84, 110).

The traditional generalization about the *Heroides*, that Ovid turns the women of the heroic age into "average" or "everyday" women, unsuited as it is for almost all of the poems, does have a germ of validity here. At any rate, he presents the emotions of a woman who has performed an act of great courage and nobility, then finds herself not totally able to bear the dire consequences. Yet, she feels that the level of heroism which she has gained should be maintained in her continuing behavior and so puts on a brave front, a sort of mask through which we get small but acute glimpses of the human being behind. But her situation and her compulsion to play a role not her own produce a terrible coldness; it is almost as if she is *clausa* (as she says in 3) psychologically, shut off from human relations, from warmth, from emotion. Lynceus, as we have noticed, is reflected in her mind as little more than the object of her heroism, the necessary "body" which had to be saved; he is regarded with little (or no) warmth and affection. There is scarcely recognition of his humanity.

One more facet. We probably do not hesitate on reading 5-6: *Quod manus extimuit iugulo demittere ferrum,/ sum rea; laudarer, si scelus ausa forem.* The personification of *manus* does not strike us as strange or remarkable, and even when the word recurs three lines later, *non piget immunes caedis habere manus* (8), we pass over it quickly.[21] After all, the phrase *immunes caedis manus* seems perfectly normal. "Clean hands" is a traditional metaphor of innocence, and, in fact, even occurs in ver-

---

[20] Words like *timeo, timor, tremo, tremor*, are frequent in the poem.

[21] See some interesting remarks on Ovid's exploitation of the *manus* "motif" in Fränkel 182, n. 33.

sions of the Hypermestra legend (Paus. 10.10.5; Nonnus 3.311).
So it comes as no surprise.[22] At 44, the hand reappears. In the
next distich it is once again subject, initiating the villainous act,
hesitating, and finally (50) refusing. By this point we must wonder. Consider again: *manus extimuit iugulo demittere ferrum;*
sustulit ensem . . . manus; dextra refugit opus. The *manus*, one
senses, is the operative agent, the controlling factor. Where we
expect "I Hypermestra," we get *manus.* Ovid further brilliantly
exploits a characteristic Latin usage to sharpen the effect. The
possessive adjective, when sense is manifest, is unnecessary. In
none of these passages does Hypermestra say *manus mea.* Consequently, the personification is deepened. The *manus* is, so to
speak, given independence from the person of whom it is a part.
It is, indeed, virtually anthropomorphized in verse 50 where it,
not Hypermestra, is *casta.* At 56 *manus* is again subject and at
59-60 it is nearly endowed with a will of its own: *Si manus haec*
aliquam posset committere caedem,/ morte foret dominae
sanguinolenta suae. Finally, as if a guarantee of its importance,
manus recurs one last time as subject in the final line: her hand
grows weary and calls an end to the poem.

What is this all about? There is, in short, a virtual dissociation
of her hand from herself; the organ, as it were, gains an existence
independent of Hypermestra. The point is this. The night of horror and particularly her own actions on that night have taken on
an existence all their own, disengaged from the persons involved.
Hypermestra now conceives those events as external to herself;
she herself virtually has no part in them. She is to them not much
more than horrified spectator. This is why there is no sense of
communication or relationship between herself and Lynceus,
who has now become in her mind little more than a fragment of
that objectified night. This is also why she is in a way alienated
from herself; and it is a concrete manifestation of this alienation
that she sees the act of that night as committed by her *manus* almost independently of herself. The whole letter sounds as if writ-

22 Some (e.g., Loers) have also seen a personification of *manus* in 19-20,
taking *quam = manum* (or better, *dextram*). This would find an interesting parallel in 12.117. It seems preferable, however, to take *quam = Hyper-*
mestram, as do Ehwald and, if I read him right, Palmer. The presence of
mariti suggests that the subject of the infinitive is Lynceus' wife and the
immediately following *sed tamen experiar* (21) indicates that Hypermestra
was subject of *timet* (20).

ten in a trance, and in a sense it is. Hypermestra is hypnotized or rather paralyzed emotionally.

And this is why the lengthy "digression" on Io (85-108) is both suitable and wonderfully effective.[23] To be sure, the introduction of Io into a Danaid context is scarcely original with Ovid. We need delve no further than Aeschylus' two plays, the *Prometheus Bound*, in which the formal situation is the reverse—Io is present on stage and by means of prophecy we look ahead to Hypermestra and the Danaids—and the *Supplices*, in which, as in Ovid, the Danaids hold the stage and we look backward to Io's fate.[24] The motivating factor for Io's appearance here is clear and simple. Io, an ancestor of Hypermestra, has suffered grievously and undeservedly, and therefore the latter identifies herself with the mistreated victim.[25] We might note that, whereas the flashbacks to Io in the *Supplices* often mention Io's ultimate redemption, Ovid's heroine makes but passing allusion to that story's happy ending (86), for, quite clearly, this would, for her, vitiate the cogency of the identification. But psychologically there is deeper value to this digression. Herein we find the emotion, the pathetic and angered outbursts, the complaints, the interjections of feelings which are missing elsewhere in the poem: the highly charged apostrophe to Io (93), the warmth and empathy for her ancestor (94-106) which she is unable to demonstrate for herself and her own plight.[26] Thus, the digression is a vicarious psychological outlet. Hypermestra, unable to respond to her own actions, her husband, and herself with anything but a cold remove

[23] J. C. Scaliger and D. Heinsius were the first of many to question either the authenticity or the place of these lines. Even Fränkel is troubled. He writes (210, n. 17) that the section is "patently out of place where it stands," yet proceeds to defend it.

[24] I note some similarities between the *Supplices'* Io and Ovid's. Both describe her eating vegetation (*Supp.* 538-540; Ovid 96; so too in Calvus' *Io* (*FPL*, p. 85, fr.9). In each her appearance generates fear and astonishment (*Supp.* 565-570; Ovid 92, 97-98). Whether these parallels are of significance may be questioned.

[25] A. Salvatore, *Atti* 2.242, well remarks that the introduction of the Io tale here "serva ad illuminare la dolorosa realtà di Ipermestra." R. D. Murray, *The Motif of Io in Aeschylus' Suppliants* (Princeton 1958) *passim*, has shown how Aeschylus similarly uses Io as a kind of reflection of the Danaids, particularly of Hypermestra, "the new Io" (86).

[26] At *AA* 1.289ff, esp. 303ff, Ovid uses a similar shift from narrative to apostrophe, strangely enough in a context like the Io story, that of Pasiphae and the bull, with reference made to Io (323).

and a numb aloofness, is better able to work herself into her distant ancestor's life and fate and respond to it. There are, by the way, a number of touches which enrich this section and enhance its place in the poem: the way in which Hypermestra plays down, virtually avoids, the perverse sexuality of the Io-Zeus-Hera relationship, just as she has avoided all mention of love and sex in recounting her own fate; the way in which she fashions herself in the image of Io (or vice-versa) with respect to the abnormality, the unnaturalness of their conditions: Io is puzzled and terrified by her new state (91-94), just as Hypermestra is horrified by the strangeness of hers (55-56; note especially how the similar use of *facere+ ad* occurs at 56 and 94). To this Ovid cleverly appends the *telum* motif. Both heroines find themselves equipped with weapons unusual, indeed alien, to them and are astonished (65-66, 98). If Io must be careful not to inflict accidental injury, *te ne feriant quae geris arma times*, so must Hypermestra, *paene manus telo saucia facta tua est* (70).[27] Finally, we may wonder whether, when Hypermestra describes her family *eiectos ultimus orbis habet* (112; scarcely true) and herself *exul* (129), she is still retaining the association of herself with Io.[28]

A few words on how the style reinforces the character of the poem. One cannot but be struck by the simplicity of the language and its easy fluidity. Quite straightforward, the sentences are short, there is little enjambement, little syntactical carry-over from distich to distich, even more striking, from hexameter to pentameter. Observe how often pentameters begin with *et* or enclitic *que*, how often full stops punctuate the ends of hexameters. It is almost as if every line were independent. The style is, in other words, emotionless, removed, almost hypnotic and trancelike in its phonographic type of stylistic similarity and re-

[27] At 103-106 Ovid views the Io tale from the perspective of the common philosophical topos of the inability to escape oneself. See Hor. *Epist.* 1.11; Sen. *Ep.* 28; Lucr. 3.1057-1070.

[28] Here comparison with Aeschylus is very fruitful. In the *Supplices* Danaus and his daughters leave of their own free will, they go to Argos (not exactly *ultimus orbis*), and conceive of it as the return to their homeland, a delightful place. Ovid's Hypermestra intensifies her plight with her peculiar description. Birt's view (418, n. 1), that *ultimus orbis* refers to Africa, and that *exul* is not meant literally, is unacceptable, both because it distorts the natural sense and because it violates the Latin. Ehwald's interpretation (25) of *pellimur* and *eiectos*, forced and unnatural, results from a wrongheaded desire to establish uniformity between Ovid and Aeschylus.

petitiveness. Toward the end, with the introduction of the Io theme, there is perhaps a slight change. A few sentences are more complex, the presence of rhetorical questions, often in staccato style (93-94, 103, 105), and the use of anaphora and polyptoton (100, 106)[29] inject a more emotional quality commensurate with the contextual and psychological changes here involved.

Here I should like to take up the second half of Palmer's remark quoted earlier, "this poem presents many marks of want of finish" (*ad* verse 5). On the contrary, I would suggest that in its abundance of small but superbly realized points this poem is an indisputable success.[30] One reason, we cannot deny, is its brevity which, on the one hand, keeps the whole tightly knit and smooth-flowing, and also makes rather impossible the various kinds of repetition which populate most of the poems. Let me here note merely some of the highlights of the wedding-night narrative.[31]

The description is superb in the atmosphere of gloom it conjures up. Beginning with the chronological designation, *modo facta crepuscula terris,/ ultima pars lucis primaque noctis erat* (21-22), it not only sets a tone of gloom with its stress on darkness, but it also proves a very precise metaphor, thanks to the common association of *lux* with life and *nox* with death (in this poem, see 74): this was the end of their lives, the beginning of their doom. The irony of *conlucent* (25) is calculated, as is the παρὰ προσδοκίαν effect of the adjectives in 26, *impia tura, invitos focos*. A whole story is comprehended in one word *armatas* (24), and the impending horror is embodied in the juxtaposition of *armatas* and *accipit*. There is a macabre irony in the elation and joy of the grooms (29-32),[32] grimly sharpened by the brilliant choice of *feruntur* (31; rather than, e.g., *ruunt* or *eunt*) which quickens the funereal imagery,[33] coming hard upon *thalamos sua busta*.

In the entire account—the entrance of the brides, the cere-

---

[29] For parallels to nudā nudă see Ehwald 23. One might add Lucr. 2.310.

[30] I agree with Salvatore (supra n. 25) who writes of the poem's merit "per il soffio di poesia che vi spira e l'assenza quasi assoluta di motivi retorici."

[31] Which even D'Elia (152-153) praises!

[32] There is a pathetic irony in the doomed grooms wearing *flore novo* (30). For parallels to the *thalamos/busta* theme, see *Antigone* 891; *AP* 7.188.7-8. One might think also of the play on marriage/doom at Lucr. 1.95-100. Ovid plays on the theme earlier (9-12) where the ritual paraphernalia of the wedding ceremony become the weapons which will punish Hypermestra.

[33] *Fero = effero*. See e.g., *AA* 3.20; *Tr.* 1.3.89.

mony, the arrival of the grooms at the bedchambers, their murder (23-36)—Hypermestra does not designate the grooms even once, that is, she does not use a single noun to denote them. They are a series of adjectives, verbs, participles, which recount their changing states, *mero dubii, frequentes, laeti, graves, morientum.* It is, I think, the horror of the event that prevents her from naming the victims. So terrifying is the deed that Hypermestra herself almost becomes a corpse too, *Sanguis abit, mentemque calor corpusque relinquit/ inque novo iacui frigida facto toro* (37-38). The complexity of the conflicting emotional claims on Hypermestra is revealed in the contradiction at 43-44; *excussere metum/ tremente manu.*[34]

This internal conflict, to commit the crime or to refrain, is constructed in precise and ordered form, in fact, as a virtual dialogue between two inner voices, or between Hypermestra and an inner voice. The latter urges her to the crime in one distich (53-54), she opposes it in one distich (55-56). The voice argues (57-58), Hypermestra replies (59-60). At this point the text raises some problems. I suspect 61-62 represents the voice again urging her to act, while in the following distich Hypermestra again responds.[35] That she has now won the argument is symbolized

---

[34] What about 42: *quaeque tibi dederam vina soporis erant?* Emendation aside, can we claim that this is Latin? Ehwald (17) thought it sufficient to refer to *AA* 1.292, *cetera lactis erant.* This is close, but as Palmer has argued, is not really parallel. G. Giangrande, *Eranos* 64 (1966) 153-157, has made a valiant attempt to defend the reading, but I find neither his theoretical explanation nor his alleged parallels convincing. Even if Ovid could have used *sopor* in the sense "sleeping potion" (which is by no means certain), to allege that *vina soporis = sopor vineus* on the analogy of *saxa columnae = saxea columna* is incredible. *Saxa columnae* makes sense precisely because the *columna* is a total entity of which the *saxa* are the component parts. This cannot be carried over to *vina soporis.* Let me say initially that I do not understand how *vina soporis* can come to mean "wine that induces sleep." But I think I can adduce a more helpful parallel than those heretofore proffered. Lucretius 2.467-468 evidently (the text is somewhat problematic before the key words) speaks of *doloris corpora,* "atoms that cause pain." I can see no objection to considering this construction precisely what we are facing in *Her.* 14.42. One hesitant suggestion: might this usage be archaic Latin? This would be typical of Lucretius, while Ovid might be echoing some early Latin reference to this episode, as e.g., he echoes Ennius' *Alexander* at *Her.* 17.237-238. See *Phoenix* 22 (1968) 299-303. For the most recent attempt at emendation, see J. Diggle, *PCPS* 198 (1972) 35-36.

[35] Housman's interpretation (*CR* 11 [1897] 287-288) of the train of thought, irrespective of the relationship of 113-114 to 61-62, seems to me eminently reasonable.

by the addition of another distich, sealing the dispute. Only here does one side receive more than a sole distich.

Iamque patrem famulosque patris lucemque timebam (71). Abruptly we realize that the events of the past 50 lines have occupied the whole night; dawn is approaching. The next twelve lines (73-84) are strikingly effective in their dramatic power, wonderfully compact, elliptical, tense. Lynceus' flight passes straightway into morning. Transition is ignored (*ipsa moror/ mane erat*). The account is stark in its brevity: Danaus the calculating villain (*dinumerat*—he counts the bodies one by one!), the pleading of Hypermestra merely implied in the need to drag her away, the simple summary: *carcer habet.*[36]

Ovid knew Horace's treatment of the Hypermestra myth (*C.* 3.11) and traces of this familiarity are clear in the letter.[37] But, as Tescari has remarked, the differences are crucial, for the tone

---

[36] I suspect that Ovid has modeled his entire account of the wedding-night on Vergil's account of another night of horror, the fall of Troy. Like Aeneas, Hypermestra begins with a prefatory remark on the pain caused her by recollection, yet declares she will describe the event (*Her.* 17-18, 21; *Aen.* 2.3, 6-8, 12-13). Both narratives commence with "symbolic" descriptions of the descent of night (*H.* 21-22; *A.* 2.250-252). In each there is much joy and performance of religious ritual (*H.* 26, 30-31; *A.* 2.239, 248-249). Both sets of victims are come upon when asleep and drunk (*H.* 33-34; *A.* 2.253,265. Austin *ad* 265 gives a list of parallel passages. He misses this one in Ovid.). Each hero can hear the sounds of death around him (*H.* 35-36; *A.* 2.298-301) and, taking up arms, prepares to act (*H.* 44; *A.* 2.314). In passing we may note the use of *excutio* at key points in both (*H.* 43; *A.* 2.302), which is not likely coincidence since Ovid repeats the Vergilian phrase *excutior somno* verbatim and in the same position in the line at *H.* 13.109. In addition, each hero is virtually paralyzed by fear (*H.* 37-40; *A.* 2.303-308) and his condition is compared to a phenomenon from the rustic world of nature. Though the similes are different, most notably in that Ovid finds the analogue in nature itself rather than in the human response to it, they are strikingly alike. Finally, we may wonder whether the following are mere coincidence. *Belidae* (*Belide*) occurs at *H.* 73 and *A.* 2.82; *Pelasgi* at *H.* 23 (gen. sing.) and *A.* 2.83 (nom. pl.). *Ecce* (*H.* 29), found twice in this poem, only three other times in the remaining fourteen letters, is found no less than eight times in *A.* 2. It is surprising that A. Zingerle, *Ovidius und sein Verhältnis zu den Vorgängern* (Innsbruck 1869 and 1871), can find no parallels between *H.* 14 and *A.* 2. One could, I imagine, find a good many more echoes of *A.* 2 scattered through the *Heroides*. I note here only *H.* 1.33-35/ *A.* 2.29-30; *H.* 9.7/ *A.* 2.104. See Zingerle's *indices*.

[37] For reminiscences, see O. Tescari, *Convivium* 6 (1934) 79-81. They had previously been noted by Wickham in his introduction to *C.* 3.11 and by Zingerle.

and aims are discrepant.[38] Horace's Hypermestra appears as a kind of *exemplum*. His interest in her is limited to her achievement of a difficult and virtuous deed. There is neither complexity in the character nor hesitation in the act.[39]

Let us turn for a moment to the little we know of Aeschylus' Hypermestra.[40] If, as most scholars today hold, the *Aigyptioi* ended at nightfall with the wedding and the *Danaides* opened the following morning to reveal the results of the night's activities, then the nocturnal scene depicting Hypermestra and Lynceus would not have had a place in the trilogy, unless Hypermestra delivered a speech in the *Danaides* reporting the events.[41] Further, we cannot be quite certain why Hypermestra spared Lynceus. The crucial line in the *Prometheus Bound* (865; assuming that the motivation was the same in the *Danaides*, which need not be the case), is subject to two interpretations. She spared Lynceus either (1) out of love[42] or (2) because she desired

[38] An interesting change is Ovid's adaptation of the epitaph motif. Ovid's Hypermestra speaks of her own epitaph, Horace's of Lynceus': so it seems better to understand Horace, as does, e.g., G. Williams, *The Third Book of Horace's Odes* (Oxford 1969) 83. Wickham, however, does disagree.

[39] One is inevitably compelled to fall back on descriptions like Fraenkel's (*Horace* 197) "dignity of thought and expression" or Williams' "the poet's picture of her is charming."

[40] I have no intention of rehashing the arguments over Ovid's use of Aeschylus in this letter. Wilamowitz' categorical dismissal of the very possibility that Ovid could have used Aeschylus is difficult to accept (*Aischylos: Interpretationen* [Berlin 1914] 20). As far as I am concerned, the fact that much of the argumentation of both Birt and Ehwald is forced and weak does not invalidate the substantial number of indications that there is, at least, some Aeschylean influence here. Be this as it may, I should like to point out two neglected items which just may provide some clues as to "sources." (1) *Rea* occurs nowhere else in the *Heroides*, three times in this poem. Might this reflect a source in which Hypermestra was, in the end, put on trial? Whether she was in Aeschylus' trilogy remains a matter of contention. (2) Verses 61, *aut meruere necem patruelia regna †tenendo†*, and 111-112, *Bella pater patruusque gerunt; regnoque domoque/ pellimur*, seem to look to a source in which the dispute between Aegyptus and Danaus arose over the question of rule (as attested at, e.g., Serv. *Aen.* 10.497; Hyg. *Fab.* 168; schol. Aesch. *PV* 853). This is almost surely not Aeschylus' version.

[41] G. Hermann's view (*Opusc.* [Leipzig 1827] 2.326) that the murder took place during the play has, it seems, found little support.

[42] The views of Birt, that Aeschylus would never have introduced an "erotic" theme into the very body of the play, and of Ehwald, that ἵμερος has no erotic connotation, have fortunately not been taken very seriously

children. I myself incline to the former because (1) the scholiast *ad loc.* so interprets the line. (2) Schol. Eur. *Hec.* 886 offers an elaboration, but with the same point. (3) There is no indication elsewhere of a version in which Hypermestra spared Lynceus out of a desire for children. (4) Aphrodite's climactic speech in the *Danaides* on the cosmic nature of love suggests that she saved him because of love.

At any rate, there are in general two versions of Hypermestra's motives: (1) love; (2) because Lynceus made no attempt to sleep with her.[43] In Horace's Ode, motivation—or circumstances—is unclear. Kiessling interprets *virgo* (35) as virgin, a recollection of motive 2. Heinze-Burck disagree, with, it seems to me, good reason when one considers *Venus* in 50. *Virgo* in *Her.* 14.55 is equally indecisive. *Femina sum et virgo natura mitis et annis*; the balance of the verse suggests that *femina* corresponds to *natura mitis*, and *virgo* to *mitis annis*. Thus, *virgo* would stress her youth, nothing else.[44] Regardless of the question of Hypermestra's virginity, we cannot miss that often in the myth love was of major importance: Aeschylus' Aphrodite, Horace's Venus, a late cup-painting showing Hypermestra sword in hand, Lynceus fleeing, all in the presence of a Pothos.[45] Thus, the total neglect of *Amor* in Ovid's poem becomes more conspicuous and more obviously calculated.

But why does Ovid take this tack? It may be the simplest application of psychology. The circumstances in which Hyper-

---

by scholars. Of late, the *Supplices* has been afforded psychoanalytic interpretation. See R. S. Caldwell, *TAPA* 101 (1970) 86-88.

[43] E.g., Apollod. 2.1.5; schol. *Il.* 4.171. If Austin's implied reconstruction of the prologue papyrus of Euripides' *Archelaus* is correct (supra n. 3), then we have our first example of this version in a Greek literary source.

[44] I am not convinced by Giangrande's argument (supra n. 33, 154) that the wine at 42 is tied up to the *virgo* of 55, i.e., the wine put Lynceus to sleep before intercourse could take place. Oppel (126, n. 6) argues much the same. While on the subject of virginity lost, I cannot resist suggesting that verse 17 contains a double-entendre, *Cor pavet admonitu temeratae sanguine noctis.* The prime—and surface—reference is to the bloody murder of the bridegrooms. But since it is also a multiple wedding-night, *temeratae sanguine noctis* could allude to the sexual initiation of the virgin brides, especially since *temero* is often used, especially by Ovid, of sexual "violation." In the *Heroides* see 5.101, 9.49.

[45] See Friedrich (supra n. 3, p. 6), who gives a reproduction: fig. 2, facing p. 4.

mestra is married to Lynceus are scarcely ripe for love and affection. Exile, flight, wandering, and a compelled marriage to a man who has been, to some degree, responsible for her misery are not fertile soil for love. But I suspect there is more. Ovid's motive is by way of response. He tends to reject simplistic psychological characterization and motivation. The notion that Hypermestra, out of a sense of love, decided not to kill Lynceus might have appeared to him too easy, too pat a resolution of a complex psychological situation, one of large conflict with questions of morality, pragmatism, and psychology all intertwined. And, of course, so simplistic a turn to the legend would naturally deprive Hypermestra of genuine psychological interest, would dissipate the potential the myth has for a rich and complicated character development. So Ovid makes it clear to us, by his total rejection of the love motif, that he has gone off in a new direction. There is no easy and empty resolve by Hypermestra to act nobly. On the very verge of murder she is beset by qualms and forced to argue the merits of each side. It is just barely that the "just cause" wins out. And then Ovid presents us with the post-*noctem* Hypermestra, suffering the consequences of her act, justifying herself, a Hypermestra in sum whose character has now been shaped by the actions of that dire night.

In conclusion, aside from the virtues of this poem which I trust have been by now made abundantly clear, Ovid's achievement in adapting this myth can be seen in three areas: (1) He may well have been the first to attempt a psychologically realistic portrait of Hypermestra on the occasion of the murder (which Horace's, for instance, certainly is not). (2) He is likely the first to represent Hypermestra after the deeds of that night, to present her feelings and thoughts in the daylight hours of retrospect and doubt, suffering and self-vindication. Finally, what we can be quite sure of (3), Ovid must have originated the treatment of the two main episodes of the myth, the wedding-night and the ensuing events, from the perspective of Hypermestra.

VIII

Heroides 4: Phaedra

The historians and the tragedians, in the words of Plutarch
(*Thes.* 28), are in agreement when it comes to the misfortunes of
Hippolytus and Phaedra. The critic, as he approaches Euripides,
Sophocles, Ovid, and Seneca, can only smile bitterly and wonder.
Without further ado, we must admit that the student of *Heroides*
4, charting the relationship between Ovid and the Greek sources,
must run aground on the rocks of conjecture and insufficient evidence.[1] Barrett has gone a long way in sorting out the bits and
pieces of information, but in the end progress is slow and meager. For Ovid, it would not be hard, by a careful perusal of the
relevant texts, to "prove" that he knew and used both of Euripides' plays and Sophocles'. Many verbal echoes have been noticed.[2] More can be added to the sum. Thus, when Phaedra

[1] The following works will be cited in this chapter by author's name or in
other abbreviated form: W. S. Barrett, ed. *Euripides Hippolytus* (Oxford
1964); T. Birt, *RhM* 32 (1877) 403ff; R. Bürger, *De Ovidi Carminum Amatoriorum Inventione et Arte* (Braunschweig 1901); G. Carugno, *GIF* 4 (1951)
151-155; L. Castiglioni, *A&R* 6 (1903) 245-247; P. Grimal, *REL* 41 (1963)
297-314 (= Grimal, *REL*); P. Grimal, ed. *L. Annaei Senecae Phaedra* (Paris
1965) (= Grimal, *Phaedra*); H. Herter, *RhM* 89 (1940) 273-292 (with a good
bibliography up to 1940 on 273-274); J. Ilberg, "Phaidra," in Roscher, *Lex.
d. gr. u. röm. Myth.*; A. Kalkmann, *De Hippolytis Euripideis Quaestiones
Novae* (Bonn 1882); F. Leo, *De Senecae Tragoediis Observationes Criticae*
(Berlin 1878); M. Mayer, *De Euripidis Mythopoeia Capita Duo* (Berlin
1883); E. Paratore, *Dioniso* 15 (1952) 199-234; G. Peters, *Observationes ad
P. Ovidii Nasonis Heroidum Epistulas* (Leipzig 1882); O. Ribbeck, *Geschichte der Römischen Dichtung* (Stuttgart 1900), vol. 2; B. Snell, *Scenes
from Greek Drama* (Berkeley and Los Angeles 1964); U. von Wilamowitz-
Moellendorff, *Analecta Euripidea* (Berlin 1875 = Wilamowitz, *Analecta*);
id., *Euripides Hippolytos* (Berlin 1891 = Wilamowitz, *Hipp.*); T. Zieliński,
Tragodumenon Libri Tres (Cracow 1925); C. Zintzen, *Analytisches Hypom-
nema zu Senecas Phaedra* (Meisenheim/Glan 1960).

[2] See e.g., Birt 404-405; Eggerding *passim*; Mayer 66; the commentaries of
Loers and Palmer *passim*.

recognizes her need for *salus* (1), why not think of Sophocles' reference to her "disease" (Fr. A Barr. = 680P.)? When she makes pleasure her ultimate criterion (133), consider this a response to Soph. Fr. C (= 677P.). When she describes the rule of Eros over men and gods (11-12), we may think of Soph. Fr. B (= 684P.). Similarly, our scholar may proceed, Ovid made abundant use of the First *Hippolytus* (here, in fact, he will probably be on more solid ground). Again, the power of Eros and the futility of fighting against him (Fr. C = 430N²), the references to αἰδώς (Fr. H = 436N²) and *pudor* (9), the notion that Phaedra's new love is motivated by or in retaliation for the escapades of Theseus (Fr. B = 491 N²; Ovid 111-112), the fire imagery (Fr. J = 429N²; Ovid 33), the arguments against piety (Fr. D = 434N²; Ovid 131ff) and against sexual abstinence (Fr. F = 428N²; Ovid 85ff), the role of deceitful rhetoric (Fr. N = 439N²; Ovid 137ff), the defense by way of claiming the inevitability of god-sent evils (Fr. S = 444N²; Ovid 53ff).

Moreover, if we turn to the *Metamorphoses*, the Hippolytus episode there (15.492ff) seems derivative from the First *Hippolytus*:[3] the locale is Athens, Phaedra is villainous and is apparently still alive when Hippolytus is accused. Further, some have seen in a peculiar statement at *RA* 743 a reflection of the First *Hippolytus*.[4] Neither of these is certain evidence for *Heroides* 4, but they do perhaps indicate Ovid's familiarity with Euripides' earlier play. The scene of *Heroides* 4 appears to be Athens:

> Aequora bina suis oppugnant fluctibus Isthmon
> et tenuis tellus audit utrumque mare.
> Hic tecum Troezena colam, Pittheia regna;
> iam nunc est patria carior illa mea.
>
> (105-108)

Barrett (32, n. 4) has rightly rejected the view that *hic* implies Phaedra's present residence in Troezen and decides *non liquet*. But we should go further. The description of the location of Troezen implies that Phaedra is talking of a place where she

---

[3] Though the Virbius aspect may make us wonder whether Ovid is drawing on a later Italianized version. Barrett, to be sure, thinks the Hippolytus-Virbius association may have been in Callimachus. W. H. Friedrich, *Euripides und Diphilos* (Munich 1953) (= *Zetemata* 5) 115-116 suspects a post-Euripidean source for Ovid's treatment in the *Metamorphoses*.

[4] Leo 174-175.

presently *is not*, and the *illa* of 108 supports this. Therefore, the scene is Athens, as in the First *Hippolytus*.[5]

The absence of Theseus is here explained by his sojourn in the land of Pirithous (if the text of 110 is sound and correctly understood).[6] In the extant *Hippolytus* his absence is motivated by a journey to an oracle, in Sophocles' *Phaedra* by an adventure in Hades. Perhaps, then, if Ovid is not innovating, his source may be Euripides' first treatment of the myth.

Most decisive is the overall set of circumstances. The direct and willful attempt by Phaedra to overthrow the traditional bounds of morality and seduce Hippolytus seems to be found only in the First *Hippolytus*.[7] The fact that in all Ovid's poetry Phaedra is condemned outright, never extenuated, suits best the first Phaedra Euripides portrayed.[8]

To complicate matters all the more, there are numerous echoes in Phaedra's letter of the Second *Hippolytus*. For example, Phaedra's falling in love with Hippolytus on seeing him at the Mysteries, the description (or implication) that Phaedra is "sick" and also possessed, the opinion that Theseus may be faithless, a lengthy passage describing Phaedra's newly found outdoor interests, references to the competition between Hippolytus and Phaedra's sons for the right to inherit from Theseus, the notion that Hippolytus is a bastard, the theme of inherited family curse, the designation of Phaedra as παῖ Κρησία (372; *Cressa puella*, 2), the αἰδώς/ *pudor* theme, Phaedra's original determination to fight

---

[5] The following have argued for Troezen: Birt 403; Kalkmann 115, n. 1; Leo 179; Paratore 214. The following for Athens: Eggerding 209ff; Herter 282; Mayer 71; Peters 25-26; Ribbeck 245; Wilamowitz, *Hipp.* 46, n. 1. For the usage of *hic* as I have argued, see *ThLL* s.v. 2759-2761.

[6] For various views, see: Barrett 32, n. 3; Birt 405; Eggerding 215-216; Grimal, *REL* 306; Herter 282, n. 18; Kalkmann 36-37; Leo 179; Mayer 67-69; Peters 26; Ribbeck 245-246; Wilamowitz, *Hipp.* 46, n. 1; Zintzen 12.

[7] Paratore (201-214) has argued that the first *Hippolytus* may not have represented a direct approach by Phaedra. As for Lycophron's *Hippolytus*, we know nothing about it.

[8] Parts of Seneca's *Phaedra* which are thought by many derivative from the First *Hippolytus* (because they are certainly not from the Second and probably not from Sophocles' play) are sometimes coincident with Ovid's letter. Unless Seneca is in these places drawing on Ovid's original ideas, it may be possible that both go back to the First *Hippolytus*, e.g., the role of Helios and Venus in the family curse (Ov. 53-54; Sen. 124-127), references to Theseus and Pirithous as homosexual lovers (Ov. 111-112; Sen. 97-98 [perhaps]).

her passion, arguments revolving around the same mythological models, references to the power of love, Hippolytus' hatred of all women.

Clearly some of this could be coincidental or simply the inevitable result of the same subject matter; but just as clearly some parallels are so striking either in their substance or in their verbal similarity that they must be echoes. Ovid, we must apparently conclude, knew and was using both of Euripides' plays (and, just possibly, Sophocles' too).[9] We know enough of Ovid's technique to judge this neither strange nor unlikely. It may, however, be possible that some of the seeming echoes of the Second *Hippolytus* are in fact echoes of the First, passages which Euripides retained and repeated in his second version.[10] Be this as it may, even if Ovid was interested primarily in the First *Hippolytus*, we must recognize that he actively acknowledges and exploits the backdrop of the later play as well. When Phaedra

[9] The following believe Ovid used the First *Hippolytus* and, at least in some measure, the Second also: Birt 405, n. 2; Carugno 151; Castiglioni 245-247; Eggerding *passim*; Herter 281; Ilberg 2223; Kalkmann 24; Kraus, *Wege der Forschung: Ovid* 91 (so I hesitatingly interpret him. His citation of Leo, who argues that the First *Hippolytus* was Ovid's main source, but the Second was also used, reinforces this interpretation. But I wonder whether he may mean that the First *Hippolytus* was the exclusive source.

"Beruhen auf Homer Penelope and Briseis, auf der Tragödie Phaedra [zugrunde liegt wie auch bei Seneca der verlorene ältere Hippolytos des Euripides, dem aus dem erhaltenen zweiten Stück dieses Namens einzelne Züge beigemischt sind: Leo, Seneca I 173], Hermione, etc.")

Leo 176ff; Mayer 66ff; Oppel 12; Ribbeck 245; Wilamowitz, *Analecta* 154; id., *Hipp.* 46, n. 1. (So I understand his note. Later scholars invariably, it seems, attribute to Wilamowitz the view that Ovid drew only on the First *Hippolytus* [e.g., Birt 403, Carugno 151].

die minder spärlichen als inhaltlosen reste des ersten Hippolytos genügen zum beweise, dass Ovid und Seneca subsidiär zu dem erhaltenen den ersten Hippolytos herangezogen haben.)

I presume that when Wilkinson (93, n.) refers to the earlier *Hippolytus* as the source for *Heroides* 4, he does not mean to exclude completely the later play. F. G. Welcker, *Die griechischen Tragödien* (Bonn 1839) 402, argued that Sophocles' *Phaedra* was the source for the *Phaedra* letter. He has been followed by Peters (26, n. 1). Paratore (214) thinks it possible that Sophocles' play influenced Ovid's letter.

[10] A point made by Bentley. See his *Epistola ad Joannem Millium*, ed. G. P. Goold (Toronto 1962) 280-281. He was followed by L. C. Valckenaer, *Euripidis Tragoedia Hippolytus* (Leiden 1768) pp. xviii-xix.

writes, *Perlege quodcumque est. Quid epistula lecta nocebit?*(3), a sentiment not expressed elsewhere in the *Heroides* (5.1-2 is closest), this must be deliberate irony, for the reader at once responds that in fact the reading of a letter will in the end kill Hippolytus, but only if one thinks of the Second *Hippolytus*. Perhaps this also partially explains why Ovid has Phaedra write at a very different time from most of his heroines, before the critical moment when she finds herself betrayed. For, within the context of the Second *Hippolytus*, having her write after her rejection would have entailed the assumption that she then writes two letters, one to Hippolytus, one to Theseus.[11] This Ovid may have wished to avoid and so set the letter earlier.

In sum, given our state of knowledge (or ignorance), it is a futile task to seek to determine with precision just how well Ovid knew each of the major treatments of the myth or to what degree he relied on each of his predecessors. Still, the echoes to which we can point are sometimes useful in determining the direction of Ovid's originality and aims.

The opening distich, typically Ovidian in its wit, is suggestive. The double-entendre on *salus* is perhaps unparalleled, certainly very rare, in the other fourteen letters (11.1-2 is spurious, but 13.1 may be a play on the two senses of *salus*), and, though it is

[11] Such an objection would not exist within the framework solely of the First *Hippolytus*, where Phaedra probably accused Hippolytus directly to Theseus. The question of whether there existed a Greek version of the myth in which Phaedra wrote Hippolytus a seduction letter is much vexed. The fact that Roman art sometimes represents the nurse bringing such a letter to Hippolytus (the letter's content is manifest from Hippolytus' reaction) makes it difficult to disbelieve in the existence of such a Greek literary treatment. When Barrett (37, n. 2) tries to explain the iconographic evidence away by seeing in it the visual art's transformation of a verbal message into a written one, he seems to be clutching at straws. Leo even suggested (178-179) that the Greek source which had Phaedra send Hippolytus this letter was Euripides' First *Hippolytus*. Though this is not likely, one wonders whether the writer who originated this approach (assuming one did exist) got the germ of his idea from the letter Phaedra writes in the Second *Hippolytus*. At any rate, see now A. Erdelyi, *Acta Antiqua* 14 (1966) 211-223, with a basic bibliography of the problem at 212, n. 2. For various views, see Castiglioni 246; Fränkel 191, n. 5; Ilberg 2223, 2231-2232; Kalkmann 65ff; Ribbeck 245; E. Rohde, *Der griechische Roman³* (Leipzig 1914) 38, n. 6; Webster 71, n. 50; Zieliński 81-84. Also Procopius' *Ekphrasis* in P. Friedländer, *Spätantiker Gemäldezyklus in Gaza* (Vatican 1939) p. 11, #19; p. 13, #23. On the general subject of the Hippolytus myth in art, see A. Kalkmann, *Arch. Zeitung* 41 (1883) 38-79; Eitrem in *RE* s.v. *Hippolytos* 8 (1913) 1870-1872.

not uncommon elsewhere,[12] Ovid utilizes it here because of the obviously pathological nature of Phaedra's behavior. A topos is made of immediate significance within its context. Even more interesting is the designation of the writer and recipient: *Amazonio Cressa puella viro.* Note the juxtaposition of the "geographical" adjectives; Phaedra comes from Crete, Hippolytus is of Amazon lineage, lines of descent quite disparate and far-removed. The current relationship, wife and son of Theseus, virtually mother and child, is completely obscured. So too *puella viro* is calculated to distort relationships. Each noun is sharp with erotic-elegiac overtones, the available young girl and her lover.[13] In a sense, the social or legal ranks are blurred and the two, stepmother and stepson, stand together on one level, potential erotic-elegiac lovers. So the opening lines may be seen in one of two ways. In her attempt to seduce Hippolytus, Phaedra tries to forestall his objection that, after all, this may be incest (I use the term for economy's sake), by showing that, in fact, the two are very far from being related. Or else this is self-deceit.[14] In her desire to win Hippolytus, Phaedra can even see herself a young girl in love with a young man (note that although she admits adultery at 17, it is not till 127ff that the additional factor of incest is even mentioned).

It is not long, however, before her self-portrait changes. She becomes a middle-aged woman looking for a youthful lover to replace her husband:

> Non ego nequitia socialia foedera rumpam;
>   fama—velim quaeras—crimine nostra vacat.
> Venit amor gravius quo serior. Urimur intus,
>   urimur et caecum pectora vulnus habent.
>
> (17-20)

It is more than a little surprising to hear our *puella* talking in such terms (e.g., *serior*): her love for Hippolytus is all the

[12] It goes back at least to Eur. *Bacchae* 1379-1380, *Hec.* 426-427. For other examples see Bürger 36-37.

[13] Kirfel (93) needlessly defends *puella* here by various examples of its use of married women. But the point resides in the word's erotic connotation. *Puella* is calculated; it needs no defense. It is part of Phaedra's posture. What is, by the way, implicit in this distich, that the writer chooses designations which obscure the illicit relationship, is explicit at *Met.* 9.528ff, where Byblis writes *soror*, then emends it to *amans*.

[14] Oppel (93) stresses the role of self-deceit in this letter.

stronger because it comes to her late in life and she has not known such feelings before. This passage (17-32) is strange in two ways. First, it not only ignores Theseus by name (references to her marriage at 17 and 34), but it presents Phaedra as one who has never before been in love. Theseus, it appears, never appealed to her at all! Even more striking is the language with which Phaedra describes herself, imagery traditional to be sure, but unusual—or impossible—for one in Phaedra's condition. *Teneros laedunt iuga prima iuvencos, de grege captus equus, primos rude pectus amores, nova . . . carpes libamina, plenis . . . ramis, primam . . . rosam.* This is, of course, sexual imagery, but beyond this it is virgin imagery.[15] Hippolytus is, in effect, invited to be the first to enjoy the fruits of Phaedra's sexuality, a rather striking and surprising profession for one already the mother of several children! Thus, two "incompatible" motifs interlace. Phaedra's passion is great because love has come to her late in life, but her attractiveness and desirability are enhanced by her being a "puella" who has never really lost her virginity.

This whole play on motifs and imagery is pure Ovid, be it joke and parody or an attempt at representing Phaedra's confused vision of the situation. Surely parodic is Phaedra's account of the tongue-tied lover (7-10), which also serves to explain why Phaedra sends a letter when Hippolytus is right there (a circumstance unusual in the *Heroides*). *Ter tecum conata loqui, ter inutilis haesit/ lingua, ter in primo destitit ore sonus* (7-8). The epic antecedents of these lines are immediately recalled (e.g., *Od.* 11.206ff; *Aen.* 2.792-793). The tragic actions of great heroes are transfigured into a lover's paralysis.[16] The next passage abruptly lifts us out of the world of epic or tragedy and unceremoniously deposits us into that of erotic elegy:

> Qua licet et †sequitur, pudor est miscendus amori;
>   dicere quae puduit, scribere iussit amor.
> Quidquid Amor iussit, non est contemnere tutum;
>   regnat et in dominos ius habet ille deos.

---

[15] E. Merone, *Studi sulle Eroidi di Ovidio* (Naples 1964) 120-121, appears to be the only scholar to have even noticed this.

[16] Apollonius' epic lover (3.654, 683-687) represents a middle ground. Note how Apollonius refrains from using the "thrice" motif of the tongue-tied girl. When Ovid uses the *ter . . . ter* theme at 14.45-46, it is almost an epic situation. He uses the motif in parodic fashion also at *Am.* 1.7.61-62.

4. Phaedra

Ille mihi primo dubitanti scribere dixit:
  "Scribe! Dabit victas ferreus ille manus."

(9-14)

The power of Eros, phrased in just about these terms, was a commonplace and did occur in earlier versions of the Hippolytus
myth. But Ovid's is not the Eros (or Aphrodite) of Euripides; this
is the Hellenistic-Ovidian figure who can only recall for us the
Cupid who stands over Ovid and instructs him to choose elegy
over epic, or, we might appropriately add, over tragedy, here
guiding Phaedra in much the same way.[17] The image of Cupid
and his elegiac vocabulary destroy any expectation of a tragic
version of the myth of the sort Euripides (or Sophocles) would
have produced.

Exaggeration as an element of parody can be seen in Phaedra's
account of her new aspirations (37ff). So taken with Hippolytus
is Phaedra that she develops an attachment to his rustic interests.
Now this is, as scholars have often observed, taken directly from
the Second *Hippolytus* (208ff). But whereas Euripides' heroine
merely expresses a spontaneous wish (note the optatives and imperatives), Ovid's indicates a new and established state of mind.
This is now her character.[18] When she proceeds to call herself
mad and describe her possessed condition (47-52), there are
again echoes of Euripides (141ff), with allusions to Cybele and
the rustic deities. But what is in Euripides speculation by the
chorus concerning Phaedra's strange behavior (self-starvation)
becomes in Ovid Phaedra's account of her own wild activities—
which in the end she must report second-hand (51-52).

Often we sense Ovid's Phaedra going one step beyond Euripides'. Each bemoans her fate and sees herself as continuing the
family curse, but Ovid's senses herself fulfilling her fate more
than suffering it (61-62). Each recalls the examples of Pasiphae
and Ariadne, but Euripides' heroine recalls Ariadne in her role as
paramour of Dionysus (339), Ovid's in her role as lover of
Theseus. In so doing, Ovid's Phaedra is able to double the element
of fate: *Hoc quoque fatale est: Placuit domus una duabus;/ me
tua forma capit, capta parente soror* (63-64).

---

[17] Procopius' *Ekphrasis* (supra n. 11) suggests that this scene may have
had a Hellenistic precedent. But this is not necessarily so, in part because of
the possible (and common) metaphorical use of Cupid in artistic representation.

[18] This is essentially Eggerding's view (201).

Like Euripides' Phaedra, Ovid's fell in love with Hippolytus at Eleusis—almost: *tunc mihi praecipue (nec non tamen ante) placebas* (69). Eleusis was only the high point; she'd been impressed even before!

Phaedra's description of Hippolytus (71ff) strikes two notes.[19] It reminds us of the *Ars* or *Medicamina*, but is at heart a variation on what was probably a topos of erotic composition, especially comedy, namely, the distorted manner in which a lover can visualize his beloved (see, e.g., *AA* 2.657ff; Lucr. 4.1157ff; cf. *AA* 1.509-512).[20] Moreover, the description bears so many resemblances to the earlier one of herself that we realize that the latter was a Phaedra drawn in the image of Hippolytus.[21]

In short, for better or worse, Ovid has no intention of competing with Euripides on the tragedian's own ground. In a sense this poem anticipates the *Ars*. The obviously erotic symbolism at 91-92, *arcus (et arma tuae tibi sunt imitanda Dianae)/ si numquam cesses tendere, mollis erit,* is humorously witty counterpoint to the character of Hippolytus. *Nequitia*, a key word in the *Amores*, occurs only here (17) in the fifteen letters. The arguments of 137-146, with their elaboration of deceitful techniques to dupe the husband and his *ianitor* (or, more exactly, the absence of any need to do so), make us think of the *Ars* or the *lena*'s speech on the ease of a liaison—except that here the seducer, the instructress of the *Art* is the woman herself.

As if to emphasize the great difference of this poem from the other *epistulae*, Ovid deliberately inverts or distorts themes which tend to occur in a fairly regular pattern through the *Heroides*. For example, when Phaedra writes *Praeposuit Theseus, nisi si manifesta negamus,/ Pirithoum Phaedrae Pirithoumque tibi* (111-112), she varies on two counts the common Heroidean motif whereby the heroine condemns her lover for preferring a rival. First, Phaedra's rival is not a woman, but a man, and, second, rather than using the rival theme to chastise

---

[19] The structural pattern of 79-84 is typically Heroidean. Hexameter describes a fact or situation, pentameter the writer's response.

[20] The presence here of this topos has by and large gone unnoticed. But see Bürger and his parallels. For another list of examples of the topos, see Gow *ad* Theoc. 10.20, 27.

[21] Note the deliberate echoes: *levis . . . pulvis // leves in pulvere; ferocis equi luctantia colla // ora fugacis equi; lentum valido torques hastile lacerto // tremulum excusso iaculum vibrare lacerto.* Also, the repeated *sive* (*seu*) recalls the repeated *aut*.

the addressee, she makes use of it to win him over. Interconnected with this is another variation. Ovid's heroines commonly describe their female rivals in nasty terms. But when Phaedra speaks of Theseus' old flame, the Amazon mother of Hippolytus, it is with great praise (117-118).

Phaedra's generous offer of her "virginity" reminds us of the many heroines who also allude to their loss of virginity—but in complaining tones.

The substance of the poem is to a large degree shaped and determined by the situation or moment which Ovid has chosen. It would be fairly accurate to say of this letter, in contrast to most of the *Heroides*, that it is a *suasoria*.[22] Certainly most everything in it is calculated to persuade Hippolytus. As a consequence, the structure is more rational—or at least more easily discerned—more direct, less complex than that of nearly all the other epistles. The poem begins with a real introductory section, an appropriate salutation, an explanation of her reason for writing (rather necessary in the situation), a description of her feelings as she begins to write (1-16). At the same time, these lines implicitly reveal to Hippolytus, without ever saying so, that she is in love with him. The next 68 lines (17-84) present the situation, describe Phaedra's feelings, behavior, and attitude toward Hippolytus, and explain how and why the circumstances have so evolved. But they simultaneously proffer varied unstated arguments to convince Hippolytus, by showing him how desirable Phaedra is (27ff), by flattering him (35-36), by depicting herself as a female version of Hippolytus (37ff). Having been carried away by this account to a final statement of her Bacchant-like activity, she pauses, considers her own insane behavior and for a few moments turns to introspection. She contemplates her fate (53ff) and ends with regrets that she ever saw Hippolytus at Eleusis (67-68). But this recollection immediately rekindles her passion and she goes off in reveries (71ff), a lovesick account of Hippolytus' looks and activities, concluding with—one step closer to desperation—mild pleas, but in broad and general terms (85ff): love is salutary, indeed necessary for one's well-being. That point made, she professes her willingness to run off with Hippolytus (105-108).

Persuasion then continues in a new vein. Liaison is *facile*: The-

---

22 As does, e.g., Wilkinson (105). Oppel, in his justified eagerness to reject the general view of the *Heroides* as rhetorical exercises, underestimates, I think, the *suasoria* element in this poem (59, 89-90).

seus is away (109-110). More, it is *iustum*, for Theseus has mistreated both of us and deserves to be repaid in kind (111-124). Anyway, such behavior is not sinful; moral standards have changed (127-136). Finally, we come full circle to the *facile* argument: there is no problem in getting away with all this (137-146).[23]

The pleas then become more urgent and personal (147ff), begging, outrageous, concrete, and vehement. Phaedra is more direct, more specific, and finally more desperate, ending not on a note of persuasion, but with pleas for kindness and sympathy toward a poor weeping woman.[24]

In sum, a rather well-developed, orderly, rational structure, without the repetitions, the complex interwoven patterns, that characterize many of these poems. In contrast, here we perceive a movement that is forward and linear. This is undoubtedly the result of the nearly exclusive emphasis on argument and persuasion.

In addition to those we have noticed, other elements of the poem are probably also parodic. Such is, for example, Phaedra's representation of herself as a female Hippolytus, virtually an Amazon. But this play on the two as counterparts is carried further than we've detected. Thus, Phaedra is driven mad by the rustic deities (49-50); Hippolytus may be blessed by them (171-174). Is there, by the way, a deliberate antithesis between Bacchus-wine (47-48) and Nymphs-water (173-174)? It is easy to discount the rustic-animal sexual imagery with which Phaedra describes her plight (21ff) as "traditional." Let us not be too eager to do so. Consider Hippolytus' affection for the outdoors, ani-

---

[23] See Eggerding 221-222.

[24] As has long been recognized, *perlegis* in the poem's final line is problematic. E. J. Kenney (*HSCP* 94 [1970] 176-177) has recently argued strongly against it and has convinced Dörrie, who adopts what Kenney considers the lesser of two possible emendations, *qui legis*. Might it be possible to defend *perlegis* as written from Phaedra's perspective, not Hippolytus', i.e., the moment when she concludes the epistle is still prior to Hippolytus' receiving the letter and so she can think, perhaps a bit illogically, of Hippolytus yet reading the letter through? At all events, when Kenney writes, "what does not appear to have been noticed is that the very next Epistle begins with the word *perlegis*," he goes wrong. For this very argument was used by N. Heinsius *ad Her.* 4.176, "certe illud *Perlegis* subnatum videtur ex primo verbo sequentis epistolae." See too W. Schmitz-Cronenbroeck, *Die Anfänge der Heroiden des Ovids* (Diss. Köln 1937) 18, n. 84.

mals, flowers, etc. (note especially the reference to the breaking of the horse at 22; Hippolytus is the "horse-breaker"). The imagery, in other words, is geared to Hippolytus' own interests. Finally, Phaedra invents a point of identity for herself and Hippolytus vis-à-vis Theseus (111ff): he has rejected and harmed them both.[25]

> Clarus erat silvis Cephalus multaeque per herbam
> conciderant illo percutiente ferae;
> nec tamen Aurorae male se praebebat amandum;
> ibat ad hunc sapiens a sene diva viro.
>
> (93-96)

The echo of *Hippolytus* 454-456 is obvious. The nurse, to persuade Hippolytus, adduces the examples of Cephalus-Eos and Zeus-Semele (453-454): even the gods are susceptible to love. Ovid, typically, adopts the mythical *exempla*, but makes far different use of them. The allusion to Cephalus-Eos looks not to Eos, the goddess who succumbed to the allurements of love, but to Cephalus, the hunter who enjoyed the practice of love (as, Phaedra implies, so should Hippolytus). The example of Zeus (sans Semele) is also transfigured. The point becomes not that Zeus loved, but that he loved Juno, his own sister (133-134), thereby becoming a model for the incestuous relationship of Hippolytus and Phaedra.[26]

The section on mythological precedent (93-100) has additional fascination. The story of Cephalus and Eos (and Procris), as familiar to Ovid, ends, precisely because of the hunt, in disaster (see *Met.* 7.839ff); *Multaeque per herbam/ conciderant illo percutiente ferae* could almost be an ironic hint to the accidental killing of Procris. Catastrophe is also the result of the relationship between Venus and Adonis. Here Ovid may be recalling the allusion at *Hipp.* 1420-1422. Finally, the tale of Meleager and Atalanta also ends in calamity (and, as with Adonis, Artemis is again, at least in part, responsible). In short, Phaedra proposes three examples of hunters who have deigned to love women, but

---

25 Is the reference to the slaying of Phaedra's brother (the Minotaur) here (115-116) more parody?

26 Like Freud, Ovid was perceptive enough to recognize how incest is permitted to the gods of mythology, but not to their human worshipers. Cf. S. Freud, *A General Introduction to Psychoanalysis* (Washington Square Press, New York 1962) 344.

in each case the issue is disaster. Perhaps irony is involved, for Hippolytus too will fall victim, but certainly there is an element of wit or parody in Phaedra's use of arguments which in effect fight against herself.

Then there is the lengthy argument from the "new morality" (127ff). It has no basis in the extant *Hippolytus* wherein the nurse's arguments neatly skirt the moral questions involved; nor do we have any indication that it was present in the First *Hippolytus*.[27] Ovid's Phaedra, who began with qualified professions of her own virtue (17-18), now proceeds to redefine moral standards, with perhaps a humorous and prophetic allusion to Ovid himself: *Ista vetus pietas aevo moritura futuro* (131). There is, in the end, no attempt at justifying herself or her values, but perfect recognition that what she desires is wicked and immoral (e.g., 138, 145). But when she calls the *vetus pietas rustica*,[28] she again defeats her own purpose, since presumably *rustica* are precisely what have appeal for Hippolytus (a joke even clearer at 102, *si Venerem tollas, rustica silva tua est*, since a forest is and by definition properly should be *rustica*).

Iuppiter esse pium statuit quodcumque iuvaret (133). This is far too close to formulations like τὸ θεοφιλὲς ὅσιόν ἐστιν and τοῦτο εἶναι τὸ ὅσιον, ὃ ἂν πάντες οἱ θεοὶ φιλῶσι and τὸ ὅσιον ἂν διὰ τὸ φιλεῖσθαι ὅσιον ἦν[29] to be anything but parody of ethical theory, especially since *iuvaret* has become absolute, qualified by no *deis* or the like, and the following verse, *et fas omne facit fratre marita soror*, sounds like a distorted exploitation of Plato's condemnation of the mythic-poetic tales of the gods.

Hippolytus, Phaedra next pleads, should have respect for her lineage (157-162). But the value of such a request must be estimated in light of her earlier allusions (53ff) to the pathological character and fate of these ancestors. And, although she now turns to the male side of the family, she does little better. Minos is none too reputable a figure (and, as Theseus' son, Hippolytus would know the story of the Minotaur); Zeus is not only the incestuous lover of his sister but also the seducer of Europa; Helios is in a sense responsible for the disastrous fate of her family (cf.

---

[27] Fr. N (= 439N²) is presumably not relevant. Of course, Euripides was capable of such an argument. We need but remember the famous motto of moral relativism from his *Aeolus* (19N²).

[28] For the argument, cf. *Am.* 3.4.37ff.

[29] Plato, *Euthyphro* 10D, 9E, 11A.

53-54). One doubts that such forebears are likely to elicit either respect or pity from a Hippolytus.

> Flecte, ferox, animos! Potuit corrumpere taurum
> mater; eris tauro saevior ipse truci?
>
> (165-166)

One cannot restrain the thought that there is a touch of irony here, since a bull will ultimately destroy Hippolytus. But surely these lines, so gross in their exaggeration, must be deliberate caricature. And the final verses of the poem,[30] pathetic in the triviality of the good wishes Phaedra confers upon Hippolytus, particularly the final one "may you have water to drink,"[31] leave us with a sense of parody of high tragedy.

Perhaps in this poem we hear Ovid's own voice, not his personal voice but that of the *persona* he adopts in the *Amores* and the *Ars*. The master seducer marshals his arguments, constantly aware—too aware—of what he is doing, and touching everything with self-parody.

However much we stress the qualities which distinguish this poem from its sisters, we cannot but observe the many techniques and devices which make it akin to them. Aside from some already noted, there is the distortion of relationships and events as seen through Phaedra's eyes. She begins to wonder whether Theseus' unusual closeness to Pirithous may reflect a homosexual relationship (probably not attested before Ovid).[32] Such is clearly the implication of verses 111-112.[33] Ovid's Phaedra scorns and rejects Theseus, indeed, hints that she never loved him. How different is Euripides' heroine (at least in the second *Hippolytus*) who

---

[30] Lines 169-175 are grievously distorted by D'Elia when he describes them as a declaration of absolute fidelity (139, n. 68).

[31] Is this ironic? In the end, water will play an important part in destroying Hippolytus. See *Met.* 15.508ff for a good description of the role of water in causing his death (note especially *cumulus immanis aquarum*).

[32] On the question of the homosexual relationship of Theseus and Pirithous in Ovid, Seneca, and perhaps elsewhere, see Herter 287, n. 25; Mayer 67-68; Paratore 229, n. 10; Grimal, *Phaedra ad* 97.

[33] If 75-76 might be taken as a veiled allusion to her husband Theseus, we could see in them further hints of his homosexuality. At 96, the implication may be that Theseus is an old man, too old to satisfy Phaedra. In Euripides' play, all indications are that Theseus does in fact love Phaedra. Is it just a coincidence that Ovid has his Phaedra condemn her husband as a homosexual and then seek out as a lover a youth who is, at the least, a misogynist?

maintains her love, or at least affection and respect, for her husband. Similarly, Phaedra's children now incur their mother's hatred, who regrets ever having borne potential enemies and rivals of Hippolytus.[34] Whereas in the *Hippolytus* Phaedra's love and concern for her children not only remain intact and strong, but prove a guide for her behavior.

Some additional examples. Phaedra's account of the Amazon's death (119-120)[35] is shaped to serve her own purposes, as is also her novel interpretation of Hippolytus' bastardy (121-122).

Phaedra's view of her ancestors (55-60) subtly mirrors her own nature. Each of the three sets of lovers she presents is seen as a relationship of deceit (*dissimulante, decepto, perfidus*), as if to underscore the presence of deceit in her own attempt to win Hippolytus. What is, so to speak, inherited from the relationships of one generation by those of the next is moral corruption.

It is not surprising, given the general patterns within the *Heroides*, that Phaedra avoids, till the very last moment, mention of Hippolytus' misogyny, and then introduces it, but parenthetically (173-174), as if to avoid the reality of the obstacles that lie before her.[36]

Finally, we must take special note, here as elsewhere in the *Heroides*, of Ovid's ability to see a myth through from its beginnings to its end, and to work out the implications of the varied, often discrepant and dissociated aspects and phases of a myth. In the case of Phaedra, Euripides himself made effective use of the pathological family history, seeing Phaedra within the context of a series of perverse love affairs. But Ovid sees more widely, if not necessarily more deeply. Not only does he fix Phaedra within a vertical continuum, but also within a horizontal one. Phaedra is married to Theseus who treacherously betrayed Ariadne, her sister (59-60, 116), and who murdered her "brother," the Minotaur (115-116), connections which seemingly had never been made (contrast Euripides on Ariadne, *Hipp*. 339), at

---

[34] Paratore (226) has an excellent insight into the deeper reasons for Phaedra's sudden hatred of her own children. Their very existence, he observes, serves to tie her more closely to Theseus.

[35] It is possible that Ovid knew a tradition in which Theseus did kill her (cf. Hyg. *Fab*. 241), but the parallel at 7.83-84 indicates clearly that this need not necessarily be so.

[36] Is Hippolytus' intense misogyny original with Euripides' extant *Hippolytus*?

any rate not in such a way as to be a motivating factor in the psychology of Phaedra. Ovid seems to consciously tie it in, meaning us to see a causal link between Phaedra's hatred for Theseus and Theseus' crimes against her close kin.

In sum, when Ovid decided to essay the character and the myth of Phaedra, he immediately realized that he had lost the common ground which underpins most of the letters in the corpus. In the first place, he could not (as explained earlier) choose the critical moment of the heroine's life as the time of writing. Moreover, if, in general, the *Heroides* are a poetic form which enables the inner person to be reflected in the narrative of concrete and external events, that is, affords a psychological insight into the depths of a character through that person's own words and especially through her peculiar transformation of reality, Euripides had, to a degree, done this already for Phaedra, not, to be sure, in the same manner as Ovid would have or with the same results, but with such perfection and conciseness as to make another attempt to render her character through her words virtually an exercise in futility (Ovid was sharp enough to perceive this; Seneca was not). And so, the lack of complexity in Ovid's characterization, attested most graphically by the absence of any real internal conflict or psychical pain (of course, we do not know what Euripides' first Phaedra was like, but we can surmise that Euripides portrayed some internal struggle within her also) is deliberate.[37] Ovid seized the opportunity to do something different, very different, though within the framework he had adopted. The whole tale is transformed into a joke with Phaedra as the butt. The psychological and dramatic power of Euripides' tragedy dissolve away into the rhetoric of a middle-aged woman, dissatisfied with a husband who appears to have no interest in her, striking out on her own in search of a young lover, who happens to be her stepson—which merely complicates the matter but enhances the rhetorical possibilities. The moral qualms which so afflict Euripides' second Phaedra are dissipated in a cloud of obfuscating but devilishly clever semantics; who can but admire the brilliance of the argument that because of their special rela-

[37] Paratore (223ff) has some excellent observations on this aspect of *Heroides* 4. (I am, however, not in complete agreement with him). I fail to understand Oppel's assertion (89-93) that the Euripidean theme of internal psychical conflict plays an important part in this poem.

tionship they can carry on their affair with ease and even win approval (137-140),[38] when it is precisely this relationship that makes their affair all the more sordid? The whole becomes a rather rational attempt, if posed in mythological terms, at ridiculing the total conglomeration of ethical standards and values that beset the sexual relations between man and woman, much after the style of the *Ars*.[39]

[38] Interestingly enough, there is a parallel to this argument at *Song of Songs* 8.1-3, where the girl wishes her lover were her brother, so that their liaison would be easy to accomplish.

[39] Ovid's rendering of another perverse love, that of Byblis for her brother (*Met.* 9.450ff), takes off (as has often been noted) from *Heroides* 4. The language is similar, the moral-semantic issues are much the same, there is a seduction letter. But the Byblis story is given a much more serious, "Euripidean" treatment. Perhaps this is a reflection of Ovid's confidence in his mature powers, perhaps the result of Byblis not being Phaedra and, consequently, the absence of an eminent precedent like Euripides' Phaedra to intimidate Ovid's ambitions and inclinations.

IX

Heroides 11: Canace

The letter of Canace has long been judged among the most successful and appealing of the *Heroides*. Palmer's appraisal (381), "the poem is the most finished of the whole series" was supported by his exposition that "the subject was one of those in which the soft genius of Ovid luxuriated, and there is nothing forced or unnatural in it." In his introduction Purser sympathetically wrote that "the agony of the mother's grief for her innocent little one . . . is the greatest achievement of the *Heroides*" (p. xix). Even Wilamowitz, in a passing mention, deigned to call the poem "ein gutes Gedicht."[1] Recently, it has earned Ruiz de Elvira's extravagant praise, "verdadera obra maestra de emoción y de verdad poética, casi unánimemente juzgada como la mejor de las *Heroidas*"; he then proceeds to laud the poem in the most lavish terms, even comparing it to Sophocles' *Oedipus Tyrannus*.[2] Yet it is an easy task to elicit sympathy for the innocent victim of a fate almost artificially cruel: the naïve young girl, seduced into an illicit relationship, harried and condemned by the stern conventions of society, faced finally with the prospect of her own death and that of her even more innocent infant child. Who could be heartless enough not to commiserate with, even shed a tear for, the wretched girl? Ovid does not lose the advantage inherent in such a tale, but it is especially to his credit that the obvious pathos never degenerates into nauseating mawkishness. The poem is testimony to Ovid's ability, which he did not often exploit, to profit from tact, restraint, and self-control.

[1] *SB Berlin* (1925) 43, n. 4 (= *Kl. Schr.* 5^2 [Berlin 1937] 57, n. 3). Similar words of praise from Otis (17 and 264) and Salvatore, *Atti* 2.253-255. Ovid himself liked this poem. He reuses material from it at *Fast.* 2.401ff, 3.221ff, and in the Myrrha episode of the *Metamorphoses*: the wise old nurse (10.408ff), the illicit sex and pregnancy, and many verbal echoes.

[2] *Emerita* 38 (1970) 305.

The publication in 1961 (*POxy* 2457) of an ancient hypothesis to Euripides' *Aeolus* shed substantial and unambiguous light, for the first time, on the plot of a play which was evidently, if not the only serious literary treatment of the story of Canace and Macareus,[3] at least the most important and widely known, as Aristophanes' jibes[4] and various comedies which probably parody Euripides' drama demonstrate.[5] The intricacies brought about by the evident interweaving of distinct myths and different Aeoluses remain, however, problematic, nor have I any intention of attempting to unravel the skeins and analyze how and when they became intertwined. Fortunately, these considerations have little relevance to our understanding of Ovid's treatment of the myth. It seems indisputable, on the basis of the limited evidence at hand, that Ovid must have known the Canace myth from Euripides' tragedy and must have, in some sense, used that work as a starting point for his own adaptation. To be sure, this has long been the traditional view (e.g., Grauert, Palmer, Purser, Robert, Welcker),[6] though some dissent and qualification have been voiced.[7] Rohde argued that Ovid used only a Hellenistic source; Kalkmann and Scherling modified this to allow for Ovid's use of

[3] In fact, the only possible testimony to any other is the Suda's reference s.v. *Lycophron* to two plays by that poet, an *Aeolus* and, if the text is right, an *Aeolides*. It is very difficult to draw conclusions about the literary tradition from the iconographic one, which included, e.g., a fifth century Lucanian vase-painting showing Canace's suicide (A. D. Trendall, *The Red-Figured Vases of Lucania, Campania, and Sicily* [Oxford 1967] p. 45, no. 221; A. D. Trendall and T.B.L. Webster, *Illustrations of Greek Drama* [London 1971] 74 and pl. III.3, 4). See A. Kalkmann, *Arch. Zeit.* 41 (1883) 51-62.

[4] Though no names are mentioned, the references at *Nubes* 1371-1372 and *Ranae* 1081 are clearly to Canace. Perhaps also *Ranae* 850.

[5] Aristophanes' *Aeolosikon*, Antiphanes' *Aeolus*, perhaps Eriphus' *Aeolus*. Ovid's allusion (*Tr.* 2.384) to a tragedy about Canace and Macareus, following immediately upon a reference to the *Hippolytus*, most likely refers to Euripides' *Aeolus*. One wonders whether Martial's poem (11.91) on the death of a girl Canace, daughter of Aeolis, at the age of seven is designed to exploit additional sympathy by the association with the tragic, mythological Canace. Also, does the very fact that the girl was named Canace, being daughter of Aiolis, testify to the popularity of the story?

[6] Grauert, *RhM* 2 (1828) 53 and *passim*, 50ff; Palmer (381); Purser (p. xv); Robert, *Die griechische Heldensage* (Berlin 1920) 383, n. 4; Welcker, *Die griechischen Tragödien* (Bonn 1839) 860-872.

[7] E.g., E. Rohde, *Der griechische Roman*[3] (Leipzig 1914) 108, n. 2. Wilamowitz (supra, n. 1) thinks it "zweifelhaft" whether *Heroides* 11 goes back to Euripides.

160

both Euripides' play and a Hellenistic model.[8] I do not, however, see either need or reason to so argue, especially since we do not have any guarantee that there were any Hellenistic versions of the myth (perhaps Lycophron). Phillippson's theory (strangely adopted by Robert)[9] that Callimachus treated the myth, a hypothesis constructed with much ingenuity and little plausibility out of a mutilated fragment of Philodemus' περὶ Εὐσεβείας, has been described by Pfeiffer as being "sine ulla specie veritatis."[10]

The view that Ovid is derivative from Euripides has always been and today remains far and away the most probable, but, to be fair, the recent attempt by Lloyd-Jones (approved by Garvie)[11] to buttress this conjecture by an appeal to the newly found hypothesis is weak. He suggests that Macareus' confidence that he will marry Canace (63-64; his citation of 123 seems rather pointless to me) reveals Euripidean influence, but the hypothesis makes clear that the lot fails to award Canace to Macareus. We might then want to assume that Macareus is confident just because he has managed to convince Aeolus to marry the sisters to the brothers. But it is just as plausible that Macareus' visit to Canace was invented by Ovid and, consequently, even his "confidence" may not go back to Euripides. Nor does dependence on Euripides, as Lloyd-Jones argues, explain the references to the marriage of Canace's sisters (101-108). In fact, there is no reason to believe that Ovid's description even implies an imminent marriage. The marriage torches need reflect no more than Canace's frustrated desire for marriage, especially if we consider how frequently in the *Heroides* the presence of (wedding) torches is imagined (e.g., 6.45-46). Further, the wish expressed as an imperative *nubite felices Parca meliore sorores* may have reference to a distant and unseen future, a simple wish that her sisters fare better in "marriage" than she has.[12]

---

8 A. Kalkmann, *De Hippolytis Euripideis* (Bonn 1882) 104-106; Scherling, *RE* s.v. *Kanake*, vol. 10 (1919) col. 1854.

9 R. Phillippson, *Hermes* 55 (1920) 249. Robert (supra, n. 6).

10 Vol. 1, p. 484 *ad* fr. 783.

11 *Gnomon* 35 (1963) 443-444; A. F. Garvie, *Aeschylus' Supplices* (Cambridge 1969) 170, n. 1.

12 It is little more than a farewell prayer that those close to her have the good fortune that she has not. Perhaps we might compare how Ajax wishes, before his death, better luck for his son (*Ajax* 550). At any rate, surely the imperative need not imply an imminent event. When Briseis writes, *Mittite me, Danai* (3.127), we do not assume that she will shortly be sent to Achilles.

In sum, I am in substantial agreement with Lloyd-Jones that *Heroides* 11 looks back to Euripides' *Aeolus*,[13] but I doubt whether arguments from *POxy* 2457 will convince anyone who did not already believe this.[14]

The direction that Ovid takes in the poem becomes clear from one novel turn that he appears to have introduced. The precise relationship between Canace and Macareus in Euripides is hard to define because of ambiguities in the Greek and slight discrepancies from source to source. Thus, Turner and Webster[15] offer varying versions of the events at *POxy* 2457, the former translating διέφθειρεν "seduced," the latter paraphrasing the papyrus, "Macareus raped his sister." Here resides the problem. Did Macareus rape his sister, i.e., physically force her, or did he seduce her, that is, in some way overcome her reluctance and persuade her to sleep with him, so that in the end there was at least some degree of willingness on her part? Presumably, διαφθείρω (and the other forms of the verb, simplex and προφθείρω, found elsewhere in versions of the story)[16] could allow either, but would much more likely mean seduce. Antiphanes' account,[17] if at all to be trusted as evidence for Euripides' treatment, with its description of the drunk Macareus "getting what he wanted," even

---

Very illuminating is a parallel passage noted by Loers, Prop. 3.19.25, *at vos, innuptae, felicius urite taedas*. This has much the same sense as Ovid's verse and certainly does not require us to think that a wedding is actually about to take place.

[13] L. Castiglioni, *RIL* 70 (1937) 60 has observed that *Her.* 11.113 clearly echoes Eur. *Rhes.* 896. It is possible that Euripides, who so often imitates himself, utilized the same sentiment in his *Aeolus* and Ovid took it from there.

[14] Lloyd-Jones suggests that Euripides may have represented the child as surviving, since Canace is known to have been mother of Triopas. This ignores two things: (1) Euripides might have felt no obligation at all to bring this story of Canace and Macareus in tune with the other tradition. (2) At any event, Poseidon, not Macareus, was the father of Triopas by Canace; and so the only way to justify this hypothesis would be to argue, with Webster (159), that Euripides also changed the father—all of which is quite unnecessary; the person of Triopas probably had no place in Euripides' treatment. In passing, I note that Webster implies (157) that Plutarch made Macareus the oldest son. This is wrong. Like *POxy* he calls him the youngest.

[15] Turner *ad POxy* 2457 (1961); Webster 157.

[16] Plutarch *Parallela Min.* 28; schol. Aristoph. *Nubes* 1371; Tzetzes *ad Nubes* 1371.

[17] *Aeolus* fr. 18 Kock.

162

should we ignore the intoxication, would seem to imply forcible rape. This finds support in Stobaeus' ἐβιάσατο (*Flor.* 64.35), which should mean rape, not seduction.[18]

What is at all events fairly clear is that rather than a love affair between brother and sister, a mutual relationship, Euripides had represented a forceful and aggressive brother and a sister who is either compelled or simply acquiesces.[19] This set of circumstances is subject to, in general terms, an approach found in a good number of the *Heroides*, a letter whose concern is, in large or in small, the berating of the man by the woman for somehow having betrayed her or having caused her to be placed in a miserable and dangerous plight. Here, on the contrary, is Ovid's Canace: *Cur umquam plus me, frater, quam frater amasti/ et tibi, non debet quod soror esse, fui?* (25-26). This is not the opening gambit in an ever-intensifying sequence of rebukes; these gentle, even tender, understated words of complaint are the farthest Canace gets in the language of chastisement. In fact, these are the only lines in the poem which imply any rebuke of Macareus at all. But examine the next distich: *Ipsa quoque incalui qualemque audire solebam,/ nescio quem sensi corde tepente deum* (27-28). The brilliant *quoque* tells all; no reason to find fault with Macareus, this was reciprocated love. She too felt the flame of love and passion. Any responsibility, any guilt, she shares—and understands that she shares. Insofar as the evidence goes, this is pure Ovid. We have no indication that Canace was ever before depicted as being in love with Macareus (though Ovid maintains the dominant role of the brother).

It is this shift which allows Ovid to develop Canace along his desired lines: loving, gentle, delicate, pitiful, yet with a carriage of dignity, quiet resolve, and resignation. In his *Tristia* (2.383-384) Ovid juxtaposed the tales of Phaedra and Canace. Following his example so have I, for it is illuminating how Ovid could take two tales of incest and develop them in such strikingly different

---

[18] Presumably Aristophanes' ἐκίνει (*Nubes* 1371-1372) is just an obscenity for intercourse.

[19] Hyginus 243, Canace killed herself *propter amorem Macarei fratris*, is probably evidence for nothing. The genitive may be subjective (so too at *Tr.* 2.384, *fratris amore sui*, and Plin. *NH* 35.99 [if, indeed, the allusion is to Canace], *propter fratris amorem*). Even if one doubts this (the neighboring references to Byblis and Calypso clearly speak of their own feelings), the precision of the phrase cannot be pressed. It may mean simply "an experience of love resulted in Canace's suicide."

fashions. The lewd and brazen shamelessness of Phaedra stands in sharp contrast to the simple acceptance of Canace. Yet, as we shall see later, the two could have been very similar, and, in fact, the character of the two Euripidean plays (*Aeolus* and First *Hippolytus*) was in all probability much closer one to the other than are Ovid's two poems.

Yet, anger and rebuke are not totally absent from the poem, but are, from the point of view of most of the letters in the *Heroides*, redirected. Aeolus, the father who has inflicted so cruel a punishment on his own daughter, bears the brunt:

> Haec est Aeolidos fratri scribentis imago;
> sic videor duro posse placere patri.
> Ipse necis cuperem nostrae spectator adesset
> auctorisque oculis exigeretur opus.
> Ut ferus est multoque suis truculentior euris,
> spectasset siccis vulnera nostra genis.
> Scilicet est aliquid cum saevis vivere ventis;
> ingenio populi convenit ille sui.
> Ille Noto Zephyroque et Sithonio Aquiloni
> imperat et pinnis, Eure proterve, tuis.
> Imperat, heu! ventis; tumidae non imperat irae;
> possidet et vitiis regna minora suis.
>
> (7-18)

This is an interesting and perhaps important passage. Ovid wittily takes full advantage of the conflation of Aeolus, Canace's father, with Aeolus, ruler of the winds, a conflation which, thanks to *POxy* 2457, we now know was made by Euripides,[20] though to what effect we are ignorant. Although the paradox of a person who is able to exercise some form of control over others but not over himself was a topos common in many and varied manifestations ("physician, heal thyself" being a common one; cf. also *Her.* 12.167-168, 173-174), the association of the character of Aeolus with his function and environment is, as far as I know, found nowhere else, and is certainly typical of Ovid's wit and psychology.[21]

[20] Consequently, Servius *ad Aen.* 1.75 is either in error or thinking of some non-Euripidean treatment.

[21] The closest example I find is the *anonym. de Ulixis erroribus* (332.3 μυθογράφοι Westermann) which describes Aeolus as δεινόν τινα καὶ κακότεχνον, but this personality trait is, as the author himself says, Αἴολον τοὔνομα ὥσπερ δὴ καὶ τὸν τρόπον, built around the etymology of the name Aeolus, not around his role as ruler of the winds.

In this passage and at 101-102 the bitterness is manifest and explicit (we should not miss at verse 9 the choice of *nex* rather than *mors*; also at 111). But throughout the indictment is low-keyed, perhaps the more bitter and effective for its understatement. Even in a moment of joy and revivification, the lovers must face the prospect of the hostile father: *Quid tibi grataris? Media sedet Aeolus aula* (67). He reacts to the discovery with insane rage (76, 81-82). His impetuosity and madness stand in close and deliberate juxtaposition to the silent paralysis of his daughter (83-84). The straightforward and calm description of his ensuing command is in terrifying contrast to the substance of his order: *Iamque dari parvum canibusque avibusque nepotem/ iusserat in solis destituique locis* (85-86). The striking language and arrangement intensifies the horror: the chiastic order *parvum canibusque avibusque nepotem*, with the central position of the agents of death embraced by two highly charged words. The victim is *parvum*, just a tiny infant; and he is *nepotem*, sent to his death by his grandfather. The same effect is obtained in 88 where Canace describes the baby wailing in his small voice (in contrast to Aeolus who is so good at shouting, 76, 81) and pleading, so to speak, with his murderer who is his *avus*.[22] And it is this unthink-

[22] I suspect that verse 87 may reflect unconscious Lucretian influence (5.226-227). *Vagitus* is not a common word and found, outside this letter, only once in Ovid. The notion that the baby's wailing manifests some awareness of his plight is peculiarly common to these two passages. I also wonder whether verses 69-76 recall the Lucretian Magna Mater passage (2.600ff). There is of course the casual similarity in the descriptions of ritual and procession. But it is again the coincidence of *vagitus* in both that is striking (*Her.* 11.73; Lucr. 2.634). In each case an elaborate plot seeks to conceal the existence of a baby from a cruel father (grandfather). The Curetes are successful in drowning out the wailings of the baby Zeus; Canace's son unfortunately betrays himself by his cries (cf. too Lucr. 4.1019). The story of Saturn, as mythical archetype of the cruel father and his children, is, as we shall later see, relevant to the relationship here established between Canace and Aeolus. Ovid, as E. J. Kenney has observed (*Ovidiana* [Paris 1958] 201), "Knew his Lucretius well, and drew on him too." He also notes a number of Lucretian echoes in the *Ars, Remedia & Medicamina* (202-203). While on the topic of influence, I note here that Ovid's familiarity with the *Aeneid* is again displayed in this poem. *Media sedet Aeolus aula* (67) recalls *celsa sedet Aeolus arce* (1.56) and *se iactet in aula Aeolus* (1.140-141); *tumidae non imperat irae* (17) is in obvious contrast to the Vergilian Aeolus who *temperat iras* (1.57). *Ipse necis cuperem nostrae spectator adesset* (9) is a bitter echo of 10.443 (noted by Loers) *cuperem ipse parens spectator adesset*: Turnus, about to kill Pallas, wishes the latter's father were present to witness the murder; but in Ovid the father is also the killer.

ing, irresistible impetuosity of Aeolus that is mirrored in vocabulary and verbal tense. In the distich 85-86 both *iam* and the pluperfect display the haste with which Aeolus acts. There is no thought for his daughter, no concern for his grandson. His is an immediate response to the situation. Once again at 93 the rapidity of his actions is reflected in the pluperfect, *exierat thalamo*.[23]

When Aeolus' attendant enters to give the fatal sword to Canace, he is described in terms that also set off the harshness of Aeolus. For, though he is Aeolus' man, his sympathies, as intimated by Canace, lie clearly with the aggrieved daughter: *Interea patrius vultu maerente satelles/ venit et indignos edidit ore sonos* (95-96).[24] The chiastic order is again effective, as *patrius* is unexpectedly followed by *vultu maerente*.

At 110 the grotesque horror of Aeolus' behavior is illuminated in the juxtaposition of *vix bene natus/ avum*. Not only is the child so young that he must be innocent, but he falls prey to his own kinsman.

There is, however, something more to the role of Aeolus in this poem than is reflected in the bare fact that he is about to have Canace and her son killed, a cruel deed which makes her duly bitter. One cannot but discern that somehow Aeolus' importance is all-pervasive, that it is almost Aeolus to whom this letter is addressed and around whom it revolves. It is, I think, no coincidence that the poem ends with the word *patris*; it may, though this remains disputed, begin with the words *Aeolis Aeolidae*, which would manifest his presence, if indirectly, also at the start.[25] More definite is the constancy with which Aeolus' name

[23] This is not to deny that pluperfects were occasionally used as equivalent to perfect or imperfect; see M. Platnauer, *Latin Elegiac Verse* (Cambridge 1951) 112-114. But here the pluperfects are effective and deliberate. At 93 Dörrie reads *plangi* and points to the parallel at 15.113 (already noted by N. Heinsius). I add that the strange shift is also exemplified at 13.31-32.

[24] A technique used in Tragedy. Witness how Hephaestus, though Zeus' man, opposes him in the *Prometheus*. So too Haemon, though Creon's son, argues against him in the *Antigone*.

[25] Kirfel (71-74) thinks the opening distich spurious, Kenney thinks it genuine (*CR* 84 [1970] 196). See too Dörrie 210 and Luck 26-29. I am inclined to doubt its authenticity. The third person is possible, but hard; the play on *salus* is obvious and not nearly as well-used as in *Heroides* 4; the description of Canace simply repeats what she says a few lines later (5-6; Kenney says this is no objection. I think it is when the lines do not adumbrate something which is later developed, but merely paraphrased as here); the distich does not serve very logically before *tamen* (3), though explanation is pos-

(three times), the noun *pater* (nine times), and the adjective *patrius* (twice) recur, and the emphasis which is sometimes placed on him by the use of *ipse* (9, 72). Twice allusion is made to the "presence" of Aeolus: *Ipse necis cuperem nostrae spectator adesset/ auctorisque oculis exigeretur opus* (9-10); *Media sedet Aeolus aula;/ crimina sunt oculis subripienda patris* (67-68). He is, almost literally, the overseer. For Canace, Aeolus is the authoritarian father, supervising and controlling his subjects (= children), subjecting them to constant and powerful scrutiny. One final touch, surely deliberate, contributes. Canace never calls herself Canace. She is one of only two heroines in the *Heroides* who never make mention of their own names.[26] Rather, we hear over and again of *Aeolis*, the daughter of *Aeolus*. Nor is this a common designation of Canace. In fact, only once in extant sources is she called *Aeolis* and that not in isolation but in association with her name: Αἰολίδος Κανάκας (Callim. *Cer.* 99). Nowhere else is she termed *Aeolis*; Ovid himself calls her Canace at *Tr.* 2.384 and *Ibis* 357. In brief, Canace is so dominated by thoughts of her father that she can scarcely see herself as more than an extension of him.[27]

Such a conclusion, I think, is inevitable, given the enormous role Aeolus plays in the poem and the language with which Canace speaks of him and herself. I am not inclined to attach psychological tags nor to introduce complexes, neuroses, and the

---

sible; *armata verba notata manu* seems to me a somewhat absurd remark based on verse 5, for, after all, one hand holds the sword, the other, which does the writing, the pen. So the words are not written with *armata manu*. And it is hard not to hear these words as a scribal introduction to the poem. As far as beginning the poem with *tamen*, I note, what seems not to have been remarked in this connection, that we do have parallels for a letter and for a poem beginning with *tamen* which may be more relevant than *tamen* at Cic. *Att.* 12.2.1 (see Kirfel 73, n. 201; Shackleton Bailey, to be sure, prefers the emendation *tantum*) or at *Fam.* 9.19.1, namely Sen. *Ep.* 96 and *Epigrammata Bobiensia* 39 (though some think the poem's opening lost and others seek to emend away *tamen*). As for the abruptness of the opening, we might point to Prop. 1.8.1 *tune igitur demens*; 1.17.1 *et merito*; 2.22B. *aut si es dura* (which Butler-Barber and Camps take as the start of a new poem); also, *Heroides* 5, *Perlegis? an. . . .*

26 The other is Ariadne. But Ovid, though often mentioning her in his poetry, only once calls her Ariadne (*AA* 3.35).

27 The very simile Canace uses to describe her panic is the product of his role: she is shaken just as the sea or a tree is shaken by the wind (77-78). A comparable image at 10.139 is much less elaborate.

like. Nor do I understand why Ovid chose to create such
a Canace. But could he have seen in Canace's love for her brother a transference of some sort of "Electra complex."[28] This seems
far-fetched, but perhaps we might recall here Seneca's Phaedra
(646ff), whose love for Hippolytus in a sense represents her love
for a young version of his father, Theseus. Perhaps it is more reasonable to see this as Ovid's attempt to understand the effect on
a daughter's personality of having a father of such great, indeed
supernatural, power and authority. Be this as it may, the fact—
and I think "fact" is the right word—remains. Ovid means
Canace's relation to her father and her perception of this relationship to be striking, probably crucial elements in his approach
to the myth, whether we are ready to see in them profound psychological insights or merely understand them as manifestations
of (to use contemporary jargon) "generation gap" or "lack of communication" between parent and child.

The simplicity of Canace is throughout reflected in her language and her modes of description. She is so modest that she
virtually avoids all mention of a lovers' relationship. Macareus
is *frater* and *germanus*, once delicately *frustra miserae sperate
sorori* (123). At 128-129 *amantis, amans,* and *dilectae nimium* get
closer to the truth. She never recounts why Aeolus gets so angry.
Indeed, from her narrative (elliptical, to be sure; 69-88) there
seems to be no time (or way) for Aeolus to learn that the father
is Macareus, only that Canace has borne a child by someone. Her
account, in other words, is controlled by her unwillingness to
speak of her love affair with Macareus. Only once does she allude
to their sexual liaison (23-26) and this in terms which almost completely lack physical colors. Moreover, instead of a direct statement of fact, this solitary account is framed as a wish and a question. When Canace does turn to narrative (27ff), she succeeds in
minimizing, almost concealing, their sexual connection. In the
distich 27-28 almost every word is put to good effect. *Qualemque*

---

[28] S. Freud, *An Outline of Psychoanalysis,* tr. J. Strachey (W. W. Norton,
New York 1949) 99, points out that a woman with an "Electra complex" will
"choose her husband for his paternal characteristics," an insight Ovid clearly
exploited in his tale of Myrrha (*Met.* 10.363-364). Even more relevant is
Otto Fenichel's observation, *The Psychoanalytic Theory of Neurosis* (W. W.
Norton, New York 1945) 93, that in Oedipal (or Electral) circumstances
"siblings may also serve as objects for the transference of love."

audire: for Canace knowledge of love has been but a matter of hearsay, but talk on this subject is common enough, *solebam*. *Nescio quem* displays her ignorance, while the unexpected occurrence of *deum*, long delayed, reveals the innocence and inexperience of the young girl for whom the strange and exciting feelings within her manifest some supernatural force. *Sensi* too projects emotional engagement, not intellectual awareness. Within the routine description of the symptomatology of love that follows[29] there is yet a sense of modesty, *at illud eram* (34); she is ashamed to say outright, "I was in love." Finally, the knowing suspicions of the old nurse bring a blush to her face and a guilty silence to her lips.[30] The diminutive *ocellos* (37; only once elsewhere in the *Heroides*, 5.45) reinforces the youthful, even childlike, color of naïveté.

So commonplace is this account of the growing pangs of love that one almost forgets that underneath it all there lies an already consummated sexual relationship. Suddenly, however, the shocking reality is unavoidably present: *Iamque tumescebant vitiati pondera ventris/ aegraque furtivum membra gravabat onus* (39-40). But even the way she describes her condition is suggestive, with a sense of remove, almost awe, not "I was pregnant" but *tumescebant pondera*, as if surprised at the physical changes in her body and almost attaching responsibility to her body, not herself: *vitiati ventris, furtivum onus*.

Ovid strives in various ways to represent the youthful naïveté of his heroine. Indirect questions (not to mention many direct ones) and words expressing ignorance or knowledge recur: *Nec*

[29] Palmer translates *ora coacta* (30) "forced to eat." I am not sure this makes much sense. At this point no one has yet recognized her condition. Who then is forcing her to eat? Does she compel herself? Of more importance is the fact that the whole context makes us expect a physiological phenomenon. Might not Burman, whose views were rejected by Loers and Palmer, have been on the right track: "contracta, minora facta per maciem?" Perhaps what we would call "pinched lips." Though I know no other use of *cogo* + *ora*, we might compare Ovid's use of *cogo* + *rugas* of the forehead. Perhaps Quintilian's description (11.3.80f) of various facial expressions (e.g., *corrugare nares, labra adstringuntur*) lends support to the possibility that *ora coacta* may be a physiological picture. And it might be important to note that *cogo* is used not infrequently in medical contexts.

[30] The wise old nurse who recognizes the signs of an "illicit" love affair is found also at *Ciris* 220ff. It is probably a Hellenistic theme which developed and grew out of Euripides' characterization of the nurse.

169

cur haec facerem, poteram mihi reddere causam/ nec noram quid amans esset (33-34). Often the simplicity of Canace is contrasted to the worldly-wise sophistication of the old nurse. So here: *Prima malum nutrix animo praesensit anili;/ prima mihi nutrix "Aeoli" dixit "amas"* (35-36). Canace's failure to understand what is happening at the onset of labor, *nescia, quae faceret subitos mihi causa dolores* (49), is set off against the alert and knowing nurse (51-52).[31] With Canace at a loss what to do after the birth, it is again the nurse who contrives a plan (69ff).[32] Ironically, when Canace is finally able to respond to a situation with understanding, it is the question of her death: *"Aeolus hunc ensem mittit tibi"—tradidit ensem—/ "et iubet ex merito scire quid iste velit."/ Scimus et utemur violento fortiter ense* (97-99), an irony sharpened by *violento fortiter,* words so unsuitable for this poor young girl.[33]

Wilkinson (99) cites verses 113-120 as an example of a rare occasion in the *Heroides* of "genuine feeling or pathos, when the poet forgets himself and his audience." Amar (quoted by Loers) goes further: (on 109ff) "Hi versus et qui sequuntur ad v. usque 124 (= 126) ex animo vere materno effluunt, nullo apparatu, ambitione nulla infucati; et quod apud Nasonem rarius, nullus hic poetae locus; totum mater occupat." It is not merely the maternal feelings that he has so vividly portrayed, but the emotions of a new mother in so strange and desperate a condition. There is a fine description at 41-46 of the conflict in a woman who feels it necessary to abort, yet cannot but help feeling strongly for her child. The success she hopes for in the "operation" cannot conceal an affection for, nay even a pride in, her unborn baby who successfully manages to fight against the threat to his life. Canace may prove to be a *rudis . . . et nova miles* (50), but the baby is certainly a good battler, *tutus ab hoste fuit* (46). For the mother, the unborn baby has a personality, an existence, an identity of his own: *nimium vivax, restitit,* he is already *infans.*

---

[31] The contrast inheres within the context, regardless of whether we take *conscia* with *anus* (as Showerman does), or with *ora* (as does ThLL s.v. *conscius* col. 371).

[32] Is the irony of concealing a grievous religious sin by a feigned religious ceremony Ovidian, or might it go back to Euripides? And is the explicit mention of the *vittae,* frequent symbol of chastity, deliberate?

[33] The brutal paradox of the delicate lover become genuine soldier is also present at 21-22. Cf. too 50.

The sympathetic description of the doomed infant (85-88) is in stark counterpoint to her attitude toward her father.[34] The sense of unity between mother and child (perhaps adumbrated in 62)[35] is emphasized in the use of *mea viscera* = my child at 91-92,[36] and tragically alluded to at 126, where the two again become one: *urnaque nos habeat quamlibet arta duos!* The pathetic tenderness of 109ff is colored by a mother's guilt (112) and enhanced by the paradox of the coincidence of the first and last day of life (116). But the magnitude and horror of the tragedy remain to be suggested in the following verses (117-120). After eight verses (109-116) filled with lamentation for an infant who dies on the day of his birth, one is emotionally prepared to hear the other side of Hermione's plaints (8.91ff), namely, "I was deprived of the chance of raising my child, tending him, loving him, caring for him as he grew, by his awful premature death."[37] But in gruesome and grotesque stead, this mother must bewail, because of her own impending death on the heels of her child's, that she has been deprived of the chill duty of offering her son his funeral rites. The grimly brilliant oxymoron *oscula frigida* (119) speaks mountains, as does the recollection in these lines of themes previously appropriated for the birth scene: *lacrimae* (56, 117), *coma* (59, 118), *incumbo* (59, 119), *pressa refovisti pectora* (60)/ *non oscula frigida carpsi* (119).[38] The doom which was earlier avoided

---

[34] Wilamowitz (supra n. 1), in his attempt to stress the primacy of the maternal feelings, suggested emending *nam* (90) to *non*. But this is unnecessary and out of character for Canace. The question is rhetorical (= you know how I feel) and on this the *nam* depends.

[35] It is, of course, possible that *duos* (62) means "yourself and the unborn baby" (cf. 7.137-138). I am, however, inclined to agree with Palmer that it means "yourself and me." See the discussion in chapter XXI, "*Variatio*," n. 25.

[36] *Ad Her.* 1.90 Palmer writes, "Ovid often uses *viscera* for a son or daughter," and then casually cites a series of instances. He is right, yet misses the essential character of this usage. At *Rem.Am.* 59 the allusion is to Medea killing her own children, at *Met.* 8.478 to Althaea killing (indirectly) her own son, at *Met.* 6.651 to Tereus eating his own offspring, at *Met.* 10.465 to Cinyras sleeping with his own daughter. In other words, on each occasion the use of *viscera*, "ones own flesh and blood," is deliberately and cogently pointed.

[37] Cf. Eur. *Medea* 1025-1027 where Medea laments that she has lost the opportunity to see her children grow, marry, etc.

[38] My objection may be ludicrous, but I wonder whether the text at 59-60 is correct. The posture described is reasonable for lovers; cf. *AP* 5.128.1, στέρνα περὶ στέρνοις, μαστῷ δ' ἐπὶ μαστὸν ἐρείσας, but is it possible or likely

in the act of childbirth has tragically come to pass not long after. The mother now recognizes that the embraces, tears, and kisses that in one place are the substance of love and creation are also the emblems of death. In the end, she must seek reunion with the ashes of her child (126). For in life she is isolated. As mother she is cut off from her son, as sister from her brother, as "wife" from her "husband," as daughter from her father. All natural ties are destroyed.

The structure and movement of the poem are at one with the simplicity of the writer. The first twenty verses provide a general view of Canace's situation. Then, she recounts the love affair, from its earliest beginnings through pregnancy, birth, discovery, and imminent punishment (23-98). Verse 99 brings us full circle back to the moment of the poem's opening verses. The final thirty verses are apostrophe, question, and declaration, consisting, as it were, of the victim's reactions to her present state. They are, in tone as well as in substance, different from the earlier part of the poem which, on the whole, is straightforward, lacking emotionally charged words, almost clinically descriptive, punctuated only here and there with expletives or exclamations.

The poem's orderly structure in conjunction with the general absence of highly-charged rhetoric and abandoned emotionalism collaborates to lend a quiet dignity, a calmness, an imperturbable quality to the poem and the character. But we should not be misled into seeing Canace as a resolute Stoic hero. True, she shows herself ready to die; perhaps too ready. Death proves almost a leitmotif, from the graphic *caede* of line 4 (= *sanguine*) to the concrete visions of her corpse at the poem's end. The motif of the tear-stained letter is transformed: tears are now replaced by blood. The picture of herself with pen in one hand, sword in the other, leaves nothing to the imagination; she even must report that the weapon is already unsheathed.

At 11-12, *Ut ferus est multoque suis truculentior euris,/ spectasset siccis vulnera nostra genis,* Loers writes that the pluperfect is equivalent to an aorist. I rather suspect the choice is precise and deliberate. We are presented with a Canace who is already dead, or at any rate offering an image of herself already dead. Shortly thereafter follow references to *funebria munera*

for a woman in labor? Do not sense, logic, and the parallel at 119 suggest that instead of *pectora* we should have a word meaning mouth, lips, or kisses?

(21) and *leto . . . meo* (24). Later, she portrays herself on the
verge of death in childbirth (57-58, 65), but almost magically resurrected by the words of Macareus, *vive . . . vive* (61-62).[39] One
confrontation with death is followed quickly by the next, and in
graphic language Canace visualizes the act of suicide, *pectoribus
condam dona paterna meis* (100), then her death, cremation, and
burial (121ff).

Of course, this is a myth of horrible deaths, the infant's, the
mother's, perhaps too the father's. But Ovid has elaborated the
theme, with the attempted abortion, the almost fatal childbirth,
the vision of the baby's death and funeral, and finally the mother's. The preoccupation with death is part of the characterization
of Canace. The terror of death lies deep in the mind of one much
too young to be subjected to imminent doom. For all the outward
show, we see through the veneer: death is always in her
thoughts.

In a poem so concerned with life and death, with birth and
destruction, it is not surprising that Time plays so important a
role. First days are paradoxically last days (116). One can be a
mother one moment, bereft the next, and nothing immediately
thereafter (122). Memory alone proves capable of maintaining
life (108, 127). Time is responsible for sin and death (23-24). Yet,
Time itself is subservient to love (31). It is Time that brings sex
to fruition (47-48),[40] and Time that makes the baby's death so pathetic (109-110). Finally, it is the artistic and linguistic use of
Time that makes much of this poem effective. Events of Canace's
tragic life are so deeply emblazoned on her mind that at critical
moments past and present seem to merge; temporal distinctions
are blurred. The pluperfect at 12 we have noticed. Equally interesting is the account of her labor (51ff). After normal usage of
past tenses, we suddenly hear *Quid faciam infelix* (53). For a second it appears that we have returned to the present, with Canace
bewailing her fate. Only as we read on do we realize that the past
has become present for Canace, a sort of mental flashback pro-
jected verbally. Again, at 65ff, the delivery successfully accom-

---

[39] Verse 58 is fine. The naïve Canace is concerned with her reputation even
on the brink of death. At 61, *soror o carissima* is patently ironic, for this sister
has been much too *cara* to her brother.

[40] Is there something of significance in the marking of time by the cycles
of the moon (goddess) at 47-48. Diana, after all, sometimes played the role
of a goddess of childbirth. See Frazer *ad Fasti* 3.267.

plished: *positum est . . . onus*, the present intrudes, *Quid tibi grataris?* a question which smacks of Canace's present crisis, until we read further and perceive that here too the critical moment of the past has merged with the disaster of the present. More, Canace is constantly concerned to point out carefully the movement of time. Twice we are told that the nurse was first to have suspicions (35-36). Soon suspicions are made unnecessary by Canace's physical appearance (*iamque*, 39). The nine months fly by (*iam*, 47). The plot develops; success is close at hand (*Iam*, 73). It takes no long time for Aeolus to react (*iam*, 85). Efficiently cruel as he is, he is able to attend to several tasks at once (*interea*, 95). The fluidity of events, the rapidity of fate, the narrow borderlines between life and death are all seen as functions of Time.

A final broad look at the versions of Euripides and Ovid will heighten our understanding and appreciation of Ovid's achievement. In the first place, we do not know whether Canace even appeared in the play. Perhaps she did,[41] but even so her part must have been a minor one. The available evidence indicates that most of the play took place after the birth of the child. This does not preclude a speech by Canace describing her feelings and experience, but it does make it unlikely that she was more than a peripheral character, tangential to the major conflict between Aeolus and Macareus. One wonders whether anyone had, before Ovid, depicted Canace with any depth and thoroughness.[42] Be this as it may, the fragments of the *Aeolus* are clear enough to suggest that Ovid's treatment of the myth deviated enormously from Euripides'. The latter's play was largely concerned with the immediate moral-legal issue and the broader problem of morality in general. The play's most famous line was one of antiquity's best-known promulgations of moral relativism: Τί δ' αἰσχρὸν ἦν μὴ τοῖσι χρωμένοις δοκῇ; (fr. 19N²). Yet, this approach, the very argumentation that Ovid's Phaedra uses so blatantly and shamelessly, is totally absent from Canace's letter. Nowhere the slightest attempt to justify her deed. This heroine is too young, too naïve, too modest, or perhaps simply too upright

---

[41] That she may have appeared in the play is perhaps suggested by her presence on a Lucanian vase (see supra n. 3) and by Euripides' use of a female chorus (note the vocative κόραι in fr. 18N²).

[42] For whatever reason, the scene of childbirth seems to have gained popularity, at least if Nero's affection for it is indicative: *cantavit Canacen parturientem* (Suet. *Nero* 21. See too Dio 63.10).

to question the criminality of her incest. She may question and implicitly deplore the severity of the punishment and the merci- lessness of her father, but she will not attempt extenuation of her actions, defense of herself. What other letter in the *Heroides* can make this claim? Undoubtedly, the absence of those pleas, cries, and claims which abound elsewhere must, if for no other reason than the temporary relief from grating and carping women, be among the factors, if a minor one, that make this letter so appealing.

X

Heroides 5: Oenone

With the exception of *Heroides* 5 and the tenth book of Quintus Smyrnaeus (259-489)[1] no literary treatment of the myth of Paris and Oenone has survived. Our pre-Ovidian sources for this Romance are largely scholia and mythographic accounts, purely of a narrative nature, generally schematic and concerned with the bare exposition of the plot.[2] Thus, the kind of comparative analysis that is fruitful in, e.g., the letters of Briseis, Phaedra, Dido is not possible here. We are compelled to take the poem in virtual isolation, though, to be sure, a degree of insight is provided by our access to information in two areas where Ovid has manifestly diverged from the traditional accounts. The violent, even malignant jealous anger that characterizes Oenone in virtually every source we have, whether taking its form in her re-

---

[1] It is no longer possible to conclude that, because of their similarities, both go back to a common Greek source. On the question of the use by late Greek writers of Latin poets, see now J. Diggle, *Euripides Phaethon* (Cambridge 1970) 180-200, with specific reference to Quintus (199).

[2] For a good survey of the Oenone myth, see T.C.W. Stinton, *Euripides and the Judgement of Paris* (London 1965) 40-50. He also has some valuable insights into Ovid's letter. Although we have no definite evidence for the pre-Hellenistic existence of the Paris-Oenone myth, there are a sufficient number of hints to make it very likely. Thus, Hellanikos (*FGrHist* 4F29) seems to have told of Corythos, the son of Paris and Oenone, and his love affair with Helen and subsequent murder by Paris. A fragment of Bacchylides may tell of Oenone's suicide or her last-minute attempt to help Paris. This was suggested, then rejected, by Lobel *ad POxy* 2362 fr. I, col. 2, line 2. Snell, *Bacchylides*[3] (1961) 101 fr. 20D, leaves the question in the air. H. Maehler, *Bakchylides* (Berlin 1968) fr. 20D, accepts Lobel's original suggestion that this refers to Oenone (130-131, 152), and Stinton seems to think it likely (42-43). F. G. Welcker, *Die griechischen Tragödien* (Bonn 1841) 1146-1148, argued that a lost Greek tragedy (Hellenistic) treated the myth, and he found followers in U. Hoefer, *Konon* (Greifswald 1890) 45-47, and E. Rohde, *Der griechische Roman*[3] (Leipzig 1914) 117-120. Welcker also suggested, *Der epische Cyclus* (Bonn 1842) 2.92, that Oenone may have appeared in the

jection of the mortally wounded Paris and her refusal to heal him,[3] or in her betrayal of Troy by sending her son to help the Greeks,[4] is absent from this poem.[5] Nor should we seek to explain this away by noting that chronologically the time of this letter much antecedes those events which will display the violence

Cypria, but evidence is lacking. At all events, in the Hellenistic period accounts seem to have proliferated. There is an elaborate allusion in Lycophron's Alexandra (57-68), a passing mention in Bion (2.10-11), and we know of versions by Hegesianax (FGrHist 45F2, 6) and Nicander (FGrHist 271-272F21, 33), the latter two reported at Parthenius Amat.Narr. 4 and 34. H. Wulfius, "De Quintae Heroidis Ovidianae Fontibus," in Žurnal: Ministerstva narodnogo prosveščenija 273 (1891) 8ff, argues that Euphorion's Alexander treated the myth of Paris and Oenone and that this indeed was Ovid's source. The suggestion is intriguing, but in no way persuasive.

PAnt 56 (1960) gives the bare remains of a [Hellenistic?] hexameter poem. Fr. C. recto, line 4 has: οινω[; verso, line 3: πηγαιη[. If the former be Oenone and the latter a reference to springs (cf. Pegasis in Her. 5.3; see infra n. 11), might we have a poem about Oenone—or at least one which touched on her myth? We might perhaps compare the phrase νύμφαι πηγαῖαι (Orphicorum Fragmenta, ed. Kern, fr. 353.1). It is surprising—indeed unaccountable—to me that Oenone is hardly mentioned in Latin poetry, not even in comedy or elegy. She is in Ovid, Heroides 5 and Rem.Am. 457-458, and perhaps never elsewhere in elegy. Prop. 2.32.35-36 may refer to Paris and Oenone (so Camps; Butler-Barber and Enk disagree). There is a reference to Oenone at Lucan 9.972-973, and Suet. Dom. 10.4 reports a scaenicum exodium on Paris and Oenone. I notice a garbled scholium at Pers. 1.134 which reports a comedy by one Atines Celer about a nymph Callirhoe (does he mean Oenone?) whom Paris had loved before Helen, then deserted. As far as I know, nobody has ever heard of an Atines Celer. F. Buecheler, RhM 34 (1879) 346, suggested Asinius Celer, who was put to death by Claudius. Do we have any indication that he wrote comedies? Further sources of importance with respect to the details of the myth are: Apollod. 3.12.6; Tzetzes ad Lycoph. Alex. 57, 61; Conon, FGrHist 26F1 #23; Dictys 3.26 and 4.21 is typically peculiar and inconsequential; Commenta Bernensia ad Lucan 9.973, ed. H. Usener (Leipzig 1869) is, at least in its first account, equally strange. Oenone also appears to have been fairly popular among Hellenistic artists; see O. Jahn, Archäologische Beiträge (Berlin 1847) 330-351, and Weizsäcker s.v. Oinone in Roscher Lex. pp. 786-791. F. H. Grantz, Studien zur Darstellungskunst Ovids in den Heroides (Diss. Keil 1955), has a lengthy and elaborate study of Heroides 5. Unfortunately, I have been able to make only very limited use of this work.

3 See Apollodorus, Nicander, Hegesianax, Conon, all cited supra in n. 2.

4 See Lycophron, Tzetzes, Comm. Bern., all cited supra in n. 2.

5 We might strain to see irony founded in these aspects of the story at 89, tutus amor meus est, and at 145-150 (allusion to her medical skills), but the avoidance of such implications elsewhere in the poem, and the vagueness of these make it unlikely.

of which Oenone is capable. We know too well that such temporal boundaries and restrictions do not bind Ovid at all. He is perfectly willing and able to incorporate within his letters the whole spectrum of events and emotions that define a particular myth. "Anachronistic" allusions to future happenings are often skillfully embraced within the seemingly confined bounds of the letter-form. At the least, Oenone could curse or threaten Paris in such a way as to foreshadow the disaster which will overtake him. Nothing of the sort is forthcoming. The implications of this deviation are great and will provide us with an acute sense of Ovid's aims in this poem.

Second, our sources are almost unanimous in endowing Oenone with the mantic art.[6] In most versions this is an important point in the development of the relationship between Oenone and Paris. Ovid has quite ignored it. More, he has not hesitated to call this omission to our attention. Not only is there no indication within the poem that Oenone is a seer, but much emphasizes, to the contrary, her lack of simple foresight. Commonly, Oenone predicts to Paris that he will desert her and, in so doing, produce disastrous results. Ovid's Oenone, no different from the rest of us, must derive her information from Cassandra:

> "Quid facis, Oenone? Quid arenae semina mandas?
>   Non profecturis litora bubus aras!
> Graia iuvenca venit, quae te patriamque domumque
>   perdat! Io prohibe! Graia iuvenca venit!"
>
> (115-118)

precisely those events which Oenone usually foresees on her own. It is no surprise to hear Oenone cursing her rival Helen, *Sic Helene doleat desertaque coniuge ploret,/ quaeque prior nobis intulit, ipsa ferat!* (75-76), but a seer would do much better. For Helen suffers none of this. These two lines are of special note when we think of Hypsipyle who curses her rival in much the same terms (6.153ff), but with success. Hypsipyle's forecast of Medea's future is strikingly accurate, though she possesses no magical gifts of the prophet. Oenone's is far off the mark. The same appears true when Oenone foresees (note the vivid indicative, *clamabis* 103) Paris' reversal of fortune:

---

[6] Apollodorus, Nicander, Hegesianax, Conon, all cited supra in n. 2.

5. Oenone

Ut minor Atrides temerati foedera lecti
    clamat et externo laesus amore dolet,
tu quoque clamabis. Nulla reparabilis arte
    laesa pudicitia est; deperit illa semel.
Ardet amore tui; sic et Menelaon amavit;
    nunc iacet in viduo credulus ille toro.

(101-106)

Again she goes astray. Helen will not betray Paris.[7] This aspect of futility and vanity in Oenone's reflections on the future is worth immediate notice. It is, as we shall see, relevant to Ovid's characterization of her.

Thus, in these two areas our sources provide us with useful contrasts to the poetic conception Ovid has formulated in *Her.* 5. And these differences dovetail, for each serves to enhance the simplicity of the character while at the same time eliminating both the propensity for hostile action and the shrewdness necessary to contrive it. Here, no hard soul to act violently, but also no seer gifted with foresight; instead, a simple girl who is struck by the unexpectedness of the events that befall her.

But an angry girl. The opening distich, perhaps unparalleled in the *Heroides* in abruptness and tone, shows us that: *Perlegis? An coniunx prohibet nova? Perlege! Non est/ ista Mycenaea littera facta manu.*[8] The unexpected *perlegis* (somewhat strange at the letter's outset), replayed in *perlege*, urgent questions followed by an imperative strengthen the impression. And the bitter context! Perhaps Paris is not reading the letter, Helen will not allow him; or he may be afraid it contains some threat from Menelaus (not of course meant seriously). Paris' cowardly disposition is traditional,[9] but the significance here lies in Oenone's

[7] There is, however, a version in which Corythus evidently seduced Helen. See Conon, Hellanikos, Hegesianax, supra. One doubts that Ovid had this in mind since the allusion would be far too vague, and, in truth, quite inexact. Helen does not abandon Paris and leave him *in viduo toro* as she did Menelaus.

[8] I have little doubt that *perlegis* begins the epistle. Kirfel's argument (54-58), though not equally cogent on all points, effectively and decisively destroys Dörrie's view (208) that distich a-b (*Nympha suo* etc.) is likely genuine. Dörrie himself condemns a-b in his edition. F. W. Lenz, *PP* 18 (1963) 373-376, had already argued strongly against Dörrie's position. See too n. 13 infra.

[9] See e.g., Hor. *C.* 1.15.13ff, with Janus' excursus *ad C.* 1.15 in his edition of Horace (Leipzig 1778) pp. 269-270.

willingness to exploit it. These are delectably nasty lines. But
they are also exemplary in their marvelous economy. Not only do
they reflect with clarity Oenone's bitter anger toward Paris, but
they effortlessly identify and define the whole situation. In
coniunx nova we see the traditional triangle and immediately
realize that a betrayed woman writes to her disloyal husband. In
Mycenaea the details are adumbrated: the man has done something to offend the Mycenaeans and had better beware the
Greeks. One knows who are involved even before the formal
epistolary introduction is set in the next distich: *Pedasis Oenone,
Phrygiis celeberrima silvis,/ laesa queror de te, si sinis, ipsa
meo.*[10] Of Paris there is no mention by name, but Oenone presents herself—displays herself, we might say—with ornamental
splendor scarcely to be found elsewhere in these poems. The
exotic adjective *Pedasis,*[11] the superlative *celeberrima,* the use of
the whole hexameter as an epithet for Oenone, are all suggestive.
We shall see that throughout the poem Oenone describes herself
in grandiose—in fact, overstated, scarcely merited—terms. Even
here: *Phrygiis celeberrima silvis;* Who, Oenone? Since when?
The next distich plunges from heaven to earth, as Oenone suggests first that her ill fate must be the work of some malignant
deity, and then—with a rare sense of reality—wonders whether
she might in some way have merited such treatment from Paris.

[10] So the text of Dörrie, Giomini, Palmer. Dörrie had earlier (208) accepted *te, si sinis ipse, meo* and Lenz (supra n. 8) 374, n. 1, had approved.
Reading *ipsa* seems to me to lose the desired point, which is not "I will
complain about you, if you allow it" (a statement perfectly in tune with
Briseis' character, cf. 3.5-6, but not with Oenone's), but "I am yours, if you
will only have me." (Perhaps cf. 153-158.) I agree with Kirfel (57-58).

[11] Micyllus' emendation of *Pegasis* (which would be equally or even more
exotic), apparently approved by Kenney, *CR* 84 (1970) 196-197, and adopted
by Dörrie. I am not convinced by Kenney's objection to *Pegasis* (197, n. 1)
on the grounds that Oenone is "not a fountain-nymph, but the daughter of
a river-god." This is true, but Oenone *is* a nymph (she says so herself, 10)
and classes of nymphs are often confused, e.g., at Prop. 1.20.12 spring-nymphs
and wood-nymphs are confused (see Butler-Barber *ad loc*; cf. Ovid *Fasti*
4.231-232) and at *AP* 6.189.1 a daughter of the river is designated a wood-
nymph (see Gow-Page, *Hell. Epig. ad* 2679). We might note that Rhesus, the
son of a muse and a river, is nursed by πηγαῖαι κόραι (Eur. *Rhesus* 929) and
that, in Callimachus (*Dian.* 170-171), nymphs inhabit the springs of a river.
In sum, given the general confusion (or flexibility) in the designation of
nymphs, I see little reason for refusing to believe that Ovid could have
called the daughter of a river-god a fountain nymph.

Broad generalizations, almost proverbial in nature, are common in the *Heroides*. Verses 7-8 fall into this category,[12] but are nonetheless mirrors of Oenone's self. They reflect a naïve ideal, as if there is something naturally, inherently, wrong about undeserved suffering. This is an idealized, almost idyllic, moral view of the world.

> Nondum tantus eras, cum te contenta marito
> edita de magno flumine nympha fui.
> Qui nunc Priamides (absit reverentia vero)
> servus eras; servo nubere nympha tuli!
>
> (9-12)

On the one hand, we have come full circle. As at the very start Oenone draws on her arsenal of invective. On the other, we have now gone off in a new direction. From mild abuse Oenone turns to questions of social status and prestige, ungenerously recalling Paris' days of yore. But these sharp and witty verses also continue Oenone's self-aggrandizement. *Te contenta marito* is condescending; Paris, she implies, barely met her standards and that only by virtue of an act, perhaps we might say, of noblesse oblige on her part. *Edita de magno flumine* follows the exaggerative pattern begun earlier. Who is this *magnum flumen* who fathered Oenone? Cebren, but no great river he; more rather of a stream. The climax is *nympha*; Oenone is no mere human being like Paris. She claims semi-divine nature.[13] I suspect further that the language is calculated to produce another ostentatious effect. *Edita de magno flumine* nearly turns our nymph into an Aphrodite, sprung from the sea (cf. 7.60: Aphrodite is *edita aquis*),[14] perhaps a meaningful association when we contemplate Aphrodite's role in Paris' life. A last point. The distich (9-10) has a built-in potential for ambiguity that also reflects Oenone's attempt to create a grand image for herself, particularly at Paris' expense. The separation of *fui* from *contenta*, remarkable in itself, is even more so given the intervention of the participial *edita*. But the

---

[12] Note the second person *patiare* and the masculine *indigno*, which seems in order to me (*contra* Dörrie). The sentiment may remind one of Hor. *C.* 1.24.19-20.

[13] Here lies further justification for condemning a-b. If first here, *nympha* has forceful dramatic effect. This is lost if it had already occurred.

[14] The primary sense is of course genealogical. But *de* can describe upward movement, e.g., Lucr. 6.884; *Ciris* 514-515; Sen. *QNat.* 7.6.3.

order thereby allows *edita fui* with *contenta* as participial (adjectival), something like this (granted, rather illogical): "I, content with you as a husband, was born a nymph from a great river." In other words, the structure suggests seeing the sentence as a strong contrast: "You were not yet so important, while I was a river-born nymph (and yet satisfied with you)." I do not mean that this is what the sentence says, only that it deliberately allows for some such secondary understanding in order to reinforce the sense of antithesis between the statuses of the two lovers. This is certainly supported by the apparent semantic and syntactic independence of the pentameter.

Finally, Oenone carries her condescension to its ultimate stage: the actual discrepancy between them was even larger than human/ nymph. For Paris was, so to speak, less than a human being, just a *servus*. Oenone, not yet content, rubs it in. Once again, she was a *nympha*, who generously lowered herself to Paris' level: *nubere tuli*. More, *qui nunc Priamides* is both humorous and pointed. *Priamides* is a patronymic; how does one suddenly become someone's son in the middle of life? Less directly the words imply that for Oenone Paris can never change his past—to her he shall always be the servant shepherd.

And so the course of the letter continues. Oenone glorifies herself, belittles Paris. Paris, it seems, would have found it hard to survive the rustic life without her practical aid (17-20).[15] In the following verses two traditional motifs are modified. The lover who carves some appropriate inscription in a tree is found in Theocritus, Callimachus, Vergil, Propertius, and elsewhere. In most cases it is little more than a graphic (no pun intended!) expression of love. It may, however, have its meaning deepened. Vergil is apposite: *crescent illae, crescetis, amores* (*Ecl.* 10.54). The inscription symbolizes their love. Ovid is clearly imitating Vergil (*crescunt . . . crescite*, 23-24), but with much different results. It is not the love which is mirrored in the tree, but Oenone's ego, *servant . . . mea nomina* (21), *legor Oenone* (22), *mea nomina crescunt* (23), *in titulos surgite recta meos* (24). Paris' inscription is emblematic, as far as she is concerned, of her glory.[16]

---

[15] Verses 15-16 are striking. The clearly deliberate shift of construction (see Palmer) is calculated to represent the lovers first lying on top of the hay, then sinking into it.

[16] Oppel (27) strangely says that Oenone carved the inscription. This, of course, is wrong (see 21). I note in passing, but pertinently, that only one

The inscription itself is the common rhetorical device, the ἀδύνατον. Yet, here too the common theme yields to unique treatment:
"*Cum Paris Oenone poterit spirare relicta,/ ad fontem Xanthi
versa recurret aqua*" (29-30). I do not know of any other ἀδύνατον
so constructed.[17] In general *ante* or *prius quam* are utilized. But
the essential thing is that ἀδύνατα usually work the other way
round, "sooner will a supernatural event happen than that . . . ,"
that is, a situation or relationship is secured by the consistency
and impeccability of Nature (perhaps even more obvious in the
variation on the theme which goes, "as long as this natural phenomenon occurs, so long will . . ." [e.g., Verg. *Ecl.* 5.76-78; Hor.
Epod. 15.4ff]). Here where naïveté is rife and self-assurance su-
preme, the reverse is arrogantly the case. Paris' love is so sure
that he can make the natural processes of the universe contingent
on it. The steadfastness of his love guarantees the natural
world.[18] As always in the *Heroides* we are left with a residue of
doubt as to the objective validity of what we have been told. Are
we meant to understand this inscription as a concrete reality or
perhaps as the product of Oenone's imagination? Here some literary source might well have shed light.[19]

Narrative opens with epic solemnity: *illa dies fatum miserae
mihi dixit* (33). The tragedy of Dido is recalled (*ille dies primus
leti*, etc., *Aen.* 4.169); we may think of the agony of Hecuba and
the Trojan women (Eur. *Hec.* 629ff) who retrace their plight to
Paris' building of his ship.[20] But Oenone is more intimately in-

---

other heroine speaks her own name as often as Oenone, Phyllis (seven times).
Though, if we count both Dido and Elissa, then Dido surpasses them both.

[17] Hor. *C.* 1.29.10ff seems closest, but there the effect is lost by the enclosure
within the question and by the humorous tone. Compare the list in H. V.
Canter, *AJP* 51 (1930) 34.

[18] Is the substance of the ἀδύνατον significant? Paris' betrayal of his oath
is in fact the cause of the Trojan war and therefore, in a sense, responsible
for the preternatural behavior of the Xanthos = Scamandros in *Iliad* 21.

[19] Parthenius' account (*Amat.Narr.* 4) may indicate some oath of eternal
faithfulness on Paris' part, but the details are ignored. Particularly interesting
is the reference in Lucan to the place where Oenone grieved. There the
sentence occurs, *nullum est sine nomine saxum* (9.973), which the scholiast
(ed. C. F. Weber [Leipzig 1831]) interprets (he need not be right; at least
one other possibility exists) to mean that Paris had inscribed Oenone's name
on every rock. This is similar to Ovid's version. Might it reflect a common
source or tradition?

[20] Cf. also *Il.* 22.115-117.

volved with the beginnings of the war; so she thinks back to the judgment of Paris. But her attempt to invest the beauty contest with a mood of tragic-epic grandeur is short-circuited when she reaches the relative clause (35-36). Her naïve but caustic *sumptisque decentior armis* followed by *nuda* completely undercuts the lofty tone.[21]

Still, Oenone persists with the elevated style: *Attoniti micuere sinus gelidusque cucurrit,/ ut mihi narrasti, dura per ossa tremor* (37-38). Indeed, I wonder whether these lines may be a close adaptation (imitation, translation) of verses in a tragedy (Euripides' or Ennius' *Alexander?*) which described *Paris' fear on seeing the divine trio*,[22] and thus serve here as parody of the grand claims Oenone makes for herself by transferring to her Paris' response. The language looks two ways. *Ut* virtually allows for two interpretations: (1) "when" which is primary; (2) "as" which is secondary, i.e., *ut mihi narrasti* is then parenthetic, "as you told me" sc. about yourself. Certainly, the immediate expectation after 35-36 is that *attoniti micuere sinus* should refer to Paris. The absence of any defining possessive adjective or pronoun, itself not unusual (cf., e.g., 1.45; 9.135-136; 14.17-18), assists the ambiguity.[23] So does the phrase *dura ossa*. Palmer, though later retracting, suggested *dure* and Sedlmayer voiced approval.[24] In fact, to the best of my knowledge, *durum os* (outside of medical-physiological contexts) elsewhere always refers to men, which supports the view that the original of this passage referred to Paris and that Ovid deliberately creates ambiguity by retaining the "masculine" phraseology.

[21] The sense of *hiems* (34) is disputed: storm (so Palmer) or winter. No argument has been decisive. I suspect "winter" is correct, since the context demands a state, a continuing condition. Perhaps the implication of 15-16 is relevant to the image here: their love wards off the coldness of winter.

[22] Cf. Colluthus 124-127; Ovid *Her.* 16.67. In the latter *gelidus . . . horror* parallels *gelidus . . . tremor* here. To be sure, this sort of language is commonly used in descriptions of fear, especially by Ovid. For examples, see Bömer *ad Fasti* 3.331; A. Turyn, *Studia Sapphica* (*Eos* Suppl. 6 [Leopoli 1929]) 98.

[23] For the motif of a woman listening with fear to the narrative of a story, cf. 1.45-46. I note that my view of the parenthetic nature of *ut mihi narrasti* has been anticipated by U. Fischer, *Ignotum hoc aliis ille novavit opus* (Diss. Berlin 1968) 35.

[24] Palmer *app. crit. ad loc.* H. S. Sedlmayer, *Kritischer Commentar zu Ovids Heroiden* (Wien 1881) *ad* 5.38.

The narrative at an end, Oenone resumes her argument. Again, she vilifies Paris' past (*pauper*, 79, 80), and contrasts to Paris' present behavior her willingness to accept him for what he was (79-80). But now there is a difference. The supercilious scorn earlier prominent has faded into insecurity; the lengthy recapitulation of past events has given Oenone at least some realistic insight into her plight. The tables have been turned. No longer can she evince a superior condescension. To the contrary, she now feels the need to establish her own equality: "I am good enough for the lordly Paris!" (83-88). Of course, as scholars have noted and often attempted to emend away, *et cupio* (85) is quite inconsistent with Oenone's earlier declarations (e.g., 81-82). But consistency is not one of Oenone's virtues here. Perhaps this is a subconscious strain emerging: at heart she does like the idea of playing royalty. Or it may simply be that she sees this ploy as enhancing her argument: don't think I have no more interest in you since you became a prince. I do; in fact, I'd like to be a royal lady. At any rate, much the same is present at 88: *purpureo sum magis apta toro.* The latter distich (87-88) is profound in its insight: *Nec me, faginea quod tecum fronde iacebam,/ despice; purpureo sum magis apta toro.* Oenone is a part of the trappings of Paris' past life; she is a concrete objectification of his past, an ever-present reminder of his old servility of which he now wishes to be free, mentally and psychologically as well as physically. This Oenone realizes and so feels that she too must divest herself of this past, and this she does by now creating herself in a new—a regal— image.

To the most controversial lines in the poem, 135ff. Palmer followed Merkel in condemning 140-145 and later regretted not having bracketed all of 135-148 and 151-152 as well. Kenney notes that 140-145 are "intolerable on grounds of sense: it is almost inconceivable that Ovid could have written anything so fatuous," and Luck has grave doubts about much of the section from 135-152.[25] Once again, it were futile to argue that these verses are consistent with the rest of the poem, or, for that matter, with their most immediate neighbors. Throughout Oenone proclaims her own virtue and chastity. She finds one of her major supports in the obvious differences between the seductive, faithless Helen and the pure, loyal Oenone. Suddenly, the very foun-

25 See Luck 20-21, who also quotes Kenney's communication on the subject.

dation of all her arguments is destroyed. Oenone becomes the seductive, at least highly attractive, interest of the passionate Satyrs, of Faunus, and ultimately of Apollo himself, who, it turns out (Paris would undoubtedly be shocked to hear this), was the first to take pleasure with Oenone.[26] Scholars have also objected that an amour between Oenone and Apollo is nowhere else attested, but this objection seems clearly self-defeating. Is it more likely that Ovid would have ventured a novel touch to the myth or that some interpolator would have so dared? Surely the former. In the end the case must rest on the contradiction engendered by these lines. And here I must again assert that such inconsistency may well be integral to the character of Oenone as reflected in the present awkward situation.[27] Earlier Oenone had realized that she was arguing in completely inappropriate terms and abruptly shifted her ground (*dignaque sum et cupio*, 85); so here also. To argue from purity and chastity in the face of a rival like Helen will avail nothing. To win Paris back she must seek to present herself as an *altera Helene* or at least as Helen's equal. This she suddenly becomes, pursued by Satyrs, sought by Faunus, won by Apollo. If the affair with Apollo does not represent a minor and otherwise lost tradition, whence did Ovid get the idea?[28] The Satyrs and Faunus are obvious suitors for a rustic nymph. Perhaps, as has been suggested, the association with Ida which Oenone and Apollo have in common (cf. *Il.* 21.448-449) induced Ovid to invent the liaison. But I suspect a different avenue of approach is more useful. Ovid (or is it Oenone?) turns Oenone into a virtual Cassandra, object of Apollo's affections (see, e.g., Hyg. *Fab.* 93; Aesch. *Agam.* 1202ff).[29] This also helps to explain another difficulty, the endowment by Apollo of Oenone with

---

[26] Why is Apollo called *Troiae munitor* (139)? Is this irony, since the events in progress are precipitating the fall of Troy? Further, why is he *fide conspicuus* (presumably this has more purpose than to differentiate him from Poseidon)? What relevance here is his fame as a musician? Is it at all possible that Ovid is playing here on fidĕ/ fidē, given the role in the poem of faithfulness/ faithlessness? Callimachus does call Apollo εὔορκος (*H.* 2.68).

[27] See too Stinton (42, n. 1).

[28] I do think that Ovid invented this liaison, but one small argument to the contrary might be founded in Oenone's role as a seer, since female prophets seem to have often been Apollo's concubines. See K. Latte, *HThR* 33 (1940) 13-17.

[29] See Welcker (supra n. 2) 1147, n. 3.

medical skills, clearly patterned on Cassandra's receipt of the "gift" of prophecy from Apollo. It is worth noting that Ovid avoids exact correspondence, because his Oenone is no seer. Probably the love affair between Oenone and Apollo is to be understood as Oenone's invention. She seems to get carried away by her imagination, beginning—a mere ploy—with examples of lovers who desired her (but seemingly got no further: *tecta latebam, quaesierunt*), suddenly reporting fulfilled love with Apollo.[30] Having been carried by her imagination into unexpected areas, she sees that she has now ruined her earlier claims: *manet casta* (133) has evaporated in the embraces of Apollo. A last resort is available; she takes it: *id quoque luctando* (141), trying at once to maintain her virtue and her allure. Ironically, she thus ends with the same kind of self-defense she had previously denied Helen, "it's all a matter of semantics" (cf. 131-132).[31]

The relationship between past and present is a crucial element in virtually all the *Heroides*, but nowhere else in quite the same manner as here. Narrative of the past, memory is integral to all, but especially to this poem. Throughout, the past is seen through a wistful haze. The description of the tree, with its dreamlike pastoral quality (21ff), reflects memory grasping at straws in the wind, an attempt to recover by recollection a past which is lost forever, irretrievably gone. It is a search to regain a lost Utopia, which in fact has been destroyed by the realities of human passion, "love," and in the end war. A world, a love which now have their existence and reality solely in the bark of a tree.[32] Verses 87-88 decisively reveal that what is at issue here is not simply the betrayal of a lover, but, more important, the question of the in-

---

[30] W. Kraus, *Ovid* (*Wege der Forschung*) 94, says that Oenone unhesitatingly tells of her affair with Apollo. This is misleading, for it ignores both the fact that Oenone is virtually swept into this "confession" unwittingly and also that she immediately seeks to qualify it.

[31] There is an interesting parallel to the argument of 132 in Hdt. 1.4. We should note the progression through the poem in the argumentation: (1) I am a famous nymph. (2) I was your benefactor. (3) My love, in contrast to Helen's, is safe. (4) I was desirable enough for Apollo. (5) I have a special talent, the gift of Apollo.

[32] It is generally agreed that verses 25-26 are spurious (Dörrie 202-203; see too Luck 19-20). *Memini* and *memor* would do well in this poem. If the distich is spurious, the interpolator has the virtue of having felt to the heart of the poem.

compatibility of two kinds of worlds and two kinds of persons that have been created by the circumstances.[33]

Parting scenes are common in the *Heroides*. But Oenone's depiction is unique and instructive: *Flesti discedens. Hoc saltim parce negare;/ praeterito magis est iste pudendus amor* (43-44). All that Oenone has left are memories of the past, memories which have become surrogates for the events themselves, with substantial reality and existence in their own right. Should Paris dispute the validity of her recollections, deny that her memories are well-founded, then all is gone—nothing remains. And it is this illusion, for illusion it surely is, that Oenone maintains, defying experience and reality to the very end. For a brief while, confronted with her plight, she bewails her inability to rectify her grief: *quod nec graminibus tellus fecunda creandis/ nec deus, auxilium tu mihi ferre potes* (153-154). Neither the earth, symbol of her rustic and pastoral habitat and way of life, nor any god (reflecting her status as semi-deity) can give her help in this all too real world, and, consequently, she must beg Paris to have consideration for her: *Et potes et merui. Dignae miserere puellae!/ Non ego cum Danais arma cruenta fero* (155-156). But the realization that, if her hopes rest in Paris alone, they are futile indeed sends her right back into the dream world in which all somehow turns out for the best: *Sed tua sum tecumque fui puerilibus annis/ et tua, quod superest temporis, esse precor* (157-158). *Tua sum* is hardly a realistic evaluation. When she again recalls the past *tecumque fui*, she acts as if her past intimacy with Paris guarantees her present and future relationship to him; only a *precor* prevents this from being stated as fact. Nor does Oenone visualize Paris as her lover for all her life, but in fact for all of time, *quod superest temporis*.[34] We might compare Penelope's letter which also stresses the theme *tua sum* (with, obviously, different point), but derives from a realistic perspective and ends with a pessimistic view of the future. In a sense, as long as Oenone can retain the images of her past, Paris will remain hers.

This is a poem of serious wit. It is, one might say, a commen-

---

[33] This is the kind of problem that Vergil's *Eclogues*, which clearly influenced this poem, sometimes focus on.

[34] Note too *tua permaneam* (6). Oenone thinks of enduring, lasting relationships. Perhaps the recurrent *saepe*'s and *quotiens*' in the poem, aside from stressing Oenone's services to Paris, are intended to give their relationship a sense of longevity.

tary on the *Heroides*, one of those rare pieces of ancient poetry that manages to be both poetry and about poetry, or about Art. Oenone is a relatively minor character associated with, though but tangentially, one of history's greatest episodes. Ovid's heroine rebels against her own insignificance. Deserted by Paris (and, as it were, by the mythical tradition), she seeks to rescue herself from oblivion, attempting to prevent the ensuing events from blotting her out altogether. The war, Ovid takes pains to indicate, is already breaking out (89-92); history has begun to obliterate Oenone. Consequently, she re-creates, indeed, resurrects Paris' forgotten past in which she occupies a crucial place, and struggles to keep it—and herself—alive. We are witness to the efforts of one of history's lesser figures to keep herself from being written out of history's textbook. But, of course, neither the bark of the tree nor the heroine's own memory can achieve this end; ironically, however, and significantly, this letter, this poem, this work of art accomplishes precisely that.

All has not yet been said on Ovid's interesting characterization of Oenone. She is, for Ovid, a *rustica* heroine in all its senses and with all its implications. She is at the opposite end of the spectrum from the urban and urbane Phaedra. While the latter sees the ambiguities of language as a useful tool in the arsenal of the practitioner of deceit, Oenone vehemently opposes the obfuscation of moral guilt by such devious means (4.137-138; 5.131-132) and demands simplistic realities and simplistic evaluations. She is, in short, a severe moralist and moralizer. Most telling is her strident and relentless attack on Helen. Through most of the epistle Paris seems a virtual innocent while Helen receives the brunt of Oenone's vituperation. In contrast our sources for the Oenone myth stress Paris' guilt and Oenone's anger toward him, while tending to make relatively little of Helen. Even when Ovid's Oenone does rebuke Paris, it is more from the perspective of a sermonizing moralist than a betrayed lover: *pudendus amor* (44), *turpe* (97), *pudenda* (98).

Though she repeatedly vilifies Helen, Oenone refuses to mention her name[35] (perhaps because it will defile her lips) with one exception, and that perhaps dictated by the need for precise designation in a curse (75). Usually Helen is branded in Victorian

---

[35] Compare Euripides' Medea who, in the quarrel scene with Jason, never calls him by name (446ff), and perhaps Vergil's Dido who, after 4.329, never mentions Aeneas' name.

terms. She is a *dira paelex* (60), a *turpis amica* (70). She is, by implication (note emphatic *ego*), only interested in Paris for his wealth and prestige (81-82; perhaps also 143-144), rather unlikely (and to my knowledge nowhere attested) for the wife of Menelaus and queen of Sparta. She is also *fugitiva* (91; a word not found otherwise in Ovid), a low-bred runaway, and, in Cassandra's words (and Oenone's) a *iuvenca* (117, 118, 124; nowhere else in the *Heroides*). The latter word must be (esp. in 124),[36] in spite of views that, like πόρτις of Helen in Lycophron (102), it represents the traditional use of animal metaphors in oracular language,[37] as Ciofani says, a "probrosa metaphora." Lastly, Helen is *adultera* (125). In contrast, Oenone is the model of respectability and propriety, worthy of being called a good Roman *matrona* (85; a word not present in the other fourteen letters).

True to this moralistic tendency, Oenone displays an almost pious righteousness or rather a naïve sort of faith. If Paris persists in his faithlessness, he will end as Menelaus has; Helen shall repay him in the same coin.[38] After all, a whore is a whore is a whore: *tu quoque clamabis. Nulla reparabilis arte/ laesa pudicitia est; deperit illa semel* (103-104), an interestingly witty and moralistic notion, rooted in the objective datum that virginity, once lost, is irretrievable. Oenone extends it: virtue, once lost, can never be regained—and evidently must be lost again and again. Oenone is a true puritan. At 125 Oenone's sense of righteousness is amusing: *Sit facie quamvis insignis, adultera certe est.* Addressed to Paris, scarcely anything could be more irrelevant, less persuasive.

Similarly, the following lines, *Illam de patria Theseus, nisi nomine fallor,/ nescioquis Theseus abstulit ante sua./ A iuvene, et cupido, credatur reddita virgo?* (127-129), reflect the overactive puritanical mind. Once again there is no feeling for the practical realities involved. Should Paris care whether long ago The-

[36] Verse 124 is particularly effective in its obvious and pointed recollection of 17. One might perhaps compare the biblical phrase, "cows of Bashan" (Amos 4.1), also pejorative, though with a different sense. I note, for whatever it might be worth (if anything), that a variant reading at *Met.* 12.609 recalls this phrase, *Graiae iuvencae*, also of Helen.

[37] *LSJ*'s reference s.v. πόρις to Eur. *Supp.* 629, "of a girl," is misleading since Io actually *was* a heifer.

[38] An argument I know elsewhere only at Eur. *Electra* 921-924.

seus raped Helen? Menelaus, no doubt, but Paris? Finally, one last proclamation from the preacher *ex cathedra*: *turpiter ingenuum munera corpus emunt* (144).

Nor perhaps does any other heroine so stress her merits. She has done no wrong (6, 8); she delights in "proper" words: *digna sum* (85), *decere manus* (86), *sum . . . apta* (88). She is *digna* again (145), and, finally, *et merui. Dignae miserere puellae* (155).

So too her values are proper. Her respect for elders and betters is commendable. She consults the appropriate authorities to receive a correct reading of the judgment (39-40) and advises Paris to do the same (93-96), describing the authorities in deferential language: *quid gravis Antenor, Priamus quid suadeat ipse, / consule, quis aetas longa magistra fuit.* There is a show of patriotism too (97). But, all in all, respect for person must take a back seat to respect for the truth, *absit reverentia vero* (11).

I suspect that the rustic background of Oenone has deeply influenced Ovid's characterization, even beyond the fact that she is rendered *rustica* in habitat and *rustica* in personality. The affection with which Oenone chooses similes and metaphors from Nature should open our eyes. Her outlook on life is in general the product of her relationship to and understanding of Nature—and is therefore misguided. She fails to distinguish between natural processes and human realities. Time may guarantee the growth of her tree; it will not, as she hopes, secure the growth of her fame or Paris' love. Nor does the embrace of the lovers reflect the close knit dependence of the vine and elm, as she seems to think (47-48).[39] The very next distich (49-50), witty though it be, is a barometer of the distinction between the determinate character of Nature and the fluctuating, relative perspectives of human beings. But where Nature and human circumstances coincide, in the evanescence that dominates both, she fails to learn a lesson. Even mountains erode (61-62), but she cannot grant the decay of human affairs. Though she utilizes a traditional motif, *tu levior foliis* (109), and even expands it with suggestive precision (109-112), she proves incapable of perceiving the hard reality conveyed by it. When even Nature shows itself powerless to heal human ills (147-149, the last verse Oenone's only glimpse of the hard truth that love is not a part of the natural world; 153-154),

[39] But urbane Ovid knows better. Cf. *Am.* 2.16.41-46.

Oenone in her delusion falls back on the most unstable and unreliable support of all, Man (154-156).[40]

Oenone's naïveté, her foolishness, her silly optimism are evident. These are brought out in ways other than I have already noted: for instance, in the juxtaposition of Oenone to characters who are knowledgeable, pessimistic, experienced, realists. Such are the *anus* and *senes* (39-40) who easily recognize the ominous nature of the judgment episode, and Cassandra who sees the catastrophic character of the coming events to which Oenone is blind. Then there is the rustic girl who writes, *Theseus nisi nomine fallor* (127) and reiterates, *nescioquis Theseus* (128). What worldly person could fail to know who Theseus is? Oenone out in the backwoods is a different story.

In brief, Ovid's Oenone is not "soft and gentle," as Palmer would have it (325). Dörrie is more accurate when he describes this letter as "einer der temperamentvollsten der Sammlung."[41] Palmer's notion is quite incompatible with Oenone's vituperation toward Helen and slander of Paris. Nevertheless, she is a nymph, and, "consequently," rustic, naïve, foolish, optimistic, and, by and large, blind. The violence is gone; she is not the sort to let loose destructive forces of a Phaedra or Medea. Gone also is her function as prophet. This would destroy the naïveté and ignorance which is hers. Ovid's Oenone has no understanding of human relations, of love, of human existence. *Tutus amor meus est* (89), she declares, blind to the erotic world whose realities she cannot apprehend, in which *militat omnis amans*, in which the phrase *tutus amor*, itself virtually an oxymoron, could only be the product of a pastoral naïveté.

A brief note on a point of structure. Ovid does not often go in for artistic structural effects, so it is a bit surprising to find a symmetrically constructed example of circular composition in the midst of this poem, the narrative of Paris' departure and return:

> 43-46, 71-74: tears (with ironic differences)
> 47-48, 69-70: lovers' embraces (in the former, Paris and
>   Oenone, in the latter Paris and Helen)

[40] For some attractive and insightful ideas (with many of which I do not agree) on the role of Nature in this poem, see E. Bradley, *CJ* 64 (1969) 158-162.

[41] P. 208.

5. Oenone

49-54, 67: description of the winds
54, 65: visual emphasis, with references to colors
55-56, 63-64: Oenone looking after the departing ship, and
eagerly watching the returning one

All in all, a balanced pair of descriptions, constructed, one might say, according to the scheme: ABCDE transition (57-62) EDCBA. From a broader panorama, the narrative begins with an event centering around women, which is terrifying to Oenone (33-40), and ends on the same note (65-70). Thus, in the first *attoniti, tremor, terrebar*; in the second, *pertimui, tremente.*

While on the subject of the narrative passage, we should note the effective account of the ship's arrival (63ff) from the perspective of a person on shore: first, only the massive sail is visible (63), then some details of color (65-66), then human faces (68).[42] It is a technique typical of the *Heroides* that to each successive stage in the advance of the ship there corresponds an intensification in the emotional response of Oenone (64, 66, 68, 71-74).

Some passing remarks on the judgment scene and the ensuing events. The problems here are to some extent inextricable from the general turn of the myth. As they apply generally, Stinton has catalogued them well and I refer the interested reader to his able discussion.[43] In brief, the question is simple: How does the poor shepherd of the judgment adventure suddenly turn into the royal prince wooing Helen? The problem inheres in Ovid's version also, but in the main he simply skirts it. But there are other difficulties which seem unique to Ovid's treatment, or at least that Ovid's tends to bring out (though, in fact, it seems likely that they are original here, the result of Ovid's innovations). Traditionally, Oenone's foresight allows her to see the future role of Helen in Paris' life. Here, however, deprived by Ovid of this gift, she remains ignorant. Thus, whereas our other sources for the myth never mention Paris' report of the judgment to Oenone,[44] in Ovid

---

42 Might there be influence here of Accius' *Medea* in which evidently the shepherd climbs a tree (cf. Oenone, who climbs the cliff) and describes the ship as it progressively approaches land. The fragments, however, do not give evidence of verbal similarities.

43 *Op. cit.* (supra n. 2) 51ff.

44 In fact, there is a relief which depicts Oenone present at the judgment scene. See Jahn (supra n. 2) 334-336 and Weizsäcker (supra n. 2) 787. There is also a relief which may show Oenone at Paris' departure, arguing with him (presumably since she knows his purpose). See Jahn 348-350; Weizsäcker 789-790.

he relates the episode to her. But it was traditional that Aphrodite won the contest by making an explicit promise to Paris that Helen would be his.[45] So Ovid contrives a very shadowy ambiguous episode with faint undertones of danger, suspicion, betrayal, but leaves it at that. What does Paris tell Oenone? A frightening story, that is clear, but certainly not the whole truth.[46] That he passes over all mention of Helen is clear from Oenone's need to consult the elders, and from their answer, *constitit esse nefas* (40), which is no sage response if Helen has already been mentioned. Further, toward what end is the immediate preparation of the ship? Oenone must be given some reason, but certainly not the true one (witness her shock when she sees a woman returning with Paris). Undoubtedly, the question has no answer. Ovid did not have to conceive of some specific tale told Oenone by Paris; it is enough for him to hint that Paris tells her something, with implications of potential danger to Oenone, but nothing more—and certainly not the whole truth.

[45] So the *Cypria* (*EGF*, p. 17K); Eur. *Helen* 23-30; *Tro.* 929-931; Hyg. *Fab.* 92; Ovid *Her.* 16.85-86.

[46] The vagueness of the account led Riese (cited by Sedlmayer [supra n. 24] *ad* 5.34) to posit a lacuna in which Paris expounded his plans in detailed clarity.

XI

Heroides 13: Laodamia

We seem to know so much about the myth of Laodamia and
Protesilaus, from the broad anthropological and religious implications that inhere in it to the smallest details of action and motivation, that it comes as something of a shock to contemplate how
little we know of the myth's literary history. We are regularly
told that Euripides' *Protesilaus* is the turning point in the literary
development. This play, elaborating on the vague shapes of the
folktale while also tightening them to dramatic succinctness,
proved the model and standard for all its successors. Yet, we
would be hard-pressed to tell exactly what elements of the myth
came down to Euripides, how the post-Euripidean versions reflected and altered Euripides' presentation, and, most crucially,
what in fact did take place in Euripides' tragedy. This is not to
say that scholarly hypotheses do not exist. They do, numerous
and elaborate; but here *quot docti tot sententiae*. Nor is this surprising, given the nature and quality of the available evidence.
The extant fragments of the *Protesilaus* are so few and indecisive as to offer little solid help. The two scholia which, by virtue
of explicit reference to Euripides, seem potentially definitive and
clear-cut are simply too brief and schematic for our needs.[1] To
complicate matters, attention has recently been called to problems in textual tradition which may even cast some suspicion on
the reliability of at least one of them.[2] In general, we are compelled to rely on the testimony, abundant but discrepant, of

[1] Schol. Ael. Aristid. 3.671-672D.; schol. Lucian *Charon* 1. λέγεται in the
latter makes it less than certain that the scholiast is recounting the Euripidean plot. I do not know why the scholium on Lucian is commonly ignored
(as by, e.g., Nauck-Snell: *TGF*; G. Radke in his *RE* article *Protesilaos*, Mayer
[infra n. 3], Lenz [infra n. 2]). H. J. Mette, *Lustrum* 12 (1967) 216, does
make reference to it.

[2] F. Lenz, *Mnemosyne* ser. 4, 21 (1968) 163-170.

Hyginus, Apollodorus, Tzetzes, and Eustathius.[3] The attempts of many scholars to sort out the various strains of the myth, to separate literary from preliterary or nonliterary versions, have produced only a degree of consensus, and, sometimes, even where general agreement has been reached, one cannot help noting that the conclusion attained is merely consistent with and allowed by the evidence, but by no means necessitated by it.

As for other treatments, the *Iliad*'s account (2.698-702) is neat and clean, but rather allusive and may suggest acquaintance with a more comprehensive story than its few lines explicitly recognize. The *Cypria* (p. 19K. and fr. 14K.), even our fragmentary evidence makes clear, clarified and expanded the brief mention in Homer. Thus, the nameless wife of Protesilaus is identified (Polydora), as is the δάρδανος ἀνήρ who killed him (Hector).[4] Hesiod's allusion (fr. 199MW) has no bearing on the main Protesilaus-Laodamia tradition, and there is no reason to believe that Sophocles' ποιμένες was at all concerned with it.[5] For Euripides' successors, how Anaxandrides' *Protesilaus* (*CAF* Kock 2.150ff) was related to the myth is unclear, while of the works entitled *Protesilaus* by Heliodorus (whose identity is even unsure; was he post-Ciceronian?)[6] and Harmodius of Tarsus[7] we know nothing. On the Roman side, the plays of Pacuvius and Titius, if they ever existed,[8] are total mysteries, while Laevius' *Protesilaodamia*, in

---

[3] Hyg. *Fab.* 103-104; Apollod. *Epit.* 3.30; Tzetzes *Chil.* 2.52.762ff, *AnteHom.* 221ff, *ad* Lycoph. *Alex.* 245, 246, 279, 528, 530; Eust. *Il.* 325. For virtually complete coverage of the primary evidence and the scholarship thereon, see the following studies, with the bibliographical information found in their notes: M. Mayer, *Hermes* 20 (1885) 101-134; F. Jouan, *Euripide et les Légendes des Chants Cypriens* (Paris 1966) 317-336; L. Séchan, *BAGB* 1953, 4 (Lettres d'humanité 12) 3-27. These will henceforth be cited by author's name alone.

[4] It is commonly asserted on the basis of Paus. 4.2.7 that the *Cypria* described Polydora's suicide (see e.g., A. Severyns, *La Cycle Épique dans L'École d'Aristarque* [Paris 1928] 301-303). The case does not seem to me clear-cut. Pausanias mentions the suicide, but it is difficult to tell whether he means that the *Cypria* reported it.

[5] Pearson, *Fragments* . . . 2.148, thinks it "barely possible" that it was.

[6] See A. Meineke, *Analecta Alexandrina* (Berlin 1843) 384; Jouan 318, n. 4.

[7] Not, as Séchan (17) and Jouan (318, n.4), write, Harmodius of Tralles. This was evidently a first century B.C. satyr play. See Dittenberger, *Syll.*[2], 699, and Christ-Schmid-Stählin II.1[6] (1920) 335.

[8] The lone testimony is Antonius Vulscus' prologue to *Heroides* 13 and even it is not altogether direct. Forcellini-Perin s.v. *Protesilaus* reports the existence of a play about Protesilaus by Livius Andronicus. I imagine this is

spite of the expressiveness of a few solitary remains, is lost to us, both in its overall contours and in its particular details.

The unfortunate fact is that, from the perspective of literary history, we are in the dark about the basic elements which shape and indeed constitute this myth. At what stage did the return of Protesilaus from the dead enter the story? We are fairly sure that his resurrection was a major part of Euripides' drama, but are we certain that Euripides did not invent it? Similarly, the image which Laodamia constructs. Fr. 655N² seems primary evidence for the role of the figure in Euripides' *Protesilaus* (though the meaning of the fragment has been disputed),[9] but can we ascertain whether it is his innovation? Equally important, where in the sequence of events does the episode of the image stand? Further, how and under what circumstances does Laodamia die? Here too a Euripidean fragment (656N²) speaks in favor of suicide, but the originality of this climax, the role of Protesilaus in bringing it about, Laodamia's own attitude are all somewhat in question. Problematic also is the length of Protesilaus' return, not solely because of the obvious conflict between reports of "one day" and "three hours" (which is specially interesting in terms of speculation as to how this difference arose and what its significance is),[10] but also for the possibility that there was a version that did not limit the return to so brief a period. If so, the question of who effectively restricted Protesilaus' return becomes important. Then, there is the oracle—or rather oracles. Most familiar is the prophecy that the first Greek to disembark on Troy must die.[11] Yet, the earliest guaranteed reference to it is Ovid's (91-92),[12] and whether the verses quoted by Eustathius (*Il.* p. 325) on the oracle

---

simply an error. Presumably Macer's epic related the story of Laodamia and Protesilaus (see Ovid *Am.* 2.18.38).

[9] See A. Kiessling, *Analecta Catulliana* (Greifswald 1877) 11.

[10] One day: Lucian *Dial. Mort.* 23, *Charon* 1; Stat. *Silv.* 2.7.120-123, 5.3.273; schol. Ael. Aristid. 3.671-672D.; Ael. Aristid. 2.300D. (by implication); Ausonius *Cup. Cruc.* 35-36 (one night). Three hours: Hyg. *Fab.* 103-104; Min. Felix *Oct.* 11.8 (a few hours).

[11] There seem to have been variant versions of the substance of the oracle (or oracles). See Eust. *Od.* p. 1697.60f; Cat. 68.73-86.

[12] Though, if the attribution at Eust. (supra n. 11) is correct, Phainias of Eresos (fourth century B.C.) seems to imply a similar oracle. See F. Wehrli, *Die Schule des Aristoteles*, vol. 9 (Basel 1969²) fr. 51 with commentary on p. 43.

actually derive from Euripides' prologue is again uncertain. Some would even argue that the oracle appeared in the *Cypria*.[13]

From this great jumble of evidence we turn to Ovid's epistle with the realization that talking about sources here must be at best conjecture, at worst wasted labor. Some scholars have been bold enough to assert that Ovid's main source was Euripides' play,[14] but one suspects that, correct though the assumption may be, it rests on two foundations that are by no means firm: first, that we know so few literary treatments of the myth other than Euripides'; second, that Ovid clearly did utilize Euripides' tragedies elsewhere in the *Heroides*. But, reasonable as the position seems, it is little more the product of taut argumentation and sound evidence than the view that Ovid's treatment is a descendant of Hellenistic Epic or Epyllion.[15]

All this is not to say that we should be ungrateful for the large amount of mythographic evidence that has survived. Though the manifest conflation and confusion may render us incapable of seeing the different traditions clear and uncontaminated, nevertheless, our knowledge of these variations can illuminate by showing what kinds of versions Ovid rejected, what he adopted and perhaps originated. Selectivity often clarifies the direction originality takes.

Merklin's 1968 essay is important on two counts.[16] First, for his specific insights on the nature and purpose of this poem; second, for the model critical stance which the author adopts toward the *Heroides*. Unwilling to explain away or cast off the poem as a mere example of Ovidian wit and facility, he considers it a serious artistic endeavor both poetically and psychologically. Adopting what is essentially a Fränkellian perspective, Merklin sees the heart of the poem in verse 78, *ne meus ex illo corpore sanguis eat*. In spite of the lively debate that Fränkel's concept of "fluidity of

---

13 E.g., Jouan 329.

14 E.g., Mayer 130 (who thinks the use may be indirect), Séchan 18-19. One common observation is that Ovid 35-36 reflects the chorus of Euripides' play (see e.g., F. G. Welcker, *Die griechischen Tragödien* [Bonn 1839] 495; Mayer 131; Jouan 321). I note that the context does sound Euripidean. The chorus in his *Electra* (191-192) urges much the same of that heroine. Professor Calder notes the similarity of verses 135-146 to Eur. *Tro.* 374ff and suggests that Euripides may have given some such lament to his Laodamia, which Ovid then adapted.

15 The possibility is suggested by Kiessling (supra n. 9) 12.

16 *Hermes* 96 (1968) 461-494.

identity" has engendered, it is hard to dispute the evidence when it stares one in the face so squarely. To argue, as Merklin does, that this verse epitomizes the love between Laodamia and Protesilaus, so deep that the two become one, seems eminently right, the more so in a myth which in its very events plays up the physical union of the couple that transcends the limits of life and death.[17] The theme is enhanced in Laodamia's vicarious identification of herself with Protesilaus:

> Scilicet ipsa geram saturatas murice vestes,
>   bella sub Iliacis moenibus ille gerat?
> Ipsa comas pectar? Galea caput ille prematur?
>   Ipsa novas vestes, dura vir arma ferat?
> Qua possum, squalore tuos imitata labores
>   dicar et haec belli tempora tristis agam.
>
> (37-42)

Her demeanor and behavior are all the more striking for being rather common in the *Heroides*. For, whereas elsewhere such symptoms are the product of a betrayed or false love and are self-centered, here they are emblematic of Laodamia's love for and empathy with Protesilaus.[18] Similarly, at 23, *lux quoque tecum abiit*, the association of Protesilaus with light and therefore life is equivalent, as Merklin observes, to a declaration that his departure means her death. With these passages as a starting point, Merklin proceeds to argue that the whole poem is a kind of symbol of this devout love and unbreakable union. Little needs to be added to his arguments on this score, but some light may be shed from a different perspective, the poem as contrast to the rest of the corpus. Thus, we cannot overlook the themes prevalent elsewhere, but missing here, most notably castigation of the hero and jealous suspicion combined with aggressive hostility to-

17 Ovid delights in calling Laodamia *comes*: *Am.* 2.18.38, *AA* 3.17, *Pont.* 3.1.109-110 (by implication), *Tr.* 1.6.20. One wonders about Laevius' *Protesilaodamia*. Séchan (19) has suggested interestingly that the title is Laevius' way of symbolizing the union of the lovers. This is seductive, but Laevius' obvious delight in such verbal compounds must make us hesitate to attribute such symbolic import. Further, the seriousness which such an interpretation implies seems, from the little we know of Laevius, out of character. Is it possible that Ovid took a clue from what was for Laevius simply another playful display of his ability to manipulate words and names?

18 As always, Ovid cannot give up a clever play on words: *geram . . . vestes/ bella . . . gerat* (37-38).

ward a rival, real or imagined. Other themes are pointedly altered, e.g., the *fama* motif which usually is attached to a report of the lover's faithlessness; the departure scene which commonly reflects the hero's deceit. The directness and straightforwardness of Laodamia's feelings for Protesilaus are sharpened by the lack of artifice. The letter is almost completely bare of simile, metaphor, and images.

The absence of jealousy is particularly interesting since it is a theme which Laevius clearly did use in his handling of the myth (*FPL* fr. 18), and which, according to a few scholars[19] (though, to be frank, on the basis of no evidence at all), may have been present in Euripides' play. To be sure, it is present here, but so transformed as to achieve completely different results. Laodamia's jealousy is directed toward a Trojan woman, but she is no rival: *Troasin invideo* (135). Like Laodamia, this imaginary wife has achieved an idyllic relationship with her man; unlike Laodamia, she is able to act out, express, and display her feelings. This is an envy which asserts rather than denies the firmness of the bonds between the lovers. After this fashion castigation too is present: Paris is rebuked for causing the war (43ff), Menelaus for initiating it (47ff), the Greeks for their eagerness in pursuing it (129ff). But again this all reflects love and concern, not anger and distrust.

Thus, Merklin is correct in his emphasis on the depths of the love evinced by Ovid's Laodamia. We are unfortunately unable to assess how far Ovid carried this beyond other poets. Certainly the fidelity and affection of the couple was of great importance before Ovid. Perhaps it was in his metaphorical extension and expression of this love that Ovid surpassed his predecessors. But even here we are guessing. It is, at any rate, quite likely that Ovid felt the cogency of his treatment to be in this realm. Still, there are a good number of determining characteristics of the poem which remain untouched and here I should like to take cognizance of some of them.

It is a commonplace of Ovidian criticism that the cornerstone of the *Heroides* is "irony," in the sense of that effect produced by the discrepancy in knowledge and awareness between the reader and the heroine. By and large this is not true. Many of the *Epistulae* do indulge a bit in irony, but one would be justified in saying that *grosso modo* Ovid deliberately avoids the irony

---

[19] Schmid-Stählin I.3 (1940) 354, n. 1; Séchan 19.

which is so easily available to this genre. But not here. Not only does this letter make extensive use of irony, but it almost seems to exist for the irony and the consequent pathos.[20] It is not simply the brutal fact that Laodamia loves Protesilaus deeply and desires his safe return while we know that he must die at Troy that is at issue, but rather that nearly every line here in some fashion plays upon, with variation on top of variation, our awareness of Protesilaus' fate. For instance, the urgent rhetorical questions of 113-116,

> Quando ego te reducem cupidis amplexa lacertis
> languida laetitia solvar ab ipsa mea?
> Quando erit, ut lecto mecum bene iunctus in uno
> militiae referas splendida facta tuae?,

cannot but make the reader respond to the pathos of *quando . . . quando,* "*numquam numquam.*" Equally, her cautious reminders to beware of Hector are sharpened for an audience which knows too well that Hector will prove to be Protesilaus' killer; and the pathetic irony is enhanced by the *nescio quem* (63), *quisquis is est* (65).[21] The final touch here is *hunc ubi vitaris* (67), wasted words: Protesilaus will never get past Hector. Laodamia urges Protesilaus to circumvent the oracle:

> Sors quoque nescio quem fato designat iniquo,
> qui primus Danaum Troada tangat humum:
> Infelix, quae prima virum lugebit ademptum!
> Di faciant, ne tu strenuus esse velis!
> Inter mille rates tua sit millesima puppis
> iamque fatigatas ultima verset aquas!
> Hoc quoque praemoneo: De nave novissimus exi!
> Non est, quo properas, terra paterna tibi.

(91-98)

---

[20] Wilkinson argues (87-88) that Ovid could not really solve the problem of finding an appropriate moment for Laodamia to write, since the major interest of the myth begins with Protesilaus' leap. Consequently, the best he could do was "elaborate tragic irony." But this falsely assumes that Ovid had to write a Laodamia letter. The truth is that Ovid saw the problem and felt he could turn it to his advantage. He could give the myth a new shape by conceiving it *in toto* at this particular time.

[21] What this tells us about Ovid's source is hard to circumscribe more narrowly than that it reported Hector as Protesilaus' killer (so too at *Met.* 12.67-68). But, though we know a number of alternative versions (see Eust. *Il.* p. 326 and schol. *Il.* 2.701), we are ignorant of what specific literary sources identified some hero other than Hector as the killer.

Every detail of her hopes is played off against the reality that will take place and will be just the opposite in all respects. Protesilaus turns out to be most *strenuus* of all the Greeks (this is commonly emphasized in the sources where almost invariably Protesilaus—whom Homer calls ἀρήιος—in deliberate contrast to Achilles and the other Greek heroes, sometimes even embarrassed by their cowardliness, vigorously challenges the oracle and in its spite disembarks first), his boat shall lead the way, he shall be the first to touch soil. The miserable girl who will be the first to grieve will be Laodamia herself and *nescio quem* will be Protesilaus.[22] The juxtaposition of *primus* and *Danaum* likely takes advantage of the common etymology (πρῶτος λαοῦ) and hammers home the inevitability of the doom and the blindness and futility of Laodamia's prayers.[23]

If the poem closes on a note of implicit resignation, the irony, here bittersweet, is not to be missed: *si tibi cura mei, sit tibi cura tui!* (164). Protesilaus will not display *cura sui*, and for a last time their fates will prove inseparable and intertwined.

This review does not exhaust the way Ovid capitalizes on the reader's awareness of the hero's impending doom, but instances need not be multiplied. Instead we take note that the poem's irony is not limited to this one facet of the myth. A single example: the elaborate buildup of Paris, with the reverent description of his great train and personal self-confidence (55-60) is an effective contrast to the traditionally weak-kneed and cowardly Paris. Nevertheless, it is the former mode of irony that dictates the shape of the poem. For the important thing about this irony is how, by virtue of the vast gulf between the feelings, hopes, and deserts of the lovers on the one hand and their ultimate catastrophic fate on the other, it effectively generates a sense of pathos and an aura of tragedy.

It is Laodamia's profound involvement with Protesilaus that sharpens a common Heroidean technique to perhaps its keenest edge in this poem, namely, the peculiar vision of the whole great external world through the narrow lens of the heroine. Interna-

---

[22] Line 93 is a typically fine Heroidean verse. The oracle is seen as it affects the woman; note how *prima* picks up *primus* (92).

[23] In part, the poem's pathetic irony is the result of the virtual refrain-like recurrence of words compounded of re-, and meaning or implying return —for Protesilaus will never return: *redux* (50, 113), *redire* (76, 128), *reditus* (157), *revoco* (83, 133), *revertor* (88, 125, 141), *refero* (142, 150, 160) [*respicio* (144)].

tional affairs and military strategies are reduced to egocentric concerns. The complex mythic structure that is the famous episode at Aulis (3) becomes an ill wind that delays—Protesilaus![24] The grief that Menelaus' vengeance will inflict on many (48) is narrowed to a prayer on behalf of one (50). The whole Trojan war is effectively seen with Protesilaus as its pivotal point, the center with many individual radii emanating outward (e.g., 63-68). The focus of the war—or Laodamia's view of it—is limited to one man (77-78). The illogic of 125-128, product of lover's distortion, has almost an Aristophanic flavor: a woman in love proposes strategies and theories of waging war and peace (cf. *Lys.* 574ff). From *quo ruitis* Laodamia jumps easily to *redite*, though logic dictates simply *manete*: wait till the storm passes, which, as she herself has admitted, the Greeks are doing. But such straightforward, dull, and cool logic is alien to the emotional Laodamia. Perhaps we might compare 63-68 which begins with the proposition that Hector is someone special and ends with the idea that everyone is a Hector—which is true for Laodamia, since every Trojan is potential slayer of Protesilaus.

But the strange new appearance which the war takes on in Laodamia's description is also a tragic one, for while it reflects the "distortion" of a spectator who is irreconcilably at once distant and involved it also implies, by way of the feelings of remoteness and distance from the war itself, the deep grief experienced by those immediately affected which may remain unknown to those far off:

> Troasin invideo, quae si lacrimosa suorum
> 　　funera conspicient, nec procul hostis erit;
> ipsa suis manibus forti nova nupta marito
> 　　imponet galeam Dardanaque arma dabit;
> arma dabit, dumque arma dabit, simul oscula sumet
> 　　—hoc genus officii dulce duobus erit—
> producetque virum dabit et mandata reverti
> 　　et dicet: "Referas ista fac arma Iovi!"
> Ille ferens dominae mandata recentia secum
> 　　pugnabit caute respicietque domum.
> Exuet haec reduci clipeum galeamque resolvet
> 　　excipietque suo corpora lassa sinu.
>
> 　　　　　　　　　　　　(135-146)

---

[24] Perhaps this personal perspective is also reflected in the use here of the traditionally erotic-elegiac word, *morari* (3).

The wish implicit in these lines, that Laodamia were present at the battlefront to perform such services for her husband is, of course, sincere. More than that, the description here functions for Laodamia as a vicarious fulfilled joy. Thus, the loving tenderness, the gentle affection that infuse the verses. This Trojan couple are not merely conceptual counterparts for Laodamia and Protesilaus; they virtually are Laodamia and Protesilaus. Hence the wife is a *nova nupta*; here are the kisses which Laodamia was prevented from bestowing in abundance (7), kisses mingled with the instruments of war just as Laodamia earlier imagined the mixture of heroic narrative and kisses for herself (117-118); here are the instructions which she was unable to give (7), the delaying tactics which she can no longer execute, the direct command (142) which she can only phrase indirectly (50), and finally, the return of the husband, which she can only pray for, and the physical union of the lovers which she must fantasize for herself (113-116). We ought not to miss the splendid *forti* (137). Laodamia's anxiety for Protesilaus is mingled with pride in him. Thus, at the same time that she urges Protesilaus to caution, she cannot forbear from calling him *fortis* (the Trojan soldier here is Protesilaus' counterpart; when she calls him *fortis*, she means her own husband). The same psychological dynamics are at work at 115-116, where in spite of her exhortations to Protesilaus to leave the warfare to others, she proudly dreams of his becoming—at the same time—a warrior-hero.

Yet, the whole picture (135-146), probably calculated to recall the moving Hector-Andromache scene of *Iliad* Six, not only produces, in its revelation of Laodamia seeking to realize her vain hopes in a world of fantasy, sympathy for her, but also betrays the naïveté—or at least limitations—of her perspective. One who remembers the sorrow and pathos of the relationship between Hector and Andromache, one who has read Euripides' *Troades*, one who has directly experienced war would not so glibly utter *Troasin invideo* or paint a scene between wife and battle-bound husband with such bright colors and cheerful strokes. The tragedy is, of course, Laodamia's, but her insensitivity to the misfortune of others sets her own fate in a broader perspective.

The tragedy of Protesilaus and Laodamia, from the Homeric version down, was one of unfulfillment. Homer's ἡμιτελής is echoed centuries later in Catullus' *inceptam frustra* (68.75) and surely the motif was regular. It could hardly be otherwise, given the barest essentials of the tale. Ovid seized on and elaborated this theme so that it permeated every facet of the myth. No longer is the lack of fulfillment generated merely by the death of Protesilaus, the fatal separation of the lovers, but it is a constant element in their relationship. The myth is not seen as tragic because one fact, one event renders it so, but because it is tragic in its very character, even before the death of the hero, which will be but the climax in a series of frustrations, failures, and unfulfillments. The following passage is instructive:

> Incubuit Boreas abreptaque vela tetendit
> iamque meus longe Protesilaus erat.
> Dum potui spectare virum, spectare iuvabat
> sumque tuos oculos usque secuta meis;
> ut te non poteram, poteram tua vela videre,
> vela diu vultus detinuere meos.
> At postquam nec te nec vela fugacia vidi,
> et quod spectarem, nil nisi pontus erat,
> lux quoque tecum abiit tenebrisque exsanguis obortis
> succiduo dicor procubuisse genu.

(15-24)

We should be wary of dismissing this as just another variation, brilliant though it be, on the common departure-scene motif.[25] The many good touches cohere and point in the same direction. We are, so to say, watching the scene through a telescope and rotating the lens in the "wrong" direction. In other terms, the visual focus shifts from a well-defined concrete point to a vague, indefinite, almost infinite area of space.[26] From a point where the lovers can stare intently into each other's eyes (17-18), we reach a stage where the ship has faded away into the panorama of the sea (22). But the visual effect subserves—or goes hand in hand with—the psychological. The ship's gradual movement out of Laodamia's sight and away from her perceptual control is characteristic and symbolic of the way things slip away from Laodamia. As intensely as she tries (note *usque, diu*), she is unable to hold on to what she wants. Observe how Protesilaus is described—with some exaggeration—*raptus es hinc praeceps* (9), the suggestive verb then repeated in *abrepta vela* (15). For Laodamia the *vela* are *fugacia*; ultimately she must lose them,

25 So Otis (236-237).
26 This is effectively the opposite of what Ovid does at 5.63ff.

and, with them, everything. Even at this point in the proceedings, before Aulis, before Troy itself, she is, in her own mind, dead. The metaphor is blunt and clear: *lux, tenebris, exsanguis* (which often = *mortuus*),[27] all carrying implications of death,[28] the light/darkness metaphor having all the more power immediately pursuant upon a passage concerned exclusively with visual phenomena of virtually symbolic proportions: physically we move from sight to darkness, from consciousness to oblivion, psychologically from hope to utter despair.

But from the beginning it was this estrangement between what was at hand and seemed attainable and what was actualized and accomplished that Laodamia embraced to color the events of her life. Unfulfillable wishes are common stock in the repertoire of Ovid's heroines, but their quality and contexts in this letter make them here of major rather than subsidary importance. The pervasive irony turns the poem into one pathetically frustrated wish. Even the initial epistolary salutation, with its play on *salus*, is colored as nowhere else in the *Heroides* by the qualifying wish which betrays the fear of failure.[29] An early distich intensifies the mood: *Oscula plura viro mandataque plura dedissem/ et sunt quae volui dicere multa tibi* (7-8). The sense of an achievement left undone is managed not only by the pluperfect subjunctive, but by the futile yearning of the repeated comparatives and most strikingly by the tense usage in verse 8. The present *sunt* enhances the sense of loss effected by the perfect *volui*. If the chance was lost at that particular moment when Protesilaus left, nevertheless the loss, the need is still felt deeply at the present. Shortly thereafter, the separation itself: *solvor ab amplexu, Protesilae, tuo/ linguaque mandantis verba imperfecta reliquit* (12-13). Two lines encapsulate essential themes of the poem. *Solvor*

---

[27] *ThLL* s.v. *exsanguis* col. 1825.

[28] Contrast the language of Phyllis' faint (2.129-130). Is the light/dark, day/night imagery, rather recurrent in the poem, related to the chthonic and fertility aspects of the myth?

[29] Many have thought the opening distich spurious (see the recent discussions by Luck 30-31, and Kirfel 96-98). I am not quite convinced (neither, evidently, is Dörrie). None of the arguments seems conclusive. Moreover, the interlocked order with the triple juxtaposition of Protesilaus to Laodamia and the designation of each by the same adjective suggest the indivisibility of the two lovers (just as does the balanced phraseology of the letter's last verse). Further, the use of *vir* to emphasize the legitimacy of their relationship may be virtually a theme of the poem (e.g., 50).

decisively embodies both the unwillingness to be separated and the act of separation itself.[30] Even her words are *imperfecta*,[31] cut off in mid-course, a reflection of all their life and love. For Laodamia this poem is a statement of "what might have been." Its hallmarks are obstacles, hindrances, frustrations, futility, incompleteness. The structural brilliance of these two verses is noteworthy. It is extremely rare in the *Heroides* for a thought to begin in the pentameter and conclude with the following hexameter. Here the anomaly is wonderfully effective. This is structural counterpoint, with the form played off against the substance. The pentameter struggles on, seeking continuity, fighting against interruption, against pause, while the words themselves declare separation and finish. When, a little later, Laodamia again returns to that day of leave-taking to fill in some details, the keynote is the same, *volui revocare* (83). Once more achievement falls short of intention. Impediments of one sort or another constantly present themselves. Laodamia can even see her death as a desideratum which she is unable to obtain, *indignor miserae non licuisse mori* (28).

The sense of futility and abortiveness is also generated in other ways. I will only touch on them. *Dum* (= while) is itself a constricting word, casting a shadow of impermanence and temporality on all it embraces. And so it is a recurrent word in Laodamia's vocabulary (17, 132), sometimes with ironic undertones (106, 149). The frequent verbs denoting preventing, hindering, and the like (*detineo, obsisto, resisto, prohibeo, veto*) are reinforced by negative equivalents, e.g., *non praebet* (127) and the many instances where *possum* is negated (or virtually negated), 14, 19, 156, 160. Thus, through the poem, there is a current of desire and hope beaten down to futility and frustration.

In a way this describes certain dynamics of the poem. Hope alternates with realism or rather is constantly confronted and defeated by it.[32] Laodamia's hope is consistently embodied in

[30] *Solvo* with a personal object (or in a virtually middle usage) occurs in the *Heroides* only in this poem, here and in the bitterly ironic echo at line 114, for this *solvor* (12) is irrevocably final.

[31] A word which occurs only here in the fifteen poems.

[32] Another aspect of the poem's dynamics is discernible in Laodamia's attitude toward Helen. First, she is *rapta* (47) and Paris is a *malus hospes* (44), then she is somewhat more responsible (61-62), and finally, a *turpis adultera* (131). Observe also the chronological and psychological develop-

fantasy. She constructs her own world (77ff) in which Protesilaus is no soldier at all and fancifully proclaims, *bella gerant alii: Protesilaus amet!* (82). But the exuberance and wishful fantasies are suddenly opposed by the stark realities. The key, one might say, changes. The realities are even worse than they have seemed: there is not only the oracle, but also a bad omen (83ff). Subsequent dreams of the return of Protesilaus (99ff) dissolve from erotic fantasies[33] to objective evaluation (105-106) and finally to the all too indicative ominous visions (107ff). But again erotic delusions return (113ff), only to have reality intrude once more, *sed cum Troia subit* (121). The lengthy description of the Trojan bride cuts two ways: it is, of course, another mode of fantasy for Laodamia who seeks vicarious identification, but at the same time it is a clear index of Laodamia's actual condition and so is followed by the reality (147-148).

The themes of fantasy and unfulfillment climax and unite in the waxen image of Protesilaus. On the one hand, the statue serves for Laodamia as almost a second Protesilaus, more than simply a memento (153-154), but in the end she must be aware that it is not Protesilaus, only a poor substitute, and all her attentions to it are unfulfilled and unfulfilling.[34] *Tamquam possit* (156) returns her to reality and to her prayers for Protesilaus' safe return and declarations of her love and loyalty (157ff).

One final aspect of Ovid's characterization deserves mention: Laodamia's susceptibility to irrational phenomena, her "superstition." To be sure, the myth of Protesilaus and Laodamia has built in all kinds of supernatural or irrational events and actions: the oracle, the strange image, the ghost. But Ovid has made all this a facet of Laodamia's character, a reflection—or at least reflector—of her internal state. It is an extension of her tendency to fantasize. Clearly of most note here is the omen:

---

ment of 85ff: departure (85-88), on the seas (95-96), landing (97-98), return (99-100). The movement is broadly paralleled in 137-146.

[33] The motif of the erotic dream, lascivious and sensual in Sappho's letter (123ff), becomes genteel, decorous, and discreet here. I note that the emendations suggested for 102 by Bentley (*veni*; see Palmer 516) and Fränkel (*celer*, 191, n. 8) were anticipated by C. Heumann, *Actorum Eruditorum Supplementa* 6 (1717) 80.

[34] The anaphora, *illi . . . illi . . . (illa)*, the sharp *tibi debita*, the recollection in *amplexus* of *amplexa* (113) make 151-152 a powerfully effective distich.

Nunc fateor: Volui revocare animusque ferebat;
    substitit auspicii lingua timore mali.
Cum foribus velles ad Troiam exire paternis,
    pes tuus offenso limine signa dedit.

(83-86)

To our knowledge, this has no precedent in the myth. Doubtless it is Ovid's invention.[35] But to what end? Perhaps Merklin is right in viewing it from a purely formal or technical perspective, arguing that Ovid invents the omen to give the letter dramatic motivation. Whereas the oracle is vague, the omen is *ad hominem*. Now Laodamia has a cogent reason for writing. That this could have been Ovid's primary motive seems, however, unlikely. Throughout the *Heroides* Ovid needs little more than the general fact that the relationship between the lovers has reached a crisis to motivate the writing.

In general, one feels that the fact of the separation, heightened by the oracle, would be quite sufficient to stimulate Laodamia's writing (and, to be sure, the vague anxieties produced by the oracle might even be more suggestive and effective in their irony). Moreover, if Ovid was simply interested in increasing the rationale for the letter by making Protesilaus' situation even more precarious in Laodamia's eyes, he might simply have turned to an alternative version of the myth according to which there was an *ad hominem* oracle directed at Protesilaus.[36] Consequently, I suspect that the innovation is meant to shed additional light on Laodamia herself, a view which may be supported by the manner in which Laodamia responds to the occurrence: *Ut vidi, ingemui tacitoque in pectore dixi:/ "Signa reversuri sint, precor, ista viri!"* (87-88). Not only is Laodamia ready to see omens easily enough, she is equally ready to ward them off in some accepted formulaic fashion. Another example:

Tu qui pro rapta nimium, Menelae, laboras,
    ei mihi! quam multis flebilis ultor eris.
Di, precor, a nobis omen removete sinistrum,
    et sua det reduci vir meus arma Iovi!

(47-50)

---

[35] The influence of Tib. 1.3.19-20, also a departure scene, seems clear. In addition, Ovid's *Mandata dedissem* (7) echoes the phrase in this Tibullan poem (15).

[36] So, apparently, Phainias (supra n. 12). Catullus 68.85-86 perhaps implies such an oracle.

Quam multis flebilis ultor eris amounts to an evil omen in Laodamia's mind, and it too must be warded off or deflected. Yet
another:

> Dum licet, Inachiae vertite vela rates!
> Sed quid ago? Revoco? Revocaminis omen abesto
> blandaque compositas aura secundet aquas!
>
> (132-134)

The wish for the immediate return of the Greek fleet becomes for
her a bad omen which must be cancelled. And it is on a similar
note that the poem draws to an end: *me tibi venturam comitem,
quocumque vocaris,/ sive . . . quod heu! timeo—sive superstes
eris* (161-162). Even the mention of the alternative to Protesilaus'
survival must be avoided, for to say *morieris* or the like would
constitute an evil omen. More: the episode at Aulis, suggesting
at first Didonian kinds of arguments (125-126) rapidly moves to
supernatural interpretation (127-130). Finally, there is the nocturnal vision (107-108). Laodamia believes in apparitions. Of
course, the *pallens imago* may simply be Ovid's way of suggesting that Protesilaus is already dead; but I rather think it is the
concrete embodiment of Laodamia's fears and anxieties. The
ghost is the materialization of her psyche. Her response is characteristic, *simulacraque noctis adoro;/ nulla caret fumo Thessalis
ara meo* (109-110). All the modes of counteracting portentous
supernatural phenomena are common knowledge to Laodamia.

This then is Ovid's Laodamia. What can we say about the originality of his characterization and its relationship to Euripides'
play and to other versions of the myth? Unfortunately, not very
much, especially because the major treatments seem to have been
chiefly concerned with the events after Protesilaus' death, while
Ovid's poem, from a strict chronological viewpoint, never
reaches that stage. Catullus mentions the wedding, Laevius may
have described the marriage-night,[37] but details are elusive.
Thus, for example, whether there was a precedent for the departure scene[38] or for Laodamia's concern over the turn of events at
Aulis remains a mystery to us. But some things are clear and im-

---

[37] *FPL* fr. 15, though this might equally refer to the night of Protesilaus'
return.

[38] We do know of an iconographic representation of the scene. See Türk
in Roscher *Lex.* s.v. *Protesilaos* 3171 (fig. 5b).

portant. Ovid has, in keeping with his practice throughout these poems, successfully incorporated two of the substantial elements of the myth which were both, strictly speaking, chronologically outside the limits of this letter: the waxen image and the return of Protesilaus' ghost. How has he managed this, with what effect and to what end?

Séchan assumes[39] that Ovid's chronological displacement of the image in the sequence of events is the result of his yielding to the exigencies of the genre. This, however, is to grossly underestimate the poet. He did not have to introduce this part of the myth at all. To be sure, Ovid does like to work in important features of the myth at hand, but as a rule only when he can use them to his own advantage, to foster his own particular poetic concepts. It is tolerably certain that no version of the myth represented Laodamia as making such an image shortly after Protesilaus' departure. One version places this after the report of Protesilaus' death,[40] another still later, after his second "death."[41] Which Euripides followed is still disputed.[42] By introducing the image at this point, Ovid increases the irony and the attendant pathos (does Laodamia feel the inevitability of Protesilaus' death?), while concurrently sharpening the pathological (or at least peculiar) character of his heroine, who, with husband still alive, seeks vicarious sexual pleasure with his statue.[43]

Finally, there is the ghost: *Sed tua cur nobis pallens occurrit imago? / Cur venit a verbis multa querela tuis?* (107-108). The problem of how traditionally Protesilaus' ghost appears to Laodamia is beyond our scope, but there seem to have been two versions. In one he reappears restored and whole[44] (so, it is generally

[39] P. 15, n. 87.

[40] Tzetzes *Chil.* 2.52.773-777. Apparently also Apollod. *Epit.* 3.30.

[41] Hyg. *Fab.* 104.

[42] Séchan 15: after the news of his death; Webster 97: after the second death.

[43] The sexual element is, I think, clearly present; cf. Apollodorus' προσ-ωμίλει (*Epit.* 3.30). See too Eust. *Il.* p. 325. This is quite different from the motif of recalling one's lover through a picture or image of him (see E. K. Borthwick, *CP* 64 [1969] 173-175). Ovid's perception of the morbid pathology of the relation between Laodamia and the image is probably evident also at *Rem.Am.* 723-724, which seems to make sense only when understood psychologically. For a different interpretation of the significance of the image in Laodamia's letter, see Oppel 97.

[44] Apollod. *Epit.* 3.30; Lucian *Dial. Mort.* 23.

held, Euripides), in the other as a ghostly revenant.[45] It is obvious that Ovid was in no position to follow the "Euripidean" version here, but we must all the same affirm Ovid's uniqueness, for no other treatment had Protesilaus appear as a ghostly dream to Laodamia while she still thought him alive.[46] Again, one might argue that this was the only way for Ovid to incorporate the "return of Protesilaus" theme, or, more generously, that this is Ovid's way of foreshadowing the future return. But there is more here than this. By turning a concrete "ghost" into a mere nightmare Ovid has with one stroke revamped the myth. Once more, as so often with Laodamia, we are in the realm of fantasy. The ghost is the product of the lover's imagination oppressed by anxiety. Indeed, in this Ovidian reinterpretation, the ghost, nay, the myth, becomes the projection of Laodamia's mind. In other words, to assume that Ovid is here eliciting an expectation of the ultimate return of Protesilaus' ghost is wrong. This is Ovid's myth, in 164 lines; the "ghost" has returned, in the special sense effected by the poem. The introduction of the statue is similar; it needs no external motivation like Protesilaus' death or his return and subsequent departure. All it requires is the mind and psyche of Laodamia. This is why the veiled allusion to Laodamia's suicide can be worked in so effectively (161-164). Other poets had needed the external impetus, Protesilaus' death or his request that Laodamia join him in death. Ovid needs nothing else than the psyche of his heroine. At this point—Protesilaus is, as far as she knows, alive— she is already prepared for, seemingly on the verge of, suicide.[47] The act cannot be, in Ovid's presentation, far off.

[45] Prop. 1.19.7-10; Stat. *Silv.* 5.3.273; Serv. *ad Aen.* 6.447; *Myth. Vat.* 1.158.

[46] The only other possibility is the strange report in Tzetzes *Chil.* 2.52.778-779, but this is quite unclear and indecisive. Jouan's suggestion (321) that Euripides showed Laodamia upset over the appearance of Protesilaus' ghost to her in a dream is totally without foundation and based purely on the hypothesis that Ovid's treatment replicates Euripides'.

[47] I disagree with Oppel (97), who feels that Ovid does not think of Laodamia committing suicide.

XII

Heroides 10: Ariadne

It is routine, if not totally reasonable, to relate Ovid's Ariadne-Epistle to Catullus 64 and assume that this takes care of the problem of sources. This is the position that I will, by and large, adopt, and consequently I think it only fair to notice its deficiencies. When Palmer (373) writes that Catullus 64 is Ovid's source and he probably had none other, he is no doubt thinking along the same lines as Anderson who states that (1) Catullus' was the best-known treatment of the myth in Ovid's day and (2) Ovid always used the best-known source.[1] Neither premise is foolproof. Not to mention the numerous versions of the myth that were found in prose authors (e.g., the Atthidographers), there is ample reason to believe that the myth was familiar in poetry. In the *Cypria* (p. 18K.), Nestor told τὰ περὶ Θησέα καὶ ᾿Αριάδνην; we know there were *Theseides*;[2] there is evidence that Simonides may have portrayed the story in some detail.[3] The Tragedians probably retold the myth: It is not likely that Euripides' *Kretes* involved Theseus and Ariadne, but his *Theseus* almost surely did;[4] probably Sophocles' *Theseus* (or perhaps his *Minos*, depending on one's attribution of *POxy* 2452) also.[5] The remains of these three plays are, however, so fragmentary as to make discussion futile, but this does not lessen the possibility of Ovid's familiarity with and use of them. And, as for Hellenistic versions, the possibilities seem limited only by self-imposed checks on the

[1] P. 76. F. H. Grantz, *Studien zur Darstellungskunst Ovids in den Heroides* (Diss. Kiel 1955), has a long chapter on the Ariadne Epistle. Unfortunately, I have been able to make only very limited use of it.

[2] See F. Jacoby, *Atthis* (Oxford 1949) 219-220; also Huxley 113ff.

[3] See *PMG* 550.

[4] See Webster 87-92 (*Kretes*), 105-109 (*Theseus*).

[5] See Turner on *POxy* 2452 (1962); Lloyd-Jones, *Gnomon* 35 (1963) 434-436. Webster disagrees with both (106) and thinks *POxy* 2452 may belong to Euripides' *Theseus*.

wings of one's imagination. Ever since Riese, Maass, and Reitzenstein, the notion of a full-blown Alexandrian treatment of the Ariadne myth of which Catullus' was a translation, or which, at the least, served as a model for both Catullus and Nonnus (7.265ff), has been a commonplace.[6] Scholars have run the gamut from Reitzenstein, who modestly refused to identify the precise poem and author, to Barigazzi, who, in an involved disquisition, comes to the conclusion that Euphorion's *Dionysus* is the poem in question (though it is only right to note that he never satisfactorily demonstrates that the story of Ariadne and Theseus was even included in Euphorion's poem).[7] Though scholars are willing to reject Reitzenstein's view that Catullus' version is a mere translation (witness, e.g., Pfeiffer's disparaging note *ad* Callim. fr. 732), they have been less ready to heed the words of caution proclaimed by Perrotta,[8] who argues that the evidence is not at all sufficient to justify positing a Hellenistic poem on the Theseus-Ariadne myth which served Catullus and Nonnus; he would suggest that Catullus' Ariadne actually grew out of Apollonius' *Argonautica*.[9] Be this as it may—and, as words of caution, they certainly merit a hearing—one cannot refuse to admit that there were Hellenistic poems touching on the myth, whether or not Catullus was influenced by them.[10] The question is why scholars have burdened Catullus' "Epyllion" with the weight of problematic Quellenforschung and have, on the whole, allowed Ovid's poem to go scot-free.[11] The answer, I imagine, must reside in the

[6] A. Riese, *RhM* 21 (1866) 498-509; E. Maass, *Hermes* 24 (1889) 528-529; R. Reitzenstein, *Hermes* 35 (1900) 101-102.

[7] A. Barigazzi in *Miscellanea di Studi Alessandrini in Memoria di Augusto Rostagni* (Torino 1963) 416-454.

[8] G. Perrotta, *Athenaeum* 9 (1931) 177-222, 370-409, esp. 370-382.

[9] *Op. cit.* 382-394. F. Klingner, *Studien zur griechischen und römischen Literatur* (Zurich 1964) 192ff, similarly argues that Catullus' Ariadne is modeled on speeches of Medea in Euripides and Apollonius, not on any lost Hellenistic source.

[10] E.g., Theolytus' *Bacchica* (one fragment in Powell, *Coll. Alex.* p. 9); Euanthes' *Hymn to Glaucus* (Athen. 7.296c); perhaps Callimachus treated it: note the associated references at *Del.* 307-315, *Aet.* fr. 67.13-14; possibly too fr. 732. There are suggestive allusions at A. R. 3.997-1004, 1097-1100; 4.431-434. The great general popularity of the myth is attested by the abundance of artistic representations. See O. Jahn, *Archäologische Beiträge* (Berlin 1847) 251-299; T.B.L. Webster, *G&R* 13 (1966) 22-31.

[11] Not all, of course. Wilkinson (94, n.) believes the source of *Heroides* 10 a lost Hellenistic poem and D'Elia (132) thinks it goes back to Catullus and some Hellenistic treatment.

relative ease of so doing, given the overall (and superficial) similarities between *Heroides* 10 and Catullus 64. But aside from the simple and important fact that Catullus' poem did exist for Ovid, there is really no stronger rationale for seeking out Greek sources for Catullus' poem than for Ovid's. Thus, my ensuing neglect of these possible sources should not be construed as willingness to admit that Ovid did not know or deliberately ignored them. On the contrary. There is no good reason to believe that Ovid was not familiar with them; he very likely was. My treatment, however, is dictated by the fact that it serves no purpose to assume that Ovid did use these sources, whether early epic, lyric, tragic, or Hellenistic, since we know so little of them. True, we know very many discrepant versions of the myth, but we can scarcely define a single individual literary treatment. And even using these numerous versions for comparative purposes becomes a bit futile, precisely because at each layer of the myth so many alternatives appear.[12] Patterns of selectivity are obscured by the plethora of possibilities. On the other hand, comparison with Catullus 64, whether or not we call it Ovid's main source, is fruitful (it needs no argument that Ovid knew this poem nor indeed that he "used" it. There are sufficient instances of clear-cut borrowing or adaptation, as we will see later), precisely because the overall framework and the basic details are the same in the two, and, against this similar background, the crucial differences stand out and are distinguished more sharply. That is to say, each assumes a tale in which Ariadne helps Theseus in his plight, accomplishing this with a ball of thread; she willingly leaves Crete with him, against the will of her parents; they stop at an island where Theseus abandons her while sleeping; on awakening, Ariadne finds herself deserted and vociferously laments her fate. Let me here point out, to forestall the objection that this seems, after all, the "standard" story—which is, in a vague fashion, true, though at what point in the chronological development is unclear —that for every one of these narrative elements there is at least one alternative version. That so much of the story is the same supplies a large amount of common ground for these two poems.[13]

First, a few passages which make clear how strongly Ovid did feel the Catullian presence and how deeply he felt the need to

[12] A glance at Plutarch *Theseus* 17ff makes this abundantly clear.

[13] I shall not, however, be concerned with the differences that are solely imposed by the difference in genres.

rebel against it or go beyond it,[14] even when expansion or redirection contributed nothing, nay, might even be detrimental, to his poem.

Dilaceranda feris dabor alitibusque/ praeda (152-153): so much for birds of prey and violent beasts in Catullus. Ovid's echo is clear, *destituor rapidis praeda cibusque feris* (96; with the gruesome addition of *cibus*), and so is his expansion: *Ossa superstabunt volucres inhumata marinae* (123).[15] But Ovid is not through so easily:

> Iam iam venturos aut hac aut suspicor illac,
>   qui lanient avido viscera dente lupos.
> Forsitan et fulvos tellus alat ista leones?
>   Quis scit an haec saevas tigridas †insula habet.†
> Et freta dicuntur magnas expellere phocas;
>   Quis vetat et gladios per latus ire meum?
>
> (83-88)

To be sure, this passage has some interesting things: the hesitancy with which Ariadne concocts the imaginary terrors (*venturos, suspicor, forsitan, quis scit an, dicuntur, quis vetat*), the way in which the names of the animals are withheld to the last position in the line (or close: 86) to enhance the suspense and excitement, the small touches like *avido*. But it were a hard task to defend the obvious rhetoric, the gross exaggeration, in terms of their place, suitability, and poetic value in the poem. We could take refuge in the extremity of Ariadne's situation, but that is probably to avoid rather than to meet the difficulty.[16] With the climax, which introduces the element of human dangers, Ovid moves effortlessly into an adaptation of Catullus 158-163:

> si tibi non cordi fuerant conubia nostra,
> saeva quod horrebas prisci praecepta parentis,
> attamen in vestras potuisti ducere sedes,

---

[14] One need not go through the poems pointing out possible borrowings or influences. Anderson *passim* 78-90 has done that with typical diligence, but with commensurate failure to distinguish between the highly probable and the rather unlikely, the important and the trivial. See too A. Zingerle, *Ovidius und sein Verhältnis zu den Vorgängern*, vol. 1 (Innsbruck 1869) 50; also J. Hutton, *CW* 36 (1943) 243-245.

[15] This is a play on a proverb. See S. F. Bonner, *Roman Declamation* (Liverpool 1949) 155.

[16] Some scholars have gone so far as to condemn verses 83-88, e.g., H. S. Sedlmayer, *Kritischer Commentar zu Ovids Heroiden* (Wien 1881) 39-40.

quae tibi iucundo famularer serva labore,
candida permulcens liquidis vestigia lymphis,
purpureave tuum consternens veste cubile.

Tantum ne religer dura captiva catena,
   neve traham serva grandia pensa manu,
cui pater est Minos, cui mater filia Phoebi,
   quodque magis memini, quae tibi pacta fui!
(89-92)

Ovid's heroine will have nothing of the servile life, princess that she is. The idea in itself is reasonable and supportable, but the manner in which it has been joined to the other Catullian motif violates its whole frame (not to say "logic"). In the first place, fear of pirates is more than irrational when, as she herself has declared, no humans are evident on land or sea (60-62). But, even granting the possibility of such an arrival, to complain about it when her major problem is the lack of any human being (as she herself says) is little short of ludicrous. To go from this to a refusal to be slave to these adventurers is ridiculous and only compounded by her proud account of her lineage, which means little enough on an uninhabited island and, moreover, with its mention of father, mother, and fiancé, calls to mind the less than noble betrayal by Ariadne of her parents and her abandonment by Theseus. The only defense here is that this is an intentional joke, for which I see little motivation.

Put to somewhat better use is Catullus' *saxea ut effigies Bacchantis* (61). Ovid analyzes the twofold nature of this simile, for Catullus the happy result of a Bacchant paradoxically frozen in a static work of art, and writes:

Aut ego diffusis erravi sola capillis,
   qualis ab Ogygio concita Baccha deo;
aut mare prospiciens in saxo frigida sedi,
   quamque lapis sedes, tam lapis ipsa fui.
(47-50)

which, apart from its elaboration of the Catullian verse, also serves to partake in the metaphorical and thematic value of the poem. But more on this later.[17]

[17] One wonders whether the bizarre description of Ariadne standing on the shore, shouting, waving arms, raising "semaphores" (37-42) is a de-

Contrarily, Ovid will avoid or tone down an elaborate motif of Catullus. Thus, Catullus' heroine:

> quaenam te genuit sola sub rupe leaena,
> quod mare conceptum spumantibus exspuit undis,
> quae Syrtis, quae Scylla rapax, quae vasta Carybdis,
> talia qui reddis pro dulci praemia vita?
>
> (154-157)

This becomes in Ovid *auctores saxa fretumque tui* (132). Here, too, however, the delimitation is part of a broader plan.[18]

Thus, Ovid knew, used, and felt compelled to strive against Catullus, sometimes indiscriminately and without consideration for the possible unhappy results. The larger implications of the relationship between the two poems will be considered later.

For the reader of *Heroides* 10 the poem is a study in strange contrasts of tone and color. The obvious rhetoric of 83-92 looks almost subtle in comparison with the grotesque, if clever, variation on the "heart of stone and steel" motif:

> Non equidem miror, si stat victoria tecum
>   strataque Cretaeam belua texit humum.
> Non poterant figi praecordia ferrea cornu;
>   ut te non tegeres, pectore tutus eras.
> Illic tu silices, illic adamanta tulisti,
>   illic qui silices, Thesea, vincat, habes.
>
> (105-110)

Not much better is *qui superant* (147); we are evidently to assume that Ariadne has pulled out most of her hair! Yet, contrast the delicacy and gentle effectiveness of these lines:

---

liberate antithesis to Catullus' heroine who perforce must stand on the shore watching Theseus sail away and do nothing whatsoever (61-67). By the time Catullus has broken the restraints of the pictorial setting, Theseus' ship is long gone (124ff).

[18] I suspect that line 31, *aut vidi aut fuerant quae me vidisse putarem* (as Dörrie reads), also illuminates Ovid's deliberate deviation from Catullus, *necdum etiam sese quae visit visere credit* (55), but the textual problem here (see Dörrie's *ap. crit.*) makes certainty impossible. If Ovid's line means either that her very thought of Theseus' betrayal, her imagined sighting of his ship sailing away paralyzed her, or that her desire to see him resulted in her "seeing" him, then Ovid has turned what is little more than a rhetorical turn in Catullus ("she can't believe her eyes") into a psychological phenomenon.

Tempus erat, vitrea quo primum terra pruina
   spargitur et tectae fronde queruntur aves;
incertum vigilans a somno languida movi
   Thesea prensuras semisupina manus.[19]

(7-10)

Not only is the time defined but the ambience is tuned to the events taking place: the quiet is sharpened by its being broken only by the plaint of birds; the coldness is crisp and emblematic, and the still-life is broken by the agitation of *spargitur*. Ariadne herself is captured in a brilliant phrase at the moment between sleep and wakefulness; her ineffectual grasping for Theseus is vividly presented in a long frustrated sentence in which *Thesea* appears early, but *manus* is delayed to the end, leaving us, like Ariadne, waiting and waiting for the outcome. With the awakening, physical and intellectual, the tone changes: *nullus erat* (11), as abrupt and to the point as possible. Ariadne's sudden agitation and movement presents itself in the flow of dactyls in 11 and, after more groping, the fact is ascertained and sealed: *nullus erat* (12).

Equally successful is Ovid's achievement of the sense of vast spaciousness and concomitantly empty solitude and desolation. Consider 27-28: *Ascendo; vires animus dabat; atque ita late/aequora prospectu metior alta meo*. It is not so much the bare *late* which has effect, but the striking use of words. Palmer (*ad loc.*) objects that both *prospectus* and *metior* are improperly used; rather they are used pointedly. The vastness of the seas is contrasted with the precision and exactness implied in *metior*, the great panorama of water with the limited gaze of Ariadne: the task, then, is futile.

Again, the effect is similar at 59-62 where the desolation of the all-embracing sea is echoed in the hollow reverberation of the string of negatives: *non ... non ... nusquam ... nulla*.[20]

Different but equally effective is line 146: *infelix tendo trans freta longa manus*. The vastness of *freta longa* is magnified by the semi-literal, semi-metaphorical notion involved in the paradox

---

[19] Even D'Elia (161), who rarely has a good word for the *Heroides*, approves this section (7-23), of which he writes, "Il brano ... è fra le cose migliori delle *Heroides*." Wilkinson (102) calls verses 7-36 "one of the best things in the whole collection."

[20] See the good observation by E. Merone, *Studi sulle Eroidi di Ovidio* (Naples 1964) 82.

tendo trans freta longa manus; once more the language reflects the futility of the endeavor.

The erratic quality of the poem, sparks of poetic brilliance side by side with overblown rhetoric and obvious artifice, is to some degree the product of Ovid's compulsion to prove superior to Catullus. Whether there is more to it than this I am not sure.

Ovid, it is perfectly obvious, is heavily interested, as Catullus is not at all, in setting the scene, creating an environment and establishing thereby a mood: spaciousness, desolation, solitude. This we have observed. But beyond the passages already noticed, Ovid seeks, for instance, to describe the island in terms that harmonize with this mood or expand it. Thus, whereas the mountain that Catullus' heroine climbs is nought but a common *praeruptos montes* (126), Ovid's *mons fuit; apparent frutices in vertice rari;/ hinc scopulus raucis pendet adesus aquis* (15-16). This is not mere expansion. The sparseness of the shrubbery and the erosion of the rocks by the water are concrete illustrations of the sterility and barrenness of the place. When Ariadne looks about, the island appears to be nothing but sand: *Luna fuit; specto si quid nisi litora cernam;/ quod videant oculi, nil nisi litus habent* (17-18). The barren echo of *nisi litora* in *nisi litus* shares in the sterile emptiness of the shore. Once this far, Ovid does not miss the possible implications of the setting and its poetic and psychological potential. Abandoned on a desert island, betrayed and bereft of aid, with nothing perceptible but the lonely and unfeeling island, Ariadne must sense or imagine the hostility of Nature itself.[21] At times this is explicit, even too obvious: *ventis quoque sum crudelibus usa* (29); *multa mihi terrae, multa minantur aquae* (94); *Vos quoque crudeles venti nimiumque parati/ flaminaque in lacrimas officiosa meas* (113-114). More interesting is the quasi-personification of the nonhuman or inanimate. Thus, in 20, *alta puellares tardat harena pedes*, the hostility of the sand is magnified by the pleading and pathetic *puellares*. At 117, *in me iurarunt somnus ventusque fidesque*, there is virtually conscious conspiracy. Throughout, sleep is conceived as an external phenomenon, part of the outside world which betrays and persecutes Ariadne (5, 111, 117).[22] Even her similes present a malign Nature: *adspice*

---

[21] For a discussion of the so-called "pathetic fallacy" in early Greek poetry, see F. O. Copley, *AJP* 58 (1937) 194-209.

[22] I wonder whether this has any connection to the artistic representation of Theseus leaving Ariadne while she sleeps which portrays a ὕπνος hovering over or resting upon her head. See Jahn (supra n. 10) 291-294.

... / tunicas lacrimis sicut ab imbre graves!/ Corpus ut impulsae segetes aquilonibus horret (137-139). Ab imbre not only poses a realistic possibility for the girl with no shelter, but in fact the combination of water (imbre) and wind (aquilonibus) reflect her major enemies, the sea which isolates and endangers her, the winds which carry her only hope away. It is on this note that the poem ends, if ironically: Flecte ratem, Theseu, versoque relabere vento (149),[23] for the wind will be no more cooperative to Ariadne than it has been till now; Theseus will not return.

But Ovid takes this theme to still another level. The personification of the inanimate becomes virtually the acknowledgment of their reality and personal existence, such that Ariadne can readily address them. Sleep is questioned (111), the winds are castigated (113-114), and the bed which held the lovers is chastised and interrogated (55-58).[24]

None of this, the perceived hostility of Nature, the personification of the inanimate and all it entails, has any place in Catullus 64, but it is all-important in Ovid. This difference vividly reveals the great gulf between the aims of the two poets. Catullus is concerned with the myth as a paradigm of lover's betrayal: he is concerned with the central fact of Ariadne's abandonment by Theseus, not with the peripheral adjuncts to this fact. She is betrayed and everything about her reflects simply this betrayal. Any psychological development that is present is rooted in her condition as, so to speak, one "seduced and abandoned." Catullus, to be brief and unfair, does nothing to exploit the myth's peculiar details in his characterization of Ariadne. For Ovid, in contrast, the raison d'être of his treatment lies in the uniqueness of Ariadne's situation (rather than, as for Catullus, its generality, its universality). Ovid evokes, while Catullus ignores, the sense of situation, atmosphere and mood of a place, the relationship between circumstances and person, the reality of the inanimate, indeed, the reality of nothingness, of alone-ness.[25] The relationship that Ovid's heroine establishes between herself and the non-human world around her is the result of the lack of any normal

[23] Pace Palmer and others, there is no reason to object to vento.

[24] Farewell addresses to marriage beds and similar objects can be found, e.g., Verg. Aen. 4.651; Soph. Trach. 920-922.

[25] Sola is a more important word for Ovid's Ariadne than for Catullus'. It is especially effective at 47-48 where it is set off against one's expectation of a band of Bacchants.

form of society. For Ariadne, abandoned on this desert island, Nature, the physical world around her is the only thing that does exist and in its vastness and unhelpfulness can only be conceived of as a hostile agent.[26] She perceives herself isolated in the center of the universe, struggling against all the forces of the world, animal, human, natural, animate and inanimate which conspire against her. An ironic but illuminating piece of counterpoint is Ovid's adaptation of or rather response to these lines of Catullus:

> sed quid ego ignaris nequiquam conquerar auris,
> externata malo, quae nullis sensibus auctae
> nec missas audire queunt nec reddere voces.
>
> (164-166)

For Catullus' Ariadne, Nature is there, deaf, indifferent. For Ovid's it is alive, the source of dialogue, of social intercourse, but it is also hostile, not indifferent. If Nature responds not to Catullus' heroine, it does to Ovid's: *Interea toto clamanti litore "Theseu!" / reddebant nomen concava saxa tuum* (21-22). In a passing moment of self-deceit Ariadne takes this for Nature's sympathy, *ipse locus miserae ferre volebat opem* (24), not quite seeing that the hollowness of the echo mirrors the vast empty solitude of the place.[27]

There is more to Ovid's elaboration of the theme. Of the natural elements that play so important a role in the poem, water and rock are, after wind, most important. Here reality and metaphor become one. Natural forces have conspired to betray, and now to doom, Ariadne. She clings to life as Nature shows its hostility: *Nunc quoque non oculis, sed qua potes, adspice mente/ haerentem scopulo quem vaga pulsat aqua* (135-136). (*Haerentem*, even if it means, as Palmer argues, "seated on," still carries a sense of anxiety and danger that *sedentem* would not.) Suddenly we understand why Ovid has cut the Catullian *quod mare, quae Syrtis*, etc. so drastically, has uncharacteristically

---

[26] We might compare Sophocles' Philoctetes, who, in similar straits, creates a society—or at least a sense of communion—out of the physical world around him.

[27] The poem, like the rocks, seems to echo and reecho the name of Theseus which occurs ten times, far more than that of any other addressee. This undoubtedly reflects the peculiarity of Ariadne's situation: literally stranded she must call and call again for her only help.

made the motif so neat and bare: *auctores saxa fretumque tui* (132). Theseus is himself a part of Nature, offspring of stone and sea; no surprise then either that he acts as he does or that natural forces cooperate so willingly in his cruelty. The conceit of Theseus as nonhuman natural object had, of course, been presented in 105-110, but in terms so grotesque as to obscure the connection to other thematic material in the poem. He is no more human than the winds, rocks, water, sand, and animals (1-2) that oppress Ariadne. Her description of Theseus' rival, the monstrous Minotaur, makes for a strange but probably deliberate contrast: *fratrem* (77), *parte virum, parte bovem* (102), *belua* (106), *fratrem* (115), *taurique virique* (127). The beast appears more human than Theseus ever does.[28] Catullus, on the other hand, though he also uses the fraternal theme (150, 181), calls the Minotaur *saevum . . . monstrum* (101), *saevum* (110).

Finally, if Nature is personified to interact with Ariadne, Ariadne is also depersonalized. The absence of human contact, the extremity of her condition blur the lines that divide life from death, the living from the inanimate. *Frigidior glacie semianimisque fui* (32): she is between life and death (*semianimis* only here in the *Heroides*), between the human and the insensate (*frigidior glacie*). A few lines later, *aut mare prospiciens in saxo frigida sedi,/ quamque lapis sedes, tam lapis ipsa fui* (49-50). The transformation, as it were, is complete. Ariadne becomes a piece of the physical landscape. The human and nonhuman merge. When she later ponders the ambiguity of her existence (75-76), the vividness of her description (*sepulta*) virtually places her in the tomb, an exaggeration which is made doubly effective by the later theme of the *ossa inhumata* (119-124).[29]

Allied to this aspect of the poem may be the strange sense of distance between self and body that inhabits the account of her awakening. The successive stages of her behavior are recounted in terms of her various organs as agents: hands (9-12), legs (? 13-14), chest, hands, hair (15-16), eyes (17-18), feet (19-20). This may be no more than Ovid's acute sense for visual detail, but it

---

[28] Perhaps the human/nonhuman theme is furthered by the vicarious *vestigia* motif (53-54). Objects become equal to human beings.

[29] One might, on the other hand, see the poem as a mythic elaboration of a topos or topoi, such as "born from rock," "harder than flint." The next stage is transformation and Ovid's *Metamorphoses*.

is almost as if the body reacts to the situation in a purely automatic and mechanical way. The sense of a controlling will is missing (as at 45, *me mea lumina flerent*).

It is, I think, almost undeniable that this poem is informed by a peculiar relationship between Ariadne the writer and Ariadne the mythical heroine, the subject of the poem. We sense Ariadne watching, indeed, directing herself, as if she becomes the epic poet, standing beyond, yet intensely interested in, and, after all, controlling the mythical character. Thus, a good part of the poem could be transposed from first to third person with little effect. Epic narrative devices are used skillfully, e.g., the terse scene-setting phrases like *tempus erat* (7), *luna fuit* (17), *mons fuit* (25), *haec ego* (37). There is a significant amount of role-playing. Ariadne portrays herself as the "deserted woman." Twice she presents herself on stage, so to say, quoting her own words (35-36, 56-58). Of course, the context is a factor. In contrast to most of the letters, the betrayal here is decisive and unambiguous, experienced in the clear light of day. So Ovid exploits this aspect of the context to take his Ariadne one step beyond Catullus'. The latter's Ariadne *is* the abandoned heroine, Ovid's Ariadne *plays* the abandoned heroine. She is both actress and director. This will account for some of the poem's excesses; she is a prima donna. A few additional examples will be of use. The girl perched on the rock as the threatening waves resound against it (135-136) is simple melodrama. The way Ariadne calls attention to the scene (*adspice mente*) only exaggerates the already excessive dramatization. When she pleads with the absent Theseus, she directs attention to her dramatic pose, and pose it is (note especially *has* and *hos*, 145, 147). In comparing herself to a *lugens* (137; note again *adspice*), what is the point? Not that she, who is almost *in extremis*, should be likened to someone who is merely *lugens*, but rather that she is mourning for herself.

At this point we move on to other dimensions of the poem. The experienced reader of the *Heroides* will be quick to perceive that an important part of the myth has been given relatively little notice, namely, the arrival of Theseus in Crete, his meeting with Ariadne, their falling in love, his victory, and their departure together. This is all the more surprising since such accounts are rather frequent in the *Heroides*. Or perhaps our argument needs to be reversed: having used the theme elsewhere, Ovid deliberately avoids it here. There is only a minimal recollection of those events (69-74, repeated at 99-104). Very likely, the fact that Catullus had extensively reported them (76-115) dissuaded Ovid from repeating the narrative. But even in the few lines which Ovid devotes to this episode it becomes perfectly clear that he has so constructed it—or rather the perspective from which it is seen—as to radically change its shape and role in the myth. Catullus' narrative ignores completely Ariadne's part in Theseus' success; even when the thread is mentioned—and that only at the end, briefly, and when success seems already essentially won— there is no explicit reference to the fact that it was Ariadne who supplied it to Theseus. Only in Ariadne's monologue is there some such allusion: *certe ego te in medio versantem turbine leti/ eripui, et potius germanum amittere crevi,/ quam tibi fallaci supremo in tempore dessem* (149-151). References to the slaying of the minotaur and her departure from her homeland are impassive in their neutrality: *an patris auxilium sperem? quemne ipsa reliqui/ respersum iuvenem fraterna caede secuta?* (180-181); *commemorem, ut linquens genitoris filia vultum,/ ut consanguineae complexum, ut denique matris,/ quae misera in gnata deperdita laetabatur,/ omnibus his Thesei dulcem praeoptarit amorem* (117-120). Nowhere, in other words, is there any implication that Ariadne has done wrong; nowhere the slightest sense of guilt. Contrast Ovid's heroine: *Nam pater et tellus iusto regnata parenti/ prodita sunt facto, nomina cara, meo* (69-70). The initial note of regret in *iusto parenti* is amplified in her confession that she has betrayed father and homeland, *nomina cara.*[30] Never does this Ariadne try to shirk this responsibility or transfer it to Theseus. This basic fact illuminates and is illuminated by other differences between the two poems. Catullus' Ariadne seeks to exploit her past help to Theseus (157). So in fact do many of Ovid's heroines; but his Ariadne pointedly rejects this avenue (141-142), recognizing that an appeal to her own guilt can get her nowhere. Moreover, she realizes that love is dead, that there is no sense to appeal to their former love nor to hope for its renewal. Indeed, she no longer has any interest in reviving it. Whereas Catullus' heroine will be glad to go off as Theseus' servant (160-163), Ovid's wants no part of him. Their love is not

[30] At 119-122 the familiar theme of death away from home with no close kin present to perform the final rituals (cf., e.g., Tib. 1.3.5-8; Prop. 3.7.9-12) is colored by the fact that she, by betraying family and fatherland, has brought this plight on herself.

merely extinguished; it is as if it never were. Nowhere does she indicate that she ever loved him. Certainly there is no expression of present or continuing affection. Faced with death, her concern is for life, not love, though she recognizes how extreme her condition is. While Catullus' Ariadne ends with a wish for Theseus' doom, still caught up as she is in the paradoxical tangles of the net of love, Ovid's ends with an implicit wish for her survival (133, 143-144, 149).

Schmidt's recent essay on this poem is interesting and important.[31] Unlike most of the secondary literature on the *Heroides*, this piece has the great virtue of being sympathetic to them. I am not intent on arguing with the details of his interpretation, many of which I do disagree with, but rather on evaluating his view of the poem as a whole. According to Schmidt, Ariadne is a woman who misses the loving proximity of her man. The qualifying clause *si modo vivit* (75) reflects the underlying notion that Ariadne lives only as long as she belongs to Theseus. The final line, which displays her strength to see the assembling of her bones as a reunification with Theseus, derives from her love; in the end, death is powerless against love.[32] Seductive as all this may sound, I find no substantiation for it in the text. Catullus' heroine wants reunion with Theseus, Ovid's never seeks it. The assertion that Ovid's Ariadne clings to Theseus is simply false.[33] To speak of the strength of love in a poem where there is never the slightest manifestation of love in any form seems perverse. Nor is the last line a conquering of death through love, but the recognition of the direness of her plight and the near-certainty of death. It is a sign of bitter resignation. What she seeks from Theseus is what he has metaphorically given her, burial (cf. *sepulta* 76)—nothing more. The assembling of her bones reflects the traditional concern for burial (cf. 119-124); there is no sense of reunification. When Schmidt interprets *si modo vivit* (75) as a sign of Ariadne's equation of her love with her life he does so at the expense of and by ignoring the following verse, which explicitly defines what she means: the ambiguity of her existence is not the result of the loss of her lover but of her betrayal and abandonment in a hopeless situation.

A few interesting peripheral issues. Ovid avoids all reference

---

[31] E. A. Schmidt, *Gymnasium* 74 (1967) 489-501.
[32] P. 500.   [33] P. 501.

to or hint of Ariadne's coming salvation through Dionysus.[34] I suggest that he does so because of his intense interest in keeping the frame of the poem very narrow. The sense of barrenness, the seemingly inevitable doom, the extremity of the situation and the hopelessness are the dynamic factors, the heart of the poem. Any sense of the arrival of Dionysus with concomitant wedding festivities (as in Catullus) would break the desired mood. And in this poem Ovid wants no irony.

Then there is the perplexing problem—throughout the long history of the myth—of Theseus' motivation. Why does he abandon Ariadne? Ovid offers no answer. To be sure, one can attribute this silence to the restraints of the genre—there is no room for Theseus or the narrating poet to tell us. But I suspect that Ovid could surely have incorporated such hints as he may have wanted to suggest one motive or another (e.g., another girl, or patriotic devotion to Athens, or amnesia—such traditions as did exist),[35] but he has refrained. Here too it is a question of deliberately narrowing the scope of the poem or the world which it inhabits. For Ariadne, abandoned, alone, doomed, it makes absolutely no difference why Theseus left. All that means anything is the tiny island in the middle of the vast sea—and she all alone on it. Theseus' act is self-sufficient; it maintains its all-importance—for her—irrespective of why he behaved as he did. Motivation here means nothing.

---

[34] I see no reason to believe that *timeo simulacra deorum* (95) has anything to do with or is meant to suggest the arrival of Dionysus. Though I readily admit that I do not understand the verse. The view propounded by both W. Marg, *Hermes* 88 (1960) 505-506, and G. Stégen, *Latomus* 19 (1960) 360, that Ariadne fears the punishment of the gods because of her impiety, seems to me quite unlikely, aside from the fact that it completely avoids the question of what *simulacra* means. The view is virtually condemned by Marg's admission that one must posit a lacuna after 95 to supply room for a clarification of 95.

[35] Another girl: the Hesiodic *Aigimios* fr. 298MW; patriotism: perhaps implied at Pherecydes *FGrHist* 3F148. Cf. Philostr. *Im.* 1.15. In art too Theseus was sometimes shown compelled to leave by Athena; see Webster (supra n. 10) 26. Amnesia: Theoc. 2.45-46 and schol. *ad loc.*

XIII

Heroides 9: Deianira

In recent years the Deianira letter has once again come under attack. Resurrecting the view of Lachmann, Courtney and Vessey have energetically maintained that the poem is not the work of Ovid.[1] It is, I think, indisputable that this epistle is in many ways different from the others, and that one might easily gain a consensus opinion that it is a flawed piece, inferior to many of the poems in the corpus. True as this may be, it remains important to remember that neither divergence nor inferiority is equivalent to spuriousness.[2] It is largely for this reason that Vessey's strongly presented case against the poem proves rather inconclusive in the end. The arguments are threefold: (1) There are two techniques unparalleled elsewhere in the *Heroides*: (a) the refrain (146ff); (b) the introduction of a change of circumstance (143ff: the news that Hercules is dying). (2) There are strange metrical anomalies: four cases of hiatus (one without parallel in Ovid) and one example of metrical lengthening that also has no like in Ovid. (3) The poem is inorganic in structure and shows internal contradictions, illogicalities, etc. The first set of objections is of no account *in itself*: novelty in the *Heroides* is scarcely evidence against Ovid's authorship. Moreover, as has often been noted, Ovid used a refrain in *Amores* 1.6, and, in so doing, was following in the steps of Theocritus, Moschus, Catullus, and Vergil.[3] Consequently, to lend the point some force, Vessey describes the refrain as a makeshift device to render unnec-

---

[1] E. Courtney, *BICS* 12 (1965) 63-66; D.W.T.C. Vessey, *CQ* 63 (1969) 349-361. Both will be cited henceforth by author's name alone. For Lachmann's views, see his *Kleinere Schriften* (Berlin 1876) 2.60.

[2] One thinks of Theocritus' *Syrinx*, long rejected because it was unlike the rest of his poetry and was considered unworthy of him. Its authenticity is still debated, but no longer, happily, on such irrelevant grounds.

[3] Theocritus 1 and 2; Moschus 3; Verg. *Ecl.* 8; Cat. 61 and 62.

essary a description of Deianira's grief. This is a weak argument, especially since it assumes that our *poeta anonymus* deliberately chose to pass up the opportunity for a grand rhetorical display of grief. In fact, the refrain serves as a technique of control. It evokes the inevitability of doom. It is the bell's tolling, unfeeling, relentless, inexorable. As for the shift of circumstances at 143ff, this may well argue more for Ovidian authorship than against, not only because Ovid is much more likely to have ventured on a daring innovation than some diligent imitator (an argument which applies to the refrain as well), but especially because this particular innovation reflects an awareness on the part of the poet of one of the crucial problems in the *Heroides*, the static nature imposed on the poem by its form, and is an experimental attempt to find a solution to this difficulty.[4] To whom shall we credit this insight into the heart of the *Heroides*, to Ovid or to some imitator? It is noteworthy that the change of situation at 143 is counterbalanced by the almost total absence of narrative, which is in part responsible for the overwhelmingly static quality. We have almost given up expectation of any development, when suddenly it is imposed from the outside.

As for the third class of objections, which Vessey has pressed more strongly than anyone else, their weakness lies not so much in their subjectivity as in their general insensitivity to the character of the *Heroides*. I do not mean that all Vessey's arguments along these lines are wasted—some are well-taken and sharp—but too many of them are irrelevant. A few instances: The poem is "inorganic in structure" (350). This observation is rooted in Vessey's assumption that the *Heroides* are *suasoriae*, and, from this perspective, the poem is inorganic. But in fact the letter is not a *suasoria*, an argument aimed at persuasion, and to judge it on the basis of this unwarranted assumption is unjustifiable. Indeed, the view that the *Heroides* are *suasoriae* has by and large been discarded; Oppel has recently dealt it the coup de grace.[5] When Vessey remarks that the other *Heroides* are fairly well-marshaled *suasoriae* (350), he shows an unhappy lack of familiarity with nineteenth century scholarship on the *Heroides*, which, in its de-

---

[4] Moreover, the technique has near-parallels in, e.g., Prop. 1.8, 2.28, 3.20; the *carmen Grenfellianum* (*Coll. Alex.* pp. 177-179); Theoc. 15 (though this is not a monologue). For more extended discussion of this problem, see chapter XIX, "Dramatic Structure."

[5] Pp. 37-67.

sire to buttress its dogma that the *Heroides* were *suasoriae*, felt compelled to utilize extensive transposition in order *to make them well marshaled.*

At verse 3 Deianira knows of Iole only by *fama*; at 121 she sees her with her own eyes: this is a contradiction (351). Rather, this is a kind of progression that can be paralleled elsewhere in the *Heroides*.[6]

Deianira's decision to commit suicide on the basis of a mere rumor (143-144) ignores her earlier maxim, *licuit non credere famae* (119; p. 352). I do not know what Vessey thinks this kind of argument shows.

It is ridiculous for Deianira to keep writing after hearing of Hercules' plight (352). This kind of argument fails to consider the non-epistolary aspects of the *Heroides*.

The Omphale section is a "long inorganic digression" (352). In fact, it is not a digression. It may indeed be, as I hope to show, the heart of the poem. Vessey does not even seek to understand why Deianira should be so concerned with Omphale.

The writer, Vessey remarks, ignores the messenger, Lichas, and the omen (354). I do not comprehend why this indicates that another poet, not Ovid, is the author.

The poem is "lacking in tragic intensity, although the story could have been an inspiring one" (354). Does this argue against Ovid? Why must we assume that Ovid here would have sought tragic intensity or an inspiring treatment?

In general, Vessey's assumption that an inept and incompetent poet would have been more likely than Ovid to make those kinds of "slips" which transgress reason and logic is open to grave suspicion, both on general principles and for the simple fact that such violations do occur in the *Heroides* (very good examples at 5.85 and 139ff).[7]

Finally, Vessey makes free use of pejorative epithets (e.g., jejune, pretentious, tedious, arid, confused, astounding banality, rhetorical absurdity, unusual bathos, frigid), but this will hardly convince.

Vessey well stresses the metrical arguments (358-361). These

[6] See e.g., my discussion of the progression in *Heroides* 3.

[7] Much of Vessey's denigration of this poem on esthetic grounds should have been diminished, if not removed completely, by the fine analyses in Dörrie's article (*A&A* 13 [1967] 51-53), which Vessey has indeed read (see 355, n. 3).

have always been and remain today the most cogent evidence against Ovidian authorship. I shall not pursue the problems involved, but only want to emphasize that other letters in the corpus also present metrical difficulties (see 8.71; 14.62, 113),[8] and that every major metrical peculiarity in this poem occurs in a line that has either Greek words[9] or obvious manuscript problems (or both).

Perhaps the main point is this: the metrical anomalies have been known since Lachmann and have nevertheless not been enough to convince most scholars that Ovid did not write this poem (among many others, the two great Heroidean scholars, Palmer and Housman, could not be persuaded). We can hardly help but believe that the additional considerations proffered by Vessey add very little, if anything. They will certainly not win over anyone not already convinced by the metrical evidence. If one disbelieves Lachmann, one will disbelieve Vessey.

Here I shall briefly present a few small arguments, not to my knowledge hitherto set out, in defense of Ovidian authorship (not to speak of the problems created by the assumption that the poem is spurious: who wrote it? why? how did it get into the corpus, indeed, into the very center?).

Latin poets of the late republic and early empire had a strong affection for books containing some number of poems that was a multiple of five, e.g., Vergil's *Eclogues*; Horace's *Epistles* One, *Satires* One, *Odes* Two, Three, Four; Tibullus One; Propertius Three; perhaps all three books of Ovid's *Amores*. Ovid himself, in his pre-exilic period, had a marked predilection for units of fifteen. Thus, Book One and probably Book Three of the *Amores* have fifteen poems; the *Metamorphoses* contains fifteen books. Both patterns are maintained for the *Heroides* if we grant the authenticity of the Deianira letter.

Seneca's *Hercules Oetaeus* displays clearly the influence of *Heroides* 9 (and *Met.* Nine). It is well known that his tragedies are filled with echoes of Ovid. Even if the play is not by Seneca (the debate continues), there would seem to be more reason to explain the letter's influence on its author if Ovid, not some obscure imitator, wrote it. It is, by the way, a coincidence which I

[8] *Potītur* (14.113) can be paralleled at Lucil. fr. 194 Kr. and Caecilius 109 Ribb. The verse need not be condemned.

[9] On metrical peculiarities caused by imitation of Greek models, see W. Kroll, *Studien zum Verständnis der römischen Literatur* (Stuttgart 1924) 21.

231

cannot explain that three of our four major extant literary sources on the Hercules-Deianira myth have had their authenticity called into question (Sophocles' *Trachiniae, Heroides* 9, the *Hercules Oetaeus*).

Finally, there is the question of Ovidian echoes in the poem. A good number of parallels in Ovid's poetry can be brought for phrases and lines in *Heroides* 9. Zingerle has been the most industrious in pursuing this line of reasoning and has concluded that the echoes are evidence of the poem's authenticity.[10] To this, Vessey has, not unreasonably, countered that this proves nothing other than that our unknown poet knew and utilized Ovid's work.[11] For my part, I suspect that the nature and scope of the evidence point more to Ovidian self-imitation. A brief glance at Zingerle's list of parallel passages makes it clear that one must assume a poet who was widely familiar with much of Ovid's work and could readily draw from it. "Imitations" of the *Ars* and *Fasti* are beyond all question. But the quality and versatility of the borrowings are even stronger evidence in favor of self-imitation. Zingerle has noted,[12] like Loers before him, that 9.73 is the verbatim equivalent of *AA* 2.219,[13] but has not observed how the whole section *AA* 2.215-222 is skillfully modeled upon *Heroides* 9. Thus, 2.219 = 9.73; 2.220, *creditur et lanas excoluisse rudes*, displays the shape of 9.74, *diceris et dominae pertimuisse minas*, though the former verse does little more than repeat the notion of its antecedent hexameter, while the Heroidean pentameter adds a new twist to accommodate Deianira's bitter grief. Verse 2.218, *qui meruit caelum, quod prior ipse tulit*, recalls 9.17, *quod te laturum est, caelum prius ipse tulisti* (as Loers has noted), especially in the last words of each verse. For Deianira it is no easy thing to say that Hercules *meruit caelum*. Finally, the introductory verses to the passage, 2.215-216, *nec tibi turpe puta (quamvis sit turpe, placebit)/ ingenua speculum sustinuisse manu*, are, I suspect, meant to be heard in light of 9.118, *vidit et in speculo*

---

[10] W. Zingerle, *Untersuchungen zur Echtheitsfrage der Heroiden Ovid's* (Innsbruck 1878) 21-24.

[11] 350, n. 4.

[12] P. 21.

[13] Perhaps the fact that at *AA* 2.8 Ovid also quotes from the *Heroides* (8.70; noted by Zingerle) reinforces here our sense of the direction of the borrowing.

coniugis arma sui, Omphale primping before her mirror in the garb of Hercules.[14]

At *AA* 3.155ff Ovid promotes the unadorned and unarranged hairstyle as advantageous for some women. He cites two mythological heroines as cases in point, Iole and Ariadne. Now within the few lines given to Iole in *Heroides* 9, her hairstyle is mentioned (125). It is evidently well-ordered. Perhaps Ovid is playing against this in his allusion in the *Ars*. The possibility may be reinforced by the fact that the other *exemplum* cited is Ariadne, whose epistle follows immediately upon this one and whose unkempt hair is a repeated theme of that letter.

Let me mention one more passage in the *Ars*:

> dum fuit Atrides una contentus, et illa
>   casta fuit; vitio est improba facta viri.
> audierat laurumque manu vittasque ferentem
>   pro nata Chrysen non valuisse sua;
> audierat, Lyrnesi, tuos, abducta, dolores
>   bellaque per turpis longius isse moras.
> haec tamen audierat; Priameida viderat ipsa:
>   victor erat praedae praeda pudenda suae.
>
> (2.399-406)

This is clearly, in language and thought, a recollection of *Heroides* 9. Ovid has simply transferred the theme from Deianira to Clytemnestra (it was, in fact, more suitable for Deianira; he must twist the Agamemnon-Clytemnestra story to make it fit). Note the strange phrase, *haec tamen audierat* (*tamen* is a bit peculiar). It occurs only once again in Ovid (as Loers observed), *haec tamen audieram* (*Her.* 9.119). In fact, the pluperfect indicative of *audio* occurs only in these two lines in Ovid outside the first position in the verse.[15] Further, 406 manifestly recalls the theme of *Heroides* 9 of the victor falling prey to his victim (e.g., verse 2; in fact, it is not very well suited to Cassandra's status vis-à-vis Agamemnon), while at the same time it is a clever adaptation of a line from *Heroides* 9 with somewhat different sense,

[14] It may be important that the description of Achilles at *AA* 1.689ff bears some similarities to that of Hercules here (57ff).

[15] With the possible but doubtful addition of *Fast.* 3.65, *ut genus audierunt* (*audierant?*), where, even should we read the pluperfect, the word-metrical structure is exactly the same as *haec tamen audieram*.

huic victor victo nempe pudendus eras (70). The linguistic similarities are unmistakable: the occurrence of *victor*; the effective
use of the juxtaposition of virtually identical words, *victor victo/
praedae praeda*; *pudendus* in a favorite Ovidian position, penultimate word in the pentameter. In composing this section of the
Ars after the model of *Heroides* 9, Ovid may have retained unconsciously its influence a few lines later, *concubitu prior est infitianda Venus* (414). The notion of canceling out one set of actions by another is essentially that of *Her.* 9.3-4, *fama . . . decolor
et factis infitianda tuis*; in addition these are the only instances
in the *Ars* and *Heroides* of *infitior*.

Tolkiehn has noted[16] the parallelism of 9.29 and *AA* 1.471:
Quam male inaequales veniunt ad aratra iuvenci// *tempore dif-
ficiles veniunt ad aratra iuvenci*. Once again, the nature of the
adaptation, language so close, sense and context so different, does
not suggest the random borrowings of some incompetent poet.
I suspect the same is true for the correspondence (noted by
Loers) between 9.121 and *Fast.* 3.483 (in the story of Ariadne and
Dionysus).[17]

Those who deny authenticity here find themselves in a
dilemma. The poem is obviously Ovidian, displaying Ovidian
technique and language. They are consequently compelled to attribute it to some unknown but effective *poeta Ovidianus,* though
of the *poetae Ovidiani* we really know nothing. Courtney's allusion (66) to *CIL* 10.6127 (not 6271) is quite pointless.

I imagine that one who was completely and irrevocably dedicated to the view that *Heroides* 9 is spurious could attempt to
argue that all these parallels simply manifest a wide range of
familiarity with Ovid and an extremely skillful ability to utilize,
adapt, transform, and even heighten the master's material. It is
a position that would seem to me forced and almost untenable.

16 Tolkiehn 93.
17 A few additional points. Lines 69-72 seem to me an adaptation of Eur.
Hipp. 976-980. It is, of course, possible that Vessey's anonymous poet knew
and recalled this play. We *know*, however, how familiar Ovid was with it.
I also wonder whether anyone but Ovid could have composed verse 42,
speque timor dubia spesque timore cadit. The double-entendre on *vale* (168)
seems characteristically Ovidian. Finally, is it not likely that an imitator of
Ovid would have followed fairly closely Ovid's treatment of the same myth
in the *Met.* (9.1ff)? The almost total divergence on every level, the deliberate
and pointed variations seem more likely the product of Ovid's own mind
and aims.

9. Deianira

As for the poem itself, a few preliminary remarks on sources will be in order. Hercules was perhaps the favorite mythological character of the Greeks. The amount of creative energy they expended on this quasi-divinity borders on the incredible. He was the subject of much literature (Panyassis' *Heraclea*, Pisander's *Heraclea*, "Creophylus' " Οἰχαλίας ἅλωσις,[18] numerous treatments in Greek lyric poetry, to mention but a few). Analyzing the sources of a treatment as late as Ovid's is difficult, if not impossible. Even an attempt to narrow our aims to those aspects of the myth which involved Deianira will not bring much improvement. Thus, should we lay hold of the three major events connected with Deianira (1) the suit for her hand which ends in the competition between Hercules and Achelous; (2) the attempt by Nessus to rape her and his slaying by Hercules; (3) the death of Hercules through the robe sent him by Deianira—we must inevitably come to the twofold realization that (1) all three have long histories; both the Achelous and Nessus battles go back at least to Archilochus, the poisoned robe to the Hesiodic *Catalogus*;[19] (2) during the course of lengthy development, each underwent numerous changes, transformations, variations, though by and large we are unable to identify the particular literary works which effected these alterations and modifications. The versions found in the mythographers and in scholia are astounding in their multiplicity, for instance, on the following points: the form of Achelous in his fight against Hercules, the method in which Hercules killed him, whether or not Nessus successfully raped Deianira, exactly where he was slain by Hercules, what Nessus gave to Deianira as a love-charm and what he said its function was. Even should we exclude certain of the variations as being the result of the error and imagination of the mythographers and scholiasts, the number of variations that have literary roots remains great. Even the cardinal point in Hercules' death, Deianira's motivation, may not have been uniform. Stoessl's suggestion[20] that there was a tradition of an evil Dei-

---

[18] See Huxley 86, 99-112, 177ff.

[19] Archilochus fr. 280 Tarditi = 268, 269, 270 Lasserre = 147 Bergk⁴. *Catalogus*, fr. 25.17ff.MW.

[20] F. Stoessl, *Der Tod des Herakles* (Zurich 1945) 16ff. Much the same suggestion had previously been made by T.B.L. Webster in *Greek Poetry and Life: Essays Presented to Gilbert Murray* (Oxford 1936) 164, and even earlier by T. Zieliński, *Eos* 25 (1921-1922) 61.

anira who wittingly sent Hercules the poisoned robe has been rejected by most scholars,[21] but the evidence certainly points to the existence of a very different kind of Deianira from Sophocles' heroine, indeed, a warrior-like, Amazonian figure,[22] not to mention the almost Medea-like character of Ovid's *Metamorphoses* and the *Hercules Oetaeus*.

The superabundance of mythic deviations and our inability to relate them to specific sources is all the more unfortunate in *Heroides* 9 since is it obvious that Ovid is assuming and utilizing more than one source (i.e., Sophocles' *Trachiniae*). Over and over we are faced with mythic material that is manifestly not Ovidian invention but which has no place in the *Trachiniae*. We will, however, find it impossible to assign each of these aspects to a particular model. A few examples will suffice. At 139-140 Ovid assumes the common tale of Hercules breaking off a horn of Achelous.[23] For so familiar a story there need be no specific source; but the important thing to note is that this is not in the *Trachiniae*. There are, by the way, a few peculiarities here. I am not sure whether they reflect Ovidian inventiveness or some version otherwise unknown to us. *Cornua flens legit ripis Achelous in udis* appears to mean that Hercules broke off both horns (unless *cornua* can mean "pieces of horn"). Certainly the plural is not equivalent to the singular (note *legit*). The usual version (as also at *Met.* 9.85-86) tells of one horn broken off.[24] Also, the picture of Achelous gathering up his lost horn(s) seems unique, especially since it is a routine part of the story that, after breaking the horn off, Hercules keeps it and uses it to his advantage (either exchanging it for the cornucopia or giving it as bride-price for Deianira).[25] Whether this novel approach is Ovid's own is hard to tell.

Then there is the elaborate account of Hercules' service to Omphale. This, of course, does not (could not) come from Sopho-

[21] But H. F. Johansen, *Lustrum* 7 (1962) 258 appears to accept it.

[22] See Apollod. 1.8.1; schol. A.R. 1.1212; Nonnus 35. 89-91.

[23] E.g., Pind. fr. 71 Turyn; Apollod. 2.7.5; Tzetzes *ad* Lycoph. *Alex.* 50. It was probably in Archilochus too, if μουνόκερας (fr. 255 Tarditi = 276 Lasserre = 181 Bergk⁴) came in his treatment of the battle between Hercules and Achelous.

[24] The plural version I know elsewhere only at Ovid *Am.* 3.6.35-36, and perhaps at Stat. *Theb.* 7.416-417 (but see schol. *ad loc.*).

[25] Given in exchange: see the Pindar, Apollodorus, Tzetzes references supra n. 23. As a bride-price: Philostr. Min. *Imag.* 4.

cles' tragedy, in which Hercules' servitude to Omphale is mentioned, but little more is said of it. On this part of the letter more will be said later.

The list of Hercules' labors in *Heroides* 9 is sufficiently different from that in Sophocles to merit the conclusion that Ovid was going elsewhere for this material.

But on the other hand the evidence is beyond contradiction that at the back of this letter stands the *Trachiniae*. Not merely in the movement of events, in the development of the "plot," but in many thematic and verbal echoes. These have been documented by Birt and Stoessl,[26] e.g. (references to *Her.* 9 first) 5/ 1048ff; 11/ 497ff; 25-26/ 488-489; 33/ 34-35; 35ff/ 27ff & 103ff; 47ff/ 459ff; 121ff/ 366ff.[27]

The letter itself is strangely dominated by the long description of Hercules' servitude to Omphale, a passage commonly maligned for its sometimes comic, nearly ludicrous tone. A partial explanation lies, I believe, in the literary history of the myth. By the late fifth century Hercules was becoming in the Greek mind a suitable figure for comic treatment. Tragic treatments were few,[28] while the comic proliferated. One of the favorite episodes of the saga became his enslavement to Omphale. An index is the

[26] T. Birt, *RhM* 32 (1877) 406-408; Stoessl (supra n. 20) 70ff.

[27] Indeed, the face-to-face confrontation between Iole and Deianira may be a Sophoclean invention. See S. G. Kapsomenos, *Sophokles' Trachinierinnen und ihr Vorbild* (Athens 1963) 11-12, following A. Beck, *Hermes* 81 (1953) 13ff. Stoessl also observes (73-74) that the reference to Hercules on Oeta (147) is an anachronistic slip, but based on the assumption of a Sophoclean conclusion. I should hesitate to call this a slip, since Ovid often in the *Heroides* seeks to work in anachronistic material. Here he does it less well than elsewhere. Alternatively, Ovid may not be thinking of a Sophoclean conclusion which necessitates the removal of the dying Hercules to Mount Oeta, but may have in mind a version in which he is at Mount Oeta all along, as indeed he appears to assume at *Met.* 9.165. At any rate, if one feels there is a slip here, certainly W. Kraus' solution (*AAHG* 11 [1958] 143), that the *nuntia fama* could have told Deianira of Hercules' transference to Oeta, will not satisfy, since in Sophocles the decision to move to Oeta is made after Deianira's death.

[28] It is possible that Aeschylus' *Heraclidae* was on the same theme as the *Trachiniae*. See T. Zieliński, *Eos* 25 (1921-1922) 59-68, and H. Lloyd-Jones in H. W. Smyth's Loeb edition of Aeschylus (Cambridge, Mass. 1957) 2.588ff. Webster (102), however, seems to accept the traditional view that Aeschylus' *Heraclidae* and Euripides' *Heraclidae* treated the same story. The Romans followed the Greek example. We do not know of any Republican tragedy whose main subject was the Hercules myth.

comedians' affection for designating Aspasia the "new Omphale."
Ion of Chios and Achaeus wrote satyr plays, *Omphale*, Antiphanes and Cratinus junior comedies by that name. It is a good
guess that they all depicted the base, sensuous and degrading
servitude of Hercules. Nicochares' Ἡρακλῆς γαμούμενος (if this
is the title)[29] and Plato comicus' Ξάντριαι may have treated the
same theme.[30] Perhaps it is this basically comic heritage which
has left its stamp on Ovid's poem.[31] This is, of course, explanation, not justification. The question still stands as to whether the
tradition has here overwhelmed Ovid or whether he has controlled and integrated it into his own framework. For, in the end,
it is clear that this poem is not meant to be essentially comic,
satiric, or parodic.

It is, in the first place, a mistake, fatal to the understanding of
the poem, to establish an artificial separation between the affairs
of Iole and Omphale (as does Vessey, 351-352). In fact, the
mythic tradition knits the two closely together; Sophocles' version is a good instance. Deianira learns of Iole and Omphale at
the same time, since Hercules' service to the latter has been a secret and is only revealed to her after the sack of Oichalia. Thus,
it becomes at least "reasonable" for Ovid's Deianira to speak out
against the affair of Hercules and Omphale only now. She appre-
hends these two new *crimina* together, almost as if they were two
sides of the same coin. But the connection is not the mere product of chronological propinquity. Ovid unites the two thematically by the notion of the vanquished Hercules. In each woman
Deianira sees a conqueror of her husband, Iole who is formally
a captive slave but displays by her bearing that she is no such
thing (125-130), Omphale who has debased and degraded Hercules by compelling him to activities unbecoming to his heroic
stature.[32] But why—as Vessey would rightly ask—when Deianira

[29] See A. Meineke, *FCG* 1.255.

[30] We may also wonder whether Demonicus' *Achelous* and Eubulus' *Amal-
theia* also made merry with the story of Hercules and Deianira.

[31] Prop. 4.9.47-50, Ter. *Eun.* 1027, and Ovid *Fasti* 2.303ff would seem to be
in the same comic tradition. For the obviously comic parody one may also
compare Alexis' Ὀδυσσεὺς ὑφαίνων, which evidently displayed the hero Odysseus plying the loom. Interestingly, the theme has recently been taken up by
Peter Hacks in his comedy *Omphale* (Frankfurt am Main 1971).

[32] This is a clever and effective adaptation not only of *Trach.* 488-489, but
also of Hercules' complaints (1046ff, 1058ff) that he, the great unconquered
hero, has now been defeated by a mere woman, i.e., Deianira, who has killed

is faced with so severe a crisis that threatens her very position as Hercules' wife, should the unifying thread of the poem and its central theme be the debasement of Hercules? One might, I imagine, argue that the treatment is persuasive in intent. She hopes to shock Hercules back to his senses by offering him a close account of his shameful behavior. There may be an element of truth in this, but not much more. One does not sense this poem as a document of persuasion at all.[33] One must, as so often in the *Heroides*, seek answers to key questions in Ovid's conception of his heroine's character.

The very first line provides direction, *gratulor Oechaliam titulis accedere nostris*. Palmer's comment is right to the point, Deianira is "the lawful wife of Hercules, and the legitimate partner of his glory."[34] She shares in the accomplishments of her husband. But this is not so much a question of legality as of psychology. To a degree, the sustaining tone of the poem is bitter disappointment and fallen pride. From the beginning the thrust of the poem is not Deianira's jealousy, but her aggrievedness that Hercules has not lived up to his name and reputation. One of the crucial substructures of the poem is the continuing contrast between what Hercules should be (and has been) and what he has now turned out to be. The theme of Hercules' present disgrace is varied in many ways. Words like *fama decolor* (3-4), *notitia* (19), *vitae labe* (8), *stupri nota* (20), *pudet* (66) are almost moralizing in tone. Jupiter, we are to believe, is embarrassed by his son's behavior (9-10), as are Hercules' enemies (67ff). The imagery of

him. Similarly, the theme of the effeminate Hercules may have a perverse relationship to *Trach.* 1075, θῆλυς ηὕρημαι.

[33] Even less so than most of the other *Heroides*. Might the reason be, in part, that Deianira, in contrast to the other heroines, has taken action to "persuade" Hercules, by sending him the robe? Consequently, verbal persuasion is superfluous.

[34] Heinsius preferred *vestris*, but *nostris* is certainly correct. See, recently, G. P. Goold, *HSCP* 69 (1965) 42. I note, however, en passant, that in general I have serious doubts about the validity of the "rule" that in Classical Latin *vester* cannot = *tuus*. There are too many examples (especially in Catullus and Ovid) that have to be forcibly explained away. To the instances usually adduced, *Am* 2.18.40, *a vestris in mea castra venis*, should be added. One could, I suppose, argue that *vestris* means "you and your fellow epic-poets" but the contrast to *mea* suggests otherwise. See A. E. Housman, *CQ* 3 (1909) 244-248; C. J. Fordyce, *Catullus: A Commentary* (Oxford 1961) 188-189; E. N. O'Neil, *CP* 62 (1967) 168, n. 31.

Hercules' defeat is sometimes bestial (e.g., *imposuisse iugum*, 6), perhaps ironic counterplay to his role as conqueror of beasts, sometimes literal (e.g., the victor's ritual at 12 & 103-104), always degrading, often with the clearest effeminate connotations (e.g., *lascivae more puellae*, 65; *molli viro*, 72). When Deianira recounts the achievements of the old Hercules, both pride and disappointment are present:

> Tene ferunt geminos pressisse tenaciter angues,
>   cum tener in cunis iam Iove dignus eras?
> Coepisti melius quam desinis; ultima primis
>   cedunt: Dissimiles hic vir et ille puer.
> Quem non mille ferae, quem non Stheneleius hostis,
>   non potuit Iuno vincere, vincit Amor,
>
>   (21-26)

pride in what Hercules has achieved, disappointment at his present defeat.[35] This is precisely the effect achieved by the lengthy account of his enslavement to Omphale. For Hercules' debased actions are not merely recounted, but each is seen in the light of some noble act of heroism. Hexameter is balanced by pentameter, sometimes distich by distich, sometimes the contrasts are internal to the verse (57-80). There is some sarcasm mixed in with the sense of loss. Even the recapitulation of Hercules' labors (85-100), boring as it is, reflects Deianira's absorption in the great heroic past of her husband, replete with feelings of awe and admiration.

Ovid's Deianira is a character-type rather familiar to us, though unusual in the ancient literary world. She is the ordinary, everyday woman who is married to the great man and lives through and in her husband's greatness. She is *Herculis uxor* (27) and it is in this role that her life attains significance. Denied self-fulfillment on a personal and individual basis, she finds honor and meaning in her husband's preeminence. But this mode of lending importance and identity to her own life depends on two things. The first is Hercules' maintenance of his heroic stature. Therefore, when Deianira, through most of the letter, laments the degradation of Hercules it is not irrelevant, but right to the point. For more important than a mere rival's affections is the

---

[35] The theme of discontinuity of identity (24), one person being two, is so characteristically Ovidian that one almost feels it is further evidence of the poem's authenticity. For discussion, see chapter xx, "Myth and Psychology."

loss of Hercules' glory, which now denies Deianira the vicarious self-importance she had cherished.

> Se quoque nympha tuis ornavit Dardanis armis
>> et tulit e capto nota tropaea viro.
> I nunc, tolle animos et fortia facta recense:
>> Quod tu non esses, iure vir illa fuit,
> qua tanto minor es, quanto te, maxime rerum,
>> quam quos vicisti, vincere maius erat.
> Illi procedit rerum mensura tuarum,
>> cede bonis: Heres laudis amica tuae.
>
> (103-110)

Omphale has usurped Deianira's privilege of pride in Hercules' feats, for they now redound to *her* glory. Once Hercules' *tituli* belonged jointly to Deianira, now the *tropaea* are Omphale's. If once Deianira was virtually *heres* to Hercules' glory, Omphale, by virtue of her victory over the hero, has now assumed that role.

Deianira's second requirement is that she retain her status as *Herculis uxor*. This is why the introduction of Iole into her home so upsets her (in contrast to the foreign loves which bother her less). Had Hercules preferred to treat Iole like his other loves, keeping her a *peregrinus amor*, then Deianira could have shut her eyes and made believe that Iole was nothing, as she had done with Hercules' amours hitherto: *nec mihi, quae patior, dissimulare licet* (122). But Iole's presence makes all the difference: *forsitan et pulsa† Aetolide Deianira/ nomine deposito paelicis uxor erit* (131-132). It is the name of *uxor*, the role of wife, which is the crucial factor. Loving and being loved is of small importance. Here is a crucial difference from Sophocles' treatment. Sophocles' heroine is a jealous woman, concerned with her husband's apparent love for another woman. She worries lest Hercules prove to be her husband in name, but in fact the lover of Iole (545-551). In contrast, it is the name, the status of wife that is Ovid's Deianira's concern. It is the familial and legal connection that she wants, as is also implied in her backhanded slaps at Hercules' other intrigues, all phrased in terms that reflect her desire to be the one and only mother of his children (see 48, 50, 54).

Even with the poem's shift at 143, this essential trait of Deianira remains constant. Her concern is with her status as *Herculis uxor*. Of course, at this point the threat of losing him to another is gone, so the theme takes a new direction. She must now prove herself to be a worthy *Herculis uxor*, which she will do by committing suicide: *Ecquid adhuc habeo facti, cur Herculis uxor/ credar, coniugii mors mea pignus erit* (149-150). Her final oath is sworn by *iura sacerrima lecti* (159), in effect, by her relationship to Hercules as his wife. The poem's final line, *virque—sed o possis!—et puer Hylle, vale!*, her farewell to life and the living, guarantees her claim and desire to be the wife of Hercules and the mother of his children *in perpetuum*.

Deianira's personal view of the relationship between herself and Hercules has some interesting extensions. For instance, her virtual identification of herself with Hercules by and large removes the need—so dominant in other letters—to emphasize that her husband's affairs do insult and injury to her; it is enough to point out that they injure *him* (e.g., 2). The interesting idea that Deianira partakes of Hercules' exploits becomes more than a mere metaphor. Thus, by way of contrast, Penelope worries about the dangers that may imperil Ulysses (1.11ff); Deianira, one would think, is right there with Hercules: *inter serpentes aprosque avidosque leones/ iactor et haesuros terna per ora canes* (37-38; cf. too 45-46). This distich leads the way to the irony of 73ff, *inter Ioniacas calathum tenuisse puellas/ diceris*, etc. The roles are reversed. While the great hero spends his time weaving at the loom, the housewife does battle with serpents and lions.

This is, in the end, a Deianira whose like probably did not exist before Ovid.[36] Unlike the violent and jealous wife of the *Metamorphoses* and the *Hercules Oetaeus*, unlike Sophocles' gentle, loving, and concerned wife, afflicted by Hercules' disloyalty to her, this is a Deianira created out of the peculiar circumstances generated by marriage to a super-hero, whose identity has perforce been subsumed by his, whose individuality finds expression only in his, whose very self exists only in his. Deianira herself has a measure of insight into the real depths of her plight:

> Quam male inaequales veniunt ad aratra iuvenci,
>   tam premitur magno coniuge nupta minor.
> Non honor est sed onus species laesura ferentes:
>   siqua voles apte nubere, nube pari.
>
> (29-32)

[36] Whether Ovid's particular version of the simple, unheroic Deianira has any roots in comedy is impossible to say.

XIV

Heroides 1: Penelope

There can be no doubt that Ovid's Penelope is shaped against the ever-present backdrop of the *Odyssey* and the Homeric Penelope. By the phrase "Homeric Penelope" I mean not merely Penelope as she is in the *Odyssey*, but at least equally the Penelope whom interpreters and readers of Homer generally claimed as the Odyssean Penelope, that is, περίφρων Πηνελόπεια, that paragon of wifely devotion and loyalty. It would serve no purpose here to argue whether the characterization of Penelope in the *Odyssey* fits this limited model. For all intents and purposes we shall assume it does, for, by and large, the ancients themselves so assumed.

The *Odyssey* then served as Ovid's source in two ways. First, in that it created—or was felt to have created—the characterization of Penelope which sets off Ovid's own. Second, it was the poem from which Ovid drew both the basic outline and the details which are the structure of the myth and the backbone of his treatment. The latter point doubtless seems obvious and scholars have, without exception (and without much examination), asserted that the *Odyssey* was here Ovid's source or model. In the final analysis, this is almost certainly right. But there are two facets to the problem which should at least cause some hesitation. There are, in the first place, a number of strange "errors," i.e., deviations from the Homeric account. Thus, Antilochus is reported slain by Hector (15); Memnon is the killer in the *Odyssey* (4.187-188) and in the general mythological tradition. Penelope sends Telemachus to Sparta and Pylos (37-38, 63-65); in the *Odyssey* Athena instructs him to go (1.280ff) and Penelope remains in total ignorance. Medon, a faithful confidant of Penelope throughout the *Odyssey*, is here ranked among the hostile suitors (91). Finally (at least of the relatively cogent deviations), the suitors, it seems, attempt to ambush Telemachus on his way to

Pylos (99-100), while, in the *Odyssey*, the ambush is planned for his return journey. Palmer and Wilkinson typify the prevailing tendency to take the path of least resistance:[1] Ovid was relying exclusively or chiefly on his memory, making only cursory use of the text of the *Odyssey*. This is, to be sure, possible, but the assumption raises a series of difficult questions: (1) Why should the Briseis-letter be so accurate in its reading of the *Iliad*? Did Ovid know the *Iliad* so much better than the *Odyssey*? Or did he choose to use diligently his text of the *Iliad* when writing *Heroides* 3? Why? (2) Could Ovid have forgotten the time of the ambush? He surely must have recalled that it occurs in the second half of the poem (even if conceived in Book Four), while Telemachus travels to Pylos and Sparta at the beginning. (3) Could Ovid have thought that the *Odyssey* represents Penelope sending Telemachus, when it is a relatively important point that he conceals his journey from her and that she grieves upon learning of it? (4) Why does much of the poem show close familiarity with the *Odyssey*? Shall we assume—certainly a possibility—that Ovid knew parts of the epic well, others not?[2]

At the other extreme is the view elegantly and firmly espoused by Loers (*ad* verse 63):

> Ego vero et de hoc loco v. 15 et omnino de tota illa in hac Epist. ab auctoritate Homeri discrepantia sic sentio, poetam in his Epistolis, ut in aliis carminibus . . . in fabulis tractandis singulari quadam et quam poetis concessam putaret usum esse libertate, et consulto ac scientem a fabula, qualis ab Homero traditur, discessisse, eamque consilio suo atque instituto accommodasse. Minime enim verisimile est, Ovidium, qui omnes prope res ab Homero narratas et ipsa quoque verba dictionesque, ut omnia eius carmina declarant, memoriter complexus est et *ab eo fonte perenni*, ut ipsius verbis utar, *sua ora Pieriis aquis rigavit*, ac praecipue in plurimis locis huius Epistolae,

---

[1] Palmer 277; Wilkinson 15, note.

[2] Palmer argues that the errors in the poem are the result of poor memory or careless reading, but at the same time defends the allusion to a hostile Medon (91) on the basis of the brief and singular reference to him among the suitors at 16.252, which implies an exact reading and close familiarity with the text.

item in Epistola III. XVI. et XVII. tam diligens Homeri studium probavit, hunc ipsum ne ea quidem, quae nemo, qui leviter tantum Homeri carmina attigit, ignorat, velut Telemachum a Minerva Pylon missum esse, in memoria habuisse, neque cum in plane Homerico argumento versaretur, Homeri carmina ante diligenter legisse, quotiesque ex eo fonte hauriret, eadem, ubicunque dubitaret, denuo evolvisse. Nam quod Lennepius Ovidium poetarum principis, qui iam tum habebatur, cum haec scriberet exemplar ad manum non habuisse censuit, non est credibile.

Otis has written much the same about the *Metamorphoses*:

At times Ovid changes a source, at times prefers one to various alternative versions of a myth, at times adds or subtracts only a few significant details; but all these procedures are dictated by the effect or point he wants to bring out in a special context.[3]

This approach has recently been promoted by Baca in his sympathetic essay on *Heroides* 1.[4] However, attractive as the view is in the abstract, the specific questions remain: In what way does this or that alteration conform to or further Ovid's overall purpose? Neither Loers nor Baca—nor anyone in the intervening century and a half—has addressed himself to this problem. This path will be the one I shall take, arguing that these "errors" (at least some of them; a few I find inexplicable and pointless as deliberate changes) represent conscious deviations. Nevertheless, there is a third possibility, one that is regularly ignored, that Ovid may have been availing himself of versions of the myth other than the *Odyssey* (though, even should one so conclude, the question must still be asked: to what end?).

There existed, after all, a large number of literary works on the myth of Odysseus. Many of them could have included Penelope. Some were even called by her name. Aeschylus' *Penelope* evidently dealt with the return of Odysseus. Of Philocles' tragedy *Penelope* we know nothing, while the few fragments of Theopompus' comedy of the same title tells us very little. We know nothing of the prose works περὶ Ἑλένης καὶ Πηνελόπης, περὶ Ὀδυσσέως

---

[3] P. 89.   [4] A. R. Baca, *TAPA* 100 (1969) 9-10.

καὶ Πηνελόπης (both by Antisthenes), and [ἐγκώμιον?] Πηνελόπης (attributed to Isocrates).[5]

At any rate, there were numerous works concerned with Odysseus' return and with post-Odyssean events in the life of Odysseus which may have presented various portraits of Penelope and considerable deviation, both in small points and large, from the Homeric version.[6] Let us at least be aware that the "errors" in the Ovidian epistle could be Ovid's preference for some non-Homeric treatments.

In spite of the great deficiencies in our knowledge, we are pretty well able to trace a mainstream in the literary history of Penelope. From the *Odyssey* was derived the unidimensional paradigm of virtue. Throughout Greek literature passing references to Penelope center on her virtuous devotion.[7] It is in this mold that the Romans finally froze—or should we say embalmed —her. No longer subject for literary development, she proved a marvelous and acquiescent *exemplum* for feminine virtue, especially, though not exclusively, favored by the elegists (further discussion infra).

If the "vulgate" Penelope is perfectly clear, so are the adversary alternatives. Most familiar is the association of Penelope with Pan, but the implications of the myth are obscure. Briefly, Penelope was reported to have been the mother of Pan. Traditions of the father are varied. But the tale that Pan was born of Penelope and Hermes goes back at least to Pindar[8] and undoubtedly earlier. Huxley has noted the possibility that Eugammon invented the story.[9] What the original intent and meaning of the myth were is unclear. Was it based purely on etymological similarities? Is this Penelope to be identified with the wife of

[5] See F. Blass, *Die Attische Beredsamkeit* 2 (1892[2]) 103, n. 7.

[6] For a rather full listing of such works see E. Wüst's article, "Penelope," in *RE* 19.1 (1937) 484-486. I would minimally add to his list Alexis' comedy Ὀδυσσεὺς ἀπονιζόμενος, Stesichorus' *Nostoi* (*PMG* 209), and a work by Hipponax, *POxy* 2174 (see e.g., the edition by O. Masson [Paris 1962] 143-144). Also, Wüst's *Philogelos* should be *Polyzelos*.

[7] E.g., Theognis 1126-1128; Eur. *Or.* 588-590; Aristoph. *Thesm.* 547-548; Eubulus *Chrysilla* fr. 116-117. 9-10 Kock. There is an interesting instance in a fourth century A.D. papyrus: part of a magical incantation to be spoken by a man seeking the faithful love of a woman is that she should remain chaste as Penelope did for Odysseus (*Pap. Gr. Mag.* 36.288-290).

[8] Fr. 100 Snell[3].   [9] P. 172.

Odysseus? *Non liquet.*[10] What is, however, clear is that at some point this myth did become closely bound up with that of the Homeric Penelope and became the foundation for an attempt to discredit her. Thus, the divine paramour, whose affections are no doubt inexorable and excusable, gives way to human ones. The traditional Penelope is turned into her opposite. Rather than maintaining steadfast faithfulness, she uses Odysseus' absence to indulge herself; Pan is often the result. Once again, lovers differ. In one instance Antinous seduces Penelope, and Odysseus, on his return, drives her from his home.[11] In another, Amphinomus is the lover and Penelope is then slain by Odysseus.[12] Apollodorus reports a version in which Odysseus returns home from later adventures to find Penelope having borne a child;[13] there may be an implication that Odysseus is not the father. Very common is the tale that Penelope, no better than a whore, slept with all the suitors (evidently connected to the similarity Πάν/πάντες). Such was the story in Duris of Samos.[14] Others also noted, in various fashions, Penelope's unfaithfulness and lasciviousness, most strongly perhaps Lycophron (*Alex.* 771-773, 792).[15] Clever carpers were able to expand the portrait of a wanton Penelope, sometimes even within the stretched confines of the *Odyssey.* There was probably a view[16] that Penelope's coaxing of gifts from the suitors reflected her base character. Amphinomus as lover of Penelope was undoubtedly strained out of *Od.* 16.397-

[10] Essentially neutral versions report the father as a god, e.g., Hermes: Hdt. 2.145; Cic. *N.D.* 3.56; Hyg. *Fab.* 224; or Apollo: Pindar (?) apud schol. Bern. *Georg.* 1.17, schol. Theoc. *Syrinx* 1-2a (with Schroeder's supplement), comment. Lucan 3.402; Hecataeus *FGrHist* 1F371 (unsicheres); Euphorion apud schol. Eur. *Rhesus* 36 (but text uncertain and cf. comment. Lucan 3.402). No father is mentioned at Dosiadas *Bomos* 16. In general, see the detailed citations in Wendell's edition of the Theocritus-scholia pp. 29-32, and in *FGrHist* 244F135, 136a.

[11] Apollod. *Epit.* 7.38. [12] Apollod. *Epit.* 7.39.

[13] *Epit.* 7.35.

[14] *FGrHist* 76F21 (= Tzetzes Lycoph. *Alex.* 772). Version also attested at schol. Theoc. *Syrinx* 15a; schol. Theoc. 1.3-4c, 7. 109-110b; schol. Oppian *Hal.* 3.15, which adds that οἱ νεώτεροι called Penelope a πόρνη; Serv. *ad Aen.* 2.44.

[15] See too Paus. 8.12.6; Theopompus *FGrHist* 115F354. Hermesianax' concoction of a love affair between Penelope and Homer seems irrelevant, given its context; see Ath. 13.597EF.

[16] See Plut. *Quomodo adul.* 27c.

398. Dicaearchus[17] blasted Penelope's appearance at the suitors' party as a mark of her immorality. The role that comedy played in the defamation of Penelope must have been great, but our sources are silent.[18]

Penelope, however, had ready defenders. Some argued that this was a case of mistaken identity: another Penelope was Pan's mother.[19] Others took the onus off Penelope: she was deceived by Hermes who disguised himself as a goat;[20] she was faithful, but the suitors raped her;[21] the liaison with Hermes occurred only after Odysseus' death.[22] Finally, some removed all illicit color from Pan's birth by making Odysseus the father.[23]

Two phenomena were, I think, responsible for the creation and brief popularity of the wanton Penelope. First was the all too human tendency to rebel against the superhuman ideal, the model of perfection. Penelope was too good to be true, she had to be brought down to earth—and, indeed, have her face, so to speak, rubbed in it. The other cause was culturally rather than psychologically conditioned. Rhetorical education and practice cultivated the art of the paradox. To successfully argue white black, good bad, up down was the province of the skilled rhetorician. This carried into mythology. What could be more delightful and more of a challenge than to turn the obviously loyal Homeric heroine into a slut? Thus, Polybius tells of boys writing exercises in condemnation of Penelope, while Philodemus[24] chastises the

---

[17] Apud schol. *Od.* 1.332.

[18] If Parthenius' account (pp. 154-155 West. *narr.* 3) is based on Sophocles' *Euryalus*, then there was a less than virtuous (though not here in the sexual sense) Penelope even in tragedy. As for later descriptions of a wanton Penelope (e.g., Mart. 11.104.15-16; *Priap.* 68.27ff), they probably have nothing to do with the Hellenistic tradition. The report at schol. Stat. *Theb.* 4.576, that Niobe was the daughter of Tantalus and Penelope, is presumably the result of corruption in the text.

[19] Tzetzes Lycoph. *Alex.* 772; Nonnus 14.92-94. This view has also been argued by the modern scholar, W. H. Roscher, *Philologus* 53 (1894) 368-372. However, E. Bethe, *Homer: Dichtung und Sage*, III: *Die Sage vom troischen Kriege* (Leipzig and Berlin 1927) 172f disagrees.

[20] Schol. Theoc. 7.109-110b-c; *Myth. Gr.* 381, no. 59 West.; Serv. *ad Aen.* 2.44.

[21] Schol. Theoc. 7.109-110c; *Myth. Gr.* 381, no. 59 West.

[22] *Myth, Vat.* 1.89.

[23] Schol. Theoc. *Syrinx* 1-2a; schol. Theoc. 1.123b; perhaps Euphorion *apud* comment. Lucan 3.402 (but cf. Schol. Eur. *Rhesus* 36).

[24] Polyb. 12.26b; Philodemus *Rhet.* 4, col. 35a-36a = 1.217 Sudh.

rhetoricians who violate moral standards by preferring Clytemnestra to Penelope. Even Seneca[25] notes the obsession of philosopher-rhetoricians with questions like "was Penelope unchaste?" The combination of these two factors produced a mild revolution in the literary history of Penelope.

To be sure, it was limited. One need do no more than note the many allusions to Penelope in Latin literature, most of which are directed toward her status as a model of virtue and loyalty. She had become a paradigm: virtue preserved through trickery in the face of powerful obstacles. When there is need of an example of a woman's fidelity or endurance or wiles, *Penelope excitanda est* is the rule. She is no more than a handy repository of a few significant motifs. Thus, Horace's *exclusus amator* can complain that his girl is playing the virtuous Penelope[26] and Propertius can contrast the loose Roman girls with Penelope.[27] Ovid himself, consigned to distant exile while his wife remains at Rome, finds comfort and hope in comparing her to Penelope, hopefully seeing in her a second Penelope devoted to her Odysseus, Ovid.[28] Penelope had turned into a proverb.[29] One might even think of *Heroides* 1 as a conscious attempt to free the character of Penelope from the shackles which constrained it: to turn the paragon back into a person.

But the model of a very different Penelope did exist and Ovid assuredly knew it. Yet, I think it here more important to keep in mind the processes which engendered this strange Penelope rather than the bare fact of her existence. For it seems to me that the Penelope of the *Heroides*, a far cry from Homer's, is rooted not so much in the Hellenistic model of a faithless wife as in a mode of thinking very similar to that which produced the wanton Penelope.

Ovid's Penelope, Palmer tells us (277), is in the tradition of

---

25 *Ep.* 88.8. 26 *C.* 3.10.11. 27 2.6.23.

28 E.g., *Pont.* 3.1.113; *Tr.* 1.6.22. For an interesting study of Ovid as Odysseus, see H. Rahn, *A&A* 7 (1958) 105-120.

29 See A. Otto, *Die Sprichwörter und sprichwörtlichen Redensarten der Römer* (repr. Hildesheim 1962) 272. Also see the discussion and numerous examples in H. Renz, *Mythologische Beispiele in Ovids erotischer Elegie* (Würzburg 1935) 52-53. I note, however, that Lucilius introduced Penelope into Book 17 of his *Satires* (fr. 539-540 Krenkel). If 541-547 are part of this context, we may wonder whether Lucilius depicted a wavering Penelope. This is, needless to say, mere conjecture. It is barely possible that Penelope also had a part in Book 27 and spoke (fr. 694 Krenkel).

Penelope as "the pattern 'of perfect wifehood and pure woman-
hood.'" Paratore thinks much the same: "Ecco l'espressione del
casto amore coniugale nella figura soave e dimessa della buona
Penelope."[30] Kraus and Otis[31] make similar judgments: she is the
faithful wife. This is, at the least, misleading. It is true that there
is no reason to believe that Ovid's Penelope has been wantonly
faithless to Odysseus; at least, nothing in the letter points notice-
ably that way. But such terse and stereotyped descriptions inevitably signify "Homer's Penelope." We are compelled to identify Ovid's Penelope with Homer's. And this is, without question,
wrong. Indeed, the difference must strike us in the opening
verse: *Hanc tua Penelope lento tibi mittit, Ulixe.*[32] Ulysses is introduced by an adjective, *lento*, which, as Palmer well notes,
"conveys reproach of deliberate tardiness." *Lentus* is frequently
found in love elegy, often denoting the one lover who does not
show enough interest and eagerness toward the other.[33] This is
virtually a rebuke of Ulysses for deliberately delaying his return
to Ithaca. *Lentus* in the opening line is, in musical terms, the key
signature of the poem. Penelope introduces herself as the dissatisfied lover who feels wronged by her man. The sharpness of the
verse's repeated "t"'s reinforces the effect.

Nil mihi rescribas tu tamen; ipse veni (2).[34] The impatience of
the second verse, with its strong *nil* for *ne*, emphatic pronouns,
and bold imperative advances the tone and sets the mood for the
whole letter: "don't put off coming by substituting a letter; come
in person!" To contrast this with Homer's Penelope would be superfluous. Never does she cast Odysseus in an ill-light, never hint
that he is master of his fate and willfully staying away. But here
is a different world, a different Penelope: complaints, utterances
of self-pity, ungracious allegations all issue from her mouth with

---

[30] E. Paratore in *Studi Ovidiani* (Rome 1959) 128.

[31] W. Kraus in *Ovid* (Wege der Forschung 1968) 94; Otis 265.

[32] *Hanc*, as all editors have observed, is difficult. I am not at all certain
that it is wrong, but I note, in support of Palmer's *haec . . . mittit*, an identical phrase at the beginning of Iphigeneia's letter (Eur. *IT* 770) ἐπιστέλλει τάδε.
Kirfel (85) compares *Her.* 10.3 and *Pont.* 4.14.1.

[33] E.g., Tib. 1.4.81; Prop. 1.6.12, 2.15.8; Ovid *Rem.Am.* 243.

[34] Dörrie (360) agreed with Housman that Aphthonius' quotation of this
verse with *attinet* is decisive. A decade later he does not accept this reading in
his text. I do not know why he changed his mind. On the value of the testimony of the grammarians for correct readings in Ovid, see G. P. Goold,
HSCP 69 (1965) 70.

consistent regularity. Sometimes she sounds like Aeschylus' Clytemnestra (861ff).[35] In harsh terms she condemns the Greek expedition to Troy, essentially because it conflicts with her self-interest. She is even ready to wish that Troy had not fallen and the
Greeks not won (67). She bewails her enforced life of celibacy
(7) and the nights of anxious sleeplessness (9-10). Her bed is not
viduus but *desertus* (7); she is not *sola* but *relicta* (8). *Tardos* in
verse 8 recalls *lento*; Ulysses' slowness causes time to move slowly for her. He is responsible for her wretched state.

In striking verses the boundaries between the war at Troy and
the wife at home are dissolved in laments of self-pity:

> Quando ego non timui graviora pericula veris?
> Res est solliciti plena timoris amor.
> In te fingebam violentos Troas ituros;
> nomine in Hectoreo pallida semper eram;
> sive quis Antilochum narrabat ab Hectore victum,
> Antilochus nostri causa timoris erat,
> sive Menoetiaden falsis cecidisse sub armis,
> flebam successu posse carere dolos.
> Sanguine Tlepolemus Lyciam tepefecerat hastam,
> Tlepolemi leto cura novata mea est.
> Denique quisquis erat castris iugulatus Achivis,
> Frigidius glacie pectus amantis erat.
>
> (11-22)

She feared *graviora pericula veris*, strange words, but clear in
their implications: (1) Odysseus' troubles were not, after all, so
great. (2) Penelope's suffering was even larger than his, because
of her exaggerated anxiety. The same point is made at 13 where
fingebam is no chance word. *Fingo* often carries a connotation of
untruth, the imaginary.[36] Penelope suffered in such fantasies, but
fantasies they were, products of her concerned imagination.
Ulysses never underwent these perils (perhaps the unreality of
this attack on Ulysses is emphasized in the future participle,
ituros). The generalization of 12 places the burden of suffering
on her shoulders. Just as the *amor* has been on her side, not his,
so has she, not he, been the real sufferer all these years.

---

[35] Contrast Penelope's plaints at *Od.* 19.510ff; 20.83ff.

[36] E.g., Ovid *Am.* 3.10.19; *AA* 2.631; 3.798, 801. *Fingo* is commonly so
used by Lucretius; for a list of examples, see L. Lenaghan, *TAPA* 98 (1967)
233, n. 41.

In four distichs (15-22) the whole Trojan war is encapsulated as a piece of Penelope's life. Each distich moves from the plains of Troy to the mind of Penelope. Hexameter recounts an event at Troy, pentameter reveals Penelope as its victim. The structure of 13-24 is carefully worked out. Ulysses is mentioned only in the first and last lines, which complement each other. In the first he is in danger, under attack by the Trojans; in the last he is finally safe. In this passage there are only two references to Troy (Trojans) and they too occur in the first and last lines. In contrast to Ulysses, in the first they are on the attack, while in the last they are totally destroyed. Similarly, the description of the war begins with a picture of a Hector who is alive, terrifying, and murdering (14-15), and it ends (temporarily) with a Hector who is dead, mangled, but still terrifying (36).[37]

I digress briefly to consider the problem of Antilochus' death. He was traditionally killed not by Hector but by Memnon.[38] Some have pointed to *victum* (15) and assumed that the reference is not to his death but only to a defeat, i.e., his flight from Hector (*Il.* 15.585ff).[39] However, Tolkiehn's objection[40] that this is too trivial an incident to be mentioned together with the deaths of Patroclus and Tlepolemus seems valid, especially when we consider the summary statement at 21, *quisquis erat iugulatus*. Moreover, one could scarcely say that Antilochus was *victus* in the *Iliad* passage. He merely runs off when he sees Hector coming. Others (e.g., Meziriac, Parrhasius) have argued that the error is deliberate, part of Ovid's characterization of Penelope. Though this seems more an attempt to avoid than meet the problem, we must remember that other works of literature have occasionally

[37] At 36 read with Loers, Palmer, Dörrie, and others *lacer admissos*. The alternative, *alacer missos*, which Giomini adopts, seems pointless. Perhaps the strongest support for *lacer admissos* comes from the clear imitation of this verse (often noted) at *Cons. Liv.* 319-320, where *sanguinolentus* represents Ovid's *lacer* and *admissos* is a direct echo.

[38] *Od.* 4.187f; Pind. *Pyth.* 6.28ff; *Aithiopis* (*EGF* p. 33 Kinkel). To be sure, Hyg. *Fab.* 113 reports Hector as Antilochus' killer, but the testimony seems weak indeed, coming in the midst of a series of apparent errors and following on the statement in *Fab.* 112 that Memnon slew Antilochus. Dares (34) strangely writes that Paris killed Antilochus.

[39] E.g., R. Ehwald, *BPW* 16 (1896) 1515.

[40] J. Tolkiehn, *Homer und die römische Poesie* (Leipzig 1900) 144, n. 10.

made effective use of the deliberate error.[41] Yet, here such an approach will not do, since this naïve error does not fit the characterization of Penelope. Besides, we will have to ask why Ovid them limits her naïve ignorance to this one case. One hesitates to attribute this mistake to forgetfulness or carelessness on Ovid's part, especially in view of the correct and specific designation in 19, where Ovid has been careful enough to accurately designate the nationality of Tlepolemus' killer. Yet, there seems to be no other explanation, and, in this case, there are some reasons for assuming an error. That Memnon killed Antilochus is mentioned but once in Homer, and that only in passing in the *Odyssey* (4.187f). It is not described in the *Iliad*. Further, one remembers that an important element of this letter is Telemachus' journey to Pylos (37-38, 63-64, 99-100). Thus, Ovid had his eye on the third book of the *Odyssey*. This was probably one cause of his using the example of Antilochus, for Nestor does mention the death of his son (3.111f). However, he simply states the fact of his death at Troy and does not mention his killer. Moreover, he touches on Antilochus' death immediately after he has mentioned the death of Patroclus. One must note that the deaths of these same two heroes are juxtaposed in the epistle (15-18). Thus, it seems possible that the mention of Antilochus' death together with that of Patroclus in *Od.* 3.110ff suggested to Ovid that Antilochus, like Patroclus, had been killed by Hector. Some corroboration of this view, that Ovid misinterpreted Nestor's narrative, may derive from Penelope's language. Most important is the fact that Antilochus' death is not described directly by Homer, but is mentioned second-hand by Nestor. Penelope's language suggests that Ovid was indeed looking to this passage: *sive quis Antilochum narrabat . . . victum . . . / sive Menoetiaden . . . cecidisse. Narrabat* is crucial. Contrast this with *Tlepolemus Lyciam tepefecerat hastam*. There is no report here, no indirect discourse, for Tlepolemus' death is not told second-hand in Homer, but described directly in the *Iliad* (5.628ff).

To return. At last the war ends: *Sed bene consuluit casto deus aequus amori:/ Versa est in cineres sospite Troia viro* (23-24). If earlier Penelope was war's victim, here she is its hero. The impli-

<hr />

[41] In recent times one thinks of Joseph Heller's *Catch* 22. Also, a satire called *A History of the Modern Age* (1971) by "Julian Prescott" constantly misspells Robert McNamara's name, evidently as an inside joke.

cation of 23, especially with the triple juxtaposition of divine intervention and chaste wife (*consuluit casto; casto deus; aequus amori*), is inevitable. It is Penelope's good faith that has been the determining factor: the Greeks owe her the victory.

The Greeks return. The account is spare, purely factual, but rich with understated, indeed unspoken, pathos:

> Argolici rediere duces, altaria fumant,
> ponitur ad patrios barbara praeda deos.
> Grata ferunt nymphae pro salvis dona maritis;
> illi victa suis Troia fata canunt:
> Mirantur † iustique † senes trepidaeque puellae,
> narrantis coniunx pendet ab ore viri.
>
> (25-30)

The war is over. All the world, both animate and inanimate, both mortal and immortal, once again receives what it has lacked for many years. Fulfillment is everywhere. The altars receive sacrifices, the gods booty, the nymphs gifts.[42] Most important, the old men have their sons and wives their husbands returned to them. Everything is restored to its normal state; all nature, all humankind regain what is theirs—only Penelope is excluded. Her anguish is subtly sharpened: *Grata ferunt nymphae pro salvis dona maritis* (27). Gifts are brought by wives on behalf of *salvis maritis*. Her husband too is safe (*sospite . . . viro*, 24), but she can offer no gifts for him. The inexplicability of her position magnifies her suffering. The position of *viri* at the end of 30 recalls *viro* at the end of 24 and heightens the contrast between those other wives who are reunited with their husbands and Penelope who is still alone. Perhaps there is special significance in the recollections of a veteran (30ff), for certainly the most famous recollections of a Trojan war hero were those of Ulysses in *Od.* 9-12, even if they were not actually of the war proper. If one is meant to think of this, the irony is clear. Penelope's husband is *sospes* like the others, and, indeed, he too spends much time in describ-

---

[42] Though *ferunt nymphae* is probably better taken to mean "the wives bring." For an extensive discussion, see Palmer *ad loc*. His hesitant conclusion is that the words mean "the nymphs receive." Both interpretations, however, find difficulty in *nymphae*. Professor Highet suggests to me that *nymphae* implies that the women are like new brides again, after a long separation. One wonders whether the unusual introduction of the word here has something to do with the allusive role played in the poem by the nymph Calypso.

ing his adventures—but to strangers, not to his wife. Further, the language *narrantis coniunx pendet ab ore viri*, as has often been remarked, is a deliberate echo of another Trojan war veteran's narrations: *pendetque iterum narrantis ab ore* (*Aen.* 4.79). Perhaps the verbal reminiscence points the reader to Ulysses' narrative at the court of Alcinous, which was the model for Aeneas' narrative to Dido. One further wonders whether the implication might be that Penelope considers even Dido more fortunate than she.[43]

Omnia namque tuo senior te quaerere misso/ rettulerat nato Nestor, at ille mihi (37-38). Anderson remarks, "This is a rather ingenious addition of Ovid's, drawn from his own imagination, to account for Penelope's knowledge of the events."[44] But there is a palpable difficulty here. Penelope has just described the returning veterans narrating the events of the war. Why now abandon this fact and make Telemachus' mission to Nestor the source of her information? Also, what exactly does *omnia* refer to? It might refer to verses 15-22, but the implication there seems that Penelope heard of these battles while the war was in progress. I suspect that, in fact, it refers to 25-36. In the *Odyssey* Ulysses goes to Troy with a substantial company of Ithacan citizens. Many survived the war and made the homeward journey with him. But on the trip home, all, to a man, were lost. When Ulysses ultimately does return to Ithaca, he does so as the lone Ithacan to return from the war. Thus, the Homeric situation is clear. No one returned from Troy to Ithaca. The complexion of verses 25ff is completely changed. *Argolici rediere duces*, but not the Ithacans. The smoking altars, the joyous wives and fathers—these were not scenes in Ithaca: Penelope saw none of this. The mere knowledge of the happy return of many warriors throughout

---

[43] Perhaps another ill-fated couple is also meant to be thought of, Mars and Venus. See Lucr. 1.38 where the language is very similar to that here, though the scene described is different. On this passage in the letter (31-36) Ovid seems to have written his own commentary. At *AA* 2.123ff Ulysses narrates events of the war, as the soldier does here, to Calypso. The passage clearly echoes ours. The soldier draws Troy with wine, Ulysses with a stick in the sand. *Haec . . . Troia est . . ./ hic tibi sit Simois; haec mea castra puta* (133-134) strongly recalls 33-35 of *Heroides* 1. Echoes are also present in the mention of Dolon, Rhesus, the horses. Perhaps we may take this as an allusion on Ovid's part to the fact that Penelope does indeed know of Calypso.

[44] P. 20.

Greece while she remains alone and waiting suffices to produce this vivid and pathetic tableau of self-pity.

Again, Penelope sees herself as the victim of the events at Troy: *Usque metu micuere sinus, dum victor amicum/ dictus es Ismariis isse per agmen equis* (45-46). The preceding lines are of particular value in the light they cast on Ovid's characterization of Penelope and its difference from Homer's:

> Rettulit et ferro Rhesumque Dolonaque caesos,
>   utque sit hic somno proditus, ille † dolo †.
> Ausus es, o nimium nimiumque oblite tuorum,
>   Thracia nocturno tangere castra dolo
> totque simul mactare viros adiutus ab uno!
> At bene cautus eras et memor ante mei.
>
> (39-44)

The tone is mock heroic. The description is bitingly sarcastic, even insulting, designed to show Ulysses' heroic deeds as acts of petty cowardice and baseness. How does Ulysses accomplish his feats of daring? The means he utilizes are emphasized by their position, at the end of the hemistich and at the end of the verse (40). To overcome by making use of *somnus* and *dolus* is scarcely characteristic of the heroic nature. True, *dolus* was Ulysses' forte and usually admirable, but what *dolus* was involved here? Many scholars, unable to perceive any real stratagem in the capture and murder of Dolon, emend.[45] Palmer hesitatingly accepts *dolo* and explains, "Ulysses and Diomedes hid themselves until Dolon had passed them by," but it is clear that even he doubts this explanation, for he appends, "a very elementary *dolus* indeed." The *dolus* here is most probably the fact that Ulysses gets Dolon to reveal the desired information by causing him to believe that his life is in no danger (*Il.* 10.382ff), but then allows Diomedes to kill him nevertheless. This interpretation is supported by *proditus*, which must be taken with *dolo* as well as with *somno*. Dolon was not simply tricked, he was betrayed, for he was slain after receiving a guarantee that his life was safe. With *proditus* Ulysses is now reduced to a cheap liar and false coward. This stratagem, if it may be so designated, is worthy of nothing but scorn.

Lines 41ff are heavily sarcastic, beginning with the scornful *ausus es*: it required no boldness to attack and murder sleeping

---

[45] I wonder whether *somno . . . dolo* might be a reminiscence of Medea plotting murderous revenge δόλῳ . . . καὶ σιγῇ (Eur. *Med.* 391).

men. *Mactare* is pointed: it was a slaughter no more heroic than killing an animal for a sacrifice. Ulysses killed so many men *adiutus ab uno* (43). Once again this is no error on Ovid's part nor is it a case of "Ovid [giving] Ulysses the larger share in the nightly exploit."[46] It is simply the height of disdain, for in fact all Ulysses did was pull away the dead bodies after Diomedes had done the killing (*Il.* 10.488ff). The great hero Ulysses did nothing bold; his part was so small that one could barely say that Diomedes was *adiutus ab uno*; to say that Ulysses was, when he did virtually nothing, is sheer contempt. The stress, once more, is on the illusory and false nature of Ulysses' dangers and troubles. Whatever risk there was was Diomedes'; the deed was his. The irony continues: *at bene cautus eras et memor ante mei* (44). Indeed, Ulysses was cautious enough, letting Diomedes do all the actual killing and limiting himself to the safer tasks, but was he thinking of Penelope or of himself when he did so? What Penelope thinks is evident.[47]

In short, Ovid's Penelope is only too ready to see Ulysses as considerably less than a great hero and to use this bitterly against him. What is important here is not the portrait of Ulysses,[48] but its occurrence in the mouth of Penelope. The Homeric heroine never betrays the slightest breath of doubt as to her husband's heroic character.

Once again the war is reduced to a one-to-one correspondence

---

[46] Palmer *ad loc.*

[47] If my interpretation of 39-44 needs further support, herewith two points: (1) This passage seems modeled on *Aen.* 1.469ff, wherein the murder of Rhesus and his men is depicted as a horrible and gruesome event; note *prodita somno* (470), the butchery of the slaying (*multa . . . caede cruentus*, 471), and the fact that Ulysses is not even mentioned, so small a role is his in this deed. (2) In the *armorum iudicium* episode of Ovid's *Metamorphoses* Ulysses is abused by Ajax in precisely the same fashion as he is here mocked by Penelope. Ajax too refers to the slaughter of Dolon and Rhesus and observes that it was accomplished at night, by stealth, and when the victims were unprepared. In addition, he notes that Diomedes performed the larger share of the deed (*Met.* 13.98-104). This episode may also confirm my interpretation of *dolo* (40), for Ulysses, in his speech, boasts of his success in eliciting important information from Dolon before killing him (244-246).

[48] Ulysses had received a bad press for a very long time. See especially W. B. Stanford, *The Ulysses Theme: A Study in the Adaptability of a Traditional Hero* (New York 1964²), chapters 7, 8, 12. The episode Ovid focuses on, *the Doloneia*, may have been the burden of Epicharmus' ridicule of Odysseus in his Ὀδυσσεὺς αὐτόμολος.

with Penelope (as earlier at 5ff): *Sed mihi quid prodest vestris disiecta lacertis/ Ilios et murus quod fuit esse solum* (47-48). What good does the fall of Troy, engineered by her husband, do her? The contrast in *mihi/ vestris* may be between Ulysses' lot and hers.[49] The war, victorious end notwithstanding, proves an exercise in vanity: *maneo, qualis Troia durante manebam* (49).

After this brief introverted lament, Penelope returns to Ulysses, now with more intense, less concealed rebuke: *Victor abes nec scire mihi, quae causa morandi/ aut in quo lateas ferreus orbe, licet* (57-58). *Victor abes*; the juxtaposition is sharp. Though victorious and therefore long due home, Ulysses persists in absenting himself. The theme of delay (*mora*) is common in erotic elegy, applied to the lover who stays away.[50] *Ferreus* is used in the same context[51] and *lateas* is crystal clear: Odysseus is almost hiding from Penelope. Nor should *licet* be missed, especially coming as it does at the very end of the distich which began with *victor*. Ulysses, being so powerful and successful, could somehow inform her, but he deliberately does not. This section of the poem concludes and climaxes with Penelope's outright suggestion that Ulysses has repaid her faithfulness with faithlessness (75-76) and with scorn (77-78).

The poem's final movement takes a new direction (81-116). These verses are, to a degree rare in the *Heroides*, calculated to persuade. Though this may seem only reasonable given the context and the epistolary format, the very existence of such argument is non- or anti-Homeric, for it itself implies that Penelope considers Ulysses' absence deliberate and willful. Moreover, the manner of the argument is revealing and unexpected (from a Homeric perspective). It is subtle, sophisticated, and suggestive. Her first approach is threatening. It is nothing less than an attempt to make Ulysses think that he may lose Penelope, that she cannot be taken for granted even though she is faithful, because external forces more powerful than she may compel her to marry anew. It is therefore to Ulysses' advantage to return as quickly as possible if he wishes and intends to keep her. *Viduo discedere lecto* (81) and the emphatic *cogit* (82) are explicit and sugges-

---

[49] Ulysses is, of course, included in—and indeed an important part of—the plural "you."

[50] E.g., Ovid *Am.* 1.11.8.

[51] E.g., Prop. 2.8.12.

tive.[52] In *immensas increpat usque moras* (82) there is again an implicit contrast between Ulysses' and Penelope's behavior, for the statement is ambiguous. Are the *moras* Ulysses' in not returning home or are they Penelope's in not remarrying? The ambiguity is pointed. Ulysses delays and thereby displays his faithlessness, Penelope delays and thereby demonstrates her faithfulness. But in spite of all Penelope resists her father and endures: *Increpet usque licet! Tua sum, tua dicar oportet;/ Penelope coniunx semper Ulixis ero* (83-84). These two verses have been much discussed. Purser remarks, "The constancy of Penelope leads to one fine outburst,"[53] and then quotes *tua . . . ero*. Anderson observes that, "here is where the real discrepancy between Ovid and Homer comes in, not in the conduct of Icarius but in that of Penelope herself. In Homer she is represented as hesitating, and we cannot but think that if Odysseus had only been a little later, he might have found things quite different."[54] This is to misunderstand the significance of Penelope's remark in the Epistle, and perhaps to misconstrue the situation in the *Odyssey*. Both Purser and Anderson consider these two verses a noble profession of everlasting love, the epitome of the characterization of Penelope (as they see it). Some have been so charmed by these verses that they have undertaken to rewrite the Epistle to improve it, or, to adopt their terms, to restore it to its original Ovidian state. Since these two verses represent in their eyes the apex of the letter, they quite naturally belong at the very end to provide the poem with a lofty conclusion, and so 81-84 are transferred to the end.[55] This view is, of course, based on the traditional misreading of the whole poem. Such a declaration ending the poem would tend to emphasize her dignity, loyalty, and no-

---

[52] This is a slight exaggeration of the situation in the *Odyssey* where Icarius (and other kin) κέλονται (15.16-17) and ὀτρύνουσι (19.158-159) Penelope to marry.

[53] *Apud* Palmer, p. xviii.

[54] P. 27.

[55] So e.g., H. S. Sedlmayer, *Kritischer Commentar zu Ovids Heroiden* (Wien 1880) 6-7. In Wilkinson's words (84). "The nineteenth century laid arrogant hands on the work of many ancient authors." He then cites the *Heroides* as a prime example. For a list of the many exclusions and transpositions proposed in this epistle, see Eggerding 224-225. Loers, *ad* 1.103, well states that the transpositions commonly advocated for 97-110 are proposed "maiore audacia et peiore sententia."

bility, if for no other reason than by virtue of its emphatic position. But Ovid does not end with this, because it is not his aim to do so. Rather, it is his goal to show her susceptibility to common human passions and feelings. Sellar is worth quoting, "What Penelope wants in Ovid is the quality that Ovid himself was so deficient in—dignity."[56] Though one might dispute the value judgment implicit, the description of Penelope is quite right. She does lack dignity, and it was precisely Ovid's purpose to so depict her.

But a close examination of 83-84 will reveal that these verses are not as simple as they look. They are not a heartfelt profession of eternal love. The language is rather stiff, formal, impassive, almost cold. The impersonal *oportet* with its implication, the formal *Penelope coniunx*, convey the feeling of a devotion emanating from a sense of duty and obligation, not from affection and love. *Tua sum* is equally its reciprocal, *meus es*.

The attempt at persuasion continues. Her father is an external force she can cope with, but the suitors are perhaps a different story: they are many, they are powerful, they are compelling. At first she speaks in general terms, relating where the suitors come from and what they are doing in Ulysses' house (87-90). Then comes the forceful *praeteritio* (91-94) mentioning by name some of the suitors.[57] These are no abstract and shadowy rivals, but flesh and blood men whom Ulysses probably knows himself. This is clearly an attempt to make Ulysses jealous.[58] Penelope is here no less than a disciple of Ovid himself, following the instructions set down by the *magister amoris*:[59] to assure your *vir*'s affections, remember to arouse his jealousy by making him believe that powerful rivals exist.

[56] W. Y. Sellar, *Poets of the Augustan Age, II: Horace and the Elegiac Poets* (repr. New York 1965) 334.

[57] The inclusion of Medon among the suitors is problematic. Though the *Odyssey* does represent him as a favorite of the suitors (17.172-173), he is always loyal to Penelope. I believe that the element of persuasion is here the determining factor. Penelope exaggerates her plight: even old faithful Medon has turned against me (Medon, after all, had virtually raised Telemachus [22.357-358]). Perhaps the addition of the adjective *dirum* is meant to counterbalance the expectation of his constant devotion.

[58] See the perceptive remarks of S. Mariotti, *Belfagor* 12 (1957) 618-619. His general observations also deserve attention: "In questa lettera come in quella di Briseide il materiale omerico è trasferito con abilità a esprimere un gusto ormai lontanissimo da quello di Omero" (619).

[59] See e.g., *Am.* 1.8.95ff; *AA* 3.599ff.

This argument flows imperceptibly into the next, an attempt to shame Ulysses into returning. His property is being destroyed: *quos omnes turpiter absens/ ipse tuo partes sanguine rebus alis* (93-94). The mode of expression, rather than rebuking the suitors, shifts the blame to Ulysses. They do not feed on his property; rather, he feeds them, he nourishes and maintains their activities by his delay. Nor is Penelope able to prevent them. She and the few on her side are too weak. At this point the tone changes; her appeal now is on behalf of Ulysses' son and father. Line 111 is effective: *Est tibi, sitque precor natus.* It is a virtual reminder to Ulysses that he does have a son, for he went off to the war when Telemachus was still but an infant. He has a dependent child and a responsibility to him.

The relationship between 97ff and Homer seems to have gone unnoticed, but in fact these verses are a strong indication of Ovid's familiarity with and close use of the *Odyssey*. They are an adaptation of *Od.* 14.172ff. In both passages, Penelope, Laertes, and Telemachus are listed in succession and in the same order. Laertes is modified in Homer by γέρων and in Ovid by *senex*. In both, the mention of Telemachus leads to a discussion of his journey to Pylos and the ambush by the suitors. One should note the changes Ovid makes to adapt the passage to his own purposes. Penelope, who goes without a modifier in Homer, is described as *sine viribus uxor*, and Telemachus, called θεοειδής in Homer, is here merely a *puer*. Both changes increase the emphasis placed on Penelope's helplessness. For the same reason Ovid leaves out the extravagant description of Telemachus' virtues which is present in Homer (175ff), and phrases them later simply in terms of a future hope (107).

Penelope's stratagem to stir up Ulysses' jealousy led her to enumerate the suitors. For the immediate purpose of rousing envy, simply listing them would be sufficient. Once, however, the suitors are mentioned, she cannot but remark their disgraceful occupation of Ulysses' household. To demonstrate that she is unable to prevent this, she undertakes to list her meager forces. But when she reaches Telemachus, she reacts emotionally and is led off on a digression (99-102) about his recent adventures which culminates in a wish that neatly incorporates her two desires, that Telemachus live and that Ulysses return home. Only then does she return to listing those on her side (103-104). When she has finished, she proceeds to explain how weak they are and why. Thus, Laertes is too old (105-106), Telemachus too young (107-108), and she merely a weak woman (109). This leads direct-ly to her plea to Ulysses to return and save them all.[60] But once again her recent mention of Laertes and Telemachus catches her up emotionally, and she returns to them. Now, however, she uses them as an emotional base in a new attempt to persuade Ulysses: *precor* (111), *mollibus* (111), *patrias* (112) are all calculated to play on his emotions. So too *respice Laerten* (113), with its impli-cation that Laertes too eagerly longs for his return. The ritual of 113 recalls 102, but now Penelope is completely out of the picture (unlike 102; note *meos*). She calls on Ulysses as the son of Laertes to fulfill his filial obligation. Lines 111-112 hark back to 107-108. Thus, *sitque* recalls *vivat modo; mollibus annis* contrasts with *fortior aetas; patrias artes* recalls *auxiliis . . . patris*. But the emo-tional connotations and the connection between father and son are much stronger in the later couplet. This is fine. Penelope turns away from herself and, in effect, writes herself out of the picture. If Ulysses cares too little for her to return, perhaps his concern and affection for his father and son will hit home. But in the end, for one last gasp, Penelope returns to herself, her suffer-ing, her plight, her unhappy fate: *Certe ego, quae fueram te dis-cedente puella,/ protinus ut venias, facta videbor anus* (115-116). This is the lament of a wasted life. In middle age Penelope can only see that in her long years of waiting life has passed her by. Her situation, as she has reminded us (49), has been character-ized by its sameness. For her nothing seems to have changed. But

---

[60] At 110 Dörrie follows Palmer, Bornecque, and Giomini in reading *portus et ara tuis*. I do not see much good reason for abandoning the better attested *aura*. The examples usually brought to support *ara* (Apul. *Met.* 11.15; Ovid *Pont.* 2.8.68), while conclusively demonstrating the validity of the collocation *portus et ara*, may not be quite relevant since in each case the sense-unit involved necessitates a physical, concrete refuge (*ad portum quietis et aram misericordiae; portus et ara fugae*); *aura* would be quite impossible. Here no such restrictions exist. The metaphor of the ship of love is not uncommon. Its basic elements are "ship, nautical conditions, and port." Thus, *aura* fits perfectly, while *ara* breaks down the image. If Penelope here is the floundering ship, Ulysses is both desirable breeze and harbor for her, two favorable things for a ship in danger. One might recall the metaphori-cal *flatus* (with reference to love affairs) at Prop. 2.25.27 and the analogy of endangered and wrecked ships a few lines earlier (23-24). On the "ship of love" see W. S. Anderson, *CP* 61 (1966) 93-98 (the quotation above is taken from p. 94). For the metaphor in post-Classical European literature, see D. C. Allen, *MLN* 76 (1961) 311-312.

time stands not still and *she* has changed. Even should Ulysses return forthwith—as he will—he will only find an *anus*, not the *puella* he left two decades earlier.[61] But not merely twenty years have passed; so has Penelope's life. Fulfillment is gone. For Ovid's Penelope there will not, there cannot, be a reunion of the order that Homer portrayed in the *Odyssey*'s final books.

It is nothing new to observe that the world of the *Heroides* is not the epic or tragic world in which these myths had their strongest flowerings. It is, however, not accurate to refer to Ovid's heroines as Roman women of the Augustan age in an Augustan milieu as, e.g., Sellar has done, "Penelope is not the Penelope of the Odyssey, the worthy wife of the great Ulysses, but a Roman wife of the Augustan age, longing for the return of her husband from the war."[62] The world of the heroines is not the world of Augustus; it is something closer to the world of Roman erotic elegy,[63] though this analogy should not be pressed either. D'Elia is right when he calls Ovid's Penelope a lover,[64] and Pichon's notice of "son petit mouvement de coquetterie"[65] is quite correct. And it is evident that Ovid's heroines speak the language of erotic elegy.[66] In fact, this epistle does not center around the specific epic heroic theme of a soldier off at war while his wife remains at home.[67] Rather, the crucial theme is the familiar one from Latin elegy of two lovers, one of whom no longer comes to

---

[61] The image of Penelope as *anus* Ovid may have inherited from Propertius (2.9.8). It is, of course, un-Homeric. In the *Odyssey* Penelope remains beautiful and desirable (18.187-213). Whether the conception goes back to Comedy cannot be determined; to be sure, it is not comic here. The *anus* motif is common in love poetry, e.g., Hor. *C.* 1.25, 4.13; Ovid *AA* 3.69-70 (this last verse, *frigida deserta nocte iacebis anus*, contains many of the erotic-elegiac themes present in *Heroides* 1). It occurs in an epigram by Callimachus (?) *AP* 5.23.

[62] *Op. cit.* (supra n. 56) 333.

[63] The language of the *"laudatio Turiae"* shows how far the actual world of Augustus was from the world of erotic elegy.

[64] P. 133.

[65] R. Pichon, *Histoire de la Littérature Latine* (Paris 1930¹²) 415.

[66] In addition to the examples already observed in *Heroides* 1, we might note the ironic variations on the theme of lovers using wine and gestures to communicate secretly (e.g., Tib. 1.6.19-20; Ovid *Am.* 1.4.19-20) at 31ff, and on the metaphor of "throwing to the winds" as a reflection of the fickleness of lovers (e.g., Cat. 70.3-4; Tib. 1.4.21-22) at 79.

[67] One should, however, remember that Propertius had adapted to the erotic sphere (4.3) the theme of a soldier at war away from his woman.

see the other, who naturally suspects that he (or she) is being betrayed. Ovid has attached—and well integrated—to this erotic-elegiac base the details of the heroic myth.

Once we free ourselves from the dogma of the Homeric Penelope and begin to understand the uniqueness of Ovid's character-ization, certain puzzling details can be explained. As Palmer says (*ad* 1.10), "It is strange that Ovid did not make more use of the story of Penelope's web." The absence of her web-trick is particu-larly striking, since this act of guile is one of the two basic motifs which later generations crystallized from Homer's Penelope and allude to over and again. Ovid himself can sum up the whole *Odyssey* as *tardaque nocturno tela retexta dolo* (*Am.* 3.9.30). An-derson writes,[68] "According to Homer, Penelope was to choose one of the suitors when she finished the winding-sheet. Ovid did not wish to bring this in because he represents her as unwavering in mind." This misses on three counts: (1) It misconstrues the sig-nificance of the trick in the *Odyssey*, wherein it is seen as a re-flection of Penelope's fidelity. In fact, the numerous post-Homeric references to it commonly see it as a manifestation of her virtue. (2) It assumes that Ovid's goal was to depict an unwavering pious heroine. This, as we have seen, is false. (3) It neglects the impli-cation of Penelope's weaving at verses 9-10. Had Ovid desired to leave out of account Penelope's ruse, he would have ignored all mention of weaving. As it is, once Penelope refers to her loom, it is inevitable that the reader think of her famous trick. Thus, in the very mention of weaving, Ovid has fashioned a clever irony, but in avoiding an explicit allusion to the trick he has Penelope conceal it from Ulysses. One concludes that she does not relate her act of guile to Ulysses because she does not want to establish and confirm her faithfulness toward him; she does not want to give Ulysses the impression that she has been totally and abso-lutely devoted to him. To assert in vague and general terms that she is faithful (as she does) is one thing; to give concrete evidence of the fact is something else—and it is not what Penelope wants to do.

For the reader, Penelope's account of her activity at the loom has additional point: *nec mihi quaerenti spatiosam fallere noctem/ lassaret viduas pendula tela manus* (9-10). The lonely girl wiling away time at the loom while her lover is away is familiar from Latin literature,[69] but when the woman is Penelope the scene takes on added coloring, for she works at the loom not simply to pass the hours of loneliness, but, more significantly, to preserve her marriage. One must also observe the manner in which Ovid has transferred the Homeric fact of Penelope's weaving to the erotic-elegiac milieu. In the *Odyssey* she is described as working and weaving only during the daytime (19.513ff). Ovid shifts her weaving to the night and thereby accomplishes two things: He focuses our attention on her activity at the loom at night, i.e., on her unravelling of the web in order to deceive the suitors, and, perhaps more important, by placing the woman at the loom at night, he sets us in the midst of the elegiac world, as the lonely woman eagerly awaits the nocturnal visit of her lover.[70]

We turn to the problem of Telemachus' mission: *Nos Pylon, antiqui Neleia Nestoris arva,/ misimus; incerta est fama remissa Pylo;/ misimus et Sparten; Sparte quoque nescia veri* (63-65). Given not only the Odyssean journey of Telemachus to Pylos and Sparta, but also the references in this poem at 37-38 and 100, there can be no doubt that Penelope means that she sent Telemachus in search of information. This is, of course, out of harmony with the *Odyssey* wherein Penelope knows nothing of her son's journey till much later. Palmer thought (*ad* 37) that "Ovid forgets the Homeric story." Anderson reasonably objected, "Ovid could scarcely have been ignorant that in Homer it is Athena that sends Telemachus," and argues, "Ovid wishes to make Penelope take a more active interest in Odysseus's return."[71] This explication, however, grows out of the view that Ovid wishes to increase Penelope's nobility and enhance her character as faithful wife. This, as I have tried to demonstrate, misreads the nature of the Ovidian Penelope.

Though it seems not to have been observed, one might here argue reliance on another source. Perhaps some treatment of the myth did depict Penelope as bidding Telemachus to undertake

[69] Cf. Prop. 1.3.41 and note how the whole erotic context there is similar to that of this epistle.

[70] Cf., e.g., Prop. 1.3. One wonders whether there is special significance in *spatiosam noctem* in view of the fact that the night of the reunion of Penelope and Ulysses was divinely lengthened (*Od.* 23.241-246).

[71] P. 24.

265

this mission. In support, one could point to a fifth century vase[72] which shows a standing Telemachus speaking to his seated mother. Could this not be Telemachus receiving instructions from Penelope for this journey, and perhaps have its roots in a literary version? Well, it could be, but we have no good reason to believe that it is; to be sure, there are equally plausible alternatives to this interpretation.

I do not think that Ovid is representing Penelope here as the instigator of Telemachus' journey. Rather, Penelope so represents herself; less than politely, she prevaricates. The motivation is again of a persuasive nature. In taking direct action, she has effectively marked a break with her past. No more waiting, no more dutiful sitting till Ulysses returns. She has taken a decisive act. She has actively sought Ulysses out, failed, and now. . . . Now what? Perhaps she can now feel free to marry again. At any rate, this is what Penelope wants Ulysses to believe, that she has taken an action which represents, in effect, a last resort. Anything may happen now.

Closely allied with this passage are verses 99-100: *Ille per insidias paene est mihi nuper ademptus,/ dum parat invitis omnibus ire Pylon.* Palmer (*ad loc.*) states, "This again does not quite agree with Homer, for the suitors did not know of the actual departure of Telemachus until it was accidentally learned by Antinous, *Od.* 4.632ff: nor did they oppose the project when he tells them of it, 2.319; 2.214." Palmer seems to have misread his Homer. The suitors do not object when Telemachus proposes the journey in Book Two, but only because of their firm belief that it is impossible for him to execute this mission. The fact that he goes without their knowledge, and indeed has to do so, points up their reluctance. *Od.* 4.663ff show clearly how unwilling the suitors are. As soon as they hear of his departure, they become worried and fearful and begin to plot against him. *Invitis*, consequently, is very appropriate. Ovid has read his Homer well. Loers (*ad loc.*), however, has put his finger on a real problem. He notes that *invitis omnibus* is inconsistent with Penelope's earlier statement that she sent Telemachus. Anderson and Showerman have attempted to obviate the difficulty by claiming that *omnibus* refers only to the suitors.[73] But to exclude Penelope from *omni-*

[72] J. D. Beazley, *Attic Red-Figure Vase-Painters*[2] (Oxford 1963) 1300.2.
[73] Anderson 29. G. Showerman, tr., *Ovid: Heroides and Amores* (Cambridge, Mass. 1947) 19, translates *omnibus* "all of them."

bus is very strained, probably impossible. In fact, *invitis omnibus* is a fairly accurate description of the situation in the *Odyssey*. In other words, the truth (as set forth in *Od.* 17.41ff) here slips out. Ovid gives us, so to speak, a retrospective key to an earlier puzzle. *Misimus* was a falsification; presently caught up in her anxiety for her son, Penelope forgets her previous claim. In fact, she had not even wanted him to go.

Scholars have noted that *dum parat . . . ire Pylon* (100) contradicts the Homeric story in which the attempted ambush takes place on Telemachus' return to Ithaca.[74] This is a discrepancy which one hesitates to consider an error. Ovid could hardly have forgotten that the suitors plot to kill Telemachus on his return. Why, however, he should have made such a change seems equally perplexing. I suspect that this is no more than a case of careless writing. Verses 99-100 seem to be an echo of *Od.* 17.41-43. *Dum parat . . . ire Pylon* recalls ἐπεὶ οἴχεο νηὶ Πύλονδε, *invitis omnibus* is a variation on ἐμεῦ ἀέκητι, and *ille per insidias paene est mihi nuper ademptus* may be a strong paraphrase of οὔ σ' ἔτ' ἐγώγε/ὄψεσθαι ἐφάμην. If this is so, Ovid, in adapting the Homeric lines to his own purpose, is guilty of slipshod expression, for he means to say, "I almost lost my son because of his plan to go to Pylos," but in both adhering to the Homeric original (e.g., ἐπεί/*dum*) and deviating from it, he has produced a misleading statement.

There is yet more willful distortion in Penelope's account of the mission. Telemachus' trip to Sparta, like that to Pylos, is described as having been in vain; no information was obtained. But the phraseology is peculiar: *Sparte quoque nescia veri* (65). Bentley preferred *vestri* (apparently with one manuscript).[75] Though *verum* is used in a totally objective sense, equivalent to "reality" (τὸ ὄν), it usually conveys a moral, subjective notion. But what place does that kind of nuance have here? We must return to Homer. Telemachus, in the third book of the *Odyssey*, goes to Pylos for information; he does not get much. Penelope's evaluation, *incerta est fama remissa Pylo* (64), is an accurate statement. But what of his journey to Sparta? Menelaus gives Telemachus a lengthy account of what he has heard and knows of Ulysses' adventures (4.332ff). He mentions, *inter alia*, that Ulysses is being

---

74 E.g., Palmer *ad loc.*

75 Or is this an acknowledged scribal error. See Giomini's *ap. crit.*

held on Ogygia by Calypso (555ff). Furthermore, when Telemachus returns to Ithaca, he recounts this to Penelope (17.142ff).[76] Thus, according to Homer, the trip to Sparta was not fruitless; Penelope's representation of it as being like the one to Pylos (note *quoque* 65) is simply not true. Penelope is not only well aware that Sparta did provide information to Telemachus, but she also knows that Ulysses is with Calypso.[77] Thus, *nescia veri* takes on special significance. Penelope knows the news from Sparta, but she does not believe it. She has heard, but she does not think it true, or rather, she would prefer not to believe it. Should we not be keyed in properly here, Ovid later gives us more retrospective clarification: *Haec ego dum stulte meditor, quae vestra libido est,/ esse peregrino captus amore potes* (75-76). This is no faint suspicion; Penelope knows. The scene is taken right from the *Odyssey*: *Forsitan et narres, quam sit tibi rustica coniunx* (77).[78] Odysseus tells Calypso that Penelope is a plain, ordinary woman (*Od.* 5.214ff), though he means it not in the pejorative colors Penelope lends it. Ironically—note *tantum* (78)—Penelope points to her small talent as a weaver, precisely that gift which she had utilized to maintain *her* fidelity to her husband.[79]

In the language of the poem lies another key to the characterization of Penelope. Its colors are largely sexual. Her marriage—or non-marriage—to Ulysses and her relationship to the suitors are explicit in their sexual point of reference: *Non ego deserto iacuissem frigida lecto* (7), *frigidus* with erotic overtones, by the way, only here in the fifteen letters; *Me pater Icarius viduo discedere lecto/ cogit* (81-82). There is nothing unusual here, though Homer's Penelope would never refer to herself as *frigida*. But 85-90 is another story. There is more here than meets the eye. *Vires temperat ipse suas* (86): *vires* is so peculiar that editors have not hesitated to emend it away or declare the distich

[76] I suspect that Telemachus' report to Penelope about Odysseus is also behind the neat turn Propertius gives the story at 4.5.7-8.

[77] That Penelope does know that Ulysses is alive is indicated by the fact that, unlike Homer's Penelope, she never thinks that Ulysses may be dead. This emphasizes her awareness of the true situation.

[78] Perhaps this verse is even sharper than it seems, for Ovid often uses *rustica* of sexual modesty, one might say prudery (e.g., *Am.* 2.4.13; *AA* 1.607, 2.369). Thus, Penelope would be representing Ulysses as even making fun of her chastity.

[79] Penelope's skill as a weaver is, of course, taken from the *Odyssey*. Cf. e.g., 2.117, 15.517.

spurious. But the unique usage adheres to the poem's idiosyncratic language. *Vires* is a (masculine) sexual word.[80] It is used both for the genitals and for sexual, procreative power.[81] Thus, Penelope identifies her father's authority with his masculine sexuality (perhaps then *pudicis* in 85 is pointed).[82]

There is nothing strange about *tulit* in 87, but it is, after all, a fertility metaphor. More interesting is 88, *turba ruunt in me luxuriosa proci*. *Luxuriosa* too is an image of fertility; used of the suitors it has a flavor of rank wantonness. *Ruunt in me* is a decidedly sexual picture.[83] Here one may make a comparison with the Homeric original (*Od.* 16.121ff). The erotic tone in Ovid does not exist in Homer: *luxuriosa* has no basis in the Homeric passage, and *ruunt in me* is Ovid's graphic and vivid representation of μνῶνται (though Homer could describe the suitors' feelings more expressively; see 18.212-213).

Inque tua regnant nullis prohibentibus aula (89). In erotic elegy the relationship between lovers is commonly spoken of in terms of ruling.[84] There is often a ruler and a ruled. *Inque tua regnant . . . aula* may thus be a metaphor for the suitors' usurpation of Ulysses' position vis-à-vis Penelope. He is losing his sexual prerogative. This is especially pointed when one recalls the *ruunt in me* of the preceding line and observes the specific *in tua aula*, for, anachronistically, *aula = atrium* and, to quote Horace, *lectus genialis in aula est*.[85] Elsewhere in the *Heroides* the husband whose wife is gone is described as being *vidua . . . in aula* (8.21, if genuine).[86]

Viscera nostra, tuae dilacerantur opes (90). That the imagery is thoroughly physical is clear, but the meaning of *viscera* is a problem. Palmer, citing parallels from Ovid, argues that it means

---

80 When Ovid uses the phrase at *Pont.* 3.6.23-24 of Augustus' kindness, the context does not lend the words any sexual coloring.

81 E.g., Plin. *HN* 11.19.60; Tac. *Ann.* 6.28 (in singular); *Priap.* 43.4. *Vis*, of course, was the term for rape.

82 A good parallel for the double-entendre play on *vires* is found at *Am.* 1.8.47 (coincidentally with regard to Penelope); cf. also Prop. 2.22.28. See further the discussion below on verse 97.

83 Cf. esp. Hor. *C.* 2.5.3-4, *ruentis/in venerem*, and Plaut. *Cas.* 890, *libet in Casinam irruere*.

84 E.g., Prop. 2.16.28, 3.10.18; Tib. 1.9.80.

85 *Epist.* 1.1.87.

86 It is interesting to note that the church fathers used *aula* to mean womb, e.g., Ambr. *Inst. Virg.* 6.44.

"our son."[87] Yet, in every case that Palmer cites (and in the one other example I know, Quint. 6. proem. 3) the context establishes beyond a shadow of a doubt that *viscera* = child. The inference is that *viscera* could not be used randomly = *filius* and be understood as such. This makes one hesitate to understand it here in the sense of "son," for context gives no direction this way at all. Further, the juxtaposition *nostra/tuae* suggests that *nostra* = *mea* and that Penelope speaks first of herself, then of Ulysses. To claim Telemachus as her own, in contrast to what belongs to Ulysses, is manifestly impossible. Owen[88] has defended *viscera* = estate here, but this seems open to two objections: (1) The phraseology suggests some contrast between the two halves of the verse; this offers none. In fact, it gives nothing but repetition. (2) *Nostra* must then mean "our," which weakens the contrast *nostra/ tua*. Moreover, what is the point of the distinction *nostra/ tua* if *viscera* and *opes* are basically identical in what they refer to?

I suppose that the problem's solution abides in the sexual connotations of *viscera*, which sometimes denotes the sexual organs.[89] I am not quite sure what the primary meaning of *viscera* is here; perhaps it is close to the colloquial American "guts," or, as Palmer translates but rejects, "my heart is rent." But not far below the surface lies a secondary level: "I am being sexually assaulted." Here the contrast: Penelope is losing control over her sexual life, Ulysses is losing control of his material possessions.

Tres sumus imbelles numero: sine viribus uxor/ Laertesque senex Telemachusque puer. It may be coincidence that *imbellis* sometimes has erotic overtones,[90] but *sine viribus uxor* can hardly not be deliberate. On the surface, it simply means that she is powerless. But it is pointedly a declaration of her existence without a sexual partner.[91] Along these lines, the sense of 109, *nec*

---

[87] In support of the notion of Telemachus being harassed or ruined, Palmer could have cited *Od.* 16.127-128 where Telemachus says that the suitors φθινύσουσιν ἔδοντες/ οἶκον ἐμόν· τάχα δή με διαρραίσουσι καὶ αὐτόν.

[88] *CR* 45 (1931) 98. Housman's view, *CR* 13 (1899) 176-177, which takes *viscera* as in apposition with *opes*, is not convincing either.

[89] *Viscera* = uterus: Ovid *Her.* 11.44; *Fast.* 1.624, 3.24; Quint. 10.3.4. *Viscera* = testicles: Petr. *Sat.* 119.21; Plin. *HN* 20.51.142. Perhaps there is sexual innuendo at Ovid *Rem.Am.* 105.

[90] Mart. 7.58.5; Juv. 6.366.

[91] For *vires* in sexual sense, see supra n. 81.

mihi sunt vires inimicos pellere tectis, is virtually, "I don't have a man to drive them away."[92]

Similarly, Laertes is *inutilis* (105), which may sometimes have sexual connotation,[93] and Telemachus is *mollibus annis* (111); *mollis* used sexually needs no documentation. If this does not go too far, the point may be that the house of Ulysses has no male sexual authority: Laertes is too old to be one, Telemachus too young, Penelope a woman.

To a degree the sexual overtones in the last part of this poem are part and parcel of the persuasive character of this section. Explicitly, Penelope writes that she is maintaining fidelity with diligence, but various forces are being brought to bear upon her —and she is weak and helpless. Underneath lie the hints: perhaps it is too late, perhaps the suitors already have had their way. This is typically Ovidian suggestiveness and love-strategy. Ambiguous language is a powerful weapon in the lover's arsenal.[94]

But the sexual language here is more, for it pervades the poem, occurring in places where the persuasive factor is minimal or nonexistent, where the element of suggestive strategy cannot be spoken of at all. Noteworthy is the following passage:

> Diruta sunt aliis, uni mihi Pergama restant,
>   incola captivo quae bove victor arat;
> iam seges est, ubi Troia fuit, resecandaque falce
>   luxuriat Phrygio sanguine pinguis humus.
>
> (51-54)

Such agricultural images are well-known for their sexual applications even in their barest form.[95] Here the description is particularly sensuous and the details are graphic in their potential

---

[92] I relegate to a footnote the hesitant suggestion that in *paene est . . . ademptus* (99) there may be a pun, i.e., *penis ademptus*, whether referring to Ulysses' absence or to her near loss of Telemachus, the last male hope of the family. There may be puns on *penis* and similarly sounding words elsewhere: *penis/paene*: Plaut. *Truc.* 518, *Pseud.* 1279; Prop. 2.34.2; *penis/poena*: Cat. 40.8; *penis/pinus*: Ovid *AA* 2.9. All this must, perforce, be highly conjectural. For a rather clear pun on penis, see Donne's *Air and Angels*, line 18, "love's pinnace."

[93] Cf. Ovid *Am.* 3.7.15. At *Her.* 15.93 the phrase *utilis aetas* seems clearly sexual in implication.

[94] See e.g., *AA* 1.489-490, 3.469ff.

[95] See e.g., *AA* 1.349-350, 381-382.

271

eroticism: *luxuriat* (as later *luxuriosa*) is rank and erotic, *pinguis* fertile and lush.[96] Nothing could be more illuminating than Ovid's own description of the girl who is ripe to be won: *mens erit apta capi tum, cum laetissima rerum/ ut seges in pingui luxuriabit humo (AA* 1.359-360). *Falx* (53) may not only be phallic,[97] but receives added coloring from its frequency as one of Priapus' main appurtenances. One could argue that the language here directly corresponds to the point implicit. Certainly, there is a contrast between the state of Troy and Penelope's condition. This was earlier evident: *Sed mihi quid prodest vestris disiecta lacertis/ Ilios et murus quod fuit esse solum,/ si maneo, qualis Troia durante manebam,/ virque mihi dempto fine carendus abest?* (47-50). Penelope's condition is ever the same, but even Troy undergoes change: from city to ruins to farmland. Change, any change, is better than the deadening sameness Penelope suffers. Perhaps implicit: Troy's "sexual existence," i.e., the fertility of its land, prospers;[98] Penelope, in contrast, has no sexual life. One need not press this interpretation.

One or two more examples. There is nothing strange about verse 19, *Sanguine Tlepolemus Lyciam tepefecerat hastam* (cf. *Pont.* 4.5.35). But perhaps the choice of vocabulary is not unrelated to the poem's dominant imagery. *Tepeo* and *tepidus* are common in erotic contexts.[99] Catullus 68.29 is apropos: *frigida deserto tepefactet membra cubili. Hasta* has phallic symbolism elsewhere.[100]

When Penelope mentions Paris, she refers to him solely in his sexual capacity (*adulter,* 6).

Quo tendam? you will now ask. In the first place, perception of the sexual language is indispensable if we are to understand properly certain passages in the poem. But from a broader perspective, the sexual language is, to some extent, literal or hints at the literal (e.g., 7, 87-88). It is also metaphorical (53-54). But it is

[96] Ovid calls a well-satisfied love a *pinguis amor* (*Am.* 2.19.25).

[97] Whether *falx* is used erotically is not certain. But I can scarcely believe that the metaphor at *AA* 3.322 is accidental.

[98] For the description of the ruined city Loers compares Prop. 4.10.29-30. It is worthwhile contrasting the two, for the lush flourishing sexuality and its concrete symbols are all Ovid's.

[99] *Tepeo*: Ovid *Am.* 2.2.53; *Rem.Am.* 7; Hor. *C.* 1.4.20; *tepidus*: Ovid *AA* 2.360.

[100] E.g., Priap. 43.1,4; Apul. *Met.* 10.21 (see the *app. crit.* of D. S. Robertson's Budé edition [Paris 1945] *ad loc.*).

essentially ethopoeic; that is, it is Penelope's style and as such the reflection of her inner person. Sex, we might say, is on her mind —or in her unconscious. This is probably an Ovidian contribution to the myth. His choice of the setting is relevant. Penelope has been without sex for twenty years; her husband has been absent ten years without explanation; she has recently heard that he has been having an affair with a nymph;[101] for many years she has been surrounded and sought by potential lovers. The product of this concatenation of circumstances is nothing short of a sex-starved, sex-obsessed woman.

Ovid was, as is well known, able to see sex anywhere. Later in life he (apologetically) described the *Odyssey* as nothing but a

[101] It is true that Calypso is said to detain Odysseus (*Od.* 1.55, 4.557ff) and that intervention by the gods is needed to free him (5.7ff), but an over-exacting reader—or an abandoned wife—may wonder just how she manages to keep him, especially when he does leave so easily when the time comes. And it is quite clear that he stays willingly with Circe and can go whenever he wishes (10.456ff). It seems that Dictys recognized this difficulty for he finds it necessary to supply Ulysses with an excuse for remaining, *utramque reginam . . . quibusdam illecebris animos hospitum ad amorem sui illicientes. inde liberatus* (6.5). The closest one gets to this in Homer is 1.56-57: αἰεὶ δὲ μαλακοῖσι καὶ αἰμυλίοισι λόγοισι/θέλγει, ὅπως Ἰθάκης ἐπιλήσεται. In fact, modern scholars and critics have displayed similar puzzlement, e.g., Stanford (supra n. 48) 45-46; G. DeF. Lord, *Sewanee Review* 62 (1954) 413; most recently R. Nickel, *Philologus* 116 (1972) 137-138. In this epistle Ovid (Penelope) seems to be viewing the Homeric episode with this same sort of suspicion. Indeed, it is possible that Ovid himself has given us substantial corroboration elsewhere: *Penelopen absens sollers torquebat Ulixes* (*AA* 2.355). Ulysses is described as *absens*, a repeated theme in our epistle (57, 66). Juxtaposed to *absens* is *sollers*. Both modify *Ulixes* and imply perhaps that he is shrewd in staying away from home. That this is the implication is supported by the context, wherein the thesis is propounded that a lover should stay away to increase the ardor of the woman. The manner of expression gives added weight to this view. *Absens Ulixes* for *absentia Ulixis* and the strong *torquebat* tend to make Ulysses the personal and direct author of her grief. (The expressive technique is very similar at *Her.* 4.96, *ibat ad hunc sapiens a sene diva viro*, where *sapiens* virtually modifies the action described in the sentence.) Verses 357-358 are also significant, both for the use of *mora* which is important in *Heroides* 1, and also for the idea of a new love, embodied in this epistle by Penelope's veiled threats to marry one of the suitors. One finds strong justification, if it be needed, for applying this line (355) to help interpret *Heroides* 1 in the simple fact that this passage in the *Ars* is clearly a deliberate reminiscence of the *Heroides*. Phyllis (353-354), Laodamia (356), and Penelope are all represented in the *Heroides* (as is Helen [359ff] whose treatment here is in many ways similar to the later letters of Paris and Helen [*H.* 16, 17]).

love story (*Tr.* 2.375-376). He could neatly turn the test of the bow into a sexual competition (*Am.* 1.8.47-48), and comically twist an Iliadic episode to make Agamemnon an Ovidian playboy (*Rem.Am.* 777ff). His propensity for this sort of thing should effectively ward off such critics who think sexual interpretation is an American psychopathology.[102] But this new Penelope is not simply the product of Ovid's witty affection for erotic twists. It is primarily the result of a new psychological attitude applied to the *Odyssey*. Centuries earlier, Greek artists had looked at Penelope, found her wanting in her very perfection, and responded by going to the other extreme, making her a base whore. Ovid, however, found Penelope, within the very context of the *Odyssey*, unsatisfying, because he could not perceive a psychologically necessary or reasonable connection between the complex situation and the character of Penelope. Gifted with psychological finesse and subtlety, he did not feel it incumbent, as did the Hellenistic writers, to destroy and dismantle Penelope in gross fashion. He sought, however, to reshape and re-create her within the context of the *Odyssey*, but in accord with his personal notions of psychological realism. Thus, his Penelope proves to be a dissatisfied, bitter woman, obsessed with sex, beset by self-pity, angry at her husband, and mourning for a lost life.[103]

A few comments are in order about the poem's interesting structure. We have noticed that there are shifts in tone, tenor, and "strategy" in the epistle. The first section is explicitly a recapitulation by Penelope of her old-time fears for Ulysses (1-56). The second part describes her attempts at getting information and her worries about his faithfulness (57-80). The last portion is basically a description of Ulysses' household and family (81-116). The divisions are rather clearly and sharply delineated, though not artificially, and there are overlaps in tone and tenor which are the natural results of an emotional, not a rational, approach to structure. These shifts on an emotional and tactical

[102] "The desire to find hitherto unsuspected sexual meanings in ancient literature frequently seems to blind American scholars to all considerations of relevance, style, and common sense." So M. L. West, *CQ* 64 (1970) 209, n. 3.

[103] The fragmentary and difficult remains of *Epigrammata Bobiensia* 36 make it, unfortunately, impossible to comprehend the characterization of Penelope in this late monologue (fourth-fifth centuries). One might see in it a dissatisfied, sexually frustrated woman, but this is speculative. It seems likely that there is Ovidian influence.

level are paralleled by the geographic movement of the letter. In very general terms, the epistle has three "scenes." The first (1-56) part takes place at Troy, the second is vaguely located: one could say its location is anywhere and everywhere (57-80). Thus, *quo . . . orbe* (58), *Pylon* (63), *Sparten* (65), *terras* (66). The final scene takes place in Ithaca (81-116). One must observe the contrasts. In the Troy portion of the poem Penelope describes her fears for Ulysses. In the Ithaca section she relates her fears for herself, Laertes, and Telemachus. There is the additional contrast between Ulysses' success in Troy and the helplessness of his family in Ithaca. In the Troy section it is Ulysses' opponents who are described, in the Ithaca section Penelope's are. In 88 the suitors are depicted as rushing at her, while in 13 the Trojans were pictured charging at Ulysses. In 97 (*tres sumus imbelles numero*) their small number points up their weakness, while in 43 (*adiutus ab uno*) the small number on Ulysses' side cannot keep him from proving victorious.

The center section is located anywhere in the world, though not in Troy (note 67ff). This vagueness mirrors the wanderings of Ulysses. It is only in this section that Penelope's suspicions are clear and explicit. Thus, 75-80 are centered on the islands of Circe and Calypso. Only when Ulysses wanders does she really doubt his loyalty. In Troy she knows he will devote himself to the war, in Ithaca to herself and the family, but when he roams, when he finds himself on Ogygia or in some other strange land, then she knows she must worry, that she must doubt his fidelity.

The Trojan section begins and ends with repeated mentions of Troy (3, 4, 49, 51, 53) and with images of the fallen city (3, 53). After the elaborate description of the destroyed city in 53-56, it is no longer the scene of any action. The transition from Troy to "anywhere" is neatly executed by *victor abes* (57), in which *victor* looks back to Troy and *abes* looks ahead to unknown places. The theme of absence in unknown lands is especially pointed in this section, which begins with *abes* (57), ends with *neve . . . abesse velis* (80), and is punctuated in the middle by *ubi lentus abes* (66). The transition to Ithaca is effected through the emphatic *me* at the beginning of 81. This shifts the focal point to Penelope herself and thereby to Ithaca. The main theme here is the weakness and helplessness of Penelope and the family, which consummates the contrast implicit since the poem's beginning with the constant stress on Ulysses' being *victor*. Thus, what Ovid has done in this poem is to adapt finely and sensibly Penelope's feelings and emotions to the chronological and geographical sequence of events from Ulysses' point of view: Troy—wanderings —Ithaca. Here lies one dynamic principle in the movement and structure of the poem.

Perhaps more than any other poem in the *Heroides* this one maintains the pretense of being a letter. It carries two obvious characteristics of the letter form which are rather rare in most of the poems, namely, the attempt to persuade and the conveyance of information unknown to the recipient. Moreover, it goes out of the way to apologize for or explain the peculiarity of writing to someone whose whereabouts are unknown or inaccessible: she gives a copy of the letter to everyone leaving Ithaca, in case the bearer should meet Ulysses (59-62). Not only that, she even refers to the possibility of a return-letter (2). This is also one of the most fluid and best-constructed of the poems. One notes that there is not a single apostrophe to someone or something aside from the addressee, rather unusual in the *Heroides*. Undoubtedly, Ovid took extra care to maintain formal illusions and adhere to formal techniques in this poem because of its important position as gateway to the whole corpus. Once the reader is acclimated to the world of the *Heroides* and its assumptions, Ovid then feels able to cast away most of the moorings and maintain but small contact with the formal assumptions, while he seeks more daring techniques and procedures.

XV

Heroides 15: Sappho

Of the *Heroides* the *Epistula Sapphus* has easily been the most discussed.[1] Two motives predominate, neither of which will be of great concern to us. First, the hazards of transmission have afflicted this poem with ambiguous paternity and the result has been a long-standing dispute as to its authenticity. Suffice it, for our purposes, to say that I consider the poem genuine—no courageous assertion at a time when consensus has come around to this opinion.[2] I recognize that there exist, in addition to the questions

[1] The following works will be cited in this chapter by author's name alone: C. M. Bowra, *Greek Lyric Poetry* (1st ed. Oxford 1936), 459-465; D. Comparetti, *Sulla Epistola Ovidiana di Saffo a Faone* (Florence 1876); S. G. De Vries, *Epistula Sapphus ad Phaonem* (Leiden 1885); J. Hubaux, "Ovide et Sappho," *MB* 30 (1926), 197-218; E. Malcovati, *Athenaeum* 44 (1966), 3-31; D. Page, *Sappho and Alcaeus* (Oxford 1955); D. M. Robinson, *Sappho and her Influence* (Boston 1924); M. Treu, "Ovid und Sappho," *PP* 8 (1953), 356-364; F. G. Welcker, *Kleine Schriften* vol. 4 (Bonn 1861); U. von Wilamowitz-Moellendorff, *Sappho und Simonides* (Berlin 1913); H. Dörrie, *Der heroische Brief* (Berlin 1968; Dörrie, *Brief*). The fragments of Sappho are cited from *Poetarum Lesbiorum Fragmenta*, ed. E. Lobel and D. Page (Oxford 1955).

[2] Though I note that E. J. Kenney thinks the poem spurious (*Philologus* 111 [1967] 213, n. 2). D. Vessey appears to agree (*CQ* 63 [1969] 359). Dörrie, who believes the poem genuine, seeks to explain the very peculiar transmission of the poem by arguing (*Brief* 76, n. 13; 80-81; also in his edition, pp. 287-288) that Ovid, when he published the second edition of the *Heroides* with the inclusion of the double-letters, removed the Sappho letter, either because it was out of tune with the mythological subjects of the other letters, or because he feared that it would offend Augustus. I find neither at all likely. Moreover, Ausonius (*epigr.* 23) groups Canace, Dido, Phyllis, Phaedra, and Sappho in a passage which appears to be an allusion to the *Heroides*. If this is right, the conclusion must be that in the fourth century the Sappho letter was still transmitted as an integral part of the *Heroides*. A. R. Baca's arguments (*TAPA* 102 [1971] 29-38) are essentially the same as Dörrie's.

277

of transmission, internal problems. But none of the metrical, stylistic, and syntactic obstacles seem insurmountable, and De Vries effectively demonstrated that most of the peculiarities could actually be paralleled elsewhere in Ovid.[3] The assumption of spuriousness also entails the rather unlikely set of coincidences that Ovid wrote a letter among the *Heroides* for Sappho (this is indisputable; Ovid's own testimony is decisive: *Am.* 2.18.26, 34), some later poet also wrote a Sappho-letter,[4] at some point Ovid's poem was lost beyond all trace, and somehow the *anonymi epistula* was substituted for—and accepted as—the original Ovidian poem. Of external evidence the most cogent argument seems that initiated by Loers,[5] repeated by some later scholars with insignificant variations, and almost a century later restated by Wilamowitz,[6] seemingly with no knowledge of any earlier presentation of the position, namely, that *Am.* 2.18.34 responds to *Her.* 15.181-184. Arguments to prove the opposite, that the echo disproves Ovidian authorship, have been special pleading and without foundation. However we understand *Am.* 2.18.34, whether as a token of gratitude for Phaon's response (so Loers) or for a successful lover's leap (so Comparetti),[7] it seems futile to argue that the verse does not deliberately recall the *Heroides*. The implications are inescapable, unless of course one believes that the *auctor anonymus* developed 15.181ff out of *Am.* 2.18.34 to "anticipate" it.

Equal stimulus for interest in the poem has been its wealth of information about Sappho, and, for this reason, it has concerned Hellenists as much as or more than Latinists.[8] The notion that this epistle was a translation of an actual poem of Sappho's did not long flourish, but it undoubtedly nourished the feeling that the poem was a repository of authentic biographical detail. The

---

[3] *Passim,* and 135ff.

[4] Such imitation in general appears to have been very rare. According to Dörrie, *Brief*, 97-98, we know of only one mythical epistle after the fashion of Ovid before the eleventh century, that a third century letter from Dido to Aeneas (*Anth. Lat.* 83; ed. Riese). We might, however, add *Epigr. Bob.* 36 (probably fourth or fifth century), a fragment of a monologue of Penelope which some scholars think is a letter.

[5] P. XLVI.

[6] P. 21, with n. 2. Kraus (*Ovid: Wege der Forschung* 88), Kirfel (102, n. 337), and Oppel (4), who all consider this argument decisive, appear to think Wilamowitz originated it.

[7] Pp. 14-19.

[8] Wilamowitz and Bowra are but two among many.

intriguing problem of the historicity of Phaon and his relationship, real or imagined, to Sappho enhanced the letter's appeal for Greek scholars. Even today biographical accounts of Sappho's life often have recourse to Ovid. It is, for instance, common to read that among the "facts" we know of Sappho's life is the death of her father when she was six years old. So Aly in *RE* and Denys Page.[9] The latter repeats Welcker's century-old error when he observes that, according to Ovid, Sappho was orphaned of both parents,[10] though he avoids Welcker's additional (and puzzling) mistake of making Sappho twelve at the time. In fact, one may at least wonder whether such a detail might not be a product of Ovid's imagination.[11] Malcovati's argument is not strong.[12] Ovid, she asserts, would not have invented something which sheds no light on the psychology of the character or on the action, an argument which assumes—perhaps without reason—that this detail does not serve some such poetic purpose here. Further, this generalization, if true, should perhaps then extend beyond Ovid's inventiveness to his selectivity as well, and would, in short, be self-negating.

A more concrete problem here is the identity of the parent. It seems common opinion that Ovid means Sappho's father. Why so? I suspect two reasons: (1) An undefined *parens* is more readily taken as "father" than "mother"; (2) A fragment of Sappho's (102) is clearly a plaint addressed by daughter to mother, proof for scholars that Sappho's mother must have lived at least into Sappho's teens. I am not sure that either argument is cogent—or at least decisive. *Parens* does equally well for "mother" and "father"; in fact, the *antiqui* (as Charisius and Festus inform us)[13] even used *parens* in the masculine gender for the female parent! If there was a tradition that Sappho was early orphaned of her mother, a simple *parens* would be clear enough to Ovid's audience. One might, indeed, argue that the vagueness of *parens* implies that Ovid was recalling a familiar biographical tradition. As for the Sapphic fragment, we are on slippery ground if we seek

---

9 Aly, s.v. *Sappho*, IA (1920) 2363; Page is cautious, using such adjectives as "likely" and "alleged" (132-133, n. 3).

10 Welcker 85. M. L. West, *Maia* 22 (1970) 328 appears to make the same error.

11 So Wilamowitz seems to have thought (20-21).

12 Pp. 22-23.

13 Charisius (ed. Keil) 1.102-103. Festus (ed. Lindsay) 137.

to identify the first-person speaker with the historical Sappho. The *persona* involved may well be a literary convention and have nought to do with Sappho herself.[14] In short, it is impossible either to prove or disprove the historicity of the death of Sappho's parent when she was six. Should, however, one try to do one or the other, he must be advised to pay more attention to the text than is commonly done.

Similar errors occur on other points. For example, Aly reports that Ovid, in contrast to the *marmor Parium*, motivates Sappho's journey to Sicily by her desire for Phaon. In fact, Ovid never mentions any journey by Sappho to Sicily.[15]

The critical issue, of course, is where this great wealth of material comes from. Ovidian innovation aside, the possibilities are two, one of which itself offers two alternatives. Ovid was either drawing directly on Sappho's poetry or he was utilizing some kind of Hellenistic biography of the poetess; the latter possibility then involves the question of the degree to which such a biography would itself have been derivative from Sappho's poetry. A third option would allow for Ovid's utilization of both elements. Direct use by Ovid of Sappho was promoted by Welcker,[16] but his view passed from favor and was rejected by Comparetti who argued that nothing in the poem could be shown to go back to Sappho's poetry.[17] Almost forty years later Wilamowitz added his refutation, at precisely the same time when the pendulum began to swing back toward the theory of Welcker.[18] Wilamowitz's view, stated with oracular directness and mystery, has since been interpreted and clarified by Treu as resting upon the apparent lack of familiarity with Sappho in Ovid's other writings.[19] Hubaux's important article in 1926 began to reverse the trend, and our increasing ability to study the poem in the light of more and more Sapphic fragments has benefited the new direction.[20] Hubaux listed a number of words or passages in *Her.* 15 which could indicate Ovid's familiarity with and use of Sappho's poetry, and in 1953 Treu added a few more. It seems safe to say that

[14] See A. Lesky, *A History of Greek Literature*, tr. Willis and de Heer (New York 1966) 143.

[15] Aly (supra n. 9) 2364. Comparetti (30, n. 1) was correct.

[16] Pp. 83ff.   [17] Pp. 45-46.   [18] Pp. 18-19.   [19] Pp. 358-359.

[20] Even before the many new fragments came to light, I. Luňák, *Quaestiones Sapphicae* (Kazan 1888) 13-43 had energetically attempted to show that in *Heroides* 15 Ovid made use of Sappho's own poetry.

Ovid's direct use of Sappho is now consensus opinion.[21] A priori this would seem reasonable. Ovid uses literary sources, not compendia or scholarly epitomes. He will use Briseis' words in her letter, Dido's in hers, though of course through the mediation of Homer and Vergil. We might well expect, when he had access to the heroine's *ipsissima verba*—as only with Sappho—that he would exploit the opportunity. I do not mean to imply that the substance of the letter derives essentially from Sappho. There is very little evidence—perhaps none of value—that Phaon figured *personally* in Sappho's poetry. It is generally held that the love affair between Sappho and Phaon is an invention of middle and new comedy.[22] Rather, Ovid grafted on to the essentials of the tale, which he probably took from comedy, echoes and allusions from Sappho's own writings, almost rephrasing the later Sapphic myth in the language and colors of Sappho's own poetry.[23] Wilamowitz's apparent assumption that Ovid was unfamiliar with Sappho will, as Treu has observed, simply not do. Ovid's allusions to Sappho and her poetry are too knowing and direct to make it believable that he had but a passing acquaintance with her work.[24] When he writes, *Lesbia quid docuit Sappho, nisi amare, puellas?* (*Tr.* 2.365), one almost senses that he considers her his female counterpart. Though there may be no definite evidence for Sapphic influence in Propertius or Tibullus, Ovid was certainly the most literate of the Roman elegists, perhaps indeed the best-read and most intensely involved in the poetic tradition of all the great Latin poets.[25] Horace, we may recall, was familiar

[21] Professor Calder believes that Ovid did not use an edition of Sappho's poetry, but rather a *vita* which quoted freely and extensively from her work. (One might compare the way Aristotle quotes large chunks of Solon's poetry in his *Ath. Pol.*)

[22] Most difficult to reconcile with this view is Palaiphatos 48 (= 211LP) which seems undeniably to assert that Sappho wrote of her love for Phaon. Wilamowitz (34, n.), however, condemns this passage as a "byzantinischer Zusatz" whose author knew nothing of Sappho's poetry. It is generally believed that Sappho alluded to the mythical Phaon in some such way that later readers were able to misinterpret it (willfully?) as a personal relationship; see Page 142, n. 1; Bowra 202-203 (also, 2d ed. [1961] 177 and 213-214).

[23] Curious are the views of Birt (*RhM* 32 [1877] 430-432), that *Heroides* 15 follows Callimachus, and Comparetti (52), that it is modeled on a post-Menandrian elegiac poem.

[24] Treu (361, with n. 1) misses the reference to Sappho at *Tr.* 3.7.20.

[25] Athenaeus, in the third century, claimed to know all Sappho's poetry by heart (if such is the sense of his adoption of Epicrates' words, 13.605e). This

with Sappho; Catullus had translated her. Certainly, Greek lyric was not in deep decline. Cicero's expression of scorn (Sen. *Ep.* 49.5), some years earlier, for Greek lyric was calculated for shock value and itself may well imply widespread interest. Dionysius of Halicarnassus, who has preserved for us the great Aphrodite Ode, was a contemporary of Ovid's. In the end, however, the internal evidence must be allowed to speak for itself. Let me, therefore, present some of the more striking "echoes" of Sappho's verse proffered by Hubaux, Bowra, and Treu. The words χέλυς and βάρβιτος, both of which Sappho used (frs. 118 and 176), occur only here in Ovid's writings. The latter occurs thrice in Horace, the former is not found in Latin poetry before this poem. The pejorative connotation of *agrestis* (207), nowhere else in Ovid, seems related to Sappho's use of ἀγροΐωτις (fr. 57). I would add that Demetrius' reference (*Eloc.* 167) to Sappho's mocking of the ἄγροικον νυμφίον may be even more relevant. The allusion to the love of Aurora and Cephalus (89) may recall Sappho's apparent mention of Eos (and Tithonus? fr. 58.19ff). Like Ovid (153-154) Sappho appears to have used the Itys myth (fr. 135). The most decisive piece of evidence, in Treu's eyes, is the gift of a papyrus first published in 1939. Sappho laments her inability to procure a headband for her daughter. Treu considers *Her.* 15.75-76 an indisputable echo: *Veste tegor vili, nullum est in crinibus aurum,/ non Arabum noster dona capillus habet.*

Other details may go back to Sappho's poetry, but could likely have reached Ovid through intermediate sources, e.g., her remarks on Cleis, her brother, her childhood, and her physical appearance.[26] Stylistically, Hubaux resurrected the view that the ἀναδίπλωσις of 40 imitates Sappho, while Treu noted the lyric quality of the verbal repetitions in the poem. These are important points and we shall return to them. Finally, as Bowra suggests, there is a variety of themes and motifs in the poem which "sound Sapphic" and therefore might have appeared in her poetry, e.g., the epiphany of the nymph, the comparison to a nightingale, the

---

proves nothing, but it makes it seem foolhardy to assert that Ovid was barely familiar with her work.

[26] The last point depends on whether we believe Sappho was in fact "small and ugly," still a subject of hot dispute. Recently, Malcovati (23) has argued that she was actually pretty, while Lesky (supra n. 14) 140 feels her homeliness, attested by, e.g., Max. Tyr. 18.7, schol. Lucian *Im.* 18, *POxy* 1800, may well be historical.

allusion to the sea-born Aphrodite. Even the description of the physical symptoms of lovesickness (111ff), so familiar by Ovid's time as to be almost trite, may have special significance in the mouth of the poet who made the theme famous.

To be sure, some of these points are less cogent than others, but a few are so striking as to reinforce the validity of the remainder. There is, I suspect, yet more to add. Is it coincidence that Ovid alludes to the story of Selene and Endymion (89-90)[27] which may have been invented by Sappho, which at all events is known to us first in Sappho?[28] The lavish praise of Phaon's beauty culminates in the almost humorous verses, *Sume fidem et pharetram,—fies manifestus Apollo;/ accedant capiti cornua,—Bacchus eris* (23-24). This has every appearance of being an exaggerated parody of Sappho's affection for comparing young men to mythical heroes.[29] Perhaps less concrete are certain general characteristics of the poem. For instance, Sappho's concern with physical appearance and especially with adornments of the body —clothing, jewelry, and the like—a theme of relative infrequency in the *Heroides*, has a disturbing emphasis throughout the poem. In Sappho's anxiety over her homely looks (31ff) and in her lament for her presently unkempt and unadorned state, we seem to be hearing the voices of Sappho's own world with its vainglorious concern for proper hairdos, fashionable styles, and ostentatious jewelry and perfumes. Details confirm the feeling. Words like *forma, formosus, facies* occur more often here than in other letters. Sappho appears to be the only heroine who wears jewelry and perfumes her hair (75-76). Lesbos, of course, was the home of the καλλιστεία, the beauty contest. There are possible verbal echoes too. Ovid refers to Sappho's use of myrrh (75), just as Sappho herself does (fr. 94.18). *In crinibus aurum* (76) calls to mind χρυσοστέφαν' Ἀφρόδιτα (fr. 33.1).

Our awareness of Sapphic influence on this poem is so often dependent on the chance survival of a single word or a petty fragment (e.g., we know she used βάρβιτος from a lexicographical observation in Athenaeus) that we must be inclined to accept the

[27] The strange illogic of the distich deserves notice. Ovid, who refers to Selene and Endymion also at *Her.* 18.63, likes the association of the love affairs of Selene and Aurora; see too *Am.* 1.13.35ff; *AA* 3.83-84.

[28] Fr. 199. See Luňák (supra n. 20) 30; Page 273-274. Was it in Epimenides? See Huxley 82-83.

[29] Himerius *Or.* 9.16.189ff (Colonna).

possibility that much else might well be attested as Sapphic by the happy discovery of a new fragment or two. Here we might number *candida Cydro* (17), a total enigma to us, never mentioned in the biographical accounts or the extant fragments.[30] And does it not seem likely that of the inordinate number of strange Greek proper nouns some may well be based on or adapted from Sappho? *Methymnias* (15) is a form seemingly never found elsewhere in Greek or Latin. *Pyrrhias* (15) is almost equally obscure. *Nisiades* (54 = Megarian?) is without parallel. *Pelasgis* (217) as an adjective meaning Lesbian seems not to occur elsewhere. I venture two unlikely suggestions. Might *Pyrrhiades* have something to do with Πυλαιίδεες,[31] the winners in the famous beauty contests (to which Alcaeus alludes, 130.32ff. LP)? Also, is it accident that in fr. 5 Sappho invokes Aphrodite (the supplement seems virtually certain) and the Νηρήιδες to bring her delinquent brother home, while Ovid's heroine calls upon the *Nisiades matres Nisiadesque nurus* to return her Phaon to her (53ff) and follows this up with an appeal to Venus? These parallels may seem far-fetched and perhaps they are. But when we consider the strangeness—in one case uniqueness—of the words involved together with the phonological similarities and the aptness of the contexts, it should give us pause and compel us to wonder whether Ovid is not, at the least, playing verbal games with Sapphic originals.

The similarity between verses 33-36 and Philodemus *AP* 5.132. 7-8, observed first by N. Heinsius, later by Hubaux, may lend itself to a different interpretation than the common one (that Ovid copied Philodemus, as e.g., Gow-Page *ad loc.*). The poet's love for a provincial girl who is unable to sing the odes of Sappho is justified by the example of Andromeda (now interestingly the emblem of "black pride") who was a "barbarian." Perhaps Ovid and Philodemus both go back to a poem of Sappho wherein she or some other girl is described as compensating for homeliness by musical and poetic abilities.[32] Ovid in the main adheres to the original, while Philodemus, in a veritable joke, inverts it. His girl may be provincial and have no cultured talents, but she is a striking beauty and for this he loves her! It may not be irrelevant that

[30] M. West, *Maia* 22 (1970) 327, n. 57, notes that her name may occur in the badly mutilated fr. 19.11.

[31] See Hesychius s.v. For a discussion of the Πυλαιίδεες, see G. Radke in *RE* s.v.

[32] A comparable theme is present in fr. 50.

the immediately following distich in Ovid (37-38) in effect compares Sappho to a bird, a comparison that "rings Sapphic."[33]

We must return to the issue of repetition. Merula seems to have been the first to confront verse 40 *nulla futura tua est, nulla futura tua est*, the only pentameter in Ovid in which the second half repeats verbatim the first half, with Demetrius' observation (140) that an effective characteristic of Sappho's style was ἀναδίπλωσις. He concluded that Ovid was here deliberately seeking to imitate Sappho's style. This view was, as a rule, rejected, but the peculiarity of the line did have generally one of two effects. Some used it as an argument in repudiating Ovidian authorship, others emended the text. I hasten to note that verse 184 in this poem, *Her.* 13.164, and *AA* 2.24 all come perilously close to achieving what Ovid has done here. Even those who retain the reading (e.g., Palmer) tend to deny Merula's claim on the ground that there is no true ἀναδίπλωσις here. And of course there is not, if ἀναδίπλωσις requires that neither sense nor syntax demand the repetition—but this would seem hardly to have mattered to Ovid.

Then there is the case for anaphora. Here too Demetrius testifies (141) to Sappho's affection for the device and Micyllus argued for Sapphic imitation at 199ff. Loers, however, notes that Ovid himself affects anaphora quite often, the validity of which statement for the *Heroides* is amply demonstrated by Merone's monograph.[34] But in spite of the various objections, some cogent, a reader cannot fail to be impressed by the great number of repetitions of one type or another in the poem (matched in no other, though some, e.g., *Her.* 2 and *Her.* 3, do have quite a few). Since we know that Sappho did make good use of repetition and that Ovid does seem to be reworking Sappho's poetry in other ways here, it is reasonable to assume that the elaborate utilization of the technique in this poem is a deliberate imitation of Sappho's style.[35]

Satis superque. All these details should demonstrate that Ovid was using Sappho's writings and was not content to rely solely on intermediate sources. But ultimately this is not the important inference. Parallel passages, identical allusions, similar motifs and

[33] It appears that Sappho often mentioned birds. See frs. 1.9ff, 42, 136.

[34] E. Merone, *Studi sulle Eroidi di Ovidio* (Naples 1964) 59-103.

[35] Note the following instances of one sort of repetition or another: 15-16, 17, 40, 54, 63-65, 66, 68, 87-91, 89, 93, 93-94, 101, 105, 107-108, 127-128, 130, 137, 143-145, 146, 154-155, 162-163, 184, 187-188, 198, 199-201, 199, 206, 213-214, 213, 215-216.

arguments enable us to establish a "source," as, e.g., the *Iliad* for *Her.* 3, the *Aeneid* for *Her.* 7. But the imitation of an author's style and language, as here, tells us a good deal more. After all, with but a few exceptions, Ovid's main sources in these letters are Greek, yet Greek words do not often occur nor does one poem sound more Homeric, a second more Euripidean. Here alone in the *Heroides* Ovid means to transform a second-hand poem into an original, that is to say, to eliminate the poet (himself) who intrudes between the subject (the heroine) and the object (the poem). How well he succeeded is evident from the erstwhile view that this letter was no more than a translation of a Sapphic original. Of course, the potential existed only in Sappho's letter, for here alone was there identity of poet and heroine. Still, it was Ovid's choice of Sappho, in contrast to the purely mythological ladies of his other letters, that opened up this avenue for him. Ovid, in brief, wanted this poem to ring, insofar as was possible, Greek, exotic, Sapphic.[36] This may, to be sure, reflect a desire on Ovid's part to be clever and witty or to display his manifold and varied talents, but I think a reading of the whole poem will reveal that this facet, when illuminated by the tenor and the tone of the poem, can be seen as part of Ovid's plan to say something about Sappho and her poetry, and Ovid and his poetry.[37]

That she is ἡ ποιήτρια (as she calls herself, 183) Ovid's Sappho never lets us forget. Nor, more importantly, is it something that she can forget. Is it lover or poetess who greets us at the poem's gate? Listen:

> Ecquid, ut adspecta est studiosae littera dextrae,
>   protinus est oculis cognita nostra tuis?
> An, nisi legisses auctoris nomina Sapphus,
>   hoc breve nescires unde veniret opus?

> (1-4)

[36] In verse 4 Dörrie reads *veniret*. There is also good manuscript support for *movetur*. For example of indicatives in indirect questions in Vergil, Propertius, Catullus, and Tibullus see Palmer (Purser) *ad loc.* and *KS* 2.494. Ovid, it appears, used this construction once elsewhere. If the reading *movetur* is correct, might it be an attempt to "sound Greek," by using Greek syntax? Perhaps we might even imagine an original ὅρμαται, which Sappho probably uses (fr. 44.23).

[37] I note, en passant, that this poem has run the critical spectrum from lavish praise (Jahn, cited by Welcker *Kl.Schr.* 2.117, n., called it *omnium praestantissimam*) to outright scorn.

Studiosae, only here in the *Heroides,* sets the tone.[38] Paramount here is the artist's vision of himself, arrogant and egocentric. A mere glance (*adspecta*) at the writing should suffice to identify her to the cognoscenti. Like the sculptor whose use of curves or the painter whose manipulation of light immediately reveals the hand at work, so the poet expects his style of writing (in both senses) to betray his presence at once. To require a look at the base of the sculpture, the corner of the canvas, or the epistle's salutation in order to discover the artist's identity is an affront to his achievement and ability, a denial of his claim—or hope—that his style is distinctive enough to obviate the need for external identifications. But this is not all. What does *breve opus* mean? Palmer misreads De Vries and, thinking the identical phrase present at *Pont.* 3.4.5, takes it to mean "a letter." Indeed, such was De Vries' opinion too, though he noted that the phrase at *Pont.* 3.4.5 was *exiguum opus.*[39] In fact, the context makes it clear that the latter reference has no relevance whatsoever to our *breve opus.* More to the point is *Fast.* 5.654, also noted by De Vries, in which the phrase refers to an injunction of two lines. But what of our context? Clearly Sappho means the whole letter-poem addressed to Phaon. But *breve*? In fact, this is the longest of all the *epistulae,* and, though less relevant, considerably longer than any Sapphic ode that we know complete (or nearly so).[40] But it is the character—or the typology—of Sappho that is at issue here, not the objective length of the letter: the self-centered artist who feels his own work is inevitably too short, too limited in quantity, indeed can never be long enough! By way of illumination, we might recall Ovid's tongue-in-cheek, self-belittling epigraph to the *Amores.* Sappho then proceeds, under the assumption that Phaon—and we—are necessarily interested in every last detail of her work,

> Forsitan et quare mea sint alterna requiras
> carmina, cum lyricis sim magis apta modis:

[38] There can be no doubt that it means "learned." The context is decisive. Attempts to interpret it = *te amantis* are both unnecessary and wrong. Is the occurrence in Sappho of πολύιδρις (fr. 190) just a coincidence?

[39] De Vries 37. Kirfel (103) translates *hoc breve opus* "dieser Brief," and points in support to *P.* 3.4.5.

[40] It is interesting to note that some of Sappho's poems may have been letters. For an extreme statement of this position, see J. M. Edmonds, *CQ* 16 (1922) 13.

Flendus amor meus est; elegi quoque flebile carmen;
non facit ad lacrimas barbitos ulla meas.

(5-8)[41]

From one perspective this is a clever variation on the *recusatio* motif. But from another, it is a reflection of how Sappho's life is subsumed under her art, how the quality and turns of her life are defined in accord with the categories of her art. Her life exists in —perhaps is—her poetry.

Abruptly, to work; or should we say, to play, to art: *Uror ut indomitis ignem exercentibus euris/ fertilis accensis messibus ardet ager* (9-10). The sudden unexpected shift to elaborate emotionalism following the straightforward, almost clinical, diagnosis catches the reader in all its artificiality. *Flendus amor meus est.* Yes, I must lament my love in appropriate elegiac strains; now let me show you how an expert does it, *uror* etc. Observe the transparent artiness: the lengthy words, *indomitis, exercentibus*; the rhyming "is" sounds, the numerous sibilants,[42] the contrived assonance, *accensis . . . ardet ager*. The theme is all too like *Amores* 1.1, in which, after accepting reluctantly the burden of love-poetry, Ovid gives a brief demonstration of his affliction and his newly found art: *uror et in vacuo pectore regnat Amor* (26). The poet waxes poetic.

The introduction of Phaon at 11 begins a new path, though the Sapphic muse is not far away.[43] *Nec mihi, dispositis quae iungam carmina nervis,/ proveniunt; vacuae carmina mentis opus* (13-14). The chief damage done Sappho by her relationship with Phaon is the paralyzing effect it has had on her art. This is, essentially, a topos, or a fusion of two: (1) passionate feelings render the victim unable to pursue normal activities; (2) poetry demands "leisure" (cf. Lucr. 1.41ff).[44] But in the context the distich must

[41] In point of fact, Sappho does seem to have written elegiac verse. See Suda s.v. *Sappho* and *POxy* 1800.

[42] Are they meant to represent the whistling winds and the hissing flames? Alliteration of sibilants to achieve various effects is common. Dante uses it in Francesca's speech (*Inferno* canto 5.98-99) to present an auditory image of the winds in the background.

[43] Is there a joke in 11-12? φάων = shining, while *calor* = heat. A similar play is found at 167, *Pyrrhae succensus amore* where *succensus* clearly reflects the πῦρ in *Pyrrhae*.

[44] On this motif, see Fränkel 116 and 229, n. 12.

288

be parodic. The compulsion to present herself in Sapphic garb (i.e., in the appropriate themes and topoi) overrides the concrete realities. Her inspiration for *carmina* is gone. But is only lyric *carmen*? No, for but a few lines earlier she herself has informed us that the present elegy is a *carmen* (6, 7). In fact, Sappho alone of the heroines calls her letter a *carmen*[45] and describes her activity as *cantat* (155). The intrinsic incompatibility between the topos and the very existence of the poem is invisible to the poetess.

The movement at this juncture to the details and complexities of Sappho's life and loves should not obscure the continuing presence, if in a lower key, of this concern with her role as artist. Thus, unlike the other Ovidian heroines, Sappho can affirm her desirability by pointing to her artistic talent (27ff) which, as her account does not conceal, seems quite large to her: *iam canitur toto nomen in orbe meum* (28); *Sum brevis. At nomen, quod terras impleat omnes,/ est mihi: Mensuram nominis ipsa fero* (33-34). We may detect a touch of professional jealousy in our prima donna, as she examines the differences between herself and her main competitor: *nec plus Alcaeus consors patriaeque lyraeque/ laudis habet, quamvis grandius ille sonet* (29-30).

Common themes and motifs are presented with intentionally blatant artfulness. Thus, with the oft-used topos of the tear-stained letter (97-98), it is not enough for Sappho to thrust it to our notice by unexpectedly injecting it in the middle of the letter (it usually comes toward the beginning), but in case we miss the poet exploiting the tricks of her trade, she graciously calls it to our attention, *adspice* (98). Similarly:

> Si tam certus eras hinc ire, modestius isses,
>   si modo dixisses "Lesbi puella, vale!"
> Non tecum lacrimas, non oscula nostra tulisti;
>   denique non timui, quod dolitura fui.
> Nil de te mecum est, nisi tantum iniuria. Nec tu
>   admoneat quod te, munus amantis habes.
> Non mandata dedi. Neque enim mandata dedissem
>   ulla, nisi ut nolles immemor esse mei.
>
> (99-106)

---

45 Unless 7.1 is genuine. Even if it is, the parallel is not exact since at 7.1 the *carmen* notion is essentially controlled by the analogy of the dying swan.

I should like to call these lines, so self-consciously gratuitous, a *praeteritio* of a poetic theme. Parodying the *Heroides* and Sappho's own poetry, both of which made common use of the departure scene, Ovid's Sappho complains that she—both as lover and poet—has been deprived of this staple. She has even lost the opportunity—traditional right of the heroines—to be afraid and to express this fear. In the end, the whole motif, the whole scene has neatly crept in: the parting words, the tears and kisses, the anxiety, the exchange of promises, the last injunction. Then, we are explicitly returned to the persona of the lover-poetess, in the form of an oath which is bound to the two sources of Sapphic and elegiac poetry—here again we are very close to the *Amores*— *Amor* and the nine *Musae* (107-108).

Sappho determines to attempt the Leucadian leap. After a plea for help, reasonably directed at *Aura* (177-178), she focuses on *Amor* and *Apollo* (179-184). The dedication of her lyre to Apollo is a symbolic act, virtually an acknowledgement of her own genius. Even the quasi-identification of Phaon with Apollo (23)[46] looks to Sappho as both poet and lover, for Phaon is—or can be —both handsome plaything for Sappho's affections and equally the source for her poetic inspiration.[47]

As earlier, obsession with the formalities and requirements of the genre makes havoc of the circumstances:

> Nunc vellem facunda forem! Dolor artibus obstat
>   ingeniumque meis substitit omne malis.
> Non mihi respondent veteres in carmina vires;
>   plectra dolore tacent, muta dolore lyra est.
>
>   (195-198)[48]

The paradox is again obvious. *Tacent* and *muta* almost annoy, as we approach line 200. We may feel like agreeing with the senti-

---

[46] Whether or not this has any roots in the myth itself, as the name Phaon and Apollo's role as sun-god might suggest, one cannot help believing that Ovid is deliberately playing on the association, since he calls the god "Phoebus" five times in the poem, a designation virtually equivalent to Phaon.

[47] As she writes, *Ingenio vires ille dat, ille rapit* (206). It is almost a commonplace of elegy that the beloved is the source of the poet's genius. See esp. Prop. 2.1.1-4.

[48] Note the obvious allusion to the *ars/ingenium* theme of ancient literary criticism.

ment of 197. As if to sharpen the basic inconsistency, the next verses break into language that is clearly "poetic" and "lyrical," with the anaphora, polyptoton, and three vocatives followed by descriptive phrases.

If Phaon has deprived Sappho of her poetic skills, so too he has rendered her incapable of loving and being loved by others (15ff, probably 202ff). He has destroyed her both as lover and as poet. In a last attempt at persuasion, *Qui mea verba ferunt, vellem tua vela referrent;/ hoc te, si saperes, lente, decebat opus* (209-210), the arrogance endures, *si saperes.* If Phaon has some sense, he will return to Sappho and bask in her glory.[49]

One final topos, embraced by a Sapphic repetition: *Solve ratem! Venus orta mari mare praestat amanti./ Aura dabit cursum—tu modo solve ratem!* (213-214). As Sappho earlier looked toward Aura and the deities of love to guide her leap, she now looks to them to restore Phaon, concluding with an *ad absurdum* extension of the motif—Cupid becomes captain and crew of the ship (215-216).

Before attempting to understand the emphasis here on Sappho as poet, I should like to attack another aspect of the poem which, I think, is inextricably intertwined with this problem.

Of Ovid's Sappho D. M. Robinson remarked, "a passionate and voluptuous *hetaera*."[50] I have no intention to enter the fray, still a heated one, surrounding Sappho's sexual activities, her morality or lack of it, the role of the comic poets in distorting the historical Sappho's character, and Ovid's place in the development of the "legend" of Sappho. One would, however, not deny that it is an interesting battle, in which one usually learns more about the combatants than about Sappho and her "legend."[51] Robinson, to be sure, sees Ovid as perhaps *the* villain in the genesis and publi-

---

49 So I read the distich. I imagine other interpretations are equally possible. J. Diggle, *PCPS* 198 (1972) 36-37 has recently suggested that the verse requires emendation.

50 P. 129.

51 This is what Robinson writes (263-264, n. 147): "Most of the literature on the subject is not fit to read. Cf. Richard F. Burton's . . . for a filthy, wrong interpretation of the word 'mascula.'. . . It is lamentable that as great a literary critic as J. A. Symonds should say that Sappho gave this female passion an eminent place in Greek literature." After citing Symond's book, he continues, "Fortunately the monograph was issued only in a very limited edition."

cation of the version of the immoral poetess. Whatever we may think of this, we must admit that there is something in Robinson's characterization of Ovid's Sappho. Sex, explicit lasciviousness, physical attractiveness receive a play in this poem that cannot be matched in the other *epistulae*. A brief survey of the chief points will suffice:[52]

> Nec me Pyrrhiades Methymniadesve puellae,
>   nec me Lesbiadum cetera turba iuvant.
> Vilis Anactorie, vilis mihi candida Cydro,
>   non oculis grata est Atthis ut ante meis
> atque aliae centum quas non sine crimine amavi.
>   Improbe, multarum quod fuit, unus habes!
>
> (15-20)

This is a controversial and—need it be said—touchy passage. Despite what seems to me good argument by Comparetti and De Vries,[53] some persist in reading *hic* in 19.[54] The attempt to defend Sappho is valiant, but futile. What point could *hic* have? And, after all, what does *amavi* mean anyway? Verse 20 states unambiguously that Phaon is now the recipient of the feelings Sappho formerly had for her girl friends. The implication—if implication is the word—is clear enough. The view, expressed by Giomini, that nowhere in the poem does Ovid allude to Sappho's homosexuality demands a rather naïve interpretation of some verses (e.g., 15-16) and outright distortion of others (e.g., 201), not to mention that even *hic sine crimine amavi* could refer to Lesbian love. What of the more rational argument that it is absurd for Sappho, trying to win Phaon over, to allude to her "immoral" behavior? This may be a real question (it may not be; need we assume a moral code by which Phaon would reject Sappho because she was bisexual?) but it is not a demanding one. It is not unusual for Ovid's heroines to say things that prejudice rather than further their positions. Cool, consistent and persuasive argument is not usually their forte. We might note a similar, if not exactly parallel, peculiarity later in this letter: *Nec vos decipiant blandae mendacia linguae:/ Quod vobis dicit, dixerat ante mihi* (55-56).

---

[52] Teuffel (cited by Palmer *ad* 24) thought about ten verses in the poem unworthy of Ovid. Needless to say, most are sexually oriented.

[53] Comparetti 42-45; De Vries 44-45.

[54] E.g., Giomini.

She seeks to regain Phaon by telling her rivals how faithless and deceitful he is. But the very act of arguing destroys the argument itself.

To return: Sappho mentions her Lesbian connections and enumerates certain of her lovers, acknowledging that she is unconventional in these relationships. Then, turning to Phaon, she says:

> Est in te facies, sunt apti lusibus anni,
>   o facies oculis insidiosa meis!
> Sume fidem et pharetram—fies manifestus Apollo;
>   accedant capiti cornua—Bacchus eris.
>
> (21-24)

The whole picture is physical sensuality, sexual electricity. Phaon's beauty and youth are everything. *Lusus* is what Sappho is after (a word, by the way, which occurs only here in the *Heroides*). An Apollo, nay, a Dionysus is what she wants. Sappho's interest in physical appeal is neatly played off at the other end by her attempts to completely minimize the importance of her own homeliness.

In addition to her poetic talents, Sappho is skilled at making love:

> Hoc quoque laudabas; omni tibi parte placebam,
>   sed tunc praecipue, cum fit Amoris opus.
> Tunc te plus solito lascivia nostra iuvabat
>   crebraque mobilitas aptaque verba ioco
> et quod, ubi amborum fuerat confusa voluptas,
>   plurimus in lasso corpore languor erat.
>
> (45-50)

This is the most explicit and graphic description of sex in the *Heroides*, set out with such relish that one senses a vicarious re-creation of the moment in Sappho's imagination. Again we notice that *lascivia* and *mobilitas* are not found elsewhere in the *Heroides*, nor is *voluptas* in a sexual sense.[55]

Sappho bathes herself in Phaon's beauty (see 85-96). His youthful attractiveness recurs (*primae lanuginis aetas . . . anni quos vir amare potest*, 85-86). Sappho sees Phaon more as an object of

[55] Another such word, suggestive of love as a physical activity, which occurs only in this letter among the fifteen is *deliciae* (138).

293

beauty than as a human being. Note the strange vocatives, *utilis aetas, decus, gloria* (85, 86). Of all the men in the *Heroides*, only he is addressed as *formose* (95). Most revealing is line 96, *Non ut ames oro, me sed amare sinas!* Sappho is obsessed with Phaon as an object of her sexual passions. As long as he will allow her to love him, that will suffice, for her only interest is to gratify her purely physical desires.

> Tu mihi cura, Phaon, te somnia nostra reducunt,
>   somnia formoso candidiora die.
> Illic te invenio, quamvis regionibus absis;
>   sed non longa satis gaudia somnus habet.
> Saepe tuos nostra cervice onerare lacertos,
>   saepe tuae videor supposuisse meos.
> Oscula cognosco, quae tu committere lingua
>   aptaque consueras accipere, apta dare.
> Blandior interdum verisque simillima verba
>   eloquor et vigilant sensibus ora meis;—
> ulteriora pudet narrare, sed omnia fiunt—
>   et iuuat—et siccae non licet esse mihi.

(123-134)

In their explicit lasciviousness these lines match, perhaps surpass, the earlier ones (45-50). There may be one other mention of erotic dreams in these letters (13.106).[56] The whole description— and it is unquestionably a fine one—is about as direct as possible. At 134, some editors to the contrary (e.g., Giomini), *siccae* is surely right.[57] The notions that such a brilliantly apposite error could have crept into the text or that so prurient a description would have been inserted by some scribe are unbelievable. One can hardly refrain from thinking that the numerous liquids in 129-133 are deliberate preparation for the picture in 134.

Even Sappho's description of the old trysting-place is phrased in what may be suggestive language, e.g., *cognovi* (147; cf. 129), *curvum pondere gramen* (148), *incubui* (149).

In yet another reminiscence, love is again shaped in purely physical terms:

[56] Dreams are recurrent in Sappho, though the fragments are too short or mutilated to reveal their substance (e.g., frs. 63, 134).

[57] Comments on 134 are revealing, e.g., Palmer "spurca sed certa lectio"; and Loers' description of Burman, who defends *siccae*, "qui ubique nequitias venatur."

At quanto melius tecum mea pectora iungi,
   quam saxis poterant praecipitanda dari!
Haec sunt illa, Phaon, quae tu laudare solebas
   visaque sunt totiens ingeniosa tibi

(191-194)

(I assume *haec, illa,* and *ingeniosa* all refer to *pectora*).

There is another dimension to Sappho, this revealed by her language. She is a materialist not only in her wants and needs, but also in her interpretation of the world about her. She sees events and people in terms of their capacity to prove useful to her, a virtual commodity market of goods and services. When her former girl friends are no longer pleasing to her, they are *viles* (17). A calculating auditor, she carefully assesses debits and credits: *Si mihi difficilis formam natura negavit,/ ingenio formae damna repende meae* (31-32); *mensuram nominis ipsa fero* (34). When she narrates her brother's fortunes, the economic perspective is uppermost: *inops, damna, inops, opes* (63-66). Her own life history is an accountant's ledger (69-72); note especially *accumulat* (only twice in all Ovid's poetry) and *accedis,* virtually financial terms.

Sappho's concern for materialistic luxuries speaks for itself. Verses 73-76 are exaggerations of genuine Sapphic motifs.

Phaon too is for Sappho little more than a major asset in her world of assets and liabilities: *O nec adhuc iuvenis nec iam puer, utilis aetas* (93). *Utilis* is obvious in its businesslike assessment, but equally striking is the fact that Sappho addresses Phaon by such an impersonal phrase, *utilis aetas,* for she values him merely as a source of pleasure and benefit for herself. For this lover, the magic of love is its power to turn humble places into palaces of marble, *Antra vident oculi scabro pendentia tofo,/ quae mihi Mygdonii marmoris instar erant* (141-142), a theme varied but a few lines later when Phaon is counted the *dos* which enhances the value of the *vile solum* (146).

In the end, Sappho views the whole affair as resulting in her bankruptcy, *abstulit omne Phaon, quod vobis ante placebat* (203). She has lost everything, her life as lover and her life as poet.

Reluctant though I am to carry this already lengthy discussion any further, it is important to take, at least, brief notice of certain other themes which occupy important places in the poem.

If the portrait of Sappho here presented is an unflattering one,

Ovid extends it by his incorporation of Sappho's role as mother. In marked contrast to the real Sappho's affection for her daughter, Ovid's considers Cleis a little nuisance: *Et tamquam desit, quae me hac sine cura fatiget,/ accumulat curas filia parva meas* (69-70). One wonders whether the lines are meant to mean anything more specific than that a career-woman like Sappho cannot endure the responsibility of raising a small child.[58] Similarly, when Sappho learns of Phaon's desertion, she grieves *non aliter quam si nati pia mater adempti/ portet ad exstructos corpus inane rogos* (115-116), lines which prove almost obscene in the continuing context:

> Gaudet et e nostro crescit maerore Charaxus
> frater et ante oculos itque reditque meos.
> Utque pudenda mei videatur causa doloris,
> "Quid dolet haec? Certe filia vivit!" ait.
>
> (117-120)

But over and above the perversity of this mother's feelings toward her daughter is the ludicrous light it sheds on Sappho's relation to Phaon. She is, after all, a mother; Phaon is a boy.[59] The simile at 115-116 virtually envisages her as his mother. Sappho is approaching middle age (Wilamowitz suggested around 35 years old!),[60] seeking to seduce a much younger boy (*nec adhuc iuvenis nec iam puer*, 93), and not particularly well suited to the love affairs of reckless youth.[61] It is no surprise to hear that Phaon literally flees from her, *fugiunt tua gaudia* (109).[62]

[58] There may have been a motif to the effect that a daughter was a nuisance or a burden to her parents. See Cat. 62.58 and Fordyce *ad loc.* who cites two examples in Menander (frs. 18 and 60K.). Cf. also Sirach 7.24f.; 22.3; 42.9-11; Bab. Talmud, Tract. *Kiddushin* 82b.

[59] We ought to observe the obvious allusions to Phaon's effeminateness and implications of his homosexuality, though I do not see what Ovid's purpose is here. Note e.g., the comparison to Dionysus (24) who is frequently portrayed as effeminate; also, 85-86, 92. That such explicit language could be intended merely to illustrate Phaon's youth and beauty I find hard to believe.

[60] P. 21.

[61] The idea of a middle-aged Sappho may emanate from Sappho's own poetry, but the gaucherie of Ovid's treatment twists and perverts what he found in Sappho. Note those fragments where she appears to lament her advancing age and its adverse effect on her life as lover (frs. 121 and seemingly 21). One senses the stigma involved in Sappho's defensiveness (85) and in *pudenda* at 119.

[62] It is interesting that Sappho describes the neglect of a lover in the same terms: φεύγει (1.21).

Other themes are clearly reminiscent of major conceptual trends in the *Heroides*, e.g., the attempt, bare though it be here, to establish a real connection between the events of the heroine's past, even her childhood, and her adult personality: *An gravis inceptum peragit fortuna tenorem/ et manet in cursu semper acerba suo?/ Sex mihi natales ierant, cum lecta parentis/ ante diem lacrimas ossa bibere meas* (59-62).[63] In quasi-Freudian terms, the early experience of life fixes the character which then determines and guarantees the similarity of later experiences.[64] A kind of psycho-developmentalism recurs again: *sive abeunt studia in mores artisque magistra/ ingenium nobis molle Thalia facit* (83-84). Habit or experience determines character. Still, I doubt that Ovid thought through all the psychological implications here as clearly and fully as he did in some other of the *Heroides*.

In conclusion, what do we have? First, let us try to draw the individual threads together: A Sappho who is supposed to sound authentic, by virtue of many Grecisms and characteristic themes and motifs; but, on the other hand, a Sappho who in many respects sounds like the Ovid of the *Amores*. The real Sappho, with keen esthetic sensibilities and subtle feelings for love and beauty, has degenerated into a grotesque pursuer of material luxury and corporeal lust. But why such a parody of Sappho? We can be fairly sure that Ovid did not write this poem to denigrate the Greek poetess, for whom he probably had sincere admiration. It is, I submit, not the poet Sappho who is being mocked, but the *persona* of the lover-poet of which Sappho is virtually the paradigm, or, in different terms, the emblem.[65] It is for this reason

[63] The concern elsewhere in the poem with the relationship of mother and child (e.g., 115, 153) suggests that *parentis* here may be Sappho's mother.

[64] Observe how the narrative of 61-70 takes us through the process of a generation, beginning with Sappho as a young girl, ending with her as mother of a young daughter.

[65] Note the frequent references on the one hand to *Amor* and *Venus*, on the other to Apollo and the Muses. It is surely this generalizing nature of the poem that motivates the apparently unique version of the Deucalion-Pyrrha tale, which, whether Ovid invented it (as seems reasonable) or not, appears to be a witty attempt to return the lover's leap all the way back to "Adam" and establish it as a permanent, almost inherited, strain in the human character and experience. Wilamowitz (27) appears to have realized this, at least to some extent. (I must, however, wonder whether there may be real importance in the fact that both Deucalion and Sappho are driven to the lover's leap by their relationships with two people who have similar significant names, Pyrrha and Phaon.) The Pyrrha-Deucalion myth was some-

that Ovid's Sappho sounds so much like Ovid, for this is also self-parody.[66] Ovid's choice of Sappho for the concluding poem of the corpus is pointed.[67] In one respect, this is a parody of the very notion of the lover-poet[68] (an entity built of two components which may be prima facie incompatible) who must convert his love, while yet experiencing it, into the substance of poetry. And so, the emphasis on Sappho's materialism and lust may not be so much the result of the influence of the Sapphic legend created by Comedy as it is the manifestation—gross and exaggerated, to be sure—of her *persona*. All the other heroines are different. For the lover-poet, love (or the facade of love) becomes a professional necessity; we may think of Ovid, *centum sunt causae cur ego semper amem* (*Am.* 2.4.10). It is his business. Interest lies more in love as a clinical discipline, in its pleasures and nuances, in its diagnosis and symptomatology, than in its aspect as a genuine and profound human relationship. And so, the grotesqueness of the parody. But, in another sense, the poem is, it seems to me, the epitome of the corpus, reflecting its two great themes, the one externally imposed, poetry, the other, elicited, as it were, from within, love, in the role of Sappho, in her relation to Ovid, and in the parody of the genre itself. The extensive place in this last

times the subject of comedy (see *POxy* 2426 and 2427). According to tradition, Prometheus advised Deucalion to build an "ark" (Apollod. 1.7.2). Perhaps some comic poet represented Prometheus advising him to execute the lover's leap (as the nymph here counsels Sappho).

[66] I cannot emphasize enough the similarity of this poem to the *Amores*. Aside from thematic and tonal likenesses already noted, there are numerous verbal echoes, e.g.: 14/ 1.15.2; 21/ 2.3.13; 27/ 2.1.38; 28/ 1.15.8 (and *AA* 2.740; *Rem.Am.* 363); 44/ 2.4.26; 80/ 2.4.10; 96/ 1.3.1-4; cf. 133-134 to 1.5.25-26. Some, of course, are insignificant. But what needs stress is how many of these correspondences bear directly on Ovid himself in his roles as lover and poet, the two functions which Ovid and Sappho share (we might note too that Sappho's remarks on her *molle ingenium* and on the relationship between her art and her character anticipate language which Ovid was later to use of himself: 79/ *Pont.* 1.3.32; 83/ *AA* 3.540, 545-546). Each wears, so to speak, the same two hats, and this is acknowledged when Ovid has Sappho describe herself in just those terms which he uses of himself. If this be, then, parody of Sappho, it is also parody of Ovid.

[67] Ovid writes about Sappho in order to write about himself as poet and about poetry itself. We may think of Broch's *Death of Vergil* in which Broch chooses a poet as his explicit subject in order to write about art and literature.

[68] Birt's description (supra n. 23, p. 388, n. 2) of the letter's style, "sermo putide inflatus" is fairly accurate, but this is part of the parody, not the traces of some inept imitator of Ovid.

poem of the lover's leap serves as a parodic symbol for the extremes to which one can be carried by love, as so often and variously manifested in the earlier letters. When we think of all Ovid's heroines who stand at the edge of the sea and gaze vainly out over the waters, it is not hard to see the lover's leap as a culminating act which stamps a seal of finality on the corpus. In some cases, death is the product of love, but the lines are blurred, and, if death is the other side of love's remedy, it is itself also the cure for love.

Furthermore, the theme of lover's leap, to have done with love, in the very last of the *Heroides* is a metaphor for Ovid's leave-taking of the corpus. We might compare the tenth *Eclogue*, but more relevant is the specialized language and concepts of erotic elegy. The identification of the poet's farewell to love with his adieu to poetry (or a particular genre of poetry) is familiar from Propertius.[69] In a sense, love = poetry, poetry = love. The clarity of the theme here is evident in what is the last line of the *Heroides*: *ut mihi Leucadiae fata petantur aquae* (220). Sappho (or Ovid) will take the leap, say farewell to love and at the same time to poetry. This line is not simply a metaphor of leave-taking, but its execution and fulfillment as well.

We must admit that this poem is not, poetically, one of the best. Such expanse of self-parody, as commonly is the case, ultimately proves self-defeating. A larger problem, however, resides in Ovid's attempt to do too much in this one poem, goals that often set the poem at cross currents, sometimes moving in opposite directions at the same time. Within the essentially static limitations of the genre, discipline must be constantly exercised. Elsewhere Ovid succeeds in self-restraint better than here.[70] But the poem is indisputably interesting for the way in which it attacks its goals, for the witty and humorous results it sometimes achieves, and for the presence of Sappho, literary, legendary, and Ovidian.

[69] See Prop. 3.24 and 25, and E. Burck, *Hermes* 87 (1959) 191-211.

[70] There is a bare attempt—which at least indicates Ovid's awareness of the difficulties—to provide some developmental movement to the poem, but success is limited. Ovid means us to feel Sappho's final situation different from her initial one, as if transformed during the course or by the process of the letter.

XVI

The Date of the *Heroides*

Surely Wilkinson's should have been the last word on the frustrating problem of early Ovidian chronology. The difficulties, as he puts it directly, are "insuperable."[1] It needs scarcely be added that such strictures have not deterred scholars from proceeding apace in their relentless pursuit of the solution. This essay is but further testimony to the stubbornness—one resists saying blindness—of the scholarly temperament. Yet, by way of apology, let me add that my main purpose here is not to offer any strikingly original and revolutionary system, but to oppose some recent developments which seem to me to stretch the limits of credibility and set back, rather than advance, our understanding of the problem.

In brief, there are but a very few pieces of evidence, some interrelated, and each one is ambiguous, apparently not susceptible

---

[1] P. 83. The following works will be cited in this chapter by author's name (or in other abbreviated form): H. Bornecque, ed., *Heroides* (Budé; Paris 1928); A. Cameron, *CQ* 62 (1968) 320-333; H. Dörrie, *Der heroische Brief* (Berlin 1968) = Dörrie, *Brief*; S. D'Elia in *Ovidiana* (Paris 1958) 210-223 = D'Elia, *Ovidiana*; S. D'Elia, *Ovidio* (Naples 1959) = D'Elia, *Ovidio*; R. Giomini in *Atti del Convegno Internazionale Ovidiano* (Rome 1959) 1.125-142 = Giomini, *Atti*; R. Giomini, ed., *P. Ovidi Nasonis Heroides* 1 (Rome 1963²) = Giomini, *Her.*; F. Jacoby, *RhM* 60 (1905) 71, n. 2; W. Kraus in *Ovid* (Wege der Forschung 1968) 67-166; G. Luck, *The Latin Love Elegy* (London 1969² = Luck, *Elegy²*); id. in *Antike Lyrik*, ed. W. Eisenhut (Darmstadt 1970) 464-479 (= Luck, *Lyrik*); W. Marg in *Ovid* (*W.d.* Forschung) 295-312; E. Martini, *Einleitung zu Ovid* (1933; repr. Darmstadt 1970); H. Mersmann, *Quaestiones Propertianae* (Paderborn 1931); F. Munari, ed., *P. Ovidi Nasonis Amores* (Florence 1959³); R. P. Oliver, *TAPA* 76 (1945) 191-215; id. in *Classical Studies Presented to Ben Edwin Perry* (Urbana 1969 = *Illinois Stud. in Lang. and Lit.* 58) 141-142 (= Oliver, *Perry*); F. Plessis in *Philologie et Linguistique: Mélanges offerts a Louis Havet* (Paris 1909) 373-375; M. Pohlenz, *De Ovidi Carminibus Amatoriis* (Göttingen 1913); E. K. Rand, *AJP* 28 (1907) 287-296.

of definitive interpretation. What this means is that an error in the understanding of any one of the pieces of evidence spoils the precision of the whole system. But what is even worse is this: Although, from a statistical point of view, a finite—indeed probably a rather small—number of systems embracing all permutations and combinations would include the correct solution, we could never be sure which system it was. With the truth staring us in the face (and perhaps it already does in the form of one or another scholar's theories), we would not be able to recognize it and canonize it with any degree of confidence.

Insofar as the relative chronology goes, there are three major items of evidence. First is the epigraph to the *Amores*:

> Qui modo Nasonis fueramus quinque libelli,
>   tres sumus: hoc illi praetulit auctor opus.
> ut iam nulla tibi nos sit legisse voluptas,
>   at levior demptis poena duobus erit.

We know, then, that there were two editions of the *Amores*, the first in five books, the second in three. What we should like to know—and this is the subject of irresistible scholarly controversy —is whether the second edition included poems not already in the first. Some will hold Ovid to the letter. He declares that the second edition is shorter, i.e., that poems were removed, but neither says nor implies anything about additions: therefore, there were no new poems in the later edition. Others will argue that simply because Ovid fails to say that he added poems does not mean he did not. The epigraph simply describes the overall change in the nature of the work, and that is abridgment. The most recent attempt to resolve the question is D'Elia's argument[2] (followed in the main by Cameron)[3] based on Ovid's own statement: *Multa quidem scripsi, sed quae vitiosa putavi,/ emendaturis ignibus ipse dedi* (*Tr.* 4.10.61-62). This suggests, D'Elia believes, that Ovid only removed material in making his second edition. In fact, this distich proves nothing of the sort and is quite irrelevant to the question of new poems in the revised edition. All it tells us is that Ovid did away with poems, nothing more—deletion is not mutually exclusive of addition—and this we already knew from the epigraph. Moreover, there is no necessity to even think that this distich refers to poems in the *Amores*; it need have

---

2 *Ovidiana* 219; *Ovidio* 90.   3 P. 328.

no connection with the immediately preceding allusion to that work.⁴ In sum, this is a question that cannot be given a decisive answer, certainly not on the basis of the epigraph alone.

Next are two distichs in the *Ars*:

> deve tribus libris, titulo quos signat Amorum,
>   elige, quod docili molliter ore legas,
> vel tibi composita cantetur Epistula voce;
>   ignotum hoc aliis ille novavit opus.
>
> (3.343-346)

These lines provide us with a *terminus ante quem* for the *Heroides*,⁵ and perhaps for the second edition of the *Amores*. Unfortunately, the decisive phrase is botched by the manuscripts and disputed by scholars. Eminent Ovidians persist in their disagreement as to whether *tribus* is the correct reading, and there is no reason to hope for light at the tunnel's end—or, indeed, for the tunnel to have an end.⁶ If *tribus* is right, then Ovid published the second edition of the *Amores* prior to 1 B.C./A.D. 1: if not, all we can say is that the first edition preceded that date. Of the second, *non liquet*.

There is a crucial section in the *Amores*:

> vincor, et ingenium sumptis revocatur ab armis,
>   resque domi gestas et mea bella cano.
> sceptra tamen sumpsi curaque tragoedia nostra
>   crevit, et huic operi quamlibet aptus eram;
> risit Amor pallamque meam pictosque cothurnos
>   sceptraque privata tam cito sumpta manu;
> hinc quoque me dominae numen deduxit iniquae,
>   deque cothurnato vate triumphat Amor.

---

⁴ Cameron refers to (327) "the common view that a substantial number of *new* poems was first included in the second edition." This exaggerates. The common opinion might better be said to be "a small number of new poems" (Oliver is a significant exception). Indeed, some scholars already argued that no new poems were included, e.g., D'Elia supra n. 2; Mersmann 70-71; Fränkel 194 (though with some hesitation).

⁵ I ignore the long-discredited view (held by, e.g., Tolkiehn, 14) that *AA* 3.345 does not necessarily mean that the *Heroides* were finished and that the Byblis letter in *Met.* Nine is evidence that Ovid was still writing the *Heroides* while at work on the *Met.*

⁶ Kenney (*OCT*), Oliver (*Perry* 142, n. 14), and Marg (302) think *tribus* right. F. W. Lenz, *WS* 80 (1967) 195-199, and E. Courtney, *CR* 84 (1970) 10-11, vehemently oppose.

quod licet, aut artes teneri profitemur Amoris
  (ei mihi, praeceptis urgeor ipse meis),
aut quod Penelopes verbis reddatur Ulixi
  scribimus et lacrimas, Phylli relicta, tuas,
quod Paris et Macareus et quod male gratus Iason
  Hippolytique parens Hippolytusque legant,
quodque tenens strictum Dido miserabilis ensem
  dicat et †Aoniae Lesbis amata lyrae†.
quam cito de toto rediit meus orbe Sabinus
  scriptaque diversis rettulit ipse locis!
candida Penelope signum cognovit Ulixis,
  legit ab Hippolyto scripta noverca suo;
iam pius Aeneas miserae rescripsit Elissae,
  quodque legat Phyllis, si modo vivit, adest.
tristis ad Hypsipylen ab Iasone littera venit,
  dat votam Phoebo Lesbis amata lyram.

(2.18.11-34)

In a passage replete with problems, perhaps the most important
is the identification of the *artes Amoris* (19). If this be a reference
to the *Ars*, complete or in progress, the poem would have to be
dated to the last years of the century and would either have to
be assigned a place as a new poem in the second edition or else
draw down the first edition to this late a date.[7] But if the reference is to the *Amores* itself, then the distich is of no consequence
to the chronological issue. Verses 21ff make clear that this poem
is posterior to at least some of the *Heroides*, but this tells us little
if we are unable to resolve the question of this poem's status in
the first or second edition, or, in other terms, its date vis-à-vis the
Ars. We will have more to say on this later. In conclusion, one
must regretfully admit that no certainty can be attained about
the phrase *artes Amoris* and hence about the place of the poem
in the Ovidian corpus. Ovid's autobiography is some help:

---

[7] Cameron (332) writes that the phrase is "almost universally assumed" to
refer to the *Ars*. This in the face of the fact that a gallery of renowned
Ovidian scholars take it to allude to the *Amores*, among them Bornecque
(pp. vii-viii), D'Elia (*Ovidiana* 215-216), Fränkel (175, n. 4), Giomini (*Atti*
127-131), Goold (*HSCP* 69 [1965] 42), Némethy (ed. *Amores* [Budapest 1907]
212), Pohlenz (9-12), Rand (295). Tolkiehn in 1888 seems to have interpreted it as a reference to the *Amores* (10-11), but then contradicts himself
but a few pages later (15) and takes it of the *Ars*.

carmina cum primum populo iuvenalia legi,
   barba resecta mihi bisve semelve fuit.
moverat ingenium totam cantata per Urbem
   nomine non vero dicta Corinna mihi.
                                     (*Tr.* 4.10.57-60)

There are difficulties: exactly what is the temporal force of the participle *cantata*? is there a causal connection (in reverse order) between the two distichs?[8] does the phrase *carmina iuvenalia* refer to the *Amores,* as does the word *Corinna*? Whether the *carmina iuvenalia* are the *Amores* (as may be supported by the phrase at *Tr.* 2.339 and *Pont.* 3.3.29-30) or some early exercises of which we know nothing, of one thing we can be sure: they are not the *Heroides.* This idea, popularized by Bornecque in his Budé edition of the *Heroides,*[9] is absolutely untenable. Ovid took great pride in his *Heroides* and would not have passed them off, without a hint at their identity, as *carmina iuvenalia.*[10] But the reason for such contorted theorizing is not hard to find. By making the *Heroides* a neophyte work, Bornecque manages to avoid the obvious problem raised by understanding the passage correctly: if the *Amores* are Ovid's earliest poetry, how does one explain the elaborate reference to the complete or nearly complete *Heroides* in *Am.* 2.18?

Finally, much has been made of Ovid's various allusions in the *Amores* to his attempts at work in other poetic genres, notably tragedy. By determining the history of Ovid's essays into tragedy on the basis of these allusions (essentially *Am.* 3.1, 3.15, 2.18), one draws conclusions about the relative times of the *Amores* and the *Medea,* and, more important, about the dating of *Am.* 2.18. It will surprise no one that scholars cannot agree how to interpret this evidence—if evidence it is at all.

[8] See e.g., Plessis 375.

[9] D'Elia (*Ovidiana* 218, with n. 1), Munari (p. x, n. 1), and Oliver (192, n. 5) are all puzzled as to how Bornecque (p. vii) comes to such a theory. It is, in fact, taken over, with some distortion or misunderstanding, from Plessis (375). One infers from Dörrie's discussion (*Brief* 74-75) that, incredibly enough, he agrees with this interpretation.

[10] Cf. *AA* 3.346 and *Am.* 2.18.21-26. We can learn nothing from Ovid's *sanctas heroidas* (*Tr.* 1.6.33). When A.H.F. Griffin, *Gnomon* 43 (1971) 713, speaks of "the implications of the adjective in *sanctas heroidas* for Ovid's own view of the 'Heroides'" he misunderstands the phrase and the context. There are no implications here for "Ovid's own view of the 'Heroides.'"

As for dates of individual poems, the situation is a bit better, though the evidence is meager and in some instances subject to dispute. *Am.* 3.9 was written shortly after Tibullus' death, which leaves us merely to define "shortly" and establish the date of Tibullus' demise. The latter event, commonly assigned to the year 19 on the basis of Domitius Marsus' Epigram, has in the past decade been challenged,[11] but I suspect that no revision of the traditional interpretation of Marsus' verses can be accepted until someone will explain why, if the deaths of Vergil and Tibullus were not proximate, Marsus chose *Tibullus* to be *comes* for Vergil in the afterlife.[12] As long as this remains unexplained, we must assume that the two deaths were nearly contemporaneous and set Tibullus' in 19 (possibly 18). Ovid's commemorative poem should have appeared within a year of death.

Am. 1.14 alludes to a defeat of the Sygambri, which indisputably places the poem in 16 or later. The *terminus post quem* would be even later if the reference is to events of 12 or even 8, which seems equally possible.[13]

Am. 1.15, with its catalogue of poets, is generally held to fall between 19 and 8, on the reasonable assumption that the mention of Vergil and Tibullus in the absence of Propertius and Horace is the result of the former poets being dead, the latter alive. In our ignorance of Propertius' year of death,[14] we must fall back on Horace's in 8.

Finally, if *Am.* 3.15.7 can also be taken as an allusion to dead poets, this poem also was written after 19.[15]

---

11 See W. T. Avery, *CJ* 55 (1960) 205-209; E. Bickel, *RhM* 103 (1960) 104; V. Buchheit, *Philologus* 109 (1965) 104-120; Luck, *Elegy*², 70 (also in his edition *Properz und Tibull Liebeselegien* [Zurich 1964] pp. viii-ix).

12 For a defense of the traditional view, see M. J. McGann, *Latomus* 29 (1970) 774-780.

13 Cameron's allusions (331) to similar references in Propertius (4.6.77: itself uncertain in date) and Horace (*C.* 4.14.51-52, 4.2.33-34) are interesting, but they prove nothing. See Oliver, *Perry* 141-142.

14 Marg (300) writes, without qualification, 15, presumably because we have no definite evidence that any of his poetry was written later than that year. But life and creativity are not necessarily coterminous. Rossini lived forty years after composing his last opera, and a quarter of a century after his last major work, the *Stabat Mater* of 1842. Luck's statement (*Lyrik* 475, n. 21) that the *terminus post quem* for *Am.* 1.15 is 16, the earliest possible death-year for Propertius, simply makes no sense.

15 I note additionally that if, as is generally believed, *Am.* 1.8 is an imitation of Prop. 4.5, then it is probably after c. 20. Also, if *Am.* 2.12.21-22 recalls

What then can we gather from all this (ignoring for now the possibility that *artes amoris* refers to the *Ars*)? Only that Ovid probably began writing some Corinna poems in about 25 and was still working on the *Amores* at least in 16. It is, of course, unreasonable to argue that because *Am.* 1.15 has a *terminus ante quem* of 8 we ought to take the writing of the *Amores* down to 9. But it is also unreasonable to use the "datable" poems to limit the period of composition for the whole work—and this is what D'Elia and Cameron both do. The latter restricts the *Amores* to the period c. 25–c. 16, the later date for no other reason than that the reference to the Sygambri is the latest topical allusion in the *Amores*.[16] D'Elia, more conservatively, allows for the possibility that Ovid was writing the *Amores* till 10, but not that anything was written later.[17] This is faulty argumentation. The only real conclusion is that if Ovid did write some of the *Amores* after 16 (or after 10), none of these poems reveal anything of their date; and what is surprising about this when only three (or four) of the fifty poems in the corpus do give any such indication.

There are no topical allusions in the *Heroides*, while the *Ars* has two, references to an event of 2 B.C. as recent (1.171-172) and to an expedition of 1 B.C. as imminent (1.177-180). C. Caesar's presence in the East at *Rem.Am.* 155ff suggests a date of A.D. 1, but not later. It is reasonable to assume that *Ars* 1 and 2 appeared in 1 B.C., *Rem.Am.* in A.D. 1. *Ars* 3 was probably published between the two. Of the *Medicamina* we can only say that it appeared before, at the least, *Ars* 3 (see 3.205-206).

It needs to be noted that this whole discussion is further complicated by the complex difficulties involved in distinguishing between the writing of a poem, its recitation, its circulation, and its publication. This maze is, I am afraid, impenetrable.

It is obvious that in dealing with the chronology, absolute and relative, of the *Amores* and *Heroides*, we are struggling to manage evidence that may in fact be intractable. It is the wise man who will take sides with Wilkinson,[18] who concludes that the only secure view is that by 1 B.C. Ovid had published at least the first

---

the *Aeneid*, then it is after 19. M. Labate, *Maia* 23 (1971) 347-348, thinks *Am.* 1.2.23ff reflects a knowledge of *Aen.* 1.291-296, which, if right, would probably place this poem also later than the year 19. Similarly, Luck (*Lyrik* 467-468) thinks *Am.* 2.1 displays familiarity with Prop. 4.1 and therefore should be dated after 16.

[16] P. 333.   [17] *Ovidiana* 221.   [18] P. 84.

edition of the *Amores* and *Heroides* 1-15.[19] In spite of the "insuperable difficulties" scholars have tried to attain more precision. What is disconcerting is that the argumentation and conclusions of the past fifteen years seem to be less reasonable and less plausible than those which they seek to displace.

Let us begin by examining one line of argument, always popular but recently revived with energy by Giomini,[20] namely, the attempt to establish the order of composition of *Am.* 3.1, 3.15, and 2.18 based on the references therein to Ovid's experiments in more serious genres of poetry (probably tragedy throughout), and to make this the cornerstone of a coherent system. Aside from the virtual impossibility of so doing because of the vagueness and ambiguity of expression in the relevant passages (amply attested by the divergence of opinion in scholars' interpretations of them), a more serious objection is the wrong-headedness of such argumentation. For it relies on turning convention into autobiography. *Am.* 3.1 and 3.15 are respectively introductory and epilogue poems, and each is written to suit its particular function. Assume that 3.1 and 3.15 are strictly autobiographical, and one has no reason to deny equal status to 1.1, 1.15, and 2.1. The result would make Ovid's early poetic career a roller-coaster of crises, as every few years he actively debated the direction of his calling. But such "biographical" data are determined by convention, not by reality.[21] Thus, to search out the course of Ovid's career in these poems is simply misguided.

Cameron's recent piece merits a longer look, both for its intrinsic interest and because it is, in a sense, the culmination of a recent trend away from the views of Jacoby, Martini, and Kraus. To recapitulate his arguments: the second edition of the *Amores* was merely an abridgment of the first; no new poems were added. Of it we can only say that it appeared before *Ars* 3. The

---

[19] Purser *apud* Palmer (p. ix) had taken the same sensible path, putting the *Heroides* between 19 and 2, though his reasoning for the upper limit (19) was faulty.

[20] *Atti* 125-142; *Her.*, pp. v-xii.

[21] If compelled to say what I thought the most reasonable way of understanding these "biographical" data *qua* biographical, I would probably agree with Pohlenz (4-6) and Kraus (83-84) that 3.1 and 3.15 both belong to the first edition (with 3.15 probably the last poem of Book 5) and 2.18 to the second. In addition to the arguments commonly adduced, one might see 3.1.28 as an indication of an early age and 3.1.68 as appropriate for a young man.

first edition was written in the period c. 25-c. 16 (I have already indicated the flaw in asserting 16 as a lower limit). The reference in *artes amoris* is to the *Amores*; this Cameron argues from two directions: first, internal evidence favors the *Amores* (here he draws heavily on D'Elia);[22] and second, if we assume that the reference is to the *Ars*, then we must conclude that Ovid was writing the *Ars* and *Heroides* simultaneously, and, at this late date, had not yet written a tragedy. This, he suggests, is terribly unlikely. This argument, however, is faulty through and through: (1) If we must conclude, on the view that *artes amoris* = *Ars*, that Ovid had not yet completed a tragedy, then let us so conclude. Nothing precludes this possibility.[23] (2) There is, in fact, no reason to think such a conclusion necessary, for this argument rests upon the hypothesis that Ovid's *tragoedia crevit* implies incompleteness. If *tragoedia* here means "my tragedy," this is possible, though one wonders why *crevit* and not *crescebat*. If, however, *tragoedia* means "the genre of Tragedy," there can be no doubt that the reference is to a completed work. Cameron completely ignores the possibility that the phrase does indeed imply a single complete work, and fails to note that such is the position of many eminent Ovidians.[24] (3) If there is reason to conclude from *Am.* 2.18 that Ovid was working on the *Ars* and the *Heroides* at the same time, though simultaneous composition would be unusual, would it be so grotesque here as to be impossible? (4) In fact, there is no reason to draw such a conclusion. What Ovid writes is that since Amor has again won him over, he has written the *Ars* and the *Heroides*; this does not make them simultaneous. The only implication is that they were worked on during what Ovid felt was one period, of what duration impossible to say. To insist on reading the present tenses to the letter is silly and self-defeating. Literal interpretation would require us to conclude that Ovid worked on nine of the *Epistulae* at the same time.

The arguments from internal evidence are rather inconclusive:

---

[22] Cameron 332; D'Elia, *Ovidiana* 215-216.

[23] In fact, Luck has recently revised his earlier opinion (*Elegy*[2] 154) and so concluded (*Lyrik* 476-479).

[24] E.g., D'Elia, *Ovidiana* 217-218; Kraus 84; Harder-Marg, eds., *Publius Ovidius Naso: Liebesgedichte* (Munich 1956) 167; Pohlenz 6. Luck (*Lyrik* 477-478) has argued, like Cameron, that *crevit* denotes incompleteness. But he too misses the force of the perfect tense.

that the allusion, if to the *Ars*, a new work and a *magnum opus*, is too brief in the face of the lengthy one to the *Heroides* may be true, but such imbalance is typical of Ovid and he may have so chosen for some reason unknown to us (even conceivably because the *Ars* was not yet complete). Or else the elaborate description of the *Heroides* may be the result of the existence of Sabinus' response-letters and Ovid's desire to exploit the peculiar situation. As for the argument, going back at least to Rand,[25] that the didactic and "strategic" element was a part of erotic elegy before the turn to strictly didactic works, this is of course true. Capitalizing on this, Cameron tries to clinch the matter by asserting that the crucial question here is whether *artes amoris*, if *Am.* 2.18 was written before the *Ars*, could be taken to mean the *Amores*. To this he replies—and no one can disagree—that the answer must be "yes." (It is this concession that makes the question, in the last analysis, unresolvable beyond all doubt.) But, in fact, this "crucial question" should be asked only for the sake of absolute caution or because we have other reason to believe that *Am.* 2.18 predates the *Ars*—and this we emphatically do not. So perhaps we should be asking a different question: is it likely that Ovid would have referred to his *Amores* (before, of course, he wrote the *Ars*) with the words *artes profitemur amoris*, and follow this with *praeceptis meis*. To this the answer must be a resounding "no."[26] In this distich Ovid is identifying, by way of description, a specific work, and the implication from *artes* and *praeceptis* is that the work in question is generally didactic-erotic in nature. This cannot be said of the *Amores* which display such a character only in isolated sections (e.g., 1.4.1-8; 3.1.47-52). That Ovid later described the poetry of Tibullus and Propertius by the word *praecepta* (*Tr.* 2.461, 465) tells us nothing, since it is clearly an attempt by Ovid to implicate other elegiac poets in the same activities for which he suffers.[27] All this not to mention the fact

[25] P. 295.

[26] Luck, who once thought *artes amoris* might refer to either the *Ars* or the *Amores* (*Elegy*[2] 154, with n. 3), now thinks (*Lyrik* 477, n. 25) it "selbstverständlich" that the phrase refers to the *Ars* and calls the other view frivolous.

[27] Tibullus 1.4.75ff is probably the best example in Latin elegy to support Rand's view, but these lines do not necessarily prove anything for Ovid and, besides, they are conditioned by the whole poem which is a kind of *ars amatoria* in small and in which Tibullus explicitly sees himself as *magister amoris*. But to generalize from this poem to the whole corpus of Tibullus

that Ovid often, with reference to the *Ars*, calls himself *praeceptor amoris* (or *amandi*) and the contents of that poem *praecepta*,[28] while (with the single exception of *Am.* 2.18.20) *praeceptor, praecipio, praeceptum* are not found in the *Amores* nor used elsewhere by him with reference to the *Amores*. Finally, *ars* and *artes* are regularly used of the *Ars*,[29] nowhere of the *Amores*.[30] The evidence is not conclusive, but it seems questionable to prefer the recent views of Cameron, D'Elia, and Giomini to those of Jacoby, Martini, and Kraus.

We noticed earlier the problem posed by the seeming inconsistency between the elaborate mention of the *Heroides* at *Am.* 2.18 and the declaration at *Tr.* 4.10.57ff of the priority of the *Amores*. To those willing to assume additional poems in Ovid's revision and to assign *Am.* 2.18 to that second edition, all difficulties disappear. But this is an avenue closed to D'Elia and Cameron, who resort to essentially the same argument: Ovid must have written some of the *Amores* before, others after the *Heroides*. Thus, D'Elia argues[31] that Ovid wrote a few books of *Amores*, followed with the *Medea*, then resumed the *Amores* and wrote also the *Heroides* 1-15. This creates an unlikely sequence of events. In about 25 Ovid began writing *Amores*, worked on them for a few years, then left elegy and wrote the *Medea*. Then he returned to the *Amores* and continued on them till perhaps even 10. Then he left the *Amores* to write the *Ars*, and followed by once more going back to the *Amores*, this time to abridge and reorder them. Now it is not impossible that Ovid twice returned to

---

(and Propertius) is very dangerous. See, however, A. L. Wheeler, *CP* 5 (1910) 28-40. We might note that the words *praecipio, praeceptor, praeceptum* are not used by Propertius and only once by Tibullus (in the above-mentioned passage: 1.4.79) to refer to their activities as instructors of love.

[28] *praeceptor amoris: AA* 2.497; *praeceptor amandi: AA* 2.161; *praecepta: AA* 2.745.

[29] Perhaps the best example at *Rem.Am.* 487; there are many others.

[30] I am not at all sure that *Am.* 2.18.20, *ei mihi! praeceptis urgeor ipse meis*, makes sense if we take *artes amoris* to refer to *Amores*. *Praeceptis urgeor meis* means that the injunction to be a lover, which is the essence of the *Ars*, has even affected Ovid, who is impelled back to a life as lover-poet; surely the humorous irony present reflects Ovid's repute as the *magister amoris*, the writer of the *Ars*. If we take *artes amoris = Amores*, then presumably the sense must be similar to that of *Am.* 2.19.34, that Corinna uses Ovid's advice against him, which seems quite inappropriate in the context here.

[31] *Ovidiana* 216.

the *Amores* after leaving them, but it seems a rather poor way of circumventing the possibility that poems were added to the second edition—what it amounts to is that there was a second edition, but in two stages, and the final stage involved no new poems.[32] Less elaborately, Cameron simply assumes that there was some overlap in the writing of the two works and that Ovid wrote both in the period c. 25-c. 16.[33] Only if we grant all of Cameron's other (unlikely) hypotheses does this become a reasonable conclusion, though it will yet raise some doubts. It asks us to believe (as do the theories of D'Elia and Giomini) that Ovid was writing the *Heroides* and the *Amores* by and large concurrently, a striking achievement since the works are so completely different in subject, style, and intent. Indeed, it is likely that the *Heroides* represent a break on Ovid's part with the more "conventional" *Amores*, i.e., with personal erotic elegy. As such, it seems very unlikely to have been written while Ovid was also engaged on the *Amores*. The *Heroides* are, in a large sense, a rejection of the *Amores*.

Secondly, there is implicit in Cameron's view—unbeknownst to him—an unlikely notion of the date of the *Heroides*. The reference to the *Heroides* at *Am.* 2.18 is almost certainly to the completed work (Cameron seems not to realize this). That the first letter mentioned is Penelope's and the last Sappho's is good indication that Ovid had already published the work in its final form.

[32] This barely matches the almost unintelligible theory of S. G. Owen, ed., *Tristium Liber Secundus* (Oxford 1924) 3-4, who, if I understand him right, argues that *Am.* 2.18 was inserted into the second edition after it had already been published—a quasi third edition! Whether or not this is what Owen means, his system is totally confused: on p. 3 he puts the second edition of the *Amores* before the *Ars*, on p. 4 after. Nor do I understand the view of Munari (p. x) and Fränkel (193) that *Am.* 3.1 and 3.15 show that Ovid, when he left personal erotic elegy, turned to tragedy and therefore *Heroides* 1-15 must have been published before the complete first edition of the *Amores*. But what precludes Ovid's having written the *Heroides* after his venture in tragedy? Are we to assume that Ovid would not have returned to elegy after tragedy? Surely not, for Ovid did: the second edition of the *Amores*, the *Ars*, etc. Finally, I am perplexed by Kenney's statement, *Philologus* 111 (1967) 213, that the second edition of the *Amores* was published before the year 1 B.C. in which *Ars* 1 and 2 were published. What guarantees the priority of the second edition to *Ars* 1 and 2? Kenney, who reads *tribus* at *AA* 3.343, must hold its priority to *Ars* 3, but why does he specifically say *Ars* 1 and 2?

[33] P. 333.

Certainly, the response-letters of Sabinus are more likely to have been a collection of letters in answer to Ovid's rather than separate responses issued every time Ovid wrote one of his *Epistulae*. The tense *scribimus* cannot be a true present since Sabinus has already responded to Ovid's finished poems. Thus, *scribimus* etc. cannot mean, "I am busy writing the *Heroides*." Consequently, when Cameron dates both the *Amores* and *Heroides* to the period 25-16, and further argues that *Am.* 3.1 and 3.15 are closer to that lower limit than 2.18, what he is in effect saying is that the *Heroides* were completed sometime early in that period. Since Cameron does not perceive these necessary implications of his argument, he never fixes on any precise date. But it seems fair to assume that Cameron, once compelled to admit that the *Heroides* were complete before Ovid wrote *Am.* 2.18, would have to date their completion to about 19 or 20. This too, I suspect, would argue cogently against his whole system, since—as I hope to show later—it is highly unlikely for the *Heroides* to be so early.

If conclusions can be drawn from likelihoods, then we must admit that the recent assault on the stronghold of Jacoby, Martini, and Kraus by Cameron, D'Elia, and Giomini does not amount to much. In the end, we have found more rather than less reason to believe that *artes amoris = Ars*, that *crevit* probably refers to a finished tragedy, that the second edition of the *Amores* involved addition as well as deletion, that Ovid did not write the *Amores* and *Heroides* concurrently.

Notwithstanding my general agreement with Jacoby, Martini, and Kraus, I think there may be some reason for diverging from them (and from the common opinions) concerning the date of *Heroides* 1-15. First, a brief résumé of standard views:

> Bornecque: Between 20 and 16.[34]
> Cameron: Between c. 25 and c. 16.
> Clark: Between 19 B.C. and A.D. 1.[35]
> Dörrie: Between 24 and 20.[36]
> D'Elia: Published shortly after the *Medea* which appeared before 15 (i.e., between 15 and 12).[37]
> Fränkel: Probably published before 13.[38]

[34] P. viii.
[36] *Brief* 74-75, n. 6.
[38] Pp. 193-194.

[35] S. B. Clark, *HSCP* 19 (1908) 151.
[37] *Ovidiana* 216, 219; *Ovidio* 90.

Giomini: Published immediately after the appearance of the
first edition of the *Amores*, which took place around 16.[39]

Jacoby: After the *Medea* which appeared after the first edition
of the *Amores*.[40]

Kraus: Shortly after the first edition of the *Amores* and the
Medea: between 16 and 9.[41]

Loers: Published before 9.[42]

Mariotti: Composed by and large at same time as *Ars* 1
and 2.[43]

Martini: Published after the *Medea* which appeared after the
first edition of the *Amores* (the latter date being after 16).[44]

Mersmann: 18-17 B.C.[45]

Munari: Published before the first edition of the *Amores* was
complete, i.e., either before c. 15 or before c. 20.[46]

Otis: After the first edition of the *Amores*, almost simultaneous
with *Medea*.[47]

Peeters: Begun c. 25; appeared c. 15-14.[48]

Peter: Begun around 15.[49]

Plessis: Begun around 23.[50]

Purser: Between 19 and 2.[51]

Rand: Before the second edition of the *Amores* which appeared c. 12.[52]

Schanz-Hosius: After the *Medea*, which was published after
the first edition of the *Amores*.[53]

Wilkinson: Published before 1 B.C.

A *terminus post quem* can be set with some ease. *Heroides* 1-15
are filled with echoes of the *Aeneid* which testify to a wide-rang-
ing and good knowledge of that work on Ovid's part. Vergil died
in 19; the *Aeneid* was published posthumously. A substantial portion of the *Heroides* cannot, then, have been written, at the very

---

[39] *La Poesia Giovanile di Ovidio: Le Heroides* (Sulmo 1958) 14; also *Her.*,
p. x, with n. 10.

[40] P. 71, n. 2.   [41] Pp. 89-90, 154.   [42] Pp. lxxix-lxxx.

[43] S. Mariotti, *Belfagor* 12 (1957) 616, n. 23.

[44] Pp. 27, 62.   [45] P. 71.   [46] Pp. x-xi.

[47] *TAPA* 69 (1938) 201, n. 48.

[48] F. Peeters, *Les Fastes D'Ovide* (Brussels 1939) 20.

[49] H. Peter, *Der Brief in der römischen Litteratur* (Leipzig 1901) 189.

[50] P. 375.   [51] *Apud* Palmer, p. ix.

[52] Pp. 290-292.   [53] Vol. 2⁴ (1935) 210-211.

earliest, before 18 or 17.[54] One might think of private recitals, but this will not do. The familiarity with the *Aeneid* displayed in *Heroides* 1-15 is too profound and extensive to have been derived from recitals.[55] Anyway, it is hard to believe that Ovid, before the year 19, would have merited an invitation to a Vergilian reading or would have been part of the "Vergilian society" at all. His "Corinna" may have been, in his own perhaps exaggerated words, the talk of the town, but this alone would never have made him a member of that select circle. Even with Propertius, who, in contrast, was by the late twenties a successful and established poet, one wonders how much he knew of the *Aeneid* during its gestation period. His famous *nescio quid maius nascitur Iliade* and the preceding allusion to the opening lines of the *Aeneid* (2.34.63-66) are in themselves proof of very little. In fact, Ovid is here the best witness: *Vergilium vidi tantum* (*Tr.* 4.10.51). No attempt to interpret this as leaving room for the possibility that Ovid saw Vergil at the latter's recitations will be credible. Had he regularly attended them, he would have more than "seen" Vergil. The context is, at any rate, decisive. The reference to Vergil follows those to Propertius and Horace. A contrast is made. Ovid had heard Propertius and Horace read their own poetry; not so with Vergil: *Vergilium vidi tantum*. He had only seen the famous man on occasion in the streets of Rome.

We are, consequently, compelled to assume that the *Heroides* were written after the publication of the *Aeneid*. *Heroides* 7 may suggest that they were not written very soon after. This poem is nothing less than a challenge to Vergil, or better, a rejection of the moral order of Vergil's world. One wonders whether even Ovid, brazen and clumsy as he could be, would have ventured down so bold a path with the memory of Vergil's death fresh in the minds of the Romans. Would not even Ovid have waited till Vergil had become more of a classic of the past? Or would he, young talent in his early twenties, have cast modesty to the winds

---

[54] That Munari implicitly allows for the possibility of publication before 20 and Dörrie explicitly sets it between 24-20 I find perplexing indeed.

[55] For substantial evidence see my chapters III, IV, VII on *Heroides* 2, 7, 14. Among many other examples throughout the letters, we might note here a few in *Heroides* 11: 67/ 1.56, 140; 9/ 10.443. It is important to note that reminiscences derive from nearly all parts of the *Aeneid*.

and challenged Rome's foremost poetic and moral symbol? Somehow, I doubt it.[56]

I abide by the assumption that *Am.* 2.18 does contain a reference to the *Ars* and therefore (1) is not earlier than about 3 B.C.; (2) belongs to the second edition, since it is almost inconceivable that Ovid had been working on the first edition for almost 25 years.[57] If then Ovid was at work on the second edition toward the end of the century, we should not set the initiation of this project too early. It is unlikely that he began to revise the *Amores* before c. 6 B.C. What this effectively means is that the handful of "datable" poems probably all belong to the first edition. Ovid therefore began the *Amores* in about 25 and was engaged in writing it for approximately 10-15 years, perhaps down to c. 10. This is a very long period, but there are qualifying circumstances. We do not know how long the first edition was. If we assume that the second edition was about three-fifths the length of the first, then it would have been about 4,000 lines, about the same size as Propertius' four books of elegies. The latter evidently devoted all his artistic energies over some fifteen years to produce that small corpus (though, to be sure, they are poems of considerably greater depth than the *Amores*). Moreover, during this period Ovid was caught up in numerous private concerns which must have greatly diminished the amount of time he could devote to composition, e.g., travels in Asia Minor and Sicily, the death of his

---

[56] If there is anything to the story at Sen. *Suas.* 3.7, Ovid paid tribute to Vergil in his *Medea* by a deliberate echo from the latter's poetry; see S. F. Bonner, *Roman Declamation* (Liverpool 1949) 140. On the phrase involved (*plena deo*), see now F. Della Corte, *Maia* 23 (1971) 102-106.

[57] A word of caution. If one thinks *artes amoris* = *Ars*, then one should be wary of dating the publication of the first edition of the *Amores* in 20 or earlier. For this would mean that on the one hand *Am.* 3.9, a poem hard to put later than 18, was a part of the second edition, while on the other hand Ovid was still working on the second edition some fifteen years later— fifteen years for a revision which was by and large deletion and abridgment. I note this because both Munari (pp. x-xi) and Luck (153-154) grant that it is possible that *artes amoris* refers to the *Ars* and also that the first edition of the *Amores* appeared in 20, without making the important qualification that if one is true the other is almost certainly not: they are virtually mutually exclusive possibilities. The only way I see out of this is to make the assumption that when Ovid wrote *Am.* 3.9, he was *not* working on poems for the *Amores*, and this poem was a singular creation for that period, given impetus by Tibullus' death.

brother, study in Athens. He may also have been experimenting on minor *parerga*—we know of many lost Ovidian works; a number of them could have been early writings[58]—and some he may have himself destroyed (cf. *Tr.* 4.10.61-62). Recently, the view that Lygdamus was the youthful Ovid has been resurrected.[59] Indeed, it seems quite likely that between the years 25 and 20 Ovid wrote no more than a handful of poems and that it was not till about the year 20 that he began to devote himself in earnest to the *Amores*.

Having argued above that the *Heroides* were not contemporaneous with the *Amores*, we must conclude that they were probably not begun much before, if at all before, 10. We return to *Am.* 2.18. Having turned to tragedy, Ovid is again overcome and led away from that genre by Amor. He proceeds to "profess" *artes amoris* and write *Heroides*. The account should, I think, be so interpreted:[60] Ovid writes the *Amores* (5-12), then embraces a career of Tragedy (13-14). After one play, he is impelled to return to erotic elegy and writes the *Ars* and *Heroides* 1-15. The present poem is its own testimony to the resumption of the *Amores*. There is nothing literal about the presents *profitemur* and *scribimus*. They have a broad embrace, covering the period from the time when Amor resumed his control over Ovid (18) up to the present. In force, the presents say that "since that time that Amor exercised his power over me again, I have written the *Ars* and *Heroides*." The *Ars* antecedes the *Heroides* for rhetorical purposes. Ovid wishes to make his description of the *Heroides* elaborate; it would be weak and anticlimactic to allude to the *Ars* in one distich *after* a lengthy account of the *Heroides*. As it is, the résumé of the *Heroides* proves forceful and effective. Thus, verses 19-26 describe a single artistic period in Ovid's career.

Turning all this into tentative dates yields the following results: (1) The *Medea* was probably composed some time between 12 and 8. (2) *Heroides* 1-15 fall in the period 10-3.[61] (3) *Ars* 1 and

---

[58] See the lists in Martini 61-64, and Kraus 151-153.

[59] M. Swoboda, *Eos* 58 (1969-1970) 99-114.

[60] Despite my earlier strictures on confusing convention and autobiography, I do not hesitate to use this poem as evidence for Ovid's career, including tragedy, since it is obviously autobiographical and does refer to his actual writings. It seems, in contrast, impossible to make solid autobiographical fact out of the remarks at *Tr.* 2.337ff.

[61] Overlapping dates do not mean that I assume contemporaneous writing of several works, though minor overlap is always possible. They represent, rather, leeway for the period of composition of each work.

2, perhaps begun as early as 6,[62] completed in 1 B.C.-A.D. 1. (4) *Ars* 3, shortly after *Ars* 1 and 2. (5) *Rem.Am.* in A.D. 1. (6) *Amores*, second edition, probably shortly after the *Rem.Am.*: This is to be sure very tentative; it may have been considerably earlier, between 6 and 1, since all we can be sure of is that it appeared when Ovid had completed or at least was working on the *Ars*. And if *tribus* at *AA* 3.343 is correct, then it will be prior to *Ars* 3. (7) *Heroides* 16-21 were probably written in the first years of the new era.

Placing *Heroides* 1-15 in this period has certain distinct advantages. It ties them closer to the *Ars*, with which they have some special affinities, than is usually done. The *Ars* (and the *Remedium*) are filled with allusions to the myths and heroines of the *Heroides*.[63] The *Ars* shares with the *Heroides* an interest in the human psyche and the world of mythology. Moreover, this sequence brings closer together than usual the first and second editions of the *Heroides* (generally, 16-21 are separated from 1-15 by ten to twenty years). This is sensible since, if (as seems likely) Ovid got the notion of double letters from Sabinus' response-epistles, he would probably have not long delayed in writing them. D'Elia, whose absolute dates diverge considerably from mine, has also argued for moving *Heroides* 16-21 closer in date to 1-15, even granting the possibility that they antecede the *Ars*.[64] Perhaps some of the stylistic and metrical anomalies usually charged to *Heroides* 1-15 would vanish—or at least lose some cogency—if we were no longer to expect them to conform to criteria for Ovid's juvenile poetry.[65]

[62] D'Elia's notion, *AFLN* 7 (1957) 59-60, that Ovid may have been working on *Ars* 1 and 2 as early as 9 seems to me beyond belief. To justify this, he argues that the much later chronological allusions in *Ars* 1 must have been interpolated by Ovid when he added *Ars* 3 in 1 B.C.

[63] E.g., *AA* 1.509ff; 2.353ff; 3.11ff; *Rem.Am.* 55ff, 771ff. I do not think there is much to D'Elia's unsubstantiated claim (*Ovidiana* 216) that stylistic differences make it impossible for *Heroides* 1-15 and *Ars* 1 and 2 to be contemporaneous—not that I am arguing that they are.

[64] *AFLN* 7 (1957) 57-91, esp. 71, 85-86, 89-91.

[65] One is surprised to note how many of the metrical peculiarities in *Heroides* 1-15 have parallels in the *Ars, Fasti, Metamorphoses,* and even in the exilic poetry. Most of the following examples are taken from E. Courtney, *BICS* 12 (1965) 63-66. Irregular caesurae at 1.95 and 7.27 are paralleled at *Fasti* 3.863; the fifth foot elision at 10.27 is found also at *Met.* 5.214; the elision at 10.86 (if not corrupt) seems to be found twice in Ovid, at *Tr.* 4.2.54; *Pont.* 1.8.46; the hiatus at 8.71 is paralleled at *Met.* 5.312, 8.310; the fourth foot spondee in a spondaic line (also 8.71) paralleled at *Met.* 1.117; the kind

It would be invaluable if a science of allusions and influence could be developed. We might then be able to draw some hard conclusions from those clear cases of influence between numerous passages in the *Heroides* on the one hand and in datable poems in Propertius or in Ovid's other poetry on the other. But no such good fortune is ours.[66]

A final observation. Even should one persist in believing that *artes amoris* = *Amores*, this does not preclude a later date for the *Heroides* than is generally assumed. *Amores* 2.18 could still be new to the second edition, written perhaps between 10-5 (but before the undertaking of the *Ars*), and the *Heroides* might come shortly before it. Other arguments (except the proximity of the *Heroides* to the *Ars*, based on *Am.* 2.18) would stand. If, however, one is also convinced that Ovid did not add new poems to the second edition of the *Amores*, then it will be quite difficult to put *Heroides* 1-15 later than the teens, since it will strain credulity to argue that 2.18 could, under such circumstances, be much later than 10.

Probability is not necessarily truth. But when it is the only path, we must be satisfied with it, broken and erratic though it may be. If a series of likely arguments that I have here adduced proves to point in the right direction, then we will have to think long before abandoning the general system of Kraus and others, while at the same time considering seriously the possibility that the *Heroides* may be even a decade later than commonly thought.[67] If not, then we may be forced to very different conclusions on both scores. Dogmatism would be naïveté; in the end, the evidence does not allow for definitive judgment.

---

of hiatus found at 9.87 and 9.141 (reading *lotifero Eveno*) is not found in Propertius and Tibullus, and in Ovid only in *Heroides*, *Ars*, and *Fasti* (see M. Platnauer, *Latin Elegiac Verse* [Cambridge 1951] 58-59). The polysyllabic end of the pentameter at 14.62 (if genuine) is, of course, characteristic of Ovid's later poetry.

[66] The vanity of such attempts is well illustrated by the debate between Mersmann (27-67) and A. LaPenna, *Maia* 4 (1951) 45-49. The former argues that the nature of the parallels between Prop. 4.3 and the *Heroides* proves that Propertius was imitating Ovid; the latter thinks the opposite the truth. For a very different approach to the question, see E. Reitzenstein, *Philologus Suppl.* 29.2 (1936) 17-34.

[67] R. S. Radford, *TAPA* 54 (1923) pp. xxii-xxiii and *PhQ* 7 (1928) 59 refused to accept the view that *Heroides* 1-15 are the work of Ovid's early youth, dating them after 6 B.C. He did not, however, present any argumentation to support his opinion.

XVII

The Nature of the Genre: Ovid's Originality

Ovid laid claim to the *Heroides* as his own invention. Although nothing that survives of Greek and Latin literature belies this claim, his originality has commonly been questioned. The evidence and argumentation has never really gone beyond Kalkmann[1] and Dilthey,[2] who supposed Hellenistic models for the *Heroides*,[3] on the basis of (1) the existence of ancient works of art showing the exchange of letters between mythological figures;[4] (2) love letters in the Greek Romances and in other erotic narratives (e.g., Ovid's Byblis); (3) an elegiac love letter by Rufinus (*AP* 5.9); (4) a letter from Medea to Jason by the seventh century writer, Theophylactus;[5] (5) mentions of mythological letters in Plutarch[6] (to Ariadne, forged in Theseus' name) and Lucian[7] (from Odysseus to Calypso). Two assumptions are involved here: First, that the post-Ovidian examples adduced reflect Hellenistic models; this need not be true. Second, that there is no substantial

[1] A. Kalkmann, *De Hippolytis Euripideis* (Bonn 1882) 98ff, esp. 100, n. 1.

[2] C. Dilthey, *Observationum in epistulas heroidum Ovidianas particula I* (Göttingen 1884-1885) 3-5.

[3] A word, however, in defense of Dilthey. It has long been routine to father upon him the view that the *Heroides*-genre existed before Ovid. Yet, as I read him, he never meant this. What he did argue was that there were examples of mythical letters and also of free-standing love letters before Ovid and that Ovid took a hint from them to develop the *Heroides*. He does not say that there was a class or corpus of *Heroides*-type poems before Ovid. This is a view that Kalkmann seems much closer to. I note that Loers' discussion (pp. xxxiv-xxxviii) of the question of Ovid's originality is still worth reading.

[4] See too G. Erdélyi, *Acta Antiqua* 14 (1966) 211-223.

[5] Letter 54 in Hercher, *Epist. Gr.*

[6] *Thes.* 20.3-5. The source is stated to be Paeon the Amathusian, of whose work and date we know virtually nothing (see *FGrHist* 757).

[7] *Ver. hist.* 2.29, 35.

difference between letters that occur within the context of a larger work, and the *Heroides*, which are each and every one an independent and isolated entity. This is manifestly erroneous. Further, when we contemplate how extensive our knowledge is of literary forms from ancient Greece, in many cases where we know nothing more than that a particular form existed, it is difficult to believe that there was a *Heroides*-type in Alexandrian literature, but not a trace nor a mention of it has survived. Certainly—and especially in the face of Ovid's own assertions—the burden of proof rests heavily on the scholar who would posit some precedent for Ovid. But no positive evidence has yet been presented.

Those who deny Ovid's originality must confront *ignotum hoc aliis ille novavit opus* (*AA* 3.346). Three avenues lie open: (1) Ovid is exaggerating ("lying" would be too brutal, but more candid); or (2) *novavit* means "renewed," in which case there is no assertion of originality: all Ovid means is that he has renewed an obsolete genre (Eggerding[8] goes further afield by taking *novavit* as reshape, give a new twist to, which has no possibility in the Latin); or (3) Ovid is adopting the traditional pose of Latin poets who present themselves as being the first Roman to follow a particular Greek model. The first is possible but cannot be determined and denies us rational argument. The second is unlikely, since *novavit* follows on *ignotum aliis*. The third is serious and deserves examination. Might Ovid's *novavit* be a variation on the traditional *primus* motif, such as we meet in Horace, *princeps Aeolium carmen ad Italos/ deduxisse modos* (*C.* 3.30.13-14), *Parios ego primus iambos/ ostendi Latio . . . / Archilochi . . . hunc* (sc. Alcaeum) *ego, non alio dictum prius ore, Latinus/ volgavi fidicen* (*Epist.* 1.19.21-33), Propertius, *Callimachi Manes et Coi sacra Philitae/ in vestrum quaeso me sinite ire nemus/ primus ego ingredior . . . / Itala per Graios orgia ferre choros* (3.1-4), Vergil, *prima Syracosio dignata est ludere versu/ nostra . . . Thalea* (*Ecl.* 6.1-2; if *prima* does not mean "at the beginning of my career"), *ausus recludere fontes/ Ascraeumque cano Romana per oppida carmen* (*G.* 2.175-176), *primus ego in patriam mecum . . ./ Aeonio rediens deducam vertice Musas* (*G.* 3.10-11), *iuvat ire iugis qua nulla priorum/ Castaliam molli devertitur orbita clivo* (*G.* 3.292-293), Lucretius, *avia . . . loca nullius ante/ trita solo . . . integros fontes, novos . . . flores* (1.926ff), *hanc*

[8] Eggerding 193-194, n. 6.

primus . . . / in patrias vertere voces (5.336-337). The theme may go back as far as Ennius, though the evidence is fragmentary, *scripsere alii rem/ versibus quos olim Faunei vatesque canebant* (*Ann.* 213-214 v²), *nos ausi reserare* (217). It does not, however, seem right to align Ovid's declaration with these. Within the *primus* motif a twofold sense of pride is discernible: (1) The poet is the first Roman to achieve something; (2) the accomplishment is the transplanting of a Greek model to Latin soil. In other words, the *primus* motif does not entail pride in originality *per se*; quite the contrary. It embodies pride in one's good taste and in one's ability to make Latin verse receptive to a particular Greek model or genre. The pride lies, I suspect, more in becoming a Roman Hesiod or Alcaeus than in being an originator. One would not be wrong in seeing in the *primus* motif essentially a rejection of originality as an end in itself.

Propertius' testimony is valuable (3.1.1-4). The Latin elegist proudly proclaims himself the disciple of Callimachus and Philitas, the Roman Callimachus, as it were. Yet, all our evidence indicates that Propertius' poetry is very far different from theirs. What is at stake here is the primacy of the Greek poetic tradition. Though he greatly diverges from Callimachus and Philitas, Propertius, rather than claiming the creative originality which was probably due him, felt compelled—and privileged—to plant his poetry in the footsteps of great Greek predecessors.[9]

But Ovid is a different story. For him the simple act of doing something in a new way was *ipso facto* an achievement. Originality *per se* was a virtue. There is more than a grain of truth in the humor at *Rem.Am.* 466, *atque utinam inventi gloria nostra foret.* The very fact that at *AA* 3.346 Ovid neither mentions nor hints at some Greek ancestor (unlike Propertius, Horace, Lucretius, and Vergil) is itself testimony that he means this as an absolute assertion of his inventiveness, not merely of Roman adaptation.[10]

---

9 The only instances of the *primus* motif I know of wherein the explicit emphasis is not on the Greek model and one may have existed are Lucr. 1.926ff and Manilius 1.1-6. But for the first, though Parmenides and Empedocles wrote philosophy in verse, Lucretius may mean that he is the first to transfer Epicurean philosophy into Latin ⟨verse⟩ (as he explicitly writes at 5.336-337) and to *religionum animum nodis exsolvere.* As for Manilius, perhaps the very mention of Helicon implies a Greek model. On the other hand, Manilius may be considering his own very real originality.

10 Perhaps his avoidance of the traditional terminology attached to the *primus* motif is also an indication.

And the context is supportive. In this passage (*AA* 3.329ff) Ovid, instructing his female students on the necessity to be cultivated, recommends that they read Callimachus, Philitas, Anacreon, Sappho, Menander, Propertius, Gallus, Tibullus, Varro, Vergil, and concludes with a "perhaps Ovid too," mentioning his *Ars*, *Amores*, and *Heroides*, the last *ignotum hoc aliis ille novavit opus.* Coming after a long list of Greek and Latin poets, it is hard to believe that this could mean a genre which the Greeks knew of, but the Romans did not, i.e., that *aliis* includes the Roman, but excludes the Greek poets. Rather, he seems to imply that, in spite of the skill and prestige of all these great poets, Greek and Latin, only he was clever enough to create this particular poetic form.

Two points of importance here: (1) The question of a Hellenistic model for the *Heroides* is not pedantic, but crucial. For the peculiar poetic character of the *Heroides* is a function of the interplay between the precise components of the form. Thus, we can allow for the influence of various factors (e.g., Prop. 4.3, rhetoric) and still see the *Heroides* as a novel poetic conception on Ovid's part, but not so if there was exactly a Hellenistic model, that is, a collection of independent mythological epistolary love poems. (2) The word "collection" is important. Even if there were pre-Ovidian mythical epistles in art, in drama, or even individually (for which there is not a scrap of evidence), still Ovid was the first to realize that this could be seen not as an isolated phenomenon, but as a class of poetry in itself. The very transformation of the *Heroides*-type letter into a whole genre testifies to Ovid's perception in this particular poetic structure of a dynamic principle and a generalized pattern (we shall later discuss these facets of the work) which a single example of such a poetic letter would not reflect. Thus, he alone conceived it as a genre and realized its possibilities.

To be sure, the *Heroides* did not spring into being *ex nihilo*. Ovid's originality is, to a degree, that of combination and association, just as with the *Metamorphoses*. Some of the factors which may have had influence must now be considered.

* * *

Despite occasional voices of protest, it remains common to call Ovid a rhetorical poet and the *Heroides* his most rhetorical work. The whole notion is unfortunate because it promotes categorization at the expense of understanding.[11] Insofar as the general view of Ovid as rhetorician goes, a few comments and references will suffice.[12] Rhetoric was, after all, the art of verbal expression, of speaking and writing well. As such, there is little reason why one should consider the strict segregation of rhetoric from poetry an ideal state. Further, rhetoric was so pervasive a cultural force in the ancient world that it is almost impossible to speak of any literature or thought that was not rhetorical, or shaped and influenced by rhetoric. At the least, poetry and rhetoric were so mutually interconnected and interacting that it is futile to behave as if they were totally unrelated and independent entities. One of the most interesting and valuable conclusions to be drawn from Heinemann's amazingly informative monograph on love letters and Alexandrian elegy[13] is just this, that the interwoven threads of rhetoric and poetry cannot be disentangled.

Moreover, the ancient rhetoricians were themselves aware of the possibility of "rhetorical poetry" without the influence of formal rhetorical training.[14] In Latin poetry rhetoric is at least as old as Ennius, and perhaps even found in Livius Andronicus,[15] which would make the association as old as Latin literature itself.

The tendency to deplore rhetoric in poetry rests largely on the assumption that rhetoric is bad, poetry good, and rhetoric influences poetry to its detriment. This not only involves certain judgments which are not necessarily reasonable, but also fails to consider that poetry influences rhetoric as much as—or more than

11 Probably the worst example is the monograph by C. Brück, *De Ovidio Scholasticarum Declamationum Imitatore* (Diss. Giessen 1909). Along the same lines is N. Deratani, *Artis rhetoricae in Ovidi carminibus praecipue amatoriis perspicuae capita quaedam* (Moscow 1916). This work, though by no means convincing or correct in its basic methods and arguments, is nonetheless interesting and valuable. Unlike Brück's, it is written with much care, intelligence, and learning.

12 For fine and detailed statements in opposition to the common view, see especially Fränkel 167-169 (also 190, n. 1; 210, n. 12; 215, n. 41), T. F. Higham in *Ovidiana* 32-48, Oppel 32-76. I am indebted to all three. It is unfortunate that H. Naumann, *AU* 11 (1968) 69-86, has recently repeated most of the traditional views about Ovid as a rhetorical poet. He appears not to know Higham's article.

13 M. Heinemann, *Epistulae Amatoriae Quomodo Cohaerent cum Elegiis Alexandrinis* (Strassburg 1910).

14 See Quint. 2.17.5ff.

15 See J. K. Newman, *Augustus and the New Poetry* (Brussels 1967 = *Coll. Latom.* vol. 88) 422.

—rhetoric poetry. Gorgias, Aristotle tells us (*Rhet.* 1404a), developed his style on the model of poets. Centuries later, Crassus (Cic. *de orat.* 1.70) expounds on the similarity of the poet to the orator, a theme which Ovid seems to approximate when he writes, of oratory and poetry, *distat opus nostrum, sed fontibus exit ab isdem (Pont.* 2.5.65). Finally, one scarcely needs to mention the important place poetry, including poetry of an erotic nature, held in the rhetorical curriculum.[16] Quintilian constantly makes reference to the poets and his famous survey of poets in Book Ten is classic testimony to the importance of poetry to the rhetor. Similarly, Hermogenes often brings examples from Greek poets. The consistent utilization of mythical material in rhetorical exercises is additional affirmation. It has even been argued that declamations often show Ovidian or Vergilian influence,[17] nor is it unlikely that the rhetoricians learned more from Ovid than he from them. Seneca's famous critique of Ovid, *nescit quod bene cessit relinquere (Contr.* 9.5.17) comes in a context which may be relevant. Montanus, he relates, was for various reasons known as an "Ovid among orators." The major point here is the similarity of the orator to the poet, not vice-versa.

Compounding the problem is the difficulty of defining precisely what one means by "rhetoric," and especially by "rhetorical verse." It is commonplace to contrast Ovid's style with Vergil's and conclude that Ovid is the rhetorical poet. Yet, studies have been written purporting to analyze the rhetorical influence on Vergil down to the last detail—nor do other poets escape. A sympathetic critic has recently interpreted much of Propertius Book Four in terms of rhetorical exercises, and has observed the influence of the rhetorical schools on Prop. 3.22, Hor. *C.* 1.7, and Verg. *G.* 2.136-176.[18] *Heroides* 14 is a prime example of the difficulties involved. Ehwald has elaborately analyzed this poem as a full-fledged *controversia*, discerning technical rhetorical devices and structural elements throughout.[19] Salvatore, on the other hand,

---

[16] See e.g., S. F. Bonner, *Roman Declamation* (Liverpool 1949) 133ff.

[17] N. Deratani, *Philologus* 85 (1930) 106-111.

[18] W. A. Camps, *Propertius: Elegies* at vol. 4, p. 2 and vol. 3, p. 154. For a lengthy discussion of "rhetoric and elegy," with a few observations on Ovid's poetry, but attentive mostly to Tibullus and Propertius, see R. Reitzenstein, *Hellenistische Wundererzählungen* (repr. 2d ed. Stuttgart 1963) 152ff.

[19] R. Ehwald, *Exegetischer Kommentar zur xiv. Heroide Ovids* (Gotha 1900).

324

praises this poem for its almost complete abstinence from rhetorical motifs.[20] And so it goes. One reluctantly concludes that the criteria are so nebulous or idiosyncratic that discussion is almost useless.

Before turning to the *Heroides*, a few words can be spoken against the view that Ovid was a rhetorical poet,[21] that is to say, that he particularly was the product of the rhetorical schools. As a rule, we are subjected to barrages of biographical data calculated to demonstrate that Ovid was an eager and capable pupil of the rhetoricians. But the evidence really shows nothing of the sort and occasional remarks by Ovid himself show a personal disaffection with formal rhetoric.[22] The contrast he makes between his brother's propensity for rhetoric and his for poetry speaks for itself.

The rhetorical interpretation of the *Heroides* has traditionally taken one of two paths. They are either called *suasoriae* in verse or *ethopoiiae*. Of the first we need say little, since Oppel,[23] following Cunningham's lead,[24] has devastatingly exploded this view. By close comparison of these poems with extant *suasoriae* he has forever demonstrated that the gulf between them is enormous. The opinion that they are *ethopoiiae*, a much more reasoned one, goes back at least as far as Richard Bentley.[25] And his name alone lends it a respectability that merits our attention.

To be sure, anyone who promotes this theory makes himself an easy target for opponents. There is no evidence that the *ethopoiia* even existed in Ovid's time. Our knowledge of it and other *progymnasmata* derive from later sources like Theon and Hermogenes (both second century) and Aphthonius (fourth century). Seeing in them an accurate reflection of an earlier period (even as far back as Hellenistic times) rests upon the assumption (not unreasonable) of a very conservative educational tradition.[26]

---

20 A. Salvatore in *Atti* 2.242.

21 Much of this paragraph is based on Higham (supra n. 12).

22 See *AA* 1.459ff and Higham 45.

23 Pp. 37-67.

24 M. P. Cunningham, *CP* 44 (1949) 105-106.

25 *Dissertations upon the Epistles of Phalaris* (ed. Berlin 1874) 78-79. So too Heinemann (supra n. 13) 34; Reitzenstein (supra n. 18) 155, n. 1; E. Rohde, *Der griechische Roman* (Leipzig 1914³) 138, n. Similar is the opinion of E. J. Kenney, *Philologus* 111 (1967) 230, with n. 1.

26 The term *progymnasmata* occurs at Anaximenes' *ars rhetorica* 28.4, but no elaboration clarifies it for us. Moreover, M. Fuhrmann (Teubner

Let us then grant this assumption and examine how cogent this view is.

The *ethopoiia* (often used interchangeably with *prosopopoiia*; I use the former on the basis of the strict distinction of the terms as found in Hermog. *Prog.* 9 and Aphthonius *Prog.* 11) was one of the preliminary exercises of the rhetorical schools.[27] There were various classes of *ethopoiia*, but I shall restrict myself to the type which most obviously bears resemblance to the *Heroides*, namely, the τίνας ἂν εἴποι λόγους exercise involving mythological characters and situations. Here are some examples: What would Andromache say on Hector's death, Achilles' on Patroclus', Hecuba at Troy's fall, Niobe over her dead children, Cassandra seeing the Trojan horse introduced into Troy, Achilles seeing Priam in his tent, Laodamia on hearing of the return of the Greeks, Briseis on being led away from Achilles, Medea going to kill her children, Medea when Jason marries Creusa. Aristides' speech 52D. is a large-scale declamation presenting a speech of the embassy to Achilles, as in *Iliad* Nine. On the face of it, several of these seem potentially much the same as the *Heroides*. Differences there obviously are, but they need not be crucial, e.g., (1) with few exceptions these are not love relationships between men and women; (2) Most are real soliloquies, that is, they lack the sense of an "other" and all that that would entail. There are, however, exceptions and Hermogenes (*Prog.* 9) even notes a species of *ethopoiia* in which the speech is an address to another. Moreover, there may have been an epistolary form of the *ethopoiia*, though the sense of Theon's words here (*Prog.* 10) is disputed. To be sure, Nicolaus' remark[28] that *ethopoiia* is a useful exercise for the epistolary style suggests that he had no knowledge of a specifically epistolary *ethopoiia*. (3) These are prose, not verse. Yet, we know that at some point, though probably quite late, there were indeed τίνας ἂν εἴποι λόγους mythological themes in verse, amply attested by *Anth. Pal.* 9.451, 452, 457-471, 473-480, and in

---

ed. 1966) obelizes the clause in which it is found on the ground that "haec verba ab auctoris temporibus aliena sunt." Aratus' *ethopoiiae* have nothing to do with the rhetorical *ethopoiia*. Schmid-Stählin, II.1⁶ (1920) 64, n. 6, assumes they were like Theophrastus' *Characters*.

[27] There are some valuable comments in H.-M. Hagen, Ἠθοποιία (Diss. Erlangen-Nürnberg 1966) 51-64.

[28] Nicolaus: *Progymnasmata*, ed. J. Felten (Teubner 1913) 67.

papyri;[29] all however are as insignificant in substance as they are small in size.

But the relationship—if any—of *ethopoiiae* to the *Heroides* is best clarified by the principles of the "genre" and by the extant samples. Hermogenes (*Prog.* 9) and Aphthonius (*Prog.* 11) define an *ethopoiia* as μίμησις ἤθους ὑποκειμένου προσώπου. Broadly speaking, there were general and specific *ethopoiiae*. An *ethopoiia* could, further, be predominantly concerned with the πάθος, the emotion, generated by a particular situation, or with the ἦθος, the character, the mental processes, of a person in a particular set of circumstances, or with both. Theon's analysis lends additional help (*Prog.* 10). An *ethopoiia* (or *prosopopoiia*, as he calls it) is the introduction of a person speaking words suitable to himself and his particular situation. To this he adds that one must consider the kind of person the speaker is, the kind of person the addressee is, the situation, the subject to be spoken on, the speaker's age, sex, profession, etc. Then we supply suitable words.[30] Finally, as Hermogenes and Nicolaus instruct, the execution should proceed in the following manner: begin with the present difficulties, continue with the prosperity and happiness of the past, and conclude with a pessimistic look to the future.

Not a little of all this theorizing and instruction *seems* related to the *Heroides*. Certainly they do display emotion (πάθος) and thought (ἦθος). And it seems apt to consider them declarations appropriate to the writer and her situation. Moreover, one could not deny that sometimes these poems move from present to past to future. Yet, all this similarity is largely illusion, for the gulf between the *Heroides* and these *ethopoiiae* is unbridgeable. A more exacting inspection of ethopoeic theory, and, most decisively, a reading of the extant *ethopoiiae* side by side with the *Heroides* establish this beyond any doubt. Nor is it a simple matter of the qualitative difference between the efforts of a fine poet and those of hack rhetoricians. Rather, the gap inheres in the vastly discrepant nature of the two genres.

The ἠθοποιία παθητική, under which category most of the female *ethopoiiae* seem subsumed, usually are little more than momen-

---

29 See O. Crusius, *Philologus* 64 (1905) 142-146 for a speech in hexameters spoken by the ghost of Achilles, probably a schoolboy's exercise (= Pack² 1843). Also see R. Reitzenstein, *Hermes* 35 (1900) 102-105 for another example (= Pack² 1844).

30 For some slightly different remarks, see Nicolaus (supra n. 28) 63-64.

tary pathetic monologues, purely strained sentimentality, self-pitying lament. Though here and there a motif or theme will strike an Ovidian note, no one could mistake, for instance, the *ethopoiia* of Niobe for one of Ovid's heroines. There is no "other" whose existence and presence conditions the thoughts of the speaker; there is no sense of an organic relationship between past and present: they exist only as the hinges on which turns the continuous contrast between yesterday's happiness and today's despair. There is, in fact, no real characterization here—only immediate emotional response to a bad situation. And this, to be fair, is not because of the ineptness of the rhetorician, but because of the demands—or ideals—imposed by the exercise.

For at the heart of the *ethopoiia* lies the old ideal of τὸ πρέπον. The determining factor is the external situation; the goal is to construct a speech that is appropriate to that situation. As such, the underlying purpose is external, to request, to lament, to persuade, to instruct, to arouse sympathy. Of course, the *ethopoiia* is not independent of the identity of the speaker—explicit emphasis in theoretical discussions on his age, profession, sex, etc. is common—but the speaker is usually conceived of as an abstract generalization (in effect just one element of the total circumstances, of the whole environment), even when his individuality could not, on the surface, be more clear-cut. Nor is this surprising, since these are, after all, a form of *progymnasmata*, preparatory exercises, and, as a pedagogical principle, focus on the general, in spite of their claim to be as particular as possible. Thus, the rhetorician aims, even in specific cases, at general suitability. Ovid, in contrast, seeks in each poem the uniqueness of the heroine.[31] Or, in other terms, the *ethopoiia* strives for suitability and appropriateness in a specific situation, not for psychological realism and depth. The very fact of similarity of situation throughout the *Heroides* directs attention to the variety of characterizations. The *ethopoiia* accepts the character and the situation as given and set, and proceeds to the task of framing an appropriate monologue. Whereas Ovid uses the speech-epistle form as a means to

---

[31] L. Winniczuk's comment, "Ovid's Elegie und die epistolographische Theorie," in *Publius Ovidius Naso* (Bucharest 1957) 59, that Ovid's heroines argue convincingly because their arguments are suited to their characters and situations is misguided. In the *Heroides* the arguments are not convincing nor meant to be so. The characterization does not subserve the argumentation.

illuminate and define the character. The broad compass of a myth is totally lost in the *ethopoiia*, but is basic to the *Heroides*. Thus, for instance, Peleus' speech, as sketched in Nicolaus (ed. Felten, 65-66), on hearing of Achilles' death, could in fact be any man's speech on learning of his son's death, with the single exception that particular details of past blessings and present and future sorrows would be different. The tenor of the speech, the character of Peleus is in no way affected by the peculiar and individual realities of the Peleus-Achilles myth. Such an approach is totally at odds with the *Heroides*. Related to this is the role of narrative; in the *ethopoiia* it is meager and insignificant, in the *Heroides* often elaborate and crucial.

Finally, there is the matter of structure. The *ethopoiiae* are, by the theorists' prescription, intended to pursue a fixed pattern and, in truth, most do so successfully. No one could say this of the *Heroides*. One might compare *Heroides* 13 with the Laodamia *ethopoiia* in Nicolaus (ed. Walz, 11.14). Like most *ethopoiiae* this is, though sentimental, well ordered, it proceeds rationally and concludes decisively, a far cry from the deliberately confused substance and structure of Ovid's letter. "The method of rhetoric," as Baldwin wrote, "is logical; the method of poetic, as well as its detail, is imaginative."[32]

Conclusions fall in two directions: To call the *Heroides* *ethopoiiae* rests upon a willingness to ignore the nature and purpose of Ovid's work and of these rhetorical exercises. It was once common to call the monologues of the *Metamorphoses* *ethopoiiae*; Heinze put an end to that.[33] We must now do the same for the *Heroides*. But to strenuously deny this identification does not necessarily mean that Ovid could not—or did not—derive some ideas for his *Heroides* from these rhetorical exercises. If the *progymnasmata* did exist in his day, if he did take part in them, there is no reason to doubt that they may have provided some impetus; they were, at least in many cases, mythological monologues of heroines. Quintilian (3.8.49ff) remarks the usefulness of the *ethopoiia* (he calls it *prosopopoiia*) to the future poet; it is perhaps of note that he does not equate any particular poetry with the *ethopoiia*. But any causal relationship between the

[32] C. S. Baldwin, *Ancient Rhetoric and Poetic* (repr. Gloucester, Mass. 1959) 134.

[33] R. Heinze, *Ovids elegische Erzählung* (Leipzig 1919 = *Sachs. Akad. Wiss. Phil.-hist. kl.* 71, 7) 70-73.

Heroides and the *ethopoiia* would be minimal and nebulous. What Heinze said about the monologues in the *Metamorphoses* goes as well for the *Heroides*: literary art-forms do not owe their existence to elementary exercises.[34] If we are inclined to see some kind of ancestor of the *Heroides* in these *progymnasmata*, then we should only marvel at the artistry which turned a sow's ear into a silk purse.

The same is valid for other forms of *progymnasmata* in which we might discern the seeds of the *Heroides*. Thus, e.g., the διήγημα, exercises in the narrative of mythological episodes, the σύγκρισις, often the comparison of two persons (sometimes mythological), the ἀνασκευή, in which one sought to overturn a traditional myth, e.g., it's unbelievable that a mother (i.e., Medea) would harm her children (Theon 6). The *Heroides* often involve large chunks of "*narratio*"; a frequent theme is the comparison by the writer of herself with a rival; certainly the *Heroides* are often concerned to "revise" a traditional myth. There is then no reason—assuming again that these *progymnasmata* did exist in Ovid's day—why we should be reluctant to admit that these too may have exerted some influence on the poet. But even a rapid glance at extant examples of these exercises will deter one from calling these the progenitors of the *Heroides*; so vast is the gap between them, or, perhaps, so radical the transformation of these exercises in Ovid's hands. If the *Heroides* are "rhetorical," it is because there is an element of rhetoric inherent in the form. But this is not the same as saying that the composition is, to any degree, determined by rules or standards of rhetorical composition. Finally, it is worth a brief mention to note here that the tendencies found in the various rhetorical exercises mentioned often existed in poetic models before they found their way into the schools of rhetoric.

Thus, even should we conclude that the *Heroides* reflect some influence from the rhetorical schools, such a conclusion is without much value since influence is not essence. The *Heroides* are, after all, poetry and make abundant use of the resources of poetry: peculiar conception of myth, wit, poetic irony, ambiguities of language, imagery, metaphor, imaginative fancies, and the like. These are not the stock in trade of the rhetorical exercises.

* * *

[34] *Op. cit.* 120, n. 1.

We turn next to the role of epistolography.[35] To delineate the issues, let us begin by breaking down those elements of the *Heroides* which relate to their character as letters: (1) They are presented as formal letters; (2) the writer and recipient are both mythological persons;[36] (3) the letters are fictitious, that is, the real writer and the presented writer are not one and the same; (4) the letters are in verse; (5) the letters are free-standing poems; (6) they are, in a sense, love letters. Taken together, these produce a literary creation which has no model in antiquity. Three questions concern us: (1) Where would Ovid have received impetus for each of these factors? (2) In what way and to what degree are the *Heroides* really letters? (3) Why did Ovid choose the epistolary format?

That love letters existed in antiquity needs no demonstration. Ovid often alludes to the role of epistolary communication in affairs of the heart.[37] The large number of comedies entitled ἐπιστολή or the like, at least some of which must have revolved around the role of a letter in a love affair, is ample testimony.[38] We can probably assume that mythic literature (epic, tragedy) on occasion embraced love letters. Iphigeneia's letter (Eur. *I.T.* 770ff), though not a love letter, bears an obvious, though superficial resemblance to the *Heroides*, in that it too is written by an abandoned heroine to a hero. And, as noted earlier, Plutarch and Lucian testify to letters from "Theseus" to Ariadne and Odysseus to Calypso, though we are unable to date them.[39] Similarly, we

---

[35] For important discussions of ancient epistolography, see H. Koskenniemi, *Studien zur Idee und Phraseologie des griechischen Briefes bis 400 n. Chr.* (Helsinki 1956); H. Peter, *Der Brief in der römischen Litteratur* (Leipzig 1901); J. Sykutris, "Epistolographie," *RE* supp. 5 (1931) 185-220; M. Van den Hout, *Mnemosyne* 4th ser. 2 (1949) 19-41, 138-153; K. Thraede, *Grundzüge griechisch-römischer Brieftopik* (Munich 1970 = *Zetemata* 48), which reached me too late for consideration. For some important discussion with reference to the *Heroides*, see too A. La Penna, *Maia* 4 (1951) 67-69. I have not seen P. Cugusi, "Studi sull'epistolografia latina, I: L'età preciceroniana," *AFLC* 33, 1 (1970).

[36] By Ovid's time Sappho hovered between the worlds of history and myth.

[37] E.g., *AA* 1.455ff, 3.469ff; *Rem.Am.* 715ff. See too Prop. 3.23.

[38] By Alexis, Euthycles, Machon, Timocles, L. Afranius, Caecilius, and perhaps Novius' *Tabellaria*. There are also love letters in extant comedy, e.g., Plaut. *Pseud.* 41ff.

[39] T. Zieliński's theory, *Tragodumenon Libri Tres* (Cracow 1925) 116-117, that Sophocles' *Hermione* had a letter from Hermione to Orestes, is ingenious, but not convincing.

are unable to determine whether paintings of mythical personages with letters and a literary example like Ovid's Byblis reflect
earlier models.

But to reiterate earlier strictures, a letter within the larger context of a play or narrative poem is not the same as a free-standing
letter in a collection of the same. Autonomous love letters can be
traced back to Lysias, but the remains are too meager to allow
for an estimate of their nature. Similar collections are attributed
to Lesbonax (see discussion below), Melesermus, and Zonaios, all
probably of the second sophistic. It would be valuable if one
could guarantee the attribution of a statement recognizing the
erotic epistle as a genre to Clearchus of Soli. Unfortunately, this
is dubious.[40] Nor is it clear that Athenaeus' attestation (639a) of
a genre of literary love letters refers to verse letters, though some
have so argued.[41]

Love letters aside, what of the history of individual letters or
collections of them? Most, of course, have nothing to do with the
Heroides. Thus, for instance, Cicero's epistles probably taught
Ovid nothing (vis-à-vis the *Heroides*), nor will they help us to understand Ovid's mythical epistles. The epistle was a catch-all
form in antiquity, utilized to contain the most divergent subject
matters and for quite distinct purposes. We need only mention
the philosophic-didactic letters of Plato and Epicurus, the scholarly and encyclopedic epistolary treatises of Varro (*epistolicae
quaestiones* and *Epistulae*), the moral essays of Seneca (*Epistulae
Morales*), and, on the side of poetry, the witty and biting epistolary satires of Lucilius[42] and Horace. In truth, these too have
little to do with Ovid, though severe critics might harshly see a
kinship in the common superficiality of the epistolary form. The
most notorious view of this sort with respect to the *Heroides* is
Eggerding's,[43] who peculiarly argued that some of the *Heroides*
were not even written as letters, but as declamations, and, after
the fact, Ovid patched on some epistolary tags. But this general
attitude is mistaken on two counts. First, by resting on contempo-

---

[40] Athenaeus 639a. F. Wehrli, *Die Schule des Aristoteles: Klearchos* (Basel
1969²) fr. 33 does not accept the statement as Clearchus'.

[41] See A. La Penna (supra n. 35) 67, n. 1, who argues the reference is to
prose letters.

[42] See 5.182-189Kr., 9.376-385Kr. (with an interesting reference to the verse-
epistle at 376ff), and Krenkel's remarks at pp. 17, 67.

[43] *Passim.*

rary notions of what a letter is, can be, and should be, it makes false assumptions about the nature and function of the ancient epistle.[44] Second, it ignores the peculiar ways in which Ovid does exploit the epistolary form.

What we are most interested in are free-standing letters (preferably in verse) in which the supposed writer and the actual writer are different people. But even this needs qualification. For we should probably differentiate between those letters whose writer intends to deceive his audience (virtual forgeries),[45] and those in which a degree of the writer's purpose and the reader's pleasure and appreciation inheres in the knowledge of the absence of identity between the real and the supposed writer. Thus, we should probably exclude from consideration such things as the letters of Phalaris and letters written in the names of Plato and Isocrates. One feels less sure of how to handle letters allegedly written by Sarpedon (Plin. *NH* 13.88) and by Priam.[46] Merkelbach's revelation of an epistolary form of the Alexander romance in late Hellenistic times may yet be of relevance.[47] What of letters where the schism between real and feigned writer is manifest? Menippus wrote a series of letters in the name of the gods, of which we know nothing,[48] and Lucian a group of four Ἐπιστολαὶ Κρονικαί, consisting of humorous letters from (1) Lucian to Kronus; (2) Kronus to Lucian; (3) Kronus to the rich people; (4) the rich to Kronus, all on the subject of the distribution of wealth among mortals. Perhaps a similar divine letter was

[44] Actually, broader perspectives would be illuminating, even within the limited area of "modern" literature. We might think of a number of large-scale epistolary works ("novels"), e.g. (I mention only works not noticed by Dörrie in his *Der heroische Brief*), Dostoevsky's *Poor Folk,* C. S. Lewis' *The Screwtape Letters,* Sterne's *Journal to Eliza,* V. Shklovsky's *Zoo, or Letters not about Love* (1923; translated into English by R. Sheldon [Ithaca, N.Y. 1971]). Wilder's *Ides of March* is a variation on the epistolary novel. Thus, the willingness to utilize and extend the letter-form in literary works does, in fact, continue into our own age.

[45] Sometimes, of course, not easy to determine. For discussions of pseudonymous epistolography, see F. Susemihl, *Geschichte der griechischen Litteratur* 2 (Leipzig 1892) 579-601; W. Speyer, *Die literarische Fälschung im heidnischen und Christlichen Altertum* (Munich 1971) *passim,* esp. 21ff, 79-81, 137f, 163f.

[46] *FGrHist* 49F6, 93F1, 687aF6, 688F1.

[47] R. Merkelbach, *Die Quellen des griechischen Alexander-Romans* (Munich 1954 = *Zetemata* 9), esp. 32-55.

[48] Diog. Laert. 6.101.

that written by Tiberianus (fourth century A.D.), *superi inferis salutem*.[49] By the second sophistic such feigned letters were not unusual. Witness Alciphron's letters of fishermen, peasants, etc; Aelian's letters of peasants; and, much later, Aristaenetus' fictional "love letters." But none of this is eloquent testimony for pre-Ovidian times. Rohde argued that Lesbonax was the first to write fictional love letters.[50] If this were the case and the writer in question were the Augustan Lesbonax, then we would have a very interesting potential source of influence. But neither is true. It is now generally believed that this Lesbonax belongs to the second sophistic, and, at any rate, we have no evidence that his love letters were "fictional" in the Ovidian sense. In the end, one example of the fictional love letter is conspicuous, that, of course, being Prop. 4.3, which we will discuss later. This poem is not merely the only fictional love letter, but also the only definitely fictional letter in verse prior to the *Heroides*.[51]

In sum, though the individual configurations of the epistolary form as conceived by Ovid in the *Heroides* had precedents, there is no evidence for any integration of these elements in a way that approximates his. This does not preclude the possibility that Ovid was influenced by one or another of these prior experiments with the epistolary genre, but it certainly must make any such influence, in the last analysis, relatively insignificant.

In the last decade or so, Winniczuk[52] and Kirfel[53] have well argued against the hackneyed view that the *Heroides* are not really letters at all. To be sure, the traditional question (as is always asked, for instance, of Horace's *Epistles*), whether or not these letters were actually dispatched, makes no sense for the *Heroides*. We must be willing to inquire—and be satisfied—whether or not these poems could, on ancient criteria, be considered letters, in the freest and broadest sense. The *prima facie* evi-

---

[49] See Serv. *ad Aen.* 6.532.

[50] *Op. cit.* (supra n. 25) 367-368, with n. 3.

[51] K. Deichgräber, *Hermes* 99 (1971) 67-68, with 68, n. 1, wonders whether Cinna may have composed an elegy in epistolary form in which a lady writes to her lover off at war. This is bold and suggestive, but really quite without a thread of evidence. We might consider fr. 18 of Laevius' *Protesilaodamia* where Laodamia appears to address the absent Protesilaus. Was this a letter? More likely it was a soliloquy in which Laodamia imagined her absent lover in her mind's eye.

[52] *Op. cit.* (supra n. 31) 39-70.

[53] Pp. 11-36, 112-119.

dence is highly important. Ovid calls these poems *Epistulae* (*AA* 3.345); it seems reasonable, if he did, that his contemporaries could accept them as such. Winniczuk's research shows clearly that one who seeks to find in the *Heroides* those characteristics which one expects in a letter can do so:[54] they inform, are conversational in tone, are persuasive, etc. But Winniczuk fails to see that her approach does not meet the genuine difficulties. For few of Ovid's critics would doubt that elements suitable to letters can be found in the *Heroides*. The stumbling blocks are those elements which seem so alien to the form: the tendency to tell the recipient much information he already knows,[55] addresses to persons other than the recipient, references to the latter in the third person, introspective deliberations which all but forget the addressee. In the end it will be hard to deny that in much of this Ovid was giving new shape and direction to the letter-form, perhaps even new life. The very introduction of mythic personages into a verse letter inevitably wrought novelties. But this is not equivalent to saying that he wrenched the epistle-form out of recognition.[56] As if to hammer this point home, Ovid begins and ends the *Heroides* on emphatically epistolary notes: *Hanc tua Penelope lento tibi mittit, Ulixe./ Nil mihi rescribas tu tamen; ipse veni!; hoc saltem miserae crudelis epistula dicat,/ ut mihi Leucadiae fata petantur aquae.* The elasticity of the epistle-form, especially as a receptacle for literary creation, had been long recognized by the Romans.

Perhaps we can get some help from the epistolographic theorists. It is now fairly certain that by the Augustan period there was a rather elaborate theoretical system of letter-writing among the Greeks. Of extant works it is possible that the τύποι ἐπιστολικοί was written as early as the second century B.C., likely that it is no later than the first century A.D. Demetrius' περὶ ἑρμηνείας, which contains a classic treatment of the epistolary genre, has recently been dated by Grube to c. 270 B.C.[57] Moreover, we know of trea-

---

[54] Pp. 44ff.

[55] Here we might see some parallel in Catullus 50, which, if a letter (see discussion infra), does relate much information the recipient clearly knows already.

[56] *Heroides* 9, the most atypical on epistolary criteria, is discussed in chapter XIII.

[57] G.M.A. Grube, *A Greek Critic: Demetrius on Style* (Toronto 1961 = *Phoenix* Suppl. 4) 56.

tises which dealt with problems of epistolography by Artemon of Cassandreia who anteceded Demetrius, and by a Dionysius.[58] This does not, of course, mean that the Romans either knew of or themselves had similar theoretic structures. It is a matter of dispute, for example, whether Cicero himself had a unified theory of letter-writing. On the other hand, it does not require such a theory to have a common consensus as to what a letter was or could be. It is not hard to find in Latin poetry quite explicit observations that coincide with those found in the Greek theorists, e.g., the theoretical notion that the letter makes the person who is absent present finds a good parallel in Ovid's reminder that in writing a letter one should strive *praesens ut videare loqui* (*AA* 1.468) and perhaps (if we can take the words as a reference to an epistle) in Turpilius (213 Ribb.), *sola res quae homines absentes ⟨nobis⟩ praesentes facit*. Such remarks need not rest on theoretical treatises. But this notion, together with the common idea, apparently first expressed by Artemon, that the letter is one side of a dialogue, means that the letter carries a double nature: (1) the physical reality that it is written by a distant, separated individual and as such is the product of isolated, unimpeded, and free floating (vis-à-vis the addressee) mental processes; (2) the imaginative reality that the writer is in the presence of and interacting with the addressee. Inextricably linked with the double nature is the function or the nature of the letter as, in Demetrius' words, εἰκὼν τῆς ἑαυτοῦ ψυχῆς, the reflection of the writer's psyche. What more is there to say? Very few, if any, letters of antiquity so effectively and strikingly achieve this as do the *Heroides*. And it is precisely from this perspective that the most problematic aspects of the *Heroides* must be understood, e.g., the emotional apostrophes, the forgotten addressee. Perhaps in this achievement Ovid reversed some traditional priorities. Commonly it may have been felt that letters were written primarily for external purposes, to inform, to persuade, to tie closely the bonds of friendship, but out of all this, from the undersurface, as it were, was revealed something of the psyche of the writer. Whereas in the *Heroides* the letter is primarily εἰκὼν τῆς ψυχῆς. To an extent, we must recognize that this subversion of the external in favor of the internal is here the very essence of the di-

---

[58] Schol. Aristoph. *Plut.* 322 gives nothing more than his bare name. He is usually identified with the first century A.D. grammarian, Dionysius of Alexandria.

chotomy between the real and the supposed writer. But such a rationale need not be limited to imagined letters. One might think of Cicero writing, *ego, etsi nihil habeo quod ad te scribam, scribo tamen quia tecum loqui videor* (*Att.* 12.53). This is the merest glimmer of what takes place in the *Heroides*.

At this point we can begin to understand why Ovid chose the letter-form. In the first place, it has the advantages of both the monologue and the dialogue. Simple monologues, however, would not do. By ancient standards they might be difficult to account for, in a poetic collection, as independent items. They would, in effect, be undefined mythic monologues existing in a vacuum. Much more significantly, they would lack the sense of interplay with an "other." From the formal perspective, we might see a twentieth century parallel to Ovid's choice of the epistolary form in Cocteau's use of modern technology's version of the letter, the telephone conversation, as a vehicle for a female lover's monologue (*La voix humaine*). Second, the choice of the letter-form amplifies the generic possibilities rather than restricting them, for while it does make very concrete demands with respect to its nature and function, it dictates very little as to the substance of the contents. Thus, boundaries can easily be overpassed. The substance can successively border on tragedy, comedy, parody, or erotic elegy as Ovid moves from poem to poem. Third, regarding the corpus as a whole, the epistolary format provided the medium in which to treat virtually the whole world of myth within 2,000 lines. In a moment of delicious insight Ovid must have realized that with the *Heroides* he could in one fell swoop take on a great number of the favorite myths of antiquity and also challenge on their ground, but after his own manner, many of the poetic masters of the past (Homer, Callimachus, Sophocles, Euripides, Aeschylus, Sappho, Catullus, Vergil). He must have scanned the possibilities of the genre with delight and enthusiasm.

Finally, we touch on an issue which will be amplified later. The letter-form applied to mythic characters crystallizes a whole complex series of dramatic events into one critical moment of potentially grand rhetoric and psychology. Thus, what makes the epistolary form integral, not peripheral, determining, not insignificant, is its special application to myth. For it freezes time. Here we can profitably compare how other writers of literary letters (e.g., Horace and Seneca) are quite blind to this capacity of

337

the form. Past, present, and future all come together, or perhaps all disappear, as the boundary lines dissolve and, with them, the world of cause and effect, of actions and events, of history as an external force upon men. All-importance devolves upon the psyche, the mind, the subjective. For the *Heroides* are timeless, by virtue of having no context, no traditional limits in time. They are usually a temporal panorama of a whole myth seen from what is specifically a very precise and limited focus in time. But it is this calculated choice that produces as well one of the *Heroides'* major artistic problems, the imposed static nature, the lack of movement. So, whereas on the one hand the new genre-form is what makes for the poetic and cognitive innovations in the *Heroides* (e.g., subjectivity as determinant, the role of memory), it also proves a large and difficult obstacle.

* * *

I suppose that there is sufficient reason to assume that in conceiving and composing the *Heroides,* Ovid did receive, here and there, ideas from the worlds of rhetorical training and strictly epistolographical writing that begot or influenced particular elements which go into the constitution of these poems. This is reasonable and probably right. Yet, one cannot help wondering if Ovid might not have written the *Heroides* even without these "models." For in the end the best way to view the whole question of the conception, originality, and nature of the *Heroides* is by seeing the poems as within the continuum of Greek and Latin poetry, particularly Latin elegy, but as rejecting old directions for new ones. Hence, it should be valuable to assess the relationship of the particular elements that comprise the *Heroides* to that Greek and Latin poetry which Ovid would have known.

The whole question of elegiac or lyric (by which I artificially mean to incorporate verse of a "personal" nature and to exclude e.g., Horace's *Epistles* which are more subject-centered than self-centered) epistles is confused by the apparent compulsion among ancient poets to address such poetry to others. Although in many cases the convention is transparent, there are a goodly number of instances in which the absence of a formal epistolary salutation does not suffice to preclude the poem's being a "letter." An example is Catullus 50, which, as Fraenkel has argued,[59] Catullus

[59] *WS* 69 (1956) 281-282.

probably dispatched to Calvus on the next morning, while also having in mind a wider public audience. We can observe how this poem does fulfill the dual epistolographic functions of communicating information (much of it, however, known to Calvus; this, of course, is meant for the reading public) and psychologically uniting the writer and the addressee.[60] Others that might fall into the same category are Catullus 13, 15, 32, 38; Prop. 1.11, 3.12, 3.22; the Sulpicia poems of the corpus Tibullianum (4.7-12). All these Kirfel has noted.[61] We might add Catullus 49, Hor. *C.* 1.20 and perhaps 4.12; Prop. 1.6, 2.7, 2.20, 2.22a, 2.22b; Tib. 1.3. But the problem of definition here is so great that one feels hesitant to attribute any epistolary character to most of these. Thus, to choose but a few, Prop. 1.6, 1.11, 2.7, though containing substantial material which could occur in a letter, advice, requests, information, they contain nothing which guarantees an epistolary nature. Prop. 3.12, 3.22, and Tib. 1.3 at least bear the one additional factor which may lend more justification to the "epistle" label, that the addressee is presumably far away from the poet. In the end, the complexities of the problem baffle us. We are foiled on the one hand by our inability to dissociate completely our contemporary sense of a letter, on the other by our inclination to draw clear lines where perhaps none existed. Nor do we know whether the criteria for a letter in verse should differ from those for a prose letter. Finally, one wonders whether even the dispatch of a poem to its addressee, a criterion commonly used as the court of final and decisive appeal, should be considered significant evidence. There seems good reason to distinguish between a poem of epistolary nature (i.e., which fulfills whatever functions an epistle has) and a poem which contains a proper name in the vocative and is sent to that "addressee" (but may not fulfill the epistolary functions). Perhaps a workable distinction could be evolved between a verse letter, in which the immediate interpersonal functions are primary, and a poetic letter, in which the artistic goals, as in any other poem, are uppermost. But even

---

[60] For general discussions of the problem of the addressee in Latin poetry, see W. Abel, *Die Anredeformen bei den römischen Elegikern* (Diss. Berlin 1930); W. Kroll, *NJbb* 37 (1916) 98-101; F. Leo, *GGA* (1901) 322-325; W. S. Teuffel, *Geschichte der römischen Literatur*, rev. by Kroll-Skutsch 1 (Berlin-Leipzig 1916) sect. 25, pp. 43-44. See too B. Otis, *HSCP* 70 (1965) 41, n. 16.

[61] Pp. 17-18.

here hard and fast lines would be difficult—and probably inadvisable—to draw.[62]

Somewhat clearer than the poems enumerated are Catullus 35 and 68 (probably 65 too). It will be readily noted that of these poems many are erotic, i.e., written by lover to lover or chiefly concerned with love affairs. Thus, Ovid had no lack of precedents for poems that were, at the least, loosely epistolary in form, and which were concerned with love.

On the Greek side epistolary poetry may have memories in Aeolian lyric, for many of Sappho's poems look as if they could easily have been, loosely, letters to friends abroad.[63] We have, moreover, illuminating evidence from Herodotus about Alcaeus' famous poem on the loss of his shield in flight; for he reports that Alcaeus sent this poem to a friend to inform him of the event.[64] Thus, even without epistolary format—the messenger who brought the poem would have sufficed for such introduction— this is to be considered an epistolary poem. Though there is no considerable body of extant evidence, Proclus (*Chrest.* sects. 37 and 99, Sev.) mentions a class of borderline, occasional melic poetry called the epistolary (ἐπισταλτικά) which he defines, ὅσα κατ' ἐντολὰς πρός τινας ποιοῦντες διέπεμπον. He notes also a similar class, the ἀποσταλικά (sect. 96).

Two kinds of epistolary poems were evidently common in the Hellenistic epigram: (1) invitation poems (see Philodemus *AP* 11.44 and cf. Cat. 13, Hor. *C.* 1.20, 4.12, *Epist.* 1.5);[65] (2) poems accompanying presents, e.g., Crinagoras *AP* 6.227 (first century B.C.); Theocritus *Id.* 28 (though it is surely strained to call this a letter); later examples at *AP* 5.74, 91.

Such is basically the evidence for poetic epistles which, in some way, could have influenced Ovid. I have not bothered to mention, so irrelevant are they, verse epistles of Spurius Mummius.[66] I

[62] Compare A. Deissmann's (*Licht vom Osten* [Tübingen 1923⁴] 193-196) classic distinction between *Epistel* and *Brief*, which, however, I find quite inadequate to the complexities of the problem. My own tentative distinction is drawn along different lines.

[63] J. M. Edmonds, *CQ* 16 (1922) 12-13, suggested, without further definition, that much of Sappho's poetry was in the form of letters.

[64] Hdt. 5.95; Strabo 600; = Z 105 LP. See D. Page, *Sappho and Alcaeus* (Oxford 1955) 153.

[65] See Nisbet-Hubbard, 244-246.

[66] See Cic. *Att.* 13.6.4.

know no substantial reason to assume that Aratus' letters were in verse, as Kroll says.[67]

Two notes from the vast repository of "la litterature inconnue." The Tibullan vita mentions that *epistolae quoque eius amatoriae, quamquam breves, omnino utiles sunt.* Interpretation is difficult, since the statement is terse and no obvious material to suit the description exists. We have no guarantee of the reliability of the *vita* anyway. Perhaps the reference is not to Tibullus but to, e.g., the Sulpicia poems. Or perhaps it represents a peculiar view of some of the addressed Tibullan elegies (though one then wonders at *breves*). Most striking, if most hazardous, would be to see in these *epistolae amatoriae* poems of Tibullus that have not survived. Such was evidently the opinion of the fifteenth century humanist, Sicco Polenton, though his exposition of the nature of these *epistolae* will obviously not do.[68] This is, however, probably a rash conclusion and Bardon, if his silence is testimony, evidently refuses even to entertain the possibility.

The Suda lists among the works of Theocritus a Ἡρωῖναι. The testimony is unique and Gow thinks the list generally suspect.[69] He does, however, suggest that the title may allude to Moschus 2 and 4 (which were sometimes attributed to Theocritus) and *Idyll* 26, all of which have to do with female characters of myth, none of which is even vaguely epistolary nor at all similar to the *Heroides*. (Moschus' *Megara*, 4, is closest, two female monologues, but still very distant). Again, we must admit the possibility of a lost work, but that it should have had any resemblance to the *Heroides* other than some similarity of title is beyond belief.

Propertius 2.20 merits a closer look. The poet defends himself before his girl's accusations of infidelity and professes eternal faithfulness and love. What is *prima facie* unusual is that the routine tables are turned: it is the poet who, rather than berating Cynthia (?) for her deceit, is compelled to play defendant. In this there is a common tie with many of the *Heroides* which show the woman as betrayed and accusing. But particularly striking is the

[67] *NJbb* 37 (1916) 98.

[68] See L. Alfonsi, *Riv. Fil. Cl.* 25 (1947) 180-181. For Sicco's text, see the edition of his *Scriptorum Illustrium Latinae Linguae Libri xviii* by B. L. Ullman (Rome 1928) 65.

[69] Vol. 1, 2d ed., pp. xxiv-xxv.

implied platform for Cynthia's complaints. She has, it appears likely, presented them to Propertius in the form of a letter: *nec tu supplicibus me sis venerata tabellis:/ ultima talis erit quae mea prima fides* (33-34).[70] This makes for a virtual *"Heroide."* Thematically the complaints—to an extent, of course, conventional—do resemble those in the *Heroides*, e.g., she cries (or perhaps describes her tears in writing, as do Ovid's heroines), invokes the justice of the gods (3), complains of the male's lack of *fides* (4). Propertius, in turn, like Ovid's heroes, takes oaths of eternal faith (14ff) and invokes curses upon himself (29ff). All this does not mean that there actually existed a letter of complaint (in elegiacs?) from Cynthia to Propertius. But this does not matter. What does is that Propertius has imagined such a letter (perhaps then we might even take this poem as a letter of response). We leave it at that. One can only guess whether Ovid, with his fine eye for the development of raw material, his clever imagination, and his delicious sense of malproportion saw in this poem the seeds for a whole genre of poetry.

Ethopoiia was discussed above as a branch of rhetorical training. But in fact the adoption of a foreign voice and identity was much earlier a literary and particularly a poetic posture: Homer speaking in the voice of Achilles, Sophocles in that of Oedipus, and most obviously relevant to the *Heroides*, Euripides in those of numerous mythological heroines.[71] But neither epic nor drama is free-standing *ethopoiia*, that is, an *ethopoiia* upon which nothing external impinges. For in epic the narrative, in drama the plurality of voices acts to mold and qualify the individual *ethopoiia*, to provide a context external to the individual monologue.[72] This, among other reasons, suffices to invalidate the fairly common identification of the *Heroides* with monologues of drama.[73] Equally important, monologues in drama are only a

---

[70] So Butler-Barber (224) seem to understand verse 33, "send me no more letters." One might take it merely as a reference to a possible future letter. But this makes little difference, since presumably this hypothetical letter would be a catalogue of complaints intermingled with pleas.

[71] The growth of the judicial system at Greece and Rome turned speechwriting into a professional art which was really just another form of *ethopoiia*.

[72] Similarly, in Moschus' *Megara* each monologue becomes the external context for the other.

[73] Made by, among others, D'Elia (130-131); Fränkel (190, n. 1); Peter (supra n. 35) 191; E. K. Rand, *Ovid and His Influence* (Boston 1925) 18; Wilkinson (86).

part of a whole in which the actions and events (loosely defined) that precede and follow are also of major importance. The monologue mirrors one moment in a continuing series of moments; it has no independent integrity, being but a piece of an "action." In contrast, each Ovidian epistle seeks to be the whole myth. That is why, in fact, no monologue in extant Greek tragedy resembles the *Heroides*.[74]

Of particular relevance to the *Heroides* are poems which in their totality speak in a voice not the author's. There is no lack of these and, to an extent, they can even be classified.[75] A valuable piece of evidence is a fragment of Alcaeus which appears to be the earliest instance of this kind of poem, A-10 LP.[76] Its poor condition prevents us from asserting positively anything more than that it is a monologue of a woman bewailing her misfortunes (very likely, misfortunes in love). But even this enables us to see the potential similarities to the *Heroides*: beyond the monologue-form we have a female speaker, lamenting her plight, possibly even love lost. There is, however, a distant possibility that should be taken into account, namely, that the poem's narrative setting has been lost. Perhaps once the monologue was done the poet proceeded to say, "such were the words of so and so, who . . ." and went on, either briefly or at length, to describe the situation. Horace's second *Epode* about the restless businessman does precisely this. On the surface, Milton's *Lycidas* appears also to utilize the same technique. Nor, in general, do we lack examples of lengthy monologues incorporated within a larger lyric or elegiac poem (see below for discussion), although the descriptive narrative will usually precede the monologue.

Whether any other early Greek poem can be called a freestanding monologue in another's person is debatable, largely because so much of the extant poetry is no more than fragments of wholes. But Sappho 102 LP may be.

Instances are easier to come by in the Hellenistic period. In the

74 Perhaps closest is Eur. *Medea* 465-519. In fact, monologues in Romance tend to be more like the *Heroides* than do those of tragedy (see e.g., Chariton, 1.14.6-10; 3.10.4-8; 5.1.4-7; 5.10.6-9; 6.6.2-5).

75 Such poems are frequent in modern literature, usually designated dramatic monologues. Much of Eliot's poetry (e.g., *Prufrock*) can be so classed. For a study of this genre in nineteenth and twentieth century English poetry, see R. Langbaum, *The Poetry of Experience* (London 1957) 75-108. A number of his insights are equally valid for the ancient form.

76 See Page (supra n. 64) 291-294.

epigrammatic literature there were occasionally erotic poems written by men in female voices, e.g., a girl's complaint that her lover has deserted her and is unfaithful (Asclepiades *AP* 12.153; Meleager [Philodemus?] *AP* 5.8). There are also other forms of the female point of view (e.g., Philodemus *AP* 5.120, 306).

More interesting are two lyric poems. The first, elaborate, skillfully wrought and metrically complex, is the so-called *carmen Grenfellianum* (Powell, *Coll. Alex.* 177-179), a highly dramatic female lament not later than the second century B.C. Notwithstanding the fact that the character of this poem is quite different from that of the *Heroides*, especially because of the substantial absence of narrative and of myth, there are some important points of contact: the lament on a lover's desertion, fluctuating emotions, imaginative preconstruction of the future, comparison of past to present, shifts from second to third person. Of passing interest is the fact that this *carmen* is likely a *hilarodia* or *magodia* and intended therefore for musico-dramatic stage presentation. This may be evidence to support Cunningham's opinion[77] that Ovid meant the *Heroides* for public singing performance. I would not, however, take this to mean that Ovid exclusively— or even primarily—so conceived them or that this is what Ovid was alluding to when claiming originality for the *Heroides*.

The *Helenae Querimonia* of c. 100 B.C. (Powell, *Coll. Alex.* 185) has little intrinsic poetic merit, but is of interest chiefly for its unique version of the Helen-Menelaus myth. For a student of the *Heroides* it has additional significance. *If* we can assume that it is a free-standing monologue, we then have an example—a single solitary example—of an independent poetic monologue in the mouth of a mythological figure prior to the *Heroides*. Of complementary interest is that it too is a woman's complaint of her lover's disloyalty. We may then have here a tiny but precious piece of testimony for a poetic-mythological-erotic-*ethopoiia* before the *Heroides*. Yet, no one could mistake one for the other. Resemblances are totally on the surface.

One final example: Theocritus' *Pharmaceutria* (2) in hexameters. This is very different from the *Heroides*, but nonetheless important as a monologue of a betrayed female lover.[78]

In Latin one must mention Horace's puzzling Ode 3.12, if we

[77] *Op. cit.* (supra n. 24) 100-106. But cf. W. Allen, Jr., *TAPA* 103 (1972) 12.
[78] Much bucolic poetry is ethopoeic in the sense I have been using the word, though most often in dialogue form. The same is true for the Mime.

344

choose to see this neither as a dialogue nor as an address by Horace to Neobule, but, with Wickham, Kiessling-Heinze, and Williams, as a monologue spoken by Neobule herself. There are also the "pseudo-Sulpicia" poems (Tib. 4.3 and 5). More important is Propertius' Cornelia-elegy (4.11), the "queen of elegies," a much overvalued poem, praised often more for its sentimental appeal than for its literary merit. Surprisingly, it shows more kinship to the *Heroides* than the bare generic similarity, e.g., the tendency to gnomic expression, the rhetorical questions, apostrophes to inanimate objects, defense and vindication of one's actions, review of one's past life, and, what is so characteristic of the *Heroides*, persistent shifts in the persons addressed. Here, then, is a poem which may well have planted an idea in Ovid's head (if, of course, as I believe, it anteceded the *Heroides*).

I want to glance briefly at a slightly different form of this ethopoeic poetry, essentially for the purpose of distinguishing it from the *Heroides*, since there is *prima facie* much to recommend identifying the two. Such poems contain lengthy monologues within a larger context. Again Propertius is most important (though we should at least note Verg. *Ecl.* 2 and Hor. *C.* 3.5) and, probably not coincidentally, again we must turn to his fourth book, that vast repository of poetic experimentation which also appears to have been an important impetus for Ovid's embarking on didactic erotic poetry (Prop. 4.5) and on aetiological poetry (Prop. 4.2, 4, 6, 9, 10). Thus, Tarpeia's soliloquy (4.4) has certain superficial similarities to the *Heroides*. But the crucial distinction is that it is enclosed within a narrative frame which endows the whole situation with a sense of concreteness, of objective existence, which the *Heroides*—soliloquies which, so to speak, hang in undefined space and time, lacking clear-cut beginning and end —reject. It is this absence of objective limits, of the concrete frame that defines and limits the poem and situation, that is peculiar to the *Heroides*. (We might see a dim analogy in the way some contemporary art rejects the traditional art-form by doing away with the frame that would give it singular existence as a work of art, thus making it simply part of the total undefined environment.) In the *Heroides*, then, each poem has total integrity and autonomy as a function of the woman's mind.

Then there is the diatribe of Cynthia's ghost (4.7). Certain of the erotic themes are the same as in the *Heroides*, but the tone is quite different and, once again, a decisive difference is how this monologue is controlled and shaded by its narrative setting. But in spite of the very real and important differences that distinguish these poems from the *Heroides*, we can be quite certain that Propertius' late obsession with the female monologue (4.3, 4.4, 4.7, 4.11) fascinated, impressed, and influenced Ovid.[79]

Smaller in scope and less literary in nature is the genre of the sepulchral epigram. The many examples in Book Seven of the *AP* are sufficient indication of the popularity of the ethopoeic first person epitaph. Of more note are the few cases of literary development of the genre. Undoubtedly Ovid would have appreciated how Horace especially (*C.* 1.28)[80] and Propertius too (1.21) expanded and developed, with wit and sympathy, this class of epigram into important poetry.

Finally, brief mention of a different form of ethopoeic verse monologue, that in which the speaker is an inanimate object. Fairly common and relatively insignificant are the epigrammatic cases, e.g., a dedicated object describes itself and the occasion of the dedication (e.g., *AP* 6.49, 107, 148, 149), a gift speaks to the recipient (*AP* 5.80), epigrams spoken by trees, etc.[81] More significant are elaborate poems like the famous *coma Berenices*, in its Callimachean and Catullian forms, full-blown *prosopopoiiae* (in the strictly technical sense), but in fact expansions of the genre of the dedicated object. Particularly interesting—once again we look toward Propertius—is his elegy 1.16, a lengthy soliloquy of a door (perhaps suggested by Catullus 67, which is, however, a dialogue between the poet and a door). What fascinates here is the way the ethopoeic monologue is the frame for the poet's words (the poet being identified—though not biographically—with the *exclusus amator*), a reversal of the usual state of affairs.

From all this we are able to conclude that the *Heroides* do not necessarily presuppose the existence of the rhetorical *ethopoiia*. This form of imaginative expression was sufficiently common, complex, and variegated in Ovid's poetic predecessors that one easily can apprehend how the *Heroides* might have been con-

[79] A substantial female monologue within a larger setting *may* have been the format for Calvus' important, but lost, elegy on the death of his wife. See E. Fraenkel, *WS* 69 (1956) 282-288.

[80] For interpretation, see now Nisbet-Hubbard 317-320.

[81] For a discussion of poems in which dedicated objects speak and of Priapus poems, see Fraenkel, *Horace* 121-122.

346

ceived and shaped in the reflection of much Greek and Latin poetry, particularly that of Propertius.

At last to Propertius 4.3. Traditionally, this poem is seen as the
immediate impetus for the *Heroides*. If, as appears likely to me,
the *Heroides* postdate Propertius' fourth book, this may be true.
But even so its importance is regularly exaggerated. By now we
have seen that many other factors lent their influence to the genesis of the *Heroides*, both as distant and as proximate motivations,
including a number of Propertius' poems beside 4.3. Anyway,
Prop. 4.3 is so essentially different from the *Heroides* that Ovid
could have gotten from it no more than the idea of a single letter
in elegiacs from a woman to her separated lover—which is, no
one will deny, a good deal, but in itself is a long way from the
Heroides. Examine Prop. 4.3 with the *Heroides* as a frame of reference.[82] The sole impetus for Arethusa's writing is her separation from Lycotas. Given such, she has virtually no individuality.
She is a separated lover writing to her beloved, nothing more,
completely unidimensional. Any one of Ovid's heroines has more
character than she. Also, the whole sense of a world seen through
and reduced to the perspective of one person, the whole aspect
of subjectivity has no place in Prop. 4.3 (here I am briefly antici-
pating later discussions of these facets of the *Heroides*). Of
course, Propertius' poem lacks the Ovidian "faults": the exaggerated wit, the verbal games, the sense of remove and occasional self-parody, the grandiose similes and metaphors, the repeti-
tiveness, the "rhetoric," the emotional extremes. In short, it lacks
the boldness, the willingness to take—even delight in taking—
poetic risks, the energy, the daring, the extension—even violation
—of limits everywhere present in the *Heroides*. Finally, all those
elements that flow from the poetic ambience of the mythical
world and bestow upon the *Heroides* many of its peculiar characteristics are no part of the landscape of Prop. 4.3.

Two areas of relative mystery bring this discussion to an end.
First, whether the poetry of the great Latin elegist, Gallus, may
have some role in the genesis of the *Heroides*. I ignore the extrav-

---

[82] For an interesting evaluation of the extensive differences between the
Heroides and Prop. 4.3, quite different from mine, see H. Merklin, *Hermes*
96 (1968) 461-494. Also see Oppel 34. I am in total disagreement with F.
Solmsen's appraisal of Ovid's adaptation of Prop. 4.3 in the *Heroides*; see
CP 57 (1962) 88, n. 71.

agant theory—which has no basis whatsoever—that he invented the epistolary elegy.[83] We know that he wrote erotic elegies and evidently made abundant use of myth in them.[84] On the surface, this could yield poems like the *Heroides*. But it is perfectly possible that his elegies were essentially mythological narratives in the Hellenistic fashion, or personal poems with mythological *exempla*, à la Propertius. In either of these likely cases, we would have to admit that the kinship to the *Heroides* would be minimal indeed, virtually nil.

Secondly, there is the Hellenistic prose romance. With its combination of erotic narratives, female character analysis, and occasional retrospective monologues, there is certainly a possibility that they made some contribution to the development of the *Heroides*.

Let this chapter end on a note of important qualification. The fact that the *Heroides* can be viewed as a mix of various factors (rhetorical exercises, epistolographical tradition, Greek lyric, Hellenistic poetry, Latin elegy, etc.)[85] does not necessarily imply causality or direct influence. Nor, even should we grant such influence, does this in any way suffice to explicate or analyze the *Heroides*. The whole is surely much more than the sum of its parts. The very association and integration of numerous elements is itself an act of creation which affects and changes the nature of these very components. In the *Heroides*, form, we must remember, is formative.

[83] See Winniczuk (supra n. 31) 51.

[84] Parthenius' collection of mythological *narrationes* was written especially for Gallus' use in his ἔπη καὶ ἐλεγείας.

[85] See W. Kraus, *WS* 65 (1950-1951) 57ff.

XVIII

The Role of Perspective

The *Heroides* are subjective poetry as is perhaps no other work of antiquity. Although it is commonplace to call Latin erotic elegy subjective, in fact we mean little more than personal. But Ovid's introduction of mythic material within the exclusively first-person format creates the necessary duality: "objective" events and individual perspective. The role of narrative is transformed. Formerly the province of the poet at one remove from his characters, once the objective mode of literature par excellence, Vergil had infused it with a degree of subjectivity and empathy. But in the *Heroides* Ovid radically transformed it into a mirror of the relative nature of reality. The world of myth is no longer reality or a symbolic reflection of reality, but to a large degree projections or extensions of individual minds. This is why Ovid chooses to create a work in which very similar situations, indeed, the very same myths recur again and again. For, given the insight that mind is itself a part of reality, one and the same event becomes a multi-faceted thing depending on who sees, experiences, and recounts it. Now all this does not make Ovid a profound or conscious philosopher, an ancestor of Kant or Berkeley. But when we consider all the philosophical schools of antiquity which in one way or another disputed the existence of a stable reality or distinguished between the real and the seemingly real or denied that knowledge was possible (e.g., Heraclitus, the Eleatics, Plato, the Academics), it is not surprising to find in Ovid an awareness of the problem. In general, the artist has always been (even without the benefit of formal philosophy) interested in the nature of reality. Pirandello and—an even more extreme case—the analytic cubists are notable examples from our own century. Whereas the philosophers will tend to see the question as cognitive or epistemological, the *Heroides* shift it largely to an emotional arena, where the involvement in, not merely the

349

perception of, the event by the writer may be a determining factor in the shape of its representation. The role of Time is central. The identity between the narrator and the participant in the events means that there is a time-lag between occurrence and description and that, consequently, the creative force at work is Memory, subject of course to the control and modification generated by the present circumstances. Here, furthermore, is the mechanism which largely governs the vexed area of Ovid's accuracy or rather his faithfulness to sources.

Here are a few examples, some of which have already been noticed in the essays on the individual poems. Briseis describes the arrival of Talthybius and Eurybates:

> Nam simul Eurybates me Talthybiusque vocarunt,
>   Eurybati data sum Talthybioque comes.
> Alter in alterius iactantes lumina vultum
>   quaerebant taciti, noster ubi esset amor.

$$(3.9\text{-}12)$$

To be sure, there is nothing of the sort in Homer, and we might be content to call it a neat expansion by Ovid. But this will really miss the point. For the behavior of the two heralds is so clearly a projection of Briseis' own feelings that we must in the end be unsure as to whether the heralds in fact so reacted. Is this "fact" or "interpretation?" The question is unanswerable; which is precisely Ovid's point. A similar instance at 11.95-98:

> Interea patrius vultu maerente satelles
>   venit et indignos edidit ore sonos:
> "Aeolus hunc ensem mittit tibi"—tradidit ensem—
>   "et iubet ex merito scire quid iste velit."

Here, unlike at *Her.* 3, we are not so fortunate as to have Ovid's source; it would be decisive to know how Euripides depicted this angel of death. But when Canace describes him *vultu maerente* we are again entitled to wonder whether this is anything more than the projection of her own feelings about herself and toward her father, especially since the messenger's explicit words do not evince any sympathy at all.

The same kind of question is raised by Deianira's description of Iole.

> Non sinis averti: Mediam captiva per urbem
>   invitis oculis adspicienda venit.

Nec venit incultis captarum more capillis:
    Fortunam vultu fassa tegente suam
ingreditur late lato spectabilis auro,
    qualiter in Phrygia tu quoque cultus eras;
dat vultum populo sublimis ut Hercule victo:
    Oechaliam vivo stare parente putes;

(9.123-130)

So different is Sophocles' Iole that Deianira even has pity for her. Is it, then, Ovid who has drastically altered Iole's carriage and appearance? Or is this account a reflection of Deianira's innermost feelings? As often, nothing allows for the "truth" to be established.

In contrast to traditional versions of the myth, Ovid's Demophoon arrives shipwrecked on Thrace and Phyllis, not her father, takes charge of caring for his affairs and welfare. Is the alteration Ovid's or are the events shaped in Phyllis' retrospective imagination?

When Vergil's Aeneas quits Carthage, it is pointedly made clear that he has left no heir. In contrast stands Ovid's Dido:

Forsitan et gravidam Didon, scelerate, relinquas
    parsque tui lateat corpore clausa meo.
Accedet fatis matris miserabilis infans
    et nondum nati funeris auctor eris.
Cumque parente sua frater morietur Iuli,
    poenaque connexos auferet una duos.

(7.135-140)

Observe how the hesitant subjunctives give way before decisive indicatives. Is Dido pregnant, or is it even possible that she may be? Or is the pregnant Dido merely product of her own wish-fulfillment, or perhaps no more than another weapon in her arsenal of persuasion? Once more the lines between objective reality and subjective truth are nowhere to be discerned.

A passage in Penelope's letter that has perplexed many becomes understandable in this light:

Nos Pylon, antiqui Neleia Nestoris arva,
    misimus; incerta est fama remissa Pylo;
misimus et Sparten; Sparte quoque nescia veri.

(1.63-65)

351

The *Odyssey* is clear: Penelope neither sends Telemachus nor even knows of his intention to go. Some scholars assume faulty reading of Homer by Ovid, forgetfulness or the like; others argue that Ovid changes the story to increase Penelope's interest in Ulysses' return. But, as before, it is equally suitable to see Penelope's claim as a product of her present mental disposition. Does she now imagine that, after all, she did send Telemachus? Or does she perhaps want Ulysses to think so? Or did she really? Questions not meant by Ovid to have answers.

Instances of this sort can readily be multiplied. But these suffice to make a point: it is of the essence of the *Heroides* that we never know whether changes in the myths are Ovid's (i.e., objective, factual) or simply reflections of the peculiar condition of the heroine's mind, e.g., anger, self-defense, need to persuade,[1] or other more complex psychic functions.[2] The form precludes any sense of objective truth such as might be produced by the presence of an external commentator who directs and establishes "reality" (e.g., the poet in epic), or by the interaction of voices (as in drama).

A second major characteristic generated by the subjective nature of the *Heroides* is the reduction of great, sometimes cataclysmic, events and myths to the narrow egocentric world of the heroine. A case in point: the judgment of Paris is traditionally the harbinger, indeed the cause, of the Trojan War, nothing less. Yet, when we encounter that famous event in Oenone's epistle, the scope of its import has been drastically reduced:

> Illa dies fatum miserae mihi dixit, ab illa
>   pessima mutati coepit amoris hiems,
> qua Venus et Iuno sumptisque decentior armis
>   venit in arbitrium nuda Minerva tuum.

> (5.33-36)

It is merely the beginning of the end for the love affair between Paris and Oenone. Similarly, Cassandra's great prophecy warning of the coming war becomes largely, for Oenone, a forecast of her own personal calamity (115-124). And the war itself? To

---

[1] A fine example of the coloring of past events in a speech attempting to persuade is *Aen.* 10.63-95.

[2] In my interpretive essays on the individual poems, I have occasionally chosen in specific cases either the "subjective" or the "objective" view, but usually more for simplicity's sake than because I felt the distinction definable.

Oenone it is little more than an inconvenience, while also being a good argument she can muster in her attempts to regain Paris:

> Denique tutus amor meus est; tibi nulla parantur
> bella nec ultrices advehit unda rates.
> Tyndaris infestis fugitiva reposcitur armis;
> hac venit in thalamos dote superba tuos.
>
> (89-92)

The devout comradeship of Theseus and Pirithous, culminating in their heroic attempt to assault the very barriers of Hell, looks rather different to Phaedra: it represents Theseus' rejection of her for a homosexual lover: *Praeposuit Theseus, nisi si manifesta negamus,/ Pirithoum Phaedrae Pirithoumque tibi* (4.111-112).

To Briseis, the lyre and girl which occupy Achilles' time are good targets for her barrage of insult with which she seeks to shame him back to his former self (3.113-122). But in these and earlier remarks (13-14, 55-56) Briseis reveals that she is totally incapable of understanding the spirit of the *Iliad* and the "larger" principles involved in Achilles' struggle.

When Penelope recounts particular episodes of the war, each is seen solely in its effect on her (13-22). And because of her enduring aloneness, the overriding success of the Greeks' expedition to Troy is as nought to her: *Diruta sunt aliis, uni mihi Pergama restant* (51).

The delay of the Greek army at Aulis, with all its great and ominous implications and consequences, is described by Laodamia: *Aulide te fama est vento retinente morari* (13.3). *Te* is wonderful. The whole Greek expedition has been reduced to Protesilaus. And the latter, who traditionally must have been a keen and distinguished warrior, is in her myopic perspective not even suited for warfare, only for lovemaking:

> Non es quem deceat nudo concurrere ferro
> saevaque in oppositos pectora ferre viros.
> Fortius ille potest multo, quam pugnat, amare.
> Bella gerant alii: Protesilaus amet!
>
> (79-82)

Again, examples could, but need not, be multiplied. These are sufficient to draw the necessary and important conclusions. This reductionist tendency, so to speak, is not the result of the transference of epic and dramatic material to elegy, a genre—one

353

often hears—incapable of sustaining the broader scope and implication of the serious subject matter. This is to confuse cause
and effect. Ovid's treatment is not a degradation of heroic myth.
In one sense, it is an elevation of it; or better, it is a translation of
it to a completely different dimension. For the *Heroides* set all-
importance in the individual, the seemingly insignificant individual who is obscured by the dazzling glare of massive events and
great principles. But when the validity, indeed, the very reality
of these events is made contingent on the perspective of the individual, we can understand that it is with the individual that significance really rests. Historically, this view takes on extra importance when we place the *Heroides* against the backdrop of
Augustus and Vergil's *Aeneid*, a world in which the individual
is a mere sacrificial lamb on the altar of community and
principle.

In general, individual perspective controls the *Heroides*. On
a large scale one thinks of the lengthy description of the fateful
wedding night told completely from Hypermestra's point of
view. On a smaller scale is the frequent motif of *crimen* (*scelus*)
= *meritum*, where the paradox is manifestly the function of the
the governing point of view. Sometimes perspectives are played
off one against another from poem to poem. Thus, for instance,
the theme of mother's separation from child. In *Heroides* 8 we
are presented with the theme from the viewpoint of the heart-
broken and deprived child (75-100), in *Heroides* 11 from that of
the grieving, mistreated mother (109ff), in *Heroides* 12, by way
of anticipation, from that of the child-killer herself, Medea
(189-214).

A complementary facet. By treating many events or myths
more than once in the course of the *Heroides*, Ovid compels us
to see that a myth or an event must be understood not as an absolute entity in itself, but as the sum of the individual perspectives
that bear upon it. The Trojan War is probably the best example,
viewed from at least half a dozen different perspectives: the
wives of the first Greek to die and the last to return, the war's
first victim (Oenone) and, in a sense, its last (Dido), two captive
women, one held by Achilles, the other by Achilles' son. For Penelope the war, while fought, was a source of constant anxiety;
now that Troy has fallen, she sees the whole thing as a waste
(1.51). Laodamia, who views the war with trepidation, can with
naïveté write enviously of the "fortunate" Trojan women. In

354

sharp contrast stand Hermione and Briseis. The former cites the Trojan War as a paradigm of honor and glory, and strives to mold Orestes in the images of his father and uncle who directed it. In similar fashion, Briseis spurs on Achilles to fight that honorable war, naïvely supposing that his withdrawal signals a rejection of her. For Oenone the war has significance merely as an obstacle to her relationship with Paris, but, set off against the background of a peaceful pastoral life, it looms as a vehicle of terrible havoc and destruction. To Dido the war seems very far off; yet it is the source of Aeneas' inexplicable attitudes and behavior which will ultimately destroy her.

Closely allied to the war is the figure of Helen. Her character and actions are variously portrayed. At one end of the spectrum she is almost innocent victim of the villainous Paris (*Her.* 8.19ff, 73ff), at the other, she is guilty not only of running off with Paris, but also of chronic depravity, having previously taken up with Theseus (*H.* 5.125-132). Midground is Laodamia who also condemns Helen, but is equally ready to blame Paris (*H.* 13.43-48, 131).

Another myth that receives elaborately divergent treatments is that of Jason and Medea. Both Medea and Hypsipyle recount Jason's labors at some length. Medea's main interest is in representing herself as a frightened and concerned girl (12.95-104). Thus, she describes the tasks in rather terrifying terms, shows herself an awestruck and scared spectator, and plays down her own role in the execution of the great feats. What a difference in Hypsipyle's version of the same events (6.9-14, 32-37)! This is all matter-of-fact narrative. The emotion, awe, fear, dread colors with which Medea paints the scene are all gone. Moreover, the deeds seem to do themselves; at the least, Jason here has no role at all. Hypsipyle, of course, knows how everything has turned out and is unwilling to give Jason any credit. But Medea, too, when her feelings of bitterness and anger become uppermost, sees the feats in the same light: she, not Jason, has accomplished them (109-110, and esp. 165-174). There is added irony in the recollection of 6.97-98 in 12.165-174. Hypsipyle imagines that Medea's powers over animals extend to men also; Medea learns that they do not.

A similar pattern resides in the two descriptions of the meeting of Jason and Medea. In retrospect Medea considers that she was overwhelmed by Jason's beauty, almost bewitched by him (33-40, esp. 38). Quite the contrary in Hypsipyle's eyes. For her there is only one possibility: Medea bewitched Jason (83-84, 93-94, 97-98). The whole portrait of Medea is similarly reversed. While Medea cannot cover over all her guilt, she does attempt a picture of innocence corrupted. She is the naïve girl who happens to possess special skills. To Hypsipyle, she is the full-blown witch, equipped with all the traditional, unnatural abilities and the propensity for evildoing.

So too a particular ambience may prove profoundly ambiguous. The juxtaposition of the letters of Phaedra and Oenone is a case in point. In the one an idyllic love is tuned to the rustic life and corrupted by the allurements of an urban civilization. In the other, it is the rustic life which stands as implacable enemy to love, and seductions are presented in sophisticated terms—power, possessions, and the violation of the "rustic" morality.

In the *Heroides* myths are internalized. Everything exists in the mind of the heroine, that is all we are given to know. It is a world not of concrete events, but of psychic projections, emotions and thought. This is why the letters can end without any real resolution of the complicated external situations in which the women are found.[3] Final resolutions are invariably internal, made stable by their frequent allusions to "terminal" states: death, old age, eternity. That so many of the poems end with hints of death where the mythic tradition did not entail the heroine's death makes abundantly clear how meaningless the external circumstances are.

It is in the narrative of the past that the subjective coloration is most obvious and blatant. Often factual accounts are interrupted by vocatives or interjections which belie or contradict the immediate statement. Rhetorical questions often break a narrative flow and reflect a vacillation in the writer's evaluation of a particular circumstance. Parenthetic phrases, pointed adjectives and adverbs, and notably impossible wishes in past time, which by their nature incorporate both description of the past and reaction of the present, achieve similar effects. Seemingly objective conditions take on shades and nuances of significance that attach themselves to the events only after they have lost their independence as facts and become part of the mental and emotional world

[3] The one probable exception is *Heroides* 9, but this is part of Ovid's experiment in that poem. For discussion, see chapter XIII.

of the heroine: the past is re-created—or created—in the light of the present.

Several examples. Demophoon's oath of eternal fidelity to Phyllis is replete with formal devices of language that render it *ab initio* an act of bad faith (2.31ff): the "proleptic" use of *falso*, the periphrastic future, *iturus eras*, the parenthetic *nisi fictus et ille*. This portrait of Demophoon, the smooth and treacherous talker, is shortly thereafter reinforced: *credidimus blandis, quorum tibi copia, verbis* (49), *credidimus lacrimis. An et hae simulare docentur?* (51). Similarly, by conjoining all of Demophoon's actions on his departure as infinitives dependent on *ausus es* (93), he is again presented as brazenly insincere and deceitful, having no intent ever to keep faith.

Much of Medea's letter works the same way. Jason, one gets the impression, never meant a word of what he told Medea: *linguae gratia ficta tuae* (14). All along he took advantage of the naïve young girl: *Perfide, sensisti! Quis enim bene celat amorem?* (39). Like Demophoon, he spoke *infido ore* (74) and made villainous use of feigned tears (93). And so, poor Medea was tricked, *sic cito sum verbis capta puella tuis* (94; *capta* is a double entendre).

Deianira is so stunned by the latest of Hercules' escapades that her accounts of his great deeds and lineage are sometimes so phrased as to cast a doubt on their validity. Thus, the question *tene ferunt* (31) and the nasty *si creditur* (9).

Such examples, a handful among many, serve to clarify the way narrative is colored in the *Heroides*.

However one is disposed to Hermann Fränkel's picture of a quasi-Christian Ovid, we should have no hesitation in accepting his delineation of Ovid's concern with the ambiguous nature of reality or with different levels of reality. The *Metamorphoses* alone is substantial testimony. Ovid's interest in metamorphosis is doubly motivated, both reasons touching on his interest in what constitutes reality: first, there is the paradox of something being other than it is; second, the consequent implication is that there is a close connection, perhaps a continuum of identity, between the human and the nonhuman, the animate and the inanimate worlds. Ovid's infatuation with the verse *semibovemque virum semivirumque bovem* (*AA* 2.24) stems not merely from its violent control of language, but equally from its concomitant reflection, in its linguistic mirror, of the paradox of the reality involved. There is evidence, even in the *Amores*, of such interest in Ovid's youth. *Am.* 2.16, though partially made up of commonplaces, does reflect an appreciation of the changes wrought by one's frame of mind on the "objective" world. *Am.* 3.14, a stunning example of Ovidian erotic wit, is at the same time evidence of Ovid's understanding of the power of mind to deflect reality— or rather, to deflect the subject matter of perception. Along similar lines is the incisive verse at *Rem.Am.* 504, *qui poterit sanum fingere, sanus erit.* For the *Heroides* and *Metamorphoses*, Ovid's declaration at *Am.* 3.12 may be particularly relevant, wherein poetry (myth) is presented as the agent through which a world, other than the "normal" one, has its existence.

In short, the unique form which is the *Heroides* has a threefold set of consequences, all of which are repeated by later writers, and have in particular been consciously elaborated by literary artists of this century. First, the *Heroides* present familiar stories and personalities from new and unexpected perspectives, a strategy recently adopted with success by Tom Stoppard in his *Rosencrantz and Guildenstern are Dead*, and by James Saunders in his *Travails of Sancho Panza*. Second, the *Heroides* represent the same events from a variety of perspectives, a technique perhaps best known from Akutagawa's *In a Grove* and Browning's *The Ring and the Book*, lately utilized by J. Hopkins in his *Talking to a Stranger*. Finally, the *Heroides* create a world in which objective and subjective realities are incapable of being distinguished. Of our contemporaries, Pirandello and Ionesco, each in his own way, have fashioned their works after the same image.

Seneca's masterpiece of pithy understatement could stand as a motto for the *Heroides: non tantum quid videas, sed quemadmodum, refert* (*Ep.* 71.24).

The role of perspective in the *Heroides* cannot be isolated from that of Time and Memory. After a fashion, the *Heroides* are autobiographies, "reconstructions of the self through memory,"[4] and are subject to principles that often determine the nature of autobiographies. We can do no better than quote from Meyerhoff's brilliant book, *Time in Literature*:

> Memory relations exhibit a *nonuniform, dynamic order* of events. Things remembered are fused and confused with things feared and hoped for. Wishes

[4] H. Meyerhoff, *Time in Literature* (Berkeley and Los Angeles 1955) 56.

358

and fantasies may not only be remembered as facts, but the facts remembered are constantly modified, reinterpreted, and relived in the light of present exigencies, past fears, and future hopes.

The objective order of temporal sequences, therefore, forms only a partial, though indispensable, aspect of our memory structure; it is an order partial, as it were, to the world of clocks, dates, and physical records. A major portion of the contents of our memory does not exhibit this kind of uniform, serial order but rather a quality by which past, present, and future events are dynamically fused and associated with each other.[5]

Meyerhoff is speaking, to be sure, of modern literature, but it takes no stretch of the imagination to see the application of his words to the *Heroides*—without feeling the need to see in Ovid a Roman Proust, Valéry, or Joyce. Though literally the expression of a particular moment in time, the *Heroides* incorporate into themselves past, present, and future; simplistically, we might say as narrative account, emotional response, and fears and hopes respectively. But the chronological strands are often so complexly intertwined that it becomes impossible—not to say misguided —to disentangle them. "All the elements comprising the self," as Meyerhoff says,[6] "are potentially co-present at any time," and this means the future also, the future as conceived, irrespective of whether this proves identical with the future as ultimately realized in "true" time. For the *Heroides*, to be sure, which are feigned autobiographies in which the identity of autobiographer and writer are divided, there is room for wit and humor in the possibility, sometimes exploited, of intentional irony and foreshadowing. Both Phyllis and Ariadne can vividly conceive of themselves as dead; that their fates will probably prove far different one from the other matters not at all. Deianira can imagine the coming marriage of Hercules and Iole; its reality in her mind is not contingent upon its abortion in "objective" time. Similarly, Laodamia can virtually experience her future reunion with Protesilaus, which is never to materialize (in life).

But more important—and more pervasive—is the constant interplay of present and past. Even the casual reader will recog-

[5] *Ibid.* 21-22.   [6] *Ibid.* 56.

359

nize how rapidly past and present alternate, interchange, and fluctuate; further, layers of the past often overlap. It is for this reason that attempts to analyze logical structural patterns in the poems almost always founder. Though it goes too far, it is not totally without foundation to see in the *Heroides* a distant, very distant, ancestor of the interior monologue, the stream of consciousness. It is superfluous to enumerate instances of this fluctuation, confronting us, as it does, on every page of the *Heroides*. Less immediately evident are other peculiarities related to the role of time. Here are a few examples: *Numen ubi est? Ubi di? Meritas subeamus in alto,/ tu fraudis poenas, credulitatis ego* (12.121-122). The sense is obviously jumbled, conditioned by Medea's present hindsight applied to her immediately preceding allusion to their escape from Colchis by sea. It is as if she has thrown herself back into the past while simultaneously maintaining the knowledge and experience of the present. Similar are these two verses from *Heroides* 11: *Quid faciam infelix* (53), *Quid tibi grataris* (67). In each case the present tense in combination with the applicability of the sentiment to the actual present situation obscures the temporal definition of the question. For each cry could be either Canace's response to her immediate calamitous plight, or else a translation to the present of her earlier perplexity. Only the ensuing remarks offer clarification.

Different, but equally interesting, is the way Ovid exploits the built-in temporal ambiguity of the inscribed-tree motif (5.21-32). Here past, present, and future inevitably coalesce. The inscription testifies to the act of inscribing and therefore to the former love of Paris for Oenone, while at the same time it ironically perpetuates, by its continuing existence, Paris' treachery.

A striking example of the blurring—indeed obliteration—of temporal demarcations is Hypermestra's account of the Io tale. What opens in ordinary fashion (14.85-92) takes on a striking turn:

> Quid furis, infelix? Quid te miraris in unda?
> Quid numeras factos ad nova membra pedes?
> Illa Iovis magni paelex metuenda sorori
> fronde levas nimiam caespitibusque famem;
> fonte bibis spectasque tuam stupefacta figuram
> et, te ne feriant quae geris arma, times.

Quaeque modo, ut possis etiam Iove digna videri,
  dives eras, nuda nuda recumbis humo.
Per mare, per terras cognataque flumina curris;
  dat mare, dant amnes, dat tibi terra viam.
Quae tibi causa fugae? Quid, io! freta longa pererras?
  Non poteris vultus effugere ipsa tuos.
Inachi, quo properas? Eadem sequerisque fugisque;
  tu tibi dux comiti, tu comes ipsa duci.

(93-106)

It is not the apostrophe that is noteworthy; this is common enough technique in the *Heroides*. But rather the fact that Hypermestra and Io suddenly become contemporaries. The past becomes vividly present for Hypermestra, who *sees* the whole myth before her eyes.

What often puzzles is the way these poems, though literally the products of particular moments, seem to lack any sure fix on a given present. It is not often that the reader feels secure as to where, chronologically, each poem is—or indeed each portion of a poem. Often one feels the need to ask, "Where are we now?" For the present is rarely stable, that is, at different occasions in one poem we seem to be standing at different presents, at distinct temporal vantage points. We look backward and forward from what appear to be drifting presents. Time is at once fluid and static. This facet of the *Heroides* is discussed in more detail elsewhere.[7] Herewith just a few observations.

After some introductory lines of a chastising nature, Ariadne proceeds to recount her bitter awakening (10.7ff). After brief histrionics she runs back and forth along the shore. The present tenses of 19-20 allow us, for a moment, to assume that this activity immediately preceded the writing of the letter. But no; *interea* and the imperfect in 21-22 explode this possibility. Later, she sights the boat. Once again the presents (33-36) deceive us, for the following lines set this scene back into the past. Finally, we are secure at line 58 as Ariadne returns to the lovers' bed and berates Theseus. The address to the bed (56-58) passes imperceptibly into the following tirade which could almost be part of it. So here, at last, is where we are—or is it? Come the poem's end and the reader's focus has again been transplanted, for at

---

[7] See chapter XIX, "Dramatic Structure."

some point Ariadne has removed herself to the cliff overlooking the sea (135-136).

Medea's letter is similar. From the outset the tone makes clear that "now" is after Jason has decided to cast off Medea and by verse 27 we know that he intends to marry Creusa. But at 137ff "now" is pushed ahead; for Jason has not only decided, he has acted: Medea has been literally thrown out of the house and the wedding ceremony has already taken place. However, it is not long before this "now" also recedes. The wedding over, *noctes vigilantur amarae* (171), and so we finally are left with a "now" that is at least a few days after the marriage.[8] Thus, before our eyes the present moment changes, "now" becomes "then," and the sense of a fixed moment disappears.

Briefly put, in their incorporation of Time and Memory as central, dynamic, and generating principles, the *Heroides* may well be a landmark in ancient literature.[9]

[8] Contrast the time span in Euripides' *Medea*.

[9] For some interesting observations on Ovid's manipulation of Time in the *Amores*, see D. Parker, *Arion* 8 (1969) 80-97.

XIX

Dramatic Structure

In the epistolary form Ovid was able to achieve his desired poetic goals, including a number of novel effects. But he also encountered the one great disadvantage that the genre-form inevitably entailed. In freezing the poem at one particular moment, he seemingly condemned it to bear a static character. Neither unexpectedly nor without reason, critics have often found fault with the *Heroides* on just these grounds. Otis' comment is well-put and representative:

> The chief inspiration of the *Heroides* is the neoteric short epic, and the device of the letter served to enhance and focus the fundamental weakness of this model—that is, its lack of real dramatic quality, its reduction of a story to one or two disconnected moments of static pathos. After all, Ovid's Ariadne is only a repetition of Catullus' Ariadne: in the one case the tapestry setting, in the other the artificial letter-form, fixes her in one emotional spot and compels her to heap up and reiterate her feelings in a long tirade that advances neither the emotion, the thought nor the action.[1]

Yet, I think that an examination of the problem will help us see that Ovid himself was aware of the difficulty and, even if he was never able to find a fully satisfactory solution, he experimented with a variety of approaches and sometimes came remarkably close to resolving what appears to be an irreconcilable incompatibility.

The basic problem is twofold. The constriction of the poem to the temporal duration of the writing of the letter precludes—or

[1] Otis 17.

363

on the surface appears to preclude—the passage of time within which things can happen. Second, the fact that the *Heroides* are internal—that is, the contents of the letter are the representation of the mind at work and consequently the only situation is the letter-writing itself, with nothing external to it—tends to render it impossible for them to be dramatic in the sense that much other ancient poetry is. Or so, at least, it would seem.

A few examples of quasi-monologue poems which strive to be dramatic will clarify the avenues which were available for adaptation. The simplest is to blatantly change the scene within the monologue. Theocritus' third *Idyll* begins with the poet's declaration that he is going off to serenade Amaryllis. Spontaneously, the scene shifts and he is now in her very presence. The *carmen Grenfellianum* (Powell, *Coll. Alex.* 177-179) does the same thing, but in considerably less obvious a manner. Here, as the monologue begins, the girl is evidently at home. The scene then shifts: she is out walking in the street. Finally, she reaches the home of her lover.[2] This mode clearly lies without the range of possibilities open to Ovid. Other instances are more subtle than these, but on the whole not much better as viable possibilities for the *Heroides*. Two from Propertius (1.8 and 2.28). In the first, Propertius bemoans the imminent departure of Cynthia. Suddenly, something happens and the situation is reversed: the poet is now ecstatic that she will, after all, stay. Similarly in 2.28. Cynthia is very sick; Propertius describes and responds to the crisis. Then, unexpectedly, all is well. Cynthia has regained her health and Propertius is thankful. Scarcely anyone will be surprised that numerous editors refuse to accept these poems as integral units and divide them up: 1.8A, 1.8B;[3] 2.28A, 2.28B (2.28C). But the technique is transparent. There is an imagined lapse of time during which something happens to alter the circumstances. To pull this off within the letter-form context of the *Heroides* would be difficult and clumsy. Horace is not averse to this technique, using it a few times in the *Odes* and perhaps once in the *Epodes*. *C.* 3.19 may be a poem in two scenes, with a break in the middle,

---

[2] This is the traditional view. P. Händel, in his revision of A. Körte, *Die hellenistische Dichtung* (Stuttgart 1960) 303-305, disagrees, suggesting that the shifts of scene are actually in the girl's imagination. See too E. Fraenkel, *Elementi Plautini in Plauto* (Florence 1960), 317, n.

[3] O. Skutsch, *CP* 58 (1963) 238-239, with 239, n. 4, divides 1.8 for different reasons.

as we move from pre-party banter to the party itself.[4] *C.* 1.27 is, on the other hand, without question dramatic, the high point coming when the reader must imagine Horace questioning a young man, receiving a whispered response, and reacting in turn. *Epode* Nine, if Wilkinson is correct,[5] may be a monologue in which one must imagine a progression of military events paralleling the movement of the poem.[6] None of this could have been immediately useful to Ovid, but the idea that the dramatic quality might inhere in the nature of the writer's response to the changing situation, as manifest in some of these poems, could ultimately prove adaptable to Ovid's own format.

To take an extreme case first. Nowhere in the *Heroides* does Ovid so openly acknowledge the problem of the static poem as in Deianira's letter, where he, so to speak, meets it head on and overwhelms it by sheer force. Bluntly at line 143: *scribenti nuntia venit/ fama virum tunicae tabe perire meae*; a message has come to Deianira while writing her letter that Hercules is close to death. The report sharply changes the course of the poem and it now proceeds in a new direction. To be sure, this letter was in need of some such drastic innovation, since it is otherwise extremely static, consisting almost completely of complaints and sardonic descriptions of Hercules' exploits.[7] So Ovid tried this once, but never again; for he must have realized that the imposition of dramatic character by an external impetus was out of tune with the essentially self-contained, internal nature of these poems.

In examining the structural dynamics of the *Heroides*, certain (overlapping) questions must be kept in mind: (1) Does anything happen, is there any development within the poem? (2) If there

[4] This is the common view. It has recently been disputed by J.F.G. Gornall, *G&R* 18 (1971) 188-190.

[5] L. P. Wilkinson, *CR* 47 (1933) 2-6.

[6] I list a few more examples: Catullus 42, Ovid *Am.* 1.13 (see D. Parker, *Arion* 8 [1969] 80-83), Asclepiades *AP* 5.181, Meleager *AP* 5.182, 184. Somewhat different are those monologues which purport to describe the progress of a ritualistic event taking place, e.g., Tib. 2.1, 2.2, Catullus 61. Dialogues, of course, are another story. Frequently they are by their very nature essentially dramatic, e.g., some of Vergil's *Eclogues* (see P. Steinmetz, *A&A* 14 [1968] 115-125), Hor. *C.* 3.9, Theoc. 15. For a seminal article on the dramatic aspects of some monologue poetry in antiquity, see F.R.B. Godolphin, *AJP* 55 (1934) 62-66.

[7] One wonders whether there is progression at 121: *Ante meos oculos adducitur advena paelex*. It would seem so if *fama pervenit* in line 3 implies that Iole has not yet appeared.

is, is the development external, i.e., the circumstances of the heroine change during the poem or there is a change in the external stimulus reflected in the heroine's response; or internal, i.e., something happens within the poem psychologically (e.g., an emotional state is intensified, relaxed, or altered) or cognitively (the writer reaches a decision)? (3) Contrariwise, is it the case that the psychological and cognitive situations are much the same at the end as at the beginning, only that a state of mind when turned into words must occupy a spatially extending area and cannot be compressed into a point of space? (4) In slightly different terms: is the substance of the entire poem meant to appear preexistent vis-à-vis the act of writing it down, or is the poem, in a sense, sequentially and immediately generated by the poem itself, and therefore the final mental state is the product of the evolving poem?

To be sure, certain poems make hardly an attempt to break out of the static mold. Thus, in Hermione's letter the combination of pleas, arguments, and accounts of past history produce no dramatic movement of any sort. Even the hint of suicide at the end is no new resolve or psychological development, but rather a final ploy in her endeavors to persuade Orestes. Similar are the epistles of Canace and Ariadne: nothing happens, externally or internally. Canace's succeeds in spite of its static quality. Ariadne's makes an attempt at external drama, with small success.[8] Of note is the change in the description of Ariadne's posture toward the end. Between line 135 and line 145 there is a visual transformation from near paralysis to earnest pleading with outstretched arms. This is of real interest since, for once, dramatic and real time coincide.

Nothing much happens in Phaedra's letter either, except that the argument progresses, becoming more extreme during the course of the letter. She turns, on the one hand, to outright brazenness, on the other, to pitiful begging. But it is only the rhetoric of the argumentation that develops. We do not feel that anything is happening to or within Phaedra.

No more successful in this area are the letters of Oenone and Hypsipyle. The former displays little more than a shift from anger to pleading, while the latter transforms an initial sarcastic ire into a final violent anger.

---

[8] See chapter xviii "The Role of Perspective."

A number of the *Heroides* are structurally built around the fluctuations of the mind and are, as it were, psychic dramas. In these there may not be substantial development and the state of mind, after all its vacillations, may end much the same as it began. A brilliant example, to go outside the *Heroides*, is Catullus Eight, in which the reader senses that the mental struggle has gone for nought and the poet remains, at the end, in the same condition. None of the *Heroides* can match the intensity Catullus achieves here through the compactness of the poem. Of Ovid's, probably Dido's letter best fits this mold. She is at the outset intent on suicide. But she still moves a limited spectrum of emotions and arguments, from anger to love, from professed acceptance of Aeneas' departure to attempts at inducing him to remain a brief period to arguments that he completely forget Italy and establish his empire at Carthage. Most striking is how halfway through the poem Dido evidently dismisses Aeneas, turns to her dead husband Sychaeus with assertions of faithfulness and seeks forgiveness for her affair with Aeneas. But then Sychaeus is forgotten and Dido again pleads with Aeneas to stay. In the end, she returns to the beginning, her resolve to commit suicide. Thus, the psychic drama is played out on the epistolary stage with no ultimate consequence. But there is another possibility. For the constant wavering may be both a sign that the initial resolve was no more than a weak pose and a medium through which the conflicting emotions are worked out and which makes possible a final decisive resolve. In other words, the initial intent to commit suicide and the final one may be very different indeed.

In the same class belongs, most probably, Phyllis' letter. Again, the generating principle is largely the fluctuation of emotion. Moving from love to condemnation, from hope to despair, from the profession that Demophoon has maliciously betrayed her to the expectation that he will yet return, Phyllis appears no closer to a stable resolution at line 130 than at line 1. Then, abruptly, she is planning suicide; the resolve is sealed with the epitaph of the final distich. But the development is not completely satisfactory. It is mechanically imposed rather than organically derived from what preceded. We may, however, choose to see it as the product of the impress made on Phyllis' mind by the whole anterior conflict. In other words, it is produced by, rather than growing out of, everything that preceded. Difficulties still remain. What do the *saepe*'s of 139 refer to? Can they possibly refer to the immediate moment? Or must we, unexpectedly, throw back the contemplation of suicide to an earlier moment? As so often in the *Heroides*, Time proves a complicating, indeed a perplexing, factor.

The nature of the dramatic movement, so obviously present, in Sappho's letter is difficult to pinpoint. Through two-thirds of the poem there is no hint, no thought of impending death. Suddenly Sappho recalls the nymph's epiphany and from this point on there is a movement toward a death-resolve. Again, however, this is wavering rather than serial, and, to the very end, she retains a glimmer of hope that she will be able to avoid the fatal leap. At any rate, the death motif grows out of the nymph's appearance. So much seems clear. The tenses in 161-163 would indicate that the episode lies in the past; yet, there has been no sign of its effect on Sappho till the present moment. Is this another case of the artificial imposition of psychological development: the episode is withheld to this moment precisely for its effect? Yet, this may be to see things from an improper perspective. For perhaps the resolve to die initiated at 175ff is generated not by the appearance of the nymph, but rather by the recollection of it at this point. If so, the development is indeed internally, organically determined.

The poem which is most oriented to a cognitive development is also, happily, the most limpid in its movement, *Heroides* 12. For it clearly displays the progress of Medea's intent to take active revenge. When the letter opens, Medea is set on expressing her anger, vilifying Jason, and perhaps persuading him. She has no thoughts of action. But her increasing anger and the growing realization of the futility of her attempts beget a plan to take drastic measures.[9] Although it is never spelled out, the references to swords, poison, and her children leave nothing to the reader's imagination. The poem concludes with vague threats, but the reader knows that the plot is now but one step away from its terrible fruition.

Hypermestra's epistle, with its lengthy narrative, unusual apostrophe to Io, and massive self-defense looks very much like a poem that, dynamically speaking, goes nowhere. Yet, there is, I think, a subtle psychological development, keyed by the brilliant last distich: *Scribere plura libet. Sed pondere lassa catenae/*

---

[9] For some qualifying observations, see chapter VI "*Heroides* 12."

est manus et vires subtrahit ipse timor. As often in the *Heroides,*
physical states or activities mirror psychological ones. The poem
concludes with a feeling of anxious mental fatigue which is generated by Hypermestra's elaborate recounting of her trauma and
by her arduous attempt to present herself as a heroic martyr.
Thus, at the poem's end, there is a mental and psychological
weariness unknown at the beginning: Hypermestra cannot bear
the burden she places upon herself.

The dynamics of the psyche is probably best realized and exemplified in Laodamia's letter. The psychological development
is here organically and systematically fulfilled. As more and more
"repressed" factual matter comes to the fore, we go deeper and
deeper into Laodamia's mind. First, the omen of the threshold;
then, the oracle; finally, the dream-vision. Concomitant is the
gradual revelation of the depths of Laodamia's anxiety, till at last
we understand that somehow Laodamia knows and accepts in
her heart that Protesilaus is dead. The waxen image is virtual
metaphor for her inner awareness that Protesilaus is gone.

Finally, the Homeric heroines. Coincidentally, there are similarities in the dramatic character of these two epistles. In brief,
Penelope's letter breaks into three sections: in the first (1-56) she
describes her fear and anxiety while Ulysses was in Troy; in the
second (57-80) she complains about Ulysses' prolonged absence;
in the last (81-116) she describes her plight in Ithaca. The structure is therefore keyed to geographical-chronological coordi-
nates. Her mind turns from one temporal-local interest-area to
the next, on the one hand from Troy to Mediterranean wanderings to Ithaca, on the other, from distant past to recent past to
present and future. The structure may then be called dramatic
in that the flow of the letter is the progress of Penelope's emotions over a period of twenty years. But nothing really happens
from within the poem itself. That is, the dynamics of the poem do
not generate any such movement. It is merely the fairly straightforward chronological advance that proves determinant.

Briseis' letter is launched from the same principle, but seeks to
do what *Heroides* 1 did not, make the temporal determinant
seem internal to, not imposed on, the poem. Initially, the letter
appears written soon after the abduction and describes Briseis'
reaction to that event (1-16). Then we realize that it is a matter
of days, not hours (*saepe,* 17; *tot noctibus absum,* 21), and Briseis
rebukes Achilles for not reclaiming her (17-24). We cannot but

be shocked when immediately thereafter we learn that the embassy to Achilles has already been rejected (25ff). Finally, some thirty lines later, we hear that Achilles is even threatening to return home (57-58). Thus, as in the letter of Penelope, the poem progresses chronologically to give, as it were, a history of Briseis' emotions. The main difference is that in this poem the chronological movement and the poem's movement are meant to appear coeval. This is one small step beyond the technique of *Heroides* 1. Nevertheless, the course of the poem is basically conditioned by the external development, i.e., by the adaptation of the progress of Briseis' mental processes to the progress of external events which impinge upon them in succession—though not in immediate succession. For the time differential is telescoped within the poem. Interesting as the attempt is, that the structuring is highly artificial and in part directed by rhetorical considerations is all too obvious.

In sum, because it is easy to condemn many of these epistles as static does not make the accusation fair or just. To be sure, a good many are so and do not even seek to mask this "fault." But Ovid did perceive the difficulty and strove, in a variety of ways, to break the static mold. At times he attempted—the most difficult task—to have the poem, i.e., the mental processes reported, be itself the source of the poem's movement. More often he allowed concrete elements, whether from within or without the poem (the latter only in *Heroides* 9), generate the dramatic movement. By and large he was not terribly successful. But the least we can do is remember that creating dramatic monologues was not Ovid's purpose. When he did seek to introduce the dramatic element it was only because he realized that it might, from an overall point of view, be to the esthetic advantage of the poem. But peripheral it certainly was to his major concerns, and it is a gross disservice to Ovid to evaluate the *Heroides* by the criterion of success at creating poems of a dramatic character.

XX

The *Heroides*: Myth and Psychology

A. The Heroines

The *Heroides* are not rarely praised as acute portraits of the female psyche. Ovid's main goal in the *Heroides* was, according to Giomini, "l'approfondito studio dell'animo femminile nelle sue varie manifestazioni,"[1] and, as Dörrie has recently written, in reading these poems "erregt zweierlei Staunen und Bewunderung: Erstens, mit welcher Einfühlungskraft Ovid die seelische Situation von Frauen zu schildern vermag, die—sei es durch eigene, sei es durch fremde Schuld—in ihren *amor*, und das heisst in ihrer Existenz bedroht sind."[2] That they are indeed studies, so to speak, in psychology cannot be reasonably denied. That is determined by—or perhaps determines—the form. Ovid presents highly expressive utterances by women in what Bettelheim calls "extreme situations," utterances which usually have little or no external value for the writer herself. Even such practical purpose that they possess for the heroine must generally be seen on the psychic level. The explicit declarations of Medea and Hermione serve well, *mutatis mutandis,* for most of the women: *Est aliqua ingrato meritum exprobrare voluptas;/ hac fruar, haec de te gaudia sola feram* (12.23-24). Medea acknowledges that her words have no other purpose than as a psychological outlet, as a vehicle for pleasurably discharging her emotions. Also Hermione:

---

[1] R. Giomini, *La Poesia Giovanile di Ovidio: Le Heroides* (Sulmo 1958) 21.

[2] *Der heroische Brief* (Berlin 1968) 77. Among many other encomiums of Ovid's psychological portraits in the *Heroides*, I note here a relatively old one, Loers, p. LXX and a very recent one, A. R. Baca, *TAPA* 100 (1969) 10. E. Paratore, *Ovidio nel Bimillenario della Nascita* (Sulmo 1958) 14-20, happily goes beyond bare words of praise and seeks to gain some understanding of Ovid's psychological insights.

371

Hermione coram quisquamne obiecit Oresti?
  Nec mihi sunt vires nec ferus ensis adest!
Flere licet certe; flendo diffundimus iram
  perque sinum lacrimae fluminis instar eunt.
Has semper solas habeo semperque profundo.
                                          (8.59-63)

Here is almost a motto for the *Heroides*: powerless women who
are helpless to influence their own lives must resort to vicarious
(and futile) acts to provide psychic satisfaction in the absence of
potency, be it weeping, complaining, or verbal expression. In
other words, the very act of letter-writing is itself little more than
an attempt at psychic gratification.[3] This is also one reason why
the recollection of past events is so important in the *Heroides*. In
a sense these poems are self-administered psychotherapy. As in
psychotherapy one "frees oneself" from the emotions and experiences of the past by reexperiencing them, so in the *Heroides* the
women recall, relive, and reexperience their past in efforts to liberate themselves psychologically.

It is, however, as psychological portraits that these poems are
particularly striking and innovative. But we can—and must—go
beyond the bland and rather inconclusive assertion that Ovid
understood the female psyche. I have attempted, in preceding
chapters, to show exactly how Ovid's understanding—or creation
—of the psyche worked in the individual poems and here should
like to offer some summary generalizations. In the first place, we
should have no reluctance to interpret the *Heroides* psychologically. By which I do not mean to promote psychoanalytic interpretation as a tool for understanding the *Heroides*, that is, the
kind of interpretation (commonly found in, e.g., *American
Imago*) which too often assumes that the work of art exists in a
psychoanalytic (usually Freudian) mold and then proceeds (in a
clear case of circular argument) to shape it after this pattern.[4]
Nor do I approve the clinical approach which virtually assumes
that literary representations are medically accurate portraits of
psychopathological states.[5] Rather, my assumption is that Ovid

---

[3] When Ovid finds himself helpless in exile, he writes of himself in the
same terms (*Tr.* 3.2.19).

[4] For valuable criticism of psychoanalytic interpretation, see C. Morrison,
Freud and the Critic (Chapel Hill 1968) 99-100, 140.

[5] For such an example see G. Devereux, *CQ* 64 (1970) 17-31. Cf. now M.
Marcovich, *CQ* 66 (1972) 19-32.

was interested in the psyche and that we must therefore seek to understand what notions of psychology informed his art. This does not imply that Ovid had a complete, well thought-out, and ordered system of psychology or theory of personality, only that he was more concerned than most ancients with why people behave as they do. He was also deeply interested in the problem of the continuity of the individual person⟨ality⟩—i.e., that we call someone one and the same person at very different stages in the organism's life—questioning in what way this is true and what precisely it means. Consequently, our interest in the psychological characteristics of the *Heroides* is merely a reflection of Ovid's interest.

Freud, as is well known, recognized poets as acute observers of the human psyche:

> Creative writers [Freud wrote "Die Dichter"] are valuable allies and their evidence is to be prized highly, for they are apt to know a whole host of things between heaven and earth of which our philosophy has not yet let us dream. In their knowledge of the mind they are far in advance of us everyday people, for they draw upon sources which we have not yet opened up for science.[6]

Conversely, an insightful critic saw in Freud's studies, yet at a very early stage, "nothing but a kind of psychology used by poets."[7] Ovid's is no depth psychology, but it is nonetheless significant as a milestone in the understanding of the continuity of the person. It may, in a way, be related to behaviorist-environmentalist theories of our century. To quote a leading figure, "A person's behaviour is determined by a genetic endowment . . . and by the environmental circumstances to which as an individual he has been exposed."[8] What is crucial to the *Heroides* is the notion that character is determined, it is the product of something specific and definable. In these poems, character is either: (1) inborn, which means for Ovid that it is genetically deter-

---

[6] *Delusions and Dreams in Jensen's Gradiva*, Standard Edition; ed. J. Strachey, vol. 9 (London 1959) p. 8.

[7] Alfred von Berger in a review of Breuer and Freud's *Studies in Hysteria* published in the Viennese newspaper *Neue Freie Presse*, December 2, 1895 (quoted by E. Kris, *Psychoanalytic Explorations in Art* [New York 1952] 265).

[8] B. F. Skinner, *Beyond Freedom and Dignity* (New York 1971) 101.

mined, result of one's hereditary endowment. This is, I think, what makes it possible for Ovid to utilize the old theme of the family curse. For, in effect, he sees it as a metaphor of the ineluctability of one's inherited nature.[9] Or (2) it is the result of the impress of early childhood experiences (a simplistic version of the profound theory made famous by Freud); Hermione is the outstanding case; her lack of trust is conceived of as the effect of having been abandoned as a child by her parents.[10] Or (3) it is the result of critical circumstances, an acute trauma. This is rather common. Among many, Briseis may stand out, whose personality is stamped by the violent loss of family and homeland. There is Canace, put suddenly face to face with the terror of death. Penelope's condition, by way of contrast, is the product of twenty years of anxiety-filled loneliness. Others belong in their own way to this category. Or (4) it is the result of a mixture of two or more of the above factors. There is no uniform approach to Ovid's heroines because Ovid's conception of any given one is also his conception of the totality of the myth to which she belongs; each must be taken on her own.

This is perhaps what is essentially unique about Ovid's characterizations. He begins with the history of his subject and builds the present character upon it, what we can aptly call "psychosynthesis."[11] He weaves the past and present of a myth together into a whole fabric, making the character organic from one phase of the myth to another. Thus, on the one hand, he develops the character of Briseis in accord with her earlier history; on the other, he ensures (in spite of her professions) a youthful Medea in tune with the later villainess. Ovid's psychosynthesis is a kind of psychological realism that proceeds beyond, for example, that of Euripides. The latter may sometimes strive for a subtle and consistent psychodynamics within the restricted frame of the

---

[9] See esp. 4.53ff; also 8.65ff; 9.153ff; 14.85ff. Consider too the illuminating distich 16.293-294, particularly if *avorum* is the correct reading. To be sure, Euripides had already extended the application of the motif to hereditary character traits. As R. P. Winnington-Ingram (in Fond. Hardt, *Entretiens*, vol. 6, *Euripide* [1958] 175) well writes of *Hipp.* 336ff, "It is not a question of inherited guilt, but of inherited sexuality."

[10] Perhaps we are meant to see something of the sort in Sappho's mention of her parent's death at 15.61-62.

[11] The reverse, so to speak, of psychoanalysis, where the analyst begins with the present, the personality of the patient, and from this re-creates the past history.

events and circumstances of a limited period, that of a play. In other words, the psychodynamics are circumscribed by the temporal and dramatic limitations of the literary form.[12] Ovid seeks a psychodynamics which embrace and comprehend the life of the individual. Meyerhoff's observations are eminently relevant to the *Heroides*: "The quest for disclosing some sense of continuity, identity, and unity within the context of the personal past of the individual has engaged great literature everywhere."[13]

For Ovid there is a life-long self which can with reason (though not always easily) be perceived as continuous: in the adult Hermione, one can recognize the child; in the filicide Medea, one descries the fratricide; in the bitter and defeated rival of Medea, one discerns the Hypsipyle who was unable to adopt the Amazonian behavior of the Lemnian women.[14] Past life and present character are bound up with each other. Here one might fruitfully recall Ernest Jones' classic analysis of Shakespeare's characterization of Hamlet. He sees Hamlet's personality as determined by events and relationships of his past life. This, however, as Jones himself acknowledges,[15] commits the "documentary fallacy" because it depends on the acceptance of Hamlet's existence outside the play itself (an existence in many ways identified with Shakespeare's own life). But it takes no such contortions to see in the *Heroides* a dynamic psychology at work in which past and present are tied together. For, by virtue of the unique form Ovid has created, the past has become an integral part of the poem, not something (as in *Hamlet*) external to it.

It need hardly be added that if we consider the *Heroides* studies in psychology, we cannot but help observing that they almost constitute a casebook of abnormal psychology. Ovid is, by and large, presenting psychopathology.[16] It could hardly have been otherwise, given the extreme circumstances which afflict

12 Though Euripides will sometimes break the confining bonds. For example, Hippolytus' psychopathology is tied closely to his illegitimate birth from the Amazon. See G.M.A. Grube, *The Drama of Euripides* (London 1941) 184ff.

13 H. Meyerhoff, *Time in Literature* (Berkeley and Los Angeles 1955) 42.

14 An explicit example of concern with the puzzling question of identity is Deianira's description of Hercules, *Dissimiles hic vir et ille puer* (9.24). As far as she can tell, the identity is discontinuous.

15 *Hamlet and Oedipus* (New York 1949) 19-22.

16 For some interesting if exaggerated remarks on the *Heroides* as studies in psychopathology, see E. Paratore, *Dioniso* 15 (1952) 224 and 226.

most of the heroines. But even in those cases where the plight seems less than final, or not severe at all, Ovid maintains the abnormal quality. Most strikingly, Phaedra, whose crisis is none other than her psychopathology itself. Or consider Hypsipyle, whose abandonment by Jason is never taken so hard that she contemplates suicide—contrast, for instance, Phyllis—but whose pathology is manifest in the strangeness and extremity of her attitude toward Medea. Or Laodamia, whose behavior while Protesilaus is still alive (as far as she knows) is quite bizarre. That Ovid had a peculiarly intense interest in the abnormal is clear in much of his writing. It is important to note that in this respect the single letters are far removed from the double letters which are scarcely (if at all) concerned with the pathology of the writers.

B. The Patterns of Myth

The view that the *Metamorphoses* consists of a long series of essentially independent episodes tied together in superficial ways to produce an artificial unity has in recent years been sufficiently exploded. That this epic is indeed a *carmen perpetuum* is now generally understood and accepted. It would be a harder task—and, to be sure, a less reasonable one—to seek to demonstrate that the *Heroides* are, in a way, a single, continuous, and unified composition. But, far-fetched as this is, it does contain an element of truth. The many significant interconnections between the poems in the corpus render it clear that a reader who considers the *Heroides* a group of fifteen isolated and unrelated poems tied loosely together by nothing more than vaguely similar settings and the common epistolary form goes far astray. In a strange fashion Ovid would have considered the *Heroides* a unified work in which the various parts interact in the service of the whole. Each poem should—and must—be taken by itself, but it was not Ovid's intention that the meaning of the whole work be apprehended without recognizing the relationships among the particular poems.

Moreover, it is only through an interpretive focus which encompasses the whole work that one can perceive Ovid's insight into the structural similarity of myth, the patterns—one almost feels the need to say, "archetypal structures"—that pervade, or rather constitute, myth. If poetry represents, in Day Lewis' words, "the perception of the similar in the dissimilar," if the poet's task is "to recognize pattern wherever he sees it,"[17] then Ovid, as poet-mythographer, is a representative of the art on a grand scale. On the one hand, he perceives these mythic patterns; on the other, he exploits them. The Heroidean technique of isolating out similarities, of realizing patterns within myth, or better, in the events that occur within the broad scope of a particular myth, on both vertical (i.e., chronological) and horizontal planes, thereby establishing or at least bringing to the fore their unifying elements, may perhaps be compared to Lévi-Strauss' method of myth-analysis by isolating out thematic patterns in a mythical continuum.[18]

An illuminating example is Ovid's treatment of Jason. Ovid realizes—and highlights—how the two phases of this hero's myth conform to similar patterns. In each, Jason is involved with a woman who has a peculiar relationship with her father. Hypsipyle proves utterly devoted to her father, while Medea is faithless in the extreme to hers. Jason proceeds to desert both, leaving each with children. Finally, each ends in exile, deprived of her children. These features are developed and heightened by Ovid's choice of the same chronological moment for each poem: both heroines have but recently found out about Jason's new liaison. Thus, each compares herself with her new rival, calls the latter *paelex* (6.81; 12.175), and expresses malignant anger toward the affair. There is almost a sense of justice when, in reading Medea's diatribe against Creusa, we recall Hypsipyle's against Medea. Each expresses in similar terms the regret she now feels for having saved Jason, only to have another woman benefit:

> Adde preces castas immixtaque vota timori
> nunc quoque te salvo persolvenda mihi!
> Vota ego persolvam? Votis Medea fruetur!
>
> (6.73-75)

> Quos ego servavi, paelex amplectitur artus
> et nostri fructus illa laboris habet.
>
> (12.175-176)

Of her entrapment each writes *me fata trahebant* (6.51; 12.37). When Medea calls upon Jason to consider their children, she repeats the experience and language of Hypsipyle. Even more

---

[17] C. Day Lewis, *The Poetic Image* (New York 1948) 35, 36.

[18] See, e.g., *JourAmerFolklore* 68 (1955) 428-444.

striking, she utilizes the same argument: beware a stepmother, she will be violent toward them. Medea's description of the children recalls, with a twist, Hypsipyle's: *Et nimium similes tibi sunt et imagine tangor/ et quotiens video, lumina nostra madent* (12.191-192); *Si quaeris, cui sint similes, cognosceris illis:/ Fallere non norunt, cetera patris habent* (6.123-124). Like Hypsipyle, Medea envisions herself inflicting corporeal injury on her enemies (6.149; 12.157-160). Like Hypsipyle, Medea makes extensive use of the *dos* motif (6.117-118; 12.105-106, 199ff).[19]

When Hypsipyle curses Medea measure for measure, that she suffer what she has condemned Hypsipyle to suffer, Ovid "fulfills" this wish by revealing a Medea who has fallen into much the same situation and must employ the same language and arguments. In this Ovid has added a formal element to highlight the remarkable way in which the tale of Jason and Hypsipyle is reborn in that of Jason and Medea. Both stories are, so to speak, cut to the same pattern; one is virtually a mythical doublet of the other. The patterning is, in a way, recognized by Medea herself, who carries it one stage further: *Hoc illic Medea fui, nova nupta quod hic est* (12.27), a verse which epitomizes Ovid's perception of the (sometimes ironic) interconnections between myths, the strange way in which myth repeats itself, the ways roles and relationships change.

I have chosen one instance as illustration. The *Heroides* is replete with similar cases, and, in many instances, the idea that myth consists of repeated thematic patterns is quite explicit. The theme of role-playing in *Heroides* 8 may reflect Ovid's sense of the identity of Achilles and Pyrrhus and of their mythic apparatus.[20] Demophoon is mythically as well as biologically the son of Theseus, *Thesei criminis heres*, as Ovid elsewhere remarks (*AA* 3.459). Hippolytus, half-brother of Demophoon and son of Theseus, destroys women in a different fashion. Ariadne's fate, to fall in love with and be rejected by Theseus, is repeated by her sister, Phaedra, who falls in love with and is rejected by Theseus' son (cf. 4.63-66). Nor does Ovid fail to descry and capitalize on the kinship between Hypsipyle and Ariadne (granddaughter/ grandmother); each notes her proud descent from Minos, as does

[19] Note how Hypsipyle's *emeruit virum* (138) is echoed verbally, though the tone is quite the opposite, by Medea's *quem merui* (199).

[20] On the myths of Achilles and Pyrrhus, see J. Fontenrose, "The Cult and Myth of Pyrros at Delphi," *UCalPubClArch* (1960) 4.3. 207ff.

Ariadne's sister, Phaedra (6.113-116; 10.91; 4.157). Hermione, like her mother Helen, is carried off (8.73-82), while Orestes, like his uncle Menelaus, must seek to regain a stolen wife (8.19).

Nor are patterns limited by the bonds of kinship. We have noticed how Ovid plays on the repetition of mythic patterns in Hypsipyle and Medea. One could, though not to the same degree, do the same for the relationships Ovid creates between Phyllis and Dido (who both save shipwrecked sailors), Hypsipyle and Hypermestra (who are both isolated and alienated from their female peers and have intensely peculiar and significant relationships to the males in their lives [fathers and husband]), Ariadne and Medea (who both betray home and family for their lovers).

Even when large patterns do not obtain, Ovid often struggles to interrelate poems by introducing details that perforce link them. Thus, Hermione's letter virtually asks to be seen in the light of Briseis' (8.83-86). The motif, present in a number of poems, of favorable or unfavorable winds, and the reference to Aeolus as moderator of the winds at 10.66 are reflected anew in the image of Aeolus in *Heroides* 11. References to Meleager (3.92ff; 4.99) reach a significant culmination in Deianira, Meleager's sister (9.151ff). Both Medea and Phaedra, pathological each, are granddaughters of the sun and both invoke his authority (4.159-160; 12.80).

These are, of course, small details, yet there are many like them throughout, in effect, cross-references from letter to letter. Ovid surely meant them to be unifying connectives, and if they are often no more than imposed, still, many a time they reflect basic and profound similarities. No other poet of antiquity was as acute an observer of the common form that underlies so much of ancient myth.

From one perspective, the sense of mythical pattern, the persistent cross-allusions, and the modified repetition of certain motifs all serve to afford the *Heroides* something of a sense of unity. From a second perspective, they may imply a coherence in the whole world of myth: in geometrical terms, a series of similar forms so arranged that none does not overlap at least one, often several, of the others. But as myths, not geometric forms, the interconnections not only trespass spatial bounds, but temporal and thematic ones as well.

A final suggestion. Given the subject matter of the *Heroides* and taking into consideration Otis' view of the *Metamorphoses* as an epic of Love, we might ponder the possibility that the *Heroides* are a poetic statement to the effect that the world of Myth is at bottom the world of Love in its many manifestations, the world of the many faces of Eros, to use a mythic metaphor favored by Freud and Ovid.[21]

[21] It is easy—too easy and too superficial—to note in this context that Ovid explicitly presented a view of much Greek mythic poetry which perceived it in terms of the love-theme: see *Tr.* 2.361ff wherein the *Iliad, Odyssey, Aeneid,* and much Greek tragedy are all reviewed in terms of their erotic content. To be sure, one will note that Ovid is defending his own integrity as love poet and this colors his survey of literature here. But in fact Ovid was capable of similar perspectives much before his exile: see *Am.* 2.18.35-40.

XXI

Variatio

The *Heroides* are in two important respects the precursors of
the *Metamorphoses*. They are the earliest manifestation of Ovid's
special interest in the world of myth which attains its culmination
in the *Metamorphoses*, and they are, in one sense, the same kind
of composition as the later epic. Each work is a collection of "variations on a theme" (so too are the *Tristia* and *Epistulae ex Ponto*,
but these more by necessity than choice), but each in its own
way. In the *Metamorphoses* the theme, miraculous transformation, is often submerged and subservient to larger issues, while
the theme of the separated and grieving woman is constantly at
the forefront of the *Heroides*. This thematic uniformity is potentially fatal to the poetic interest of the work and much of the adverse criticism directed at the *Heroides* fixes on its monotony:
"Le genre est monotone, chacune de ces *Héroïdes* étant d'un sentiment trop semblable à l'autre";[1] "La lettura delle *heroides* produce un senso di noia."[2] These remarks are typical. Perhaps
Fränkel is right when he says that, "it is our own mistake if we
read elegies in bulk,"[3] but I doubt that the *Heroides* need such
weak extenuation. For there is something basically inexplicable
in condemning the *Heroides* for their sameness. Could Ovid, of
all poets, have been blind to the danger of ennui in a series of letters all written by lonely women? Look to the *Metamorphoses*.
Otis has ably shown how Ovid, in the face of myths that were
"very much alike and abounded in stock motifs and characters,"
achieved an incredible variety and diversity of treatment and
was able to "overcome the intrinsic monotony of such themes."[4]
What then was wrong with the Ovid of the *Heroides*? Why has
he failed to surmount the obstacle posed by the fact that the

1 E. Ripert, *Ovide: Poète de l'Amour, des Dieux et de l'Exil* (Paris 1921) 84.
2 G. Carugno, *GIF* 4 (1951) 155.   3 P. 41.
4 Otis 78; see esp. 77-80.

381

heroines' "loves are after all remarkably similar"[5] (a remark which is not quite true, anyway)? Why do the *Heroides* typically consist of, in Otis' words, "the wearisome complaint of the reft maiden, the monotonous iteration of her woes"?[6] I am afraid that the fault here lies more with Ovid's readers than with the poet himself. For the more similar poems are from a gross perspective, in their general shape and themes (and these surely are similar), the more subtle must be the distinctions which mark and identify each one as unique. Consequently, appreciation of this variety depends upon a close and studied reading of the poems, not a cursory one. Casual perusal will inevitably leave one with the impression that the letters are all more or less the same, since only the contours are apprehended.

But in fact common sense, aside from the poems themselves, points in the opposite direction. That Ovid chose to treat one theme fifteen times is itself an indication that he was interested in finding and displaying difference where there seemed to be only sameness. Ovid did not have to write fifteen poems in the same generic format, i.e., the letter-form, which would probably compel him to repeatedly adopt some motifs and techniques of that genre. Once done, he did not have to make the author in each case a woman. That decided, he did not have to make each woman a lover; finally, he did not have to make each lover strikingly separated, either physically or emotionally, from her man. Let us remember that at every turn Ovid *chose* to increase and multiply the levels and degree of sameness. His intention is manifest: to set a challenge to his skill, to display his talent in accomplishing variety and diversity in the midst of apparently overwhelming uniformity. As usual, Ovid fully knew what he was doing; paucity of imagination and invention was not one of his faults. In fact, the *Heroides* are a tour de force of *variatio*.[7]

"There is, of course, a difference between the 'heroines,' but it is a difference of external situation rather than of intrinsic content."[8] This is simply not accurate. The differences between the heroines is equally, nay more, of intrinsic content. Certainly there

---

[5] *Ibid.* 17.   [6] *Ibid.*

[7] The article by T. Zieliński, "Topika i Typika Heroid Owidjusza," *Acta II Congressus Philol. Class. Slav.* (Prague 1931) 31-43, which is known to me only through later references, seems to have been directed against the view that all the *Heroides* are alike.

[8] Otis 265.

are variations in the external situations. Penelope's condition is unique; only Laodamia's even slightly resembles hers. Phyllis, Hypsipyle, Ariadne, Sappho, Oenone, Dido, Medea have all been deserted by lovers or husbands; in a sense, so too has Deianira. Yet, it takes no great effort to distinguish between the external situations of all eight. The situations of Briseis and Hermione—both have been stolen by their lovers' rivals—are quite unlike those of the other heroines, but at the same time are vastly different from one another. Canace and Hypermestra are differentiated from the rest in their suffering at the hands of their fathers. But the reasons for their incarceration are so different as to clearly distinguish their positions. Phaedra's state is so different that in her case she has not even yet embarked on a love affair with her "lover" Hippolytus.

So the situations do differ. But to argue, with Otis, Peter,[9] D'Elia,[10] and others that this is what essentially, indeed solely, differentiates these poems is to misread—or perhaps "miss reading" is more accurate—them. For it is the internal substance which ultimately gives each poem its unique character.[11]

One striking example to make a point. As far as we know, the tale of Hypsipyle and Jason was never deemed a love story in which the heroine was betrayed by the hero. Ovid took the story and fashioned it into the mold of the *Heroides*, making it, in fact, markedly similar to Phyllis' situation. The astounding number of echoes of *Heroides* 2 in *Heroides* 6 make it perfectly clear how Ovid's version of the Jason-Hypsipyle affair is shaped in the image of his rendition of Phyllis and Demophoon.[12] But having taken the myth and given it a sameness, a likeness to the *Heroides* which it did not have in the first place, he then went about brilliantly differentiating it within the common pattern so that the poem is quite unlike any of the other fourteen. In other words, Ovid is so intent on exhibiting his powers of *variatio* that

9 H. Peter, *Der Brief in der römischen Litteratur* (Leipzig 1901) 191.

10 P. 141.

11 Some brief but valuable remarks on the internal variation within the *Heroides* are to be found in L. Haley, *CJ* 20 (1924-1925) 15-25. See now Fr. Della Corte in *Mythos: Scripta in Honorem Marii Untersteiner* (Genova 1970) 157-169.

12 Note the following "parallels" (first reference of each pair is to *Her.* 6, second to *Her.* 2): 41f/31ff; 43ff/115ff; 59ff/98; 63f/95f; 69ff/121ff; 74f/98f; 115f/79f; 117/111f; 141ff/135ff; 95/93; 137f/28.

he even refashions a myth so as to make it *prima facie* more similar, not less, to the others.[13]

As *tema con variazioni*, the *Heroides* are a double tour de force. First—and most significantly—each poem, on the surface much like the others, is a unique creation with its own individual personality, revolving usually around the characterization of the particular heroine. This I only mention here; it is, I hope, made clear in my analyses of the individual poems. Second, numerous motifs recur over and again, appearing to him who reads and runs sickeningly repetitious and boring, the product of poverty of imagination. Here I should like to select a number of these recurrent motifs and show how, on the contrary, they manifest a startling talent on Ovid's part to variegate and diversify a single motif.

A few preliminary observations. Variation on a theme can be accomplished at different levels. Least significant is mere verbal or stylistic alteration, i.e., variation for its own sake. Certainly, Ovid is adept at this and will at times repeat a motif, leaving sense and effect intact while totally changing its shape and vocabulary. More difficult and correspondingly more productive is to vary the motif in accord with the demands of the immediate context and the specific poem. Ovid often meets this difficult challenge with success. It is especially important to realize that variation does not necessarily inhere in the language utilized. Traditional or repeated motifs may be shaped extrinsically, that is, they *become* different by the way they appear, shaped and influenced by different contexts, situations, adjacent images, etc. Thus, a motif can even be varied when it is repeated verbatim. Conversely, verbal alterations can prove to be no change of consequence at all. Finally, that certain motifs are found frequently in many poems is perhaps not so important as is the way Ovid will, in a given poem, elevate one or two of these and make them a central force in the particular poem. Thus, though many poems share a commonality of motifs, the emphasis on one rather than the others will often sharply distinguish one letter from its sisters. On the other hand, the fact that a theme or motif is common does not preclude its bearing special value, meaning, intent, and significance in a particular passage or poem.

Some concrete examples.[14] One of the most frequent pieces of

[13] For further discussion of this poem, see chapter v "*Heroides* 6."
[14] The third chapter in F. H. Grantz, *Studien zur Darstellungskunst Ovids*

384

thematic material in the *Heroides* is the departure scene, the depiction of the moment of the lovers' separation. Here are the versions of Phyllis and Oenone:

> Illa meis oculis species abeuntis inhaeret,
>   cum premeret portus classis itura meos.
> Ausus es amplecti colloque infusus amantis
>   oscula per longas iungere pressa moras
> cumque tuis lacrimis lacrimas confundere nostras,
>   quodque foret velis aura secunda queri,
> et mihi discedens suprema dicere voce:
>   "Phylli, fac expectes Demophoonta tuum!"
> Expectem, qui me numquam visurus abisti?
>   Expectem pelago vela negata meo?
>
> (2.91-100)

> Flesti discedens. Hoc saltim parce negare;
>   praeterito magis est iste pudendus amor.
> Et flesti et nostros vidisti flentis ocellos;
>   miscuimus lacrimas maestus uterque suas.
> Non sic appositis vincitur vitibus ulmus,
>   ut tua sunt collo bracchia nexa meo.
> Ah quotiens, cum te vento quererere teneri,
>   riserunt comites—ille secundus erat.
> Oscula dimissae quotiens repetita dedisti!
>   Quam vix sustinuit dicere lingua "Vale!"
> Aura levis rigido pendentia lintea malo
>   suscitat et remis eruta canet aqua.
> Prosequor infelix oculis abeuntia vela,
>   qua licet, et lacrimis umet arena meis.
>
> (5.43-56)

Similar scenes, to be sure. The boat is prepared, the winds are
favorable, the lovers exchange embraces, kisses, and tears; then
the final word of farewell. A spectator would surely find it difficult to differentiate between the two scenes. Yet, the descriptions
are very different. *Amplecti colloque infusus amantis* becomes a
vivid simile (47-48); *tuis lacrimis lacrimas confundere nostras* is
elaborated to four lines (43-46). Demophoon manages a last dec-

---

in den Heroides (Diss. Kiel 1955) is evidently also concerned to show how
the motifs display a manifold variety, though his treatment is quite different in nature from mine.

385

laration of faithfulness, *fac expectes Demophoonta tuum*, which Phyllis keys on, *expectem*, while Paris, overwhelmed by his emotions, can barely utter a final *vale*. More significant is the twist on the wind-motif. Demophoon can only regret that the winds now make it opportune for him to leave (96). Oenone's version is humorous, but nonetheless significantly relevant (49-50). So strong is Paris' love that he pretends the winds are unfavorable. And, to be sure, there are witnesses: his companions realized his ploy and were amused. Here lies the clue. The controlling factor in Phyllis' account is the introductory *ausus es*; the whole description is in the form of a rebuke. Thus, she can immediately cry, *expectem, qui me numquam visurus abisti?* Implicit in the description is Demophoon's treachery. Kisses, embraces, tears— all, we must conclude, were a false show. Oenone's account is virtually a polar opposite. At every point she seeks to demonstrate— and persuade—that Paris was sincere, that all his show of affection was genuine. No accusation here; rather, an attempt to recall both to Paris and to herself how true a love their's was.

Hypsipyle's variation reads as follows:

> Tertia messis erat, cum tu dare vela coactus
>   implesti lacrimis talia verba tuis:
> "Abstrahor, Hypsipyle. Sed dent modo fata recursus;
>   vir tuus hinc abeo, vir tibi semper ero.
> Quod tamen e nobis gravida celatur in alvo,
>   vivat et eiusdem simus uterque parens!"
> Hactenus. Et lacrimis in falsa cadentibus ora
>   cetera te memini non potuisse loqui.
> Ultimus e sociis sacram conscendis in Argon;
>   illa volat, ventus concava vela tenet.
>
>   (6.57-66)

We miss here the embraces and kisses. Jason's final speech is elaborate, though he ends tongue-tied. That he boards last is an interesting variation on Paris' delaying tactics. But other aspects lie deeper. The coolness of the narrative is momentarily but decisively shattered by *falsa* and the bitterly ironic *memini*. Consider especially how unilateral this separation scene is. Where is Hypsipyle? Were it not for Jason's vocative in 59, we would not notice her presence till verse 68, when the boat has already departed. The focus is so narrowly directed that she is, in effect, read out of the scene. There is only the blatant liar Jason in all his deceit and arrogance.

Variatio

Laodamia's account is the other side of the coin:

> Tum freta debuerant vestris obsistere remis;
>   illud erat saevis utile tempus aquis.
> Oscula plura viro mandataque plura dedissem
>   et sunt quae volui dicere multa tibi.
> Raptus es hinc praeceps et qui tua vela vocaret,
>   quem cuperent nautae, non ego, ventus erat.
> Ventus erat nautis aptus, non aptus amanti;
>   solvor ab amplexu, Protesilae, tuo
> linguaque mandantis verba imperfecta reliquit;
>   vix illud potui dicere triste 'vale.'
> Incubuit Boreas abreptaque vela tetendit
>   iamque meus longe Protesilaus erat.
>
> (13.5-16)

Everything is Laodamia; there is scarcely a trace of Protesilaus, beyond his simple presence. It is she who kisses. Strikingly, it is she who complains of the winds, she who utters the only words (*mandata plura dedissem*), she who bids the fond farewell, *vale*. One almost gets the feeling that Protesilaus is too eager to rush off, that it is only Laodamia who is concerned with delaying the departure. The context too is crucial. In contrast to other departure scenes, there is no retrospective hindsight: no oaths of faith broken by a treacherous lover. And so, the shape of the account becomes very important, *tum freta debuerant, oscula plura viro mandataque plura dedissem*. In the "contrary to fact" terms, there is present already a sense of imminent catastrophe, despair, finality. Now it is too late; the opportunity will prove to be gone forever. Laodamia senses the doom that is upon her.

Finally, Sappho and Phaon:

> Si tam certus eras hinc ire, modestius isses,
>   si modo dixisses "Lesbi puella, vale!"
> Non tecum lacrimas, non oscula nostra tulisti;
>   denique non timui, quod dolitura fui.
> Nil de te mecum est, nisi tantum iniuria. Nec tu,
>   admoneat quod te, munus amantis habes.
> Non mandata dedi. Neque enim mandata dedissem
>   ulla, nisi ut nolles immemor esse mei.
>
> (15.99-106)

What departure scene, one may wonder! There is none; and that, of course, is precisely the point. The component motifs are all present: the farewell *vale*, the tears, the kisses, the final *mandata*. This is parody of the *Heroides'* departure motif. Sappho complains that she has been cheated, deprived of that familiar scene properly due to the deserted heroine. Phaon could, at least, have had the courtesy to treat her according to the "rules" of the genre.

On the periphery of the motif are certain other examples. The Argonauts hear the harsh injunctions of Aeetes and in gloom prepare to leave the palace: *Tristis abis. Oculis abeuntem prosequor udis/ et dixit tenui murmure lingua: 'Vale!'* (12.57-58). The language clearly recalls the departure scene: the hero leaves, the girl weeps, she follows him with her eyes (cf. 13.17-18; 6.71-72; 5.55-56), there is a one-word farewell, *vale*. But it makes all the difference in the world that Medea and Jason have not even met. In Medea's perspective, the lovers are separated without ever having been united.

What of the seizure of Briseis?

> Nam simul Eurybates me Talthybiusque vocarunt,
>   Eurybati data sum Talthybioque comes.
> Alter in alterius iactantes lumina vultum
>   quaerebant taciti, noster ubi esset amor.
> Differi potui; poenae mora grata fuisset.
>   Ei mihi! discedens oscula nulla dedi!
> At lacrimas sine fine dedi rupique capillos;
>   infelix iterum sum mihi visa capi.
>
> (3.9-16)

Again, the hope for delay, the tears, the (frustrated) kisses; but the context is critical. Briseis goes, Achilles stays. More important, he allows her to be taken from him against both their wills.[15]

Let us turn now to another motif. The tear-stained or written-in-tears letter is familiar to any reader of Latin love poetry.[16] Ovid turns it to good and varied use: *Quascumque adspicies, lacrimae fecere lituras;/ sed tamen et lacrimae pondera vocis habent* (3.3-4). It is rather direct here, and the apologetic tone is characteristic of Briseis. Contrast the identical theme in Sappho:

[15] One might see more remote variations on the general motif at 7.41ff, 177f; 8.5-10, 75ff; 10.3ff; 13.125ff. For a discussion of Ovid's transference of the departure motif from the *Heroides* to his exilic poetry, see H. Rahn, *A&A* 7 (1958) 110-111.

[16] See Cat. 68.1-2; Prop. 4.3.3-4.

Scribimus et lacrimis oculi rorantur obortis;/ adspice quam sit in hoc multa litura loco (15.97-98). No apology, quite the contrary. This is almost a touch of humor. The tears well up in Sappho's eyes and lo! we nearly see the drops fall upon the page and stain it—right here! The unexpected imperative actually calls attention to the motif: *adspice quam sit*, virtually a sense of proud delight; and that, after all, is what it is: Sappho, conscious of her status as lover-poet par excellence, takes pride, as poet, in fulfilling a traditional motif as lover, and is only too ready to show it off.

Elsewhere the motif undergoes more basic transformation:

> Siqua tamen caecis errabunt scripta lituris,
> > oblitus a dominae caede libellus erit.
> Dextra tenet calamum, strictum tenet altera ferrum
> > et iacet in gremio charta soluta meo.
>
> > > (11.3-6)

The motif takes on more grievous proportions. The blots on Canace's page will be blood stains. Immediately on closing the letter she will kill herself. A variation of this form is Dido's:

> Adspicias utinam quae sit scribentis imago;
> > scribimus et gremio Troicus ensis adest;
> perque genas lacrimae strictum labuntur in ensem,
> > qui iam pro lacrimis sanguine tinctus erit.
>
> > > (7.185-188)

Quite obviously, the posture differs. Also, the letter has disappeared. It is the sword which, now bathed in tears, will soon be washed in blood. On the one hand, the picture here is less decisive, less final than Canace's who already holds the sword poised for slaughter; Dido's yet remains dormant in her lap. On the other, it is more gruesome, for the vision of the sword dripping blood produces an attendant picture of the act of suicide itself.

Played off against these two representations is Hermione's:

> Hermione coram quisquamne obiecit Oresti?
> > Nec mihi sunt vires nec ferus ensis adest!
> Flere licet certe; flendo diffundimus iram
> > perque sinum lacrimae fluminis instar eunt.
> Has semper solas habeo semperque profundo;
> > ument incultae fonte perenne genae.
>
> > > (8.59-64)

Unlike Dido and Canace, she possesses no sword (which, unlike them, she would not use on herself). So her tears drip down from her cheeks and fall not upon her sword nor upon the letter, but aimlessly and fruitlessly into her lap. All she can do is cry, and, perhaps as psychological outlet, she takes full advantage, *fluminis instar*.[17]

A less obvious recurrent theme is the relative status of the lovers, what I shall loosely call the motif of the *dignus amor*. In its most straightforward form it occurs at 5.83-88:

> Non tamen ut Priamus nymphae socer esse recuset
> aut Hecubae fuerim dissimulanda nurus.
> Dignaque sum et cupio fieri matrona potentis;
> sunt mihi quas possint sceptra decere manus.
> Nec me, faginea quod tecum fronde iacebam,
> despice; purpureo sum magis apta toro.

Finding herself a mere rustic in the face of Paris' newly discovered royal status, Oenone must argue that she is worthy of, indeed well-suited to, the royal purple. At 12.85 the relationship is essentially reversed: *Quodsi forte virum non dedignare Pelasgum*; it is the male who is forced to argue—or at least courteously imply—that he is not unworthy of the princess' love.

For Phaedra the theme functions quite otherwise:

> Si tamen ille prior, quo me sine crimine gessi,
> candor ab insolita labe notandus erat,
> at bene successit, digno quod adurimur igni;
> peius adulterio turpis adulter obest.
> Si mihi concedat Iuno fratremque virumque,
> Hippolytum videor praepositura Iovi.
>
> (4.31-36)

Unlike Oenone and Jason, she claims not that *she* is *digna*, but that her lover is *dignus*; and *dignus* of what? Why, of partnership in adultery and (quasi) incest. The immoral behavior is excused, nay, even justified by Hippolytus' attractiveness. As throughout the letter, semantics are a powerful weapon in Phaedra's arsenal of sophism. *Dignus* is cleverly and ironically perverse, not quite the adjective that suits her intentions.

[17] Might 10.137-140 and 14.67-68 be considered extreme variations of the motif?

Dido's *dignus amor* is subtly different:

> Da veniam culpae; decepit idoneus auctor;
>   invidiam noxae detrahit ille meae.
> Diva parens seniorque pater, pia sarcina nati,
>   spem mihi mansuri rite dedere viri.
> Si fuit errandum, causas habet error honestas:
>   adde fidem, nulla parte pigendus erit.
>
>   (7.107-112)

She too makes the claim for her lover, not for herself. But Dido
is not Phaedra. She recognizes her guilt (if guilt it even be; guilty
conscience would be more accurate), and seeks to excuse it, not
deny it. How different are her criteria. Hippolytus' physical appeal justifies anything Phaedra might do, while Dido merely ex-
tenuates her guilt by pointing out Aeneas' honorable lineage and
his pious behavior toward his father.

Deianira's description of the state of her marriage and her relationship to Hercules appears to me a variation on the basic
theme of *dignus amor*, but with a real twist. If Oenone argues
that she is worthy of Paris, while Phaedra and Dido argue that
Hippolytus and Aeneas are deserving of their love, Deianira surprisingly indicates that she is not *digna* enough, or perhaps that
Hercules is too *dignus*. Marriage to the great man proves too
much for the simple Deianira, *non honor est sed onus*, as she par-
anomasiacally puts it;[18] *Quam male inaequales veniunt ad aratra
iuvenci,/ tam premitur magno coniuge nupta minor* (9.29-30). To
sum it up, a word of advice: *nube pari* (9.32).

A last twist in the typically Sapphic-Ovidian vein:

> Candida si non sum, placuit Cepheia Perseo
>   Andromede patriae fusca colore suae.
> Et variis albae iunguntur saepe columbae
>   et niger a viridi turtur amatur ave.
> Si nisi quae facie poterit te digna videri,
>   nulla futura tua est, nulla futura tua est!
>
>   (15.35-40)

Sappho readily concedes that her looks are no match for Phaon's,
but if Phaon requires that his girl be *digna facie*, then surely he

---

18 The play on *honor-onus* seems impossible to put into English. One
might do better in German using *Last* and *Lust*, as in *deine Last ist Lust*.

will be left empty-handed. Not merely a striking accommodation of language to rhythmic obligations, and a fine instance of playful wit, but withal an effective piece of flattery which nearly turns Sappho's traditional homeliness into a rhetorical asset.

Certainly one of the most immediately captivating motifs in the *Heroides* is that of the inauspicious "wedding"-night.[19] Thrice it appears essentially the same, in the letters of Phyllis, Hypsipyle, and Dido. Surface diversity is transparent. The presence of the baleful deities is acknowledged in varied phraseology:

> cui mea virginitas avibus libata sinistris
> castaque fallaci zona recincta manu.
> Pronuba Tisiphone thalamis ululavit in illis
> et cecinit maestum devia carmen avis.
> Adfuit Allecto brevibus torquata colubris
> suntque sepulchrali lumina mota face.
>
> (2.115-120)

> Non ego sum furto tibi cognita. Pronuba Iuno
> affuit et sertis tempora vinctus Hymen.
> At mihi nec Iuno nec Hymen, sed tristis Erinys
> praetulit infaustas sanguinolenta faces.
>
> (6.43-46)

> Illa dies nocuit, qua nos declive sub antrum
> caeruleus subitis compulit imber aquis.
> Audieram voces, nymphas ululasse putavi:
> Eumenides fatis signa dedere meis.
>
> (7.93-96)

[19] The ill-omened marriage is a Greek motif with, most probably, a fairly long history. Eur. *Tro.* 308-352 seems close to the motif, while Lloyd-Jones, *HSCP* 73 (1969) 103-104 has argued its presence at Aesch. *Agam.* 744ff. The earliest certain example I know is Erinna *AP* 7.712. It is also at Meleager *AP* 7.182. However, the earliest (certain) elaborate version in Greek, i.e., with a fury presiding, is Thallus *AP* 7.188, and may well be later than Ovid. Significantly, these three examples all deal with the death of a girl on her wedding-night; none have the notion of a marriage which will, in the future, prove to be ill-fated. It is possible that the beginnings of such an application of the motif rest with Vergil, who has Juno condemn the marriage of Aeneas and Lavinia by declaring *Bellona pronuba* (*Aen.* 7.319) and by identifying their marriage torches with funereal ones (7.322). From here Ovid expanded and elaborated the motif in numerous ways. One might note that Prop. 4.3.13-16, a specially fascinating turn of the motif, may play a role here also. For a tentative—and weak—attempt at relating certain examples of the motif to a common Alexandrian source, see T. P. Wiseman, *Catullan Questions* (Leicester 1969) 19-20.

If Phyllis' is most elaborate, it is also simplest and most direct, being little more than a metaphorical account of an event in terms of a retrospective vision. Hypsipyle's, however, grows directly out of an implied contrast of herself to Medea. When she alludes to the presence of Juno and Hymen, it is not as testimony to the auspiciousness of their "marriage," but rather to its legitimacy. But suddenly, in the light of hindsight, she realizes that questions of legitimacy are irrelevant and futile, for Jason is lost to her. Juno and Hymen become now symbols not of legitimate, but of happy, love and as such they must make way for the *tristis Erinys*, symbol of ill-omened love.

Dido's version cannot be understood without recourse to the *Aeneid. Nymphas ululasse putavi* is clearly a rejoinder to Vergil's *summoque ulularunt vertice nymphae* (4.168). Equally suggestive is how Ovid does without the traditional trappings, no Juno, no Hymen, no torches; but unlike elsewhere, he turns the metaphorical wail into concrete reality. The rustic scene, the heavy storm, nature itself becomes—or proves identical to—the metaphor. There really is an audible noise that accompanies the consummation, but it is nothing else than the thundering of heaven—which Dido first takes as sympathetic, later as hostile, Nature.

At 14.27-28 the motif manages without the deadly goddesses: *Vulgus "Hymen Hymenaee" vocant. Fugit ille vocantes;/ ipsa Iovis coniunx cessit ab urbe sua.* Here at last a real wedding ceremony. The multitude invokes Hymen, but Hymen knows better. He flees and Juno with him, the last a neat touch: the extremity of the horror even constrains Juno to leave her sacred city. Here the wedding and the catastrophe are contemporaneous, with the violence so great that *Hymen fugit.* In other words, instead of the absence of Hymen being a symbol of the marriage's destined disaster, it is literally precipitated by the atrocity the wedding will entail.

Form and context transform the motif at 11.103-106:

> Tolle procul, decepte, faces, Hymenaee, maritas
> et fuge turbato tecta nefanda pede!
> Ferte faces in me quas fertis, Erinyes atrae,
> et meus ex isto luceat igne rogus!

Pathos resides in the fact that here no marriage will ever take place. Hymen himself is frustrated, participating in Canace's grief. The latter calls down upon herself the agents of her own

393

doom. Not least, the common metaphorical identity of marriage torch and funeral torch is the unfortunate literal truth.

The motif lies beneath the surface and is again transformed by the context of 12.139-146:

> Ut subito nostras Hymen cantatus ad aures
> venit et accenso lampades igne micant
> tibiaque effundit socialia carmina vobis,
> at mihi funerea flebiliora tuba,
> pertimui nec adhuc tantum scelus esse putabam,
> sed tamen in toto pectore frigus erat.
> Turba ruunt et "Hymen" clamant "Hymenaee" frequenter;
> quo propior vox haec, hoc mihi peius erat.

No ominous goddesses here, but no need. For the circumstances invert, as it were, the motif. Here the *Hymen cantatus* is the bad omen, here the marriage song itself has funereal connotations (142), here the very name *Hymen* is dire (146).

Perhaps Hermione's account of her nights with Pyrrhus also belongs here:

> nox ubi me thalamis ululantem et acerba gementem
> condidit in maesto procubuique toro,
> pro somno lacrimis oculi funguntur obortis
> quaque licet fugio sicut ab hoste viro.

$$(8.107\text{-}110)$$

Certainly the association of *ululantem* with *thalamis* vividly recalls the ominous shriek of the fury presiding over the wedding. For Hermione, who realizes and in her own voice bewails her dire connection with Pyrrhus, every night is an ill-omened experience.

Three heroines compose their own epitaphs.[20] Those of Phyllis and Dido are quite similar, each intended to condemn the hero for his beloved's death, yet the small differences are significant: "*Phyllida Demophoon leto dedit, hospes amantem;/ ille necis causam praebuit, ipsa manum*" (2.147-148); *Praebuit Aeneas et causam mortis et ensem./ Ipsa sua Dido concidit usa manu* (7. 197-198).[21] The shape of the lines, the use of epithets provide the

---

[20] Ovid may have derived the idea of an epitaph dramatically and pathetically composed prior to death from some predecessor. Cf. e.g., Eur. *Tro.* 1190f; Tib. 1.3.55-56; Prop. 2.13.35-36, 2.1.78.

[21] I pass over *et ensem* which is obviously dictated by the different circumstances.

clue. Dido's statement is direct, even cold in its resigned objectivity. She has now emotionally dissociated herself from Aeneas; their names are separated far from one another, no epithets tell anything about their relationship. Only the name Dido is an index (rather than Elissa).[22] Where Dido will not let Aeneas be detached from herself is in his guilt. In death she will not be *Elissa Sychaei*; let responsibility fall where it belongs—on Aeneas. Contrast Phyllis, who cannot so neatly sever herself from Demophoon. To the end she calls herself *amantem* and, as at the letter's beginning, so at its end, she persists in setting herself and her lost lover in juxtaposition, *Phyllida Demophoon, hospes amantem.*

Very different is Hypermestra's epitaph: *"Exul Hypermestra pretium pietatis iniquum,/ quam mortem fratri depulit, ipsa tulit"* (14.129-130). It is, of course, a terse summation of the letter's major theme, a proclamation by Hypermestra of her heroic martyrdom. But especially determinant here is the placement of the epitaph. We expect it to end the poem, as at *Heroides* 2 and 7. To our surprise, it does not, and thereby the sense of finality that would inhere in the epitaph's role as "last words" dissolves and disappears. No final resolve here, just a further attempt by Hypermestra to persuade herself of the ultimate merit and rightness of her behavior.[23]

That many of Ovid's heroines mention or recount their nocturnal activities scarcely comes as a surprise. But they do it in illuminatingly different fashions. Penelope, the great web-weaver, wiles away the long anxious hours of the night at the loom (1.9-10). Deianira, with husband away fighting all brands of monsters, suffers nightmares (9.37-40). Medea, infatuated with the newly come young hero, has visions of the terrifying tasks Jason must confront and cries the whole night through—what Deianira is too experienced to do (12.59ff). Years later, in anxiety this time over her own plight, Medea cannot sleep (12.171-174). And her sleeplessness finds a witty correlative in the mythic material: *Quae me non possum, potui sopire draconem* (173). In Canace's case, insomnia is a symptom of her love-sickness (11.31-32, esp. *nox erat annua nobis*). These sleepless heroines owe their condition to the absence of their men; they sleep alone. Hermione's

---

[22] This point is well made by H. Rupprecht, *Gymnasium* 66 (1959) 250, who brings out the significance of Ovid's deliberate and skillful use of the two names in this poem.

[23] Perhaps a variant of the epitaph motif is that of the "inscription," as at 2.73f, 5.29f.

insomnia is caused by the man with whom she is compelled to sleep (8.107-110). Laodamia manages to sleep and seeks vicarious pleasure in erotic dreams. But she fails and instead sees ghostly visions which arouse her (13.105-110). Sappho is more successful. In fact, so real are her dreams that her physical satisfaction is equal to that of making love (15.123-136). Her solitary complaint is that they do not last long enough. A turn to the motif is given by Hypsipyle who wonders how Jason can peacefully sleep the night with the sorceress Medea (6.95-96).

Of all the heroines the only one who sleeps soundly by her lover is Ariadne. Ironically, of course, it is this sound sleep which proves her undoing: *Crudeles somni, quid me tenuistis inertem?* (10.111).

Finally, night and sleep are center stage in Hypermestra's letter. All revolves about the wedding/murder-night. Night, in the company of one's lover, should have been a source of joy and pleasure: *Nox grata puellis,/ quarum suppositus colla lacertus habet*, as Laodamia observes (13.103-104). But here night and sleep are at once agents of death and metaphors of it (see esp. 14.22, 33-34, 42, 74).

An interesting offshoot of this general motif is the theme of groping, grasping, touching while asleep. Three instances: Hermione, forgetting her plight and thinking it Orestes by her side, reaches out, touches a body and suddenly recoils in horror, recalling that the body she feels is the hated Pyrrhus (8.111-114). Lynceus, in his drunken sleep, reaches out to embrace his beloved Hypermestra—and is nearly stabbed in the hand by the sword she wields (14.69-70). Ariadne too reaches out for her mate. She gropes once: nothing; a second time, nothing. Frightened, she is roused from sleep to discover the truth: Theseus is gone (10.9-14). It is plain that all three examples follow a basic pattern: groping in one's sleep that proves frustrated or futile. Yet, the three cases are distinct, each one perfectly suited to the circumstances of the individual heroine.

The next motif is, in its most basic form, a sort of paradox or oxymoron, what I shall call the "virtuous crime." It has a distant ancestor in Sophocles' Antigone, who describes herself as ὅσια πανουργήσασα (*Ant.* 74). In the *Heroides*, it is the very backbone of Hypermestra's letter, she whose crime is the refusal to commit a crime: *est mihi supplicii causa fuisse piam* (14.4), *laudarer, si scelus ausa forem* (6), *rea laudis agar* (120). In less literal and less dominant forms the motif is common elsewhere too. So Phyllis:

Dic mihi, quid feci, nisi non sapienter amavi?
  crimine te potui demeruisse meo?
Unum in me scelus est, quod te, scelerate, recepi;
  sed scelus hoc meriti pondus et instar habet.

(2.27-30)

Her kindness to Demophoon is sarcastically reinterpreted in the light of his subsequent behavior (though it is possible to see some feelings of genuine guilt on Phyllis' part; note *turpiter* in 57). Similar are Dido's words: *Quod crimen dicis praeter amasse meum?* (7.166); but these take on their own interest in the light of Dido's earlier admission that her love for Aeneas was indeed a crime—toward Sychaeus (105-108). The same motif is underplayed by Oenone, *ne tua permaneam, quod mihi crimen obest?* (5.6), who in fact has not only loved Paris, but also taught him the means of survival in the rustic life; by Canace, who pathetically calls her baby her *crimen* (66, 68), and questions, *Quid puer admisit tam paucis editus horis?* (109); and by Medea in her allusion to the daughters of Pelias, *pietate nocentes* (12.131). A number of times the motif is, so to speak, reversed: *Tutus eris mecum laudemque merebere culpa* (4.145), *crimine dotata est emeruitque virum* (6.138), *Ut culpent alii, tibi me laudare necesse est,/ pro quo sum totiens esse coacta nocens* (12.133-134). Here the crimes are real, but the return—actual or sought—is honor and happiness.

Let us next pursue a motif which, though not as frequent as others, may be in itself of special import in Ovid's poetry. This I shall call, "one life in two" (or "two lives in one"). Its importance vis-à-vis Hermann Fränkel's conception of Ovidian poetry is patent, but this facet I shall not discuss. Let me, however, observe that this notion is not so peculiar to Ovid as Fränkel maintains, though it is particularly difficult to determine when the idea represents a quasi-mystical sense of union and when it is little more than a neat rhetorical posture. Euripides, for instance, has Theseus remark of Phaedra's death, με κατθανοῦσ᾽ ἀπώλεσεν (*Hipp.* 810), and Vergil's Anna says similarly, of Dido's death, *extinxti te meque* (*Aen.* 4.682).[24] So Macareus pleads: *vive nec unius corpore perde duos* (11.62).[25]

---

[24] Somewhat different is Admetus' remark to Alcestis (Eur. *Alc.* 277f): οὐκέτ᾽ ἂν εἴην · ἐν σοὶ δ᾽ ἐσμὲν καὶ ζῆν καὶ μή. For other examples from Sophocles and Euripides, see Pease *ad Aen.* 4.682.

[25] I agree with Palmer that *duos* are the lovers, Canace and Macareus, though it might appear more obvious to take it as Canace and her unborn

A different shape of the motif is exemplified by the proverbial definition of φιλία: μία ψυχὴ ἐν δυοῖν σώμασι κειμένη (Porph. *ad Hor. C.* 1.3.8; cf. Cic. *Lael.* 92: *unus quasi animus fiat ex pluribus*) and is not infrequently found in Hellenistic epigram in the explicit or implicit designation of one's beloved as ἥμισυ ψυχῆς.[26] Horace as well calls Maecenas *te meae . . . partem animae (C.* 2.17.3-5) and Vergil, *animae dimidium meae (C.* 1.3.8). It is in these terms that Ariadne's cry must be understood: *pars nostri . . . maior ubi est?* (10.58).

Of course, the most striking instance of this concept in the *Heroides,* if not in all ancient literature, is Laodamia's prayer: *Parcite, Dardanidae, de tot, precor, hostibus uni,/ ne meus ex illo corpore sanguis eat!* (13.77-78).

Finally, Ovid insightfully transfers this abstract motif to the physical reality of sexual union: *et quod, ubi amborum fuerat confusa voluptas,/ plurimus in lasso corpore languor erat* (15. 49-50).

"I am your wife, if you will marry me; if not, I'll die your maid. To be your fellow you may deny me; but I'll be your servant, whether you will or no" (*Tempest* 3.1.83-86). Miranda's commonplace goes back as far as Euripides and Ovid knew it, if not elsewhere, at least from Catullus 64.16off. But he varies its use: *Victorem captiva sequar, non nupta maritum:/ Est mihi, quae lanas molliat, apta manus* (3.69-70). Interestingly, there is little concession here, for, in fact, Briseis already is *captiva*. But Dido is queen and she can go no further than *si pudet uxoris, non nupta, sed hospita dicar,* following it by the totally vague *dum tua sit Dido, quidlibet esse feret* (7.169-170). She will not deign to call herself *captiva* or *serva*.

---

baby. Against the latter view we can argue: (1) Presumably Canace's death does not necessarily entail the baby's also. (2) The point made is quite weak. Canace knows as well as Macareus that the baby is involved. The words are more effective and make better contextual sense if they come as a supportive declaration of Macareus' love at this critical moment. (3) At *Am.* 2.13.15f Ovid writes: *in una parce duobus:/ nam vitam dominae tu dabis, illa mihi.* Such is the poet's prayer to Isis to heal the (pregnant) ill Corinna (cf. too Prop. 2.28.42). This clearly supports taking *duos* here as the two lovers. E. Bréguet in *Hommages à Léon Herrmann* (Brussels 1960 = *Coll. Lat.* 44) 205-214, discusses the motif and thinks *duos* at *Her.* 11.62 is pointedly ambiguous (213).

[26] See Meleager *AP* 12.52; Callimachus *AP* 12.73. Cf. Asclepiades *AP* 12.166. That Theoc. 29.5-6 is relevant is doubted by Gow.

A bitter contrast to both these is Deianira. Unlike the "typical" abandoned heroine, she does not yearn for the title of *uxor* while professing willingness to be satisfied with the role of *hospita* or *serva*. For she *is uxor*, but it does her no good: *At bene nupta feror, quia nominer Herculis uxor . . . premitur magno coniuge nupta minor* (9.27-30).

A contrast of different dimensions is Ariadne's use of the motif not as an expression of love and devotion, but of fear and pride, with reference not to her lover but to some unknown enemy. Abandoned on an unknown island, she is filled with fears for her welfare: wolves, tigers, murderers; but the worst of all: *Tantum ne religer dura captiva catena,/ neve traham serva grandia pensa manu,/ cui pater est Minos, cui mater filia Phoebi,/ quodque magis memini, quae tibi pacta fui* (10.89-92). By its transference to a novel context, the motif is essentially reversed.

Hoping that my point has been made, I shall forbear from pursuing additional motifs at such length and rest content to touch on a few interesting areas. The motif of "worthy ancestors" occurs at least half a dozen times, ranging from efforts by the heroine to persuade her lover of her own worth (e.g., 6.113ff) to an attempt to convince the hero of his worth (8.43ff). One particularly intriguing instance (or "non-instance") is the way language and form prepares for the motif at 8.27, *quid quod avus nobis* (*nobis* is initially ambiguous), but one word, *idem*, unexpectedly makes it vanish.

The proverbial "physician, heal thyself" is utilized occasionally (e.g., 5.149-152; 12.167-174). It is commonplace in classical literature, though almost always of intellectual, not medical, proficiency.[27] Interestingly, both Oenone and Medea do use the motif in an extended medical character: *amor non est medicabilis herbis*, as Oenone writes. Medea's variation is wittily accommodated to the details of the myth: *flammae* literal of the fire-breathing dragons, metaphorical of Medea's passion; *sopire* of both the wakeful serpent and the insomniac anxious lover, Medea.

A common theme is the fearful lover. There are fears for one's self, fears for one's lover, real fears, imagined fears. Here I note merely the interplay of three examples: *Quando ego non timui*

---

27 See e.g., Eur. fr. 905N²; Aesch. *PV* 469-475; Plato *Hipp. Mai.* 283B; Ennius *Medea* 221; Tib. 1.4.81-84.

graviora pericula veris?/ Res est solliciti plena timoris amor
(1.11-12); *Quid timeam ignoro; timeo tamen omnia demens*
(1.71). This is the basic motif: the concerned lover fears everything. But Penelope recognizes the irrational and imaginary
nature of many of her worries. In contrast, Laodamia: *Nos sumus
incertae, nos anxius omnia cogit,/ quae possunt fieri, facta putare
timor* (13.147-148). Circumstances make the difference; in her case
the worst fears shall materialize. The plight of the youthful Jason
arouses Medea's pity and fear; here the motif is, with good psychological insight, quite inverted: *ipsum timor auget amorem*
(12.63), the converse of the motif which, in its usual shape, might
be rephrased: *amor auget timorem*.

Almost as common is the motif of the "rival," sometimes real,
sometimes imagined. Often she is compared—to her disadvantage, of course—with the writer. Of note is Dido's invention of
a rival for Aeneas' affections, who of course, regardless of who
she may be or whether she exists at all, cannot be any match for
Dido herself (7.19-24). Then there is Phaedra who professes to
be jealous of Theseus' lover—Pirithous! (4.109-112). Sometimes
the roles are shifted. Thus, at 8.43ff, the motif is rearranged. The
rivals are two men, Pyrrhus and Orestes, while Hermione is the
bystander making the comparison. Many other variations occur
(e.g., 13.131; 15.29-30).

In this discussion I have often belabored the obvious, but
sometimes the obvious must be spoken. It has become virtually
an accepted, though unexamined, critical commonplace that the
Heroides abound in stock themes and motifs that occur again and
again. Only rarely is it even noted that these motifs undergo
astounding and multifarious transformations in almost direct
proportion to their frequency of occurrence. Of recent critics
most guilty is D'Elia who evidently supposes that the essence of
the *Heroides* can be captured in a seven-page summary of the
themes and motifs that recur in the poems.[28] In his own words:

[28] Pp. 136-142. I am compelled to add that D'Elia's method of briefly describing a particular motif and then citing numerous instances in footnotes
is, while rhetorically effective, not quite fair. Checking out his citations reveals a goodly number of "examples" that require a generous stretch of the
imagination to see as examples, and some examples that unquestionably
do not belong at all. Aside from this, he makes no effort to discern the variations of the particular motifs.

> Alla somiglianza delle situazioni si accompagna il re-
> petersi continuo, prolisso, di alcuni motivi, in una
> forma espressiva tipica, quasi sempre approssimativa,
> dolcemente e genericamente melodiosa, coerente ma
> "decorativa," molto raramente atta a raggiungere
> l'assolutezza dell'espressione poetica.
>
> (137)

The fact of the matter is that a study of many other recurrent
motifs would reveal a diversity similar to that displayed by those
examined above.[29]

One final area of *variatio* is in the presence of *exordia*. As letters, there is a certain similarity between the openings of the
poems, yet most important is their purposeful differentiation. Indeed, much of the scholarly concern with the problem of the
epistolary openings has unfortunately been misspent effort, because it has been predicated upon the unacceptable assumption
that the *exordia* should conform to a fairly uniform pattern.[30]
The truth is that a number of the openings are in no sense epistolary in nature. In beginning each letter Ovid's major interest is
to immediately distinguish between the relationships and feelings
of the various heroines, to provide at the outset a sense of the
character involved and to foreshadow thematic patterns which
will prove of importance in the given letter. Thus, the opening
distich of Penelope's epistle prepares the tenor of the poem with
its manifestation of the writer's suspicions of Ulysses. The first
word in Phyllis' letter, *hospita*, prefigures the theme of unre-
quited help and love, while the precision of *Rhodopeia Phyllis* is
retrospectively clarified by the ensuing accusation (105-106) that
Demophoon probably no longer remembers who she is.[31] The
apologetic character of the opening verses of *Heroides* 3 sets the
dominant tone of the entire letter. The nearly formal introductory distich of *Heroides* 4 turns the traditional *salus* into a witty
play on words which discloses the pathological nature of Phaedra's desires. In the designation *Amazonio Cressa* the employ-

---

[29] I simply note a few which would repay study: dowry, self-injury, self-
deceit, abandoned homeland, helplessness (what can I do, etc.?), false oaths,
impossible wishes, rebuke, neglected appearance, return to trysting place.

[30] For discussion of the problems surrounding the opening distichs, see
the appendix to this chapter.

[31] Kirfel's objections (89-90) to the opening distich are without foundation.

ment of adjectives in place of actual names is an attempt by Phaedra to obscure the incestuous relationship by displaying the disparity in family backgrounds and concealing their kinship. In the same way *puella viro* places the two on the same level, rather than on that of stepmother-stepson. The use of language as a tool of concealment and obfuscation is of prime significance through this poem.

Oenone's forthright beginning proves characteristic of this direct and frank rustic, and her biting *an coniunx prohibet nova?* initiates the recurrent theme of the rivalry between Helen and Oenone (e.g., 89-92). *Mycenaea . . . manu* forebodes the fatal consequences of the Helen affair, while *Phrygiis . . . silvis,* we will learn, alludes to the prior love of Paris and Oenone in the woodlands of Phrygia. Finally, *te, si sinis ipse, meo* reveals her strong affection abiding in spite of the anger.

The sixth epistle's first finite verb, *diceris,* introduces the theme, afterwards developed (9-16), of the affront to Hypsipyle on Jason's part in not directly informing her of his exploits. In the next poem, the image of the dying swan, Dido's resolve, sets the mood of helplessness and impending death, while placing all Dido's pleas and hopes in a frame of futility and vanity.[32]

The opening distich of *Heroides* 8 is straightforward, a description of Hermione's present plight.[33] But it is more, for in the patronymic and the portrait of Pyrrhus, *animosus imagine patris,* the important theme of paternal heritage is begun (e.g., 43ff); and in *contra iusque piumque* another theme takes root (e.g., 31ff).

Both the sarcasm and the paradox of *victorem victae subcubuisse* (9.2) set the stage for the continuing tone and for a thematically important and recurrent element.

Ariadne's initial remarks are, of course, castigation, but the unusual terms are dictated by her unique circumstances.[34] The abruptness of Canace's first words is, to be sure, strange, but it may, as Giomini has argued, be tuned to her character.[35] The

---

[32] The tone is the same—actually reinforced—if we accept the preceding distich, *Accipe Dardanide,* etc.

[33] I am inclined to agree with Dörrie (216-217), against Kirfel (65-67), that the distich *Alloquor Hermione* etc. is spurious.

[34] I am not convinced by Kirfel's arguments (69-71) against the distich, *mitius inveni* etc.

[35] R. Giomini, *Stud Urb* 39 (1965) 89-103.

tone of quiet gentleness, yet tragic sorrow and approaching doom, is the same that pervades the entire letter.[36]

Medea opens with a reference to her help to Jason in Colchis, an episode which recurs often in the poem. The tone, as throughout, is bitter. Her self-delineation as *Colchorum . . . regina* effectively foreshadows her later comparison of herself to the present princess in Jason's life and her contrast of her current condition to her old life. In *ars mea* the motif of the failure of Medea's art is prefigured.

Laodamia offers a direct prayer couched in formal epistolary language for the welfare of Protesilaus. It is a product of her true and enduring love which proves a dominant strain in the poem. Reinforcing this is *amans* and the intermingling of their names in the second verse, a symbol of their indissoluble love.[37]

Very striking in Hypermestra's opening, which superficially sets the scene, is her designation of her husband as *de . . . fratribus uni*. This lack of affection, indeed absence of emotion, shall prove to permeate the letter. And when she writes *est mihi supplicii causa fuisse piam*, we have our first indication of the poem's dominant theme.

Sappho's initial expectation that Phaon should immediately recognize her hand, her notion of herself as *studiosa* (lit. *studiosae . . . dextrae*), and her immediately pursuant remarks on the poem itself all manifest the ego-centeredness which characterizes her, essentially in her large concern for her role and status as poetess.

In brief, the *exordia* (a term which we should not even use) are very different from one another, this because they are not conditioned by a common generic role as introduction or salutation for letters, but rather by the character of the particular poems of which they are an integral part. Many do, to be sure, help to set the scene, but this is a minor function. The trap here is the tendency to conceive of the poem's opening as virtually a self-standing unit, independent of the poem itself, present for little else than to establish the situation and the identity of the characters.[38]

---

[36] Kirfel's transposition (71-74) of the first two distichs seems unnecessary to me.

[37] One must take note of Kirfel's arguments (96-98) which, if accepted, would compel us to reject this distich.

[38] See Kirfel's good remarks (35).

In fact, quite the opposite is true. Each opening is an organic part of the poem to which it belongs and its character is determined essentially by the nature of its particular poem. As each poem is uniquely its own creation, so too will each opening be. That the openings are different is to be expected and we go far astray if we seek to force them into a common mold.

The *Heroides*, I think it fair to say, are a masterwork of *variatio*. Not merely in the broadest strokes, i.e., in the characterizations of the heroines and in the individuality of each poem, but down to the component details: the recurrent themes and motifs which to a large degree comprise the work. Wherever there is sameness there is differentiation; wherever a possibility of monotony there is variety. Always the same, yet always different. For Ovid, this was surely one of the most noteworthy achievements of the *Heroides*.

Appendix on the Openings of the Heroides

The century-long debate, initiated by Vahlen,[39] over the authenticity of many opening distichs in the *Heroides* is now nearing its end. The recent work of Dörrie, Kenney, and most notably Kirfel has seen to that. Here I want only to make a few, I hope not superfluous, points.

What caused most of the difficulty was the twofold assumption that, as letters, these poems should have formal epistolary *exordia* and—an obviously overlapping hypothesis—that, as mythical poems with no larger defining context, they must reveal the identity of writer and recipient at the very outset.[40] The former is simply a totally unwarranted assumption, failing to distinguish between real private letters and poetic literary ones. The latter has more cogency and a solid foundation in common sense. For instance, Phaedra's letter tells us in the second verse *mittit Amazonio Cressa puella viro*. A sharp and learned reader would have perceived Hippolytus and Phaedra here, but surely many readers would have been at a loss. And it is not till line 36

[39] J. Vahlen, "Ueber die Anfänge der Heroiden des Ovid," *AbhBerl* (1881).

[40] Vahlen might have thought twice about his whole approach to the question had he considered Loer's typically acute comments on Ovid's practice in opening these poems (*ad Her.* 8.1-2).

that an explicit mention is made. Similarly, the reader of *Heroides* 6 will not discover till verse 8 that Hypsipyle is the writer, unless he manages to infer it—no easy matter—from the allusion to the golden fleece. No reader of *Her.* 11 will recognize the writer before line 7 (actually the fifth verse), most not before 23. The same difficulty, though in varying degrees, may be present in 8, 9, 13. The solution, as Kenney has suggested acutely but not forcefully enough,[41] is that Ovid must have prefixed to each letter a superscription of the order *Penelope Ulixi, Dido Aeneae,* etc. Thus, the reader knows, before beginning the letter proper, who writer and recipient are, and consequently has no need of being told at the poem's beginning. Eduard Fraenkel's strictures[42] against the idea that a superscription might be an indispensable element of an ancient poem (he is talking about Horace's *Odes,* but seems to hold the principle valid for ancient poetry in general) will fail here, mainly because of the epistolary nature of these poems.

There is, in addition, one piece of positive evidence, the opening of Sappho's poem:

> Ecquid, ut aspecta est studiosae littera dextrae,
> > protinus est oculis cognita nostra tuis?
> An, nisi legisses auctoris nomina Sapphus,
> > hoc breve nescires unde veniret opus?

The first verse may imply that Phaon has already had something to read before *ecquid.* Be this as it may, verse 3 certainly indicates that Phaon has already read Sappho's name. The implications are large and seem obvious. Yet, Kirfel, who has analyzed these lines and well compared *Pont.* 2.10.1-4, misses them (or refuses to acknowledge them).[43] If I read him correctly, he understands the allusion to refer to an *imagined* seal or address bearing Sappho's name, i.e., Ovid simply pretends this is an actual letter, addressed, sealed, dispatched. But this is a blind alley for the reader. It is easier—and more effective—to take the reference as one to a real mention of her name, accessible equally to the reader. When Sappho writes *nisi legisses auctoris nomina Sapphus,*

---

[41] See *CR* 84 (1970) 196. Kenney seemed more certain a decade earlier (see *Gnomon* 33 [1961] 485).

[42] *Horace* 208-209.

[43] Pp. 102-103.

she then alludes to the prescript which would come initially to the attention of Phaon and the reader, *Sappho Phaoni*.[44]

A last point. A number of the *Heroides* begin with indisputably genuine verses that do identify the writer and present some sort of salutation (1, 2, 3, [4], [5], 13, 14, 15). Why, one might object, is this necessary or even desirable, given the existence of informative prescripts? The answer is two-edged. In the first place, such duplication is by no means impossible. It was, in fact, present in real letters. One form of external address was τῷ δεῖνι παρὰ τοῦ δεῖνος. Use of such an address did not, however, eliminate an apparently superfluous internal salutation. Second—and more important—these "salutations" that form the opening verse or verses are never used by Ovid for purposes of identification. As we have seen earlier, in every case the salutation effects some goal relevant to the total conception of the letter, e.g., to define the nature of the relationship. None can, by any stretch of the imagination, be viewed as solely or chiefly intended to identify the characters.

[44] One might compare *Tr.* 4.7.7-8, though the fact that the letters there referred to are real makes a difference.

Appendix

The Order of the Heroides

It has become rather fashionable to search out conscious and intricate patterns in the arrangement of poems within individual books of the Latin poets. Propertius has probably been the greatest beneficiary. Having struggled with the material, I am unable to discern any overriding scheme in the order of the *Heroides* without resorting to extreme violence. Thus, playing with chiastic patterns (1/15, 2/14, 3/13, etc.) offers nothing nor does dividing up the corpus into groups, e.g., three groups of five, five of three, etc. Thinking in terms of sources works no better than in terms of substance. Using the most simplistic view of the sources, Ovid sometimes juxtaposes (8 and 9: Sophocles; 11, 12, 13: Euripides), sometimes separates (1 and 3: Homer; 4 and 6: Euripides), General schemata seem absent. Nevertheless, there are limited facets of the arrangement which seem manifestly significant and deliberate. The alternation of 1, 3, 5, 7 appears intentional. Each revolves around the Trojan War: One is the Odyssean, Three the Iliadic face. Five depicts the world of Troy before the war, Seven the Trojan aftermath. To be sure, the principle is not watertight. Why is Laodamia's letter thirteenth? Could not Eight (Hermione) also be considered part of the Trojan affair? Dörrie has perceived another, more pervasive, pattern of alternation,[1] noting that the writers of 1, 3, 5, 6, 8, 10, 12, 14 survive, while those of 2, 4, 7, 9, 11, 13, 15 die as a result of their loves. But this approach also is, to a degree, flawed. As Dörrie observes, the scheme breaks down at one point: Oenone and Hypsipyle (5 and 6) both survive. Nor will Dörrie's attempt to circumvent the difficulty satisfy anyone, arguing as he does that Ovid wanted to juxtapose the two queens, Dido and Hypsipyle

---

[1] H. Dörrie, *A&A* 13 (1967) 45.

(6 and 7). First, we are given no reason as to why Ovid wanted to juxtapose the two. Second, even if we grant that he did, surely he could have done so and still maintained the general alternation by e.g., removing the Oenone letter from the fifth position. There are other problems. It is not always easy to determine what the outcome of the epistle will be. For instance, Dörrie believes that Ovid's Oenone will live on, though traditionally her death followed soon after Paris'. He argues[2] that the final distich proves that Ovid thinks of her as surviving: *Sed tua sum tecumque fui puerilibus annis/ et tua, quod superest temporis, esse precor.* But if we take these lines at face value, we should also have to imagine a reunion of the two lovers, which is certainly out of the question. Furthermore, the allusion to her future life no more proves that she will survive the whole business than Briseis' or Hypermestra's mentions of possible death indicate that they will shortly die.

A different sort of objection: it seems rather perverse to consider the upshot of Medea's letter that she survives rather than that she kills her enemies and children. This puts the trivial before the critical.

But the serious problem with Dörrie's view is a more general one. He makes the determining factor in the order of the poems a condition of very little importance, whether the girl lives or dies. The fate of the heroine is both external to the poem and often irrelevant to it. To assign it such import seems an error of judgment.

In spite of these objections, we must admit that there is something to the theory. It works at too many places to be purely a coincidence. At one point we might vary it a bit. The order of 11, 12, 13 seems related to the future of the heroine: Canace will be murdered, Medea will be murderer, Laodamia will prove a willing suicide.

If there is some vaguely general principle at work, I suspect it is a form of *variatio.* Ovid avoids juxtaposing two poems which are similar in both mythic story-line and poetic treatment. The separation of 1, 3, 5, 7 has been noticed. Similarly, the poems concerned with Theseus and his sons are separated (2, 4, 10), as are Jason's two loves (6, 12). In 3, 8, and 14 the heroine is held captive and calls on her lover for help. In 2, 6, 10 the hero has literally gone off and abandoned his girl. Both 11 and 14 involve

2 *Ibid.* n. 5.

kinship marriages and heartless fathers. In 1 and 13 wives lament the separation inflicted on them by the Trojan War. If there is something to all this, it is simply that, after a loose fashion, Ovid sought to keep poems that were thematically similar apart. There is not much surprise in this.

There is, however, one aspect of real significance in the arrangement of the poems. This is the frame, the opening and closing poems. We can have no doubt that Ovid was careful in setting Penelope's first and Sappho's last. A minor but suggestive fact is that the first is shortest, the last longest of the poems. Ovid begins with Penelope because she represents the beginning of mythic literature, Homer (Briseis would not do because of her lack of stature in the mythic tradition). He ends with Sappho because, through her persona as poet-lover, he can speak of himself as poet-lover too. It is, after all, a common habit in Latin elegy to utilize the last poem of a book to express one's self on the subject of poetry, "one's art," e.g., *Amores* One and Three, Propertius Two.[3] But the movement from Penelope and the other heroines to Sappho is a serious one, for it marks a passing from the world of myth into that of history (with mythic qualifications), a format that Ovid was to utilize again in the *Metamorphoses*, where the epic's final section crosses the border of myth into the realm of history (again with mythic overtones). Thus, the *Heroides* open with the beginning of poetry, Homer; the *Metamorphoses* with the beginning of philosophy, the creation of the world. Both end in historical-poetical worlds. The epic concludes with the apotheosis of both Caesar and Ovid; the elegy finds appropriate conclusion in Sappho, the concrete embodiment of the union of mythology, poetry, and love.

[3] For more detailed discussion, see chapter xv, "*Heroides* 15."

Select Bibliography

Since the reader will have ready access to Dörrie's recent edition with its ample bibliography, I have been content to offer a relatively short list of editions, books, and articles.

I. The Heroides: *Some Editions and Commentaries*

Bornecque, H. (ed.) and Prévost, M. (trans.). *Ovide: Héroides* (Paris 1928).

Burman, P. *Publii Ovidii Nasonis Opera Omnia*, 1 (Amsterdam 1727).

Dörrie, H. *P. Ovidii Nasonis Epistulae Heroidum* (Berlin and New York 1971).

Ehwald, R. *P. Ovidius Naso,* 1 (Leipzig 1903).

Giomini, R. *P. Ovidi Nasonis Heroides,* 1 (Rome 1963²); 11 (Rome 1965).

Heinsius, N. *P. Ovidii Nasonis Opera Omnia,* 1 (Leiden 1670).

Loers, V. *P. Ovidii Nasonis Heroides* (Köln 1829-1830).

Palmer, A. *P. Ovidi Nasonis Heroides with the Greek Translation of Planudes* (Oxford 1898).

Sedlmayer, H. S. *P. Ovidi Nasonis Heroides* (Vienna 1886).

Showerman, G. *Ovid with an English Translation: Heroides and Amores* (repr. Cambridge, Mass. and London 1947).

II. Collections of Articles on Ovid

Atti del Convegno Internazionale Ovidiano. Two vols. (Rome 1959). (Henceforth cited as "Atti.")

Ovid. Edited by M. v. Albrecht and E. Zinn (Darmstadt 1968; *Wege der Forschung* 92). (Henceforth cited as "Ovid: WF.")

Ovidiana: Recherches sur Ovide. Edited by N. I. Herescu (Paris 1958). (Henceforth cited as "Ovidiana.")

Publius Ovidius Naso (Bucharest 1957). (Henceforth cited by title alone.)

Studi Ovidiani (Rome 1959). (Henceforth cited by title alone.)

III. Books, Monographs, and Articles

Agostino, V. d'. "Introduzione alla lettura delle Eroidi ovidiane," *RSC* 3 (1955) 107-120.

Amerio, R. "De Ovidi Didone cum Vergili comparata disputatio," *Mondo Classico.* Suppl. 5 (1936) 1-39.

Anderson, J. N. *On the Sources of Ovid's Heroides I, III, VII, X, XII* (Berlin 1896).

Arnaldi, F. "La 'Retorica' nella Poesia di Ovidio," *Ovidiana* 23-31.

Baca, A. R. "Ovid's Claim to Originality and *Heroides* 1," *TAPA* 100 (1969) 1-10.

———. "Ovid's Epistle from Sappho to Phaon: *Heroides* 15," *TAPA* 102 (1971) 29-38.

———. "The Themes of *Querela* and *Lacrimae* in Ovid's *Heroides*," *Emerita* 39 (1971) 195-201.

Bergmann, J. H. *De Didonis epistula Ovidiana* (Diss. Leipzig 1922).

Birt, T. "Animadversiones ad Ovidi heroidum epistulas," *RhM* 32 (1877) 386-432.

Bradley, E. M. "Ovid *Heroides* V: Reality and Illusion," *CJ* 64 (1969) 158-162.

Brück, C. *De Ovidio scholasticarum declamationum imitatore* (Diss. Giessen 1909).

Bürger, R. *De Ovidi carminum amatoriorum inventione et arte* (Braunschweig 1901).

Cameron, A. "The First Edition of Ovid's *Amores*," *CQ* 62 (1968) 320-333.

Capecchi, E. "L'Allitterazione nelle 'Heroides' Ovidiane," *SIFC* 39 (1967) 67-111 and *SIFC* 41 (1969) 95-127.

Carugno, G. "Due Note," *GIF* 4 (1951) 151-159.

Castiglioni, L. "Intorno alle Eroidi di Ovidio," *A&R* 6 (1903) 239-249.

Clark, S. B. "The Authorship and the Date of the Double Letters in Ovid's Heroides," *HSCP* 19 (1908) 121-155.

Cola, M. de. *Callimaco e Ovidio* (Palermo 1937).

Coletti, M. L. "Un nuovo contributo al problema delle Heroides di Ovidio," *StudUrb* 31 (1957) 247-251.

Comparetti, D. *Sulla Epistola Ovidiana di Saffo a Faone* (Florence 1876).

Courtney, E. "Ovidian and Non-Ovidian Heroides," *BICS* 12 (1965) 63-66.

Cugusi, P. "Studi sull'epistolografia latina, I: L'età preciceroniana," *AFLC* 33, 1 (1970).

Cunningham, M. P. "The Novelty of Ovid's *Heroides*," *CP* 44 (1949) 100-106.

Damsté, P. H. "Ad Ovidii Heroides," *Mnemosyne* N.S. 33 (1905) 1-56.

Deferrari, R. J. et al. *A Concordance of Ovid* (Washington 1939).

Della Corte, Fr. "I Miti delle *Heroides*," in *Mythos: Scripta in Honorem Marii Untersteiner* (Genova 1970) 157-169.

———. "Perfidus Hospes," *Coll. Lat.* 101 (1969) = *Hommages à Marcel Renard*, 312-321.

Deratani, N. *Artis rhetoricae in Ovidi carminibus praecipue amatoriis perspicuae capita quaedam* (Moscow 1916).

Diggle, J. "Notes on the Text of Ovid, *Heroides*," *CQ* 61 (1967) 136-144.

———. "Ovidiana," *PCPS* 198 (1972) 31-41.

Dilthey, C. *Observationum in epistulas heroidum Ovidianas particula I* (Göttingen 1884-1885).

Döpp, S. *Virgilischer Einfluss im Werk Ovids* (Diss. Munich 1968).

Dörrie, H. *Der heroische Brief* (Berlin 1968).

———. "Die dichterische Absicht Ovids in den *Epistulae Heroidum*," *A&A* 13 (1967) 41-55.

———. "Untersuchungen zur Überlieferungsgeschichte von Ovids Epistulae Heroidum," *NAkG* (1960).

Dziatzko, K. "Brief," *RE* 3 (1899) 836-843.

Eggerding, F. "De Heroidum Ovidianarum Epistulis quae vocantur commentationes," *DPhH* 18 (1911) 133-252.

Ehwald, R. *Exegetischer Kommentar zur XIV. Heroide Ovids* (Gotha 1900).

Elia, S. d'. "Il Problema Cronologico degli Amores," *Ovidiana* 210-223.

———. "Lineamenti dell'Evoluzione Stilistica e Ritmica nelle Opere Ovidiane," *Atti* 2.377-395.

————. *Ovidio* (Naples 1959).

————. "Problemi Ovidiani: Cronologia e Autenticità di Her. XVI-XXI," *AFLN* 7 (1957) 57-91.

Fargues, P. "Ovid, l'homme et le poète: Les Héroides," *RCC* 40[1] (1938-1939) 354-365.

Ferguson, J. "Catullus and Ovid," *AJP* 81 (1960) 337-357.

Fischer, U. *Ignotum hoc aliis ille novavit opus* (Diss. Berlin 1968).

Fisher, E. "Two Notes on the *Heroides*," *HSCP* 74 (1970) 193-205.

Fränkel, H. *Ovid: A Poet Between Two Worlds* (Berkeley and Los Angeles 1945).

Garvie, A. F. *Aeschylus' Supplices: Play and Trilogy* (Cambridge 1969).

Giangrande, G. "Latin Contributions," *Eranos* 64 (1966) 153-160.

Giomini, R. "L'epistola XV delle Heroides nel manoscritto Cors. 43 F 5," *Maia* 6 (1953) 185-207.

————. *La Poesia Giovanile di Ovidio: Le Heroides* (Sulmo 1958).

————. "Ricerche sulle due Edizioni degli 'Amores,'" *Atti* 1.125-142.

————. "Sul distico introduttivo di Ovid. 'Her.' XI," *StudUrb* 39 (1965) 89-103.

Grantz, F. H. *Studien zur Darstellungskunst Ovids in den Heroides* (Diss. Kiel 1955).

Haley, L. "The Feminine Complex in the *Heroides*," *CJ* 20 (1924-1925) 15-25.

Heinemann, M. *Epistulae amatoriae quomodo cohaereant cum elegiis Alexandrinis* (DPhA, Strassburg, 1910).

Herescu, N. I. "Le Sens de l'Epitaphe Ovidienne," *Ovidiana* 420-442.

Higham, T. F. "Ovid and Rhetoric," *Ovidiana* 32-48.

Horváth, I. K. "Impius Aeneas," *Acta Antiqua* 6 (1958) 385-393.

Housman, A. E. *The Classical Papers of A. E. Housman.* Edited by J. Diggle and F.R.D. Goodyear. Three vols. (Cambridge 1972) 1.380-421; 2.470-480; 3.1052-1055, 1262.

Hross, H. *Die Klagen der verlassenen Heroiden in der lateinischen Dichtung. Untersuchung zur Motivistik und zur dichterischen Form* (Diss. Munich 1958).

Hubaux, J. "Ovide et Sappho," *MB* 30 (1926) 197-218.

Hutton, J. "Catullus and Ovid," *CW* 36 (1943) 243-245.

Jacobson, H. "Ovid's Briseis: A Study of *Heroides* 3," *Phoenix* 25 (1971) 331-356.

Kalkmann, A. *De Hippolytis Euripideis quaestiones novae* (Bonn 1882).

Kenney, E. J. "Liebe als juristisches Problem," *Philologus* 111 (1967) 212-232.

———. "Notes on Ovid: III," *HSCP* 74 (1970) 169-185.

———. "Ovid and the Law," *YCS* 21 (1969) 243-263.

Ker, A. "Notes on Some Passages in the Amatory Poems," *Ovidiana* 224-228.

Khan, H. Akbar. "Dido and the Sword of Aeneas," *CP* 63 (1968) 283-285.

Kirfel, E.-A. *Untersuchungen zur Briefform der Heroides Ovids* (Bern and Stuttgart 1969 = *Noctes Romanae* 11).

Knaack, G. *Analecta Alexandrino-Romana* (Greifswald 1880).

Kraus, W. "Die Briefpaare in Ovids Heroiden," *WS* 65 (1950-1951) 54-77.

———. "Ovidius Naso," *Ovid: WF* 67-166 (revised version of *RE* 18.2 [1942] 1910-1986).

Lachmann, K. "De Ovidii Epistulis," *Kleinere Schriften zur classischen Philologie* 2 (Berlin 1876) 56-61.

Lamacchia, R. "Ovidio Interprete di Virgilio," *Maia* 12 (1960) 310-330.

La Penna, A. "Properzio e i poeti latini dell'età aurea," *Maia* 4 (1951) 43-69.

Latta, B. *Die Stellung der Doppelbriefe (Heroides 16-21) im Gesamtwerk Ovids* (Diss. Marburg 1963).

La Ville de Mirmont, H. de. *La Jeunesse d'Ovide* (Paris 1905).

Lee, A. G. "The Originality of Ovid," *Atti* 2.405-412.

Lenz, F. W. "Bemerkungen zu Ovids Carmina Amatoria," *PP* 18 (1963) 364-377.

Luck, G. *The Latin Love Elegy* (London 1969²).

———. *Untersuchungen zur Textgeschichte Ovids* (Heidelberg 1969).

Lueneburg, A. *De Ovidio sui imitatore* (Jena 1888).

Luňák, I. *Quaestiones Sapphicae* (Kazan 1888).

Malcovati, E. "La Fortuna di Saffo nella Letteratura Latina," *Athenaeum* N.S. 44 (1966) 3-31.

Marg, W. "Ovid, Heroides 10, 95/6," *Hermes* 88 (1960) 505-506.

Mariotti, S. "La Carriera Poetica di Ovidio," *Belfagor* 12 (1957) 609-635.

Martini, E. *Einleitung zu Ovid* (Brünn, Prag, Leipzig, Wien 1933 = Schr. der Philos. Fak. der Deutschen Univ. Prag, vol. 12).

————. "Ovid und seine Bedeutung für die römische Poesie," Ἐπιτύμβιον *Heinrich Swoboda Dargebracht* (Reichenberg 1927) 165-194.

Means, T. "A Comparison of the Treatment by Vergil and by Ovid of the Aeneas-Dido Myth," *CW* 23 (1929) 41-44.

Merklin, H. "Arethusa und Laodamia," *Hermes* 96 (1968) 461-494.

Merone, E. *Studi sulle Eroidi di Ovidio* (Naples 1964).

Mersmann, H. *Quaestiones Propertianae* (Paderborn 1931).

Naumann, H. "Ovid und die Rhetorik," *AU* 11 (1968) 69-86.

Naylor, H. D. "The Alleged Hyperbaton of *Heroides* 3.19," *CR* 25 (1911) 42.

Nissen, T. "Übersehene Lesarten zu Ovids Heroiden," *Hermes* 76 (1941) 87-93.

Oliver, R. P. "The First Edition of the *Amores*," *TAPA* 76 (1945) 191-215.

Oppel, E. *Ovids Heroides: Studien zur inneren Form und zur Motivation* (Diss. Erlangen-Nürnberg 1968).

Otis, B. "Ovid and the Augustans," *TAPA* 69 (1938) 188-229.

————. *Ovid as an Epic Poet* (Cambridge 1966; second ed. 1970).

Paratore, E. "L'influenza delle *Heroides* sull'episodio di Biblide e Cauno nel L. ix delle Metamorfosi ovidiane," in *Studia Florentina A. Ronconi Oblata* (Rome 1970) 291-309.

————. "Ovidio nel Bimillenario della Nascita," *Studi Ovidiani* 113-131. (Also published separately, Sulmo 1958.)

————. "Sulla 'Phaedra' di Seneca," *Dioniso* 15 (1952) 199-234.

Peter, H. *Der Brief in der römischen Litteratur* (Leipzig 1901 = *AbhLeipz* 20, 3).

Peters, G. *Observationes ad P. Ovidii Nasonis Heroidum Epistulas* (Leipzig 1882).

Plessis, F. "Quelques Mots sur les Héroides," *Philologie et Linguistique: Mélanges Offerts à Louis Havet* (Paris 1909) 373-383.

Pohlenz, M. *De Ovidi Carminibus Amatoriis* (Göttingen 1913).

Radford, R. S. "The Order of Ovid's Works," *TAPA* 54 (1923) xxii-xxiii.

————. "Ovid's *Carmina Furtiva*," *PhQ* 7 (1928) 45-59.

————. "Tibullus and Ovid," *AJP* 44 (1923) 230-259.

Rahn, H. "Ovids elegische Epistel," *A&A* 7 (1958) 105-120.

Rand, E. K. "The Chronology of Ovid's Early Works," *AJP* 28 (1907) 287-296.

Rand, E. K. *Ovid and his Influence* (Boston 1925).

Reitzenstein, E. "Wirklichkeitsbild und Gefühlsentwicklung bei Properz," *Philologus* Suppl. 29, 2 (1936).

Renz, H. *Mythologische Beispiele in Ovids erotischer Elegie* (Würzburg 1935).

Ripert, E. *Ovide: Poète de l'Amour, des Dieux et de l'Exil* (Paris 1921).

Rupprecht, H. "Dido oder Elissa," *Gymnasium* 66 (1959) 246-250.

Salvatore, A. "Motivi Poetici nelle 'Heroides' di Ovidio," *Atti* 2.235-256.

Schmidt, E. A. "Ariadne bei Catull und Ovid," *Gymnasium* 74 (1967) 489-501.

Schmitz-Cronenbroeck, W. *Die Anfänge der Heroiden des Ovid* (Diss. Köln 1937).

Sedlmayer, H. S. *Kritischer Commentar zu Ovids Heroiden* (Vienna 1881).

Sicherl, M. "Vermeintliche Versinterpolationen in Ovids Heroides," *Hermes* 91 (1963) 190-212.

Stégen, G. "Ovide, *Her.*, x, 94-95," *Latomus* 19 (1960) 360.

Stinton, T.C.W. *Euripides and the Judgement of Paris* (London 1965).

Stoessl, F. *Ovid, Dichter und Mensch* (Berlin 1959).

———. *Der Tod des Herakles* (Zürich 1945).

Sykutris, J. "Epistolographie," *RE* Suppl. 5 (1931) 185-220.

Tescari, O. "De Ovidi epistulis, quae Heroides inscribuntur, adnotatiunculae," *Convivium* 6 (1934) 79-81.

Thraede, K. *Grundzüge griechisch-römischer Brieftopik* (Munich 1970 = *Zetemata* vol. 48).

Tolkiehn, J. *Homer und die römische Poesie* (Leipzig 1900).

———. *Quaestionum ad Heroides Ovidianas spectantium capita VII* (Leipzig 1888).

———. "Zur XII Heroide Ovids," *WKPh* 23 (1906) 1208-1214.

Treu, M. "Ovid und Sappho," *PP* 8 (1953) 356-364.

Vahlen, J. "Ueber die Anfänge der Heroiden des Ovid," *AbhBerl* 1881.

Vessey, D.W.T.C. "Notes on Ovid, *Heroides* 9," *CQ* 63 (1969) 349-361.

Vries, S. G. de. *Epistula Sapphus ad Phaonem* (Diss. Leiden 1885).

Wilkinson, L. P. "Greek Influence on the Poetry of Ovid," in *L'Influence Grecque sur la Poésie Latine de Catulle à Ovide* (Fond. Hardt, Entretiens, vol. 2, 1953) 223-254.

416

Bibliography

————. *Ovid Recalled* (Cambridge 1955).

Winniczuk, L. "Ovid's Elegie und epistolographische Theorie," *Publius Ovidius Naso* 39-70.

Winsor, E. J. *A Study in the Sources and Rhetoric of Chaucer's Legend of Good Women and Ovid's Heroides* (Diss. Yale 1963).

Wulfius, H. "De quintae Heroidis Ovidianae fontibus," *Zŭrnal: Ministerstva narodnogo prosveščenija* 273 (1891).

Zieliński, T. "Topika i Typika Heroid Owidjusza," in *Acta II Congressus Philol. Class. Slav.* (Prague 1931) 31-43.

Zingerle, A. *Ovidius und sein Verhältniss zu den Vorgängern und gleichzeitigen römischen Dichtern.* Three vols. Innsbruck 1869 and 1871.

Zingerle, W. *Untersuchungen zur Echtheitsfrage der Heroiden Ovid's* (Innsbruck 1878).

Zoellner, F. *Analecta Ovidiana* (Leipzig 1892).

Index Locorum

Index Nominum et Rerum

Index

Index

Gallus, 322, 347-348

Gorgias, 324

Gower, 3

Grenfellianum carmen, 229 n. 4, 344, 364

guilt (survival), 37

Hacks, P., 238 n. 31

Hamlet, 375

Harmodius, 196

Hecataeus, 124 n. 3

Hecate, 117

Hector, 196, 201, 203, 204, 326

Hecuba, 326

Hegesianax, 177 n. 2

Helen, 65, 178-179, 189, 344, 355, 402

Helenae Querimonia, 344

Heliodorus, 196

Hellanicus, 176 n. 2

Heller, J., 253 n. 41

Heraclitus, 349

Hercules, *passim* 228-242, 357, 359, 391

Hermes, 246

Hermesianax, 247 n. 15

Hermione, 34 n. 49, *passim* 43-57, 118, 127 n. 9, 171, 331 n. 39, 355, 371-372, 374, 379, 383, 389-390, 394, 395, 396, 400, 402, 407

Hermogenes, 324-327

Herodorus, 94 n. 1

Herodotus, 340

Heroides, date of, 300-318; faults of, 7-8, 81; imitation of in Middle Ages, 278 n. 4; as immoral literature, 7; Ovid's feelings about, 4-5; as serious poems, 4; as simple or complex work, 4; sung, 344; as a unified composition, 376

heroines as Augustan women, 263

"Hesiod," 44, 125 n. 3, 196, 227 n. 35, 235, 321

hilarodia, 344

hints in the *Heroides*, 64-65, 100

Hippolytus, *passim* 142-158, 375 n. 12, 378, 390-391, 404

Hipponax, 246 n. 6

Homer, *passim* 12-42, 44, 65, 196, 202, *passim* 243-276, 326, 337, 342, 352, 380 n. 21, 407

homosexuality, 296 n. 59, 353

Hopkins, J., 358

Horace, 138-139, 140, 249, 269, 281-282, 314, 320, 321, 332, 340, 343, 344-345, 346, 398, 405

Hyginus, 196

Hymen, 393-394

Hypermestra, *passim* 124-141, 354, 360-361, 379, 383, 395, 396, 403, 408

Hypsipyle, *passim* 94-108, 178, 355-356, 375, 376, 377-378, 379, 383, 386, 392-393, 396, 402, 405, 407

Ibycus, 44 n. 2

inanimate speakers, 346

"inauspicious marriage" motif, 64, 136, 392-394

inconsistency, deliberate, 82, 185, 186, 230

indicative in indirect questions, 286 n. 36

internal struggle, 137-138, 157

Io, 134-135, 360-361

Iole, 237 n. 27, 238, 241, 350-351, 359

Ion of Chios, 238

Ionesco, 358

Iphigenia, 331

irony, 102-104, 136, 200-202, 206, 211, 227

Isocrates, 246, 333

Itys, 282

Jason, *passim* 94-123, 319, 355-356, 357, 362, 376, 377-378, 383, 386, 388, 390, 395-396, 400, 402, 403, 408

Jones, E., 375

Joyce, J., 65, 359

Juno, 393

kallisteia, 283

Kant, 349

Laevius, 196-197, 199 n. 17, 200, 210, 334 n. 51

language, Ovid's use of, 8

Laodamia, *passim* 195-212, 326, 329,

433

Library of Congress Cataloging in Publication Data

Jacobson, Harold, 1940-
  Ovid's Heroides.

  Bibliography: p.
  1. Ovidius Naso, Publius. Heroides. I. Ovidius
Naso, Publius. Heroides. 1974. II. Title.
PA6519.H7J3   871'.01   73-16754
ISBN 0-691-06271-4